Praise for
Mental Health Practice with LGBTQ+ Children, Adolescents, and Emerging Adults in Multiple Systems of Care

"We are living in dark times for LGBTQ+ children, youth, and their families as restrictions on education, health care, sport, and access to public spaces continue to intensify. Against that backdrop, this book serves as a beacon for clinicians at all career stages who are committed to providing excellent care for young LGBTQ+ people. Grounded in psychological science, the text takes a refreshing resilience-based, strengths-focused approach to filling the need for rich interdisciplinary information and practical skills uniquely tailored to work with LGBTQ+ children and youth. It is an essential tool for clinicians who work with children, youth, and emerging adults, especially those in interdisciplinary spaces."

—**Douglas Knutson, PhD, LHSP, associate professor,
School of Community Health Sciences,
Counseling and Counseling Psychology,
Oklahoma State University**

"In today's climate, mental health practitioners and those in related fields need as many resources and tools in their toolbox as they can possibly have, particularly when it comes to serving LGBTQ+ children and adolescents. This text will be a priceless addition for all those wanting to serve the LGBTQ+ population. I truly appreciate that it covers such a broad spectrum of issues and concerns impacting children, adolescents, and those in emerging adulthood. It is a must for training programs and clinicians."

—**Tonya Renee Hammer, associate professor,
School of Community Health Sciences,
Counseling and Counseling Psychology,
Oklahoma State University**

"This is an ambitious and comprehensive project. It is grounded in important theoretical frameworks, yet also promises information relevant to a diverse group of clinicians, youth workers, educators, and service providers."

—**Sean Cahill, PhD, Director of Health Policy Research,
The Fenway Institute**

"The collection of papers in this book come at a crucial moment for LGBTQ+ youth in the United States. As societal conflict around the rights and well-being of LGBTQ+ youth mounts, every mental health provider working with this population will benefit from the insights found in this book. These essays will be a rich resource for providers who are interested not only in building their practice but also in building their praxis."

—**Carl Waitz, PsyD, licensed psychologist**

"This groundbreaking new volume offers a much-needed guide for mental health professionals working with LGBTQ+ youth in a variety of contexts. The text provides a comprehensive and intersectional framework for understanding the unique mental health needs of LGBTQ+ youth and offers evidence-based strategies for meeting those needs in culturally competent ways. With chapters by a stunning list of world-leading experts, this book is an essential resource for scholars, practitioners, and advocates alike."

—**Thomas J Billard, executive director,
Center for Applied Transgender Studies and
assistant professor of communication studies and sociology
(by courtesy), Northwestern University**

"This book is a long-needed addition to the burgeoning field of affirmative mental health practice with LGBTQ+ individuals. Many of the complex systems that LGBTQ+ youth, their families, and their providers must navigate are still improving LGBTQ+ cultural competency. Practitioners, organizations, and agencies across disciplines will benefit greatly from this accessible yet nuanced view of the needs of LGBTQ+ youth across systems of care."

—**Jayme L. Peta, instructor, Palo Alto University**

"Providing an opus of mental health care for LGBTQ+ youth, the editors of this book are meticulous in crafting a compendium connected by an intersectional, decolonial, multisystemic paradigm, with particular attention to include writings that discuss theory and practice structures in an accessible language for clinicians and clients alike. The book's undeniable strength further lies in its efforts to bridge the translation from theory to practice with the presentation of concrete and actionable items across the chapters, which fills a dire gap that other collections often overlook with a tool kit that may be readily employed to improve care."

—**Jacks Cheng, PD, EdM, counseling psychologist**

Mental Health Practice with LGBTQ+ Children, Adolescents, and Emerging Adults in Multiple Systems of Care

Diverse Sexualities, Genders, and Relationships

Series Editors

Richard Sprott, California State University, East Bay
Elisabeth Sheff, University of Tennessee,
Chattanooga and Sheff Consulting Group

The Diverse Sexualities, Genders, and Relationships Series highlights evidence-based approaches to understanding and serving diverse individuals and families whose relational or sexual practices or identities have been marginalized and understudied; reports of emerging empirical research on these topics; and analyses of the latest trends in cultural and societal developments on the status and place of diverse sexualities, genders, and relationships. Books in the series emphasize the intersections of race, culture, age, social class, (dis)ability, and other factors that shape the social locations of relational, sexual, and gender minorities as they intersect with institutions in fields such as education, law, medicine, religion, and public policy.

The books in this series will serve as sound and critical resources for the training and continuing education of professionals directly serving diverse communities, in professions such as counseling, marriage and family therapy, social work, healthcare, criminology, human services, and education. They will also be useful for educators teaching undergraduate and graduate level university courses in anthropology, cultural studies, gerontology, psychology, sexuality studies, sociology, and women's and gender studies. Finally, these books will interest educated laypeople who wish to better understand diversity among relational, sexual, and gender minorities.

TITLES IN SERIES:

Love and Freedom: Transcending Monogamy and Polyamory by Jorge N. Ferrer
Please Scream Quietly: A Story of Kink by Julie L. Fennell
The Handbook of Consensual Non-Monogamy: Affirming Mental Health Practice
    edited by Michelle D. Vaughan and Theodore R. Burnes
Mental Health Practice with LGBTQ+ Children, Adolescents, and Emerging Adults
    in Multiple Systems of Care edited by Cristina L. Magalhães, Richard Sprott,
    and G. Nic Rider

Mental Health Practice with LGBTQ+ Children, Adolescents, and Emerging Adults in Multiple Systems of Care

Edited by

CRISTINA L. MAGALHÃES, PhD, LMHC
California School of Professional Psychology at Alliant International University

RICHARD A. SPROTT, PhD
California State University, East Bay

G. NIC RIDER, PhD, LP
Institute for Sexual and Gender Health at University of Minnesota Medical School

ROWMAN & LITTLEFIELD
Lanham • Boulder • New York • London

Executive Acquisitions Editor: Mark Kerr
Assistant Acquisitions Editor: Sarah Rinehart
Sales and Marketing Inquiries: textbooks@rowman.com

Credits and acknowledgments for material borrowed from other sources, and reproduced with permission, appear on the appropriate pages within the text.

Published by Rowman & Littlefield
An imprint of The Rowman & Littlefield Publishing Group, Inc.
4501 Forbes Boulevard, Suite 200, Lanham, Maryland 20706
www.rowman.com

86-90 Paul Street, London EC2A 4NE

Copyright © 2023 by The Rowman & Littlefield Publishing Group, Inc.

All rights reserved. No part of this book may be reproduced in any form or by any electronic or mechanical means, including information storage and retrieval systems, without written permission from the publisher, except by a reviewer who may quote passages in a review.

British Library Cataloguing in Publication Information Available

Library of Congress Cataloging-in-Publication Data

Names: Magalhães, Cristina L., 1966– editor. | Sprott, Richard A., 1965– editor. | Rider, G. Nic, 1983– editor.
Title: Mental health practice with LGBTQ+ children, adolescents, and emerging adults in multiple systems of care / edited by Cristina L. Magalhães, PhD, LMHC (California School of Professional Psychology at Alliant International University), Richard A. Sprott, PhD (California State University, East Bay), G. Nic Rider, PhD, LP (Institute for Sexual and Gender Health at University of Minnesota Medical School).
Description: Lanham : Rowman & Littlefield, [2023] | Series: Diverse sexualities, genders, and relationships | Includes bibliographical references and index.
Identifiers: LCCN 2022034532 (print) | LCCN 2022034533 (ebook) | ISBN 9781538154465 (cloth) | ISBN 9781538154472 (paperback) | ISBN 9781538154489 (epub)
Subjects: LCSH: Sexual minority children—Mental health services—United States. | Sexual minority youth—Mental health services—United States. | Transgender children—Mental health services—United States. | Transgender youth—Mental health services—United States. | Sexual minority children—Mental health—United States. | Sexual minority youth—Mental health—United States. | Transgender children—Mental health—United States. | Transgender youth—Mental health—United States.
Classification: LCC RJ507.S48 M34 2023 (print) | LCC RJ507.S48 (ebook) | DDC 362.2086/7—dc23/eng/20221007
LC record available at https://lccn.loc.gov/2022034532
LC ebook record available at https://lccn.loc.gov/2022034533

♾️™ The paper used in this publication meets the minimum requirements of American National Standard for Information Sciences—Permanence of Paper for Printed Library Materials, ANSI/NISO Z39.48-1992.

Brief Contents

Acknowledgments xix

Introduction: Health Disparities, Resilience, and Interdisciplinary Care for LGBTQ+ Youth and Emerging Adults 1
G. Nic Rider, PhD, LP, Cristina L. Magalhães, PhD, LMHC, & Richard A. Sprott, PhD

SECTION I: THEORETICAL APPROACHES

1   Minority Stress Theory and Resilience-Building Practice 11
    Eunice V. Avilés Faría, PsyD, LMHC, LPC
2   Intersectionality, Culturally Sensitive Care, and LGBTQ+ Youth 31
    *Kayden J. Schumacher, BA, MSc, MSEd, LSC,
    Leonardo E. Candelario-Pérez, PhD, LP,
    Eunice V. Avilés Faría, PsyD, LMHC, LPC, & G. Nic Rider, PhD, LP*
3   Interdisciplinary Healthcare for Transgender Youth: An Application of the Gender Affirmative Lifespan Approach (GALA) 41
    Katherine G. Spencer, PhD, LP, CST, & Nova Bradford, LGSW

SECTION II: DEVELOPMENTAL CONSIDERATIONS

4   The Youngest Part of the Rainbow: Clinical Care for Gender Diverse Children 65
    Dianne R. Berg, PhD, LP, Caroline Maykut, PhD*,
    Rachel Becker-Warner, PsyD, LP, Catherine Schaefer,
    MS, & Jennifer J. Connor, PhD, LMFT (*Co–First Authors)*
5   Risk and Protective Factors among LGBTQ+ Adolescents 95
    *Amy L. Gower, PhD, Marla E. Eisenberg, ScD, MPH, &
    G. Nic Rider, PhD, LP*
6   Not a Teen, Not Yet an Adult: Health Risk and Protective Factors among LGBTQ+ Emerging Adults 113
    *Caleb Esteban, PhD, Alixida Ramos-Pibernus, PhD,
    Luis X. Díaz-Medero, MS, & Astrid Irizarry-Rodríguez, MS*

SECTION III: SYSTEMS OF CARE

7   Pre-K–12 Schools   137
    Molly M. Strear, PhD, NCC, & Matthew J. Beck, PhD, LCPC, NCC, ACS
8   Serving LGBTQ+ Students at University and College Campuses   157
    Jan E. Estrellado, PhD, & Saeromi Kim, PhD
9   Medical Care Centers as Beacons of Hope for LGBTQ+ Youth   183
    *Hiram Rivera-Mercado, PsyD, Kevin Carrión, PsyD, &
    Taymy J. Caso, PhD*
10 Improving Child Welfare and Foster Care Outcomes for LGBTQ+ Youth   197
    Kellen Grayson, PsyD, LMFT, & Mira Krishnan, PhD, ABPP
11 LGBTQ+ Youth Experiencing Homelessness   211
    Catherine Forbes, PhD, Carrie Mounier, LCSW, & Kaitlin Venema, PhD
12 Gender Expansive and Sexual Minority Youth and the (In)Justice System   239
    Macy Wilson, PsyD, Jessica Ward, MA, & Roberto L. Abreu, PhD
13 Services for Youth and Emerging Adults at LGBTQ+ Centers and
    Other Community-Based Organizations   261
    Tangela Roberts, PhD, Zari Carpenter, MA, & Kat Schuette, MA
14 Independent Practice   285
    Gary Howell, PsyD, Arlene Noriega, PhD, & Julie Williams, MSEd, MA

Conclusion: Increasing Health and Well-Being of LGBTQ+ Youth
and Emerging Adults: Lessons Learned, Questions Unanswered   305
*Richard A. Sprott, PhD, G. Nic Rider, PhD, LP, &
Cristina L. Magalhães, PhD, LMHC*

Appendix: List of Resources   311

Bibliography   315

Index   377

About the Authors   399

Contents

Acknowledgments — xix

Introduction: Health Disparities, Resilience, and Interdisciplinary Care for LGBTQ+ Youth and Emerging Adults — 1
G. Nic Rider, PhD, LP, Cristina L. Magalhães, PhD, LMHC, & Richard A. Sprott, PhD
    Rationale for this Book — 2
    Target Audience — 2
    Useful Frameworks — 3
        Minority Stress Theory — 4
        Intersectionality Theory — 4
        Resilience-Based and Strength-Focused Approaches — 5
        Interdisciplinary and Whole-Person Approaches — 5
    Overview of the Book — 6
    Conclusion — 7
    References — 8

SECTION I: THEORETICAL APPROACHES

1 Minority Stress Theory and Resilience-Building Practice — 11
    Eunice V. Avilés Faría, PsyD, LMHC, LPC
    Author's Note — 11
    Minority Stress Theory — 11
    Minority Stress Processes — 12
    Minority Stress Processes and Transgender and Nonbinary Individuals — 12
        Distal Stressors — 13
        Proximal Stressors — 14
    The Impact of Minority Stress on Mental Health — 15
    The Impact of Minority Stress on Physical Health — 16
    Resilience — 17
        Individual Resilience — 17
        Community Resilience — 18

	Resilience-Building Practice: Interventions That Can Enhance Resilience	19
	Societal Level Interventions	19
	Community- and Group-Level Interventions	19
	Individual-Level Interventions (ILI)	19
	Empirical Support for the Minority Stress Model	21
	Gaps in the Literature and Future Directions for Clinically Relevant Research	21
	References	22
2	Intersectionality, Culturally Sensitive Care, and LGBTQ+ Youth	31
	Kayden J. Schumacher, BA, MSc, MSEd, LSC, Leonardo E. Candelario-Pérez, PhD, LP, Eunice V. Avilés Faría, PsyD, LMHC, LPC, & G. Nic Rider, PhD, LP	
	Practice Considerations	34
	Advocacy Considerations	35
	Conclusion	36
	References	37
3	Interdisciplinary Healthcare for Transgender Youth: An Application of the Gender Affirmative Lifespan Approach (GALA)	41
	Katherine G. Spencer, PhD, LP, CST, & Nova Bradford, LGSW	
	Introduction to Transgender Health	42
	History of Gender Affirmative Healthcare for Youth	43
	Minority Stress	44
	The Gender Affirmative Lifespan Approach (GALA)	45
	Philosophical Foundations of GALA	45
	Core Components of GALA	46
	Interdisciplinary Approach	47
	Connections to Medical Interventions	47
	Case Studies	48
	Case Study A: Research—Unicorn Youth	48
	Case Study B: Advocacy & Policy—Health Insurance Advocacy in Minnesota	50
	Case Study C: Clinical Example—Sexuality and Agency	52
	Case Study D: Youth Homelessness	54
	Conclusion	56
	Key Knowledge Points	56
	Recommendations for Professionals	57
	References	57

SECTION II: DEVELOPMENTAL CONSIDERATIONS

4	The Youngest Part of the Rainbow: Clinical Care for Gender Diverse Children	65
	Dianne R. Berg, PhD, LP*, Caroline Maykut, PhD*, Rachel Becker-Warner, PsyD, LP, Catherine Schaefer, MS, & Jennifer J. Connor, PhD, LMFT (*Co–First Authors)	

Social and Historical Context of Research with Gender Diverse Children	67
Gender Identity Development	68
Mental Health in Gender Diverse Children	70
Clinical Implications of Mental Health Research	72
Resilience in Gender Diverse Children	72
Interpersonal Contexts	73
Peer Group	73
Family	73
Community Contexts	74
Schools	74
Healthcare Settings	75
Medical Settings	75
Mental Health Settings	75
Case Study	77
Andi's Gender Journey	78
Sessions 1–3 Assessment: Age 4.11–5.0	79
Sessions 4–5 Feedback and Collaborative Treatment Planning with Parents Only: Age 5.1–5.2	79
Sessions 6–11 Early Therapy Process: Age 5.3–6.1	80
Sessions 12–16 Ongoing Therapeutic Process: Age 6.2–6.7	82
Sessions 17–24 Ongoing Therapeutic Process: Age 6.8–7.5	82
Sessions 24–35 Ongoing Therapeutic Process: Age 7.6–9.0	83
Sessions 36–44 Present Therapeutic Process: Age 9.3–10.5	84
Case Reflection	84
Future Directions	85
Key Knowledge Points	86
Recommendations for Practitioners and Professionals	87
References	88
5 Risk and Protective Factors among LGBTQ+ Adolescents	**95**
Amy L. Gower, PhD, Marla E. Eisenberg, ScD, MPH, & G. Nic Rider, PhD, LP	
Interpersonal Relationships	97
Friendships	97
Romantic Relationships	98
Parent/Family Relationships	99
The School Context	100
Community Support	101
Online/Internet Support	102
Developmental Considerations	103
Case Study	104
Practice Considerations	104
Conclusions	106
References	106

6	Not a Teen, Not Yet an Adult: Health Risk and Protective Factors among LGBTQ+ Emerging Adults *Caleb Esteban, PhD, Alixida Ramos-Pibernus, PhD,* *Luis X. Díaz-Medero, MS, & Astrid Irizarry-Rodríguez, MS*	113
	LGBTQ+ Emerging Adults	113
	Institutional Challenges	114
	Family	114
	College	114
	Religious Institutions	115
	Healthcare	115
	Government	116
	Interpersonal Challenges	116
	Relationships	116
	Marriage	116
	Peers	117
	Religious Affiliation	117
	Personal Challenges	118
	Physical Health	118
	HIV/STIs	119
	Healthcare	119
	Substance Abuse	119
	Mental Health	120
	Depression and Anxiety	120
	Suicide	120
	Protective Factors for LGBTQ+ Emerging Adults	121
	Resilience	121
	Social Support	122
	Community Engagement and Connectedness	123
	Gaps and Future Direction for Studies	124
	Clinical Implications	125
	Case Study	126
	Case Study Discussion	126
	Key Knowledge Points	127
	Recommendations for Mental Health Clinicians	128
	References	128

SECTION III: SYSTEMS OF CARE

7	Pre-K–12 Schools *Molly M. Strear, PhD, NCC, & Matthew J. Beck, PhD, LCPC, NCC, ACS*	137
	SBMHPs Working with LGBTQ+ Youth: Review of Literature	140
	School Counselors	140
	School Social Workers	141
	School Psychologists	142
	SBMHP Collaboration	142
	Recommendations for SBMHPs	143

Coordination of Services through MTSS		145
Tier 1—Universal Support		146
Tier 2—Supplemental Support		148
Tier 3—Intensified Support		149
Family/Community Engagement		150
Implications and Future Directions		151
Conclusion		152
Key Knowledge for Students		152
Recommendations for Practitioners and Professionals		153
References		153

8 Serving LGBTQ+ Students at University and College Campuses ... 157
Jan E. Estrellado, PhD, & Saeromi Kim, PhD

Challenges Facing LGBTQ+ College Students	157
Mental Health Disparities	157
Identity Development as a Major Task of Late Adolescence and Emerging Adulthood	158
Acceptance and Visibility of LGBTQ+ Students on Campus	159
Intersectionality and Marginalized Identities	160
The Need for Affirming LGBTQ+ College Student Services	161
Student Support Services	161
Relationships with Faculty	162
Relationships with Peers	163
Health Services on Campus	164
Gaps in Research	165
First-Generation Students	165
Bisexual and Fluid Students	166
Transgender, Nonbinary, and Gender Expansive (TNBGE) Students	166
STEM Students	167
Immigration Status	167
International Students	168
Clinical and Policy Recommendations When Working with LGBTQ+ College Students	168
University or College Counseling Centers	168
Coming Out	169
Language	171
Complexity of Identities	171
Depathologizing Symptoms	172
Advocacy	172
Policy Recommendations	173
Data Collection	173
Institutional Policies	173
Feedback Loops	173
Inclusivity	174
Dialogue Spaces	174
Intersectionality	174

	Community LGBTQ+ Services	174
	Community Colleges	174
	Protective Factors	175
	Health Providers	175
	Counseling Centers	175
	Academic and Career Advisors	175
	Conclusion	175
	Key Knowledge Points	176
	Recommendations for Practitioners	176
	References	176
9	Medical Care Centers as Beacons of Hope for LGBTQ+ Youth	183
	Hiram Rivera-Mercado, PsyD, Kevin Carrión, PsyD,	
	& Taymy J. Caso, PhD	
	Role of Hospitals in Serving LGBTQ+ Youth and Emerging Adults	184
	Some Services Included	184
	Primary Care	184
	Pediatric Endocrinologist	185
	Behavioral Health and Mental Health Services	186
	Obstetrics and Gynecology	187
	Policies and Their Function	188
	Training of Personnel	189
	Community Partnerships and Resources	190
	Creating a Welcoming Environment	191
	Physical Environment	191
	Registration and Documentation Processes	192
	Language and Communication	192
	Conclusion	193
	References	193
10	Improving Child Welfare and Foster Care Outcomes for LGBTQ+ Youth	197
	Kellen Grayson, PsyD, LMFT, & Mira Krishnan, PhD, ABPP	
	Family Rejection, Abuse, and Homophobia	198
	LGBTQ+ Youth and Polyvictimization	199
	Poverty and LGBTQ+ Youth Vulnerability	200
	Overrepresentation of LGBTQ+ Youth in Child Welfare Services	201
	The State of Foster Care and Child Welfare Systems	201
	Policies and Practices in Child Welfare Services	201
	Training and Oversight of Foster Parents and Child Welfare Workers	203
	Gaps in Care	203
	Transition-Age Youth	203
	The Landscape for Change	204
	Religious Freedom Restoration Acts and Child Welfare	205
	Considerations for Clinicians	205
	Conclusion	206
	References	207

11 LGBTQ+ Youth Experiencing Homelessness 211
    Catherine Forbes, PhD, Carrie Mounier, LCSW, & Kaitlin Venema, PhD
    Literature Review and Gaps in Research: LGBTQ+ Youth
        Experiencing Homelessness 211
    Figure 11.1. Risk Factors for Homelessness Shared with Cisgender/
    Heterosexual Youth and Unique for LGBTQ+ Youth 213
    Clinical Considerations and Recommendations for Practice
        in Mental Health and Substance Abuse Treatment 215
            Trauma-Informed Care 216
            Interdisciplinary Programs for LGBTQ+ YEH 218
            Evidenced-Based LGBTQ+-Affirming Therapeutic Services 219
            Group Therapy Approaches 220
            Alternative Programming for LGBTQ+ YEH 221
            Medical Interventions 221
    Structural Competency and Service Systems for LGBTQ+ YEH 222
    Impact of Structures on Patient Health 224
            Influence of Structures on the Clinical Encounter 225
            Respond to Structures in the Clinic 226
            Respond to Structures beyond the Clinic 227
            Structural Humility 228
    Practice and Policy Recommendations 228
            Healing-Centered Engagement and Structural Violence 228
            Restorative Justice and Structural Violence 229
            Positive Youth Development and Structural Violence 230
            Harm Reduction and Structural Violence 230
    Gaps and Future Directions 231
    References 232

12 Gender Expansive and Sexual Minority Youth and the (In)Justice System 239
    Macy Wilson, PsyD, Jessica Ward, MA, & Roberto L. Abreu, PhD
    Incidence and Prevalence 239
    Risk Factors 239
    School-to-Prison Pipeline 240
    "No Promo Homo" Laws and a Heterosexual-Cisgender
        School-Based Curriculum 241
    A Failed Welfare System 242
    The (Il)legal System 242
        Disproportionate Representation 242
        Unequal Injustice 243
        Gender Differences 243
        Youth of Color 244
        Microaggressions 244
        Mediating Factors 245
    Mental Health Behaviors While Incarcerated 245
        Self-Harming Behaviors 246
        Aggression toward Others 247

	Toward a Socially Just System: Ensuring Safety for LGBTQ+ Youth	249
	Incorporating a Holistic Approach to Care	250
	Constitutional Rights	252
	Legal Rights of LGBTQ+ Youth in the Justice System	253
	Recommendations	254
	Key Knowledge Points	256
	References	256
13	Services for Youth and Emerging Adults at LGBTQ+ Centers and Other Community-Based Organizations	261
	Tangela Roberts, PhD, Zari Carpenter, MA, & Kat Schuette, MA	
	Authors' Note	261
	LGBTQ+ Youth and Emerging Adults of Color	262
	Transgender and Gender-Nonconforming (TGNC) Youth and Emerging Adults	262
	Challenges for LGBTQ+ Youth and Emerging Adults	263
	Health Care Challenges	263
	Mental Health	263
	Sexual Health	264
	Interpersonal Challenges	264
	Coming Out	264
	Building Community	266
	Dating and Relationships	267
	Intimate Partner Violence	268
	Vocational Challenges	269
	Career Development	269
	Employment Discrimination	269
	Workplace Identity Management	270
	Method	270
	Sample of LGBTQ+ Community Centers	271
	Table 13.1: Number of LGBTQ+ Community Centers in the United States by State	272
	Results	273
	Physical Health Services	273
	Mental Health Services	274
	Services for Queer Youth and Emerging Adults of Color (QYAOC)	274
	Services for Transgender and Gender-Nonconforming (TGNC) Youth and Emerging Adults	275
	Emotional Support	275
	Social Support	275
	Services Related to the Provision of Basic Needs	275
	Housing Stability	275
	Food Insecurity	276
	Services Related to Educational and Vocational Assistance	276
	Auxiliary Services	276
	Discussion	277

Areas of Improvement in Serving LGBTQ+ Youth		
and Emerging Adults		277
Availability of Services by Geographical Region		277
Access to LGBTQ+ Community Centers		277
LGBTQ+ Youth and Emerging Adults of Color		278
Considerations for Clinical Practice		278
Policy Recommendations		279
References		279
14	Independent Practice	285
	Gary Howell, PsyD, Arlene Noriega, PhD, & Julie Williams, MSEd, MA	
	Independent Practice	285
	Solo Practices	285
	Group Practices	286
	Integrated Practices	286
	Nuances with LGBTQ+ Affirmative Practices	287
	Consultative Roles	288
	Barriers to Care	288
	Healthcare Disparities	289
	Sociopolitical Factors	289
	Social Determinants of Care	290
	Eliminating Barriers to Care	290
	Cultural Competence	291
	Intersectional Approach	292
	Centering Marginalized Voices	292
	Advocacy	293
	Integrated Approach	293
	Impact of the Affordable Care Act	294
	Impact of COVID	294
	Successes	296
	Challenges	296
	Research Gaps and Future Directions	297
	Considerations for Practice	298
	Key Knowledge Points	298
	Recommendations for Practitioners	299
	References	299

Conclusion: Increasing Health and Well-Being of LGBTQ+ Youth and
Emerging Adults: Lessons Learned, Questions Unanswered   305
Richard A. Sprott, PhD, G. Nic Rider, PhD, LP, & Cristina L. Magalhães, PhD, LMHC

Summary of Findings and Lessons	305
A Possible Agenda for Research, Clinical Treatment, and Policy	307
More Resources and Funding	307
Train Mental Health Providers	307
Systems-Based Approach Refinement	308

Summary	308
Reference	309
Appendix: List of Resources	311
Bibliograpy	315
Index	377
About the Authors	399

Acknowledgments

Cristina L. Magalhães, PhD, LMHC, Richard A. Sprott, PhD, & G. Nic Rider, PhD, LP

The idea of this book originated in 2019, in conversations among members of the Committee on Children, Youth, and Families of Division 44 (the Society for the Psychology of Sexual Orientation and Gender Diversity) of the American Psychological Association. The group had been working on several initiatives, so writing a book seemed like a natural extension of the tasks we wanted to accomplish to further the mission of the committee and of the division. Since that time, much has changed locally and globally. We have experienced a COVID-19 pandemic, have seen social uprising and mobilizing in response to police violence and murders in local communities, and are witnessing an intense new wave of anti-LGBTQ+ legislation that threatens the civil rights of LGBTQ+ people and families in many parts of the United States. This last development has heightened the need for professionals to urgently fill in gaps in the literature and to document current challenges and best practices for working with LGBTQ+ children, adolescents, and emerging adults, who have been especially targeted in the culture wars of our times. For this reason, we believe this book is timely, and we hope it will serve to support the training of mental health professionals who want to work with this incredibly rewarding and underserved population.

This book could not have been written without the support, collaboration, and shared enthusiasm of several people. We start with acknowledging our ancestors and elders who paved the way for us to do this work and the young people who are the focus of this book, as they give us hope for the future. We also want to note a few names here but recognize that many others not mentioned have also contributed in meaningful ways. First, we acknowledge Dr. Roberto Abreu and Dr. Jillian Scheer for providing conceptual insights and practical suggestions that helped consolidate our ideas for the book proposal. We also acknowledge the Committee on Children, Youth, and Families of Division 44, which provided a "home base" for us to collaborate, organize symposia presentations on topics addressed in the book, and connect with national experts within the American Psychological Association. We thank Mark Kerr at Rowman & Littlefield for believing in our vision, sharing our conviction in the importance of this work, offering encouragement to keep us moving along, and providing much needed guidance in the publication process. We also acknowledge all chapter authors for their dedication and commitment to this project and for producing great writing while tending to personal and family needs and the demands of a busy work life during unprecedented times. We express much gratitude for their willingness to share their expertise with all of us. We learned so much from them, and without their dedication, this book would not have been possible. We are excited to share the co-authorship of this book with such an incredible community of dedicated mental health professionals who are not only competent in their areas of expertise but also so passionate and inspiring. Lastly, we acknowledge our life partners, families, and friends who supported us along this journey. Their love and encouragement nourished us daily.

Introduction

HEALTH DISPARITIES, RESILIENCE, AND INTERDISCIPLINARY CARE FOR LGBTQ+ YOUTH AND EMERGING ADULTS

G. Nic Rider, PhD, LP, Cristina L. Magalhães, PhD, LMHC, & Richard A. Sprott, PhD

Casey is a 17-year-old Asian American who, along with a twin sibling and their mother, has been unstable in housing for the past year due to the economic downturn related to the COVID-19 pandemic. Casey is pansexual, meaning that for them, they are emotionally, physically, romantically, and sexually attracted to people of all gender identities and expressions. They are also nonbinary, meaning that they don't identify exclusively as a man or a woman. School has not felt safe, and Casey receives no affirmation for their sexual and gender identity from their mother. Casey has been spending time at the LGBT center in their community, which has become a safe space for them. A teen group facilitator reports that Casey has discussed nonsuicidal self-injurious behaviors in the group support meetings, and the facilitator has suggested that Casey seek mental health care. This teen group facilitator is the only person who has suggested mental health care to Casey within the various microsystem contexts where Casey spends their time. Casey is reluctant and wary but approaches a psychologist who provides care through the LGBT center. Casey doesn't want anyone from the center to contact their mother.

- How can mental health professionals address the needs of this adolescent?
- What sociocultural and institutional factors need to be taken into consideration with this case example?
- Working within the center's policies, limitations, and obligations, what are the challenges to providing effective and culturally responsive care to this adolescent? What can be done about such policies?

The above case example presents some clinical and ethical considerations that need to be addressed by care providers and is also not an uncommon scenario for many clinicians. The multiple systems of care accessed or experienced by Casey and their family are mostly siloed and function separately, but their cumulative neglect and missed opportunities for coordination can have a negative effect on Casey's health and well-being. Casey may be experiencing family rejection/lack of support (Mother does not affirm their identities), exposed to intersectional stigma-based bullying at school (given they don't feel safe at school), navigating housing instability and anti-Asian harassment, feeling complex emotions about the sociopolitical climate (due to multiple anti-LGBTQ+ policies), and learning to manage stigma related to accessing mental health services. Casey also demonstrates resilience by finding support through a community-based organization where they feel safe, likely have been able to self-define their identities, and likely have found a sense of belonging.

Rationale for this Book

The overall purpose of this book is to support the training of mental health professionals who work with LGBTQ+ children, adolescents, and emerging adults within different systems of care, and to emphasize the importance of integrated care when working with LGBTQ+ young persons in these contexts. Other books have also addressed the topic, at least in part. When we began thinking about starting this writing project, we looked for training resources to see what was available and found approximately 44 books and resources that focused on health disparities for LGBTQ+ populations. Twenty of these books addressed health and healthcare for elderly LGBTQ+ individuals specifically; and the remaining 24 books that addressed the subject of LGBTQ+ health disparities had only a small section, or sometimes one chapter, on LGBTQ+ youth and emerging adults. We also noted most of these books addressed the topic from a public health perspective with little attention paid to psychological science, and not all of them touched on issues related to mental health practice in more than a cursory way. Few provided practice-relevant information that could serve to support care delivery. Thus, our examination of the literature gave us the impression that health disparities and related issues impacting LGBTQ+ children, adolescents, and emerging adults were getting some attention in the field; however, going beyond the surface impression, we found there was a dearth of discussion about issues that are directly relevant to mental healthcare providers who work with LGBTQ+ children, adolescents, and emerging adults specifically. Since then, a few books about young LGBTQ+ populations have been published targeting mental health professionals, but greater attention has been given to transgender and gender diverse youth compared to other groups under the larger LGBTQ+ umbrella. This book speaks to mental health professionals about important matters that impact care delivery for all groups of young LGBTQ+ persons seeking care in a range of health service settings.

Target Audience

The primary target audience for this book are mental health professionals at any stage of their career who want to expand their knowledge base and improve their skill level for working effectively with LGBTQ+ children, adolescents, and emerging adults. Mental health clinicians in training at the master's or doctoral level may find the book especially helpful since the initial chapters focus on describing foundational principles of clinical practice, while the remaining chapters focus on describing how these principles can be applied in a range of settings. Specifically, when we developed a proposal for this book, we envisioned a volume that could be used to support the training of graduate and post-graduate students who are taking a clinical elective in LGBTQ+ mental health or a similar topic; those who are completing a practicum rotation, internship, or post-doctoral training at a site that serves young LGBTQ+ clients; those who are conducting translational research on clinical issues with the goal of improving care for young LGBTQ+ individuals and families; or those who are seeking to expand knowledge of gender and sexual diversity on their own to improve multicultural competencies more broadly. Psychology instructors teaching undergraduate courses in sexuality, gender and women studies, transgender studies, LGBTQ psychology, human diversity, human development, clinical or counseling psychology, and other related topics will find throughout the book thought-provoking material that can inspire their students to pursue a career in mental health.

Children, adolescents, and emerging adults who identify as LGBTQ+ are seeking care in a variety of clinical settings and have become increasingly more visible to service providers in recent years. As educators, we also have seen an increased demand for LGBTQ+ training in recent years, which is very exciting to us, as this suggests more clinicians are recognizing the need for specialized training in LGBTQ+ mental health. While graduate-level LGBTQ+ electives we taught in the past attracted primarily LGBTQ+ students interested in learning how to better serve their own communities, they are now filled with students who have very little experiential knowledge of the community, and those who are eager to learn how to effectively engage clinically with LGBTQ+ individuals and families and how to competently address issues they know little about aside from tidbits of information they acquire via mass media. We've also experienced an increased demand for post-graduate training for mental health professionals with master's and doctoral degrees seeking certification in LGBTQ+ mental health to better serve their clients. Their willingness to seek additional training at the post-graduate level illustrates the point made earlier about increased recognition that specialized training is indeed needed for competent care.

Useful Frameworks

It is in this spirit, thinking how we can best help entry-level and seasoned mental health clinicians strengthen their skills for working with young LGBTQ+ clients and their families, that we developed this book and organized its content. We begin with a review of relevant frameworks that experts in LGBTQ+ mental health find useful for conceptualizing the clinical work they do with LGBTQ+ children, adolescents, and emerging adults before we introduce chapters that focus on more applied content. This review is not meant to be comprehensive or representative of the entire breadth of frameworks that can be applied effectively to the work of clinicians whose clients are LGBTQ+ children, adolescents, and emerging adults. Our purpose is to offer a place of departure for clinicians where there is consensus among experts; a beginning strategy grounded in principles that are theoretically sound and empirically supported by literature. Assuming clinicians are already familiar with the concept of "affirmative care," which we do not explicitly cover, we note that it is also foundational in the field of LGBTQ+ mental health and described in many other excellent texts.

MINORITY STRESS THEORY

Since first introduced in the literature (Brooks, 1981), the concept of minority stress has become a widely adopted framework for understanding the impact of sociocultural factors in the lives of LGBTQ+ individuals and their families (Meyer, 1995, 2003; Testa et al., 2015). Minority stress is linked to a host of poor outcomes for LGBTQ+ people of all ages (e.g., high rates of behavioral and emotional problems, psychiatric disorders, poor overall health, low academic achievement, unemployment, homelessness), and a large body of empirical literature supports this assertion (see chapter 1). The book starts here, describing minority stress theory, to help clinicians understand the range of contextual factors that can make LGBTQ+ individuals more vulnerable to psychological distress and at risk for developing a host of diagnosable mental health conditions that require targeted intervention. Minority stress theory principles are especially important for clinicians to grasp because the theories of personality and psychotherapy most clinicians are trained to use in case conceptualization and treatment tend to overemphasize the role of intrapersonal factors over external factors in the development and maintenance of behavioral problems, emotional distress, and psychiatric disorders. Minority stress theory doesn't negate the importance of attending to intrapersonal dynamics in clinical assessment and psychotherapy but stresses that there are contextual roadblocks for clients that are external to them and difficult to overcome. These need to be acknowledged first when working with young LGBTQ+ clients and their families.

INTERSECTIONALITY THEORY

The book also calls attention to intersectionality theory as an important framework for clinicians who deliver care to LGBTQ+ children, adolescents, and emerging adults (see chapter 2). It is not uncommon for clinicians unfamiliar with the LGBTQ+ community to assume that certain issues that impact the community at large (such as prejudice, discrimination, and marginalization) affect all LGBTQ+ individuals and families equally, which is not the case. The LGBTQ+ community is composed of people of all genders, ages, sizes, races, ethnicities, socioeconomic backgrounds, immigration statuses, ability statuses, religious backgrounds, and all other factors used to describe a person's identity or status in society (Bowleg, 2012; Aguayo-Romero, 2021). LGBTQ+ people with multiple marginalized identities or statuses are exposed to different combinations of minority stressors, and through exposure to intersectional stigma and discrimination, they have differing access to resources and supportive, affirming networks (Salerno et al., 2020). There is consensus in the field regarding the importance of diversity training for clinicians, and intersectionality theory has become an essential part of the diversity training curriculum. Clinicians who take the time to understand the constellation of sociodemographic factors, cultural backgrounds, and life experiences that impact each of their clients' uniquely—and use that understanding to craft individualized treatment plans that account for those factors and experiences—are more likely to be successful in developing therapeutic relationships that lead to positive clinical outcomes for young LGBTQ+ clients and their families.

RESILIENCE-BASED AND STRENGTH-FOCUSED APPROACHES

The book also highlights contemporary frameworks in mental health that are resilience-based and strength-focused (as opposed to problem-focused or disease-focused), as there seems to be consensus in the field among clinicians that many clients respond well to interventions that are geared toward accentuating positives, amplifying strategies that worked for the client in the past, and building new capacities for better coping. Encouraging health-promoting behaviors the client already engages in, supporting the pursuit of natural interests and activities that the client enjoys and that are life-enhancing, nurturing positive self-talk as means to manage distressing emotions, and helping the client build or expand existing support systems are examples of resilience-based and strength-focused interventions many clinicians use in their practice, regardless of the clinical population they treat. Grounded in principles of positive psychology (Rashid, 2015), we find this approach especially relevant for working with LGBTQ+ children, adolescents, and emerging adults because it helps counteract the negative impact of social stigma associated with marginalized sexual and gender identities on the young person's developing sense of self.

INTERDISCIPLINARY AND WHOLE-PERSON APPROACHES

The book also stresses the importance of adopting an interdisciplinary (aka interprofessional) approach to care when working with LGBTQ+ children, adolescents, and emerging adults (Bidell & Stepleman, 2017). While the relevance of this approach is clear to mental health clinicians who provide specialized gender care to transgender and nonbinary clients (McIntosh, 2016), and to those who work in health care settings where interprofessional collaborations are common (American Psychological Association, 2013), we argue that a whole-person, holistic approach to care that involves referring to, consulting with, and or working alongside professionals from other disciplines is essential for supporting the healthy development of all young LGBTQ+ clients across physical, cognitive, and socio-emotional domains, and no matter where services are sought. From a case conceptualization perspective, adopting a whole-person approach to care as a mental health clinician is about remaining attuned to the fact that mind and body are not separate entities, that psychological and physical wellness are interdependent (e.g., dietary considerations are important in the treatment of anxiety, physical exercise is important in the treatment of depression, adequate sleep is important for optimal cognitive performance), and that clinicians better serve their clients when they participate in formal or informal care teams for improved coordination of services. Chapter authors provide illustrations for how interdisciplinary and whole-person approaches can be applied to the care of young LGBTQ+ clients in a range of settings.

Overview of the Book

This book is unique in bringing together three approaches to the topic, which we organized under three different sections: (1) overview of relevant and productive theoretical frameworks that support the delivery of culturally sensitive and effective clinical services to LGBTQ+ children, adolescents, and emerging adults; (2) overview of issues that are common among LGBTQ+ youth at three developmental stages (children, adolescents, and emerging adults); and (3) overview of issues and information relevant to particular agency/organizational contexts where mental health clinicians are likely to interact with LGBTQ+ children, adolescents, and emerging adults.

In section I, the first chapter by Eunice V. Avilés Faría, "Minority Stress Theory and Resilience-Building Practice," reviews the roots and the scope of minoritized stress theory, which is an expansion of the social stress theory applied to minority groups that have been marginalized by mainstream societies. The second chapter, by Kayden J. Schumacher, Leonardo E. Candelario-Pérez, Eunice V. Avilés Faría, and G. Nic Rider, "Intersectionality, Culturally Sensitive Care, and LGBTQ+ Youth," examines how systems of care are part of an interlocking system of oppression and privilege, affecting the health of people who have multiple marginalized identities. The third chapter, "Interdisciplinary Healthcare for Transgender Youth," by Katherine G. Spencer and Nova Bradford, discusses approaches that integrate mental and medical health by providing an extended example of whole-person, holistic care for transgender youth.

The second section discusses considerations for working with LGBTQ+ persons at three different stages of development: childhood, adolescence, and emerging adulthood. Chapter 4, "The Youngest Part of the Rainbow," by Dianne R. Berg, Caroline Maykut, Rachel Becker-Warner, Catherine Schaefer, and Jennifer J. Connor, articulates contemporary theories about gender identity development and highlights mental health issues facing gender diverse children. Chapter 5, "Risk and Protective Factors among LGBTQ+ Adolescents," by Amy L. Gower, Marla E. Eisenberg, and G. Nic Rider, addresses the development of LGBTQ+ adolescents with a special emphasis on radical healing. The last chapter in section II (chapter 6), "Not a Teen, Not Yet an Adult," by Caleb Esteban, Alixida Ramos-Pibernus, Luis X. Diaz-Medero, and Astrid Irizarry-Rodríguez, examines the interpersonal and institutional struggles that confront LGBTQ+ emerging adults and their effects on mental health.

Section III presents a series of chapters that each focus on a particular system of care as the context for mental healthcare practice. Molly M. Strear and Matthew J. Beck address issues that are relevant to clinicians working with LGBTQ+ children and youth in "Pre-K–12 Schools" (chapter 7), and Jan E. Estrellado and Saeromi Kim examine issues for emerging adults in the context of higher education in a chapter titled "Serving LGBTQ+ Students at University and College Campuses" (chapter 8). In chapter 9, by Hiram Rivera-Mercado, Kevin Carrión, and Taymy J. Caso, "Medical Care Centers as Beacons of Hope for LGBTQ+ Youth," special attention is paid to interdisciplinary care in medical healthcare settings. Mental healthcare practice in the context of the foster care system is the focus of chapter 10, "Improving Child Welfare and Foster Care Outcomes for LGBTQ+ Youth," by Kellen Grayson and Mira Krishnan. Chapter 11, "LGBTQ+ Youth Experiencing Homelessness," by Catherine Forbes, Carrie Mounier, and Kaitlin Venema, addresses the range of mental health issues in a system that is not generally affirming of LGBTQ+ populations but where LGBTQ+ youth are overrepresented. Macy Wilson, Jessica Ward, and Roberto L. Abreu provide an overview of care in the context of detention centers and the juvenile justice system, with an analysis of the school-to-prison pipeline and particular mental health issues that get exacerbated by involvement in these systems for LGBTQ+ youth and emerging adults (chapter 12, "Gender Expansive and Sexual Minority Youth and the (In)Justice System"). Chapter 13, "Services for Youth and Emerging Adults at LGBTQ+ Centers and Other Community-Based Organizations," by Tangela Roberts, Zari Carpenter, and Kat Schuette, examines a range of issues addressed by community centers when serving LGBTQ+ youth and emerging adults, including vocational issues, mental health challenges, and physical health. The last chapter in this section (chapter 14), "Independent Practice," by Gary Howell, Arlene Noriega, and Julie Williams, discusses issues relevant to mental health practitioners who have a practice outside of a system of care but interact with a number of these systems as they provide care to their LGBTQ+ adolescent and emerging-adult clients.

In our conclusion, we provide an overview of the main points articulated in the book and highlight gaps and needed steps in the development of the field. Challenges in both theory and practice face our field as we attempt to provide high-quality mental health services for LGBTQ+ children, adolescents, and emerging adults.

Conclusion

We intend this book to address the needs of mental health clinicians and clinicians-in-training for knowledge and practical strategies for working effectively with LGBTQ+ children, adolescents, and emerging adults wherever they are being served, across multiple systems of care. It is our hope that this book will help improve the delivery of integrated care to young LGBTQ+ persons by encouraging clinicians to adopt a strengths-based, holistic approach to treatment that will promote the optimum health and well-being of young clients across all domains of human development (socioemotional, cognitive, and physical). We also intend this book to impress upon clinicians the importance of adopting an intersectional lens in case conceptualization and of recognizing the impact of multiple levels of minority stress on individuals and families. We hope you will get as much from reading this book as we have learned from working with all clinicians who contributed a chapter. Their expertise has enriched our clinical practice and our teaching of graduate students in mental health fields.

References

Aguayo-Romero, R. A. (2021). (Re)centering black feminism into intersectionality research. *American Journal of Public Health, 111*(1), 101–103. https://doi.org/10.2105/AJPH.2020.306005

American Psychological Association. (2013). Guidelines for psychological practice in health care delivery systems. *American Psychologist, 68*(1), 1–6. https://www.apa.org/pubs/journals/features/delivery-systems.pdf

Bidell, M. P., & Stepleman, L. M. (2017). An interdisciplinary approach to lesbian, gay, bisexual, and transgender clinical competence, professional training, and ethical care: Introduction to the special issue. *Journal of Homosexuality, 64*(10), 1305–1329. https://doi.org/10.1080/00918369.2017.1321360

Bowleg, L. (2012). The problem with the phrase women and minorities: Intersectionality—an important theoretical framework for public health. *American Journal of Public Health, 102*(7), 1267–1273. https://doi.org/10.2105/AJPH.2012.300750

Brooks, V. R. (1981). *Minority stress and lesbian women*. Lexington Books.

McIntosh, C. A. (2016). Interdisciplinary care for transgender patients. In K. L. Eckstrand & J. M. Ehrenfeld (Eds.), *Lesbian, gay, bisexual, and transgender healthcare* (pp. 339–350). Springer Cham. https://doi.org/10.1007/978-3-319-19752-4_18

Meyer, I. H. (1995). Minority stress and mental health in gay men. *Journal of Health and Social Behavior, 36*(1), 38–56. https://doi.org/10.2307/2137286

Meyer, I. H. (2003). Prejudice, social stress, and mental health in lesbian, gay, and bisexual populations: Conceptual issues and research evidence. *Psychological Bulletin, 129*(5), 674–697. https://doi.org/10.1037/0033-2909.129.5.674

Rashid, T. (2015). Positive psychotherapy: A strength-based approach. *Journal of Positive Psychology, 10*(1), 25–40. https://doi.org/10.1080/17439760.2014.920411

Salerno, J. P., Devadas, J., Pease, M., Nketia, B., & Fish, J. N. (2020). Sexual and gender minority stress amid the COVID-19 pandemic: Implications for LGBTQ young persons' mental health and well-being. *Public Health Reports, 135*(6), 721–727. https://doi.org/10.1177/0033354920954511

Testa, R. J., Habarth, J., Peta, J., Balsam, K., & Bockting, W. (2015). Development of the gender minority stress and resilience measure. *Psychology of Sexual Orientation and Gender Diversity, 2*(1), 65–77. https://doi.org/10.1037/sgd0000081

Section I
THEORETICAL APPROACHES

CHAPTER 1

Minority Stress Theory and Resilience-Building Practice

Eunice V. Avilés Faría, PsyD, LMHC, LPC

Author's Note

The concept "minority" is part of the theoretical framework used in this chapter as a basis for competent interventions. I recognize the social evolution of language and the importance of using concepts such as marginalized, underrepresented, or underserved to depict the reality of oppression and discrimination.

Minority Stress Theory

The minority stress framework proposes that, given their social and minority status, individuals who are part of stigmatized groups are subjected to additional stressors beyond those experienced by people who belong to dominant groups (Brooks, 1981; Meyer, 1995, 2003). In her book, *Minority Stress and Lesbian Women*, Brooks (1981) conceptualized minority stress as the chronic stressors that individuals face due to the cultural designation of certain groups as being of lesser status and defective based on their sexual orientation, race, or other traits. These stressors are a result of systematic prejudice and inequality imposed by the dominant culture (Brooks, 1981), which, through political and economic power, imposes its values and behavioral norms on the subordinate culture (Scott & Marshall, 2009). Consequently, the dominant culture devalues and marginalizes those who deviate from their cultural expectations. What has been conceptualized as "minority stress," therefore, occurs because of the adverse events and experiences that stigmatized individuals encounter in society (Meyer, 1995).

The minority stress model was further developed by Ilan H. Meyer, creating a foundation for evaluating evidence-based research and for the development of recommendations, interventions, and policies regarding LGB individuals (Meyer, 2003; Meyer & Frost, 2013). Currently, the minority stress model assists with understanding the high prevalence of mental health and medical issues among LGBTQ+ individuals (Meyer et al., 2021; Poteat et al., 2021).

Minority Stress Processes

Meyer (2003) described minority stress processes as a continuum that considers how external social events and social structures affect the individual. The continuum encompasses "distal stressors," described as "objective events" and circumstances beyond the individual, such as life experiences and negative social attitudes expressed by others (Meyer 2003, p. 5; Meyer, 2015). It also includes "proximal personal processes," defined as "subjective" because these depend on the person's evaluation of the stressor (Meyer, 2003, p. 5). Distal stressors can turn into proximal personal stressors and, consequently, affect important aspects of the individual's psychological experience. This can happen through socialization and cognitive appraisal (Meyer, 2003; Meyer, 2015), a process through which an individual evaluates the reason and the degree to which interactions with the environment cause stress (Lazarus & Folkman, 1984). Given the subjective nature of the proximal stressors, they can be linked to the individual's identity with regard to their sexual orientation and gender (Meyer, 2003; Meyer, 2015).

From distal to proximal, the minority stress processes in LGB populations include: (a) enacted stigma, events that are acute and chronic, such as discrimination, violence, and other external stressful events; (b) expectation or anticipation of rejection, discrimination and violence, or felt stigma, and the experience of vigilance due to such anticipation; (c) internalized homophobia, the internalization of society's negative attitudes about one's sexual orientation; and (d) concealment of the sexual orientation (Gray, 2002; Meyer, 1995; Meyer, 2003; Meyer, 2015).

Minority Stress Processes and Transgender and Nonbinary Individuals

The minority stress model (Meyer, 2003) applied to the experiences of transgender and nonbinary individuals holds some parallels with previous versions that focused on sexual minorities. For instance, it incorporates the notion of distal and proximal stressors and acknowledges the impact of stressful events on the individual's mental and physical health (Hendricks & Testa, 2012; Poteat et al., 2021). Distinctly, to describe the experiences of this part of the LGBTQ+ community, it integrates the unique issues encountered by gender diverse individuals.

"Nonaffirmation" was proposed as a distal stressor to describe the experience of one's gender identity not being affirmed or validated by others (Testa et al., 2015). Internalized transphobia (i.e., the internalization of society's negative attitudes about one's gender identity) was incorporated as a proximal stressor (Hendricks & Testa, 2012). Three specific aspects of gender identity concealment were also described. First, given the fact that gender is frequently and visibly communicated through physical characteristics (i.e., the shape of the body), the decision to reveal the gender identity can be partly motivated by aspects such as genetic traits, the developmental stage when the person began their gender affirmation, the gender affirmation stage, and the person's access to health care services. Second, under some circumstances, there isn't an option not to disclose the gender identity. Third, disclosure or concealment of the gender identity can shift dramatically throughout the process of social and medical gender affirmation. For example, before the social and/or medical affirmation, the person will have to decide if they will reveal their gender identity. After social and/or medical affirmation, the person will have to determine if they will disclose or not their sex assigned at birth to those around them (Testa et al., 2015).

DISTAL STRESSORS

LGBTQ+ individuals around the world experience a host of stressful events, including life-threatening experiences, and are frequently invisible to social institutions (Herek et al., 2012; Lee & Ostergard, 2017). Interpersonal and structural stigma, discrimination and violence, rejection, anti-LGBTQ+ political environment, and negative religious messages are some of the distal stressors experienced by LGBTQ+ individuals of all ages (Felner et al., 2020; Hafeez et al., 2017; Schmitz, Robinson, & Sanchez, 2020).

LGBTQ+ individuals can experience stress from diverse sources, especially those that have multiple minority statuses (i.e., sexual orientation, gender identity, and race) (Wong et al., 2014). Intersecting minority statuses can determine distinct stigma and discrimination experiences. Systemic racism, white privilege, and white supremacy can intersect with transphobia and/or homophobia and increase the individual's risk of exposure to prejudice and violence. For example, given their race, the experience of discrimination will be different for a Black gay man when compared to a white gay man (McConnell et al., 2018).

Young LGBTQ+ individuals, and specially LGBTQ+ youth of color and those who do not conform to social norms regarding gender expression, are uniquely impacted by distal stressors. Stigma, discrimination, and violence coming from peers, disparities in the health care system, as well as rejection from the family are some of the stressors experienced by young LGBTQ+ individuals (Hafeez et al., 2017; Klemmer et at., 2021). Young LGB individuals, particularly girls and young women of color, are overrepresented in correctional facilities and are more often victims of sexual assault than their heterosexual peers (Wilson et al., 2017). Younger transgender individuals who disclose their gender identity are more vulnerable to experiencing physical violence at home or to become homeless (Lombardi et al., 2001).

Social approval and cultural insertion of sexual minority individuals have not helped the mental well-being of young LGBTQ+ people who suffer a persistence of homophobic and transphobic sociocultural ideologies, discrimination, and violence (Meyer et al., 2021). Multiple studies have found that LGB teens and adults experience more physical and sexual violence and harassment than non-LGB individuals (Saewyc et al., 2006; Smith et al., 2016). Additionally, compared to LGB individuals, transgender and nonbinary individuals are especially impacted by discrimination and violence (Blondeel et al., 2018). Anti-LGBT homicides, especially of transgender and nonbinary individuals of color, is a severe issue that impacts this community (Gruenewald, 2012; Human Rights Campaign, 2021). Transgender and nonbinary individuals report recurrent negative experiences in health care settings, including refusal of treatment or having to teach the provider about their needs to receive proper care (James et al., 2016; Puckett et al., 2018). Individuals who do not identify in the binary report higher levels of victimization and discrimination than those who do (Lefevor et al., 2019).

Research has shown how transgender status is associated with socioeconomic outcomes. Transgender and nonbinary individuals report substantially greater levels of unemployment and poverty and "lower household income" when compared with cisgender individuals (Carpenter et al., 2020). Astonishing disparities exist between transgender and nonbinary individuals and the US population with regard to having a place to live, ability to obtain a job, access to medical services, and benefit from family and community support (Grant et al., 2011; James et al., 2016; Xavier et al., 2007). This reflects a problem with economic discrimination, which has been found to predict incidents of violence motivated by gender-related stigma (Lombardi et al., 2001).

Transgender individuals of color, including Latinx, American Indian, multiracial, and Black individuals, experience more discrimination than white individuals due to structural racism. These individuals are more likely to be living in poverty, unemployed, experiencing health disparities, and living with HIV. Undocumented and disabled transgender individuals will most certainly struggle with severe financial difficulties and violence (Grant et al., 2011; James et al., 2016).

PROXIMAL STRESSORS

Proximal stressors (anticipated and perceived stigma, vigilance, internalized stigma, and identity concealment) impact individuals at an inner and personal level. Given the enacted stigma that is present in society at large, which all LGBTQ+ individuals experience either directly or indirectly by learning individuals in the community have been targeted, LGBTQ+ individuals may live in a constant state of hypervigilance as they anticipate stigma, rejection, and victimization (Meyer, 1995; Meyer, 2003; Meyer, 2015). Furthermore, when an LGBTQ+ individual assimilates into their belief system society's negative attitudes about their sexual orientation and/or gender identity, the person experiences internalized homophobia and/or internalized transphobia, which become proximal stressors impacting the individual from within (Meyer, 1995; Bockting, 2015). Internalized homophobia is one of the reasons why a person might reject their sexual orientation (Meyer & Dean, 1998). Likewise, internalized transphobia could lead to a person concealing their gender identity (Testa et al., 2015). Concealment of the sexual and gender identity can directly impact the LGBTQ+ person's mental health. Repressing and hiding these important aspects of the human experience can lead to the development of depression and high levels of stress, anxiety, and substance use (Brennan et al., 2021; Riggle et al., 2017; Rood et al., 2017). These outcomes are particularly significant for LGBTQ+ youth who may feel unable to express their authentic selves in different contexts including at home, in school, or online, due to experiences of stigma, abuse, and bullying (McDermott et al., 2018).

Proximal stressors mediate the impact of distal stressors on psychological and physical well-being. For example, the LGBTQ+ individual's subjective understanding (perceived stigma) of structural stigma has been associated with psychological distress (Jackson et al., 2020; Mereish & Poteat, 2015; Ouch & Moradi, 2019; Rood et al., 2016; Schmitz, Robinson, Tabler et al., 2020). For instance, for transgender and nonbinary individuals, experiencing discrimination because of their gender identity (distal stressor) can be correlated to suicidal ideation and suicidal behaviors through the mediation of internalized transphobia (proximal stressor) (Cogan et al., 2021). In other words, the transgender person can be exposed to negative ideas about their gender identity through experiences of discrimination and victimization. When these ideas are evaluated, recognized as true, and internalized, the person can experience emotional distress that is so severe that it could lead to the experience of suicidal ideation and behaviors.

The Impact of Minority Stress on Mental Health

LGBTQ+ individuals report higher levels of stress compared to the general population (American Psychological Association, 2016). The high levels of stress compound their risk of suffering mental health problems, including anxiety disorders, mood disorders, post-traumatic stress disorder, substance use disorders, eating disorders, and suicidality (Livingston et al., 2020; Mustanski et al., 2016; Nagata et al., 2020; Puckett et al., 2020; Smith et al., 2016; Tebbe & Moradi, 2016; Villarreal et al., 2020). Furthermore, compared to heterosexual and cisgender individuals, LGBTQ+ individuals are more likely to have a history of suicidal ideation and attempts (James et al., 2016; Silenzio et al., 2007).

The high levels of victimization experienced by LGBTQ+ youth from adolescence to adulthood increase their risk of developing depression and post-traumatic stress disorder (Mustanski et al., 2016). They are at greater risk than non-LGBTQ+ youth of using substances as a coping mechanism, practicing self-harm, and experiencing suicidality, suggesting that stressors specific to this community have a detrimental impact on their mental health (Almeida et al., 2009; Felner et al., 2020; McDermott et al., 2018; Ream, 2019). For instance, concealment of the LGBTQ+ identity can be a source of stress and suicidality among LGBTQ+ youth (McDermott et al., 2018).

Compared with the general population, transgender and nonbinary individuals present with an exponentially greater incidence of psychological distress, psychiatric disorders, and suicidal thoughts and attempts (Beckwith et al., 2019; Bockting et al., 2013; James et al., 2016; McNeil et al., 2017; Meyer et al., 2021). In fact, transgender and gender diverse youth, whose gender presentation does not conform with expectations of their sex assigned at birth, are more likely to report poorer general health and long-term mental health concerns (Rider et al., 2018). Distress is heightened when the person experiences higher levels of discrimination (Puckett et al., 2020), a common occurrence for those who belong to multiple marginalized groups (Borgogna et al., 2018; Casey et al., 2019; Puckett et al., 2020).

The Impact of Minority Stress on Physical Health

LGBTQ+ youth battle with major healthcare problems, including increased incidence of disease (Hafeez et al., 2017). Transgender individuals' risk for health issues has been described as "ultra-high" (Juster, 2019). The first national probability sample of transgender individuals in the United States exposed that the likelihood of a fair or poor health self-rating is higher among transgender individuals and lesbian, bisexual, and queer cisgender females than among gay, bisexual, and queer cisgender males (Meyer et al., 2021). Compared to cisgender males, transgender men and nonbinary individuals report lower levels of self-perceived exceptional or very good health (Lagos, 2018). Nonbinary individuals report poorer health outcomes when compared to cisgender individuals, possibly due to the level of discrimination they experience in health care settings (Cicero et al., 2020; Lagos, 2018; Rider et al., 2018). Healthcare discrimination, limited health insurance coverage, and lack of trained providers to address the needs of transgender and nonbinary individuals create barriers for accessing preventative health care treatments and gender-affirming care (Cicero et al., 2019; James et al., 2016; Reback et al., 2018).

Studies have shown an association between minority stress and physical health issues among LGBTQ+ individuals. For LGB individuals, the health-related problems include respiratory infections, alterations in cardiovascular function, hypertension, AIDS-related symptoms and mortality, and cancer prevalence, among others (Flentje et al., 2020; Frost et al., 2015). A high incidence of HIV and myocardial infarction has been recorded among transgender and nonbinary emerging adults and adults (Grant et al., 2011; Meyer et al. 2017). Distal stressors, including adverse childhood experiences (i.e., sexual, physical, and emotional abuse) and discrimination, as well as psychological stressors, have been linked to higher chances of cardiovascular issues among transgender individuals (Poteat et al., 2021).

The allostatic load framework can facilitate some understanding of poor physical health outcomes for LGBTQ+ individuals. Allostasis is the process that physiological systems undergo to adjust to change, which allows for the stability of the organism (McEwen, 2004; McEwen & Stellar, 1993; Sterling & Eyer, 1988). Allostatic overload takes place as a result of recurrent exposure to challenging situations in the environment that are interpreted by the individual as stressful. Persistent dysregulation of the organism, due to chronic stressors such as discrimination, leads to "wear and tear of the body" (McEwen, 1998; McEwen, 2004; McEwen & Stellar, 1993; Van Dyke et al., 2020). The accumulation of stressors can also add to the allostatic overload (Pearlin et al., 2005), and greater allostatic overload has been associated with increased risk for disease (Guidi et al., 2020).

The practice of behaviors that promote health, including restful sleep, social interactions that are positive, as well as being in spaces that are green and that promote safety, are recommended to decrease the allostatic overload and prevent disease (McEwen, 2020). These recommendations fail to take into consideration how the experiences of discrimination, marginalization, and violence impact the LGBTQ+ community. Recommendations should also target interpersonal, community, and societal factors (National Institute on Minority Health and Health Disparities, 2018; National Institute of Health, Sexual and Gender Minority Research Office, 2021). Aiming to mitigate the impact of these factors is essential to addressing the social determinants of health; that is, "the conditions in the environments where people are born, live, learn, work, play, worship, and age that affect a wide range of health, functioning, and quality-of-life outcomes and risks" (World Health Organization, 2012). Furthermore, this is the way to reduce health disparities and improve physical health outcomes for all LGBTQ+ individuals.

Resilience

The interactive process to adapt or recover and succeed in life through or after stressful experiences that may be life threatening is known as resilience (Masten, 2007; Masten et al., 2009). Resilience, an essential component of the minority stress framework, acts as protection from stress (Meyer, 2015) and supposes the capacity to live a meaningful life despite challenges (Zautra et al., 2010). Resilience can be conceived as a progressive development that begins during childhood and is strengthened through the impact of socialization and the individual's thought process. It can develop or manifest at different points of a person's life (Buikstra et al., 2010; Masten & Tellegen, 2012). Resilience has also been viewed as common and emerging from protective factors and adaptive systems (Masten, 2014b). Protective factors moderate and mitigate the effects of risk (Masten, 2014a; Masten & Tellegen, 2012).

INDIVIDUAL RESILIENCE

Meyer (2015) defines individual resilience in the context of minority stress according to Turner and Roszell's (1994) concept of personal agency, which refers to individuals' characteristics that can assist or impede the ability to cope with stress and consequently be "more or less resilient" (p. 210). The literature has been consistent at exposing the personal and life characteristics of the youth that manifest resilience. The "short list" of such characteristics developed by Masten (2014b) include "effective caregiving and parenting quality (received by caretakers), close relationships with other capable adults, close friends and romantic partners, intelligence and problem-solving skills, self-control, emotion regulation, planfulness, motivation to succeed, self-efficacy, faith, hope, belief life has meaning, effective schools, effective neighborhoods, [and] collective efficacy" (p. 148).

For some LGBTQ+ individuals, the characteristics of youth who manifest resilience, for example those related to the quality of the parenting received, are not always available (Asakura, 2019). This is significant when considering that parental support and acceptance are particularly important protective factors that safeguard the LGBTQ+ youth's mental health (van Beusekom et al., 2015). Issues with the family of origin, as well as environmental and social structure inequality, limits the support and buffer they can receive to protect their well-being, exemplifying how not everyone has the same chances to be resilient (Meyer, 2015; Zautra et al., 2010). For this reason, Meyer (2015) urges us to be cautious about hyperfocusing on individual resilience as this emphasis places pressure on the person to be resilient and takes away the responsibility from the social structures.

COMMUNITY RESILIENCE

From a minority stress perspective, community resilience has been conceptualized as "minority coping" or "group level resource"; that is, the marginalized group's capacity to build the necessary self-reinforcing tools to reduce or neutralize the effects of stigma for the community. It considers the individual's ability to assume and implement the ideals and tools developed by the group, not the individual's own ability to cope, and implies chances to receive social support (Meyer, 2003; Meyer, 2015).

Among LGB youth, access to social support has shown to help in the development of a positive sexual identity despite experiences of concealment of their sexual orientation (Bruce et al., 2015). For transgender and gender nonbinary individuals, access to social support, including mental health providers, support groups, community resources, and support from friends, partners, and family, is a protective factor against suicide (Moody et al., 2015).

Self-identification and affiliation with the LGBTQ+ community provides individuals with the opportunity to take advantage of group-level resilience possibilities (Meyer, 2015). For example, affiliation with the House and Ball community[1] is a resource that has allowed BIPOC MSM to receive support, as well as guidance for the prevention of high-risk sexual behaviors (Schrager et al., 2014). The experience of being accepted and valued by others, trans community connectedness, identity pride, and general social support are protective factors for transgender and gender nonbinary individuals. These factors shield them from psychological distress, including anxiety and depression symptoms (Bockting et al., 2013; Moody et al., 2015; Pflum et al., 2015). Thus, the development of friendships and peer support are crucial minority coping tools to address the impact of discrimination (Bockting et al., 2013; Tebbe & Moradi, 2016).

LGBTQ+ community tangible resources that help foster resilience include access to community centers for LGBTQ+ individuals, specialized support groups and health centers, a "hotline," education, mentors, and policies and laws that protect them. Intangible resources consist of the application of a minority perspective and rearticulation of sociocultural values, rules, and standards (Meyer, 2015).

---

1. The House and Ballroom community are concrete and abstract (symbolic) houses for members of the LGBTQ+ community. The houses are chosen family systems where members of the LGBTQ+ community, in the past only Black and Latinx individuals, receive support and guidance that they do not receive from their family of origin. They are organized in ways that transcend cultural norms. For example, the mother can be a transgender female. The guidance helps overcome stereotypes and fight transphobia, homophobia, and white supremacy. The houses organize and take part of ballroom performances, where they compete with other houses or individuals, and can express who they are in an emotionally and physically safe space.

Resilience-Building Practice: Interventions That Can Enhance Resilience

Resilience-building interventions assist with strengthening individuals and communities to lessen the impact of minority stressors. Interventions should consider the individual's or the community's access to resources (i.e., in person, online) and be conducted at different levels and contexts. Moreover, interventions should take into account factors that are known to augment resilience, including environmental and economic factors, infrastructure, and support services (Buikstra et al., 2010; Masten, 2014b).

SOCIETAL-LEVEL INTERVENTIONS

Societal-level interventions address the social structure and environmental aspects impacting the LGBTQ+ community. These include public education initiatives to change stigmatizing ideology about the LGBTQ+ community, increase awareness and acceptance of their needs, and inform social advocacy initiatives, policies, and the law.

COMMUNITY- AND GROUP-LEVEL INTERVENTIONS

Community- and group-level interventions incorporate tangible LGBTQ+ resources that promote affiliation and connectedness to the community, as well as social and family support. This level entails access to spaces where the LGBTQ+ individual's sexual and gender identity are validated and their biopsychosocial needs are satisfied. These can be delivered at schools, workplaces, neighborhoods, healthcare centers, within family contexts, and in LGBTQ+ specific spaces. The family context can be addressed through family and couples therapy and support groups. Education should be incorporated to promote understanding of the history of the LGBTQ+ community and individual experiences to increase validation and support.

INDIVIDUAL-LEVEL INTERVENTIONS (ILI)

Individual-level interventions (ILI) are especially important in the context of clinical work. These interventions focus on the psychological and physical needs of the person at an individual level. ILI are intended to be developed and used in the context of mental health and medical services. There is consensus in the field that interventions should be person-centered (Rogers, 1957), should be trauma-informed (Harris & Fallot, 2001), and should consider the individual's intersecting identities. Additionally, a holistic approach should be taken by incorporating interventions that target the physical, psychological, emotional, sociocultural, and spiritual needs of the person (Tjale & Bruce, 2007). Furthermore, an approach to diagnosis and treatment that considers a variety of healing alternatives from different traditions, chosen according to the needs of the person, must be taken. It may include pharmacotherapy and surgeries, as well as lifestyle changes and complementary treatments (Academy of Integrative Health and Medicine, 2021).

Coming out growth, or stress-related growth, has been documented among LGBTQ+ individuals. This construct refers to the emotional growth one may experience after facing a stress-provoking situation, such as disclosing one's sexual orientation and/or gender identity. For some people, this stress can trigger growth as the individual converts the difficult situation of coming out into one of development, evolution, and progress (Antebi-Gruszka et al., 2021; Brownfield et al., 2018; Vaughan & Waehler, 2009). Stress-related growth facilitates intrapersonal (i.e., improved mental health) and interpersonal (i.e., increased ability to support other members of their community) growth (Brownfield et al., 2018; Vaughan & Waehler, 2009). Among bisexual individuals, it has been documented that it enables critical growth, the awareness of their own privilege, as well as recognition of the oppression experienced by other marginalized groups, not only those marginalized due to their sexual orientation (Brownfield et al., 2018). For transgender women, the availability of emotional and cognitive resources, as well as social support, is crucial for stress-related growth to take place (Antebi-Gruszka et al., 2021). In view of these findings, and considering that the resources available to the individual can facilitate the coming out growth (Antebi-Gruszka et al., 2021; Brownfield et al., 2018), clinical spaces should facilitate the process of exploration of sexual orientation and gender identity and enable coming out for LGBTQ+ individuals and gender affirmation for transgender and gender nonbinary individuals. Before doing so, psychoeducation is recommended to facilitate the understanding of the impact of minority stressors on well-being and how resilience-building interventions can help buffer their effects.

In mental health settings, cognitive strategies can help the person identify and challenge irrational cognitions that trigger distress and that can also inhibit access to and enjoyment of social support and community connectedness. Mindfulness-based interventions (Kabat-Zinn, 2013) can help address the impact of chronic stress on psychological and physical well-being, and Dialectical Behavioral Therapy (Linehan, 2014) can help address self-harming and suicidality specifically. Information about community resources should be provided to address the need for social support and community connectedness.

Medical interventions must be culturally competent and clinically relevant and tailored to fulfill the specific healthcare needs of LGBTQ+ individuals. Services should emphasize prevention strategies for high-risk conditions and the evaluation and treatment of medical problems that are common among LGBTQ+ people due to the impact of minority stress. For transgender and gender nonbinary (TGNB) individuals, ILI includes medically necessary gender-affirming interventions.

The mental health and medical needs of LGBTQ+ individuals must be addressed from an interdisciplinary perspective, calling for coordination of different specialties and approaches, as well as for collaborative care between various providers (Strelnik & Strelnik, 2020). Health care systems that have an interdisciplinary approach to care build teams that form collaborations between providers from various disciplines (e.g., psychotherapist, primary care provider, case manager, gender-affirming surgeon, etc.). When all disciplines and services are not available under one service umbrella, collaboration and partnership among providers from different settings are of utmost importance.

Empirical Support for the Minority Stress Model

As described by Meyer (2003; 2015), the minority stress model can be used as a framework to conduct research and explain the health outcomes of stigmatized "minorities," including the LGBTQ+ community. Empirical data supports the use of this model for those purposes. The minority stress model explains health outcomes among LGBTQ+ individuals, including adults and adolescents (Bockting et al., 2013; Breslow et al., 2015; Goldbach & Gibbs, 2017; Lehavot & Simoni, 2011; Poteat et al., 2021; Testa et al., 2015). When utilized in conjunction with an intersectional theoretical approach, it has helped explain the effects of minority stress, as well as resilience factors, among LGBTQ+ individuals of diverse racial and ethnic groups (Jemal, 2017; McConnell et al., 2018; Schmitz, Robinson, & Sanchez, 2020; Wong et al., 2014) and of transgender youth of low socioeconomic status (Hatchel & Marx, 2018). The use of the minority stress model to understand health outcomes among transgender and gender nonbinary individuals is supported especially when it factors in their experiences with stigma and discrimination, includes cultural considerations, and incorporates an intersectional approach (Tan et al., 2020; Testa et al., 2015).

Gaps in the Literature and Future Directions for Clinically Relevant Research

Studies about minority stress and the LGBTQ+ community have mostly focused on adult populations and individuals who identify as LGB and in the gender binary. More research is needed with regards to the impact of minority stress on LGBTQ+ children, youth, and emerging adults, as well as gender nonbinary, agender, pansexual, demisexual, and asexual individuals of all ages. Studies should evaluate the specific minority stressors experienced by these marginalized populations considering characteristics such as (but not limited to) their race, ethnicity, cultural background, religion, migratory status, disability, and family dynamics. Future research should also aim to inform the development of resilience-building strategies for LGBTQ+ children, adolescents, and emerging adults, particularly from an intersectional lens.

Limited studies have focused on the effects of minority stress on the physical health of young LGBTQ+ individuals and transgender and gender nonbinary individuals. Additional studies are needed to understand the physical impact of stress processes on these demographic groups. More research is needed to study the validity and applicability of the model internationally, and particularly in countries outside the Western world.

References

Academy of Integrative Health and Medicine. (2021). AIHM core values. https://aihm.org/vision

Almeida, J., Johnson, R. M., Corliss, H. L., Molnar, B. E., & Azrael, D. (2009). Emotional distress among LGBT youth: The influence of perceived discrimination based on sexual orientation. *Journal of Youth and Adolescence, 38*(7), 1001–1014. https://doi.org/10.1007/s10964-009-9397-9

American Psychological Association. (2016). Stress in America: The impact of discrimination. Stress in America™ Survey. https://www.apa.org/news/press/releases/stress/2015/impact-of-discrimination.pdf

Antebi-Gruszka, N., Cain, D., Millar, B. M., Parsons, J. T., & Rendina, H. J. (2021). Stress-related growth among transgender women: Measurement, correlates, and insights for clinical interventions. *Journal of Homosexuality*, 1–24. https://doi.org/10.1080/00918369.2021.1921511

Asakura, K. (2019). Extraordinary acts to "show up": Conceptualizing resilience of LGBTQ youth. *Youth & Society, 51*(2), 268–285. https://doi.org/10.1177/0044118X16671430

Beckwith, N., McDowell, M. J., Reisner, S. L., Zaslow, S., Weiss, R. D., Mayer, K. H., & Keuroghlian, A. S. (2019). Psychiatric epidemiology of transgender and nonbinary adult patients at an urban health center. *LGBT Health, 6*(2), 51–61. https://doi.org/10.1089/lgbt.2018.0136

Blondeel, K., de Vasconcelos, S., García-Moreno, C., Stephenson, R., Temmerman, M., & Toskin, I. (2018). Violence motivated by perception of sexual orientation and gender identity: A systematic review. *Bulletin of the World Health Organization, 96*(1), 29–41L. https://doi.org/10.2471/BLT.17.197251

Bockting, W. O. (2015). Internalized transphobia. In A. Bolin & P. Whelehan (Eds.), *International encyclopedia of human sexuality*. https://doi.org/10.1002/9781118896877.wbiehs236

Bockting, W. O., Miner, M. H., Swinburne Romine, R. E., Hamilton, A., & Coleman, E. (2013). Stigma, mental health, and resilience in an online sample of the US transgender population. *American Journal of Public Health, 103*(5), 943–951. https://doi.org/10.2105/AJPH.2013.301241

Borgogna, N. C., McDermott, R. C., Aita, S. L., & Kridel, M. M. (2018). Anxiety and depression across gender and sexual minorities: Implications for transgender, gender nonconforming, pansexual, demisexual, asexual, queer, and questioning individuals. *Psychology of Sexual Orientation and Gender Diversity*. Advance online publication. http://dx.doi.org/10.1037/sgd0000306

Brennan, J. M., Dunham, K. J., Bowlen, M., Davis, K., Ji, G., & Cochran, B. N. (2021). Inconcealable: A cognitive–behavioral model of concealment of gender and sexual identity and associations with physical and mental health. *Psychology of Sexual Orientation and Gender Diversity, 8*(1), 80–93. https://doi.org/10.1037/sgd0000424

Breslow, A. S., Brewster, M. E., Velez, B. L., Wong, S., Geiger, E., & Soderstrom, B. (2015). Resilience and collective action: Exploring buffers against minority stress for transgender individuals. *Psychology of Sexual Orientation and Gender Diversity, 2*(3), 253–265. https://doi.org/10.1037/sgd0000117

Brooks, V. R. (1981). *Minority Stress and Lesbian Women*. Lexington Books.

Brownfield, J. M., Brown, C., Jeevanba, S. B., & VanMattson, S. B. (2018). More than simply getting bi: An examination of coming out growth for bisexual individuals. *Psychology of Sexual Orientation and Gender Diversity, 5*(2), 220–232. https://doi.org/10.1037/sgd0000282

Bruce, D., Harper, G. W., & Bauermeister, J. A. (2015). Minority stress, positive identity development, and depressive symptoms: Implications for resilience among sexual minority male youth. *Psychology of Sexual Orientation and Gender Diversity, 2*(3), 287–296. https://doi.org/10.1037/sgd0000128

Buikstra, E., Ross, H., King, C. A., Baker, P. G., Hegney, D., McLachlan, K., & Rogers, C. C. (2010). The components of resilience-Perceptions of an Australian rural community. *Journal of Community Psychology, 38*(8), 975.

Carpenter, C. S., Eppink, S. T., & Gonzales, G. (2020). Transgender status, gender identity, and socioeconomic outcomes in the United States. *ILR Review, 73*(3), 573–599. https://doi.org/10.1177/0019793920902776

Casey, L. S., Reisner, S. L., Findling, M. G., Blendon, R. J., Benson, J. M., Sayde, J. M., & Miller, C. (2019). Discrimination in the United States: Experiences of lesbian, gay, bisexual, transgender, and queer americans. *Health Services Research, 54*(6), 1454–1466. https://doi.org/10.1111/1475-6773.13229

Cicero, E. C., Reisner, S. L., Merwin, E. I., Humphreys, J. C., & Silva, S. G. (2020). The health status of transgender and gender nonbinary adults in the United States. *PloS one, 15*(2), e0228765. https://doi.org/10.1371/journal.pone.0228765

Cicero, E. C., Reisner, S. L., Silva, S. G., Merwin, E. I., & Humphreys, J. C. (2019). Health care experiences of transgender adults: An integrated mixed research literature review. *Advances in Nursing Science, 42*(2), 123–138. https://doi.org/10.1097/ANS.0000000000000256

Cogan, C. M., Scholl, J. A., Lee, J. Y. and Davis, J. L. (2021). Potentially traumatic events and the association between gender minority stress and suicide risk in a gender-diverse sample. *Journal of Traumatic Stress, 34*(5), 977–984. https://doi.org/10.1002/jts.22728

Felner, J. K., Wisdom, J. P., Williams, T., Katuska, L., Haley, S. J., Jun, H. J., & Corliss, H. L. (2020). Stress, coping, and context: Examining substance use among LGBTQ young adults with probable substance use disorders. *Psychiatric Services, 71*(2), 112–120. https://doi.org/10.1176/appi.ps.201900029

Flentje, A., Heck, N. C., Brennan, J. M., & Meyer, I. H. (2020). The relationship between minority stress and biological outcomes: A systematic review. *Journal of Behavioral Medicine, 43*(5), 673–694. https://doi.org/10.1007/s10865-019-00120-6

Frost, D. M., Lehavot, K., & Meyer, I. H. (2015). Minority stress and physical health among sexual minority individuals. *Journal of Behavioral Medicine, 38*(1), 1–8. https://doi.org/10.1007/s10865-013-9523-8

Goldbach, J. T., & Gibbs, J. J. (2017). A developmentally informed adaptation of minority stress for sexual minority adolescents. *Journal of Adolescence, 55*, 36–50. https://doi.org/10.1016/j.adolescence.2016.12.007

Grant, J. M., Mottet, L. A., Tanis, J., Harrison, J., Herman, J. L., & Keisling, M. (2011). Injustice at every turn: A report of the national transgender discrimination survey. Washington: National Center for Transgender Equality and National Gay and Lesbian Task Force. https://www.transequality.org/sites/default/files/docs/resources/NTDS_Report.pdf

Gray, A. J. (2002). Stigma in psychiatry. *Journal of the Royal Society of Medicine, 95*(2), 72–76. https://doi.org/10.1258/jrsm.95.2.72

Gruenewald, J. (2012). Are anti-lgbt homicides in the United States unique? *Journal of Interpersonal Violence, 27*(18), 3601–3623. https://doi.org/10.1177/0886260512462301

Guidi, J., Lucente, M., Sonino, N., & Fava, G. A. (2020). Allostatic load and its impact on health: A systematic review. *Psychotherapy and Psychosomatics*, 1–17. Advance online publication. https://doi.org/10.1159/000510696

Hafeez, H., Zeshan, M., Tahir, M. A., Jahan, N., & Naveed, S. (2017). Health care disparities among lesbian, gay, bisexual, and transgender youth: A literature review. *Cureus, 9*(4), e1184. https://doi.org/10.7759/cureus.1184

Harris, M., & Fallot, R. D. (Eds.). (2001). *Using trauma theory to design service systems.* Jossey-Bass/Wiley.

Hatchel, T., & Marx, R. (2018). Understanding intersectionality and resiliency among transgender adolescents: Exploring pathways among peer victimization, school belonging, and drug use. *International Journal of Environmental Research and Public Health, 15*(6), 1289. https://doi.org/10.3390/ijerph15061289

Hendricks, M. L., & Testa, R. J. (2012). A conceptual framework for clinical work with transgender and gender nonconforming clients: An adaptation of the Minority Stress Model. *Professional Psychology: Research and Practice, 43*(5), 460–467. https://doi.org/10.1037/a0029597

Herek, G. M., Chopp, R., & Strohl, D. (2012). Sexual stigma: putting sexual minority health issues in context. In: I. H. Meyer & M. E. Northridge (Eds.), *The health of sexual minorities: Public health perspectives on lesbian, gay, bisexual, and transgender populations* (pp. 171–208). Springer.

Human Rights Campaign. (2021). Violence against the transgender and gender nonconforming community in 2021. https://www.hrc.org/resources/fatal-violence-against-the-transgender-and-gender-non-conforming-community-in-2021

Jackson, S. D., Mohr, J. J., Sarno, E. L., Kindahl, A. M., & Jones, I. L. (2020). Intersectional experiences, stigma-related stress, and psychological health among Black LGBQ individuals. *Journal of Consulting and Clinical Psychology, 88*(5), 416–428. https://doi.org/10.1037/ccp0000489

James, S. E., Herman, J. L., Rankin, S., Keisling, M., Mottet, L., & Anafi, M. (2016). The report of the 2015 U.S. Transgender Survey. National Center for Transgender Equality.

Jemal, A. (2017). Critical consciousness: A critique and critical analysis of the literature. *Urban Review, 49*(4), 602–626. https://doi.org/10.1007/s11256-017-0411-3

Juster, R. (2019). *Sex × gender and sexual orientation in relation to stress hormones and allostatic load.* SAGE Publications. https://doi.org/10.1177/2470289719862555

Kabat-Zinn, J. (2013). *Full catastrophe living: Using the wisdom of your body and mind to face stress, pain and illness.* Delacorte.

Klemmer, C. L., Rusow, J., Goldbach, J., Kattari, S. K., & Rice, E. (2021). Socially assigned gender nonconformity and school violence experience among transgender and cisgender adolescents. *Journal of Interpersonal Violence, 36*(15–16), NP8567-NP8589. https://doi.org/10.1177/0886260519844781

Lagos, D. (2018). Looking at population health beyond "male" and "female": Implications of transgender identity and gender nonconformity for population health. *Demography, 55*(6), 2097–2117. https://doi.org/10.1007/s13524-018-0714-3

Lazarus, R. S., & Folkman, S. (1984). *Stress, appraisal, and coping.* Springer.

Lee, C., & Ostergard, C. R. (2017). Measuring discrimination against LGBTQ people: A cross-national analysis. *Human Rights Quarterly, 39*, 37–72.

Lefevor, G. T., Boyd-Rogers, C. C., Sprague, B. M., & Janis, R. A. (2019). Health disparities between genderqueer, transgender, and cisgender individuals: An extension of minority stress theory. *Journal of Counseling Psychology, 66*(4), 385–395. https://doi.org/10.1037/cou0000339

Lehavot, K., & Simoni, J. M. (2011). The impact of minority stress on mental health and substance use among sexual minority women. *Journal of Consulting and Clinical Psychology, 79*(2), 159–170. https://doi.org/10.1037/a0022839

Linehan, M. M. (2014). *DBT training manual.* Guilford Press.
Livingston, N. A., Berke, D., Scholl, J., Ruben, M., & Shipherd, J. C. (2020). Addressing diversity in PTSD treatment: Clinical considerations and guidance for the treatment of PTSD in LGBTQ populations. *Current Treatment Options in Psychiatry*, 1–17. Advance online publication. https://doi.org/10.1007/s40501-020-00204-0
Lombardi, E. L., Wilchins, R. A., Priesing, D., & Malouf, D. (2001). Gender violence: Transgender experiences with violence and discrimination. *Journal of Homosexuality, 42*(1), 89–101. https://doi.org/10.1300/j082v42n01_05
Masten, A. (2007). Resilience in developing systems: Progress and promise as the fourth wave rises. *Development and Psychopathology, 19*(3), 921–930. doi:10.1017/S0954579407000442
Masten, A. S. (2014a). Global Perspectives on Resilience in Children and Youth. *Child Development, 85*, 6–20. https://doi.org/10.1111/cdev.12205
Masten, A. S. (2014b). *Ordinary magic: Resilience in development.* Guilford Press.
Masten, A. S., Cutuli, J. J., Herbers, J. E., & Reed, M. G. (2009). Resilience in Development. In Lopez, S. J., & Snyder, C. R. (Eds.), *Oxford handbook of positive psychology* (pp. 74–88). Oxford University Press
Masten, A. S., & Tellegen, A. (2012). Resilience in developmental psychopathology: Contributions of the Project Competence Longitudinal Study. *Development and Psychopathology, 24*(2), 345–361. https://doi.org/10.1017/S095457941200003X
McConnell, E. A., Janulis, P., Phillips, G. II, Truong, R., & Birkett, M. (2018). Multiple minority stress and LGBT community resilience among sexual minority men. *Psychology of Sexual Orientation and Gender Diversity, 5*(1), 1–12. https://doi.org/10.1037/sgd0000265
McDermott, E., Hughes, E., & Rawlings, V. (2018). The social determinants of lesbian, gay, bisexual and transgender youth suicidality in England: A mixed methods study. *Journal of Public Health (Oxford, England), 40*, e244–e251.
McEwen, B. S. (1998). Protective and damaging effects of stress mediators. *New England Journal of Medicine, 338*(3), 171–179. https://doi.org/10.1056/NEJM199801153380307
McEwen, B. S. (2004). Protection and damage from acute and chronic stress: Allostasis and allostatic overload and relevance to the pathophysiology of psychiatric disorders. *Annals of the New York Academy of Sciences, 1032*, 1–7. https://doi.org/10.1196/annals.1314.001
McEwen, B. S. (2020). The untapped power of allostasis promoted by healthy lifestyles. *World Psychiatry: Official Journal of the World Psychiatric Association (WPA), 19*(1), 57–58. https://doi.org/10.1002/wps.20720
McEwen, B. S., & Stellar, E. (1993). Stress and the individual: Mechanisms leading to disease. *Archives of Internal Medicine, 153*(18), 2093–2101.
McNeil, J., Ellis, S. J., & Eccles, F. J. R. (2017). Suicide in trans populations: A systematic review of prevalence and correlates. *Psychology of Sexual Orientation and Gender Diversity, 4*(3), 341–353. https://doi.org/10.1037/sgd0000235
Mereish, E. H., & Poteat, V. P. (2015). A relational model of sexual minority mental and physical health: The negative effects of shame on relationships, loneliness, and health. *Journal of Counseling Psychology, 62*(3), 425–437. https://doi.org/10.1037/cou0000088
Meyer, I. H. (1995). Minority stress and mental health in gay men. *Journal of Health and Social Behavior, 36*(1), 38–56. http://www.jstor.org/stable/2137286
Meyer, I. H. (2003). Prejudice, social stress, and mental health in lesbian, gay, and bisexual populations: Conceptual issues and research evidence. *Psychological Bulletin, 129*(5), 674–697. https://doi.org/10.1037/0033-2909.129.5.674
Meyer, I. H. (2015). Resilience in the study of minority stress and health of sexual and gender minorities. *Psychology of Sexual Orientation and Gender Diversity, 2*(3), 209–213. https://doi.org/10.1037/sgd0000132

Meyer, I. H., Brown, T. N., Herman, J. L., Reisner, S. L., & Bockting, W. O. (2017). Demographic characteristics and health status of transgender adults in select US regions: Behavioral risk factor surveillance system, 2014. *American Journal of Public Health, 107*(4), 582–589. https://doi.org/10.2105/AJPH.2016.303648

Meyer, I. H., & Dean, L. (1998). Internalized homophobia, intimacy, and sexual behavior among gay and bisexual men. In G. M. Herek (Ed.), *Psychological perspectives on lesbian and gay issues, Vol. 4. Stigma and sexual orientation: Understanding prejudice against lesbians, gay men, and bisexuals* (pp. 160–186). Sage Publications, Inc. https://doi.org/10.4135/9781452243818.n8

Meyer, I. H., & Frost, D. M. (2013). Minority stress and the health of sexual minorities. In C. J. Patterson & A. R. D'Augelli (Eds.), *Handbook of psychology and sexual orientation* (pp. 252–266). Oxford University Press.

Meyer, I. H., Russell, S. T., Hammack, P. L., Frost, D. M., & Wilson, B. (2021). Minority stress, distress, and suicide attempts in three cohorts of sexual minority adults: A U.S. probability sample. *PloS one, 16*(3), e0246827. https://doi.org/10.1371/journal.pone.0246827

Meyer, I. H., Wilson, B. D. M., & O'Neill, K. (2021). LGBTQ People in the US: Select findings from the generations and transpop studies. Los Angeles: The Williams Institute. https://williamsinstitute.law.ucla.edu/publications/generations-transpop-toplines/

Moody, C., Fuks, N., Peláez, S., & Smith, N. G. (2015). "Without this, I would for sure already be dead": A qualitative inquiry regarding suicide protective factors among trans adults. *Psychology of Sexual Orientation and Gender Diversity, 2*(3), 266–280. http://dx.doi.org/10.1037/sgd0000130

Mustanski, B., Andrews, R., & Puckett, J. A. (2016). The effects of cumulative victimization on mental health among lesbian, gay, bisexual, and transgender adolescents and young adults. *American Journal of Public Health, 106*(3), 527–533. https://doi.org/10.2105/AJPH.2015.302976

Nagata, J. M., Ganson, K. T., & Austin, S. B. (2020). Emerging trends in eating disorders among sexual and gender minorities. *Current Opinion in Psychiatry, 33*(6), 562–567. https://doi.org/10.1097/YCO.0000000000000645

National Institute of Health, Sexual and Gender Minority Research Office. (2021). Sexual & gender minority health disparities research framework. https://dpcpsi.nih.gov/sites/default/files/NIH-SGM-Health-Disparities-Research-Framework-FINAL_508c.pdf

National Institute on Minority Health and Health Disparities. (2018). National institute on minority health and health disparities research framework. https://www.nimhd.nih.gov/about/overview/research-framework/nimhd-framework.html

Ouch, S., & Moradi, B. (2019). Cognitive and affective expectation of stigma, coping efficacy, and psychological distress among sexual minority people of color. *Journal of Counseling Psychology, 66*(4), 424–436. https://doi.org/10.1037/cou0000360

Pearlin, L. I., Schieman, S., Fazio, E. M., & Meersman, S. C. (2005). Stress, health, and the life course: Some conceptual perspectives. *Journal of Health and Social Behavior, 46*(2), 205–219. https://doi.org/10.1177/002214650504600206

Pflum, S. R., Testa, R. J., Balsam, K. F., Goldblum, P. B., & Bongar, B. (2015). Social support, trans community connectedness, and mental health symptoms among transgender and gender nonconforming adults. *Psychology of Sexual Orientation and Gender Diversity, 2*(3), 281–286. https://doi.org/10.1037/sgd0000122

Poteat, T. C., Divsalar, S., Streed, C. G. Jr., Feldman, J. L., Bockting, W. O., & Meyer, I. H. (2021). Cardiovascular disease in a population-based sample of transgender and cisgender adults. *American Journal of Preventive Medicine*, S0749-3797(21)00350-0. Advance online publication. https://doi.org/10.1016/j.amepre.2021.05.019

Puckett, J. A., Cleary, P., Rossman, K., Newcomb, M. E., & Mustanski, B. (2018). Barriers to gender-affirming care for transgender and gender nonconforming individuals. *Sexuality Research & Social Policy: Journal of NSRC: SR & SP, 15*(1), 48–59. https://doi.org/10.1007/s13178-017-0295-8

Puckett, J. A., Maroney, M. R., Wadsworth, L. P., Mustanski, B., & Newcomb, M. E. (2020). Coping with discrimination: The insidious effects of gender minority stigma on depression and anxiety in transgender individuals. *Journal of Clinical Psychology* 76: 176–194. https://doi.org/10.1002/jclp.22865

Ream, G. L. (2019). What's unique about lesbian, gay, bisexual, and transgender (LGBT) youth and young adult suicides? Findings from the National Violent Death Reporting System. *Journal of adolescent health: Official Publication of the Society for Adolescent Medicine, 64*(5), 602–607. https://doi.org/10.1016/j.jadohealth.2018.10.303

Reback, C. J., Clark, K., Holloway, I. W., & Fletcher, J. B. (2018). Health disparities, risk behaviors and healthcare utilization among transgender women in Los Angeles county: A comparison from 1998–1999 to 2015–2016. *AIDS and Behavior, 22*(8), 2524–2533. https://doi.org/10.1007/s10461-018-2165-7

Rider, G. N., McMorris, B. J., Gower, A. L., Coleman, E., & Eisenberg, M. E. (2018). Health and care utilization of transgender and gender nonconforming youth: A population-based study. *Pediatrics, 141*(3), e20171683. https://doi.org/10.1542/peds.2017-1683

Riggle, E. D. B., Rostosky, S. S., Black, W. W., & Rosenkrantz, D. E. (2017). Outness, concealment, and authenticity: Associations with LGB individuals' psychological distress and well-being. *Psychology of Sexual Orientation and Gender Diversity, 4*(1), 54–62. https://doi.org/10.1037/sgd0000202

Rogers, C. R. (1957). The necessary and sufficient conditions of therapeutic personality change. *Journal of Consulting Psychology, 21*(2), 95–103. https://doi.org/10.1037/h0045357

Rood, B. A., Maroney, M. R., Puckett, J. A., Berman, A. K., Reisner, S. L., & Pantalone, D. W. (2017). Identity concealment in transgender adults: A qualitative assessment of minority stress and gender affirmation. *American Journal of Orthopsychiatry, 87*(6), 704–713. https://doi-org.colby.idm.oclc.org/10.1037/ort0000303

Rood, B. A., Reisner, S. L., Surace, F. I., Puckett, J. A., Maroney, M. R., & Pantalone, D. W. (2016). Expecting rejection: Understanding the minority stress experiences of transgender and gender-nonconforming individuals. *Transgender Health, 1*(1), 151–164. https://doi.org/10.1089/trgh.2016.0012

Saewyc, E. M., Skay, C. L., Pettingell, S. L., Reis, E. A., Bearinger, L., Resnick, M., Murphy, A., & Combs, L. (2006). Hazards of stigma: The sexual and physical abuse of gay, lesbian, and bisexual adolescents in the United States and Canada. *Child Welfare, 85*(2), 195–213.

Schmitz, R. M., Robinson, B. A. & Sanchez, J. (2020). Intersectional family systems approach: LGBTQ+ Latino/a youth, family dynamics, and stressors. *Family Relations, 69*, 832–848. https://doi.org/10.1111/fare.12448

Schmitz, R. M., Robinson, B. A., Tabler, J., Welch, B., & Rafaqut, S. (2020). LGBTQ+ Latino/a young people's interpretations of stigma and mental health: An intersectional minority stress perspective. *Society and Mental Health, 10*(2), 163–179. https://doi.org/10.1177/2156869319847248

Schrager, S. M., Latkin, C. A., Weiss, G., Kubicek, K., & Kipke, M. D. (2014). High-risk sexual activity in the House and Ball community: Influence of social networks. *American Journal of Public Health, 104*(2), 326–331. https://doi.org/10.2105/AJPH.2013.301543

Scott, J., & Marshall, G. (2009). *Dominant culture. A Dictionary of Sociology*. Oxford University Press. https://www.oxfordreference.com/view/10.1093/acref/9780199533008.001.0001/acref-9780199533008-e-634

Silenzio, V. M., Pena, J. B., Duberstein, P. R., Cerel, J., & Knox, K. L. (2007). Sexual orientation and risk factors for suicidal ideation and suicide attempts among adolescents and young adults. *American Journal of Public Health, 97*(11), 2017–2019. https://doi.org/10.2105/AJPH.2006.095943

Smith, C. P., Cunningham, S. A., & Freyd, J. J. (2016). Sexual violence, institutional betrayal, and psychological outcomes for LGB college students. *Translational Issues in Psychological Science, 2*(4), 351–360. https://doi-org.colby.idm.oclc.org/10.1037/tps0000094

Sterling, P. & Eyer, J. (1988). Allostasis: A new paradigm to explain arousal pathology. In S. Fisher & J. Reason (Eds.), *Handbook of life stress, cognition, and health* (pp. 629–649). John Wiley & Sons

Strelnik, O. N., & Strelnik, S. N. (2020). Interdisciplinary research of self-consciousness on the base of phenomenology of Karl Jaspers. *RUDN Journal of Philosophy, 24*(3), 410–418. doi: 10.22363/2313-2302-2020-24-3-410-418

Tan, K. K. H., Treharne, G. J., Ellis, S. J., Schmidt, J. M., & Veale, J. F. (2020). Gender minority stress: A critical review, *Journal of Homosexuality, 67*(10), 1471–1489. doi: 10.1080/00918369.2019.1591789

Tebbe, E. A., & Moradi, B. (2016). Suicide risk in trans populations: An application of minority stress theory. *Journal of Counseling Psychology, 63*(5), 520–533. https://doi.org/10.1037/cou0000152

Testa, R. J., Habarth, J., Peta, J., Balsam, K., & Bockting, W. (2015). Development of the gender minority stress and resilience measure. *Psychology of Sexual Orientation and Gender Diversity, 2*(1), 65–77. https://doi.org/10.1037/sgd0000081

Tjale, A. A., & Bruce, J. (2007). A concept analysis of holistic nursing care in paediatric nursing. *Curationis, 30*(4), 45–52. https://doi.org/10.4102/curationis.v30i4.1116

Turner, R. J., & Roszell, P. (1994). Psychosocial resources and the stress process. In W. R. Avison & I. H. Gotlib (Eds.), *Stress and mental health, contemporary issues and prospects for the future* (pp. 179 –210). Plenum Press

van Beusekom, G., Bos, H. M. W., Overbeek, G., & Sandfort, T. G. M. (2015). Same-sex attraction, gender nonconformity, and mental health: The protective role of parental acceptance. *Psychology of Sexual Orientation and Gender Diversity, 2*(3), 307–312. https://doi.org/10.1037/sgd0000118

Van Dyke, M. E., Baumhofer, N. K., Slopen, N., Mujahid, M. S., Clark, C. R., Williams, D. R., & Lewis, T. T. (2020). Pervasive discrimination and allostatic load in African American and white adults. *Psychosomatic Medicine, 82*(3), 316–323. https://doi.org/10.1097/PSY.0000000000000788

Vaughan, M. D., & Waehler, C. A. (2009; 2010). Coming out growth: Conceptualizing and measuring stress-related growth associated with coming out to others as a sexual minority. *Journal of Adult Development, 17*(2), 94–109. https://doi.org/10.1007/s10804-009-9084-9

Villarreal, L., Charak, R., Schmitz, R. M., Hsieh, C., & Ford, J. D. (2020). The relationship between sexual orientation outness, heterosexism, emotion dysregulation, and alcohol use among lesbian, gay, and bisexual emerging adults. *Journal of Gay and Lesbian Mental Health.* Advance online publication. https://doi.10.1080\\19359705.2020.1809588

Wilson, B., Jordan, S. P., Meyer, I. H., Flores, A. R., Stemple, L., & Herman, J. L. (2017). Disproportionality and disparities among sexual minority youth in custody. *Journal of Youth and Adolescence, 46*(7), 1547–1561. https://doi.org/10.1007/s10964-017-0632-5

Wong, C. F., Schrager, S. M., Holloway, I. W., Meyer, I. H., & Kipke, M. D. (2014). Minority stress experiences and psychological well-being: The impact of support from and connection to social networks within the Los Angeles House and Ball communities. *Prevention*

Science: The Official Journal of the Society for Prevention Research, 15(1), 44–55. https://doi.org/10.1007/s11121-012-0348-4

World Health Organization. (2012). What are the social determinants of health? Retrieved from http://www.who.int/social_determinants/sdh_definition/en/

Xavier, J. M., Bradford, J., & Honnold, J. (2007). *The health, health-related needs, and life course experiences of transgender Virginians.* Virginia Department of Health.

Zautra, J., Hall, J. S., & Murray, K. E. (2010). Resilience: A new definition of health for people and communities. In J. W. Reich, A. J. Zautra & J. S. Stuart (Eds.), *Handbook of adult resilience* (pp. 3–29). Guilford Press.

CHAPTER 2

Intersectionality, Culturally Sensitive Care, and LGBTQ+ Youth

Kayden J. Schumacher, BA, MSc, MSEd, LSC,
Leonardo E. Candelario-Pérez, PhD, LP,
Eunice V. Avilés Faría, PsyD, LMHC, LPC,
& G. Nic Rider, PhD, LP

Adolescence and emerging adulthood may be critical developmental periods in which experiences of stigma and oppression-related stressors could have present and lifelong consequences (Gee et al., 2019; English et al., 2022; Trent et al., 2019). The COVID-19 pandemic undoubtedly re-illuminated disturbing inequities across the United States that significantly affect the health and well-being of marginalized youth and adults. Historical and ongoing structural oppression, such as anti-LGBTQ+ policies, and little to no protections for racial/ethnic marginalized LGBTQ+ youth accessing homeless services provide additional context for the exacerbation of social, economic, and health inequities for these young people (English et al., 2022).

Bowleg (2020) critiqued the phrase, "We are all in this together," noting the realities of how historically marginalized/excluded groups carry the intersectional burden of structural inequities. With ongoing structural oppression and the COVID-19 pandemic, LGBTQ+ youth at multiple social positions (e.g., undocumented LGBTQ+ adolescents; LGBTQ+ adolescents of color) have experienced nuanced challenges related to access to care. In some cases, these young people did not have access to resources (e.g., internet, computers, health insurance, financial assistance) to be able to participate in teletherapy, online groups, or web-based chat services for mental health, social support, or crisis intervention (Salerno et al., 2020). Some, particularly transgender and gender diverse youth of color, may have also been concerned with transphobia and racism, which could lead to social rejection within and outside of LGBQ spaces (Truszczynski et al., 2020).

In previous oppression-related research and scholarship, the primary focus has been on one identity category among youth, such as sexual identity alone or gender identity alone. Further, most quantitative research aggregate particular marginalized communities into one group (e.g., youth of color or LGBTQ+ youth) for analyses. LGBTQ+ youth at multiple social positions are exposed to intersecting stigma and discrimination (e.g., racism, transphobia, homophobia, sexism, etc.), which affect the resources they have access to and their health and well-being. By combining categories, critical differences and similarities in relationship to power between groups are likely overlooked, limiting the ability to create intersectionality-tailored intervention strategies. Notably, demographic changes, particularly the growth of racial and ethnic groups, have made the term "minority" obsolete (Sotto-Santiago, 2019).

A person's identities and social positions are not problematic or a source of mental health concerns; instead, the problem is the stigma, discrimination, and oppression people are exposed to in relation to their social identities and positions. As discussed in chapter 1, the minority stress model facilitates understanding of the prevalence of health outcomes among LGBTQ+ individuals (Bockting et al., 2013; Goldbach & Gibbs, 2017; Meyer, 2003; Testa et al., 2015). The initial development of this theoretical framework focused on understanding the impact of stigma, discrimination, marginalization, and victimization on a person's health due to a single aspect of the individual's identity—their sexual identity. The minority stress model has evolved, and its progression has included the integration of the intersectionality framework to better explain health outcomes among all LGBTQ+ individuals.

Intersectionality can expand minority stress theory by highlighting "how power and privilege operate on several levels at once (experiential, epistemological, political, and structural) and across (and within) categories of experience and personhood (including race, gender, sexuality, disability, social class, and citizenship)" (May, 2015, p. 23). Intersectionality includes the consideration of intersecting structural factors and systems of oppression, including racism, poverty, sexism, heterosexism, cisgenderism, ableism, colonialism, and others, in order to understand health outcomes of systematically minoritized, discriminated, marginalized, and victimized individuals and communities (Bowleg, 2012; Aguayo-Romero, 2021). An "intersectional minority stress framework" has been used to create awareness of the processes that influence mental health problems among specific marginalized groups such as Latinx LGBTQ+ young adults (Schmitz et al., 2019).

Both the minority stress model and an intersectional perspective have also informed the development of studies that have explored stressors and resilience among LGBTQ+ individuals of different racial and ethnic backgrounds. For example, considering the intersection of sexism, racism, heterosexism, and cultural values, Noyola and colleagues (2020) documented distinct minority stressors (e.g., sexual objectification, intersectional invisibility, and misrepresentation in the media) experienced by sexually diverse Latinx people and the specific strategies they used to cope with the stressors. Coping strategies involved the management of their identities (sexual and racial) depending on the context, creating psychological separation from minority stress in response to their family's reaction to their sexual identity, and the use of social support from individuals with similar cultural and sexual identities. As such, use of the intersectionality framework when studying sexual and gender minority stress has facilitated the understanding of health-related factors and disparities within the LGBTQ+ community (Williams et al., 2020).

Importantly, the focus of intersectionality is not simply about "multiple identities" but instead a focus on power and multiple interlocking structural inequities

(Bowleg, 2021). The movement toward a matrix perspective and away from thinking about identities as single, discrete categories that can be added or ranked (Crenshaw, 1989) is foundational to an intersectional lens. In other words, intersectionality embraces the complexities inherent across individuals' multiple social identities and positions, acknowledges that one identity (e.g., gender) must be understood in relation to other social identities (e.g., race, class, age), and that socio-structural factors create and exacerbate social, economic, and health inequities based on interlocking oppressive systems (Bowleg, 2017). An example of structural racism and LGBTQ+ oppression is the increased likelihood of entry into the school-to-prison pipeline for youth living at the intersection of multiple marginalized social positions (see chapter 12 for a more detailed discussion). It is important to critically examine the complex factors that perpetuate intersectional oppression that not only affect individuals' psychological health but also the stress experiences on community and population levels (English et al., 2022).

For those in schools, LGBTQ+ youth with multiple marginalized positions may face intersectional stigma-based bullying and harassment from their peers. In general, stigma-based bullying (also known as bias-based bullying) is a frequent occurrence in the school setting and has been shown to affect mental, physical, and social health and well-being and academic engagement and performance (Gower et al., 2018; Rosenthal et al., 2015; Russell et al., 2012). LGBTQ+ youth often are faced with significant societal pressures to conform, which may contribute to the internalization of negative perceptions of the self. These experiences of stigma-based bullying and pressures to conform, along with parental rejection, various forms of harassment, and hate crimes, have been described as potentially traumatic events for LGBTQ+ youth and are associated with increased rates of anxiety, depression, suicidality, substance use, and post-traumatic stress disorder for these young people (Barba et al., n.d.). Native American LGBTQ+ or two-spirit youth may experience similar potentially traumatic events as listed above, and these may be compounded by intergenerational/historical trauma (Bearse, 2012). LGBTQ+ youth of color who experience intersectional stigma-based bullying and harassment have been found to have an increased likelihood to miss school and have lower academic success (Diaz & Kosciw, 2009).

Additionally, LGBTQ+ young people are more likely to experience poor mental health in comparison to their cisgender and heterosexual counterparts (Charlton et al., 2018; Schnarrs et al., 2020). Schnarrs and colleagues (2020) found a large disparity in childhood trauma experiences among LGBTQ+ individuals, which was associated with poor mental health outcomes. The authors noted that resilience moderated this relationship and helped LGBTQ+ individuals to face these disparities and keep going. If resilience is a moderator to poor mental health associated with childhood trauma, and if community connectedness and pride in one's identity are protective factors against poor mental health and adverse outcomes later in life (e.g., Meyer, 1995, 2003; Testa et al., 2015), then it would only stand to reason that connecting LGBTQ+ youth with one another in supportive and empowering ways would be highly influential.

Practice Considerations

Connecting youth who share LGBTQ+ identities may be particularly beneficial in that it creates cultural connectedness and shared community. It gives youth a safe space to share common struggles and experiences, such as those related to identity exploration and peer relationships, which are vital during the influential years of puberty and development, especially for youth who may be struggling with puberty. However, not including an intersectional framework in the effort to connect youth directly affects the ability to provide this opportunity for some. Social media has been a monumental discovery for youth within the past few decades. Hagai, Annechino, Young, and Antin (2020) discuss that the use of social media and finding safe spaces online can be tricky for African American LGBTQ+ youth. While white and African American youth may use internet and social media at the same rates, African American households are less likely to have quality internet (Fields, et al., 2015; Jamil et al., 2009). Therefore, finding safe spaces and community with other LGBTQ+ people, especially other LGBTQ+ youth of color, can be directly affected by the resources available to particular families and communities.

Intersectionality is a transformative framework that centers power, praxis, and social justice, and it has the potential to be beneficial across multiple levels of intervention (individual, family, community, and structural). When considering mental health services, it is important to incorporate intersectionality in conceptualizations of clients, particularly as they share about marginalization, discrimination, and inequities in their lives. Intersectional and trauma-informed approaches are critically important for the healing process. Mental health providers can work with caregivers to help their LGBTQ+ youth develop pride in their identities, which may buffer against some negative mental health outcomes. The provider can also educate families and others who the youth interacts with about the importance of support at multiple levels (peer, family, community). The use of positive LGBTQ+ messaging, family and peer support/acceptance, and LGBTQ+-affirming school environments may buffer against mental health concerns, particularly for suicidality among young men who have sex with men (Luong et al., 2018).

It is also important that organizations provide access to trainings, consultation, and/or resources to assist clinicians in being prepared to work with LGBTQ+ youth (Barba et al., n.d.) as well as focus on broader sociopolitical concerns (e.g., substance abuse; food and housing instability; providing high-quality, culturally sensitive care; access to care). English and colleagues (2022) note that transformative efforts focused on racial-, sexual-, and gender-affirming policies such as protections against bullying, harassment, and other victimization at school; access to high-quality health across their marginalized identities; and bans for conversion therapy may be particularly important to buffer against suicidality and other mental health concerns for LGBTQ+ youth of color, particularly Black sexually diverse boys and men.

Advocacy Considerations

Intersectionality can also be a framework used for building relationships, fostering community mobilization, and working toward social and systemic change—all of which are complex and directly impact LGBTQ+ youth. Ellison and Langhout (2020) used the idea of intersectional solidarity to "recognize difference, examine privilege, and understand that intersecting social structures influence experience" (Ellison & Langhout, 2020, p. 950). Intervention is needed to dismantle the multiple interlocking systems of power and oppression that maintain and perpetuate inequities and negative health outcomes (Bhattacharya, 2017; Combahee River Collective, 1977/1995; Collins, 1990; Moraga & Anzaldúa, 1983, Ellison & Langhout, 2020, p. 951), which differentially impact youth exposed to various intersectional stigma. Ellison and Langhout (2020) describe how using an intersectional solidarity framework with accountability of transgressors makes apparent the interplay of oppression that is often occurring within organizations, relationships, and systems. A lack of accountability for oppressive actions is one of the real pitfalls standing in the way of organizations' ability to create social change and operate most effectively across intersectional differences (Ellison & Langhout, 2020). In this way, it is important to collect and analyze data that captures intersections that exist within schools, businesses, and other organizations, combined with accountability and actions leading to solidarity, social justice, and effective organizing (Fletcher, 1999; Ellison & Langhout, 2020).

Currently, schools, mental health professionals, and other youth organizations, especially those working closely with marginalized youth, including LGBTQ+ youth at multiple marginalized social positions, are adopting many intervention practices that promote relationship building, calling-in, and being mindful of intersectional identities. These practices come from indigenous roots and involve inviting an individual or individuals who have caused harm back into the community after hearing from those who were harmed and working through the harm they have caused. When applied, "restorative practices improve climate and culture . . . and . . . provides responses to wrongdoing that focus on repairing harm" (International Institute of Restorative Practices, 2021). With such practices starting at young ages, children are able to learn about others' lived experiences, thereby allowing for intersectionality-informed dialogue. Through this work, ideally youth will be able to express empathy and deeper understanding for the struggles of LGBTQ+ youth and why harm caused to them can be so detrimental.

Calling-in is a process in which an individual or group works to maintain a relationship but educate and teach after a harmful incident has occurred. The process of calling-in involves being "strategic, weighing the stakes and figuring out what we're trying to build and how we are going to do it together" (Trần, 2016, p. 60), which is different from calling-out or public shaming. If youth learn the strategies of calling-in instead of calling-out, the hope is that over time, dialogue for social change and intersectional solidarity, especially for LGBTQ+ youth, will develop. However, if someone is called-in, it does not mean that there has not been harm. In the process of calling-in, it is essential that the transgressor take accountability, learn from their mistake, and work toward behavior change (Trần, 2016). Despite the laborious and somewhat energy-consuming process that calling-in is, it can be an empowering experience and a way to address oppressive acts that center relationship and community building (Ellison & Langhout, 2020). The investment in growth and change is what the therapy relationship may look like, yet, in therapy, there does not need to be harm caused to learn and grow. Hence, therapy and therapeutic interventions are vital toward protecting LGBTQ+ youth.

Regardless of which methods are used to bring about intersectional solidarity, going through this process and finding therapeutic intervention, support to recover from potentially traumatic events, and a sense of community for LGBTQ+ youth is vital. Herman (2015) asserts that the individual who has experienced trauma will initially need a safe and secure environment in order to process about and grieve the loss from the trauma. Often this first stage is where therapists and mental health professionals come in. They aid in supporting and creating a safe and secure environment for individuals (especially LGBTQ+ youth) to start to grieve and rebuild from trauma. Following this first stage, the person may want to reconnect and reintegrate into society. In this process, they may share their experience of trauma in hopes to protect others and form relational bonds of resistance and healing with others. Radical healing (discussed in more detail in chapter 5) has most often been conceptualized for communities of color who collectively identify traumatic events (e.g., exposure to racism, genderism, and transphobia) and work collaboratively to foster hope and healing (French et al., 2020). Yet, without potential therapeutic intervention and the knowledge of intersectionality, many of these communities and individuals may struggle with finding a safe environment for themselves and working through the grieving stage of recovering from trauma. Intersectionality- and trauma-informed therapy and mental health support is essential.

Conclusion

When socio-structural-level experiences that reflect interconnected systems of oppression and privilege combine with internalized views of the self, we start to get a picture of an individual that is nuanced and complex. Mental health professionals need to recognize that clients' concerns and struggles do not exist in a vacuum. The fields of social sciences and mental health are especially important and relevant for increasing cultural-responsive, trauma-informed, and intersectional considerations for research and clinical practice. The mental health burdens of LGBTQ+ clients at multiple marginalized social positions are associated with exposures to intersectional stigma and discrimination. Therefore, professionals working within psychology need to have a large and empathetically minded grasp on the ways that societal marginalization plays a role in the manifestation of mental health concerns in order to care for, support, research, and engage LGBTQ+ individuals from all walks of life.

References

Aguayo-Romero, R. A. (2021). (Re)centering black feminism into intersectionality research. *American Journal of Public Health, 111*(1), 101–103. https://doi.org/10.2105/AJPH.2020.306005

Barba, A., Mooney, M., Giovanni, K., Clarke, M., Grady, J. B., & Cohen, J. A. (n.d.). *Identifying the intersection of trauma and sexual orientation and gender identity part I: Key considerations.* National Center for Child Traumatic Stress.

Bearse, M. L. (2012). Becoming who we are meant to be: Native Americans with two-spirit, LGBT, and/or related tribal identities. In S. K. Fisher, J. M. Poirier, & G. M. Blau (Eds.), *Improving emotional & behavioral outcomes for LGBT youth: A guide for professionals* (pp. 87–109). Brookes Publishing.

Bhattacharya, T. (2017). Introduction: Mapping social reproduction theory. In *Social reproduction theory: Remapping class, recentering oppression* (pp. 1–20). Pluto Press. http://doi.org/10.2307/j.ctt1vz494j

Bockting, W. O., Miner, M. H., Swinburne Romine, R. E., Hamilton, A., & Coleman, E. (2013). Stigma, mental health, and resilience in an online sample of the US transgender population. *American Journal of Public Health, 103*(5), 943–951. https://doi.org/10.2105/AJPH.2013.301241

Bowleg, L. (2012). The problem with the phrase women and minorities: Intersectionality—an important theoretical framework for public health. *American Journal of Public Health, 102*(7), 1267–1273. https://doi.org/10.2105/AJPH.2012.300750

Bowleg, L. (2017). Intersectionality: An underutilized but essential theoretical framework for social psychology. In B. Gough (Ed.), *Palgrave handbook of critical social psychology* (pp. 507–530). MacMillan Publishers Ltd.

Bowleg, L. (2020). We're not all in this together: On COVID-19, intersectionality, and structural inequality. *American Journal of Public Health, 110*(7), 917. https://doi.org/10.2105/AJPH.2020.305766

Bowleg, L. (2021). Evolving intersectionality within public health: From analysis to action. *American Journal of Public Health, 111*(1), 88–90. https://doi.org/10.2105/AJPH.2020.306031

Charlton, B. M., Gordon, A. R., Reisner, S. L., Sarda, V., Samnaliev, M., & Austin, S. B. (2018). Sexual orientation-related disparities in employment, health insurance, healthcare access and health-related quality of life: A cohort study of US male and female adolescents and young adults. *BMJ Open, 8*(6), e020418. http://dx.doi.org/10.1136/bmjopen-2017-020418

Collins, P. H. (1990). *Black feminist thought: Knowledge, consciousness, and the politics of empowerment.* Unwin Hyman.

Combahee River Collective. (1977/1995). Combahee River Collective statement. In B. Guy-Sheftall (Ed.), *Words of fire: An anthology of African American feminist thought* (pp. 232–240). New Press.

Crenshaw, K. W. (1989). Demarginalizing the intersection of race and sex: A Black feminist critique of antidiscrimination doctrine, feminist theory, and antiracist politics. *University of Chicago Legal Forum, 139*(1), 139–167. Retrieved from http://chicagounbound.uchicago.edu/uclf/vol1989/iss1/8

Diaz, E. M., & Kosciw, J. G. (2009). *Shared differences: The experiences of lesbian, gay, bisexual, and transgender students of color in our nation's schools.* GLSEN.

Ellison, E. R., & Langhout, R. E. (2020). Embodied relationship praxis in intersectional organizing: Developing intersectional solidarity. *Journal of Social Issues, 76*(4), 949–970. https://doi.org/10.1111/josi.12402

English, D., Boone, C. A., Carter, J. A., Talan, A. J., Busby, D. R., Moody, R. L., Cunningham, D. J., Bowleg, L., & Rendina, H. J. (2022). Intersecting structural oppression and suicidality among black sexual minority male adolescents and emerging adults. *Journal of Research on Adolescence, 32*(1), 226–243. https://doi.org/10.1111/jora.12726

Fields, E. L., Morgan, A. R., Malebranche, D. J., Smith, K. C., Ellen, J. M., & Sanders, R. A. (2015). The role of virtual venues among young black men who have sex with men (YBMSM): Exploration of patterns of use from 2001–2011. *Journal of Adolescent Health, 56*(2), S118–S119. https://doi.org/10.1016/j.jadeohealth.2014.10.237

Fletcher, J. K. (1999). *Disappearing acts: Gender, power, and relational practice at work*. M.I.T. Press. https://doi.org/10.7551/mitpress/2440.001.0001

French, B. H., Lewis, J. A., Mosley, D. V., Adames, H. Y., Chavez-Dueñas, N. Y., Chen, G. A., & Neville, H. A. (2020). Toward a psychological framework of radical healing in communities of color. *Counseling Psychologist, 48*(1), 14–46. https://doi.org/10.1177/0011000019843506

Gee, G. C., Hing, A., Mohammed, S., Tabor, D. C., & Williams, D. R. (2019). Racism and the life course: Taking time seriously. *American Journal of Public Health, 109*(S1), S43–S47. https://doi.org/10.2105/AJPH.2018.304766

Goldbach, J. T., & Gibbs, J. J. (2017). A developmentally informed adaptation of minority stress for sexual minority adolescents. *Journal of Adolescence, 55*, 36–50. https://doi.org/10.1016/j.adolescence.2016.12.007

Gower, A. L., Rider, G. N., McMorris, B. J., & Eisenberg, M. E. (2018). Bullying victimization among LGBTQ youth: Critical issues and future directions. *Current Sexual Health Reports, 10*(4), 246–254. https://doi.org/10.1007/s11930-018-0169-y

Hagai, E. B., Annechino, R., Young, N., & Antin, T. (2020). Intersecting sexual identities, oppressions, and social justice work: Comparing LGBTQ Baby Boomers to Millennials who came of age after the 1980s AIDS epidemic. *Journal of Social Issues, 76*(4), 971–992. https://doi.org/10.1111/josi.12405

Herman, J. L. (2015). *Trauma and recovery: The aftermath of violence—from domestic abuse to political terror*. Hachette.

International Institute of Restorative Practices. (2021). *Restorative practices in schools*. IIRP Graduate School. Retrieved from https://www.iirp.edu/resources/restorative-practices-in-schools-k-12-education.

Jamil, O. B., Harper, G. W., & Fernandez, M. I. (2009). Sexual and ethnic identity development among gay/bisexual/questioning (GBQ) male ethnic minority adolescents. *Cultural Diversity & Ethnic Minority Psychology, 15*(3), 203–214. https://doi.org/10.1037/a0014795

Luong, C. T., Rew, L., & Banner, M. (2018). Suicidality in young men who have sex with men: A systematic review of the literature. *Issues in Mental Health Nursing, 39*(1), 37–45. https://doi.org/10.1080/01612840.2017.1390020

May, V. M. (2015). *Pursuing intersectionality, unsettling dominant imaginaries*. Routledge.

Meyer, I. H. (1995). Minority stress and mental health in gay men. *Journal of Health and Social Behavior, 36*(1), 38–56. http://www.jstor.org/stable/2137286

Meyer, I. H. (2003). Prejudice, social stress, and mental health in lesbian, gay, and bisexual populations: Conceptual issues and research evidence. *Psychological Bulletin, 129*(5), 674–697. https://doi.org/10.1037/0033-2909.129.5.674

Moraga, C., & Anzaldúa, G. (1983). *This bridge called my back: Writings by radical women of color* (2nd ed.). Kitchen Table Press.

Noyola, N., Sánchez, M., & Cardemil, E. V. (2020). Minority stress and coping among sexual diverse Latinxs. *Journal of Latinx Psychology, 8*(1), 58–82. https://doi.org/10.1037/lat0000143

Rosenthal, L., Earnshaw, V. A., Carroll-Scott, A., Henderson, K. E., Peters, S. M., McCaslin, C., & Ickovics, J. R. (2015). Weight- and race-based bullying: Health associations among urban adolescents. *Journal of Health Psychology, 20*(4), 401–412. https://doi.org/10.1177/1359105313502567

Russell, S. T., Sinclair, K. O., Poteat, V. P., & Koenig, B. W. (2012). Adolescent health and harassment based on discriminatory bias. *American Journal of Public Health, 102*(3), 493–495. https://doi.org/10.2105/AJPH.2011.300430

Salerno, J. P., Devadas, J., Pease, M., Nketia, B., & Fish, J. N. (2020). Sexual and gender minority stress amid the COVID-19 pandemic: Implications for LGBTQ young persons' mental health and well-being. *Public Health Reports, 135*(6), 721–727. https://doi.org/10.1177/0033354920954511

Schmitz, R. M., Robinson, B. A., Tabler, J., Welch, B., & Rafaqut, S. (2019). LGBTQ+ Latino/a young people's interpretations of stigma and mental health: An intersectional minority stress perspective. *Society and Mental Health, 10*(2), 163–179. https://doi.org/10.1177/2156869319847248

Schnarrs, P. W., Stone, A. L., Salcido, R., Georgiou, C., Zhou, X., & Nemeroff, C. B. (2020). The moderating effect of resilience on the relationship between adverse childhood experiences (ACEs) and quality of physical and mental health among adult sexual and gender minorities. *Behavioral Medicine, 46*(3–4), 366–374. https://doi.org/10.1080/08964289.2020.1727406

Smith, A. (2014). *African Americans and technology use*. Pew Research Center.

Sotto-Santiago, S. (2019). Time to reconsider the word minority in academic medicine. *Journal of Best Practices in Health and Professions Diversity, 12*(1), 72–78.

Testa, R. J., Habarth, J., Peta, J., Balsam, K., & Bockting, W. (2015). Development of the gender minority stress and resilience measure. *Psychology of Sexual Orientation and Gender Diversity, 2*(1), 65–77. https://doi.org/10.1037/sgd0000081

Trần, N. L. (2016). Calling-in: A less disposable way of holding each other accountable. In M. McKenzie (Ed.), *The solidarity struggle: How people of color succeed and fail at showing up for each other in the fight for freedom*. BGD Press.

Trent, M., Dooley, D. G., & Dougé, J. (2019). The impact of racism on child and adolescent health. *Pediatrics, 144*(2), e20191765. https://doi.org/10.1542/peds.2019-1765

Truszczynski, N., Singh, A. A., & Hansen, N. (2020). The discrimination experiences and coping responses of non-binary and trans people. *Journal of Homosexuality, 69*(4), 741–755. https://doi.org/10.1080/00918369.2020.1855028

Williams, S. L., Job, S. A., Todd, E., & Braun, K. (2020). A critical deconstructed quantitative analysis: Sexual and gender minority stress through an intersectional lens. *Journal of Social Issues, 76*, 859–879. https://doi.org/10.1111/josi.12410

CHAPTER 3

Interdisciplinary Healthcare for Transgender Youth

AN APPLICATION OF THE GENDER AFFIRMATIVE LIFESPAN APPROACH (GALA)

Katherine G. Spencer, PhD, LP, CST, & Nova Bradford, LGSW

Interdisciplinary care, or interprofessional collaboration, is the process whereby providers from different health and social care disciplines work together to provide clinical care (Reeves et al., 2017). Traditionally, clinicians have been largely isolated from those of other disciplines and worked in discipline-specific settings; for instance, primary care providers may have worked in clinics staffed exclusively by other primary care physicians and nurses. However, patient health needs are often complex and multifaceted in ways that are inadequately addressed in single-discipline clinical settings. As a result, there have been increasing calls for integrated care, in which clinicians from various disciplines, as well as entire organizations and health systems, work together to address complex health conditions (Institute of Medicine, 2013; World Health Organization, 2010).

In spite of significant calls for integrated care, the definition of the term has remained conceptually ambiguous. To address this, Valentijn and colleagues (2013) reviewed and synthesized existing literature to develop a comprehensive conceptual framework of integrated care at the macro, meso, and micro levels. Interdisciplinary care, which largely occurs on the micro level, must be viewed within the broader context of health systems (e.g., macro and meso levels) that facilitate or impede meaningful collaboration. The macro level includes system integration, which may include vertical integration (e.g., the integration of care across levels, such as primary care and secondary/tertiary care that are housed in the same healthcare system) as well as horizontal integration (e.g., the integration of care within a single level, such as grouping multiple primary care practices within the same healthcare system). The meso level includes organization integration, including the extent of linkage and relationships between different organizations, as well as professional integration, including partnerships between professionals both within and between organizations. This should include interprofessional partnerships based on shared competencies, roles, and responsibilities. The micro level includes clinician integration, which includes coordination of care in a single process that spans time, place, and professional discipline. Macro, meso, and micro levels of care integration are linked through two processes: functional and normative integration. Functional integration is the extent to which key supports (e.g., finance, human resources, management, medical records, etc.) are structured to enable collaboration between professionals and communications, whereas normative integration refers to a common frame of reference (e.g., mission, values, and culture) that supports integration across professionals and organizations.

As health systems become increasingly integrated, healthcare professionals are increasingly called upon to engage collaboratively across disciplines. For behavioral health professionals, such as clinical or counseling psychologists, social workers, marriage and family therapists, and clinical counselors, this may often involve developing collaborative relationships with health professionals who have dramatically different training, expertise, and clinical perspectives. In writing of interdisciplinary research, Hesse-Biber (2016) encourages individuals to "work the tensions" that lie within the space between disciplinary borders and to leave one's theoretical comfort zones in order to reimagine oneself as a part of a multidisciplinary team. We find this advice helpful for those working in interprofessional collaborative care.

This chapter explores interdisciplinary care within the field of transgender health specifically, as an extended example of how it can be applied to the work of clinicians with LGBTQ youth; and it includes historical background, theoretical orientation, and case examples in clinical care, research, and policy practice. We encourage readers to consider personal, organizational, and political factors that may facilitate or impede meaningful interprofessional collaborations and examine ways in which interdisciplinary approaches may be uniquely applicable to topics in transgender health.

Introduction to Transgender Health

The need for integrated, interdisciplinary healthcare is clear in the field of transgender health, perhaps even more so than in other subdisciplines, and decidedly so when working with gender creative youth. By nature, gender affirmative healthcare can involve professionals in disciplines ranging from endocrinology, family medicine, gynecology, dermatology, psychiatry, social work, psychotherapy, speech-language pathology, and more (Coleman et al., 2012). In recent years, team-based models and pedagogical standards for interdisciplinary transgender healthcare have been articulated by professionals in the Boston Children's Hospital (Edwards-Leeper & Spack, 2012) and the Veterans Health Administration (VHA) (Shipherd et al., 2016) and in emerging frameworks such as the gender affirmative model (Keo-Meier & Ehrensaft, 2018) and the Gender Affirmative Lifespan Approach (GALA) (Berg et al., 2017; Rider et al., 2019; Spencer & Vencill, 2017; Spencer et al., 2021) have provided increased guidance for interdisciplinary healthcare delivery for transgender people of all ages. In working with youth, there are particular concerns related to developmental needs, perceptions of autonomy, and interactions with multiple systems. In the current chapter, we contribute to this emerging body of literature through describing the GALA and exploring several applications of GALA to the interdisciplinary treatment of transgender youth.

Please note that the scope of the current chapter is limited to transgender healthcare for youth (adolescents and young adults) in the United States. The realities of interdisciplinary collaboration and basic logistics of healthcare delivery are fundamentally shaped by the structure of a nation's health system. In the United States, healthcare is largely situated in the private sector, with hospitals and clinics, pharmacies, and insurers operating independently. The unsystematic nature of this system creates a unique set of benefits and challenges for healthcare providers and clients. As such, we urge readers from countries other than the United States to exercise discretion, given that the insights discussed here may or may not generalize to other health systems.

History of Gender Affirmative Healthcare for Youth

Access to gender affirmative medical interventions, including surgeries and hormone therapy, have historically relied on psychotherapists as "gatekeepers," meaning that some degree of contact with a psychotherapist has traditionally been a prerequisite for accessing desired medical interventions (Budge, 2015). Such recommendations have been dictated primarily by the World Professional Association for Transgender Health (WPATH) through the publication of the Standards of Care for the Health of Gender Diverse People (SOC). For instance, Version 6 of the SOC outlined that transgender people must receive at least three months of psychotherapy prior to obtaining a letter from their psychotherapist that would enable access to hormone therapy (Meyer et al., 2001). Version 7 (the current version as of publication of this chapter) does not require a minimum period of psychotherapy but stipulates that referral for gender-affirming surgical interventions should be "initiated by a referral (one or two, depending on the type of surgery) from a qualified mental health professional" (Coleman et al., 2012).

It is important to note that SOC version 7 stipulates that gender-affirming hormone therapy can be initiated either by a mental health professional or other qualified health professional who can provide "documentation—in the chart and/or referral letter—of the patient's personal and treatment history, progress, and eligibility" for gender-affirming hormone therapy (Coleman et al., 2012, p. 182). Though they have become less stringent over time, such criteria have been widely criticized for myriad reasons, including the arbitrary nature of such requirements, which lack a clear empirical justification (Coleman et al., 2012), as well as ethical concerns due to the compulsory and potentially dehumanizing nature of mental healthcare as a prerequisite for medical intervention (Ashley, 2019). This also demonstrates an abject failure of meaningful interdisciplinary care—the use of mental health professionals as a barrier to medical care access runs contrary to the intent and purpose of care integration.

Autonomy and self-determination within healthcare are well-established principles in international human rights law (e.g., through the Universal Declaration of Human Rights [UN General Assembly, 1948], Convention on the Rights of Persons with Disabilities [UN General Assembly, 2006], and International Covenant on Civil and Political Rights [UN General Assembly, 1966]). In recent times, transgender community-led efforts have resulted in a proliferation of so-called "informed consent" clinics in the United States (e.g., Fenway, Howard Brown, Callen-Lorde, and many others). Informed consent is standard practice in all other areas of medicine, in which patients are granted the right to access or decline treatment as they see fit, yet the application of this well-established standard to transition-related healthcare is an improvement nonetheless. This shift has led to an increase in the availability of hormone providers, broadening access outside the traditional, highly specialized "gender clinic" and into areas such as primary care and family medicine (Schulz, 2018).

The health needs of gender diverse youth (in this case defined as adolescents and young adults up to age 25, excluding prepubescent children) are unique in several ways when compared to their cisgender, heterosexual counterparts. The advent of puberty-suppressing medications in particular has been met with much controversy within the field of transgender healthcare as well as the larger culture (de Vries et al., 2014). Adolescents and young adults with gender concerns are often met with disbelief and questions about their ability to "know" themselves and their future. This intersects with dominant cultural beliefs about youth, while also intersecting with developmental needs of youth in their own gender and sexual development. The ability of providers to be able to check their own beliefs and assumptions about youth is an important step in safeguarding the autonomy and self-determination of youth, especially with regards to gender-affirming medical interventions. Studies have found transgender youth avoid seeking primary care and do not trust providers to be gender affirming (Clark et al., 2018).

We imagine the future of interdisciplinary care in transgender health as one grounded in respect for the dignity and autonomy of transgender people. Furthermore, we hope for a future in which the expertise of mental health professionals is leveraged for a more legitimate purpose—that is, actually treating the mental health of transgender people, rather than simply providing unnecessary and burdensome assessments.

Minority Stress

It is well-established that transgender individuals report higher rates of psychological distress than their cisgender counterparts (James et al., 2016). To explain this phenomenon of elevated psychopathology in lesbian women, Brooks (1981) proposed the theory of sexual minority stress as a potential causative factor. This work was expanded by Meyer (2003), who formalized the minority stress model, which was subsequently extended to transgender individuals by Hendricks and Testa (2012). The minority stress model is an extension of the observation that stressful aspects of a social environment can have psychopathogenic effects, and it posits that the stigma and marginalization faced by LGB and transgender individuals is experienced in the form of chronic stress (Hendricks & Testa, 2012; Meyer, 1995; Meyer, 2003). Therefore, the elevated rates of psychological distress among transgender individuals can be attributed to cisgenderism, a bias that privileges and normalizes cisgender expressions and experiences over transgender ones (Ansara & Hegarty, 2012).

Three processes underlie the minority stress model, progressing from proximal to distal: first, external stressful events, either chronic or acute such as discrimination or other forms of bias; second, expectations of stressful events and vigilance toward potential bias; and third, the internalization of negative social beliefs. Distal stressors, such as objective instances of prejudice and discrimination, can occur regardless of an individual's minority identity—for instance, gender-nonconforming behaviors may result in social sanctions for individuals regardless of their gender or sexual minority identity (Rosario et al., 2011). Proximal stressors, on the other hand, may depend on an individual's minority identity; according to social identity theory (Tajfel, 1974), group memberships are represented as part of an individual's self-concept, so sanctions against behaviors associated with a minority group are likely to hold greater significance for individuals who identify with that group.

Meyer (2003) identifies resilience pathways whereby coping with minority stress results in what are considered adaptive outcomes. For instance, individuals holding marginalized identities may evaluate themselves based on the countercultural norms of their minority community rather than the norms of the dominant culture (Meyer, 2003; Pettigrew, 1967). This is reflected by Pinto, Melendez, and Spector's (2008) findings that trans women participants formed friendship networks within the clinics they frequented, which served as a catalyst for in-group identification and social support. However, Meyer (2003) notes that the ability to access such group-level coping resources depends on the circumstances of the individual, such that these resources may be systematically unavailable to certain members of marginalized communities. For instance, certain transgender individuals, such as those who are nonbinary or genderqueer, may be alienated from transgender communities and thus experience thwarted in-group identification and social support (Brooks, 2016; Farmer & Byrd, 2015; Johnson, 2016). Therefore, the same coping attempts may lead to normatively resilient or maladaptive outcomes depending on personal and community circumstances.

The Gender Affirmative Lifespan Approach (GALA)

GALA is an integrated, interdisciplinary model of psychotherapy applicable to gender development throughout the life span. This integrated, biopsychosociocultural model of psychotherapy is based on feminist and developmental theories of sexuality and gender and has emerged from the fields of psychology, social work, transgender health, gender and sexuality studies, and sex therapy. GALA was developed with a focus on clinical work with transgender and gender diverse clients, but the model is applicable to people of all gender and sexual identities. GALA consists of six philosophical foundations and five core components, which are described below.

PHILOSOPHICAL FOUNDATIONS OF GALA

The philosophical foundations of GALA provide the conceptual underpinnings of the model. The six foundations of GALA include: (1) transaffirmative care; (2) intersectionality; (3) transparency; (4) developmental differences in care across the life span; (5) an interdisciplinary approach; and (6) empiricism (Rider et al., 2019).

Transaffirmative, as an orientation within psychotherapy, means to value transgender and gender diverse identities and experiences within a spectrum of gender identities and expressions (Rider et al., 2019). Transaffirmative perspectives intentionally resist cisnormative frameworks of identity, which understand cisgender identities as "standard" or "normal" and approach transgender identities as "variant." *Intersectionality* is a rich construct that has been applied across various fields of medicine and psychotherapy that refers to the interconnectedness of all social categorizations (Crenshaw, 1997). Within an individual's gendered experience, intersectionality means a provider cannot disregard the complex ways in which the cultural context of a client's race, class, sexual orientation, ability status, and other important lived experiences overlap and interact and the ways these identities are linked to structural and systemic inequality. Additionally, GALA holds *transparency* as an essential practice. Transparency within psychotherapy involves intentional and thoughtful sharing of information, collaboration in therapeutic tasks, and breaking down opaque medical and psychiatric systems. Many LGBTQ people report enduring negative and even harmful experiences with health providers (e.g., Puckett et al., 2018), so transparency is necessary to assist clients in navigating health systems that are rooted in a historically homophobic, transphobic cultural environment. GALA highlights the importance of both generational and developmental differences in shaping individual experiences *across the life span*, particularly around gender and sexual identities. Finally, *interdisciplinary* approaches are central to GALA and critical to informing competent practice with LGBTQ clients, who frequently interact with multiple health systems from a range of professional disciplines.

CORE COMPONENTS OF GALA

GALA involves five core components central to gender affirmative psychotherapy: 1) developing gender literacy; 2) building resiliency; 3) moving beyond the binary; 4) supporting pleasure-oriented positive sexuality; and 5) making affirming connections to medical interventions. Consistent with the philosophical foundation of working across the life span, these five core components must be tailored to the developmental needs of each individual client. These five core components can be the basis for interdisciplinary care coordination and interprofessional collaboration. The components are explored in more depth below.

Developing *gender literacy* is the process of developing a more nuanced vocabulary to understand and discuss gender and sexuality. For instance, gender literacy involves understanding how sex assigned at birth, gender identity, gender expression, and sexual orientation are distinct but interconnected aspects of experience. Gender literacy also involves learning to identify and name oppressive social practices within society as they manifest in the lives of LGBTQ people. Building *resiliency* involves learning how to effectively cope with stressful and challenging situations that LGBTQ people face, including experiences of homophobia and transphobia. Resiliency-building also involves having safe social support systems, such as family, friends, and community groups, which are a key protective factor that buffers against some of the deleterious impacts of stress (Breslow et al., 2015). Moving *beyond the binary* to a spectrum or continuum perspective allows for the acceptance and celebration of the full range of gender identities and expressions. Similarly, developmentally appropriate psychotherapy aimed at developing *pleasure-oriented positive sexuality* is essential, especially considering the near-exclusive focus on negative sexual health outcomes for LGBTQ people. Finally, gender-competent psychotherapists need to possess the knowledge and skills to refer clients to *medical interventions* when appropriate.

In order to explore GALA more closely in relation to the current topic, one philosophical underpinning, interdisciplinary approach, and one core component, connections to medical interventions, will be elucidated in greater depth below.

Interdisciplinary Approach

Given that transgender youth frequently interact with many healthcare providers from a range of health professions, an integrated, interdisciplinary approach is critical to competent mental health practice with transgender clients. In practice, accessing gender affirmative healthcare is often challenging, given the shortage of competent, available healthcare providers, which can lead to delays in accessing care (Hendricks & Testa, 2012) or adverse experiences with healthcare providers (Safer et al., 2016). This is especially critical for transgender youth, considering undergoing desired medical transition is associated with improved mental health outcomes (de Vries et al., 2014). Thus, it is important for gender-affirming mental health professionals to view transgender clients from a holistic approach rather than from a purely psychological framework. Similarly, gender-affirming medical providers must consider the psychosocial context of their clients' lives, given that gender affirmative medical interventions are directly associated with mental and emotional health. It is critical for gender affirmative providers to create and consult with an interprofessional team of healthcare providers when approaching transgender healthcare. For example, gender diverse children on the cusp of puberty may or may not meet with a medical gender specialist, depending on whether they are interested in puberty suppression. Even for those children interested in puberty suppression, it is often helpful to have a gender-competent pediatrician who understands the ways routine pediatric care may or may not be impacted by puberty suppression. Communication and care coordination among providers are essential steps in maintaining relevant health outcomes. Additionally, it may also be important for health providers to advocate for transgender youth as they encounter barriers to their healthcare needs. This may include, for example, connecting patients with lawyers who can provide legal support for matters such as name/gender marker changes or insurance denials.

Connections to Medical Interventions

Traditionally, psychotherapists have served as "gatekeepers" to gender affirmative medical interventions, a widely criticized practice by laypersons and providers alike due to the barriers this creates to accessing care, the dehumanizing nature of such practices, and the deleterious impact on the psychotherapeutic process (Ashley, 2019; Budge, 2015). Many of these practices persist, including compulsory psychological evaluations for transgender people interested in accessing surgery. For example, the current WPATH Standards of Care (version 7; Coleman et al., 2012) recommends one or two letters of referral for genital surgeries and one for breast/chest surgeries. The process of acquiring these letters of referral from mental health providers is often quite complex, and it creates a barrier to healthcare access. It is important to note that SOC version 7 does stipulate the possibility that providers working within "multidisciplinary specialty team[s]" may not need a letter of referral since "the assessment and recommendation can be documented in the patient's chart" (Coleman et al., 2012, p. 183), but this recommendation still suggests that mental health assessments should be a compulsory prerequisite to accessing gender-affirming surgeries. Given this history, shifting the paradigm toward *facilitating* empowering connections to medical interventions, rather than implementing barriers, is a core component of GALA. Providers working with transgender youth provide optimal care by embedding themselves in a community of interdisciplinary gender affirmative providers, which may include surgeons, hormone providers (including pediatric endocrinologists), primary care providers (including pediatricians and adolescent medicine), speech-language pathologists, physical therapists, and any other relevant providers that may interact with their clients, including health-adjacent professions such as electrologists and laser hair-removal technicians.

Case Studies

Below are a series of case studies that outline the application of GALA, with an emphasis on the interdisciplinary philosophical underpinning and core component of connections to medical interventions. Please note that case examples are based on real clinical material, but each represents a synthesis of similar cases and thus are not specific to any individual. All potentially identifying information has been removed and details have been changed to protect confidentiality. Each case starts with an introduction and relevant demographic and clinical information.

CASE STUDY A: RESEARCH—UNICORN YOUTH

Sex education involves the communication of health information and largely occurs within the context of primary and secondary school, therefore it involves interdisciplinary collaboration at the intersection of the fields of medicine, public health, and education. Sex education is fraught with political controversy in the United States due to divergent value systems relating to youth, sexuality, and access to information (for a review, see Santelli et al., 2006). The sex education experiences of transgender youth are particularly noteworthy for three reasons: 1) the general barriers that impact the delivery of any education to trans youth, such as not being referred to by their preferred name and pronouns or being forced to use restrooms that are incompatible with their gender identity (Reisner et al., 2015; Miller et al., 2017); 2) the unique negative sexual health outcomes of which trans youth are at high risk, including higher rates of dating abuse, sexual coercion, and HIV infection when compared to cisgender youth (Dank et al., 2014; Garofalo et al., 2006); and 3) the unique dating and sexual experiences of trans youth, such as navigating gender dysphoria during sexual encounters (Riggs & Bartholomaeus, 2017). Perhaps unsurprisingly, an emerging body of research has suggested that the sex education experiences of transgender youth are frequently inadequate. For instance, trans youth have reported sex education experiences that are irrelevant to their needs (e.g., information about safer sex practices explained only within the context of cisgender, heterosexual couples) or even actively hostile toward gender diversity (e.g., discouraging gender nonconformity; Jones, 2017; Jones et al., 2016; Riggs & Bartholomaeus, 2017). As such, unique attention toward the sex education needs and experiences of transgender youth is warranted to ensure the development of culturally relevant curricula.

In order to address these questions, an interdisciplinary team of researchers at the University of Minnesota conducted a series of qualitative interviews with transgender youth to explore their experiences with sex education—a study that came to be known as the Unicorn Youth Project. The research team included the authors of this publication (a clinical social worker and a counseling psychologist/assistant professor) as well as a second counseling psychologist, a sex educator, a public health professional, and a physician. Hesse-Biber (2016) notes the manner in which interdisciplinary research calls upon researchers to "de-discipline," a process involving re-integrating research practice and identity around a collaborative model. In *working the tension* between disciplinary boundaries, researchers are empowered to step out of their theoretical comfort zones and approach research questions from new angles. We agree that this type of integrative interdisciplinary research fosters the type of epistemological creativity that is necessary when approaching complex problems in health research, and it encourages all researchers to question the ways disciplinarity may inhibit the innovation of their scholarly work.

The Unicorn Youth Project was intentionally youth-centered, as understanding the subjective experiences of trans youth in sex education is integral to providing culturally relevant curricula (to read the published report, see Bradford et al., 2018). A semi-structured online questionnaire and group interview were the most relevant research designs for these purposes. Most methodologies involve a trade-off between the depth or "thickness" of data and the sample size, as qualitative methodologies that provide rich, nuanced descriptions of subjective phenomena are labor-intensive and often cost-prohibitive for underfunded research topics. For the purposes of this study, the group interview was chosen due to its resource efficiency and usefulness in providing insights into the subjective experiences underlying social and behavioral phenomena (Frey & Fontana, 1991), and the online questionnaire for its capacity to reach a greater number of participants. These dual methodologies were designed to maximize both the depth and scope of the results within the constraints of available funding.

One of the central findings of the study, reflected in the title of the published paper, is the importance of the educator. The often-stated participatory concept of "nothing about us without us" was strongly reflected in participants' accounts, including the desire for queer and trans youth to be included both in the creation and delivery of sex education content. Participants reported a no-win situation when accessing sex education material, such that sources of information that they perceived to be accurate and reliable, such as doctors, were not perceived as affirming, whereas affirming sources of information, such as blogs, were not perceived as accurate or reliable. These results call into question the "youth-as-expert" approach, which has been favored by the majority of the youth activism movement (Garmulewicz & Ireland, 2010). This approach understands youth as experts on their own experience and has traditionally understood youth empowerment as best attained through peer support and undermined by adult authority. Participants in the Unicorn Youth study reported suspiciousness that entirely youth-curated materials might be medically inaccurate, and they desired some involvement of health professionals in the development of sex education curricula. However, the limitations of the implicit "adult as expert" model are also obvious, as participants did not perceive health professionals as possessing relevant cultural knowledge about queer and trans youth. Given the historically fractured relationships between transgender people and the medical profession (for a review, see Prunas, 2019), such reticence is understandable. The limitations of both approaches to sex education are remedied by a systemic approach (Miller, 1998), which emphasizes positive natural hierarchies, such as those between adults and youth, while simultaneously facilitating open, intergenerational collaboration (Garmulewicz & Ireland, 2010). Such an approach allows for the expertise of both youth and health professionals and provides the framework for developing sex education curricula that is both culturally relevant and medically accurate.

The imperative for sound, interdisciplinary collaboration when developing and delivering sex education curriculum is clear. Sex education cannot be understood as the purview of a single professional discipline, as no single discipline is likely to possess the necessary degrees of expertise in sexual health, youth development, education, and human diversity required for truly comprehensive sex education. The results of the Unicorn Youth study further suggest the need for an even broader conceptualization of interdisciplinarity, which encompasses service users as holding a relevant disciplinary perspective. As sexual health professionals, we are called upon to engage in critical reflexivity and participatory interdisciplinarity if we are to achieve truly culturally competent sex education.

CASE STUDY B: ADVOCACY & POLICY—HEALTH INSURANCE ADVOCACY IN MINNESOTA

An interdisciplinary approach to advocacy and policy has been essential throughout the progression of fighting for rights and access to healthcare for sexual and gender minorities. The specific context of trans youth rights is shaped in the United States by dominant cultural norms and beliefs about youth rights and LGBTQA+ rights. For example, in creating access to gender-affirming healthcare for trans and gender diverse youth, not only is the interface of the medical industrial complex and access to care significant, but also legal and policy norms of age of consent and beliefs about if/how youth should/can be able to make decisions about their own healthcare are important. In this case example, we focus on an interdisciplinary approach to building an advocacy and policy approach to advocating for healthcare access for gender-affirming treatment for trans and gender creative youth (defined as younger than 18 years old).

Kelsey (she/her) is a 13-year-old trans girl who presented to a gender care clinic seeking puberty suppression gender-affirming medical care. She had socially transitioned at age 10 and, along with her supportive parents, had been attending gender-affirming psychotherapy for several years. She met with a provider who prescribed puberty suppression, and with the support of the medical provider, her psychotherapist, and her parents, she was well informed and prepared to start puberty suppression medical treatment. When the medical provider submitted the request for insurance coverage, the claim was immediately denied. The insurance company requested a letter from both Kelsey's medical provider and her psychotherapist, attesting to Kelsey's readiness for puberty suppression and a rationale for medically necessary treatment. After consulting with WPATH, as well as a local LGBTQ-rights nonprofit, the providers submitted detailed letters to the company. At this point, the insurance company denied the claim again given the lack of clarity regarding the evidence base supporting the medical necessity of puberty suppression.

For trans and gender diverse youth, the denial of gender-affirming care is too often a reality, given the politicized nature of gender-affirming care for youth. Even as Kelsey had the support of her family and providers, she and her family then came up against barriers within insurance and policies about access to gender-affirming medical care that can vary from state to state. Puberty suppression medications can be prohibitively expensive and limited in how they can be prescribed by the medical system. In order to access her gender-affirming care, Kelsey is in need of complex collaboration and coordination between her psychologist, her family medicine physician, her family, and legal and health advocates. In order to expand access to puberty suppression care for clients like Kelsey, medical and mental health providers must serve as forceful advocates not only within their healthcare provision sites, but also on a local, state, and national level regarding policy around trans and gender diverse youth. Legislators on national and local levels continue to use gender-affirming healthcare, particularly for youth, as a divisive issue and often use misleading research to inflame transphobic and homophobic fears and intersect them with beliefs around childhood development and autonomy.

After receiving the second denial, Kelsey's psychologist and a lawyer for the state LGBTQ-rights organization involved in the case submitted letters to the insurance company. They included information from WPATH and transgender health-rights organizations in order to educate and apply pressure. The medical provider prescribing the puberty suppression medication also submitted appeals. In Kelsey's case, individual providers applying pressure to insurance companies to provide consistent coverage, state and national advocacy, and coordination with trans health organizations such as WPATH were necessary to decrease barriers to her care. Coordinated efforts to include puberty suppression medications on indexes of empirically supported treatments for childhood gender dysphoria has required a patchwork of state- and national-level advocacy. This needed level of complex policy fluency in order to access medically necessary treatments puts youth and their families and caregivers in difficult, daunting circumstances; hence the need for providers to take an active role in advocating for their patients as well as being educated in healthcare policy.

After several denials and advocacy by Kelsey's providers, and pressure from the state-level LGBT health-rights organization, Kelsey's claim was approved and she was able to begin her treatments. The denials added months of wait and uncertainty to her healthcare experience, which aggravated her gender dysphoria, increased her anxiety and depression symptoms, and increased feelings of stigmatization. Anti-LGBT policy on state and federal levels has been shown to increase negative mental health symptoms (Mallory et al., 2017).

CASE STUDY C: CLINICAL EXAMPLE—SEXUALITY AND AGENCY

The disciplinary lens of each provider shapes their approach to youth care. Social workers, child psychologists, school psychologists, pediatricians, teachers, coaches, spiritual leaders—each may operate from a particular framework when considering what is an appropriate reach and boundary for the supportive relationship. For psychotherapists working with LGBTQ youth on concerns surrounding gender and sexuality, often those frames can be expanded beyond a strict psychotherapy-room hour. In this case example, creative approaches to interdisciplinary and holistic care are demonstrated.

Nico (she/her) is a 14-year-old Korean American, middle class, trans feminine youth who presented to a gender-focused psychotherapy clinic with her adoptive white heterosexual cisgender married parents. Nico reported she had not felt like a boy as far back as she could remember. She recalled the lineup for classrooms in elementary school had been very confusing for her as she did not feel at home in either the boy's line or the girl's line, and she had always felt uncomfortable in her body. When she came out to her parents as gender diverse in seventh grade, Nico's parents were initially supportive and attempted to assist Nico in exploring her gender identity by joining a local LGBT youth and families weekly drop-in support group. They eventually became concerned about her gender dysphoria, gender identity, and sexual interests and decided to enter her into therapy.

Since early childhood, Nico's parents noticed she had sensory sensitivities and struggled with social interactions. Nico became increasingly dysphoric and distressed as she progressed in puberty, and her physical characteristics were more and more out of alignment with her ideal feminine self-image, which she reported was a "goth anime high femme." In eighth grade, Nico was diagnosed with Autism Spectrum Disorder (ASD), which led to her parents' concerns that ASD could be influencing her gender identity development and expression, and that her interest in manga and sexual material could also be related to ASD, since one of the symptoms of autism is having special interests that are unusual in their level of intensity. At the time of intake, Nico and her parents were in conflict about her gender expression and sexual interests. Her parents had started limiting her social media use and anime watching and were taking her phone away at random times to check what websites and content she was using. At the time the parents initiated therapy for Nico, she was depressed, withdrawn, and angry, and she refused to attend the support group she had joined or talk to her parents about her gender and sexuality concerns. During the first session, Nico refused to be in the room with her parents and the therapist.

The therapist began by meeting with Nico alone for the intake and initial sessions, respecting her wish not to be in session with her parents. The therapist explained to Nico that she was a minor and so her parents had access to all of her medical and therapy records. The therapist worked collaboratively with Nico to identify the boundaries of what could be discussed, especially when she was concerned a topic could be shared with her parents. The therapist and Nico agreed that the therapist would tell Nico before she reported something to Nico's parents and that she would involve Nico's parents if she became concerned about Nico's well-being or safety. After multiple sessions of building rapport and offering a container of trust and safety, the therapist encouraged Nico to invite her parents into the session for them to express their concerns. In this session, Nico became activated and angry as her parents focused on her sexual interests in manga and stated they would not support any medical interventions such as puberty suppression or hormones until their concerns about her behavior were addressed. Nico left the session and refused to return until her parents were not allowed back into session. The therapist worked with Nico to affirm her experience, clarify her own gender goals for herself, and stabilize her mood.

The therapist and Nico began exploring her sexual interests. Nico was encouraged to bring in material she was interested in and to make a list of questions she had about sex and sexuality to be discussed in sessions. The therapist and Nico then explored online sexual education information intended for teens to answer some of Nico's questions (e.g., Scarleteen) and to identify how certain sexualized images of girls and women were interesting to her. Nico brought into session imagery of her ideal femme self, and the therapist and Nico explored how aspects of her gender expression and identity could be expressed. The therapist and Nico explored sex education books such as *Girl Sex 101* (Moon & Diamond, 2018) and spent time talking through Nico's questions and understandings of gender, bodies, and sexuality. Nico struggled with binary thinking and feeling she had to fit normative binary definitions of femaleness and femininity before she could identify as her ideal self. The therapist worked with the impact of ASD cognitive rigidity to identify ways Nico could express and affirm her femininity and challenge beliefs that she must conform to normative binary cultural gender norms. The therapist referred Nico to a peer sex education training group for teens at the local LGBT sexual health clinic, which allowed her to explore her gender and sexual concerns with age-appropriate peers and receive accurate sexual health information.

After working together without her parents in session, Nico and the therapist discussed how to best move forward with bringing the parents into session to discuss Nico's gender goals. Nico discussed feeling that her parents' questions, although meant to be supportive, felt invasive at times, and that she wished her parents could educate themselves more about gender topics without using her as a primary resource. Nico and the therapist explored the dilemma of being known and receiving support within the family while also balancing privacy and not bearing the burden of managing her parents' first reactions to gender and sexuality topics. Nico decided she would like the therapist and the parents to meet alone, and Nico and the therapist discussed what she wanted the therapist to say and not to say to her parents within a transparent and consensual model of therapist-client relationship. The therapist agreed to make a list of questions or comments the parents had that she could bring back to Nico, for them to discuss prior to going back to the parents. High degrees of cooperation and transparency within the therapeutic context were necessary in order to create a safe and trusting container for Nico and to model to the parents ways to collaborate within the parent-child relationship around gender concerns. The therapist worked with the parents to normalize Nico's sexual concerns and affirm her gender identity and expression. The therapist also worked to bring the parents on board with Nico's particular developmental needs around her gender and sexual exploration while also supporting her needs around her ASD.

In this case example, the use of a youth-empowerment framework, centering transparency and collaboration with the youth, was of central importance to create a safe container for her gender and sexuality exploration. Without trust within the therapeutic relationship, Nico would likely continue to escalate in her distress and feel stigmatized as her parents focused on the sexual concerns, which escalated her gender dysphoria, distress, and feelings of alienation. An integrative approach within a sex-positive framework along with an intervention strategy that was neurodiverse appropriate allowed Nico to fully explore her gender and sexuality and feel affirmed. She also took the time she needed to be able to articulate and advocate for herself with her parents, peers, and other social contextual contacts.

CASE STUDY D: YOUTH HOMELESSNESS

Felix (they/them) was a 16-year-old African American nonbinary person who presented at an emergency youth shelter due to ongoing family conflict. Felix lived primarily with their mother, whom they described as having a bipolar disorder. It is unclear whether Felix's mother had a diagnosable bipolar condition, but Felix reported a pattern of highly inconsistent care and significant financial stress, including inconsistent income and frequent moves, which is consistent with symptoms of a bipolar disorder. At the time of contact, Felix reported significant violence in their mother's current neighborhood, resulting in elevated anxiety and limited safe recreation outside the home. Felix occasionally lived with their grandmother, who was financially stable, but Felix reported a strained relationship due to their grandmother's conservative religious identity. Felix reported that their grandmother believed that being gay was "a sin" and reported seeing advertisements for so-called "conversion therapy" posted at their grandmother's church.

Felix reported that they wanted to "be a man," but their family would not "let [them]." They reported developing a male identity at an early age but were strongly discouraged from engaging in masculine behaviors and family members did not address them by their preferred name. Felix reported that their current nonbinary identity was temporary, and they reported plans to start taking testosterone and using "he" pronouns at the age of 18. Felix reported that they were not currently "out" to their mother or grandmother and requested that staff use their legal name and "she" pronouns to refer to Felix when communicating with their family.

At the time of intake, Felix reported that they were staying in a youth shelter for the third time in several months. This type of shelter recidivism is typical in cases like Felix's; since their home environment was chronically unsafe and unsupportive in both logistical and emotional ways, the safety and reliability of life in the youth shelter (characterized by food security, freedom from violence, and close relationships with shelter staff) can inadvertently incentivize repeated runaway behavior (Staller, 2004). The primary goal of shelter staff was to facilitate family reunification and establish a plan for long-term safety, but several barriers prevented this in Felix's case. Namely, Felix's mother was chronically financially stressed. When coupled with her unstable mental health, this resulted in low capacity for engagement in family-reunification efforts. It was often impossible for Felix or shelter staff to contact her, and she would occasionally agree to participate in family-reunification conferences with Felix but fail to attend. She would often report that she was "doing her best" and did not believe she could change anything to make Felix's home life more stable. Likewise, Felix's grandmother reported that Felix was welcome to live with her if Felix was willing to "follow the rules," which included attending church and participating in religious activities. She did not report any willingness to relax her requirement for Felix's religious participation, and due to Felix's desire to conceal their sexual and gender identities, they were not open to discussing the matter with their grandmother in more depth. Neither Felix, their mother, nor their grandmother were open to participating in family therapy.

In the local jurisdictions, Felix was above the medical age of consent at age 16, meaning they were legally permitted to consent to treatment without the involvement of parents or guardians. Due to Felix's concerns about initiating medical interventions prior to attaining independent living, facilitating medical interventions at the present juncture primarily involved planning and education related to gender affirmative medical interventions and independent living skills. In order to help Felix understand the effects of testosterone and other interventions, social workers at the youth shelter facilitated an informational consultation with a nurse practitioner who provided primary care to residents of the youth shelter and was knowledgeable about gender affirmative medical interventions. This consultation was helpful in assisting Felix in planning how and when to initiate hormone therapy and correcting any possible misconceptions about the effects of testosterone. Likewise, the nurse practitioner was knowledgeable about local resources for gender affirmative care and was able to provide Felix with specific recommendations about which clinics they could contact when they were ready to initiate hormone therapy. Regarding independent living, Felix attended a variety of educational groups during their stays at the youth shelter, which provided instruction related to budgeting and personal finances, job skills like resume writing and interview skills, and finding and securing rental apartments. Through case management, Felix worked with staff social workers to create an individualized plan for specific steps that would enable independent living when they reached age 18, including plans for housing, employment, and health insurance.

Felix's case demonstrates the importance of sound, interdisciplinary collaboration when working with LGBTQ youth, particularly youth with significant resource deficits such as housing insecurity. The lack of family support in Felix's case introduces a complex dynamic, as interventions for adolescents often involve or are contingent upon the family's willingness to provide emotional, financial, and other resources needed to promote the client's well-being. For instance, many adolescents in the United States have private health insurance provided by a parent's employer, which can undermine the receipt of confidential healthcare. As such, it is essential for providers to be aware of the specific circumstances of each client's life experiences in order to provide relevant, client-centered care. Furthermore, Felix's case calls upon providers to engage in "transdisciplinarity," developing knowledge that transcends traditional disciplinary boundaries (Van Bewer, 2017). For instance, the creation of an individualized case management plan for Felix would not have been possible if social workers did not have a basic understanding of the availability and effects of hormone therapy, and tailored medical advice from the nurse practitioner would have been inadequate without an understanding of the ways housing insecurity can impact the continuity of healthcare delivery. While maintaining an appropriate scope of practice, we urge all providers working with LGBTQ youth to develop close, collaborative relationships with providers of other disciplines and familiarize themselves with these divergent perspectives.

Conclusion

In this chapter, we have presented the framework of integrated care and provided the Gender Affirmative Lifespan Approach (GALA) as a model for working with transgender youth from a holistic, integrative, interdisciplinary framework. Interdisciplinary collaboration is necessary to holistically address the health of transgender people in a coherent manner, and care integration across professionals from different disciplines provides a framework for approaching these goals.

Future research should aim to address the ways in which interdisciplinary care can be used to address the needs of transgender youth with particularly complex needs, such as those with high interaction with multiple systems and experiencing housing and economic challenges. Likewise, further research is warranted at the meso and macro levels of care integration in transgender health, such as the ways in which the operations of hospitals, health insurers, and legislative policy makers may impact the feasibility of care integration.

KEY KNOWLEDGE POINTS

- Interdisciplinary care involves the collaboration of providers across professional disciplines and sites of care.
- Holistic care considers the "whole person" from a biological, psychological, social, and environmental context.

- For interdisciplinary approaches to be most effective, interventions should be implemented at macro, meso, and micro levels of care.
- Interdisciplinary holistic approaches are integral to LGBTQ youth healthcare and can improve outcomes for these youth.
- GALA is an example of an interdisciplinary holistic model of care that can be applied to work with trans and gender diverse youth. It has five core components that rest on six philosophical foundations. GALA's five core components include: 1) developing gender literacy; 2) building resiliency; 3) moving beyond the binary; 4) supporting pleasure-oriented positive sexuality; and 5) making affirming connections to medical interventions.
- GALA's six philosophical foundations are: (1) provision of transaffirmative care; (2) consideration to intersectionality; (3) need for transparency; (4) developmental differences in care across the life span; (5) interdisciplinary approach to care; and (6) empiricism.
- Macro, meso, and micro forces impact LGBTQ youth well-being and interventions on all levels can improve outcomes. Because of the existence of systemic oppressions, implementation of individual-level interventions may not be enough, and advocacy within systems and at the macro level are needed to support individual well-being.

RECOMMENDATIONS FOR PROFESSIONALS

- Identify your own educational background and philosophical approach to care. Reflect on how that shapes your care provision, conceptualization, and treatment planning. Be able to articulate your perspective and see how it differs/is similar to others.
- Establish relationships with professionals within the systems you work and within your community. Join or start an interdisciplinary listserv or monthly community care coordination meeting.
- Identify how different disciplines work within macro, meso, and micro levels of care provision and explore how to maximize positive impact for clients through taking the best of what different disciplines can offer.
- Educate yourself about impacts of macro-level policies on individual well-being. Know the advocacy organizations in your region. Develop referral sources for addressing macro-level impacts.

References

Ansara, Y. G., & Hegarty, P. (2012). Cisgenderism in psychology: Pathologizing and misgendering children from 1999 to 2008. *Psychology & Sexuality*, *3*, 1–24. https://doi.org/10.1080/19419899.2011.576696

Ashley, F. (2019). Gatekeeping hormone replacement therapy for transgender patients is dehumanising. *Journal of Medical Ethics*, *45*(7), 480 LP–482. https://doi.org/10.1136/medethics-2018-105293

Berg, D., Spencer, K., McGuire, J., Becker-Warner, R., Vencill, J. A., & Catalpa, J. (2017, January). The Gender Affirmative Lifespan Approach: Promoting positive identity by building resiliency, increasing gender literacy, moving beyond the binary, and developing sex-positive pleasure and satisfaction. In G. Knudson (Chair), *WPATH presents: The inaugural USPATH scientific conference*. Symposium conducted at the meeting of the United States Professional Association of Transgender Health, Los Angeles, CA.

Bradford, N. J., DeWitt, J., Decker, J., Berg, D. R., Spencer, K. G., & Ross, M. W. (2018). Sex education and transgender youth: 'Trust means material by and for queer and trans people.' *Sex Education*. https://doi.org/10.1080/14681811.2018.1478808

Breslow, A. S., Brewster, M. E., Velez, B. L., Wong, S., Geiger, E., & Soderstrom, B. (2015). Resilience and collective action: Exploring buffers against minority stress for transgender individuals. *Psychology of Sexual Orientation & Gender Diversity, 2*, 253–265. https://doi.org/10.1037/sgd0000117

Brooks, V. R. (1981). *Minority stress and lesbian women*. Lexington Books.

Brooks, S. (2016). Staying in the hood: Black lesbian and transgender women and identity management in North Philadelphia. *Journal of Homosexuality, 63*(12), 1573–1593. https://doi.org/10.1080/00918369.2016.1158008

Budge, S. L. (2015). Psychotherapists as gatekeepers: An evidence-based case study highlighting the role and process of letter writing for transgender clients. *Psychotherapy, 52*(3), 287–297. https://doi.org/10.1037/pst0000034

Clark, B. A., Veale, J. F., Greyson, D., & Saewyc, E. (2018). Primary care access and foregone care: A survey of transgender adolescents and young adults. *Family Practice, 35*(3), 302–306. https://doi.org/10.1093/fampra/cmx112

Coleman, E., Bockting, W., Botzer, M., Cohen-Kettenis, P., DeCuypere, G., Feldman, J., Fraser, L., Green, J., Knudson, G., Meyer, W. J., Monstrey, S., Adler, R. K., Brown, G. R., Devor, A. H., Ehrbar, R., Ettner, R., Eyler, E., Garofalo, R., Karasic, D. H., . . . Zucker, K. (2012). Standards of care for the health of transsexual, transgender, and gender-nonconforming people, version 7. *International Journal of Transgenderism, 13*(4), 165–232. https://doi.org/10.1080/15532739.2011.700873

Crenshaw, K. (1997). Intersectionality and identity politics: Learning from violence against women of color. In M. L. Shanley & U. Narayan (Eds.), *Reconstructing political theory: Feminist perspectives*. (pp. 178–193). Pennsylvania State University Press.

Dank, M., Lachman, P., Zweig, J. M., & Yahner, J. (2014). Dating violence experiences of lesbian, gay, bisexual, and transgender youth. *Journal of Youth and Adolescence, 43*(5), 846–857. https://doi.org/10.1007/s10964-013-9975-8

de Vries, A. L. C., McGuire, J. K., Steensma, T. D., Wagenaar, E. C. F., Doreleijers, T. A. H., & Cohen-Kettenis, P. T. (2014). Young adult psychological outcome after puberty suppression and gender reassignment. *Pediatrics, 134*(4), 696–704. https://doi.org/10.1542/peds.2013-2958

Edwards-Leeper, L., & Spack, N. P. (2012). Psychological evaluation and medical treatment of transgender youth in an interdisciplinary "gender management service" (GeMS) in a major pediatric center. *Journal of Homosexuality, 59*(3), 321–336. https://doi.org/10.1080/00918369.2012.653302

Farmer, L. B., & Byrd, R. (2015). Genderism in the LGBTQQIA community: An interpretative phenomenological analysis. *Journal of LGBT Issues in Counseling, 9*(4), 288–310. https://doi.org/10.1080/15538605.2015.1103679

Frey, J. H., & Fontana, A. (1991). The group interview in social research. *Social Science Journal, 28*(2), 175–187. https://doi.org/10.1016/0362-3319(91)90003-M

Garmulewicz, A., & Ireland, L. (2010). The Canadian Youth Climate Change Conference (YC3) as a model for effective youth and adult engagement in promoting environmental and social justice. In W. Linds, L. Goulet, & A. Sammel (Eds.), *Emancipatory practices: Adult/youth engagement for social and environmental justice* (pp. 145–164). Brill. https://doi.org/10.1163/9789460911538_013

Garofalo, R., Deleon, J., Osmer, E., Doll, M., & Harper, G. W. (2006). Overlooked, misunderstood and at-risk: Exploring the lives and HIV risk of ethnic minority male-to-female transgender youth. *Journal of Adolescent Health, 38*(3), 230–236. https://doi.org/10.1016/j.jadohealth.2005.03.023

Hendricks, M. L., & Testa, R. J. (2012). A conceptual framework for clinical work with transgender and gender nonconforming clients: An adaptation of the minority stress model. *Professional Psychology: Research and Practice, 43*(5), 460–467. https://doi.org/10.1037/a0029597

Hesse-Biber, S. (2016). Doing interdisciplinary mixed methods health care research: Working the boundaries, tensions, and synergistic potential of team-based research. *Qualitative Health Research, 26*(5), 649–658. https://doi.org/10.1177/1049732316634304

Institute of Medicine. (2013). *Interprofessional education for collaboration: Learning how to improve health from interprofessional models across the continuum of education to practice: Workshop summary*. National Academies Press.

James, S. E., Herman, J. L., Rankin, S., Keisling, M., Mottet, L., & Anafi, M. (2016). *The report of the 2015 US transgender survey*. National Center for Transgender Equality. http://www.transequality.org/

Johnson, A. H. (2016). Transnormativity: A new concept and its validation through documentary film about transgender men. *Sociological Inquiry, 86*(4), 465–491. https://doi.org/10.1111/soin.12127

Jones, T. (2017). Evidence affirming school supports for Australian transgender and gender diverse students. *Sexual Health, 14*(5), 412–416. https://doi.org/10.1071/SH17001

Jones, T., Smith, E., Ward, R., Dixon, J., Hillier, L., & Mitchell, A. (2016). School experiences of transgender and gender diverse students in Australia. *Sex Education, 16*(2), 156–171. https://doi.org/10.1080/14681811.2015.1080678

Keo-Meier, C., & Ehrensaft, D. E. (2018). *The gender affirmative model: An interdisciplinary approach to supporting transgender and gender expansive children*. American Psychological Association.

Mallory, C., Brown, T. N., Russell, S. T., & Sears, B. (2017). *The impact of stigma and discrimination against LGBT people in Texas*. Williams Institute.

Meyer, I. H. (1995). Minority stress and mental health in gay men. *Journal of Health and Social Behavior, 3*(1), 38–56. https://doi.org/10.2307/2137286

Meyer, I. H. (2003). Prejudice, social stress, and mental health in lesbian, gay, and bisexual populations: Conceptual issues and research evidence. *Psychological Bulletin, 129*(5), 674–697. https://doi.org/10.1037/0033-2909.129.5.674

Meyer, W., Bockting, W. O., Cohen-Kettenis, P., Coleman, E., DiCeglie, D., Devor, H., Gooren, L., Hage, J. J., Kirk, S., Kuiper, B., Laub, D., Lawrence, A., Menard, Y., Patton, J., Schaefer, L., Webb, A., & Wheeler, C. C. (2001). Harry Benjamin International Gender Dysphoria Association's: The standards of care for gender identity disorders—sixth version. *Journal of Psychology & Human Sexuality, 13*(1), 1–30. https://doi.org/10/1300/J056v13n01_01

Miller, sj, Mayo, C., & Lugg, C. A. (2017). Sex and gender in transition in US schools: Ways forward. *Sex Education, 18*(34), 1–15. https://doi.org/10.1080/14681811.2017.1415204

Miller, J. (1988). *The holistic curriculum*. OISE Press.

Moon, A., & Diamond, K. D. (2018). *Girl Sex 101*. Lunatic Ink.

Pettigrew, T. F. (1967). Social evaluation theory: Convergences and applications. In *Nebraska symposium on motivation* (pp. 241–304). University of Nebraska Press.

Pinto, R. M., Melendez, R. M., & Spector, A. Y. (2008). Male-to-female transgender individuals building social support and capital from within a gender-focused network. *Journal of Gay & Lesbian Social Services, 20*(3), 203–220. https://doi.org/10.1080/10538720802235179

Prunas, A. (2019). The pathologization of trans-sexuality: Historical roots and implications for sex counselling with transgender clients. *Sexologies, 28*(3), e54–e60. https://doi.org/10.1016/j.sexol.2019.06.002

Puckett, J. A., Cleary, P., Rossman, K., Mustanski, B., & Newcomb, M. E. (2018). Barriers to gender-affirming care for transgender and gender nonconforming individuals. *Sexuality Research and Social Policy, 15*(1), 48–59. https://doi.org/10.1007/s13178-017-0295-8

Reeves, S., Pelone, F., Harrison, R., Goldman, J., & Zwarenstein, M. (2017). Interprofessional collaboration to improve professional practice and healthcare outcomes. *Cochrane Database of Systematic Reviews*, (6). https://doi.org/10.1002/14651858.CD000072.pub3

Reisner, S. L., Greytak, E. A., Parsons, J. T., & Ybarra, M. L. (2015). Gender minority social stress in adolescence: disparities in adolescent bullying and substance use by gender identity. *Journal of Sex Research, 52*(3), 243–256. https://doi.org/10.1080/00224499.2014.886321

Rider, G. N., Vencill, J. A., Berg, D. R., Becker-Warner, R., Candelario-Pérez, L., & Spencer, K. G. (2019). The gender affirmative lifespan approach (GALA): A framework for competent clinical care with nonbinary clients. *International Journal of Transgenderism, 20*(2–3), 275–288. https://doi.org/10.1080/15532739.2018.1485069

Riggs, D. W., & Bartholomaeus, C. (2017). Transgender young people's narratives of intimacy and sexual health: Implications for sexuality education. *Sex Education, 18*(4), 376–390. https://doi.org/10.1080/14681811.2017.1355299

Rosario, M., Corliss, H. L., Koenen, K. C., & Austin, S. B. (2011). Childhood gender nonconformity: A risk indicator for childhood abuse and posttraumatic stress in youth. *Pediatrics, 129*(3), 410–417. https://doi.org/10.1542/peds.2011-1804

Safer, J. D., Coleman, E., Feldman, J., Garofalo, R., Hembree, W., Radix, A., & Sevelius, J. (2016). Barriers to healthcare for transgender individuals. *Current Opinion in Endocrinology & Diabetes and Obesity, 23*(2), 168–171. https://doi.org/10.1097/MED.0000000000000227

Santelli, J., Ott, M. A., Lyon, M., Rogers, J., Summers, D., & Schleifer, R. (2006). Abstinence and abstinence-only education: A review of U.S. policies and programs. *Journal of Adolescent Health, 38*(1), 72–81. https://doi.org/10.1016/j.jadohealth.2005.10.006

Schulz, S. L. (2018). The informed consent model of transgender care: An alternative to the diagnosis of gender dysphoria. *Journal of Humanistic Psychology, 58*(1), 72–92. https://doi.org/10.1177/0022167817745217

Shipherd, J. C., Kauth, M. R., Firek, A. F., Garcia, R., Mejia, S., Laski, S., Walden, B., Perez-Padilla, S., Lindsay, J. A., Brown, G., Roybal, L., Keo-Meier, C. L., Knapp, H., Johnson, L., Reese, R. L., & Byne, W. (2016). Interdisciplinary transgender veteran care: Development of a core curriculum for VHA providers. *Transgender Health, 1*(1), 54–62. https://doi.org/10.1089/trgh.2015.0004

Spencer, K. G., Berg, D. R., Bradford, N. J., Vencill, J. A., Tellawi, G., & Rider, G. N. (2021). The gender-affirmative life span approach: A developmental model for clinical work with transgender and gender-diverse children, adolescents, and adults. *Psychotherapy, 58*(1), 37–49. https://doi.org/10.1037/pst0000363

Spencer, K. G., & Vencill, J. A. (2017). Body beyond: A pleasure-based, sex-positive group therapy curriculum for transfeminine adults. *Psychology of Sexual Orientation and Gender Diversity, 4*(4), 392–402. http://dx.doi.org/10.1037/sgd0000248

Staller, K. (2004). Runaway youth system dynamics: A theoretical framework for analyzing runaway and homeless youth policy. *Families in Society: The Journal of Contemporary Social Services, 85*(3), 379–390. https://doi.org/10.1606/1044-3894.1499

Tajfel, H. (1974). Social identity and intergroup behaviour. *Social Science Information, 13*(2), 65–93. https://doi.org/10.1177/053901847401300204

UN General Assembly. (1948). *Universal declaration of human rights*. United Nations.

UN General Assembly. (1966). *International covenant on civil and political rights*. United Nations.

UN General Assembly. (2006). *Convention on the rights of persons with disabilities*. United Nations.

Valentijn, P. P., Schepman, S. M., Opheij, W., & Bruijnzeels, M. A. (2013). Understanding integrated care: A comprehensive conceptual framework based on the integrative functions of primary care. *International Journal of Integrated Care, 13*, e010. https://doi.org/10.5334/ijic.886

Van Bewer, V. (2017). Transdisciplinarity in health care: A concept analysis. *Nursing Forum, 52*(4), 339–347. https://doi.org/10.1111/nuf.12200

World Health Organization. (2010). *Framework for action on interprofessional education and collaborative practice*. World Health Organization.

Section II
DEVELOPMENTAL CONSIDERATIONS

CHAPTER 4

The Youngest Part of the Rainbow
CLINICAL CARE FOR GENDER DIVERSE CHILDREN

Dianne R. Berg, PhD, LP, Caroline Maykut, PhD*,
Rachel Becker-Warner, PsyD, LP, Catherine Schaefer, MS,
& Jennifer J. Connor, PhD, LMFT (*Co-First Authors)*

Providing clinical care to children with diverse gender identities has continued to evolve as the social climate regarding gender also evolves (de Graaf & Carmichael, 2019). In this chapter, we provide an overview of the research context related to studying gender diversity in children, current gender identity development theories, mental health concerns that may be associated with childhood gender diverse identities, and resilience in gender diverse children and their social systems, and finally, we apply a model of clinical care to a case study. We aim to provide clinicians from mental health backgrounds with the foundation to assist children and their families who are exploring gender through an affirmative and empirically driven therapeutic model.

Due to children's unique stage of development, many of the concepts represented by the LGBTQ+ acronym may not apply to children (or have been assumed not to apply). As developmental theories have long posited, this could be because establishing a gender identity is a developmental task of childhood while sexual orientation is assumed to be the purview of pubescence and adolescence. However, there is also societal discomfort around sexuality-related topics in childhood, making discussions of sexuality with children confined to concepts of anatomy and/or basic education on reproduction. In addition, deeply embedded culturally based heteronormativity and homophobia impact willingness to consider certain aspects of sexuality, such as sexual orientation. The assumption is that children need to be protected from sexual identity topics aside from heterosexuality, which is compulsory and ubiquitous. Interestingly, whereas the other letters in the LGBTQ+ acronym have remained off-limits, in the past 10 to 15 years, we have seen increasing openness to the "T" being used with children, in other words, transgender children. In many ways, this is a step forward because the recognition of transgender children furthers the important societal shift toward inclusion and affirmation of diverse identities. At the same time, we believe that it is important to think critically about language and how it shapes our understanding and assumptions about experiences. The specific label of transgender, when applied to children, fails to fully encompass the broad range of gender identity and expression diversity that exists in children. Further, it suggests that gender identity is fixed in childhood, thus neglecting important developmental considerations that we will discuss in this chapter.

While it is important when working clinically with children to listen carefully to the terms they use for their own identities, including when those terms change over time, in this chapter, we will use the term "gender diverse" because we believe it captures a broad range of gender identities, expressions, and experiences that extend beyond the culturally dominant binary view of gender. This culturally dominant lens historically assumed that sex determines gender, where *sex* is defined as one's assigned status as male or female based on biological characteristics (Deaux, 1993; Ruble et al., 2006)—and *gender* is defined as one's subjective experience of characteristics and behaviors associated with sex (stereotypes, roles, and expressions of masculinity and femininity) (Fausto-Sterling, 2000; Ruble et al., 2006). Any experiences that differed were deemed abnormal (Pleak, 2011; Zucker & Bradley, 1995). What was lost in these assumptions is an awareness of differences of sexual development (DSD), of which there are many variations (Beh & Diamond, 2000; Gardner & Sandberg, 2018), as well as the legitimization of *gender identity*—one's internal and felt experience of one's gender, which may or may not align with one's sex assigned at birth (Hines, 2005). The term "gender diverse" accounts for the rich and expansive experience that exists outside of this culturally dominant binary view of gender, without assigning an identity label. This is also important because the use of these labels in young children implies that gender identity becomes fixed at some point in childhood and then has an accompanying identity trajectory. While for some children their sense of gender identity is strong and well established, there are currently no steadfast measures or fixed indicators for knowing the trajectory of a child's gender identity into adolescence. In addition, as gender diverse identities become more culturally acceptable in the United States, an increasing number of adolescents are expressing these identities (Rider et al., 2018), rendering previous research on prediction of identity into adulthood less informative.

As discussed in more detail below, the nature of childhood gender identity development leaves room for complex variations of gender identity formation and self-actualization that can continue to evolve into adolescence and adulthood. This is not to say that awareness of gender or sexual identity in childhood is misguided; instead, focusing on the child's experience, rather than the label, leaves room for evolving identity without confining the developmental process to the strict socially constructed parameters that come with identity labels that were developed from the experiences of adults (Rivas, 2015; Spencer, Berg et al., 2021). In that spirit, we will use the term gender diverse throughout this chapter to represent prepubescent children whose gender identity development differs from the developmental process that is normalized from the culturally dominant frame. If alternate terminology (e.g., "transgender children") is used in specific research studies being discussed, terminology used will be consistent with those studies. We will also use the term "presumed cisgender" rather than cisgender to describe children whose gender identity and expression aligns (or appears to align) with their sex assigned at birth, as these children may later express a non-cisgender identity. Additionally, rather than speculating about the sexual orientation development of children who may or may not eventually assume a sexual minority identity, we will focus on what is known about gender identity in children starting with what can be gleaned from the research literature.

Social and Historical Context of Research with Gender Diverse Children

Currently, empirical knowledge about the experiences of gender diverse children is limited and shaped by historical and present effects of cissexism and heterosexism (Hyde et al., 2019). While transgender identities in adulthood only recently have been recognized as valid and healthy by the fields of medicine and psychology, there remains debate with respect to children. This historical conceptualization of gender diversity as pathological not only has limited children from exploring and expressing their gender identities, but also has influenced the way that gender is measured and discussed both clinically and in research with children. In the current literature on the general well-being of all children, gender diverse children have either been assumed to be cisgender or, when identified, have been relegated to the "other," causing their experiences to be unacknowledged or erased. In cases where gender is recorded in a study or clinical practice, options often do not represent identities outside the binary. If nonbinary or transgender identities are available as identification options, small sample sizes are a common explanation for leaving out gender diverse populations in analyses and findings. Furthermore, it is important to note that the demographic field called "gender" on many research and clinical measures used with children is often intended to be answered in terms of sex assigned at birth for the purpose of comparison to established norm groups. If the child identifies (or parent/s who are filling out the measure identify the child) according to the child's affirmed gender versus their sex assigned at birth, and this is not changed prior to scoring, the child will likely be compared to an "incorrect" norm group. If the child (or parent/s) recognizes that the measure is actually asking about sex assigned at birth, the experience of selecting a marker that is incongruent with identity can be upsetting and lead to more dysphoria. For a more detailed review of these concerns in assessment overall, please see Berg & Edwards-Leeper (2018). For a discussion about these concerns specific to the Child Behavior Checklist (CBCL), please see Rider et al., 2019. Further, of those few measures of gender identity that allow for a graded scale of gender identification outside the binary, few have been adapted for use in children (Tate, 2016). In addition, although words describing diverse gender identities are making their way into societal consciousness, they can have different and changing meanings among those who use them (Zosky & Alberts, 2016), and they are not typically included in the social messages received by young children in current US culture. Unless a child has exposure to the concept of gender diversity, they are unlikely to understand the variety of identification options available on more inclusive measures. Interestingly, attempts to use language that researchers thought may be better understood by children (e.g., asking gender diverse children about who they are "inside") have shown potential for being misunderstood by children (Olson et al., 2015), and nuances in facets of gender (e.g., expression vs. identity vs. attitudes) are confusing even for adults. Because the current research on children is limited in its ability to identify gender diverse children from presumed cisgender children, our understanding of how variations in gender identity and gender expression contribute to outcomes in well-being also remains quite limited.

Within the clinical and research literature that has identified gender diverse children, research and sampling methods have contributed to the potential overrepresentation of children with binary identities (e.g., transgender boys and girls) and children who have been referred for treatment (Steensma et al., 2013; Zucker & Bradley, 1995). Nonbinary identities present challenges for quantitative research that relies on discrete gender categories, meaning that to date, much of the available information on children who have not expressed binary identities comes from qualitative methods. Inclusion in both qualitative and quantitative studies on gender diversity often requires that the child participate in some element of social transition (e.g., using chosen name and/or pronouns, wearing affirming clothing), which, in younger populations, necessitates a safe environment for doing so. And while in its most complex form, social transition is a process involving an array of choices, it is unclear the extent to which binary norms pressure children to adopt a transnormative identity, or an identity that conforms to current social expectations of how transgender people should look or identify (Johnson, 2016). Because the current social and political climate within the United States does not tend to foster safe environments for gender diverse children in schools, health care, and sometimes, families and communities, only children who are able to express their identity, access treatment, and take steps toward transition tend to be included in the literature. Thus, it is likely that we currently have an extremely limited understanding of a very small cross-section of gender diverse children because those who do not have these options are left unrepresented.

Last, in addition to heterosexism and cissexism, racism, classism, and ableism are pervasive forces that create and maintain barriers to representation in research for gender diverse children, especially for children of color and those who are neurodiverse. The systematic embedding of these factors across contexts limits access to resources essential to well-being, such as reliable sources of food and housing, and reduces the likelihood that other protective factors will be available within the child's environment. These stressors vary by demographic characteristics, and children who experience them most frequently are rarely represented in the clinical and research literature on gender diverse children that focuses on white, upper-middle-class children and families.

Gender Identity Development

Historically, theorists and researchers have asserted that childhood gender identity forms by way of a predictable developmental process that assumes an overarching goal of *gender differentiation* (i.e., "assigning social significance to biological differences of sex" [*Oxford Dictionary of Sports Science & Medicine*, n.d., definition 1]). Early developmental frameworks are rooted in Eurocentric and binary ways of thinking that marginalized and often rendered invisible anything that did not conform to the narrow view of birth-assigned sex determinism. Thus, they failed to consider the possibilities of gender identities that differed from sex assigned at birth. Recent research examining the experiences of gender diverse children has supported differing conceptual theories of gender identity development to varying degrees (de Vries et al., 2014). Some researchers have explored whether a distinctive group of gender diverse children exists whose gender identity development parallels the predictable processes modeled after presumed cisgender children (Fast & Olson, 2018; Hines, 2000; McGuire & Morrow, 2020; Olson et al., 2015; Wong et al., 2019). More and more research supports theories of gender identity development as a multidimensional "complex and dynamic system" (McGuire & Morrow, 2020, p. 36; Bockting, 2014; Diamond et al., 2011). Mental health clinicians need to have an understanding of both historical and current gender identity theories as their client's (particularly caregivers) perspective may be influenced by developmental theories rooted in either historical perspectives or current theory and research. Clinicians who understand multiple theories are able to explore the clients' viewpoints and potentially expand upon existing thoughts and/or beliefs. In this section, we explore three families of gender identity development theories.

Gender essentialism, or the "Born This Way" biologically based theory (Hines, 2009; McGuire & Morrow, 2020), privileges the most overt experiences of gender-sex incongruence commonly differentiated in literature as childhood assertions of "being born in the wrong body." Essentialist approaches posit that there is a core "essence" of a person that determines gender identity that is fixed and unchangeable. They emphasize the necessity of *gender dysphoria* (i.e., distress in response to the incongruence between sex assigned at birth and experienced gender), as operationalized in the *Diagnostic and Statistical Manual of Mental Disorders* (DSM-5; APA, 2013), as an essential indicator that biological factors (mediated by environment) are central to gender identity development (for a review of "biology of transgender identity," see Erickson-Schroth, 2013). Within an essentialist framework, children who experience their gender as in conflict with their birth-assigned sex and who may not experience gender role incongruence, body dysphoria, or strong cross-sex identification, are thought to be motivated by sexual identity development or social exploration, rather than a core transgender identity (Drescher, 2014; Wong et al., 2019).

Gender environmentalists argue that one's view of one's gender is embedded in the meaningful interactions of a person with their environment (Liben & Bigler, 2002). However, there has yet to be scientific support of environment as a stand-alone contributor of gender identity development (de Vries et al., 2014). Research supporting bans of conversion therapy due to harmful outcomes highlights this argument. It could be debated that if environment was the driving force of one's view of their identity, then conversion therapy aimed at changing an individual's gender or sexual identity would have consistent predictive outcomes (McGuire & Morrow, 2020). Similar arguments can be made when considering the fact that the majority of gender diverse children will be born in a culture that views gender and sexuality from a cisgender heteronormative frame; the same cultural frame from which the majority of their parents were socialized. When considering gender environmentalist theories, we would expect homogeneous binary gender differentiation among all children. This is clearly not the case, as a growing number of children are describing gender identities or exhibiting gender expressions that are nonbinary, defined as the experience of gender identity or expression as both masculine and feminine, neither masculine nor feminine, between masculine and feminine, or fluid over time. As of now, we know little about the unique aspects of nonbinary gender development in children, including whether differences exist from those gender diverse children who assert a binary gender experience (Diamond, 2020).

Gender constructivist theories posit that individual traits interact with one's environment to create gender schemas that inform gender attitudes, beliefs, and behaviors (Liben, 2017; McGuire & Morrow, 2020). These theories are differentiated from their most closely related gender environmentalist theories in that gender constructivists would argue that children are active agents in their gender identity development (i.e., internal aspects of one's self interact with their external environment to organize their understanding of their gender) versus the gender environmentalist view that it is solely the environmental structures (e.g., sex-typed societal practices and language) that inform one's gender distinction.

It is becoming clearer that gender diverse children who have been supported in a social transition as well as their cisgender siblings show a greater acceptance and understanding of gender identity and expression diversity. For example, Fast and Olson (2018) found that both socially transitioned children and their siblings viewed other people's gender with the potential of changing over time. These findings are similar to past studies of gender nonconforming children who tended to view the stability of their gender over time and consistency of their gender across situations as variable (Zucker et al., 1999). It is possible that the way in which gender is constructed and discussed in families who are knowledgeable and supportive of gender diversity extends beyond the binary sex-based view of gender. As such, it may be that this social influence and conditioning plays a role in the important developmental task of gender identity development. Thus, gender constructivism provides an explanation for how children's gender schemas can come to include expansive potentials for gender identity and expression.

To conclude, the theories discussed above help to provide a conceptual lens from which we understand childhood gender diverse development. At this time, constructivist theories are best able to capture the broadest range of gender experiences, given they account for the importance of the interaction of internal and external factors in the development of gender identity. In effect, gender appears to be "a pattern in time" (Fausto-Sterling, 2019, p. 405) that shifts and evolves to adapt the complex interplay of internal and external influences (Diamond, 2020). In keeping, in order to foster the positive gender development of all children, theory, research, education, and therapeutic conceptualization need to shift away from the linear and binary conceptualizations of "typical" development toward conceptualizations that accommodate the complex multidimensional nature of gender diverse identity development (Diamond, 2020; Fausto-Sterling, 2019; McGuire & Morrow, 2020).

Mental Health in Gender Diverse Children

Until recently, data on the mental health of gender diverse children was available through research with children who were referred for services at specialty gender clinics. Historically, these gender diverse children showed very high rates of both internalizing and externalizing symptoms as compared to their presumed cisgender peers and high rates of comorbid mental health disorders, particularly depression, anxiety, and externalizing disorders (see Zucker et al., 2014 for review). Gender incongruence in childhood has been found to be negatively correlated with self-worth (Rijn et al., 2013), self-confidence, and social acceptance (Egan & Perry, 2001), meaning that as feelings of gender incongruence increased, feelings of self-worth, self-confidence, and social acceptance decreased. Longitudinal data has shown that self-esteem continued to decline in children with more gender incongruence, which in turn led to more internalizing problems (Yunger et al., 2004). Predominant theories about what accounted for these higher rates of mental health concerns included the possibility that gender diverse children had more general risk factors, that their distress was a consequence of gender dysphoria, or that the distress resulted from social rejection (Zucker et al., 2014).

More recent literature, however, does not appear to support a hypothesis of increased general risk factors or a necessary distress associated with gender dysphoria. For example, research using community samples has begun to shed light on the mental health of gender diverse children who have not sought (or who do not have access to) the specialized care offered through gender clinics. The Trans*Kids Project follows a community sample of 49 families with gender diverse children ages 6 to 12 years. In their baseline data of children's well-being assessed through the CBCL (Achenbach & Rescorla, 2001), children, on average, fell within the normal range for internalizing and externalizing problems (Kuvalanka et al., 2017). Likewise, children enrolled in the Trans*Youth Project, a large-scale, national longitudinal study of more than 300 socially transitioned transgender children ages 3 to 12 years, showed depressive symptoms within the normal range and only slightly elevated anxiety (Olson et al., 2016). While there are many factors that differentiate these community samples from clinic-referred children (e.g., the status of social transition and implications this may have for family support and resources, selection bias in community samples, or the apparent need for mental health support in clinic-referred children), these data highlight that poor mental health is not inevitable for gender diverse children.

Rather, gender diverse children who experience discouragement and rejection from others on account of what the studies referred to as "gender atypicality" and/or "gender nonconformity" are at greater odds of developing a host of psychosocial adversities in adolescence and even into adulthood (e.g., depressive symptoms, low life satisfaction, self-harm, isolation, post-traumatic stress, and suicidal ideation and attempts [D'Augelli et al., 2006; Roberts et al., 2012; Roberts et al., 2013]). This suggests that the experience (or anticipation) of rejection that gender diverse children face may account for the mental health risks often observed, as opposed to gender diverse children being inherently at risk for mental health concerns. This hypothesis is further supported by qualitative data from a focus group of parents of gender diverse children. When parents were asked how four specific domains of emotional and behavioral problems (oppositional behavior, anger, sadness, and fear/worry) were characterized in the context of gender nonconformity, parents noted that oppositional behavior appeared in response to restrictions they placed on their child's gender expression and noted that their child's fear and worry was related to nonacceptance or victimization because of their gender nonconformity (Chen et al., 2017).

Clinical Implications of Mental Health Research

For gender diverse children who present to a therapeutic setting, mental health assessment may be similar to all children who present for therapy, such that both internalizing and externalizing symptoms are a component of the diagnostic assessment. However, clinicians (and researchers) need to be mindful of the limitations of many assessment measures that are commonly used in clinical settings when applied to gender diverse children. Specifically, as noted earlier, many of these measures ask children or parents to self-identify using a gender marker of M (for male) or F (for female), and they are normed according to a sex-assigned-at-birth norm group. Thus, not only do these measures conflate sex assigned at birth with gender identity, but they also do not allow for the range of gender identities that exist beyond the binary. Another unique assessment component for gender diverse children is an exploration of how their social context (e.g., family members, peers, school officials) may be either supportive or discouraging of their gender exploration and identity. The current state of the literature suggests that the mental health of gender diverse children is linked to the social systems they are a part of.

Resilience in Gender Diverse Children

We will now shift focus to the factors that promote the development of resilience in gender diverse children. Resilience is a key component of the clinical approach that will be detailed later in this chapter. By focusing on resilience, we move away from viewing gender diversity as a vulnerability and instead focus on the well-being of the child and their environment (Panter-Brick & Leckman, 2013). We use the definition of resilience offered by Ann Masten (in Southwick et al., 2014), who articulates resilience as "the capacity of a dynamic system to adapt successfully to disturbances that threaten the viability, the function, or the development of that system" (p. 3). This perspective views resilience as a process of ecological systems interacting to create opportunities for the gender diverse child, rather than a trait within the child or a desired outcome. Masten (2018) explains that this view of resilience builds upon systems theory and human ecology theory (Bronfenbrenner, 1979, 2001; Masten, 2018), which state that the developing child is embedded within both immediate systems, such as the family and school, and systems that have an indirect impact on the child, such as culture and government (Bronfenbrenner, 1979). Within each system, one can identify stressors or risks, but also protective factors. As such, we do not perceive gender diversity as a risk factor on its own, but rather, it can be a risk factor when the surrounding environments lack appropriate support. In the following sections, we will review the characteristics within the child's surrounding systems that promote and hinder resilience. Each context provides opportunities for clinical intervention and asset building; these will be highlighted throughout the following sections.

INTERPERSONAL CONTEXTS

Peer Group

The presence of a social support system can buffer the impact of stressful events (Lakey & Cohen, 2000). For gender diverse children in both community and clinical samples, peer relations are strongly correlated with well-being and fewer internalizing and externalizing symptoms (Cohen-Kettenis et al., 2003; Kuvalanka et al., 2017; de Vries et al., 2016). Unfortunately, gender diverse children often experience negative social consequences of gender nonconforming behavior. Specifically, compared with gender-conforming peers, gender diverse children (particularly those assigned male at birth) have higher rates of peer rejection and lower rates of peer acceptance (e.g., Cohen-Kettenis et al., 2003; Wallien et al., 2010). Additionally, segregation of peer groups according to the gender binary is a common occurrence in childhood relationships and is particularly notable during the early school years in research with children who were presumed to be cisgender (Rose & Smith, 2018). This segregation is particularly challenging for gender diverse children, whose experiences outside of strict gender norms can contribute to feelings of isolation. The clinician can assist the child in developing language to address questions from peers about gender, build assertiveness, identify safe people, and provide support for any negative peer interactions.

Family

Family support is a key protective factor for gender diverse children. In early childhood, families are one of the main organizing forces in children's development of gender schemas (McHale et al., 2003). This can be influenced by the way families talk about gender, for example, by acknowledging and validating gender diverse identities that extend beyond the binary. On a practical level, gender expression (e.g., clothing and hairstyle) is typically managed by the caregiver, and parents are the primary advocates as their children navigate cisnormative social and community systems. Attempts to restrict gender creativity or other types of nonaccepting responses from parents are associated with internalizing and externalizing symptoms in gender diverse children (Chen et al., 2017; Kuvalanka et al., 2019; Pariseau et al., 2019). For a clinician working with gender diverse children, working with the family to ensure their support for the child's authentic gender identity and expression is an important aspect of care.

Gender diverse children are not the only ones to experience the negative impact of minority stress. Social stigma is a common challenge among parents in fully supporting their child's gender identity (Pullen Sansfaçon et al., 2015). Parents can be subject to judgment by family or peers and experience negative societal responses to their children's gender diversity—for example, criticism about their decision to support their child's social transition (Hidalgo & Chen, 2019). Parenting stress has also been noted as a moderator between gender nonconformity and externalizing psychopathology (Kolbuck et al., 2019). Thus, an important part of building family resilience is recognizing and supporting parents' needs and experiences. Abreu and colleagues' (2019) review of 32 studies on parental reactions to children's gender diversity identified common factors that characterize parents' experience. They identified a range of *initial experiences*, including noticing gender "atypical" behavior, experiencing diverse emotional reactions (from grief and loss, to strong positive emotions), cognitive dissonance between previously held beliefs about gender and their child's experience, and lack of knowledge about gender diversity. *Transformation processes* included seeking out information, developing cognitive flexibility, and seeking support and making connections with the trans and gender diverse community. In the transformation stage, parents also described their own experience of facing barriers, including stigma and rejection from family and larger systems, and through that process, developing more awareness of discrimination and building empathy. Finally, 16 studies in this review described the *positive outcome* of having a gender diverse child, noting the positive impact on parent/child relationships and the new personal narratives that were developed.

In discussing the protective role of family support, it is important to recognize that this support extends beyond the child's parents. The Trans*Kids Project is beginning to explore how sibling or extended family responses can impact the child, particularly when those responses differ from that of the parents. For example, if parents are affirming but extended family is not, the child may still be indirectly influenced due to parents' self-doubt, anxiety, or rejection (Kuvalanka et al., 2014; Pullen Sansfaçon et al., 2015). Alternatively, if parents are nonsupportive, the child may receive vital support from other family members. Extended families can also support parents by validating their approach and engaging in their own education about gender diversity, all of which increase cohesion and bolster the resilience of the family system (Kuvalanka et al., 2019).

COMMUNITY CONTEXTS

Schools

The school environment plays a critical role in a child's social and psychological wellbeing. In considering resilience-building factors in this environment, it is necessary to consider both the interpersonal and the institutional. At the interpersonal level, having a positive relationship with adults in the school system is a protective factor, as is the belief that adults will intervene in cases of bullying or harassment (McGuire et al., 2010). School-based peer support programs such as Gender-Sexuality Alliances (GSAs) serve as an important resource for gender diverse children, particularly middle school children who experience high rates of bullying. Although middle school children are less likely than high school students to have GSAs, the 2017 GLSEN school climate survey shows that when middle school children do have them, they have higher rates of participation, including attending meetings more frequently and serving in leadership roles (Kosciw et al., 2018). At the institutional level, schools can offer protection to gender diverse children through anti-bullying policy that explicitly includes gender identity and expression, by having policies in place to support students who wish to socially transition at school (e.g., being able to change their name within the school system without requiring legal name change), and by being proactive in educating all school personnel about gender diversity. Qualitative research with teachers of gender diverse children points to the importance of flexible, student-centered curriculum, fostering an environment in which creativity and nonconformity are valued, and decreasing the number of sex-segregated activities and facilities (Meyer et al., 2016). The more supportive environments tend to be found in alternative school systems (McGuire et al., 2010, Meyer et al., 2016), although it has not yet been explored how school placement decisions may impact academic or extracurricular opportunities (McGuire et al., 2010). The clinician can assist the parents in advocating for their child within the school system. This might include guiding parents in the process of school selection (e.g., learning about the school climate with respect to gender inclusive policies, meeting with the school administrators in advance of the child's enrollment) or, when necessary, supporting the child and parents to involve school officials in cases of bullying.

Healthcare Settings

Medical Settings

Oftentimes, primary care providers or pediatricians are the first point of contact within the healthcare system for gender diverse children and their caregivers as they begin exploring gender and options for care. Although medical intervention is not a consideration for gender diverse children prior to puberty, providers can offer support to children by allowing chosen names and pronouns to be documented within their system, asking about a child's gender rather than making assumptions based on birth-assigned sex, and facilitating referrals to specialty gender care if needed. Within these conversations, families will likely receive direct or indirect messages about gender and transition from medical providers. Such messages could include dismissing gender issues (e.g., "she's just a tomboy"), making assumptions about the child's gender identity based on their gender creativity, or making assumptions about the need for future medical interventions (e.g., "he can do puberty suppression in a few years and then go on hormones"). Because the trajectory of a gender diverse child's gender identity and desired expression cannot be presumed, it is important that the language used about medical intervention reflects this. The mental health clinician can play an important role in helping children and families identify, process, and challenge messages that imply only one trajectory when appropriate.

Mental Health Settings

Although it is clear that environmental support is a critical protective factor for gender diverse children at all levels of the social system, one of the biggest debates in the field of transgender healthcare centers on the question of what constitutes appropriate support for gender diverse children, specifically, the question of whether children should be supported in an early (prepubertal) social transition. Until the last 10 to 15 years, clinical intervention for gender diverse children focused on diagnosing gender dysphoria (formerly gender identity disorder) and assessing whether dysphoria was insistent, consistent, and persistent throughout childhood as an indicator of whether the child should proceed with a social and/or medical transition from one sex to the other in adolescence. Two approaches to care broadly follow this framework. In the model of care developed at the Center for Addiction and Mental Health, which has been described as the "therapeutic model" (Dreger, 2009), as well as the *Live in Your Own Skin* approach in a critique by Ehrensaft (2020), the treatment goal was to facilitate the child's acceptance of, and identification with, their birth-assigned sex, through individual and family intervention in childhood. If the child continued to demonstrate "cross-gender identification" in adolescence, they could be supported in a gender transition (see Zucker et al., 2012, for a description of this approach). In a *Watchful Waiting* approach, the child's gender identity or expression is observed over time rather than manipulated. The use of puberty blockers could be used to stall pubertal development in order to add time for more gender identity exploration. Again, if the transgender identity persists into adolescence, the child can then be supported in social transition (see de Vries & Cohen-Kettenis, 2012, for a description of this approach). These two approaches reflect a binary framework of gender and are grounded in gender essentialism, neglecting the existence of multiple pathways of gender development and the possibility of a much broader range of gender identities and expressions. The *Live in Your Skin* approach has been challenged for its potential to harm gender diverse children, fostering a sense of shame about their gender diversity, and increasing vulnerability to mental health issues (Wallace & Russel, 2013). While no study has been done on conversion therapy for gender identity (only sexual orientation), Turban and colleagues (2020) recently asked transgender adults to recall gender identity conversion efforts in childhood and found that such efforts were associated with mental health issues and suicidality in adulthood.

Gender affirmative models of care have been most prominent in the past 10 to 15 years and developed in response to the aforementioned concerns with *Watchful Waiting* or *Live in Your Own Skin* approaches. Gender affirmative models are informed by gender development theory described earlier in this chapter, recognizing that gender variation is not disordered, that gender is influenced by the child's bio-psycho-social-cultural context, and that gender identity exists on a spectrum and is not strictly binary (see Hidalgo et al., 2013 for an overview of gender affirmative frameworks). In gender affirmative models, the therapeutic focus is on supporting the child's exploration of their gender without restricting the option of a social transition until puberty. Within a gender affirmative framework, there are many ways that therapeutic care can be approached. In other words, there is no single model of gender affirmative therapy.

Two models of gender affirmative care that promote the resilience of the child and their social systems are the Multidimensional Family Approach (MDFA; Malpas, 2011) and the Gender Affirmative Lifespan Approach (GALA; Rider et al., 2019; Spencer, Berg et al., 2021). In MDFA, parents are central to treatment, and therapeutic goals begin with facilitating parental acceptance of fluidity and increasing harmony between the gender diverse child and their immediate family environment. Then, parents are better able to advocate and promote flexibility of gender norms in social contexts, starting with schools, faith communities, neighborhoods, family friends, and extended families, and expanding outward to social and cultural messaging (Malpas, 2011). GALA, described further in the case discussion that follows, emphasizes the importance of developing gender literacy around sociocultural messages and rules about gender, exploring between the gender binary and holding space for ambiguity as children explore their gender.

Critiques of gender affirmative approaches center on the lack of empirical data on long-term outcomes for affirmative approaches, the weight given to the child's self-reported gender, and the possibility that early social transition could reinforce a gender binary and actually limit exploration (de Graaf & Carmichael, 2019). Thus, it is critical that gender affirmative approaches remain grounded in the literature on developmental theory, offering a flexible and individualized framework that affirms the child's identity while holding space for ambiguity about how the child's gender identity and expression will evolve over time. In gender affirmative approaches, social transition steps can facilitate gender exploration, rather than being an outcome of exploration once a gender diverse identity has been "solidified." This approach to social transition sets gender affirmative models apart from prior models of care. In models of care that restrict social transition until puberty when a youth's transgender identity has been more "solidified," social transition often can be treated as a process of moving from one gender "box" to another at a single point in time. This approach to social transition can indeed be problematic with prepubescent children, as it can neglect a spectrum of possible gender identities and expressions and inadvertently "lock the child in" to a specific trajectory. Instead, approaching social transition in prepubescent children as a fluid process that can evolve over time allows the child to explore and be in whatever gender identity and expression fits them at any given time. As previously noted, the available literature on early social transition indicates that it can be a protective factor in terms of mental health (Olson et al., 2016). Thus, the key question is not simply *whether* to do an early social transition, but *how* to do it in a way that promotes the optimal mental health of the child.

Case Study

The therapeutic process described in the following case has been guided by the philosophical foundations and therapeutic components of GALA (Rider et al., 2019; Spencer, Berg et al., 2021). The philosophical foundations of GALA, when applied specifically to children, emphasize the following: 1) Across the life span—the developmental context of children's gender identity and expression is different from that of adults or adolescents, meaning that specific interventions must account for these unique developmental needs (e.g., tolerating ambiguity about gender identity); 2) Transaffirmative—gender diversity in children should not be pathologized, but instead affirmed as a part of normal gender development; 3) Transparency—intentional information sharing with gender diverse children and their parent/s related to the social and historical context of approaches to care and collaborative treatment planning is encouraged; 4) Intersectionality—when addressing the child's gender identity, clinicians recognize that other cultural contexts based on identities (e.g., gendered racism) are inextricably linked and interwoven into a child's and family's lived experience; 5) Interdisciplinary—gender diverse children benefit from having a range of gender-competent providers (e.g., pediatrician, school personnel); and

6) Empiricism—the development of scholarship that centers gender diverse children's lived experiences is essential.

While not all gender diverse children need therapy, it is likely that engaging in a therapeutic process such as the one described below can be beneficial and even play a protective role in preventing the internalization of stigma and discrimination that many gender diverse children experience. Thus, GALA believes in the role of supportive therapy as one aspect of affirmative care for gender diverse children with an emphasis on the following therapeutic components: (a) Gender literacy—helping children to differentiate gender identity and gender expression as distinct from sex assigned at birth as well as to identify and externalize (rather than internalize) oppressive messages and experiences related to gender within society; (b) Beyond the binary—helping children recognize all the potential possibilities of gender identity, expression, and experience; (c) Resiliency—learning how to overcome gender-based adversity through effective coping, which includes identifying safe spaces to share these difficulties and gain support; (d) Pleasure-oriented positive sexuality—helping children to develop the foundations for sexual pleasure and satisfaction including cultivating, as much as possible, a positive sense of one's body and the existing range of body diversity; and (e) Connections to medical care—given that children do not need gender-related medical interventions prior to puberty, this component is focused on parent education, as parents may be misinformed about the need for medical intervention at this stage of development and/or may be making premature assumptions about the trajectory of their child's gender. As the process of gender identity development and gender exploration can be long-term, as shown in the case below, which spanned from Spring 2015 through Fall 2020, the role of the therapist is often one of support, guidance, and skill-building during a developmental journey. The therapist also can serve as a touchpoint for the child/family down the road if gender-related concerns arise or if medical interventions are being considered.

ANDI'S GENDER JOURNEY

Andi, a 10-year-old child of African/Columbian/Spanish descent, assigned female at birth, was adopted from Colombia at approximately one year of age by a white, cisgender, heterosexual couple. Andi and parents have attended sessions over the past five years, during which time Andi's gender expression has remained consistent while use of pronouns and self-identified gender have fluctuated. Note that in order to accurately reflect Andi's gender exploration process over time, pronouns will be changed accordingly. Sessions have typically occurred on a monthly basis, scaling up or down in frequency as needed. As parent involvement is a key component of integrated care for children, approximately one third of the total number of sessions to date have taken place with the parent(s) alone. When Andi was present, the parent(s) were always invited to check in at the beginning of each session, as well as at the end, so Andi could share what we had done together. Full family sessions also took place to have conversations about how things were going or to make important decisions together.

Sessions 1–3 Assessment: Age 4.11–5.0

Parents reported at intake that they were seeking support in "finding peace with our child's need to be a boy" and input on "when to socially transition Andi." Parents reported that from age two, Andi had indicated that she "wished to be a boy." They shared that Andi had been determined to stand while peeing and when questioned about this, had "broken down screaming 'I'm a boy!'" Around this same time period, Andi started showing preference for what would be considered masculine clothes, including "throwing a fit" when asked to wear an Easter dress. By age four, Andi began to say things like, "I feel like a boy on the inside but have girl parts." At age 4.5, Andi told her parents, "being a girl makes me sad, and I want to have a penis." While her parents had already been considering doing so, this propelled them to begin to use the name Andi (including at preschool) and Andi, happily, got a short haircut. Andi continued to request she/her pronouns.

When asked why she was at the appointment, Andi shared, "because I am a boy. I don't have a penis, but I can still be a boy." Andi referenced her "boy clothes and boy's shoes." Semi-structured interviews and drawing activities were used to understand the meaning that Andi was making of her gender experience. Andi was very engaged and expressive for a five-year-old, offering nuanced and complex responses. To a variety of questions designed to assess gender identity (albeit from a binary perspective, i.e., "Are you a girl or a boy?") Andi consistently endorsed both genders, stating, "girl and boy," or "half boy and half girl." When asked questions that were more pointed in the boy direction (e.g., "Do you ever think you are really a boy?"), Andi maintained similar responses, stating, "Yes, I like to be a girl and a boy because it feels good inside of me." However, Andi could not come up with any good things about being a girl, and to the question, "Do you think it is better to be a girl or a boy?" Andi shared "I asked if I can be a boy, and they said you'll be a boy with a 'gina.'" Andi's level of anatomical dysphoria was also assessed in a variety of ways. Andi did not express anatomical dysphoria. Andi reported being "happy" with all parts of herself and was not *unhappy* with any parts of herself. When talking specifically about "private parts," Andi consistently reported feeling okay about her "gina" with no mention of wanting a penis. Interestingly, a question about being able to choose birth-assigned sex yielded, "boy," with a "not sure" as to why.

In terms of gender literacy, Andi initially differentiated gender by differences in hair length, but when this was revisited, she also shared that "boy bodies have a penis and no [waved hand over chest area]." When given the word, "breasts," Andi said "yes, no boobs, girl bodies have boobs and a gina." In terms of the concept of gender roles and gender expression, Andi gave examples of "boy toys and girl toys," saying that she liked "both." Andi did not seem to grasp the concept of sexual orientation.

Sessions 4–5 Feedback and Collaborative Treatment Planning with Parents Only: Age 5.1–5.2

In the feedback session with parents, we discussed that while Andi demonstrated clear gender expression diversity in line with what society would consider stereotypically masculine, she did not appear to have a clear binary boy identity. Instead, she tended to consider herself to be "half girl and half boy." It was noted that what Andi shared about her gender experiences during the assessment was not as extreme as what she shared with parents, particularly around anatomical dysphoria, and that this was something we would continue to track. In addition to gender-related issues, parents raised the issue of intersectionality related to race and adoption. They expressed concerns that Andi would be subject to increased teasing in the African American community, not because of decreased tolerance, but because African American people appeared more apt to "read" Andi as a girl and therefore notice her gender nonconformity much more often as compared to white people who tended to "read" Andi as male. Parents also expressed concern about the negative climate that exists for African American males, noting that there was a much higher likelihood that Andi would face both implicit and explicit racial bias if she grew up as a boy. Parents expressed an awareness of the need to nurture Andi's racial identity combined with uncertainty of how to do that as people of white experience. They reported seeking out supportive environments but noted difficulty with finding spaces that could be supportive of both Andi's gender and racial identities.

Together, the therapist and parents discussed the pros and cons of engaging in supportive therapy from a GALA framework. The following goals were established: 1) gather more information over time about Andi's gender experience; 2) explore how best to support Andi within our culture that stigmatizes gender diversity and expects children to conform to binary identity expectations; 3) increase Andi and parents' gender literacy and resilience; 4) explore questions related to social transition; and 5) discuss ways to actively nurture Andi's racial identity development.

Sessions 6–11 Early Therapy Process: Age 5.3–6.1

In the months immediately following assessment, Andi began asking parents to use he/him pronouns and making statements like, "I am your son, right?" Parent-only sessions were provided to explore how they were perceiving and coping with Andi's gender-related assertions, as well as how to affirm his identity while also giving messages that all options remained available. Andi's mother observed that he was making more comments about not liking his vagina but felt this might be more motivated by Andi thinking he had to reject "female" things because of their connection to femaleness as opposed to not really liking them. Andi's parents also observed that identity statements appeared to be context-dependent (sometimes asserting boy identity, sometimes girl identity). In a facilitated discussion about this, Andi's mother was able to express her concern that Andi was picking up on his father's anxiety, confusion, and sadness when these gender situations arose. This topic was then brought to a family session where Andi's father was guided in communicating to Andi that his job is to be whoever he is rather than change himself to accommodate his father in some way. Andi's parents also expressed to Andi that it was the parents' job to support Andi and to take care of their own emotions.

During this time, both parents were able to open up about their fears and uncertainties about how best to support Andi in the larger social transition step of identifying and expressing his gender as a boy in all settings, which they perceived as inevitable at this time. These were often emotional sessions where empathy and safety were provided. The therapist reinforced parents' open and supportive stance and emphasized the importance of following Andi's lead in the here and now rather than becoming outcome focused. The therapist emphasized that if/when it became time to navigate this social transition step, doing it in a way that leaves the spectrum of gender identity and expression open to Andi would be most beneficial.

During this time, parents were also making decisions about school choice for kindergarten and were weighing the opportunities between a private school noted for its academic resources versus a public school with greater racial diversity and emphasis on social interaction. Parents were guided in how to assess the extent to which the schools' climates were gender affirming (e.g., meeting with school administrators to ascertain whether they had sought gender inclusive training for their teachers and whether affirming policies related to pronouns, name usage, and aspects of social transition had been written or adopted). Given Andi's recent request for he/him pronouns, parents also explored whether Andi should begin kindergarten as a boy. They ultimately decided to wait to take this larger social transition step but were encouraged to begin having discussions with Andi about what he wanted and what the potential implications of various choices might be. Time was spent processing how to introduce topics related to both racial and gender stigma and discrimination in a way that would build Andi's gender and racial literacy and increase his resilience. Parents began having conversations with Andi about his adoption as a segue to addressing the complexities of racial and gender diversity.

The early therapy process with Andi focused on building rapport, exploring beyond the binary, developing gender literacy, and increasing resilience. The name tag intervention (i.e., in each session, everyone attending makes a name tag to wear with the name and pronouns each would like to use in that session) was introduced, and over the course of sessions, Andi picked various names and pronouns (e.g., Willy with he/him, Fishy with he/him, Andi with he/him, and Andi with she/her). Children's books designed to show the spectrum of racial and gender diversity were introduced to support discussions of racial and gender literacy. Gender-affirming coloring books (e.g., Gonzalez, 2010; Labelle, 2015) depicting pictures of children, both clothed and unclothed, with varying gender identities and gender expression enjoying their bodies in all sorts of ways were used to increase gender literacy by talking about some of the "gender rules" that exist and how those rules impact children's choices about what they can/can't do and who they get to be and not be. These coloring book pictures were also important in setting the foundation for positive sexuality through body-affirming messaging. Andi was able to point out to parents how the children depicted were similar and different from himself both in terms of skin color as well as pronoun usage, sharing that some people use they/them pronouns rather than he or she. As bathroom usage at school was leading to children questioning Andi's gender in a way that made Andi uncomfortable, art-based interventions were used to help Andi express his feelings about these situations. Role-playing with potato heads and dolls allowed Andi to build resilience by practicing different ways of handling these interactions. Bathroom discussions also led to topics of underwear and private parts, which not only added much humor to sessions, but also were used to help Andi explore the ways that cultural messages reinforce the gender binary and to make distinctions between sex assigned at birth and gender identity. Throughout this time, we explicitly celebrated racial and gender diversity while acknowledging through examples occurring at school that not everyone is as accepting as Andi and his family and friends, but over time, people can grow and change.

By the end of this kindergarten year and into the summer, Andi appeared less invested in a male identity. With parents, we processed the hypothesis that Andi was "going underground" rather than truly feeling less dysphoric, and we continued to have discussions about how to tolerate the ambiguity of Andi's gender identity development and give messages that all options are to be celebrated.

Sessions 12–16 Ongoing Therapeutic Process: Age 6.2–6.7

As Andi and parents got ready for the upcoming school year, Andi's worries about being misgendered by peers resurfaced. Throughout the summer, Andi had shifted to wanting to use she/her pronouns at home but "no pronouns" out in public. Essentially, Andi was able to say that when people know her, she doesn't have to be worried about being accepted or that people are going to have a huge reaction to being told she is a girl after they have assumed, based on her gender expression, that she is a boy. Unfortunately, because of not wanting to deal with this, Andi had begun to avoid these interactions by acting like she didn't hear someone asking, "Are you a girl or a boy?" Thus, we revisited resilience strategies for coping with these gender-related questions directly and authentically and invited parents to practice these with Andi in role-plays with stuffed animals at home. In addition, we worked to identify those peers who "knew she was a girl" and were friends across different life contexts who would support her in these situations. Both parents were able to be compassionate about this struggle. They shared how proud they were of Andi for being brave and let Andi know that whenever they were present, they would help Andi to assert herself—that they were "in this together."

In the next number of sessions with Andi, we used the book *Jacob's New Dress* (Hoffman & Hoffman, 2014) to continue exploring all the different gender identities and expressions between the binary that kids can have. Andi agreed that Jacob should get to wear a dress if he wants to but questioned why there was not a book like this for girls. Following this lead, we drew a set of pictures that could be used for such a book and then used these pictures in an ongoing way to understand more about how Andi was making meaning of her gender experiences. For example, when Andi developed an interest in playing ice hockey, we looked at different pictures and discussed what type of team a given child would like to play on—all girl, all boy, or mixed gender. Andi expressed that it didn't really matter which team she played on, she just wanted to try it out.

Sessions 17–24 Ongoing Therapeutic Process: Age 6.8–7.5

The next sessions with Andi occurred in the school year and after Andi had joined a girls-only hockey program. Prior to the decision to enroll Andi in this program, the options of all girl, all boy, or mixed gender had been discussed with Andi, who was supported in making the final decision. Parents were guided to initiate a number of conversations behind the scenes with the hockey coaches and some of the other parents at an open house event to make sure that Andi's gender identity (which at this point had shifted to "girl") and expression (continued to be what would be considered masculine) would be respected and honored. We discussed how Andi's mother could strategically support Andi in the locker room before and after practices to make sure that there was no uncertainty by other parents or peers. It also became clear that there were other girls in the program who would be considered to have a more masculine gender expression and thus, for the first time, Andi had the experience of her gender identity and expression being mirrored back to her. Andi was able to make friends on the hockey team with both "girly girls" and "girls like me" and quickly grew to feel at home in this environment. At the same time, it was becoming clear to Andi's parents that Andi needed community to nurture her racial identity as well as her gender identity. News that Andi's mother in Colombia had given birth to another baby prompted further discussion about Andi's family history and about what it was like for Andi to "have brown skin when most everyone else has lighter skin." Being a gender diverse kid in a transracial adoptive home and largely white social environment was taking a toll on Andi. We focused on how to provide more opportunities for Andi to engage with people of color, including attending racially diverse programming at the local YMCA, and discussed some therapy referrals that would be able to better address the unique issues of transracial adoption and positive racial identity development.

As Andi's resilience continued to grow, she continued to do well with handling various situations arising out of ignorance or oppressive beliefs related to gender, including challenging situations at school. Despite a largely supportive environment at school, Andi continued to face discrimination by certain peers (e.g., constantly asking "Are you boy or a girl?" despite Andi's clear statements "I'm a girl."). Andi was supported by her parents and therapist in recognizing that not everyone is going to "get it," but that doesn't have to influence how she thinks or feels about herself. As Andi prepared for her first experience at summer camp (in an all-girl setting within a coed camp), parents were worried that gender-based teasing/bullying may occur around Andi wearing "boy" underwear and "boy" swim trunks and shirt. They connected with camp staff ahead of time to increase the chances of intervening quickly and appropriately. Parents were supported by the therapist in their struggle to promote the message that "you are fine just the way you are" as well as continue to gently prepare Andi for the reality that she may, unfortunately, be made fun of for her gender expression.

Sessions 24–35 Ongoing Therapeutic Process: Age 7.6–9.0

About two and a half years into therapy, there was another potential shift in Andi's gender identity. Following another bathroom event, Andi shared that she wished she had a penis. While Andi observed that having a penis would make it more convenient to pee, she was more importantly beginning to notice that boys get some status and privileges that girls do not. In an age-appropriate way, the therapist noted the inequities that exist related to gender (sexism) and helped parents to draw parallels between this and the family's ongoing discussions about race and racism. Parents also voiced their support for a shift to neutral or masculine pronouns if Andi desired. In the following family session, Andi put down "Andrea" with "he/him" pronouns during the name tag activity. Parents noted that Andi appeared to be deciding whether to identify as girl/boy depending on context. We discussed how parents could continue to communicate support for any gender identity, and in particular, introduced the idea of a nonbinary identity. The session explored Andi's beliefs about the pros and cons of living in a "girl world vs. boy world" vs. a place that is "in between." Over the next several months, Andi's choice of pronouns during the name tag activity was "he/she," and a decision was made at school, due to Andi's discomfort with peers continuing to question Andi's gender regardless of what bathroom was being used, that Andi would use a private restroom. It appeared as though a nonbinary identity was emerging, and, as with any other identity, parents continued to supportively follow Andi's lead and advocate for others to do so as well.

Sessions 36–44 Present Therapeutic Process: Age 9.3–10.5

When asked about gender identity, Andi says, "I just want to be me," and when given the opportunity, Andi does not endorse a nonbinary identity. In settings where Andi feels emotionally safe and is not worried about gender-related stigmatizing responses, Andi is comfortable being identified as a girl with she/her pronouns. Her gender expression remains traditionally masculine. Though still experiencing anxiety related to bathroom use, she now routinely is comfortable using the girl's bathroom and is confident in her ability to assert herself if there are issues. Andi continues not to express body dysphoria. Thus, in a treatment plan update, the original DSM-5 diagnosis of gender dysphoria in childhood was removed and replaced with an adjustment disorder with anxiety to capture the continued distress Andi experiences when having to handle others' reactions to her gender diversity.

In the next two sessions, discussions focused on exploring topics related to sexuality and puberty. This has provided another window into how Andi is making meaning of her gender experience. In discussions about the potential for menstruation and breast development, Andi reported that she is "fine with periods" and that she understands this means "I am becoming a woman." Andi also reported that she is fine with the breast development that is starting to happen, elaborating, "I don't want really big boobs but am happy because that means I can breastfeed." In addition, Andi shared "I want to have a baby and be a mom." Andi was able to relate this to her mother, telling her, "I like being like you." Mother gave Andi a hug and simply replied, "Awww, thanks Andi, I like you too."

CASE REFLECTION

The above case demonstrates how supportive therapeutic interventions can help explore the complexity of a child's gender and their intersecting identities, identify points of resilience within the child and their support systems, and tolerate the ambiguity of not having a set outcome based in binary thinking. As authors, the process of writing this case study also offered an important opportunity for reflection. In clinical practice with prepubescent children, it is rare to work with a child and family for five years (and counting). The pediatric gender care field is evolving due to developments in research and scholarship, as well as important shifts in the social climate related to gender (i.e., today's gender diverse children are developing in a different social climate than those just five years ago). We recognize that some of our clinical thinking at the time of Andi's initial presentation to our clinic has shifted too. For example, a more intersectional approach would have integrated therapeutic goals related to race and gender, rather than thinking of them as discrete aspects of Andi's identity. We also recognize that some of the ways in which the therapist discussed gender with Andi reflected binary thinking. For example, when Andi expressed interest in joining a hockey team and Andi's pictures were reviewed to discuss whether those children would play on "girls' teams," "boys' teams," or "mixed-gender teams," this may have inadvertently reinforced the message that all children can fit into a binary gender "box." A more nuanced conversation may have addressed why these sports team options are limited and how difficult it can be for children to have to make these choices. Finally, during the five years in which Andi's family has been seen at the clinic, conversations around prepubertal social transition have become more nuanced. At the time of Andi's intake, parents and therapist did not think of Andi as having socially transitioned, despite using the name Andi and making changes in her gender expression. This reflects a way of thinking about social transition as an "all or none" process that happens at a specific point in time. As we have discussed in this chapter, many models of gender-affirming care, including GALA, now emphasize the possibility for social transition to be a series of steps that can help a child explore their gender. Following the gender journey of a child such as Andi highlights the importance of a nuanced approach to social transition.

Future Directions

Considering the issues addressed throughout this chapter, it is imperative that future clinical work and research with gender diverse children and their families take an intersectional, inclusive, and methodologically creative approach. The development and use of inclusive and culturally relevant measures of gender identity is a foundational requirement for understanding the experiences of gender diverse children, and these measures should be part of all child development research to avoid repeating historic misrepresentation of gender diverse children. The inclusion of nonbinary identities in this body of work is essential for creating a comprehensive picture of gender development that opens opportunities for understanding well-being throughout the life course. Researchers and clinicians must consider multiple facets of gender (e.g., expression, beliefs, and identity) and consider how these aspects each relate to risk and resilience within populations of gender diverse children. Wording that is accessible, up-to-date, and comprehensive is also necessary and informs the kinds of questions that can be addressed.

Furthermore, an inclusive foundation will open up opportunities for examining gender identity development longitudinally. The lack of inclusion of well-developed measures of gender beyond the binary in longitudinal studies means that it is impossible to accurately detect shifts in gender identity in many broadscale longitudinal studies of child well-being, especially in populations that have not been clinically referred for gender-related concerns. The inclusion of comprehensive gender identity measures would help to normalize the understanding of the wide array of identities and remove barriers to understanding set by research that requires an element of social transition.

Finally, an openness to considering a broader range of gender-related information in the literature would help to shed light on the environmental and contextual factors shaping gender identity and expression. For example, research on gender literacy, or the understanding of what gender is and how it functions in society, is very limited but suggests that this could be an influential force in exploring and expressing one's gender identity. Researchers and clinicians should also question the predominant reliance on quantitative methods and explore options in qualitative and community-based research to more accurately reflect the lived experiences of gender diverse children and their families.

As mental health clinicians interested in gender-affirming care, we have the opportunity and the obligation to set things right. It is imperative that future clinicians and researchers/scholars emphasize the importance of integrated care that prioritizes intersectionality as well as actively promotes the positive development of *all* children by celebrating the diversity of experience that exists within that development. In order to accomplish this, clinicians and researchers must explicitly be thinking about the impact of racism, cissexism, heterosexism, ableism, and other systemic oppressions on children and their families. And most important, we always must be willing to critically examine ourselves and our work to determine how these forces shape our clinical conceptualizations, assessment measures, treatment plans, clinical interventions, theories, research questions, and the literature produced.

Key Knowledge Points

- The care of gender diverse children is rapidly evolving in response to growing scholarship and shifts in the societal context related to gender diversity.
- Due to developmental factors unique to childhood, the care of gender diverse children requires specialized knowledge that is distinct from that of gender diverse adolescents and adults.
- Historically, the field of child development has viewed gender identity through a binary, cisgender lens, leading to the erasure of the broad range of experiences of gender diverse children.
- There is a serious lack of representation of children of color and children with neurodiversity in the clinical and research literature on gender diverse children. Racism, classism, and ableism, in addition to heterosexism and cissexism, are pervasive forces that create and maintain barriers to representation.

- In order to foster positive gender identity development of all children, we need to move toward ways of thinking about gender development that accommodate the complex, multidimensional nature of gender diversity.
- The current state of the literature suggests that positive mental health of gender diverse children is linked to the level of support within the social systems the children are a part of. Gender diverse children who experience rejection based on societal gender stigmatization are at greater risk of developing psychosocial and mental health problems.
- Gender diverse children, as all children, are embedded in a variety of systems (peers, family, school, etc.) that can either promote or hinder resilience in terms of gender identity and gender expression. Mental health clinicians should assess the social systems that the child is a part of and identify and encourage those aspects of the system that promote resilience.
- Gender-affirming mental health therapy focused on the therapeutic components found in the Gender Affirmative Lifespan Approach (GALA) (i.e., gender literacy, beyond the binary, resiliency, pleasure-oriented positive sexuality, connections to medical care) has the potential to be a protective factor for gender diverse children and their families.
- Mental health clinicians interested in gender-affirming care need to critically examine the inherent bias in the scholarship related to gender and gender diversity, the cultural landscapes of gender in society, and their own assumptions because these influence how clinicians approach all children and their families.

Recommendations for Practitioners and Professionals

- We recommend that mental health clinicians working with gender diverse children receive theoretical and evidenced-based training in general child and family mental health as well as in gender development and gender diversity in children.
- We recommend that clinicians working with gender diverse children and families engage in continuing education related to gender diverse children and families in order to maintain up-to-date knowledge in the field.
- We recommend that clinicians working with gender diverse children who do not have specialized training themselves find gender specialists in their area whom they can consult with.
- We recommend that mental health clinicians who wish to specialize in providing care to gender diverse children become WPATH SOC7/8 certified through the World Professional Association for Transgender Health (WPATH) Global Education Initiative (GEI).

References

Abreu, R. L., Rosenkrantz, D. E., Ryser-Oatman, J. T., Rostosky, S. S., & Riggle, E. D. (2019). Parental reactions to transgender and gender diverse children: A literature review. *Journal of GLBT Family Studies, 15*(5), 461–485. https://doi.org/10.1080/1550428X.2019.1656132

Achenbach, T. M., & Rescorla, L. A. (2001). *Manual for the ASEBA school-age forms & profiles*. University of Vermont, Research Center for Children, Youth, & Families.

American Psychiatric Association. (1987). *Diagnostic and statistical manual of mental disorders* (3rd ed., revised). American Psychiatric Association.

American Psychiatric Association. (2000). *Diagnostic and statistical manual of mental disorders* (4th ed.). American Psychiatric Association.

American Psychiatric Association. (2013). *Diagnostic and statistical manual of mental disorders* (5th ed.). American Psychiatric Association.

Beh, H. G., & Diamond, M. (2000). An emerging ethical and medical dilemma: Should physicians perform sex assignment surgery on infants with ambiguous genitalia. *Michigan Journal of Gender & Law, 7*(1), 1–63.

Berg, D., & Edwards-Leeper, L. (2018). Child and family assessment. In C. Keo-Meier & D. Ehrensaft (Eds.), *The gender affirmative model: An interdisciplinary approach to supporting transgender and gender expansive children* (pp. 101–124). American Psychological Association.

Bockting, W. O. (2014). Transgender identity development. In D. L. Tolman & L. Diamond (Eds.), *APA handbook of sexuality and psychology, vol. 1: Person-based approaches* (pp. 739–758). American Psychological Association.

Boskey, E. R. (2014). Understanding transgender identity development in childhood and adolescence. *American Journal of Sexuality Education, 9*(4), 445–463. https://doi.org/10.1080/15546128.2014.973131

Bronfenbrenner, U. (2001). The bioecological theory of human development. In N. J. Smelser & P. B. Baltes (Eds.), *International encyclopedia of the social and behavioral sciences* (Vol. 10, pp. 6963–6970). Elsevier.

Bronfenbrenner, U. (1979). *The ecology of human development*. Harvard University Press.

Chen, D., Hidalgo, M. A., & Garofalo, R. (2017). Parental perceptions of emotional and behavioral difficulties among prepubertal gender-nonconforming children. *Clinical Practice in Pediatric Psychology, 5*, 342–352. https://doi.org/10.1037/cpp0000217

Cohen-Kettenis, P. T., Owen, A., Kaijser, V. G., Bradley, S. J., & Zucker, K. J. (2003). Demographic characteristics, social competence, and behavior problems in children with gender identity disorder: A cross-national, cross-clinic comparative analysis. *Journal of Abnormal Child Psychology, 31*, 41–53. http://dx.doi.org/10.1023/A:1021769215342

Coleman, E., Bockting, W., Botzer, M., Cohen-Kettenis, P., DeCuypere, G., Feldman, J., . . . Monstrey, S. (2012). Standards of care for the health of transsexual, transgender, and gender-nonconforming people, version 7. *International Journal of Transgenderism, 13*(4), 165–232.

Craig, A. (2009). How do you feel—now? The anterior insula and human awareness. *Nature Reviews Neuroscience, 10*(1), 59–70. https://doi.org/10.1038/nrn2555

Deaux, K. (1993). Reconstructing social identity. *Personality and Social Psychology Bulletin, 19*(1), 4–12.

D'Augelli, A. R., Grossman, A. H., & Starks, M. T. (2006). Childhood gender atypicality, victimization, and PTSD among lesbian, gay, and bisexual youth. *Journal of Interpersonal Violence, 21*(11), 1462–1482. https://doi.org/10.1177/0886260506293482

de Graaf, N. M., & Carmichael, P. (2019). Reflections on emerging trends in clinical work with gender diverse children and adolescents. *Clinical Child Psychology and Psychiatry, 24*(2), 353–364. https://doi.org/10.1177/1359104518812924

de Vries, A. L., & Cohen-Kettenis, P. T. (2012). Clinical management of gender dysphoria in children and adolescents: The Dutch approach. *Journal of Homosexuality, 59*(3), 301–320.

de Vries, A. L. C., Kreukels, B. P. C., Steensma, T. D., & McGuire, J. K. (2014). Gender identity development: A biopsychosocial perspective. In B. P. C. Kreukels, T. D. Steensma, & A. L. C. de Vries (Eds.), *Gender dysphoria and disorders of sex development: Progress in care and knowledge*. Springer. https://doi.org/10.1007/978-1-4614-7441-8_3

de Vries, A. L., Steensma, T. D., Cohen-Kettenis, P. T., VanderLaan, D. P., & Zucker, K. J. (2016). Poor peer relations predict parent- and self-reported behavioral and emotional problems of adolescents with gender dysphoria: A cross-national, cross-clinic comparative analysis. *European Child & Adolescent Psychiatry, 25*(6), 579–588. https://doi.org/10.1007/s00787-015-0764-7

Diamond, L. M. (2020). Gender fluidity and nonbinary gender identities among children and adolescents. *Child Development Perspectives, 14*(2), 110–115. https://doi.org/10.1111/cdep.12366

Diamond, L. M., Pardo, S. T., Butterworth, M. R. (2011). Transgender experience and identity. In S. J. Shwartz, K. Luyckx, & V. L. Vignoles (Eds.), *Handbook of identity theory and research* (pp. 629–647). Springer.

Dover, K. J. (1978 [1989]). *Greek homosexuality*. Harvard University Press.

Dreger, A. (2009). Gender identity disorder in childhood: Inconclusive advice to parents. *The Hastings Center Report, 39*(1), 26–29.

Drescher, J. (2014). Gender identity diagnoses: History and controversies. In *Gender dysphoria and disorders of sex development* (pp. 137–150). Springer.

Drummond, K. D., Bradley, S. J., Peterson-Badali, M., & Zucker, K. J. (2008). A follow-up study of girls with gender identity disorder. *Developmental Psychology, 44*(1), 34. https://doi.org/10.1037/0012-1649.44.1.34

Egan, S. K., & Perry, D. G. (2001). Gender identity: A multidimensional analysis with implications for psychosocial adjustment. *Developmental Psychology, 37*(4), 451. https://doi.org/10.1037//0012-1649.37.4.451

Ehrensaft, D. (2020). Treatment paradigms for prepubertal children. In M. Forcier, G. van Schalkwyk, & J. L. Turban (Eds.), *Pediatric gender identity: Gender-affirming care for transgender & gender diverse youth*. Springer Cham. https://doi.org/10.1007/978-3-030-38909-3_13

Erickson-Schroth, L. (2013). Update on the biology of transgender identity. *Journal of Gay & Lesbian Mental Health, 17*(2), 150–174. https://doi.org/10.1080/19359705.2013.753393

Fast, A. A., & Olson, K. R. (2018). Gender development in transgender preschool children. *Child development, 89*(2), 620–637.

Fausto-Sterling, A. (2000). *Sexing the body: Gender politics and the construction of sexuality*. Basic Books.

Fausto-Sterling, A. (2019). The dynamic development of gender variability. In A. Slomowitz & A. Feit (Eds.), *Homosexuality, Transsexuality, Psychoanalysis and Traditional Judaism* (pp. 155–182). Routledge.

Flores, A. R., Herman, J. L., Gates, G. J., & Brown, T. N. T. (2016). *How many adults identify as transgender in the United States?* Williams Institute.

Foucault, M. (1980). *The history of sexuality. Volume one: An introduction*. Robert Hurley (trans.). Vintage Books.

Gardner, M., & Sandberg, D. E. (2018). Navigating surgical decision making in disorders of sex development (DSD). *Frontiers in Pediatrics, 6*, 339.

Gonzalez, M. C. (2010). *Gender now coloring book: A learning adventure for children and adults.* Reflection Press.

Hidalgo, M. A., Ehrensaft, D., Tishelman, A. C., Clark, L. F., Garofalo, R., Rosenthal, S. M., Spack, N. P., & Olson, J. (2013). The gender affirmative model: What we know and what we aim to learn. *Human Development, 56*(5), 285–290.

Hidalgo, M. A., & Chen, D. (2019). Experiences of gender minority stress in cisgender parents of transgender/gender-expansive prepubertal children: A qualitative study. *Journal of Family Issues, 40*(7), 865–886. https://doi.org/10.1159/000355235

Hines, M. (2000). Gonadal hormones and sexual differentiation of human behavior: Effects on psycho-social and cognitive development. In A. Matsumoto (Ed.), *Sexual differentiation of the brain* (pp. 257–278). CRC Press.

Hines, M. (2005). *Brain Gender.* Oxford University Press.

Hines, M. (2009). Gonadal hormones and sexual differentiation of human brain and behavior. In D. W. Pfaff, A. P. Arnold, A. M. Etgen, S. E. Fahrbach, & R. T. Rubin (Eds.), *Hormones, brain and behavior* (2nd ed., pp. 1869–1909). Academic.

Hoffman, S., & Hoffman, I. (2014). *Jacob's new dress* (C. Case, Illus). Albert Whitman & Company.

Hyde, J. S. (2005). The gender similarities hypothesis. *American Psychologist, 60*(6), 581–592. https://doi.org/10.1037/0003-066X.60.6.581

Hyde, J. S., Bigler, R. S., Joel, D., Tate, C. C., & van Anders, S. M. (2019). The future of sex and gender in psychology: Five challenges to the gender binary. *American Psychologist, 74*(2), 171–193. https://doi.org/10.1037/amp0000307

Joel, D., Berman, Z., Tavor, I., Wexler, N., Gaber, O., Stein, Y., . . . Assaf, Y. (2015). Sex beyond the genitalia: The human brain mosaic. Proceedings of the National Academy of Sciences of the United States of America, 112, 15468–15473. https://doi.org/10.1073/pnas.1509654112

Johnson, A. H. (2016). Transnormativity: A new concept and its validation through documentary film about transgender men. *Sociological Inquiry, 86,* 465–491. http://dx.doi.org/10.1111/soin.12127

Kent, M. (2006). Gender differentiation. *Oxford Dictionary of Sports Science & Medicine.* Oxford University Press. https://www.oxfordreference.com/view/10.1093/acref/9780198568506.001.0001/acref-9780198568506-e-2832

Kohlberg, L. (1966). A cognitive developmental analysis of children's sex role concepts and attitudes. In E. E. Maccoby (Ed.), *The development of sex differences* (pp. 82–172). Stanford University Press.

Kolbuck, V. D., Muldoon, A. L., Rychlik, K., Hidalgo, M. A., & Chen, D. (2019). Psychological functioning, parenting stress, and parental support among clinic-referred prepubertal gender-expansive children. *Clinical Practice in Pediatric Psychology, 7*(3), 254. https://doi.org/10.1037/cpp0000293

Kosciw, J. G., Greytak, E. A., Zongrone, A. D., Clark, C. M., & Truong, N. L. (2018). The 2017 National School Climate Survey: The experiences of lesbian, gay, bisexual, transgender, and queer youth in our nation's schools. GLSEN.

Kuvalanka, K. A., Weiner, J. L., & Mahan, D. (2014). Child, family, and community transformations: Findings from interviews with mothers of transgender girls. *Journal of GLBT Family Studies, 10*(4), 354–379.

Kuvalanka, K. A., Weiner, J. L., Munroe, C., Goldberg, A. E., & Gardner, M. (2017). Trans and gender-nonconforming children and their caregivers: Gender presentations, peer relations, and well-being at baseline. *Journal of Family Psychology, 31*(7), 889–899. https://doi.org/10.1037/fam0000338

Kuvalanka, K. A., Gardner, M., & Munroe, C. (2019). All in the family: How extended family relationships are influenced by children's gender diverse and transgender identities. *Families in transition: Parenting gender-diverse children, adolescents, and young adults*, 102–117.

Labelle, S. (2015). *The genderific coloring book*. AssignedMale.

Lakey, B., & Cohen, S. (2000). Social support theory and measurement. In S. Cohen, L. G. Underwood, & B. H. Gottlieb (Eds.), *Social support measurement and intervention: A guide for health and social scientists* (pp. 29–52). Oxford University Press.

Liben, L. S., & Bigler, R. S. (2002). The developmental course of gender differentiation: Conceptualizing, measuring, and evaluating constructs and pathways. *Monographs of the Society for Research in Child Development, 67*(2), vii–147.

Liben, L. (2017). Gender development: A constructivist-ecological perspective. In N. Budwig, E. Turiel, & P. Zelazo (Eds.), *New perspectives on human development* (pp. 143–144). Cambridge University Press.

Malpas, J. (2011). Between pink and blue: A multi-dimensional family approach to gender nonconforming children and their families. *Family Process, 50*(4), 453–470. https://doi.org/10.1111/j.1545-5300.2011.01371.x

Masten, A. S. (2018). Resilience theory and research on children and families: Past, present, and promise. *Journal of Family Theory & Review, 10*(1), 12–31. https://doi.org/10.1111/jftr.12255

McGuire, J. K., & Morrow, Q. J. (2020). Pathways of gender development. In M. Forcier, G. Van Schalkwyk, & J. Turban (Eds.), *Pediatric gender identity*. Springer Cham. https://doi.org/10.1007/978-3-030-38909

McGuire, J. K., Anderson, C. R., Toomey, R. B., & Russell, S. T. (2010). School climate for transgender youth: A mixed method investigation of student experiences and school responses. *Journal of Youth and Adolescence, 39*(10), 1175–1188. https://doi.org/10.1007/s10964-010-9540-7

McHale, S. M., Crouter, A. C., & Whiteman, S. D. (2003). The family contexts of gender development in childhood and adolescence. *Social Development, 12*(1), 125–148. https://doi.org/10.1111/1467-9507.00225

Meyer, E. J., Tilland-Stafford, A., & Airton, L. (2016). Transgender and gender-creative students in PK–12 schools: What we can learn from their teachers. *Teachers College Record, 118*(8), 1–50. https://doi.org/10.1177/016146811611800806

Olson, K. R., Durwood, L., DeMeules, M., & McLaughlin, K. A. (2016). Mental health of transgender children who are supported in their identities. *Pediatrics, 137*(3), e20153223. https://doi.org/10.1542/peds.2015-3223

Olson, K. R., Key, A. C., & Eaton, N. R. (2015). Gender cognition in transgender children. *Psychological Science, 26*, 467–474. https://doi.org/10.1177/0956797614568156

Panter-Brick, C., & Leckman, J. F. (2013). Editorial commentary: Resilience in child development—interconnected pathways to wellbeing. *Journal of Child Psychology and Psychiatry, 54*(4), 333–336. https://doi.org/10.1111/jcpp.12057

Pariseau, E. M., Chevalier, L., Long, K. A., Clapham, R., Edwards-Leeper, L., & Tishelman, A. C. (2019). The relationship between family acceptance-rejection and transgender youth psychosocial functioning. *Clinical Practice in Pediatric Psychology, 7*(3), 267–277. https://doi.org/10.1037/cpp0000291

Pleak, R. R. (2011). Gender-variant children and transgender adolescents. *Child and Adolescent Psychiatric Clinics, 20*(4), xv–xx. https://doi.org/10.1016/j.chc.2011.08.007

Price, C. J., & Hooven, C. (2018). Interoceptive awareness skills for emotion regulation: Theory and approach of mindful awareness in body-oriented therapy (MABT). *Frontiers in Psychology, 9*, 798. https://doi.org/10.3389/fpsyg.2018.00798

Pullen Sansfaçon, A., Robichaud, M. J., & Dumais-Michaud, A. A. (2015). The experience of parents who support their children's gender variance. *Journal of LGBT Youth, 12*(1), 39–63. https://doi.org/10.1080/19361653.2014.935555

Rider, G. N., McMorris, B. J., Gower, A. L., Coleman, E., & Eisenberg, M. E. (2018). Health and care utilization of transgender and gender nonconforming youth: A population-based study. *Pediatrics, 141*(3), e20171683. https://doi.org/10.1542/peds.2017-1683

Rider, G. N., Vencill, J. A., Berg, D. R., Becker-Warner, R., Candelario-Pérez, L., & Spencer, K. G. (2019). The gender affirmative lifespan approach (GALA): A framework for competent clinical care with nonbinary clients. *International Journal of Transgenderism, 20*(2–3), 275–288. https://doi.org/10.1080/15532739.2018.1485069

Rijn, A. B. V., Steensma, T. D., Kreukels, B. P., & Cohen-Kettenis, P. T. (2013). Self-perception in a clinical sample of gender variant children. *Clinical Child Psychology and Psychiatry, 18*(3), 464–474. https://doi.org/10.1177/1359104512460621

Rivas, J. (2015). Half of young people believe gender isn't limited to male and female. Splinter. https://splinternews.com/halfof-young-people-believe-gender-isnt-limited-to-mal-1793844971

Roberts, A. L., Rosario, M., Corliss, H. L., Koenen, K. C., & Austin, S. B. (2012). Childhood gender nonconformity: A risk indicator for childhood abuse and posttraumatic stress in youth. *Pediatrics, 129*, 410–417. https://doi.org/10.1542/peds.2011-1804

Roberts, A. L., Rosario, M., Slopen, N., Calzo, J. P., & Austin, S. B. (2013). Childhood gender nonconformity, bullying victimization, and depressive symptoms across adolescence and early adulthood: An 11-year longitudinal study. *Journal of the American Academy of Child & Adolescent Psychiatry, 52*(2), 143–152. https://doi.org/10.1016/j.jaac.2012.11.006

Rose, A. J., & Smith, R. L. (2018). Gender and peer relationships. In W. M. Bukowski, B. Laursen, & K. H. Rubin (Eds.), *Handbook of peer interactions, relationships, and groups* (pp. 571–589). Guilford Press.

Ruble, D. N., Taylor, L. J., Cyphers, L., Greulich, F. K., Lurye, L. E., & Shrout, P. E. (2007). The role of gender constancy in early gender development. *Child Development, 78*, 1121–1136. https://doi.org/10.1111/j.1467-8624.2007.01056.x

Ruble, D. N., Martin, C. L., & Berenbaum, S. A. (2006). Gender development. In N. Eisenberg (Ed.), *Handbook of child psychology: Vol. 3, Personality and social development* (pp. 858–932).

Southwick, S. M., Bonanno, G. A., Masten, A. S., Panter-Brick, C., & Yehuda, R. (2014). Resilience definitions, theory, and challenges: Interdisciplinary perspectives. *European Journal of Psychotraumatology, 5*(1), 25338. https://doi.org/10.3402/ejpt.v5.25338

Spencer, K. G.*, Berg, D. R.*, Bradford, N. J., Vencill, J., Tellawi, G., & Rider, G. N. (2021). The Gender Affirmative Lifespan Approach: A developmental model for clinical work with transgender and gender diverse children, adolescents, and adults. *Psychotherapy, 58*(1), 37–49. https://doi.org/10.1037/pst0000363

Steensma, T. D., McGuire, J. K., Kreukels, B. P. C., Beekman, A. J., & Cohen-Kettenis, P. T. (2013). Factors associated with desistence and persistence of childhood gender dysphoria: A quantitative follow-up study. *Journal of the American Academy of Child and Adolescent Psychiatry, 52*(6), 582–590. https://doi.org/10.1016/j.jaac.2013.03.016

Tate, Charlotte. (2016, October). *Self-categorization dynamics for transgender spectrum and cisgender adults*. Presented at the Gender Development Research Conference, San Francisco.

Turban, J. L., Beckwith, N., Reisner, S. L., & Keuroghlian, A. S. (2020). Association between recalled exposure to gender identity conversion efforts and psychological distress and suicide attempts among transgender adults. *JAMA Psychiatry, 77*(1), 68–76.

Turner, W. B. (2000). *A genealogy of queer theory*. Temple University Press.

Wallace, R., & Russell, H. (2013). Attachment and shame in gender-nonconforming children and their families: Toward a theoretical framework for evaluating clinical interventions. *International Journal of Transgenderism, 14*(3), 113–126.

Wallien, M. S., Veenstra, R., Kreukels, B. P., & Cohen-Kettenis, P. T. (2010). Peer group status of gender dysphoric children: A sociometric study. *Archives of Sexual Behavior, 39*(2), 553–560.

Wong, W. I., van der Miesen, A. I. R., Li, T. G. F., MacMullin, L. N., & VanderLaan, D. P. (2019). Childhood social gender transition and psychosocial well-being: A comparison to cisgender gender-variant children. *Clinical Practice in Pediatric Psychology, 7*(3), 241–253. https://doi.org/10.1037/cpp0000295

Yunger, J. L., Carver, P. R., & Perry, D. G. (2004). Does gender identity influence children's psychological well-being? *Developmental Psychology, 40*(4), 572.

Zosky, D. L., & Alberts, R. (2016). What's in a name? Exploring use of the word queer as a term of identification within the college-aged LGBT community. *Journal of Human Behavior in the Social Environment, 26*(7–8), 597–607. https://doi.org/10.1080/10911359.2016.1238803

Zucker K. J. (2017). Epidemiology of gender dysphoria and transgender identity. *Sexual Health 14,* 404–411.

Zucker, K. J., Bradley, S. J., Kuksis, M., Pecore, K., Birkenfeld-Adams, A., Doering, R. W., . . . Wild, J. (1999). Gender constancy judgments in children with gender identity disorder: Evidence for a developmental lag. *Archives of Sexual Behavior, 28,* 475–502.

Zucker, K. J., & Bradley, S. J. (1995). *Gender identity disorder and psychosexual problems in children and adolescents.* Guilford Press.

Zucker, K. J., Wood, H., Singh, D., & Bradley, S. J. (2012). A developmental, biopsychosocial model for the treatment of children with gender identity disorder. *Journal of Homosexuality, 59*(3), 369–397.

Zucker, K. J., Wood, H., & VanderLaan, D. P. (2014). Models of psychopathology in children and adolescents with gender dysphoria. In: B. P. C. Kreukels, T. D. Steensma, A. L. C. de Vries (Eds.), *Gender dysphoria and disorders of sex development: Progress in care and knowledge* (pp. 171–192). Springer Science + Business Media.

CHAPTER 5

Risk and Protective Factors among LGBTQ+ Adolescents

Amy L. Gower, PhD, Marla E. Eisenberg, ScD, MPH, & G. Nic Rider, PhD, LP

Adolescence is a key developmental period for identity exploration and development, including sexual and romantic development (DeLamater & Friedrich, 2002; Morgan, 2020), increasing salience of the peer group, and the remodeling of the prefrontal cortex to gradually support logical decision making and inhibitory control (McCormick et al., 2011). All adolescents undertake these tasks to varying degrees based on the context and the individual and discover strengths and challenges along the way. For LGBTQ+ adolescents, these developmental tasks can be complicated by a variety of factors. In this chapter, we discuss common risk and protective factors during adolescence for LGBTQ+ adolescents, situating them in the socioecological model and acknowledging that sexual and gender identity are only two facets of identity that interact with other identities that may or may not be subject to stigma. It is critical to view the following research findings with an eye to variation among LGBTQ+ adolescents and contexts in which they live. For example, variation in what adolescents disclose or visible aspects of sexual and gender identity—that is, whether someone is out, whether they pass, their level of gender conformity, and so on—may be associated with increased peer victimization in the short run. However, when viewed from a longer-term perspective, integrating and living one's true self may be seen as protective (Russell et al., 2014). When combining adolescents' broader social ecology with a radical healing approach, several key areas to promote well-being among LGBTQ+ adolescents emerge.

Health risks for LGBTQ+ adolescents are well-known and established in the literature. LGBTQ+ adolescents engage in developmentally typical experimentation in risk-taking behaviors (e.g., smoking/vaping, occasional alcohol consumption), as do their straight, cisgender peers (Day et al., 2017; Reisner et al., 2015). However, in the context of minority stressors such as discrimination, family rejection, bullying, and gender dysphoria, these behaviors can become problematic, moving from experimentation to health-risking coping strategies. Rates of emotional distress, depression, and suicidality in particular are elevated among LGBTQ+ adolescents, with BIPOC (Black, Indigenous, and People of Color) LGBTQ+ adolescents bearing even higher burden (Almeida et al., 2009; Eisenberg et al., 2016; Katz-Wise et al., 2018; Mustanski & Espelage, 2020; Perez-Brumer et al., 2017; Simons et al., 2013; Taliaferro et al.,

2018; Vance et al., 2021; Veale et al., 2017). At the same time, a variety of protective factors have been identified that buffer adolescents from minority stressors. Often, these protective factors are similar to those for straight, cisgender adolescents—supportive parents, connections to school and teachers, a strong sense of self and internal assets—yet others, such as the LGBTQ+-supportive resources in a community, are unique to LGBTQ+ adolescents (Eisenberg, Erickson et al., 2020; Gower, Rider, Brown et al., 2018; Hatchel et al., 2019; Hatzenbuehler, 2011; Saewyc et al., 2020). Identifying both types of protective factors can help the clinician focus efforts on 1) ensuring general adolescent resources are supportive spaces for adolescents with marginalized identities and 2) linking adolescents to LGBTQ+-specific spaces that address relevant topics and issues.

We adopt the framework of radical healing for this chapter (French et al., 2020; Hicks Peterson, 2018; Mosley et al., 2020). Radical healing is a process rooted in collectivist ideals originally developed among communities of color in the United States; however, the strong influence of intersectionality in the framework makes it applicable to a variety of socially stigmatized groups, including LGBTQ+ adolescents. Radical healing is centered on "an unconditional desire for human dignity, meaningful existence, and hope" (Ginwright, 2015, p. 35). Connecting and leaning into radical hope and healing allows for imagining and re-imagining liberation from oppression (Brown, 2017; Suzuki et al., 2019). In short, radical healing involves the development of critical consciousness: recognizing the oppression and systems of power in which an individual lives. This consciousness must be paired with actions that work against these oppressive systems and toward liberation. Foundational to the ability to work toward change is the cultivation of radical hope (Mosley et al., 2020), or an orientation that acknowledges the possibility of a future without oppression. Radical healing is situated in the middle of critical consciousness and radical hope—balancing acknowledgment of oppressive systems with hope for a different future—and motivates agentic, strengths-focused action to achieve liberation and social change (French et al., 2020). Healing requires attending to both internal symptoms a person is experiencing and the multiple intersecting oppressive systems contributing to and maintaining distress. To take into account how oppressive systems affect a person's mental health concerns, mental health providers must also understand nuances in a young person's lived experiences as related to psychological trauma and concerns (Chavez-Dueñas et al., 2019).

In the United States, a particular challenge of adopting a radical healing approach during adolescence stems from the fact that the dominant narrative frames adolescence as a time of risk-taking and rebellion, rather than in a more holistic, agentic, and capable way. This is particularly impactful for BIPOC LGBTQ+ adolescents, whose voices are often minimized, silenced, or ridiculed. Although some prevention and health-promotion approaches, such as positive youth development (PYD), do focus on the agency of the individual, they are rooted in individualistic conceptions of society (Gonzalez et al., 2020). Further, their use in primary prevention has not historically incorporated an intersectional approach, nor sufficiently acknowledged the many identities adolescents bring to these programs. However, recent efforts to acknowledge power, privilege, and oppression in PYD theories have led to the development of critical positive youth development, which adds critical reflection, political advocacy, and critical action to the broader PYD model (Gonzalez et al., 2020). This approach holds promise because it views adolescents as capable and agentic, takes a strengths-based perspective, and acknowledges the lived experiences that come from the overlapping social positions adolescents hold.

Radical healing, and adolescents themselves, seek real, powerful involvement and change. A key implication of that desire is that professionals working with LGBTQ+ adolescents must ensure adolescent voices are heard by creating spaces where adolescents are valued for all their identities and help them access and shape these spaces. Adults working in these spaces, too, must engage in learning and self-reflection to understand their positionalities and may need training to develop their own critical consciousness and capacity for understanding the lived experiences of the adolescents around them. Adolescence can be a time to focus on core aspects of radical healing (e.g., critical consciousness building, fostering cultural exploration and authenticity, connecting with social supports, and learning about strengths and resistance). Radical healing goes beyond addressing concerns only at the individual level and focuses on interpersonal, community, and institutional/structural levels (Ginwright, 2015; Suzuki et al., 2019).

LGBTQ+ adolescents exist within multilayered, nested social-ecological contexts, beginning with interpersonal relationships (e.g., family, peers) and moving distally to organizations (e.g., schools, community groups, places of worship), communities (e.g., neighborhoods, local resources and regulations), and broad, macro-level social factors (e.g., public policy, media) (Bronfenbrenner, 1999; McLeroy et al., 1988). The minority stress model is directly applicable to this social-ecological view. Through several different conceptualizations and revisions (Hendricks & Testa, 2012; Meyer, 2003; chapter 1 this volume), the concept of minority stressors is a powerful articulation of the ways in which one's identity and experiences as a person with one or more stigmatized identities shape long-term health. When combined with a social-ecological framework, minority stressors and protective factors during adolescence can be examined with more nuance and in a comprehensive way, identifying both strengths that can be drawn on and bolstered as well as stressors, ranging from interpersonal to social/structural, that must be removed or mitigated. Social, community, and organizational processes and structures influence people at the individual level. As a result, we must move beyond conceptualizations of healing, coping, and health promotion as solely an individual-focused endeavor and shift to a holistic view that accounts for these broader processes, understanding that true health equity comes from eliminating structural discrimination and strengthening cultural and societal protection as much as it comes from individual-level factors.

Interpersonal Relationships

FRIENDSHIPS

Relationships with similar-aged adolescents are key contexts of adolescent development. The increasing salience of friends and romantic partners across adolescence and into young adulthood is well recognized; friendships and romantic relationships are often where adolescents explore their various identities and receive feedback from others, whether implicit or explicit. These relationships also provide numerous opportunities for the development of resilience against stressors, for example through supportive friendships. Friends are often among the first people LGBTQ+ adolescents come out to, and their support can be important for LGBTQ+ adolescents in ways similar to straight, cisgender adolescents (Roe, 2015). Yet LGBTQ+ adolescents have additional considerations when making friends, including assessing their peers' level of openness to their sexual and gender identities, which can complicate and slow this relationship-building process.

ROMANTIC RELATIONSHIPS

LGBTQ+ adolescents may be exploring or navigating romantic and sexual relationships, much like their cisgender, heterosexual peers. However, LGBTQ+ adolescents may experience minority stressors (e.g., biphobia, homophobia, transphobia) that can affect relationships (e.g., concealing relationships) and individual mental health. Systemic marginalization, lack of institutional support, and interpersonal challenges further contextualize the experiences of navigating romantic and sexual relationships for LGBTQ+ adolescents (Morgan, 2020). These factors are important for consideration because early relationship experiences can have a lasting impact on emotional well-being and future relationship functioning (Gillum & DiFulvio, 2012). Notably, healthy romantic relationships can help with fostering interpersonal skills, communication skills, emotional regulation, and intimacy. Relationships, in general, that are intimate build a foundation for LGBTQ+ adolescents to have social support, which may buffer against minority stressors that LGBTQ+ adolescents often experience (Morgan, 2020).

Over time, online relationship seeking has become more common among LGBTQ+ adolescents than in-person relationship seeking. For example, sexual and gender diverse youth assigned male at birth report using geospatial networking applications and social media for meeting partners (Macapagal et al., 2018, 2020). LGBTQ+ adolescents also tend to have more online romantic partners than their heterosexual peers (Korchmaros et al., 2015). LGBTQ+ adolescents may prefer relationship or partner seeking online as opposed to in-person due to having more sense of control regarding who they talk to, how much information they share (Morgan, 2020), and being able to end a conversation if they would like. Geospatial social networking applications allow for individuals to proactively disclose their sexual and gender identities (e.g., "come out" intentionally; Ma et al., 2021; Fernandez & Birnholtz, 2019), and social media methods allow for adolescents to vet and filter through potential partners (Lykens et al., 2019). Communicating online may also facilitate connections to the LGBTQ+ community that would not be possible if relying solely on in-person meetings (McConnell et al., 2017; Singh, 2013).

PARENT/FAMILY RELATIONSHIPS

While peer relationships exert important influence during adolescence, parents have a large role to play. In fact, the bulk of research on protective factors for LGBTQ+ shares the conclusion that caring, supportive, and connected relationships between a young person and a parent are among the strongest interpersonal protective factors. LGBTQ+ adolescents with more supportive parents report less emotional distress, substance use, school dropout, and a range of other health risk behaviors. (Eisenberg & Resnick, 2006; Gower, Rider, Brown et al., 2018; Hall, 2018; Hatchel et al., 2019; Ryan et al., 2009; Ryan et al., 2010). Not surprisingly then, family rejection predicts a host of health-compromising behaviors. At its most extreme, family rejection can lead to abuse and homelessness, which are both elevated among LGBTQ+ adolescents (Baams, 2018; Roberts et al., 2012). Additionally, Craig and colleagues (2020) demonstrated that LGBTQ+ adolescents report adverse childhood experiences (ACEs), including emotional abuse and neglect, at higher rates compared to their straight, cisgender peers. The highest rates of ACEs in this LGBTQ+ sample were among adolescents who were pansexual, transgender and gender diverse, Native American, Latina/x/o, and those living in rural settings (Craig et al., 2020). Thus, clinicians may observe higher rates of childhood abuse and trauma among LGBTQ+ adolescents as well as a need to support parents in efforts to educate themselves and manage their own emotions around their adolescent's sexual orientation and gender identity.

Work with the family system is a crucial route to supporting LGBTQ+ adolescents (Westwater et al., 2019). Encouraging parents to attend support groups, such as PFLAG, can be a successful intervention for parents of LGBTQ+ adolescents who live in close proximity to a meeting. These connections can support parents by reducing alienation and helping them process their own feelings about their child's sexual and gender identity without passing that grief or anger onto their LGBTQ+ children (Field & Mattson, 2016). Traditionally, attending such groups as PFLAG was not possible for some, such as those in rural areas where the closest meeting may be hours away or for families who belong to communities, religions, or cultural groups with strong homophobic and transphobic beliefs. In those cases, support for families, where it existed, may have been exclusively underground. However, in response to the COVID-19 pandemic, many existing resources moved their support online. This allowed more accessibility for people who found in-person meetings to be a barrier, such as those who live in rural areas or too far from a PFLAG meeting, parents whose children are not ready to risk being outed by having their parent seen at a meeting for parents of LGBTQ+ adolescents, or parents themselves who are not ready to be out about having an LGBTQ+ child. Although not perfect, these online groups may serve a critical need for early support when attending in-person meetings is a barrier, and at a time when parents may need support the most but not feel comfortable accessing it.

The School Context

Although schools are not a universal context for LGBTQ+ adolescents, since many miss school or drop out due to feeling unsafe at school (Aragon et al., 2014; Kosciw et al., 2019), they are one setting where a large number of adolescents can be reached for the promotion of health and well-being. It is a common place where adolescents may practice skills needed for critical consciousness and can engage in advocacy efforts. Schools are also the context where much of the research on LGBTQ+ adolescents takes place.

A large portion of adolescents' engagement activities in schools involves peers. Relationships with similar-aged peers can provide supportive experiences, such as opportunities for identity-related exploration and activism, participation in shared identity interest groups at school and in the community, and access to key sources of connection. At the same time, peers can also contribute to stressors, including stigma and bias related to personal characteristics. Bullying, teasing, and harassment are common in secondary schools and are particularly frequent experiences for adolescents with stigmatized identities. Bullying based on bias related to sexual orientation, gender identity, race, ethnicity, social class, and ability has received increasing attention because these behaviors, often called bias-based bullying, are thought to underlie health-compromising behavior and broader health disparities for LGBTQ+ people (Earnshaw et al., 2016; Gower, Rider, McMorris, & Eisenberg, 2018; Russell et al., 2012).

Understanding experiences of bias-based bullying within the broader climate of the school (e.g., personally experiencing or secondhand exposure to microaggressions, slurs, and epithets) yields a more holistic understanding of the school experience for LGBTQ+ adolescents (Kosciw et al., 2019; Ybarra, Mitchell, Kosciw et al., 2015). Microaggressions are experienced in multiple contexts and are especially common at intersecting social positions among BIPOC LGBTQ+ adolescents (Munro et al., 2019). Intersectional microaggressions are particularly insidious to long-term health and well-being because they influence self-esteem and identity development (Mereish et al., 2021). Many young people do not report microaggressions, teasing, or slurs because they perceive school personnel as either unwilling to take action or ineffective when they do take action (Eisenberg et al., 2021). As a result, bias at school can leave adolescents feeling unheard and unseen.

Importantly, schools can also function as protective factors, though some school administrators and staff may need education and professional development on how to ensure safe and inclusive schools for LGBTQ+ adolescents. Strong connections to school and caring teachers have long been associated with positive outcomes for all adolescents. While they can also serve this function for LGBTQ+ adolescents, research shows that LGBTQ+ adolescents perceive schools to be less welcoming and supportive on average than their straight peers (Gower et al., 2017; Gower, Rider, Brown et al., 2018; McGuire et al., 2010). Importantly, BIPOC adolescents also perceive schools to be less supportive and experience disparities in discipline and treatment from teachers that lead to school pushout, particularly among BIPOC boys (Baams & Russell, 2021; Chan et al., 2021; Liang et al., 2020). Preliminary evidence suggests variation in perceptions of school climate among adolescents with overlapping stigmatized social position. For example, using an innovative mixed-methods, participatory research design that engaged multiple stakeholders and perspectives, Chmielewski and colleagues (2016) added context to our understanding of disparities in discipline and school pushout/dropout for BIPOC LGBTQ+ adolescents. In qualitative focus groups addressing these issues and findings from quantitative analyses, adolescents reported both unequal application of disciplinary policies (e.g., differential sanctioning of public displays of affection) and targeting of BIPOC LGBTQ+ students by school staff and school safety agents/school resource officers (Chmielewski et al., 2016). School staff need education on how to better build rapport and create supportive environments for students with stigmatized identities, and efforts to train and hire teachers with more diverse identities are an important part of addressing this need.

More specifically, student groups or clubs within schools can provide a number of key supports for LGBTQ+ adolescents. GSAs, sometimes called Gay-Straight Alliances or Gender-Sexuality Alliances, are groups within a school, often student-led or co-led by students and staff, that provide support and advocacy opportunities for LGBTQ+ adolescents and often their allies (Poteat et al., 2015; Theodore & Chiasson, 2021). While the exact activities and leadership structure vary from one GSA to another, the functions of these GSAs generally include emotional support, connection, bridges to resources, and opportunities for advocacy within the school environment and sometimes the larger community (Day et al., 2020; Porta et al., 2017; Poteat et al., 2015; Poteat et al., 2013; Roe, 2015; Toomey et al., 2011). Importantly, GSAs can also be spaces to develop critical consciousness on a range of issues, intentionally making space for intersectional lived experiences. For example, after the 2016 US presidential election, some GSAs in Massachusetts provided rich contexts for discussion about immigration (Poteat et al., 2019). Poteat and colleagues (2019) found that GSAs naturally varied in the quantity, quality, and openness of their discussion around these topics, with GSAs where the advisor reported more comfort discussing matters of race, culture, and immigration taking up the topic more often than GSAs with leaders who felt less self-efficacy on these topics. Thus, training and resources for GSA leaders to address the intersectional needs of adolescents may be useful.

Community Support

LGBTQ+-supportive community connections are critical to healing and well-being because connection is a fundamental need. However, these community connections must be culturally competent (French et al., 2020). Communities that focus solely on supporting sexual and/or gender diversity without incorporating understanding and appreciation for race and other identities ignore the critical life experiences of many LGBTQ+ adolescents. Much of the quantitative research on community is conducted from an individual-focused perspective and operationalizes community support as the broader presence of supportive resources, policies, or practices within the community. However, when examined from a radical healing perspective, it is clear that the meaning of community support goes beyond these proxies of LGBTQ+ friendliness and requires true acceptance and belonging within a community that welcomes and respects all of a young person's identities. Still, we review here research that examines broader community climate briefly, as it is instructive.

LGBTQ+ adolescents who live in communities with more LGBTQ+-supportive political climates (Hatzenbuehler et al., 2019; Saewyc et al., 2020), community resources (Eisenberg, Erickson et al., 2020), and laws and policies (Hatzenbuehler et al., 2009) report fewer health-risk behaviors and less emotional distress. These measures are thought to be proxies for the supportiveness of community members toward LGBTQ+ adolescents. Both adolescents who participate in LGBTQ+ community-based organizations and those who live in proximity to LGBTQ+ community organizations experience protective effects in the form of reduced alcohol and marijuana use, internalizing symptoms, and suicidal ideation and higher self-esteem (Eisenberg, Gower et al., 2020; Eisenberg, Erickson et al., 2020; Fish et al., 2019). Fish and colleagues (2019) reported that adolescents who participated in LGBTQ+ community organizations were more likely to be BIPOC, assigned male at birth, transgender, and have lower socioeconomic status. In a qualitative study of BIPOC LGBTQ+ adolescents, young people described the ways in which participation in a community-based organization felt like home and provided opportunities for support, advocacy, and resistance against oppression as part of a community (Gamarel et al., 2014). These community spaces may be particularly important for adolescents without family support, and all adolescents can benefit from another context where they can be a meaningful part of a community and engage in advocacy.

Online/Internet Support

While researchers once thought that in-person support was the primary driver of well-being for LGBTQ+ adolescents, emerging research clarifies that online support and connection can also play a positive role. For example, Wagaman and colleagues (2020) found that online support significantly buffered the effects of minority stressors on self-esteem among LGBTQ+ adolescents in the southern United States, where in-person resources are scarce. Online resources, including websites and social media, can provide informational resources, support, and connection to LGBTQ+ peers, and that is particularly the case for adolescents who have less access to LGBTQ+ peers (e.g., rural adolescents) or safety concerns about revealing their sexual and gender identity (Cserni & Talmud, 2015; DeHaan et al., 2013; Shapiro & Margolin, 2014; Wagaman et al., 2020). Further, online interaction can be important when LGBTQ+ adolescents have unsupportive parents, or recently during the COVID-19 pandemic, when in-person resources were largely closed (Fish et al., 2020). Online support may also play an important role for BIPOC LGBTQ+ adolescents living in less diverse areas or looking for support from others with similar intersecting lived experiences. Yet these spaces are not without risk, as LGBTQ+ adolescents online are exposed to cyberbullying, harassment, and exposure to homophobic and transphobic rhetoric (Wagaman et al., 2020; Ybarra, Mitchell, Palmer et al., 2015). To ensure benefits from online interactions, adolescents need skills for media literacy, critical consciousness, and support from caring adults who can guide adolescents to trustworthy content and be a sounding board if LGBTQ+ adolescents encounter content or people that are hostile.

Developmental Considerations

These social-ecological factors must be considered within the broader developmental context of adolescence. Although many changes occur during this period, we highlight two salient considerations—diversifying contexts and identity development. During adolescence, many youth experience broadening participation in various social contexts, such as workplaces, organizations, sports teams, extracurricular activities, and places of worship. Often, these interactions are characterized by increased independence as well, leading adolescents to navigate a variety of new situations, people, and activities without trusted adults. While this is typical of adolescence, it poses different concerns for LGBTQ+ teens. These spaces have the ability to provide additional support, opportunities for engagement and acceptance, and critical consciousness and advocacy skills (Clark & Kosciw, 2021; Poteat et al., 2020). In fact, connecting adolescents with resources may broaden protective nets, particularly where other resources, such as family support, may be lacking. On the other hand, these contexts can be spaces where adolescents with diverse sexual and gender identities and/or BIPOC adolescents may experience microaggressions, discrimination, and harassment. Further, settings with low or no supervision may provide more opportunities for adolescents to engage in health-compromising behaviors, especially if peers are also engaged in these behaviors. Clinicians can work with adolescents to identify opportunities for engagement that fit with adolescents' interests and needs and are supportive of all their identities. Importantly, if negative experiences do arise, clinicians can work through those experiences with adolescents, developing and modeling critical consciousness and encouraging in the adolescents a sense of their own agency in the next steps. For example, a young person may attempt to address or report microaggressions, or they may decide that context is not appropriate and select another activity. Individualized considerations, such as the amount of social support, whether the adolescent is out in that setting, and the broader community context will naturally shape these discussions. The discussions allow the young person to examine their current experiences while making connections to the past (e.g., historical oppression) and building for a future that is different. The adolescent can develop skills to analyze and navigate oppressive situations. They can also develop agency that fosters a sense of control over the situation and/or motivation to challenge such oppression.

The second key aspect of adolescence is identity development. While much has been written on the topic of identity development in adolescence (i.e., regarding general aspects of identity; racial, ethnic, and cultural identity; sexual identity; and gender identity), much of this work comes from an individual perspective that does not acknowledge intersectional experiences and has been conducted primarily with white participants (Cerezo et al., 2020). Undoubtedly, a primary goal of adolescence and early adulthood is to explore, form, and integrate various aspects of identity into a coherent sense of self; but quantitative research is lacking on this topic for a number of reasons. One reason is the fact that longitudinal studies are confounded by rapid change in community attitudes toward LGBTQ+ people and LGBTQ+ adolescents' dynamic and expansive understandings of sexual orientation and gender identity. Emerging work in this area that does include more holistic approaches views the formation and integration of intersectional identities as primary acts of resistance to oppression and hallmarks of resilience (Cerezo et al., 2020; Hulko & Hovanes, 2018). These theories place identity development in specific community contexts, such as a town/rural location; integrate key aspects of culture in identity development, both in diverse conceptions of sexual and gender identity as well as openness to sexual and gender diversity; and emphasize the power and agency that come from defining a unified identity for oneself. Together, these authors argue that we must go beyond traditional milestone theories of sexual and gender identity to broadly and holistically conceptualize identity formation. This reimagining is part of a radical healing approach, emphasizing dignity and meaning in the context of critical consciousness.

Case Study

Kai is a 16-year-old Black, queer, nonbinary, trans girl who uses she/her pronouns and lives with her mom, dad, and older sibling in a rural area. The family is active in their church, and their Christian faith is important to them. The area where she lives has a small-town feeling where everyone knows everyone. The county has no mental or physical health providers who specialize in transgender and gender diverse (TGD)- or LGBTQ+-affirming care, and the county does not have legal protections for TGD people. The closest city with TGD-related resources is at a two-hour-drive distance.

Kai first told her sibling and parents that she identified as queer and then about a year later explained that she identifies as queer, trans, and nonbinary. Her family members are supportive, but they have concerns about her safety at school and in the community. Kai has a history of being bullied and does not have any friends. Her grades have started to drop, and she displays other stress-related responses, such as frequently scanning her environment for signs of a threat (e.g., aggression, rejection from others) as well as anxiety and depressive symptoms. The school does not have a GSA, and school administrators brush off the bullying as typical adolescent behavior.

Kai learned about transgender people and a little about transitioning on social media. She is interested in continuing to explore her gender and learn about options for her gender-affirming process. Her parents are also interested in learning about how to best support Kai as she works toward her gender goals. Given Kai's experiences of bullying and the impact it has had on her mental health, the family is worried that Kai will have a life full of hardship and suffering due to violence and discrimination.

PRACTICE CONSIDERATIONS

Kai has a multifaceted experience at the intersection of race, gender, sexual orientation, rural location, and age. To understand Kai from a holistic lens, providers must consider how her experiences based on her intersectional identities affect her mental, physical, psychological, sexual, and spiritual health, as well as how these experiences influence her on an individual level, and are also reflective of interpersonal, community, and social structural levels. She has supportive immediate family members who care about her and have a desire to help her by connecting her with gender-affirming providers. There is no easy access to gender-affirming care, minimal support in the school, and no legal protections in her county. Kai began showing signs of mental health problems after experiencing bullying at school and realizing she has no support in the school for dealing with these incidents.

Given that Kai has multiple marginalized identities, her bullying experiences may not be isolated to school settings. She may experience discrimination in other areas of her life (e.g., at church, out in public, etc.). These experiences of social oppression are likely not based on any of her individual minority identities (racism versus genderism versus homophobia); instead, she is likely experiencing a confluence of discrimination and negative attitudes such as gendered racism, transmisogynoir (Preston, 2020), and/or adultism combined with cissexism and homophobia. Further, her rural location creates additional considerations relevant to Kai and her family, such as not being able to easily access support and resources. Rural areas have fewer people, meaning that people who do not conform to social and cultural expectations may be more noticeable and at heightened risk for harassment, discrimination, and violence (Movement Advancement Project, 2019a; Movement Advancement Project, 2019b). Further, communities tend to overlap in rural areas (e.g., Kai's classmates may go to the same church, those classmates' parents may be a coworker of one of Kai's parents). This overlap can significantly impact one's general acceptance or rejection within a community. In Kai's case, she may experience rejection in multiple areas of life, which can contribute to her feeling isolated beyond geographic isolation (Movement Advancement Project, 2019a; Movement Advancement Project, 2019b). Kai and her family do not have rural health care providers who have LGBTQ+ cultural competence, resulting in them either having to travel long distances or rely on the availability of virtual healthcare. Lastly, in some rural states, access to health care services for LGBTQ+ individuals may be denied due to religious exemption laws (Movement Advancement Project, 2019b).

Mental health providers are in a position to help clients gain knowledge about structural and systemic inequities and oppression, which clients can then use to critically analyze situations that occur in their own lives, develop a sense of agency, and move toward actively changing things within their control, which can help them decrease self-blame and feelings of isolation (Diemer et al., 2017; Ginwright, 2010).

An LGBTQ+-affirming provider can help Kai develop language to describe how she understands her identities, share her experiences with others, and have the ability to discuss issues of inequities. By identifying barriers affecting one's life, whether related to identity exploration, access to care, or any other area, Kai can communicate her observations and discover ways to navigate or work against the oppressive forces that create or perpetuate the barriers she experiences. For example, she may be interested in discussing anti-transgender legislation, gatekeeping, and other challenges for minors to access gender-affirming medical interventions; police brutality against trans women of color; or another relevant topic. Helping Kai learn about interpersonal, institutional/structural, and internalized oppression provides a lens she can use to understand and talk about her experiences. Having the ability to name experiences of injustices that are often unacknowledged by the dominant culture can be a powerful antidote to oppression, contributing to clients feeling empowered and part of a collective movement toward social justice and assisting them with challenging the status quo and navigating oppressive systems.

Further, Kai can work with her mental health treatment provider to understand the depths of inequities, forces sustaining and maintaining inequities, and the impact of those inequities on the lives of people, including her own. These types of discussions can include, but are not limited to, conversations about policy, legislation, multiple healthcare systems, schools, churches, communities, families, and individuals. Analyzing oppression in this way can help Kai to understand how inequities occur systemically and in her own life, as well as understanding how historical violence continues to perpetuate oppression and marginalization and impacts multiple areas of health. These discussions can lead to exploring what action steps Kai and/or her family can take to address identified concerns as well as implications of such actions. For example, Kai may consider either creating or attending a nearby GSA or participating in organizations (even if virtually) to build social support and engage in activism with others with similar goals. She may feel a sense of belonging to a community, which can lead to improved mental wellness, while advocating for change beyond what she can achieve for herself at the individual level (e.g., changes in school policies, creating a GSA in school, activism against religious exclusionary laws, etc.). Overall, clients and providers collaborating in discussions as described above are some of the ways to help clients develop critical consciousness, which can foster a sense of hope for a future that is different and more equitable and just. This is a path for attaining radical healing, through action.

Conclusions

While LGBTQ+ adolescents experience a range of general and identity-specific stressors, they also have multiple avenues for support and healing. Helping adolescents build meaningful connections in their families, communities, and schools goes a long way toward increasing belongingness. At the same time, we must acknowledge the ways that broader systems and policies shape the lives of LGBTQ+ adolescents. Clinicians providing perspective and skill building around critical consciousness and cultivation of radical hope and healing provide a path for LGBTQ+ adolescents to increase feelings of agency and help create a future free from oppression.

References

Almeida, J., Johnson, R. M., Corliss, H. L., Molnar, B. E., & Azrael, D. (2009). Emotional distress among LGBT youth: The influence of perceived discrimination based on sexual orientation. *Journal of Youth and Adolescence, 38*(7), 1001–1014. https://doi.org/10.1007/s10964-009-9397-9

Aragon, S. R., Poteat, V. P., Espelage, D. L., & Koenig, B. W. (2014). The influence of peer victimization on educational outcomes for LGBTQ and non-LGBTQ high school students. *Journal of LGBT Youth, 11*(1), 1–19. https://doi.org/10.1080/19361653.2014.840761

Baams, L. (2018). Disparities for LGBTQ and gender nonconforming adolescents. *Pediatrics, 141*(5), e20173004.

Baams, L., & Russell, S. T. (2021). Gay-Straight Alliances, and mental health: Associations for students of color and LGBTQ students. *Youth & Society, 53*(2), 211–229. https://doi.org/10.1177/0044118X20951045

Bronfenbrenner, U. (1999). Environments in developmental perspective: Theoretical and operational models. In S. L. Friedman & T. D. Wachs (Eds.), *Measuring environment across the life span: Emerging methods and concepts* (pp. 3–28). American Psychological Association Press.

Brown, A. M. (2017). *Emergent strategy: Shaping change.* AK Press.

Cerezo, A., Cummings, M., Holmes, M., & Williams, C. (2020). Identity as resistance: Identity formation at the intersection of race, gender identity, and sexual orientation. *Psychology of Women Quarterly, 44*(1), 67–83. https://doi.org/10.1177/0361684319875977

Chan, C. D., Ngadjui, O. T., Jackson, T., & Steen, S. (2021). Unsettling complex inequities on school climate for males of color: School counseling applications from an intersectionality-based policy analysis. *Professional School Counseling, 25*, 1–14. https://doi.org/10.1177/2156759X211040029

Chavez-Dueñas, N. Y., Adames, H. Y., Perez-Chavez, J. G., & Salas, S. P. (2019). Healing ethno-racial trauma in Latinx immigrant communities: Cultivating hope, resistance, and action. *American Psychologist, 74*(1), 49–62. https://doi.org/10.1037/amp0000289

Chmielewski, J. F., Belmonte, K. M., Fine, M., & Stoudt, B. G. (2016). Intersectional inquiries with LGBTQ and gender nonconforming youth of color: Participatory research on discipline disparities at the race/sexuality/gender nexus. In R. Skiba, K. Mediratta, & M. Rausch (Eds.), *Inequality in school discipline.* Palgrave Macmillan.

Clark, C. M., & Kosciw, J. G. (2021). Engaged or excluded: LGBTQ youth's participation in school sports and their relationship to psychological well-being. *Psychology in the Schools* (March 2020), 1–20. https://doi.org/10.1002/pits.22500

Craig, S. L., Austin, A., Levenson, J., Leung, V. W. Y., Eaton, A. D., & D'Souza, S. A. (2020). Frequencies and patterns of adverse childhood events in LGBTQ+ youth. *Child Abuse & Neglect, 107*(June), 104623. https://doi.org/10.1016/j.chiabu.2020.104623

Cserni, R. T., & Talmud, I. (2015). To know that you are not alone: The effect of internet usage on LGBT youth's social capital. *Studies in Media and Communications, 9*, 161–182. https://doi.org/10.1108/S2050-206020150000009007

Day, J. K., Fish, J. N., Grossman, A. H., & Russell, S. T. (2020). Gay-straight alliances, inclusive policy, and school climate: LGBTQ youths' experiences of social support and bullying. *Journal of Research on Adolescence, 30*, 418–430. https://doi.org/10.1111/jora.12487

Day, J. K., Fish, J. N., Perez-Brumer, A., Hatzenbuehler, M. L., & Russell, S. T. (2017). Transgender youth substance use disparities: Results from a population-based sample. *Journal of Adolescent Health, 61*(6), 729–735. https://doi.org/10.1016/j.jadohealth.2017.06.024

DeHaan, S., Kuper, L. E., Magee, J. C., Bigelow, L., & Mustanski, B. S. (2013). The interplay between online and offline explorations of identity, relationships, and sex: A mixed-methods study with LGBT youth. *Journal of Sex Research, 50*, 421–434. https://doi.org/10.1080/00224499.2012.661489

DeLamater, J., & Friedrich, W. N. (2002). Human sexual development. *Journal of Sex Research, 39*, 10–14. https://doi.org/10.1080/00224490209552113

Diemer, M. A., Rapa, L. J., Park, C. J., & Perry, J. C. (2017). Development and validation of the Critical Consciousness Scale. *Youth & Society, 49*(4), 461–483. https://doi.org/10.1177/0044118X14538289

Earnshaw, V. A., Bogart, L. M., Poteat, V. P., Reisner, S. L., & Schuster, M. A. (2016). Bullying among lesbian, gay, bisexual, and transgender youth. *Pediatric Clinics of North America, 63*(6), 999–1010. https://doi.org/10.1016/j.pcl.2016.07.004

Eisenberg, M. E., Erickson, D. J., Gower, A. L., Kne, L., Watson, R. J., Corliss, H. L., & Saewyc, E. M. (2020). Supportive community resources are associated with lower risk of substance use among lesbian, gay, bisexual, and questioning adolescents in Minnesota. *Journal of Youth and Adolescence, 49*(4), 836–848. https://doi.org/10.1007/s10964-019-01100-4

Eisenberg, M. E., Gower, A. L., Brown, C., Nam, Y. S., Rider, G. N., & Ramirez, M. (2021). "It was never really bullying, but . . .": Stigmatized adolescents' experiences with microaggressions in school. *International Journal of Bullying Prevention.* https://doi.org/10.1007/s42380-021-00103-9

Eisenberg, M. E., Gower, A. L., & McMorris, B. J. (2016). Emotional health of lesbian, gay, bisexual and questioning bullies: Does it differ from straight bullies? *Journal of Youth and Adolescence, 45*(1), 105–116. https://doi.org/10.1007/s10964-015-0316-y

Eisenberg, M. E., Gower, A. L., Watson, R. J., Porta, C. M., & Saewyc, E. M. (2020). LGBTQ youth-serving organizations: What do they offer and do they protect against emotional distress? *Annals of LGBTQ Public and Population Health, 1*(1), 63–79.

Eisenberg, M. E., & Resnick, M. D. (2006). Suicidality among gay, lesbian and bisexual youth: The role of protective factors. *The Journal of Adolescent Health, 39*(5), 662–668. https://doi.org/10.1016/j.jadohealth.2006.04.024

Fernandez, J. R., & Birnholtz, J. (2019). "I don't want them to not know": Investigating decisions to disclose transgender identity on dating platforms. *Proceedings of the ACM on Human-Computer Interaction, 3*(CSCW), 1–21.

Field, T. L., & Mattson, G. (2016). Parenting transgender children in PFLAG. *Journal of GLBT Family Studies, 12*(5), 413–429.

Fish, J. N., Mcinroy, L. B., Paceley, M. S., Williams, N. D., Henderson, S., Levine, D. S., & Edsall, R. N. (2020). "I'm kinda stuck at home with unsupportive parents right now": LGBTQ youths' experiences with COVID-19 and the importance of online support. *Journal of Adolescent Health, 67*(3), 450–452. https://doi.org/10.1016/j.jadohealth.2020.06.002

Fish, J. N., Moody, R. L., Grossman, A. H., & Russell, S. T. (2019). LGBTQ youth-serving community-based organizations: Who participates and what difference does it make? *Journal of Youth and Adolescence, 48*, 2418–2431. https://doi.org/10.1007/s10964-019-01129-5

French, B. H., Lewis, J. A., Mosley, D. V., Adames, H. Y., Chavez-Dueñas, N. Y., Chen, G. A., & Neville, H. A. (2020). Toward a psychological framework of radical healing in communities of color. *Counseling Psychologist, 48*(1), 14–46. https://doi.org/10.1177/0011000019843506

Gamarel, K. E., Walker, J. J., Rivera, L., & Golub, S. A. (2014). Identity safety and relational health in youth spaces: A needs assessment with LGBTQ youth of color. *Journal of LGBT Youth, 11*, 289–314. https://doi.org/10.1080/19361653.2013.879464

Gillum, T. L., & DiFulvio, G. (2012). "There's so much at stake:" Sexual minority youth discuss dating violence. *Violence against Women, 18*, 725–745.

Ginwright, S. (2010). *Black youth rising: Activism and racial healing in urban America.* Teachers College Press.

Ginwright, S. A. (2015). Radically healing black lives: A love note to justice. *New Directions for Student Leadership, 2015*(148), 33–44.

Gonzalez, M., Kokozos, M., Byrd, C. M., & McKee, K. E. (2020). Critical positive youth development: A framework for centering critical consciousness. *Journal of Youth Development, 15*(6), 24–43. https://doi.org/10.5195/jyd.2020.859

Gower, A. L., Forster, M., Gloppen, K., Johnson, A. Z., Eisenberg, M. E., Connett, J. E., & Borowsky, I. W. (2017). School practices to foster LGBT-supportive climate: Associations with adolescent bullying involvement. *Prevention Science, 19*, 813–821. https://doi.org/10.1007/s11121-017-0847-4

Gower, A. L., Rider, G. N., Brown, C., McMorris, B. J., Coleman, E., Taliaferro, L. A., & Eisenberg, M. E. (2018). Supporting transgender and gender diverse youth: Protection against emotional distress and substance use. *American Journal of Preventive Medicine, 55*, 787–794. https://doi.org/10.1016/j.amepre.2018.06.030

Gower, A. L., Rider, G. N., McMorris, B. J., & Eisenberg, M. E. (2018). Bullying victimization among LGBTQ youth: Critical issues and future directions. *Current Sexual Health Reports, 10*(4), 246–254. https://doi.org/10.1007/s11930-018-0169-y

Hall, W. J. (2018). Psychosocial risk and protective factors for depression among lesbian, gay, bisexual, and queer youth: A systematic review. *Journal of Homosexuality, 65*(3), 263–316. https://doi.org/10.1080/00918369.2017.1317467

Hatchel, T., Polanin, J. R., & Espelage, D. L. (2019). Suicidal thoughts and behaviors among LGBTQ youth: Meta-analyses and a systematic review. *Archives of Suicide Research, 25*(1), 1–37. https://doi.org/10.1080/13811118.2019.1663329

Hatzenbuehler, M. L. (2011). The social environment and suicide attempts in lesbian, gay, and bisexual youth. *Pediatrics, 127*(5), 896–903. https://doi.org/10.1542/peds.2010-3020

Hatzenbuehler, M. L., Keyes, K. M., & Hasin, D. S. (2009). State-level policies and psychiatric morbidity in lesbian, gay, and bisexual populations. *American Journal of Public Health, 99*(12), 2275–2281. https://doi.org/10.2105/AJPH.2008.153510

Hatzenbuehler, M. L., Shen, Y., Vandewater, E. A., & Russell, S. T. (2019). Proposition 8 and homophobic bullying in California. *Pediatrics, 143*(6), e20182116. https://doi.org/10.1542/peds.2018-2116

Hendricks, M. L., & Testa, R. J. (2012). A conceptual framework for clinical work with transgender and gender nonconforming clients: An adaptation of the minority stress model. *Professional Psychology: Research and Practice, 43*(5), 460–467. https://doi.org/10.1037/a0029597

Hicks Peterson, T. (2018). Self-awareness and radical healing. In *Student Development and Social Justice*. https://doi.org/10.1007/978-3-319-57457-8_3

Hulko, W., & Hovanes, J. (2018). Intersectionality in the lives of LGBTQ youth: Identifying as LGBTQ and finding community in small cities and rural towns. *Journal of Homosexuality, 65*(4), 427–455. https://doi.org/10.1080/00918369.2017.1320169

Katz-Wise, S. L., Ehrensaft, D., Vetters, R., Forcier, M., & Austin, S. B. (2018). Family functioning and mental health of transgender and gender-nonconforming youth in the Trans Teen and Family Narratives Project. *The Journal of Sex Research, 55*, 582–590. https://doi.org/10.1080/00224499.2017.1415291

Korchmaros, J. D., Ybarra, M. L., & Mitchell, K. J. (2015). Adolescent online romantic relationship initiation: Differences by sexual and gender identification. *Journal of Adolescence, 40*, 54–64. https://doi,org/10.1016/j.adolescence.2015.01.004

Kosciw, J. G., Clark, C. M., Truong, N. L., & Zongrone, A. D. (2019). The 2019 National School Climate Survey: The experiences of lesbian, gay, bisexual, transgender, and queer youth in our nation's schools. www.glsen.org/research

Liang, C. T. H., Rocchino, G. H., Gutekunst, M. H. C., Paulvin, C., Li, K. M., & Elam-Snowden, T. (2020). Perspectives of respect, teacher-student relationships, and school climate among boys of color: A multifocus group study. *Psychology of Men & Masculinities, 21*(3), 345–356.

Lykens, J., Pilloton, M., Silva, C., Schlamm, E., Wilburn, K., & Pence, E. (2019). Google for sexual relationships: Mixed-methods study on digital flirting and online dating among adolescent youth and young adults. *Journal of Medical Internet Research, 5*, e10695. https://doi.org/10.2196/10695

Ma, J., Korpak, A. K., Choukas-Bradley, S., & Macapagal, K. (2021). Patterns of online relationship seeking among transgender and gender diverse adolescents: Advice for others and common inquiries. *Psychology of Sexual Orientation and Gender Diversity*. Advance online publication. http://dx.doi.org/10.1037/sgd0000482

Macapagal, K., Moskowitz, D. A., Li, D. H., Carrión, A., Bettin, E., Fisher, C. B., & Mustanski, B. (2018). Hookup app use, sexual behavior, and sexual health among adolescent men who have sex with men in the United States. *Journal of Adolescent Health, 62*(6), 708–715. https://doi.org/10.1016/j.jadohealth.2018.01.001

Macapagal, K., Kraus, A., Moskowitz, D. A., & Birnholtz, J. (2020). Geosocial networking application use, characteristics of app-met sexual partners, and sexual behavior among sexual and gender minority adolescents assigned male at birth. *Journal of Sex Research, 57*(8), 1078–1087. https://doi.org/10.1080/00224499.2019.1698004

McConnell, E. A., Clifford, A., Korpak, A. K., Phillips, G., & Birkett, M. (2017). Identity, victimization, and support: Facebook experiences and mental health among LGBTQ youth. *Computers in Human Behavior, 76*, 237–244. https://doi.org/10.1016/j.chb.2017.07.026

McCormick, C. M., Kuo, S. I., & Masten, A. S. (2011). Developmental tasks across the lifespan. In K. L. Fingerman, C. A. Berg, J. Smith, & T. C. Antonucci (Eds.), *Handbook of Lifespan Development* (pp. 117–139). Springer.

McGuire, J. K., Anderson, C. R., Toomey, R. B., & Russell, S. T. (2010). School climate for transgender youth: A mixed method investigation of student experiences and school responses. *Journal of Youth and Adolescence, 39*, 1175–1188. https://doi.org/10.1007/s10964-010-9540-7

McLeroy, K., Bibeau, D., Steckler, A., & Glanz, K. (1988). An ecological perspective on health promotion programs. *Health Education & Behavior, 15*, 351–377.

Mereish, E. H., Parra, L. A., Watson, R. J., & Fish, J. N. (2021). Subtle and intersectional minority stress and depressive symptoms among sexual and gender minority adolescents of color: Mediating role of self-esteem and sense of mastery. *Prevention Science*. https://doi.org/10.1007/s11121-021-01294-9

Meyer, I. H. (2003). Prejudice, social stress, and mental health in lesbian, gay, and bisexual populations: Conceptual issues and research evidence. *Psychological Bulletin, 129*(5), 674–697. https://doi.org/10.1037/0033-2909.129.5.674

Morgan, E. M. (2020). Same-sex relationships and LGBTQ youth. In S. Hupp & J. D. Jewell (Eds.), *Encyclopedia of Child and Adolescent Development*. John Wiley & Sons. https://doi.org/10.1002/9781119171492.wecad488

Mosley, D. V., Neville, H. A., Chavez-Dueñas, N. Y., Adames, H. Y., Lewis, J. A., & French, B. H. (2020). Radical hope in revolting times: Proposing a culturally relevant psychological framework. *Social and Personality Psychology Compass, 14*(1), 1–12. https://doi.org/10.1111/spc3.12512

Movement Advancement Project. (2019a). *Where we call home: LGBT people in rural America*. http://www.lgbtmap.org/rural-lgbt

Movement Advancement Project. (2019b). *Where we call home: Transgender people in rural America*. https://www.lgbtmap.org/file/Rural-Trans-Report-Nov2019.pdf

Munro, L., Travers, R., & Woodford, M. R. (2019). Overlooked and invisible: Everyday experiences of microaggressions for LGBTQ adolescents. *Journal of Homosexuality, 66*(10), 1439–1471. https://doi.org/10.1080/00918369.2018.1542205

Mustanski, B., & Espelage, D. L. (2020). Why are we not closing the gap in suicide disparities for sexual minority youth? *Pediatrics, 145*(3), e20194002. https://doi.org/10.1542/peds.2019-4002

Perez-Brumer, A., Day, J. K., Russell, S. T., & Hatzenbuehler, M. L. (2017). Prevalence and correlates of suicidal ideation among transgender youth in California: Findings from a representative, population-based sample of high school students. *Journal of the American Academy of Child & Adolescent Psychiatry, 56*(9), 739–746. https://doi.org/10.1016/j.jaac.2017.06.010

Porta, C. M., Singer, E., Mehus, C. J., Gower, A. L., Saewyc, E., Fredkove, W., & Eisenberg, M. E. (2017). LGBTQ youth's views on Gay-Straight Alliances: Building community, providing gateways, and representing safety and support. *Journal of School Health, 87*(7), 489–497. https://doi.org/10.1111/josh.12517

Poteat, V. P., Calzo, J. P., Yoshikawa, H., Rosenbach, S. B., Ceccolini, C. J., & Marx, R. A. (2019). Extracurricular settings as a space to address sociopolitical crises: The case of discussing immigration in gender-sexuality alliances following the 2016 U.S. presidential election. *American Educational Research Journal, 56*, 2262–2294. https://doi.org/10.3102/0002831219839033

Poteat, V. P., Godfrey, E. B., Brion-Meisels, G., & Calzo, J. P. (2020). Development of youth advocacy and sociopolitical efficacy as dimensions of critical consciousness within Gender-Sexuality Alliances. *Developmental Psychology, 56*(6), 1207–1219.

Poteat, V. P., Scheer, J. R., Marx, R. A., Calzo, J. P., & Yoshikawa, H. (2015). Gay-straight alliances vary on dimensions of youth socializing and advocacy: Factors accounting for individual and setting-level differences. *American Journal of Community Psychology, 55*, 422–432. https://doi.org/10.1007/s10464-015-9722-2.Gay-Straight

Poteat, V. P., Sinclair, K. O., DiGiovanni, C. D., Koenig, B. W., & Russell, S. T. (2013). Gay-straight alliances are associated with student health: A multischool comparison of LGBTQ and heterosexual youth. *Journal of Research on Adolescence, 23*(2), 319–330. https://doi.org/10.1111/j.1532-7795.2012.00832.x

Preston, A. M. (2020, September 9). The anatomy of transmisogynoir. *Harper's Bazaar.* https://www.harpersbazaar.com/culture/features/a33614214/ashlee-marie-preston-transmisogynoir-essay/

Reisner, S. L., Greytak, E. A., Parsons, J. T., & Ybarra, M. L. (2015). Gender minority social stress in adolescence: Disparities in adolescent bullying and substance use by gender identity. *Journal of Sex Research, 52*(3), 243–256. https://doi.org/10.1080/00224499.2014.886321

Roberts, A. L., Rosario, M., Corliss, H. L., Koenen, K. C., & Austin, S. B. (2012). Childhood gender nonconformity: A risk indicator for childhood abuse and posttraumatic stress in youth. *Pediatrics, 129*(3), 410–417. https://doi.org/10.1542/peds.2011-1804

Roe, S. L. (2015). Examining the role of peer relationships in the lives of gay and bisexual adolescents. *Children & Schools, 37*(2), 117–124. https://doi.org/10.1093/cs/cdv001

Russell, S. T., Sinclair, K. O., Poteat, V. P., & Koenig, B. W. (2012). Adolescent health and harassment based on discriminatory bias. *American Journal of Public Health, 102*(3), 493–495. https://doi.org/10.2105/AJPH.2011.300430

Russell, S. T., Toomey, R. B., Ryan, C., & Diaz, R. M. (2014). Being out at school: The implications for school victimization and young adult adjustment. *American Journal of Orthopsychiatry, 84*(6), 635–643.

Ryan, C., Huebner, D., Diaz, R. M., & Sanchez, J. (2009). Family rejection as a predictor of negative health outcomes in white and Latino lesbian, gay, and bisexual young adults. *Pediatrics, 123*, 346–352. https://doi.org/10.1542/peds.2007-3524

Ryan, C., Russell, S. T., Huebner, D., Diaz, R., & Sanchez, J. (2010). Family acceptance in adolescence and the health of LGBT young adults. *Journal of Child and Adolescent Psychiatric Nursing, 23*, 205–213. https://doi.org/10.1111/j.1744-6171.2010.00246.x

Saewyc, E. M., Li, G., Gower, A. L., Watson, R. J., Erickson, D., Corliss, H. L., & Eisenberg, M. E. (2020). The link between LGBTQ-supportive communities, progressive political climate, and suicidality among sexual minority adolescents in Canada. *Preventive Medicine, 139*, 106191. https://doi.org/10.1016/j.ypmed.2020.106191

Shapiro, L. A. S., & Margolin, G. (2014). Growing up wired: Social networking sites and adolescent psychosocial development. *Clinical Child and Family Psychology Review, 17*, 1–18. https://doi.org/10.1007/s10567-013-0135-1

Simons, L., Schrager, S. M., Clark, L. F., Belzer, M., & Olson, J. (2013). Parental support and mental health among transgender adolescents. *Journal of Adolescent Health, 53*(6), 791–793. https://doi.org/10.1016/j.jadohealth.2013.07.019

Singh, A. A. (2013). Transgender youth of color and resilience: Negotiating oppression and finding support. *Sex Roles, 68*, 690–702. https://doi.org/10.1007/s11199-012-0149-z

Suzuki, L. A., Shaughnessy, T. A. O., Roysircar, G., Ponterotto, J. G., & Carter, R. T. (2019). Counseling Psychology and the amelioration of oppression: Translating our knowledge into action. *Counseling Psychologist, 47*, 826–872. https://doi.org/10.1177/0011000019888763

Taliaferro, L. A., Gloppen, K. M., Muehlenkamp, J. J., & Eisenberg, M. E. (2018). Depression and suicidality among bisexual youth: A nationally representative sample. *Journal of LGBT Youth, 15*(1), 16–31. https://doi.org/10.1080/19361653.2017.1395306

Theodore, P. S., & Chiasson, J. (2021). Evolving strategies to counter school bullying of gender and sexually diverse students. In M. C. Lytle & R. A. Sprott (Eds.), *Supporting gender identity and sexual orientation diversity in K–12 Schools* (pp. 71–96). American Psychological Association. http://www.jstor.org/stable/j.ctv19wx7zq.8

Toomey, R. B., Ryan, C., Diaz, R. M., & Russell, S. T. (2011). High school gay-straight alliances (GSAs) and young adult well-being: An examination of GSA presence, participation, and perceived effectiveness. *Applied Developmental Science, 15*(4), 175–185. https://doi.org/10.1080/10888691.2011.607378

Vance, T. A., Klein, S. L., Nikiforova, Y., Rubin, L. R., & Lopez, F. G. (2021). The health and wellbeing of transgender and gender non-conforming people of colour in the United States: A systematic literature search and review. *Journal of Community & Applied Social Psychology*, 1–29. https://doi.org/10.1002/casp.2555

Veale, J. F., Watson, R. J., Peter, T., & Saewyc, E. M. (2017). Mental health disparities among Canadian transgender youth. *Journal of Adolescent Health, 60*(1), 44–49. https://doi.org/10.1016/j.jadohealth.2016.09.014

Wagaman, M. A., Watts, K. J., Lamneck, V., Souza, S. A. D., Mcinroy, L. B., Eaton, A. D., & Craig, S. (2020). Managing stressors online and offline: LGBTQ+ youth in the Southern United States. *Children and Youth Services Review, 110*, 104799. https://doi.org/10.1016/j.childyouth.2020.104799

Westwater, J. J., Riley, E. A., & Peterson, G. M. (2019). What about the family in youth gender diversity? A literature review. *International Journal of Transgenderism, 20*(4), 351–370. https://doi.org/10.1080/15532739.2019.1652130

Ybarra, M. L., Mitchell, K. J., Kosciw, J. G., & Korchmaros, J. D. (2015). Understanding linkages between bullying and suicidal ideation in a national sample of LGB and heterosexual youth in the United States. *Prevention Science, 16*(3), 451–462. https://doi.org/10.1007/s11121-014-0510-2

Ybarra, M. L., Mitchell, K. J., Palmer, N. A., & Reisner, S. L. (2015). Online social support as a buffer against online and offline peer and sexual victimization among U.S. LGBT and non-LGBT youth. *Child Abuse & Neglect, 39*, 123–136. https://doi.org/10.1016/j.chiabu.2014.08.006

CHAPTER 6

Not a Teen, Not Yet an Adult

HEALTH RISK AND PROTECTIVE FACTORS
AMONG LGBTQ+ EMERGING ADULTS

*Caleb Esteban, PhD, Alixida Ramos-Pibernus, PhD,
Luis X. Díaz-Medero, MS, & Astrid Irizarry-Rodríguez, MS*

The term "emerging adult" has been proposed to highlight the developmental period between the ages of 18 to 25 years. In a period where transition to adulthood (i.e., residential status, self-sufficiency) is still evolving, internal and external struggles are common. Research has found that LGBTQ+ emerging adults face even more struggles than their heterosexual and cisgender peers. They face unique organizational (e.g., being underinsured), interpersonal (e.g., discrimination), and individual (e.g., fear, guilt, shame) stressors when transitioning to adulthood and developing their sense of self that are in addition to stressors that are common at this developmental stage (Arnett, 2000). The intersection of all these factors has a direct impact on their health. Research has documented an increase in the prevalence of emotional, physical, and sexual health concerns (e.g., mental illness, substance abuse, STIs/HIV) and lack of access to affirmative health promotion (Arnett, 2000). Despite this worrisome scenario, the existing literature highlights the resilience capacity of LGBTQ+ communities, including social support and community engagement (Erickson-Schroth & Glaeser, 2017). This chapter focuses on the unique challenges LGBTQ+ emerging adults experience as they transition from adolescence into adulthood. Clinicians working with this age group must understand their unique needs and develop skills to effectively connect with and respond to their clients.

LGBTQ+ Emerging Adults

Emerging adulthood is a developmental period that exists in cultures where the assertion of independence and exploration of social roles is prolonged (Arnett, 2000). This is considered a time of transition from adolescence to adulthood where the person begins growing independent from their parents and adapting to adulthood, exploring love, work, worldviews, and life possibilities such as financial, educational, and social responsibilities (Arnett, 2000; Forster et al., 2020). This stage is characterized by identity exploration, instability, self-focus, and feelings of in-between, transformation, discoveries, and possibilities (Forster et al., 2020). It is a very important time for the formation of peer relationships, refining social skills, and enhancing emotion-regulation capacities (Richmond et al., 2020). This phase is known for the concretization of identity, relationship and intimacy exploration, residential status, self-sufficiency, career considerations, and the beginning of college and/or occupational life (Ginicola et al., 2017). In brief, individuals in this developmental period are still evolving, thus internal and external struggles are common. According to Arnett (2000, p. 469), "Emerging adulthood is a time of life when many different directions remain possible, when little about the future has been decided for certain, when the scope of independent exploration of life's possibilities is greater for most people than it will be at any other period of the life course." The first major section of this chapter discusses additional challenges for LGBTQ+ emerging adults at institutional, interpersonal, and personal levels that their cisgender and heterosexual peers do not necessarily face.

Institutional Challenges

FAMILY

The term "family" as a construct has changed over the years, influenced by the social, economic, cultural, political, geographical, and historical context. Despite the visibility and acceptance of sexual and gender diversity, more inclusivity in society for what family can mean for LGBTQ+ people is needed. For example, images represented in books, magazines, and commercials for what constitutes a couple, marriage, and/or family are often based on heterocisnormative and/or "nuclear" family visions (Orel & Coon, 2016). On the other hand, study findings indicate that some LGBTQ+ people struggle with living and spending time with their family of origin, usually because of lack of acceptance and a hostile environment due to their sexual orientation and/or gender identity. For LGBTQ+ individuals, especially, the term "family" does not necessarily refer only to biological relatives; family also can include other people who execute its roles and functions. Among this community, the terms "families of choice" and "chosen family" are commonly used to describe individuals in their lives who they identify as family members and who provide them support and care (Orel & Coon, 2016). At the same time, when LGBTQ+ individuals decide to become parents, they may experience elevated costs in the insemination and conception of a child, the need for surrogacy, discrimination during the adoption process, government services obstruction, and sometimes the disapproval of their peers and their own family (Carrión-Santiago et al., 2016).

COLLEGE

College is a difficult transition for every student; however, LGBTQ+ emerging adults who decide and can afford to pay for schooling may experience more vulnerability (Garvey et al., 2019). During this education development, LGBTQ+ individuals may simultaneously "seek acceptance while also evading harm, battling stereotypes, and potentially being ostracized due to their identities" (Garvey et al., 2019, p. 150). Studies have also documented that LGBTQ+ students experience harassment, violence, and discrimination on college campuses, including through jokes, slurs, threats, unfair treatment, physical attacks, and other forms of mistreatment (Dessel et al., 2017). Some students also experience isolation and marginalization; thus, for some of them, being *out* is not an option (Garvey et al., 2019).

RELIGIOUS INSTITUTIONS

Religious institutions have had a vast influence on how people understand sexuality, including sexual orientation and gender identities. Some non-LGBTQ+-affirming religious groups believe that being LGBTQ+ and having a religious affiliation is contradictory, which contributes to the condemnation and exclusion of LGBTQ individuals (Fuist, 2017). Unlike other "sins," some religious representatives speak against, denounce, and attack LGBTQ+ communities publicly, going so far as to produce advertisement campaigns and sometimes even speaking in the name of their God/s (Fuist, 2017), making it difficult for LGBTQ+ emerging adults to harmonize with their own and other people's religious beliefs (Wood & Conley, 2014).

HEALTHCARE

Healthcare services are key to reducing health disparities among LGBTQ+ emerging adults (Smith & Turell, 2017). Studies have documented the barriers that LGBTQ+ individuals face when accessing and using healthcare services, such as stigmatization, providers having insufficient knowledge of LGBTQ+ issues, and bias-based behaviors (e.g., microaggressions and discrimination) by staff and providers (Rosenkrantz et al., 2017; Smith & Turell, 2017). This panorama contributes to LGBTQ+ clients experiencing discomfort accessing healthcare services and mistrust of providers, which can manifest as withholding personal information, changing healthcare providers, avoiding seeking healthcare, and/or fear of repercussions for self-advocacy (Smith & Turell, 2017). Those negative incidents, lack of knowledge, and barriers to care could be worse for LGBTQ+ persons in rural regions (Rosenkrantz et al., 2017) and for transgender and gender diverse (TGD) individuals (Willis et al., 2020). For example, medical records do not always accurately document or reflect TGD emerging adults' gender identities. This can also affect people living in a favorable context where they can legally change their gender marker but are treated according to their sex assigned at birth, violating their dignity and identity (Dahlen, 2020). Some TGD young people who seek to begin physical transition need to obtain consent from their parents if they are younger than the legal age (age varies based on location) in order to be able to start gender-affirming hormone therapy, gender-affirming surgeries, and other medical procedures, even though these procedures can help improve their quality of life and mental health by their "being seen by others in accordance with one's gender identity" (Sørlie, 2019, p. 296).

GOVERNMENT

State-level policies and procedures have a significant impact on physical and mental health. Young people may be unaware of the political climate that impacts LGBTQ+ people's lives until they reach the emerging adulthood stage. Sexual and gender structural stigma creates stressors and affects LGBTQ+ people's health outcomes (Hatzenbuehler et al., 2017). This structural stigma has an effect on cultural norms, laws, and institutional policies, and it can impact equitable treatment and resource allocation for LGBTQ+ individuals (Hatzenbuehler et al., 2017). Studies suggest that lower levels of health were reported in same-sex couples living in anti-gay states (Kail et al., 2015), documenting how government decisions can negatively impact LGBTQ+ people and their families. While progress, such as depathologization of LGBTQ+ identities, legalization of same-sex marriage, more ability to make a gender marker change, and LGBTQ+ work protection, has been made, there is still a lot to do to eradicate disparities, especially for trans and nonbinary communities.

Interpersonal Challenges

RELATIONSHIPS

For emerging adults, affective and sexual relationships may be a significant part of their lives and can be beneficial for mental and physical health (Macapagal et al., 2015). For example, González and colleagues (2019) found that LGB+ emerging adults that are in a relationship report fewer symptoms of depression and half of the probability of having suicidal thoughts compared to those not in a relationship, suggesting that relationships may be an important source of support (González et al., 2019). However, for some LGBTQ+ people, relationships are not always beneficial. Sometimes, they can be unfavorable, or an additional stressor related to their minority status (Macapagal et al., 2015). For example, they can be discriminated or victimized if they hold hands, show affection, or kiss in public; they could hide their relationships due to the disapproval of their families and friends; or simply not know how a relationship works because they have seen only cisgender and heterosexual relationship models.

Trans and nonbinary individuals experience unique concerns related to stigma and struggles in their relationships. For example, some trans and gender diverse individuals report facing transphobia and cissexism by their own partners and peers (Giammattei, 2015; Twist et al., 2017). Experiences of stigmatization may contribute to challenges in relationships, including having difficulty initiating, committing, maintaining, and ending relationships (Macapagal et al., 2015).

MARRIAGE

Same-sex marriage is now legal in the United States and other countries and territories, but stigma and negative attitudes toward it remain (Hatzenbuehler et al., 2017).

Regardless of how attitudes have positively improved over the years, same-sex marriage is not recognized by society as equal to different-sex marriage (Hatzenbuehler et al., 2017; Lee & Mutz, 2019), even though same-sex couples face much of the same struggles and enjoy much of the same relationship benefits that different-sex couples do, especially in emerging adulthood. Before same-sex marriage was legalized, studies found that same-sex couples living in states with anti-gay constitutional amendments reported lower levels of health (Kail et al., 2015). Fear of discrimination has been shown to negatively affect mental health and well-being and can also disrupt intimacy in the relationship (Drabble et al., 2020). Consequently, to reduce discrimination experiences, some couples feel more comfortable being apart or "acting" like friends. Some factors that have been associated with negative views of same-sex marriage are religious intensity, homonegativity, not having contact with an LGBTQ+ person, and their generation (Daniels, 2019). Because those factors are always present in society at large, no matter how supportive an individual's inner circle might be, some LGBTQ+ persons live with constant fear of same-sex marriage political backlash (Drabble et al., 2020). Furthermore, same-sex marriage is illegal in some other countries. Although same-sex marriage is legal in all of the United States and its territories, LGBTQ+ couples face additional challenges if they decide to migrate to a country that does not recognize same-sex marriages as their relationship status can be nullified.

PEERS

At this developmental stage, peer relationships and close friendships (offline and online) become very important for support and integration into the larger LGBTQ+ community and may also become recognized as family members (DeHaan et al., 2013; Orel & Coon, 2016). LGBTQ+ emerging adults may fear being judged, secluded, victimized, mistreated, mocked, and the like when looking for friends, which may limit their social circle. Even if those feelings begin in adolescence, they can continue in emerging adulthood and have long-term impacts on an individual's capacity to form broad social networks, which can be especially important when establishing a new career path and/or forming a family of their own. Because of these difficulties, some LGBTQ+ young adults compensate for their peer limitations with online peers and friends, which, though beneficial, can be accompanied by difficulties and risks such as talking and meeting with strangers, who may put them in unsafe and otherwise harmful situations (DeHaan et al., 2013).

RELIGIOUS AFFILIATION

Due to the negative stance some religious groups and institutions have taken against same-sex behavior and minority sexual and gender identities, some LGBTQ+ young adults lose or struggle with their religiosity or spirituality. "Negative experiences with a religious leader have more impact than having negative experiences with religious peers" (Wood & Conley, 2014, p. 101), which may increase the impact on LGBTQ+

individuals given the multiple people that they may be having interpersonal struggles with. Thus, negative interactions with leaders and institutions can make it very difficult for LGBTQ+ people to reconcile their sexual and/or gender identities with their religious identities. LGBTQ+ individuals who belong to religious communities can experience distress, pain, confusion, suffering, guilt, shame, and conflict, as well as abuse, mistreatment, micro and macroaggressions, bullying, victimization, harassment, and harm (Esteban & Díaz-Medero, 2019; Gibbs & Goldbach, 2015). While LGBTQ+ people in LGBTQ+-affirming religious institutions find ways to integrate both identities, others in non-affirming institutions may feel as if they must compartmentalize or reject one aspect of themselves, increasing stress in their lives (Wood & Conley, 2014). This conflicting scenario can lead LGBTQ+ young adults to experience increased internalized stigma, which has also been linked to suicidal thoughts (Gibbs & Goldbach, 2015).

Personal Challenges

At an individual level, LGBTQ+ young adults experience numerous challenges that impact their personal well-being and overall health. Findings from previous studies indicate that LGBTQ+ individuals experience increased physical and mental health disparities when compared with their cisgender, heterosexual counterparts (Fredriksen-Goldsen et al., 2014). Healthcare disparities have been found to be associated with stigma, discrimination, violence, and lack of access to competent healthcare services (Gay and Lesbian Medical Association, 2010). In working with LGBTQ+ emerging adults, it is crucial to take into account the individual's intersecting identities (Henry et al., 2020) in order to better understand and address the disparities affecting them. The following section summarizes some of the key physical and mental health issues that significantly impact LGBTQ+ emerging adults.

PHYSICAL HEALTH

Research has documented an increase in disease prevalence and lack of access to affirmative health services among LGBTQ+ people in general (Henry et al., 2020). In the case of LGBTQ+ emerging adults, studies have identified increased health challenges largely associated with chronic and acute stressors due to their minority status (Halkitis et al., 2020). For LGB+ individuals, emerging adulthood can be a highly vulnerable time in one's life, and a combination of factors (i.e., sexual risk-taking, drug use and abuse, mental health issues, homo/bi-phobia, and discrimination) may compromise health (Coulter et al., 2018; Feinstein et al., 2019; Halkitis et al., 2020). Some health disparities that affect LGBTQ+ emerging adults include higher rates of tobacco use, higher rates of alcohol and illicit drug consumption, risky sexual behaviors, low physical activity, and obesity/overweight compared with cisgender and heterosexual peers (Halkitis et al., 2020; Wallace & Santacruz, 2017). Below are some of the factors that impact the physical health of LGBTQ+ emerging adults.

HIV/STIs

LGBTQ+ emerging adults account for a disproportionate number of HIV diagnoses, with a particularly increased risk for those at the intersection of racial or ethnic minority groups (Henry et al., 2020). Specifically, for trans emerging adults, studies have identified prevalence rates of HIV ranging between 5% to 22% (Fisher et al., 2017). Moreover, based on one recent study, Black and Latinx LGB+ emerging adults have the most new infections in contrast with other racial/ethnic groups (Halkitis et al., 2020), highlighting the syndemic between gender, sexual minority status, race/ethnicity, and HIV risk. STI (syphilis and Hepatitis B) rates are also higher among LGBTQ+ emerging adults when compared to heterosexual, cisgender individuals (Wood et al., 2016).

Healthcare

One of the principal health disparities experienced by LGBTQ+ people is access to adequate and appropriate health care services. Multiple studies have documented that LGBTQ+ patients frequently have negative experiences with healthcare providers (Macapagal et al., 2016; Padilla et al., 2016; Ramos-Pibernus et al., 2020). These negative experiences lead to avoidance of preventive and routine healthcare because of fear of mistreatment, which contributes to increased risk for multiple health conditions (e.g., cancer and cardiovascular disease) (James & Salcedo, 2017; Romanelli & Hudson, 2017). Healthcare insurance is another important factor for access to healthcare. This is particularly important during young adult years because of the transitory nature of emerging adulthood, which is when many LGBTQ+ young adults lose their family coverage and some do not have the economic means to acquire health insurance on their own (Schmitz & Tabler, 2019). Not having healthcare insurance has been associated with fewer health care visits and poor general health (Griffin-Tomas et al., 2019).

Substance Abuse

Several studies have documented that LGBTQ+ emerging adults are more likely to report substance use as a way to cope with rejection, discrimination, stigma, and sociocultural influences due to their minority status (Kelly et al., 2015; Magette et al., 2018; Oberheim et al., 2017). This stage of life has been associated with increases in the consumption of alcohol, binge drinking, and substance use (Coulter et al., 2018). The minority stress theory (Meyer, 2003) posits that marginalized groups, such as LGBTQ+ individuals, experience chronic stress due to stigma, discrimination, and victimization, which is linked to adaptive and maladaptive coping mechanisms. For example, alcohol consumption can be used to self-medicate in order to be able to cope with internalized, interpersonal, and structural stigma (Coulter et al., 2018; Felner et al., 2020). Studies have also found elevated rates of illicit drug use among LGBTQ+ emerging adults in comparison to cisgender, heterosexual peers (Parent et al., 2019). It is important to note that, even though literature identifies LGBTQ+ individuals as a high-risk population for substance use, there are differences in the patterns of disparities within subgroups (lesbian, gay, bisexual, trans, and nonbinary) that need to be considered when providing health services or designing preventive strategies. For example, a recent study identified that queer and transmasculine individuals had two times greater odds of reporting marijuana use when compared to lesbian and cisgender women (Barger et al., 2021). Factors such as social and family support, self-esteem, and family bonds could be key protective factors to reduce or avoid substance use disorders in LGBTQ+ emerging adults (Magette et al., 2018; Vaitses-Fontanari et al., 2019).

MENTAL HEALTH

Previous studies have documented that LGBTQ+ individuals are at an increased risk for substance abuse and mental health problems (Feinstein et al., 2019). Unique aspects of LGBTQ+ people's experiences, such as navigating identity disclosure, may result in overall poor mental health outcomes across the life span. Some studies indicate that LGBTQ+ people who are restricted from disclosing their sexual orientation or gender identity experience an increase in mental health symptoms (Wallace & Santacruz, 2017). Furthermore, studies have documented that LGBTQ+ people of color, including Latinx, experience higher rates of depression, anxiety, and suicide attempts in comparison with their cisgender and heterosexual peers (Russell & Fish, 2016). In this section, some of the main mental health issues affecting LGBTQ+ emerging adults are highlighted.

Depression and Anxiety

Studies have documented increased incidence of mood and anxiety disorders among LGBTQ+ emerging adults (Hall, 2018). Bullying and homophobic and transphobic comments from peers have been linked to higher rates of depression and anxiety during emerging adulthood (Wang et al., 2018). A recent review identified other risk factors that could foster depression among LGBTQ+ individuals, including experiencing abuse, negative social interactions, negative religious experiences, experiencing harassment and violence in the community, and family rejection (Hall, 2018). When compared with heterosexual, cisgender individuals, LGBTQ+ people have higher levels of both depression and anxiety (Borgogna et al., 2019). The cumulative stressors experienced by LGBTQ+ individuals from childhood to emerging adulthood, including victimization, have a great impact on their mental health and depressive symptomatology (Mustanski et al., 2016). Moreover, individuals belonging to emerging minority identities (pansexual, demisexual, and gender nonconforming) may experience even higher levels of depression and anxiety, possibly associated with experiences of discrimination and invisibility within the LGBTQ+ communities (Borgogna et al., 2019).

Suicide

LGBTQ+ emerging adults experience high frequencies of suicide ideation and attempt as well as self-harm behaviors (Peterson et al., 2016). A study with gender minorities indicates that more than one quarter have attempted suicide at least once and 41.8%

had a history of self-harm behaviors (Peterson et al., 2016). Studies with LGB+ individuals have also identified higher frequency of suicide behaviors in contrast with heterosexual counterparts (Baams et al., 2015). Some of the predictors of self-harm and suicidal ideation among LGBTQ+ emerging adults include lack of family acceptance, insufficient social support, victimization, and low level of openness regarding their sexual orientation or gender identity. Moreover, the intersection of identities may increase the prevalence of self-harm behaviors (Hill et al., 2017). Family and community support and sense of belongingness have been described as protective factors for suicide prevention efforts (Hill et al., 2017; Parra et al., 2018).

Protective Factors for LGBTQ+ Emerging Adults

Having reviewed different aspects that negatively affect or influence LGBTQ+ emerging adults, it is now important to emphasize characteristics that are highlighted through a more positive scope in recent literature. By using the term "positive," we do not aim to describe pleasurable or desired circumstances for these communities. On the contrary, we describe different coping strategies and social dynamics that are developed because of the multiple struggles LGBTQ+ emerging adults face. These strategies are vital for the development of adaptive behaviors that enable social minorities to thrive against unmeasurable odds and help them live a healthy and meaningful life.

RESILIENCE

As stated before, LGBTQ+ people are more susceptible to experiencing discrimination, victimization, and harassment throughout any developmental stage of their life (Almeida et al., 2009; Berlan et al., 2010). While it may seem reasonable to assume LGBTQ+ emerging adults who have experienced trauma, discrimination, loss, and other adverse events will experience negative outcomes like anxiety, depression, risky behaviors, and drug and alcohol abuse, among others, resilience in the face of these stressors is commonly observed (Grant Smith, 2017).

Our discussion of resilience in this section is not meant to minimize the challenges or microaggressions LGBTQ+ emerging adults experience. Even though resilience studies tend to focus on positive aspects of LGBTQ+ communities, we need to acknowledge that resilience is born from oppression. If this community was not oppressed by sociopolitical factors, we would not be discussing their resilience (Rivas, 2020). Which brings us to highlight that not all LGBTQ+ individuals experience the same adverse effects of stigma and social rejection, for these are complicated dynamics that consider not only gender and sexual orientation identities, but also race, economic resources, ethnicity, and religious or spiritual beliefs, among others. So, as you read this section, please keep in mind how unique experiences related to intersections of identities affect a person's life.

Resilience is sometimes defined as a trait, focused above all on individual characteristics; and, other times, as a dynamic process involving the complex relationship between risk factors, protective factors, and positive adaptation (Nogueira de Lira & Araujo de Morais, 2018). Fergus and Zimmerman (2005) define resilience as the process in which one focuses attention on positive contextual, social, and individual variables that interfere or disrupt development trajectories from risky behaviors, mental distress, and poor health outcomes. For emerging adults, who are finding their way through a transitional developmental stage, these protective factors are essential in the upbringing of healthy identities. In other words, resilience among emerging adults is not something that can be obtained in a definite way, but rather a state in which their thoughts, behaviors, and actions are oriented to overcoming adversity (Gil-Hernández, 2007).

Addressing the questionable approach of considering only the individual nature of resilience, Meyer (2015) argues that most LGBTQ+ literature has focused on individual-level resilience, which creates an "expectation of individual resiliency" and de-emphasizes the importance of large-scale social change. This social expectation may lead to a "blame the victim" attitude; by noting that individuals *can* be resilient, we risk expecting that individuals *ought to be* resilient (Kwate & Meyer, 2010).

Thus, how can scientifically based expectations of individual resilience affect LGBTQ+ emerging adults? At some point we might assume they must have developed effective coping skills during earlier stages of development or consider they have learned to move on from past or present adversities as adults. As we begin to focus on individual responses and resilience, we risk a shift from interventions that attempt to correct the pathogenic environment, to interventions that focus on individuals so that they can become resilient in coping with the environment (Meyer, 2015, p. 211). At this point in the discussion, it is important to introduce external factors such as social support and community engagement, which undoubtedly could help LGBTQ+ emerging adults transition in a more positive manner to adulthood.

SOCIAL SUPPORT

Social support refers to the psychological and material resources provided by an individual's social networks (Ding et al., 2020). This support is often considered as a coping strategy that produces a "stress buffering effect" that can help mediate the effects of sexual minority stigma, other forms of rejection, and sexual orientation concealment (Ding et al., 2020). Literature has also shown that social support can help reduce symptoms such as anxiety, depression, and low self-esteem among nonbinary and trans emerging adults (Thorne et al., 2018). Social support might also buffer the effects of other stressors on mental health (Wong et al., 2014), as well as reduce the negative effects of social stigma on psychological distress (Morandini et al., 2015).

Ding and collaborators (2020) found that, in some cases, individuals with higher levels of stigma and higher social support were more likely to conceal their sexual orientation. LGBTQ+ emerging adults who are living in socially conservative countries may have some form of social support that enables them to overcome adversities, and thus act resiliently. Unfortunately, if the people who compose these networks of social support are less tolerant of LGBTQ+ communities, the individual may feel the need to hide one or more aspects of their identity in order to maintain support and reduce the risk of losing friends, housing, or career opportunities (Liu & Choi, 2013).

A good example of valuable social support, which could potentially feed internalized stigma, is the role of religion or spirituality in the community. Spiritual well-being has been known for its functions as a protective factor and a predictor of adjustment (Smith et al., 2013). It has also been correlated with increased self-esteem, identity affirmation, lower internalized homophobia, and fewer feelings of alienation (Wright & Stern, 2016). Other authors have noted that involvement in accepting or affirming forms of worship can support the integration of sexual and religious identities (Esteban & Díaz-Medero, 2019). However, LGBTQ+ individuals' experiences with spiritual or religious roles may vary greatly. While spirituality refers to one's subjective, inner relationship with some higher power, religion is the externalized involvement in a standardized organization of beliefs and practices (Tan, 2005). In this sense, spirituality more than religiosity, which often promotes heteronormative norms, may help to buffer sexual identity conflicts (Carter, 2013) and result in more affirmative social support.

Another good example would be family relationships. During adolescence and emerging adulthood, most individuals develop their sexual orientation and gender identity, and some LGBTQ+ individuals disclose their identities to family during this period (Kuper et al., 2018; Zimmerman et al., 2015). Coming out to family has been associated with increasing community protective factors (Zimmerman et al., 2015). Nonetheless, family rejection can enhance self-stigma, confusion, internalized negativity, and other identity risk factors to lower collective self-esteem (Zimmerman et al., 2015). Even though family rejection can be understood as a negative experience, LGBTQ+ emerging adults can build resilience out of the structural barriers they encounter, which can lead them to view themselves as their most reliable sources (Schmitz & Tyler, 2019).

For LGBTQ+ emerging adults, it is a common experience to build social and emotional connections with others outside of the family nucleus. For example, making friends and having a steady romantic relationship has shown to be a buffer in negative situations (Schmitz & Tyler, 2019; Shilo et al., 2015). Similarly, chosen and created families allow the individual to feel accepted and to have access to role models who may have experienced similar adversities. These families provide support in helping mitigate distress related to racial, sexual, and gender identities (Wong et al., 2014).

COMMUNITY ENGAGEMENT AND CONNECTEDNESS

As mentioned before, forming and maintaining interpersonal relationships is innate among human beings and often considered a universal need (Baumeister & Leary, 1995). More so, it has been acknowledged as a protective factor among LGBTQ+ youth and emerging adults. Community engagement refers to the process of working collaboratively with and through groups of people affiliated by geographic proximity, special interest, or similar situations to address issues affecting the well-being of those people (Centers for Disease Control and Prevention [CDC], 1997). For LGBTQ+

people, the community can be understood as global and encompassing (Carney, 2017). It can also be perceived as welcoming, supportive, and accepting for some and provide a feeling of "fitting in." This can grant a sense of validation, self-worth, and be a source of resilience (Gray et al., 2015), though it is not necessarily a shared experience for all LGBTQ+ individuals. For those who adopt a more holistic self-view, engaging with the LGBTQ+ community can be perceived as unessential, as they recognize that their sexual orientation and/or gender is not something that solely defines them (Gray et al., 2015).

Before engaging and connecting with the community, one must interact with them. Community interaction is any event or action in which an individual is exposed to the community (Frost & Meyer, 2012). For example, this could be making LGBTQ+ friends in college, work, or other social gatherings. After a first interaction, a person will evaluate if said experience was pleasurable or not, if they felt comfortable, and if they desire to keep interacting with them. If the person chooses to keep socializing and getting to know the LGBTQ+ community, they can do it in formal ways or informal ways. For instance, joining an LGBTQ+ work group or college association can be identified as a formal way of getting involved with the community, while attending an LGBTQ+ bar is an informal method to get involved. Recurrent involvement may allow individuals to develop an attachment to the LGBTQ+ community even if the interactions are not consistently positive (Baumeister & Leary, 1995). When a person feels connected, a positive and mutually beneficial relationship can develop, building a shared emotional connection (Frost & Meyer, 2012). Connectedness can enhance resilience by affirming one's identity, finding other people who share similar experiences and identities, and working toward changing heteronormative and cisnormative culture (DiFulvio, 2011).

Gaps and Future Direction for Studies

We have described some of the most pressing issues impacting the health and well-being of LGBTQ+ emerging adults. In recent decades, there has been an increase in the research, understanding, and visibility of LGBTQ+ populations; however, there are still a lot of gaps in the literature. Research regarding the factors affecting the health of LGBTQ+ emerging adults is still relatively young. The documentation of their needs and experiences, though important, is not sufficient to eradicate the disparities in their everyday lives. There is a need for action and for development of structural-level interventions targeting stigma and discrimination from a social justice stance.

Moreover, due to the impact that intersecting identities have in the promotion or reduction of health disparities, it is important to conduct additional research with marginalized groups within the sexual and gender minority spectrum. For example, ethnic and racial characteristics combined with LGBTQ+ status puts them in an even more dire position in society. Understanding the impact on those intersections is crucial in order to address them both at individual and structural levels. Finally, there is a need to conduct more studies focused on protective factors and that highlight the strengths of

LGBTQ+ emerging adults. This is an important step to move toward a more positive view of LGBTQ+ communities while highlighting their virtues.

Clinical Implications

Clinicians of all sexual orientations and gender identities can work successfully with diverse sexual and gender identities, if they are accepting and free of heterosexist bias and prejudice. That is why acquiring knowledge, skills, and awareness relevant to LGBTQ+ clients is essential for working with this community. When a professional neglects to acquire these competences, they are at risk of crossing serious ethical breaches, which can include inflicting harm. Therefore, it is vital for health care professionals working with LGBTQ+ emerging adults to be up-to-date with recent terminology and guidelines.

During emerging adulthood, particular situations might arise for LGBTQ+ people, and it is relevant for mental health professionals to be aware of them. During this period, it is common for LGBTQ+ individuals to ask themselves if they want to come out to others (Logan & Carter, 2017). During the coming out process, mental health professionals can discuss with the client if it is safe or not to come out. For example, it might not be safe to come out to nonsupportive family members who financially provide for the client. Nonetheless, the decision is for the client to make—not the therapist. During the coming out process, it is also important for the clinician to validate exploration of gender identity and sexual orientation when the client feels safe to do so (Logan & Carter, 2017). Clinicians should be aware that internalized bias might be present in the client's verbalizations, and they should be able to reflect it back to clients. By doing this, clients and clinicians can safely explore it in therapy and address it. Another situation that might arise when working with LGBTQ+ emerging adults is the challenges of developing a career path (Norman et al., 2017). LGBTQ+ emerging adults might be worried about potential workplace discrimination, or they might have already experienced discrimination and are working through the negative repercussions. These concerns and/or experiences influence their decision to come out as LGBTQ+ or not in their work environments.

As previously discussed, LGBTQ+ emerging adults may have difficulties accessing health services due to several reasons; ensuring an LGBTQ+ affirmative environment in health care is key to promoting access to medical and mental health care among the community. As health care workers, we must aim to provide interdisciplinary services that are available for all, meaning that the professionals have the knowledge, competence, and experience to work with emerging adults who identify as LGBTQ+. For example, trans and nonbinary individuals may benefit from seeking care within multiple disciplines to assist with achieving embodiment and gender-affirming goals such as: speech pathology, surgery, legal issues, social work, endocrinology, physical therapy, and others. Finally, health care services must be equitable for all LGBTQ+ individuals (Hadland et al., 2016).

Case Study

José is a 19-year-old middle-class Puerto Rican male who moved to California to start college. José presented for services because he is having weekly panic attacks. José identifies as a bigender gay male and uses masculine pronouns. He is only open about his sexual orientation to his college friends. No one knows about his gender identity or sexual orientation back home. José reports he has been changing and discovering diverse identities while away at college. He identifies as a white person back home, yet his college peers correct him, saying that he is Latino or maybe Puerto Rican, but definitely not white. He also mentions that people constantly ask him if he has a green card or just a visa, because they do not know that Puerto Ricans are born US citizens.

José is not comfortable identifying as masculine, but the only gender category outside the traditional binary he knew about prior to going to college was transgender. When he moved, he discovered other identities, such as bigender, which he feels describes him very well. He now feels the pressure to explain the definition of bigender to all the people with whom he discloses his gender identity, and some of them begin questioning him about it. José thinks his anxiety is due to his fear of people questioning who he is or how he should identify. In addition, he is scared that his anxiety will get worse when he visits home and when he chooses to come out to his family and friends.

Case Study Discussion

This case highlights stressors LGBTQ+ emerging adults might face and considerations for intersectional experiences. In order to integrate the principles of resilience, we must recognize the risks and difficulties, risky behaviors, stressors, and barriers relevant for this client. First, we have multiple identities and characteristics to highlight, including sexual orientation, gender identity, language, race and ethnicity, migrant status, and culture, to name a few. Second, this case shows us that the client has several minority identities at the same time, and not everyone knows about some of these identities. Some of the identities are new for him, and other identities are constantly questioned by his peers.

From an affirmative model focused on resilience, we must make visible his strengths so he can continue to use them as a tool to manage current and future situations. When talking about resources, as professionals we can focus our help on strategies to assist the client develop a sense of empowerment and agency with exploring his identities and making disclosures about his identities (if desired). It is important that this emerging adult becomes referred to in the way he identifies himself, that even if others question his identity, he has the knowledge necessary to reaffirm himself and not question himself. This will also help him when he must face his family. In addition to the psychotherapy process, referrals to other interdisciplinary professionals would also be necessary. For example, a primary care physician or psychiatrist might give him medication to reduce panic attacks, a professional counselor might provide support and arrange to decrease anxiety with outpatient therapy, an occupational therapist might help him with tasks that make it difficult for his daily life as a migrant, among others.

Finally, culturally sensitive care is very important in all cases. In this case, we must be aware of his Puerto Rican/Latin culture, where factors such as familialism might be present. For example, for Latinx families, what family thinks of you and their acceptance is very important for the well-being of the person. At the same time, the family is willing to do anything to understand, support, and defend their family members. Thus, family acceptance is very important in this community. On the other hand, as an emerging adult gay person, his vision of life will be different, and he will have to deal with heteronormativity and homophobia in our society. As a bigender person, in addition to cisnormativity and transphobia, he will have to navigate society's lack of knowledge and the lack of legal and cultural recognition. With English as a second language, he will have to contend with the bias that exists in this regard, with constant corrections and micro/macroaggressions toward his accent simply because it is different. Finally, he will have to deal with ethnic and racial background in a Eurocentric culture and the constant implications that this brings to his life.

Key Knowledge Points

- LGBTQ+ young adults face unique challenges both at individual and institutional levels.
- Family does not refer only to biological relatives, it also includes other people who execute its roles and functions. Close peers and friends (offline and online) become very important for support, empathy, and understanding among LGBTQ+ emerging adults.
- LGBTQ+ emerging adults who go to college are often exposed to harassment, violence, and discrimination on campus. For some, being *out* is not an option.
- Physical and mental health disparities are associated to stigma, discrimination, violence, and lack of access to competent healthcare services. In working with sexual and gender minority emerging adults, it is crucial to consider their intersecting identities in order to better understand and address the disparities affecting them.
- Relationships stages are similar to cisheterosexual relationships, but being part of a stigmatized minority adds unique struggles to initiating, committing, maintaining, and ending relationships.
- Emerging adulthood is a vulnerable developmental period of life in which increased independence can lead to greater risk-taking and compromise health (e.g., substance use, unprotected sex, poor self-care).
- Experiencing abuse, negative social interactions, negative religious experiences, harassment and violence in the community, and family rejection have been linked to higher rates of depression and anxiety during emerging adulthood.
- Some of the predictors of self-harm and suicidal ideation among sexual and gender minorities emerging adults include lack of family acceptance, insufficient social

support, victimization, and low level of openness regarding their sexual orientation or gender identity.
- Social support and community engagement are considered protective factors and have been linked to resilience among LGBTQ+ emerging adults.
- When a professional neglects to acquire competences for working with LGBTQ+ emerging adults, they are at risk of crossing serious ethical breaches, which can include inflicting harm. Therefore, it is vital for health care professionals to be up-to-date with recent terminology and guidelines.

Recommendations for Mental Health Clinicians

- Begin by examining your attitudes and beliefs toward LGBTQ+ emerging adults. Reflect on your beliefs regarding their capacity to understand and describe their sexual orientation and gender identity.
- Literature, definitions, and best practices are always evolving. It is important to keep your knowledge updated and never assume you know better than your client.
- Seek supervision, when possible, from other colleagues with more experience working with LGBTQ+ emerging adults.
- It is always helpful to have a service directory at hand that includes a list of competent, well-prepared, affirming health professionals to provide adequate referrals when needed.
- Assume an active role in advocating for the rights of LGBTQ+ emerging adults in different scenarios, including with family, at school or college, in the community, and at work.

References

Almeida, J., Johnson, R. M., Corliss, H. L., Molnal, B. E., & Azrael, D. (2009). Emotional distress among LGBT youth: The influence of perceived discrimination based on sexual orientation. *Journal of Youth Adolescence, 38*(7), 1001–1014.

Arnett, J. J. (2000). Emerging adulthood: A theory of development from the late teens through the twenties. *American Psychologist, 55*(5), 469–480. https://doi.org/10.1037/0003-066X.55.5.469

Baams, L., Grossman, A. H., & Russell, S. T. (2015). Minority stress and mechanisms of risk for depression and suicidal ideation among lesbian, gay, and bisexual youth. *Developmental Psychology, 51*(5), 688–696. https://doi.org/10.1037/a0038994

Barger, B. T., Obedin-Maliver, J., Capriotti, M. R., Lunn, M. R., & Flentje, A. (2021). Characterization of substance use among underrepresented sexual and gender minority participants in the Population Research in Identity and Disparities for Equality (PRIDE) study. *Substance Abuse, 41*(1), 1–12. https://doi.org/10.1080/08897077.2019.1702610

Baumeister, R. F., & Leary, M. R. (1995). The need to belong: Desire for interpersonal attachments as a fundamental human motivation. *Psychological Bulletin, 117*(3), 497–529.

Berlan, E., Corliss, H., Field, A., Goodman, E., & Austin, S. (2010). Sexual orientation and bullying among adolescents in growing up today study. *Journal Adolescent Health, 46*(4), 366–371.

Borgogna, N. C., McDermott, R. C., Aita, S. L., & Kridel, M. M. (2019). Anxiety and depression across gender and sexual minorities: Implications for transgender, gender nonconforming, pansexual, demisexual, asexual, queer, and questioning individuals. *Psychology of Sexual Orientation and Gender Diversity, 6*(1), 54–63. https://doi.org/10.1037/sgd0000306

Carney, V. (2017). Community connectedness within the LGBT* community. *Honors Projects.* https://scholarworks.bgsu.edu/honorsprojects/240

Carrión-Santiago, K., Francia-Martínez, M., Esteban, C., & Rivera-Mercado, H. (2016). Familias homoparentales: Mitos y realidades. In M. Vázquez-Rivera, A. Martínez-Taboas, M. Francia-Martínez, & J. Toro-Alfonso (Eds.), *LGBT 101: Una mirada introductoria al colectivo* (pp. 227–246). Publicaciones Puertorriqueñas Inc.

Carter, J. W. Jr. (2013). *Giving voice to black gay and bisexual men in the south: Examining the influences of religion, spirituality, and family on the mental health and sexual behaviors of black gay and bisexual men* (Doctoral dissertation). Retrieved from ProQuest Dissertations and Theses Full Text: The Humanities and Social Sciences Collection.

Centers for Disease Control and Prevention (CDC). (1997). *Principles of community engagement.* Centers for Disease Control and Prevention.

Coulter, R. W. S., Jun, H. J., Calzo, J. P., Truong, N. L., Mair, C., Markovic, N., Charlton, B. M., Silvestre, A. J., Stall, R., & Corliss, H. L. (2018). Sexual-orientation differences in alcohol use trajectories and disorders in emerging adulthood: Results from a longitudinal cohort study in the United States. *Addiction, 113*(9), 1619–1632. https://doi.org/10.1111/add.14251

Dahlen, S. (2020). De-sexing the medical record? An examination of sex versus gender identity in the general medical council's trans healthcare ethical advice. *The New Bioethics: A Multidisciplinary Journal of Biotechnology and the Body, 26*(1), 38–52. https://doi.org/10.1080/20502877.2020.1720429

Daniels, R. S. (2019). The evolution of attitudes on same-sex marriage in the United States, 1988–2014. *Social Science Quarterly (Wiley-Blackwell), 100*(5), 1651–1663. https://doi.org/10.1111/ssqu.12673

DeHaan, S., Kuper, L., Magee, J., Bigelow, L., & Mustanski, B. (2013). The interplay between online and offline explorations of identity, relationships, and sex: A mixed-methods study with LGBT youth. *Journal of Sex Research, 50*(5), 421–434. https://doi.org/10.1080/00224499.2012.661489

Dessel, A. B., Goodman, K. D., & Woodford, M. R. (2017). LGBT discrimination on campus and heterosexual bystanders: Understanding intentions to intervene. *Journal of Diversity in Higher Education, 10*(2), 101–116. https://doi.org/10.1037/dhe0000015

DiFulvio, G. T. (2011). Sexual minority youth, social connection and resilience: From personal struggle to collective identity. *Social Science & Medicine, 72*(10), 1611–1617. https://doi.org/10.1016/j.socscimed.2011.02.045

Ding, C., Chen, X., Wang, W., Yu, B., Yang, H., Li, X., Deng, S., Yan, H., & Li, S. (2020). Sexual minority stigma, sexual orientation concealment, social support and depressive symptoms among men who have sex with men in China: A moderated mediation modeling analysis. *AIDS and Behavior, 24*, 8–17. https://doi.org/10.1007/s10461-019-02713-3

Drabble, L. A., Wootton, A. R., Veldhuis, C. B., Perry, E., Riggle, E. D. B., Trocki, K. F., & Hughes, T. L. (2020). It's complicated: The impact of marriage legalization among sexual minority women and gender diverse individuals in the United States. *Psychology of Sexual Orientation and Gender Diversity.* https://doi.org/10.1037/sgd0000375

Erickson-Schroth, L., & Glaeser, E. (2017). The role of resilience and resilience characteristics in health promotion. In K. Eckstrand & J. Potter (Eds), *Trauma, resilience and health promotion in LGBT patients* (pp. 51–56). Springer International Publishing.

Esteban, C., & Díaz-Medero, L. X. (2019). Una reflexión sobre prácticas adecuadas: Integración ética de las creencias religiosas/espirituales y las identidades sexuales y de género diversas (Sección especial). *Revista Ciencias de la Conducta, 22*(1), 97–134.

Feinstein, B. A., Dyar, C., Li, D. H., Whitton, S. W., Newcomb, M. E., & Mustanski, B. (2019). The longitudinal associations between outness and health outcomes among gay/lesbian versus bisexual emerging adults. *Archives of Sexual Behavior, 48*(4), 1111–1126. https://doi.org/10.1007/s10508-018-1221-8

Felner, J. K., Wisdom, J. P., Williams, T., Katuska, L., Haley, S. J., Jun, H.-J., & Corliss, H. L. (2020). Stress, coping, and context: Examining substance use among LGBTQ young adults with probable substance use disorders. *Psychiatric Services, 71*(2), 112–120. https://doi.org/10.1176/appi.ps.201900029

Fergus, S., & Zimmerman, M. (2005). Adolescent resilience: A framework for understanding healthy development in the face of risk. *Annual Review of Public Health, 26*, 399–419. https://doi.org/10.1146/annurev.publhealth.26.021304.144357

Fisher, C. B., Fried, A. L., Desmond, M., Macapagal, K., & Mustanski, B. (2017). Facilitators and barriers to participation in PrEP HIV prevention trials involving transgender male and female adolescents and emerging adults. *AIDS Education and Prevention, 29*(3), 205–217. https://doi.org/10.1521/aeap.2017.29.3.205

Forster, M., Vetrone, S., Grigsby, T. J., Rogers, C., & Unger, J. B. (2020). The relationships between emerging adult transition themes, adverse childhood experiences, and substance use patterns among a community cohort of Hispanics. *Cultural Diversity and Ethnic Minority Psychology, 26*(3), 378–389. https://doi.org/10.1037/cdp0000304

Fredriksen-Goldsen, K. I., Hoy-Ellis, C. P., & Brown, M. (2015). Addressing behavioral cancer risk from LGBT health equity perspective. In U. Boehmer & R. Elk (Eds.), *Cancer and the LGBT community: Unique perspectives from risk to survivorship* (pp. 37–62). Springer.

Fredriksen-Goldsen, K. I., Simoni, J. M., Kim, H.-J., Lehavot, K., Walters, K. L., Yang, J., Hoy-Ellis, C. P., & Muraco, A. (2014). The health equity promotion model: Reconceptualization of lesbian, gay, bisexual, and transgender (LGBT) health disparities. *American Journal of Orthopsychiatry, 84*(6), 653–663. https://doi.org/10.1037/ort0000030

Frost, D. M., & Meyer, I. H. (2012). Measuring community connectedness among diverse sexual minority populations. *Journal of Sex Research, 49*(1), 36–49. https://doi.org/10.1080/00224499.2011.565427

Fuist, T. N. (2017). "It just always seemed like it wasn't a big deal, yet I know for some people they really struggle with it": LGBT religious identities in context. *Journal for the Scientific Study of Religion, 55*(4), 770–786. https://doi.org/10.1111/jssr.12291

Garvey, J. C., Mobley, S. D., Summerville, K. S., & Moore, G. T. (2019). Queer and trans students of color: Navigating identity disclosure and college contexts. *Journal of Higher Education, 90*(1), 150–178. https://doi.org/10.1080/00221546.2018.1449081

Gay and Lesbian Medical Association. (2010). *Healthy people 2020: Companion document for lesbian, gay, bisexual, and transgender (LGBT) health.* https://jnccn.org/doi/10.6004/jnccn.2017.0169

Giammattei, S. V. (2015). Beyond the binary: Trans-negotiations in couple and family therapy. *Family Process, 54*(3), 418–434. https://doi.org/10.1111/famp.12167

Gibbs, J. J., & Goldbach, J. (2015). Religious conflict, sexual identity, and suicidal behaviors among LGBT young adults. *Archives of Suicide Research, 19*(4), 472–488. https://doi.org/10.1080/13811118.2015.1004476

Gil-Hernández, G. (2007). El proceso de resiliencia en el desarrollo de la identidad gay, lesbiana y bisexual. *Vector Plus: Miscelánea científico—Cultural, 30,* 64–73.

Ginicola, M. M., Smith, C., & Filmore, J. M. (2017). *Affirmative counseling with LGBTQI+ people.* American Counseling Association.

González-Rivera, J. A., Rosario-Rodríguez, A., & Santiago-Torres, L. E. (2019). Depresión e ideación suicida en personas de la comunidad LGBT con y sin pareja: Un estudio exploratorio. *Revista Puertorriqueña de Psicología, 30*(2), 254–267.

Grant Smith, N. (2017). Resilience across life span: Adulthood. In: K. Eckstrand & J. Potter, (Eds), *Trauma, resilience and health promotion in LGBT patients* (pp. 77–88). Springer International Publishing AG.

Gray, N., Mendelsohn, D., & Omoto, A. (2015). Community connectedness, challenges, and resilience among gay Latino immigrants. *American Journal of Community Psychology, 55*(1–2), 202–214. https://doi.org/10.1007/s10464-014-9697-4

Griffin-Tomas, M., Cahill, S., Kapadia, F., & Halkitis, P. N. (2019). Access to health services among young adult gay men in New York City. *American Journal of Men's Health, 13*(1), 155798831881868. https://doi.org/10.1177/1557988318818683

Hadland, S., Yehia, B., & Makadon, H. (2016). Caring for LGBTQ youth in inclusive and affirmative environments. *Pediatrics Clinics of North America, 63*(6), 955–969.

Halkitis, P. N., Maiolatesi, A. J., & Krause, K. D. (2020). The health challenges of emerging adult gay men: Effecting change in health care. *Pediatric Clinics of North America, 67*(2), 293–308. https://doi.org/10.1016/j.pcl.2019.12.003

Hall, W. J. (2018). Psychosocial risk and protective factors for depression among lesbian, gay, bisexual, and queer youth: A systematic review. *Journal of Homosexuality, 65*(3), 263–316. https://doi.org/10.1080/00918369.2017.1317467

Hatzenbuehler, M. L., Flores, A. R., & Gates, G. J. (2017). Social attitudes regarding same sex marriage and LGBT health disparities: Results from a National Probability Sample. *Journal of Social Issues, 73*(3), 508–528. https://doi.org/10.1111/josi.12229

Henry, R. S., Perrin, P. B., Sawyer, A., & Pugh, M. (2020). Health conditions, access to care, mental health, and wellness behaviors in lesbian, gay, bisexual, and transgender adults. *International Journal of Chronic Diseases, 2020,* 1–8. https://doi.org/10.1155/2020/9094047

Hill, R. M., Rooney, E. E., Mooney, M. A., Kaplow, J. B., Hill, R. M., Rooney, E. E., & Mooney, M. A. (2017). Links between social support, thwarted belongingness, and suicide ideation among lesbian, gay, and bisexual college students. *Journal of Family Strengths, 17*(2). http://digitalcommons.library.tmc.edu/jfs/vol17/iss2/6

James, S. E., & Salcedo, B. (2017). *2015 U.S. transgender survey: Report on the experiences of Latino/a respondent.* www.USTransSurvey.org

Kail, B. L., Acosta, K. L., & Wright, E. R. (2015). State-level marriage equality and the health of same-sex couples. *American Journal of Public Health, 105*(6), 1101–1105. https://doi.org/10.2105/AJPH.2015.302589

Kelly, J., Davis, C., & Schlesinger, C. (2015). Substance use by same sex attracted young people: Prevalence, perceptions and homophobia. *Drug and Alcohol Review, 34*(4), 358–365. https://doi.org/10.1111/dar.12158

Kuper, L., Wright, L., & Mustanski, B. (2018). Gender identity development among transgender and gender nonconforming emerging adults: An intersectional approach. *International Journal of Transgenderism, 19*(4), 436–455. https://doi.org/10.1080/15532739.2018.1443869

Kwate, N., & Meyer, I. H. (2010). The myth of meritocracy and African American health. *American Journal of Public Health, 100,* 1831–1834. http://dx.doi.org/10.2105/AJPH.2009.186445

Lee, H.-Y., & Mutz, D. C. (2019). Changing attitudes toward same-sex marriage: A three-wave panel study. *Political Behavior, 41*(3), 701–722. https://doi.org/10.1007/s11109-018-9463-7

Liu, J. X., & Choi, K. H. (2013). Emerging gay identities in China: The prevalence and predictors of social discrimination against men who have sex with men. In P. Liamputtong (Ed.), *Stigma, discrimination and living with HIV/AIDS* (pp. 271–287). Springer.

Logan, C., & Carter, A. (2017). Coming out and gay identity development. In C. B. Roland & L. D. Burlew (Eds.), *Counseling LGBTQ adults during life span* (pp. 3–5). American Counseling Association.

Macapagal, K., Bhatia, R., & Greene, G. J. (2016). Differences in healthcare access, use, and experiences within a community sample of racially diverse lesbian, gay, bisexual, transgender, and questioning emerging adults. *LGBT Health, 3*(6), 434–442. https://doi.org/10.1089/lgbt.2015.0124

Macapagal, K., Greene, G. J., Rivera, Z., & Mustanski, B. (2015). "The best is always yet to come": Relationship stages and processes among young LGBT couples. *Journal of Family Psychology, 29*(3), 309–320. https://doi.org/10.1037/fam0000094

Magette, A. L., Durtschi, J. A., & Love, H. A. (2018). Lesbian, gay, and bisexual substance use in emerging adulthood moderated by parent-child relationships in adolescence. *American Journal of Family Therapy, 46*(3), 272–286. https://doi.org/10.1080/01926187.2018.1493958

Meyer, I. H. (2003). Prejudice, social stress, and mental health in lesbian, gay, and bisexual populations: Conceptual issues and research evidence. *Psychological Bulletin, 129*(5), 674–697. https://doi.org/10.1037/0033-2909.129.5.674

Meyer, I. (2015). Resilience in the study of minority stress and health of sexual and gender minorities. *Psychology of Sexual Orientation and Gender Diversity, 2*(3), 209–213.

Morandini, J., Blaszczynski, A., Dar-Nimrod, I., & Ross, M. (2015). Minority stress and community connectedness among gay, lesbian and bisexual Australians: A comparison of rural and metropolitan localities. *Australian and New Zealand Journal of Public Health, 39*(3), 260–266.

Mustanski, B., Andrews, R., & Puckett, J. A. (2016). The effects of cumulative victimization on mental health among lesbian, gay, bisexual, and transgender adolescents and young adults. *American Journal of Public Health, 106*(3), 527–533. https://doi.org/10.2105/AJPH.2015.302976

Nogueira de Lira, A., & Araujo de Morais, N. (2018). Resilience in lesbian, gay, and bisexual (LGB) populations: An integrative literature review. *Sexuality Research and Social Policy, 3*(15), 272–282. https://doi.org/10.1007/s13178-017-0285-x

Norman, D., Hunter, Q., & O'Hara, M. (2017). Career development. In C. B. Roland & L. D. Burlew (Eds.), *Counseling LGBTQ adults during life span* (pp. 6–9). American Counseling Association.

Oberheim, S. T., DePue, M. K., & Hagedorn, W. B. (2017). Substance use disorders (SUDs) in transgender communities: The need for trans-competent SUD counselors and facilities. *Journal of Addictions and Offender Counseling, 38*(1), 33–47. https://doi.org/10.1002/jaoc.12027

Orel, N. A., & Coon, D. W. (2016). The challenges of change: How can we meet the care needs of the ever-evolving LGBT family? *Generations, 40*(2), 41–45.

Padilla, M. B., Rodríguez-Madera, S., Varas-Díaz, N., & Ramos-Pibernus, A. (2016). Transmigrations: Border-crossing and the politics of body modification among Puerto Rican transgender women. *International Journal of Sexual Health, 28*(4), 261–277. https://doi.org/10.1080/19317611.2016.1223256

Parent, M. C., Arriaga, A. S., Gobble, T., & Wille, L. (2019). Stress and substance use among sexual and gender minority individuals across the lifespan. *Neurobiology of Stress, 10*(December), 100146. https://doi.org/10.1016/j.ynstr.2018.100146

Parra, L. A., Bell, T. S., Benibgui, M., Helm, J. L., & Hastings, P. D. (2018). The buffering effect of peer support on the links between family rejection and psychosocial adjustment in LGB emerging adults. *Journal of Social and Personal Relationships, 35*(6), 854–871. https://doi.org/10.1177/0265407517699713

Peterson, C., Matthews, A., Copps-Smith, E., & Conrad, L. (2016). Suicidality, self-harm, and body dissatisfaction in transgender adolescents and emerging adults with gender dysphoria. *Suicide and Life-Threatening Behavior, 47*, 475–482. https://doi.org/10.1111/sltb.12289

Ramos-Pibernus, A. G., Rivera-Segarra, E. R., Rodríguez-Madera, S. L., Varas-Díaz, N., & Padilla, M. (2020). Stigmatizing experiences of trans men in Puerto Rico: Implications for health. *Transgender Health, 5*(4), 234–240. https://doi.org/10.1089/trgh.2020.0021

Richmond, J. R., Edmonds, K. A., Rose, J. P., & Gratz, K. L. (2020). Examining the impact of online rejection among emerging adults with borderline personality pathology: Development of a novel online group chat social rejection paradigm. *Personality Disorders: Theory, Research, and Treatment, 11*(5), 301–311. https://doi.org/10.1037/per0000381.supp

Rivas, D. (2020). Resiliencia: ¿Debemos hablar de ella? *Boletín Diversidad.* https://www.boletindiversidad.org/articulo3

Romanelli, M., & Hudson, K. D. (2017). Individual and systemic barriers to health care: Perspectives of lesbian, gay, bisexual, and transgender adults. *American Journal of Orthopsychiatry, 87*(6), 714–728. https://doi.org/10.1037/ort0000306

Rosenkrantz, D. E., Black, W. W., Abreu, R. L., Aleshire, M. E., & Fallin-Bennett, K. (2017). Health and health care of rural sexual and gender minorities: A systematic review. *Stigma and Health, 2*(3), 229–243. https://doi.org/10.1037/sah0000055.supp (Supplemental)

Russell, S. T., & Fish, J. N. (2016). Mental health in lesbian, gay, bisexual, and transgender (LGBT) youth. *Annual Review of Clinical Psychology, 12*, 465–487. https://doi.org/10.1146/annurev-clinpsy-021815-093153

Russell, S., Ryan, C., Toomey, R., Diaz, R., & Sanchez, J. (2011). Lesbian, gay, bisexual and transgender adolescent school victimization implications for young adult health and adjustment. *Journal of School Health, 81*(5), 223–230.

Schmitz, R., & Tyler, K. (2019). "Life has actually become more clear": An examination of resilience among LGBTQ young adults. *Sexualities, 22*(4), 710–733. https://doi.org/10.1177/1363460718770451

Schmitz, R. M., & Tabler, J. (2019). Health services and intersections of care: Promises and pitfalls experienced by LGBTQ + Latino/a emerging adults. *Journal of LGBT Youth, 0*(0), 1–22. https://doi.org/10.1080/19361653.2019.1684416

Shilo, G., Antebi, N., & Mor, Z. (2015). Individual and community resilience factors among lesbian, gay, bisexual, queer, and questioning youth and adults in Israel. *American Journal of Community Psychology, 55*(1), 215–227.

Smith, L., Webber, R., & DeFrain, J. (2013). Spiritual well-being and its relationship to resilience in young people: A mixed methods case study. *Sage Journals, 1*, 1–16. http://doi.org/10.1177/2158244013485582

Smith, S. K., & Turell, S. C. (2017). Perceptions of healthcare experiences: Relational and communicative competencies to improve care for LGBT people. *Journal of Social Issues, 73*(3), 637–657. https://doi.org/10.1111/josi.12235

Sørlie, A. (2019). The right to trans-specific healthcare in Norway: Understanding the health needs of transgender people. *Medical Law Review, 27*(2), 295–317. https://doi.org/10.1093/medlaw/fwy029

Tan, P. (2005). The importance of spirituality among gay and lesbian individuals. *Journal of Homosexuality, 49*, 135–144. http://dx.doi.org/10.1300/J082v49n02_08

Thorne, N., Witcomb, G., Nieder, T., Nixon, E., Yip, A., & Arcelus, J. (2018). A comparison of mental health symptomatology and levels of social support in young treatment seeking transgender individuals who identify as binary and non-binary. *International Journal of Transgenderism, 20*(2–3), 241–250. https://doi.org/10.1080/15532739.2018.1452660

Twist, J., Barker, M.-J., Nel, P. W., & Horley, N. (2017). Transitioning together: A narrative analysis of the support accessed by partners of trans people. *Sexual & Relationship Therapy, 32*(2), 227–243. https://doi.org/10.1080/14681994.2017.1296568

Vaitses-Fontanari, A. M., Fagundes-Pase, P., Churchill, S., Machado-Borba Soll, B., Schwarz, K., Schneider, M. A., . . . Rodrigues-Lobato, M. I. (2019). Dealing with gender-related and general stress: Substance use among Brazilian transgender youth. *Addictive Behaviors Reports, 9*(November 2018), 100166. https://doi.org/10.1016/j.abrep.2019.100166

Wallace, B. C., & Santacruz, E. (2017). Health disparities and LGBT populations. In R. Ruth & E. Santacruz (Eds.), *LGBT psychology and mental health: Emerging research and advances* (pp. 177–196). Praeger.

Wang, C.-C., Lin, H.-C., Chen, M.-H., Ko, N.-Y., Chang, Y.-P., Lin, I.-M., & Yen, C.-F. (2018). Effects of traditional and cyber homophobic bullying in childhood on depression, anxiety, and physical pain in emerging adulthood and the moderating effects of social support among gay and bisexual men in Taiwan. *Neuropsychiatric Disease and Treatment, Volume 14*, 1309–1317. https://doi.org/10.2147/NDT.S164579

Willis, P., Dobbs, C., Evans, E., Raithby, M., & Bishop, J. (2020). Reluctant educators and self-advocates: Older trans adults' experiences of health-care services and practitioners in seeking gender-affirming services. *Health Expectations: An International Journal of Public Participation in Health Care & Health Policy.* https://doi.org/10.1111/hex.13104

Wong, C., Schrager, S., Holloway, I., Meyer, I., & Kipke, M. (2014). Minority stress experiences and psychological well-being: The impact of support from connection to social networks within the Los Angeles House and ball communities. *Prevention Science, 15*(1), 44–55.

Wood, A. W., & Conley, A. H. (2014). Loss of religious or spiritual identities among the LGBT population. *Counseling and Values, 59*(1), 95–111. https://doi.org/10.1002/j.2161-007X.2014.00044.x

Wood, S. M., Salas-Humara, C., & Dowshen, N. L. (2016). Human immunodeficiency virus, other sexually transmitted infections, and sexual and reproductive health in lesbian, gay, bisexual, transgender youth. *Pediatric Clinics of North America, 63*(6), 1027–1055. https://doi.org/https://doi.org/10.1016/j.pcl.2016.07.006

Wright, A., & Stern, S. (2016). The role of spirituality in sexual minority identities. *Psychology of Sexual Orientation and Gender Diversity, 3*(1), 71–79.

Zimmerman, L., Darnelle, D., Rhew, I., Lee, C., & Kaysen, D. (2015). Resilience in community: A social ecological development model for young adult sexual minority women. *American Journal of Community Psychology, 55*(1), 179–190. https://doi.org/10.1007/s10464-015-9702-6

Section III
SYSTEMS OF CARE

CHAPTER 7

Pre-K–12 Schools

Molly M. Strear, PhD, NCC, &
Matthew J. Beck, PhD, LCPC, NCC, ACS

Schools of pre-kindergarten through 12th grade are an essential part of the development, health, and well-being of youth. In addition to academic knowledge and skills, educational stakeholders are tasked with supporting students as they develop physically, mentally, emotionally, and socially. Further, schools are integrally connected to creating and sustaining cultural norms and values of communities. For example, the ways in which children and adolescents construct and appraise sexual orientation and gender constructs are impacted by school culture and climate (Gay, Lesbian and Straight Education Network [GLSEN], 2019). An inclusive school has the capacity to affirm LGBTQ+ people, allowing space for non-dominant narratives that do not align with heterosexual or cisgender identities (Hanson et al., 2019). On the other hand, schools that do not acknowledge and value non-dominant narratives perpetuate oppression and exclusion, contributing to disproportionate educational access, attainment, and health disparities (GLSEN, 2016).

For nearly 30 years, GLSEN has contributed to increased understanding of LGBTQ+ students' experiences, elucidating the barriers that LGBTQ+ students face in schools and the school-based resources that support them (Kosciw et al., 2020). One of the first surveys conducted by GLSEN in 2001 captured the perspectives of 904 lesbian, gay, bisexual, and transgender middle and high school students from 48 states and the District of Columbia, systematically examining school climate for one of the first times (Kosciw & Cullen, 2002). Nearly 20 years later, a much larger and more diverse sample of 16,713 lesbian, gay, bisexual, transgender, and queer students between the ages of 13 and 21 "from all 50 states, the District of Columbia, Puerto Rico, American Samoa, and Guam" (Kosciw et al., 2020, p. xviii) illustrated that a lot has changed in our nation's schools, but many challenges remain for LGBTQ+ youth.

Although progress has been made to improve school climate for LGBTQ+ youth, students still report feeling unsafe at school due to anti-LGBTQ+ bullying and harassment-related concerns (Kosciw et al., 2020). Findings from GLSEN (Kosciw et al., 2020) revealed that the number of harassment-related concerns reported by LGBTQ+ youth to school personnel was greater in 2019 than in almost all previous years (from 1999 to 2019). Perhaps most significantly, the results of the survey indicated that intervention frequency by school personnel and its effectiveness were lower in 2019 compared to prior years (Kosciw et al., 2020). Additionally, GLSEN's 2019 survey found no significant improvement regarding the number of youth exposed to positive representations of LGBTQ+ individuals through curriculum material in class (Kosciw et al., 2020). Among LGBTQ+ students of color specifically, GLSEN researchers identified increasing reports of youth hearing racist statements starting from 2003 with the highest rate noted in 2019 (Kosciw et al., 2020). Similar results from a large sample (n = ~800,000) of seventh-, ninth-, and eleventh-grade students in California highlighted concerning educational and mental health disparities for LGBTQ+ students (Hanson et al., 2019). According to Hanson and colleagues (2019), LGBTQ+ students "reported significantly fewer positive perceptions of and experiences at school and of their own well-being than their non-transgender and straight peers" (p. 2) across all 14 measures under investigation (five overarching domains included school supports, school safety, mental health, school engagement, and academic performance). As such, numerous challenges related to the unique needs of LGBTQ+ students continue to be left unaddressed, and they call for a greater commitment from educational stakeholders to equitable education for LGBTQ+ youth.

Since the first National School Climate Survey conducted by GLSEN in 1999, substantive efforts have been made to diversify the ways sexual orientation and gender identities are included in educational discourse, such as the intentional inclusion of youth that identify as "pansexual, queer, transgender, nonbinary, genderqueer, two-spirit, and other non-cisgender and non-heterosexual identities" (Kosciw et al., 2020, p. xviii). However, additional attention is needed to further disaggregate the experiences of LGBTQ+ youth in schools. For example, research indicates that the experiences of transgender and gender diverse youth are unique from their cisgender peers that identify as sexually diverse (Greytak et al., 2009; Hanson et al., 2019; Movement Advancement Project & GLSEN, 2017). Transgender and gender diverse youth often report higher rates of harassment, assault, and victimization (Greytak et al., 2009) and unique challenges navigating discriminatory facilities (e.g., bathrooms, locker rooms) and state and federal laws (Movement Advancement Project & GLSEN, 2017). Hanson and colleagues (2019) found that "transgender and bisexual high school students were more likely than students of other gender identities and sexual orientations to experience chronic sadness and to contemplate suicide" (p. 2). Such attention to the complexities of within-group differences must also address other aspects of LGBTQ+ students' identities by amplifying understanding of the educational experiences of LGBTQ+ youth of color through an intersectional lens (Crenshaw, 1991; Truong et al., 2020a; Truong et al., 2020b; Zongrone et al., 2020a; Zongrone et al., 2020b). Attention to within-group differences and intersectionality (Crenshaw, 1991) is necessary for educational stakeholders to meet the needs of LGBTQ+ students given that macro social structures, such as school systems, can perpetuate power and oppression, marginalizing and privileging some students over others.

In order to improve pre-K–12 school climate and better meet the needs of LGBTQ+ youth, educational stakeholders ought to embrace an integrated, interdisciplinary, and holistic approach to education. In particular, school-based mental health professionals (SBMHPs) are well positioned and ethically obliged to lead this work. How schools provide student services outside of classrooms looks differently across the nation given the unique configurations of professional teams and resources available at each school. Therefore, for the purpose of this chapter, we will present recommendations for integrated, interdisciplinary services provided by school counselors, school psychologists, and school social workers, which will be referred to as SBMHPs in this chapter, working in conjunction with educational professionals to meet the needs of LGBTQ+ students. Our discussion about the roles and responsibilities of these unique, but complimentary SBMHPs are based on professional literature reflecting current best practice in each field and our experiences working within pre-K–12 schools and is not intended to be exhaustive. The recommendations we provide in this chapter must be adapted to reflect the specific constellation of SBMHPs available within each school. However, we believe that all schools should have access to each of these service providers in order to better meet the diverse educational and wellness needs of students. Further, students' access to SBMHPs is important for educational equity, as research clearly indicates schools with more students of color, students with disabilities, and students living in poverty have less access to student services such as SBMHPs (Whitaker et al., 2019). Such disparities were highlighted by Whitaker and colleagues' (2019) national scan finding that "14 million students are in schools with police but no counselor, nurse, psychologist, or social worker" (p. 4). This disproportionality contributes to pervasive access and achievement gaps, the school-to-prison pipeline, and health disparities (Whitaker et al., 2019).

When properly funded and fully staffed, schools with a sufficient number of school counselors, school psychologists, and school social workers have the capacity to improve the educational experiences and outcomes of all students. The effectiveness of these SBMHPs hinges on appropriate student ratios, with professional organizations suggesting 250-1 for school counselors (American School Counselor Association [ASCA], 2019) and school social workers (School Social Work Association of America [SSWAA], 2010) and 500-1 for school psychologists (Griffith, 2018). School counselors, school psychologists, and school social workers have several commonalities in their training and some overlap in scope of practice yet have unique expertise and professional identities. All of the aforementioned SBMHPs operate within equity-focused, holistic, and systemic frameworks that consider the uniqueness of each student within the context of the many social systems in which they are a part. SBMHPs must be culturally humble and responsive in order to meet the unique needs of their students and families. SBMHPs have expertise to support students' educational success, emotional and behavioral health, physical wellness, and interpersonal skills, while reducing barriers that prevent schools from being socially just. Further, all three strategically provide comprehensive services through a multitiered system of supports (MTSS). Using this framework, SBMHPs use assessment and data-driven decision making to support student success through individual, small-group, and systemic interventions, in addition to working closely with families, teachers, administrators, and the greater school community.

School counselors, school psychologists, and school social workers have a minimum of a master's degree or specialists' degree (60 graduate semester hours) in their respective fields (Cowan et al., 2013). School counselors provide services through comprehensive school counseling programs, which are often developed in congruence with the ASCA National Model (2019). The ASCA National Model (2019) provides organizational strategies to define program objectives, manage and deliver services, and assess outcomes (ASCA, 2019). Through such comprehensive programs, school counselors support the academic, social, emotional, and career development of all students (ASCA, 2019). School psychologists are educational specialists who provide behavioral health services to students, while supporting teachers and families. School psychologists "typically have extensive knowledge of learning, motivation, behavior, childhood disabilities, assessment, evaluation, and school law" (Cowan et al., 2013, p. 9). In congruence with the National Association of School Psychologists (NASP) Practice Model (Skalski et al., 2015), school psychologists provide comprehensive services across 10 domains of practice (e.g., interventions and instructional support to develop academic skills; interventions and mental health services to develop social and life skills; school-wide practices to promote learning; preventive and responsive services; family-school collaboration services; diversity in development and learning). And finally, school social workers are mental health providers with expertise in social systems theory and the connections between students, their homes, schools, and the community (SSWAA, 2010). With extensive knowledge of culture, risk assessment, and social justice, school social workers are well positioned to assess and reduce barriers preventing students from being successful in school, particularly for "vulnerable populations of students that have a high risk for truancy and dropping out of school," such as youth experiencing housing and/or food insecurity, youth in the foster care system, youth in the juvenile justice system, and students experiencing domestic violence (Cowan et al., 2013, p. 9). School social workers provide coordinated services through the School Social Work Practice Model (Frey et al., 2013) to foster home-school-community linkages, emphasizing educational rights and advocacy.

These SBMHPs are well positioned to facilitate interdisciplinary and integrated-care teams that address the emotional, behavioral, social, and physical health of LGBTQ+ youth, while ensuring these youth have access to high-quality, affirmative educational experiences. With advanced training in collaboration and consultation, SBMHPs can foster communication and action among stakeholders such as teachers, administrators, school nurses, caregivers, and community-based agencies. A clear understanding of the unique roles and responsibilities of each SBMHP can help schools establish intentional policies and practices that foster affirmative school climates and holistic services for LGBTQ+ youth.

SBMHPs Working with LGBTQ+ Youth: Review of Literature

SCHOOL COUNSELORS

In recent years, authors within the field of school counseling have prioritized research on the work of school counselors with LGBTQ+ students (Singh & Kosciw, 2017). Research clearly demonstrates the value and importance of school counselor advocacy for and with LGBTQ+ students (Beck, 2018; Beck & Wikoff, 2020; Gonzalez, 2017; Goodrich, 2017; Simons & Cuadrado, 2019; Simons et al., 2017; Strear, 2017). Simons and Cuadrado (2019), for instance, explored how and why school counselors advocate on behalf of LGBTQ+ youth in schools. Findings revealed that school stakeholder expectations can influence how LGBTQ+ topics are supported (or not) in schools (Simons & Cuadrado, 2019). Additionally, participants in the study shared that efficacy as an advocate for the LGBTQ+ community is connected to school counselors' exposure and experience with the LGBTQ+ population (Simons & Cuadrado, 2019).

Gonzalez (2017) explored school counselor advocacy with 12 high school counselors in the southeastern United States at the intersection of race/ethnicity and social class for LGBT students. Gonzalez (2017) found that low-socioeconomic status can increase barriers for LGBT youth of color and they may perceive their sexual and/or gender identity as "less salient than their race and/or class identities" (p. 45). From a systems-level advocacy lens, Strear (2017) investigated strategies employed by school counselor educators and school counselors toward deconstructing heteronormativity in schools. A key finding from Strear's (2017) Delphi study was that if "school counselors approach policy reform from a strengths-based perspective, they can begin deconstructing regulatory practices" (p. 54). For example, school counselors can advocate for changes that focus on resilience and inclusivity such as document revisions that include transgender and nonbinary gender identities and diverse family systems (Strear, 2017). Further, the school counseling literature highlights characteristics and practices that can influence advocacy for and with LGBTQ+ youth in schools, including school counselor-principal relationships (Beck, 2018), professional development (Beck & Wikoff, 2020; Mason et al., 2017; Byrd & Hays, 2013), geography, and school settings (Palmer et al., 2012).

SCHOOL SOCIAL WORKERS

School social workers, too, serve as leaders and advocates for LGBTQ+ students. According to Bullard (2020), "social work practitioners are the scaffolding with which society can build up its most vulnerable populations, and the key to maintaining and enhancing the overall wellbeing of the young LGBTQ child population" (p. 31). However, empirical studies exploring the phenomenon of school social work advocacy and LGBTQ+ students are limited (Bullard, 2020). Professional documents, as outlined by the National Association of Social Workers (NASW), also contain limited language relating to the work of school social workers for and with LGBTQ+ youth (Bullard, 2020). For example, the NASW (2015) *Standards and Indicators for Cultural Competence in Social Work Practice* includes LGBTQ+ populations within a general definition of the term culture but lacks specifics to the role and function of the school social worker with this population. In addition, the *Code of Ethics of the National Association of Social Workers* (2017) lacks detailed dispositions regarding how school social workers advocate for and deliver ethical services to the LGBTQ+ student population.

Of particular relevance to the work of school social workers and LGBTQ+ youth, Bullard (2020) used a qualitative design to document the experiences of 12 school social workers. The aim of this study was to determine what perceived challenges may inhibit school social workers' ability to advocate and provide services to LGBTQ+ students (Bullard, 2020). Participants in this study demonstrated a strong commitment and dedication to serving this student population but noted specific barriers to their work (Bullard, 2020). Participants in Bullard's (2020) study noted several challenges, including limited time to engage in advocacy, the need for LGBTQ-specific education, heteronormativity within the school system, and less-affirming geographic locations. Despite these barriers, noteworthy recommendations for school social workers were provided by Mulkern (2020), proposing a multitiered system of supports for designing and implementing advocacy strategies. For example, Mulkern (2020) suggested school social workers provide education for school staff to reduce assumptions about pronouns, include pronouns in introductions, and challenge heteronormativity and cisnormativity.

SCHOOL PSYCHOLOGISTS

The NASP developed a position statement outlining eight action steps for the work of school psychologists with LGBTQ+ students (2017). Examples include implementing anti-bullying policies and practices (i.e., sexual orientation, gender identity, and gender expression), delivering LGBTQ+-focused professional development to educators and administrators, consulting with teachers to implement inclusive curriculum, establishing a Gender-Sexualities Alliance (GSA), and providing affirmative support to LGBTQ+ students and their families (NASP, 2017). Despite this guidance from NASP, both empirical and conceptual articles that address LGBTQ+ student needs within the field of school psychology are limited.

Arora and colleagues (2016) explored current (n=162) and future (n=117) school psychologists' education, training, and attitudes toward intervening on behalf of the needs of LGBTQ+ students. Arora and co-authors (2016) reported that higher levels of education and training specific to the unique needs of LGBTQ+ students correlated with improved attitudes and high levels of preparedness to work for and with these youth. In addition, the authors found that schools with a GSA resulted in increased understanding about LGBTQ+ youth (Arora et al., 2016). Authors in the field of school psychology have also discussed the ethical responsibility of school psychologists to serve as advocates for LGBTQ+ students, calling upon school psychologists to incorporate evidence-based anti-bullying and harassment strategies into their LGBTQ+ advocacy (Murphy, 2012).

SBMHP COLLABORATION

Research on the combined experiences among SBMHPs working with LGBTQ+ students is limited. National survey research conducted by GLSEN in partnership with ASCA, the American Council for School Social Work (ACSSW), and SSWAA highlighted the LGBTQ+-focused work of SBMHPs (2019). The 2019 report, *Supporting*

Safe and Healthy Schools, investigated perspectives on school climate, graduate education and training, and self-efficacy with LGBTQ+ practices, as well as efforts and inclusive practices among 1,741 SBMHPs in US schools (GLSEN et al., 2019). The study found that 87% of SBMHPs believed that it is their role to provide school-based counseling to LGBTQ+ students (GLSEN et al., 2019). This report also documented a clear need for education and training with respect to LGBTQ+ school topics and SBMHPs. For example, 37% of study participants indicated having no formal education or professional development training on working with LGBTQ youth (GLSEN et al., 2019). Based on the results of this survey, it is unclear whether SBMHPs are equipped and providing the counseling services that align with their desired role and function working with LGBTQ+ students.

Empirical research has also explored SBMHPs' experiences working with LGBTQ+ youth. A quantitative study by Smith-Millman and colleagues (2019) examined LGBTQ+- focused experiences, perceptions, and attitudes among a sample of 157 SBMHPs in one North Carolina school district. The study found that having an LGBTQ+-identified friend was associated with positive outcomes for SBMHPs, including enhanced knowledge of youth risks (e.g., mental health and physical concerns, academic difficulties) and decreased bias toward the LGBTQ+ community (Smith-Millman et al., 2019). Additionally, the study offered insights regarding SBMHP bias toward LGBTQ+ students and the impact of providers' school grade level on personal bias. For example, Smith-Millman and colleagues (2019) found that middle and high school providers held more bias toward LGBTQ+ students than providers who worked in preschool and/or elementary schools. LGBTQ+-identified SBMHPs who participated in the study reported more obstacles (e.g., resistance from administration, parents/guardians) to their work for and with LGBTQ+ students (Smith-Millman et al., 2019). Despite professional consensus regarding the critical importance of SBMHPs' advocacy for and with LGBTQ+ students, scholarship on how these professionals collaborate and coordinate an advocacy-focused plan as it relates to LGBTQ+ students is lacking.

Recommendations for SBMHPs

It is essential that SBMHPs engage in intentional and reflexive practices to meet the needs of LGBTQ+ youth in pre-K through 12th grade schools. According to ASCA (2016), NASP (2017), and SSWAA (Paceley et al., 2018), school counselors, school psychologists, and school social workers must have knowledge of diverse sexual orientations, gender identity development trajectories, and gender expressions. A commitment to LGBTQ+ youth is embedded in ethical practice for SBMHPs, as ethical codes include the promotion of safe and inclusive schools for all students (e.g., ASCA, 2016). Further, SBMHPs must engage in holistic and intersectional practices that support LGBTQ+ students at individual, small-group, and systemic levels. In order to do so effectively, we recommend that SBMHPs assess the roles and responsibilities of each SBMHP within their school, as this varies by school, district, and state. SBMHPs are encouraged to discuss and assess their professional working relationships, which may include collaboration with supportive administrators at school and district levels and the identification of potential barriers that may impede LGBTQ+ advocacy.

Once an interdisciplinary team of SBMHPs has been established and roles and responsibilities have been clearly defined, it is essential that each stakeholder reflect on their strengths, biases, assumptions, values, experiences, and level of training on sexual orientation, gender identities, and gender expressions in order to ensure they are prepared to contribute to effective, holistic, and coordinated services that meet the needs of LGBTQ+ students. Although it can be difficult, SBMHPs need to acknowledge the ways in which they contribute to oppressive systems that have silenced LGBTQ+ people and the ways in which these systems perpetuate oppression, especially in educational settings. Grounded in the works of liberatory leaders such as Freire (1970), Chan and Mak (2020) explored the "proposed liberating and empowering effects of critical reflection on collective action in LGBT individuals (study 1) and cisgender heterosexual individuals (study 2)" (p. 67) living in Hong Kong. According to Chan and Mak (2020), critical self-reflection may look different for LGBTQ+ and cisgender heterosexual individuals depending on the ways systemic oppression has shaped their lives and the ways in which individuals must take responsibility for their participation in systemic oppression and the impact of their privileged statuses. However, the findings of Chan and Mak (2020) indicated that both LGBTQ+ and cisgender heterosexual participants committed to critical self-reflection were more likely to engage in collective action for LGBTQ+ rights. Similarly, SBMHPs will benefit from structured, intentional reflection on their own identities and positionality in order to effectively contribute to more inclusive, LGBTQ+-affirming schools.

SBMHPs may also benefit from a comprehensive understanding of each national organization's recommendations for working with LGBTQ+ youth. ASCA, NASP, and SSWAA each provide professional position statements and LGBTQ+ inclusive strategies that guide the work of SBMHPs (ASCA, 2016; NASP, 2017; Paceley et al., 2018). Further, LGBTQ+ advocacy organizations such as GLSEN, Human Rights Campaign, Welcoming Schools, and Gender Spectrum provide valuable information for establishing a foundation for this work. It is important for SBMHPs to familiarize themselves with current terminology to ensure all team members are operating within the same framework. For example, Gender Spectrum defines gender as a complex interrelationship between body, identity, and social gender, and this is consistent with current scientific and professional understanding of gender across multiple disciplines. Having clarity on construct definitions and terminology helps SBMHPs promote shared professional understandings and ensures services are provided in accordance with current best practices.

We also recommend that SBMHPs engage in conversations with all stakeholders (e.g., other SBMHPs, students, teachers, administrators, families, etc.) about sexual and gender identity development and the intersection of culture and identity for LGBTQ+ students (Simons & Beck, 2019). Bronfenbrenner's Ecological Model of Human Development is a useful, holistic framework for SBMHPs working with and on behalf of LGBTQ+ people (Bronfenbrenner, 1979). Bronfenbrenner's ecological model examines individual identity development by exploring the impact of various systemic factors that include the microsystem (i.e., immediate surroundings), mesosystem (i.e., connections between microsystems), exosystem (i.e., indirect social structures), macrosystem (i.e., cultural contexts), and the chronosystem (i.e., time) (Bronfenbrenner, 1979). Adopting an ecological approach to the understanding of LGBTQ+ youth experiences can help SBMHPs see students' challenges and resiliencies from an intersectional lens (Crenshaw, 1991) and recognize a multitude of systemic factors (e.g., organizational climate, race/ethnicity, education level, policies, practices, etc.) that contribute to identity development. These focused and intentional conversations will help SBMHPs determine their professional strengths and understand their competency in advocating for and with LGBTQ+ students, as well as pinpoint areas that could benefit from more professional development and support (Smith-Millman et al., 2019).

By acknowledging the ways in which systemic factors contribute to health and educational disparities for LGBTQ+ youth, SBMHPs can establish interdisciplinary action plans to ensure the complex needs of LGBTQ+ students are being addressed. For example, SBMHPs may be responsible for ensuring that other educational stakeholders such as teachers, administrators, and support staff are aware of the health disparities of LGBTQ+ students, which may include efforts for increased school climate assessments and student health screenings. Further, SBMHPs may collaborate with administrators and school nurses to ensure that curriculum and conversations are inclusive of LGBTQ+ health and development such as affirmative and comprehensive sex education that acknowledges the disproportionate negative sexual health outcomes of LGBTQ+ youth (Centers for Disease Control and Prevention, 2018) and provides resources to support safer sex practices. Continuous assessment of school culture and climate through a holistic, ecological framework will allow SBMHPs to identify areas for advocacy and action as school and student needs change throughout time.

Coordination of Services through MTSS

Although research is limited, it is our belief that effective coordination between school counselors, school psychologists, and school social workers is essential for meeting the needs of LGBTQ+ youth. For example, the report titled *A Framework for Safe and Successful Schools* (Cowan et al., 2013) explicitly outlines coordinated efforts among the aforementioned SBMHPs in order to improve school safety and access to mental health services. Similarly, *Fostering the Whole Child: A Guide to School-Based Mental Health Professionals* (Aragon et al., 2020) details the integration of these service providers. The following section will provide guidance for SBMHPs as they engage in collective action to support the needs of LGBTQ+ youth in pre-K through 12th grade schools.

One strategy for SBMHPs to work and collaborate intentionally on behalf of LGBTQ+ students is to utilize language and educational initiatives familiar to both stakeholders and school-based mental health colleagues (Goodman-Scott et al., 2020). Connecting LGBTQ+ advocacy priorities with existing, culturally sustaining school-wide practices and data-driven frameworks is a recommended place to start. As such, an MTSS framework is likely to be familiar to most SBMHPs and is an effective way to coordinate services to meet the needs of LGBTQ+ students. According to Goodman-Scott and colleagues (2020), the MTSS framework consists of three tiers of prevention, intervention, and resources to support and address each and every student's needs. Tier 1 is composed of general education instruction, school-wide programming, and the school counseling core curriculum (ASCA, 2019). Approximately 15% of students will need additional interventions beyond the Tier 1 universal supports (Goodman-Scott et al., 2020). Thus, students may receive services through small-group instruction and counseling at the Tier 2 level. Approximately 5% of students will require more intensive interventions and Tier 3 supports, which may consist of individualized instruction, assessment, school-based counseling services, and referrals to community-based counseling and resources (Goodman-Scott et al., 2020).

As previously mentioned, SBMHPs' roles and duties might differ according to state, district, and/or building-level procedures and practices. However, every school will benefit from an interdisciplinary team that is committed to LGBTQ+ affirmative advocacy. Given that school counselors are often an LGBTQ+ student's first contact for support (Jackson, 2017) and connect with various school stakeholders (e.g., students, administrators, educators, parents/guardians) each day, we suggest that school counselors take a leadership role on interdisciplinary teams of SBMHPs (Goodman-Scott et al., 2020). This approach will strengthen coordination of services and enhance communication between team members. In the following sections, we will illustrate how the MTSS framework can be adapted for SBMHPs and their intentional work for and with LGBTQ+ students.

TIER 1—UNIVERSAL SUPPORT

School counselors are in a unique position to provide leadership to the SBMHPs team while delivering direct services to students at the Tier 1 level (Goodman-Scott et al., 2020). Through collaboration, systemic planning, and problem solving, school psychologists and school social workers also bring expertise and specialized skills to Tier 1–level intervention. First, SBMHPs can collaboratively facilitate a needs assessment or universal screening tool by collecting data on LGBTQ+ student perspectives and school experiences (Beck, 2018). For example, the Local School Climate Survey developed by GLSEN (n.d.) may be a helpful tool for assessing climate. It is advised that Tier 1 data collection also include options for disaggregating data to explore the unique needs and experiences of transgender and gender diverse students (see Gender Identity in U.S. Surveillance [GenIUSS], 2014, for guidance) and LGBTQ+ students of color. Data gathered and analyzed from school-wide surveys can strengthen team conversations regarding how to best advocate for culture and climate activities at the Tier 1 level. For example, the SBMHPs team may discover a need to advocate for assemblies and presentations that challenge heteronormativity and cisnormativity. SBMHPs can utilize the wealth of resources provided by GLSEN to foster a more inclusive school culture, including acknowledging significant events such as the Day of Silence, LGBTQ+ history month, National Coming Out Day, No–Name Calling Week, International Transgender Day of Visibility, and so on. School-wide efforts to address microaggressions and biased language may also be a necessity, as the 2019 National School Climate Survey found that 91 to 98% of LGBTQ+ students heard microaggressions at school such as using gay in a derogatory way, negative comments about masculinity/femininity, and explicit homophobic and transphobic remarks (Kosciw et al., 2020). SBMHPs can work collaboratively to develop school-wide interventions that challenge bias such as *Speak Up at School: How to Respond to Everyday Prejudice, Bias, and Stereotypes* (Willoughby, 2018). Fostering school culture that is accepting and affirming of sexual and gender diversity is essential for all students and stakeholders, and it requires an ongoing commitment to assessment and collective action.

Another component of delivering interventions at the Tier 1 level is providing classroom lessons to all youth (Goodman-Scott et al., 2020). Although all SBMHPs are equipped to facilitate such lessons, school counselors are well positioned to lead this work through the school counseling core curriculum. School counselors can draw from resources such as GLSEN, Gender Spectrum, Learning for Justice (2021), and Welcoming Schools to deliver lessons across the developmental spectrum, teaching students about sexual and gender diversity. Lessons across all three domains of the ASCA National Model (2019)—academic, social-emotional, and career—can reinforce the history (GLSEN, 2022), positive contributions, and roles of LGBTQ+ individuals. Further, it may be beneficial for school counselors to invite LGBTQ+ individuals from the community to share their lived experiences with students (Smith-Millman et al., 2019). Learning firsthand from the LGBTQ+ community may enhance empathy and increase students' comfort and efficacy to serve as a friend and ally (Smith-Millman et al., 2019). Both school social workers and school psychologists can assist the school counselor in locating local LGBTQ+ organizations and enlist guest speakers from the community who can partner with the school. If possible, it is important to compensate guest speakers for their time to establish reciprocal and sustainable partnerships that value the contributions of the community. Further, school social workers may provide brief lessons to teach students about local resources, intentionally including LGBTQ+ organizations.

In addition to student-focused climate interventions, SBMHPs can contribute to a more inclusive school climate by supporting teachers, administrators, and school staff to better understand sexual and gender diversity. Such stakeholder collaboration is essential for fostering more inclusive and affirming school climate, as more than half (52.4%) of the LGBTQ+ students participating in the 2019 National School Climate Survey reported hearing homophobic comments from teachers and school staff, and 66.7% heard transphobic comments from teachers and school staff (Kosciw et al., 2020). In addition, only 13.7% reported that school staff intervened when homophobic comments were made and only 9% reported that school staff intervened when transphobic comments were made (Kosciw et al., 2020).

Such alarming data are evidence that all stakeholders must commit to a more accepting and affirming school climate, which can position SBMHPs as leaders in this work. School climate and needs-assessment data collected by SBMHPs can be used to inform school personnel about the current school climate and provide professional development activities such as educator workshops and teacher in-service events (Beck, 2018; GLSEN, n.d.). For example, SBMHPs can facilitate opportunities for critical self-reflection to allow the adults in the building to reflect on their own biases, beliefs, and values, while creating an environment for collective action. Professional development on intersectionality (Crenshaw, 1991) can also foster conversations about how educational stakeholders can intentionally interrupt patterns of oppression and contribute to a more inclusive school climate. Additionally, raising awareness about the negative effects of gendered (e.g., "Good morning, boys and girls!") and heteronormative (e.g., "Please have your mom or dad sign your permission slip") language is an essential aspect of professional development for all educational stakeholders (Strear, 2017). SBMHPs are well positioned to facilitate these essential conversations and manage possible resistance that may arise.

TIER 2—SUPPLEMENTAL SUPPORT

In congruence with a MTSS framework, SBMHPs provide supplemental services for students who need additional support. Supplemental support most often takes place through small-group work, which will be determined primarily through ongoing needs assessments and climate surveys conducted by SBMHPs, and student, teacher, and guardian referrals. Small-group work may take several forms, which can help determine which SBMHPs are best suited to facilitate. One way to effectively utilize the unique expertise of SBMHPs is to consider supplemental supports as preventive, responsive, or systemic. School counselors can take the lead on preventive supports, with school psychologists facilitating responsive group work, and school social workers leading systemic services.

Preventive supplemental supports can be conceptualized as small-group work for students who identify as LGBTQ+ or allies and have requested additional services or opportunities to organize. For example, school counselors can support the establishment and maintenance of student-led GSAs (DePaul et al., 2009; Frank & Cannon, 2010). The presence and benefit of GSAs is well documented and commonly associated with improved educational outcomes for LGBTQ+ youth (Kosciw et al., 2020). Results of the most recent National School Climate Survey (Kosciw et al., 2020) indicated students with an established GSA within their school reported feeling safer and more connected to their school communities, as well as reporting fewer incidents of biased language, harassment, and victimization (Kosciw et al., 2020). Similarly, school counselors may expand upon traditional approaches to a GSA, which typically refer to safe, supportive environments, to include the promotion of "GSAs as political groups where LGBTQ and ally students can learn about LGBTQ history, civil rights movements, and gain skills to advocate for improved school culture" (Cerezo & Bergfeld, 2013, p. 364). Such counterspaces can provide space for students to challenge oppression and marginalization experienced by LGBTQ+ people (Cerezo & Bergfeld, 2013). In congruence with an intersectional lens (Crenshaw, 1991), it is also possible that students may benefit from small-group work with other students with similar marginalized identities, as LGBTQ+ students who had access to ethnic/cultural clubs at school "were less likely to feel unsafe due to their race/ethnicity" and "felt a greater belonging to their school community" (e.g., Truong et al., 2020a, p. xix).

Additional preventive, supplemental support may include psychoeducational group work designed to foster resilience for LGBTQ+ students. For example, Craig (2013) outlined the Affirmative Supportive Safe and Empowering Talk (ASSET) group counseling model for LGBTQ+ youth. This small-group curriculum was designed to foster resilience and moderate stress of marginalization (i.e., minority stress theory) (Craig, 2013). Preliminary analysis of the ASSET model resulted in evidence of significant improvements in participants' self-esteem and proactive coping abilities (n = 263) (Craig, 2013). According to Craig, the eight-week, ASSET model is guided by themes of LGBTQ+ identity development, hope, and the identification of stressors, coping strategies, and personal strengths.

Some LGBTQ+ students may experience barriers preventing them from being successful in school or leading to behavioral health concerns. For these students, it may be helpful for school psychologists to facilitate responsive group work with specialized objectives. For example, if a number of teacher referrals have been identified for LGBTQ+ students indicating these students are falling behind academically, school psychologists can create a small group to discuss the unique and common challenges faced by these students, while offering academic interventions to help them be more successful in school. Similarly, if it comes to the attention of the SBMHPs team that a number of LGBTQ+ students are experiencing higher levels of anxiety or depression, for example, a small group could be created to help LGBTQ+ students acknowledge the effects of homophobia and transphobia on behavioral health (NASP, 2017). School psychologists are well positioned to support students in establishing cognitive and behavioral strategies to reduce distressing symptoms and improve well-being, while fostering universality among small groups of students to normalize that these experiences are common and often the result of navigating oppressive social systems such as schools.

Small groups facilitated by school social workers may also be a valuable resource for addressing LGBTQ+ students' needs pertaining to their families or other social systems. For example, school social workers may find it helpful to facilitate small groups with students that are preparing to or have recently come out to their families and/or friends. School social workers' expertise in systems work can support LGBTQ+ students with navigating conversations and fostering more effective communication with the various systems of which they are a part. According to Mulkern (2020), school social workers may also facilitate restorative circles to address harassment and bullying that may occur in order to facilitate learning and restoration, rather than punitive disciplinary practices that may lead to further turmoil.

TIER 3—INTENSIFIED SUPPORT

Through a MTSS framework, it is anticipated that approximately 5% of students will need individualized support in addition to Tier 1 and Tier 2 services (Goodman-Scott et al., 2020). Although this may be an accurate estimate within the student body as a whole, LGBTQ+ students face unique challenges, and SBMHPs must be prepared to address their individualized needs. In addition to the complex identity development occurring in childhood and adolescence, LGBTQ+ youth are navigating a world that does not always reflect their identities. LGBTQ+ children and adolescents are at higher risk of discrimination, stigma, harassment, and victimization than heterosexual and cisgender youth (Zaza et al., 2016). Further, LGBTQ+ youth are constantly negotiating heteronormative and cisnormative spaces, exposing them to continuous stressors. The 2015 Youth Risk Behavior Survey conducted by the Centers for Disease Control and Prevention (CDC) illustrated that LGBTQ+ youth are at elevated risk for adverse health consequences such as sexual assault, dating violence, substance use, hopelessness, and suicide-related behaviors (Frieden et al., 2016; Zaza et al., 2016). Thus, LGBTQ+ youth are more likely to need behavioral health services to support their safe and successful transition into adulthood.

School counselors are frequently the first SBMHP to come in contact with LGBTQ+ students (Jackson, 2017), therefore, school counselors must be prepared to provide short-term, culturally responsive, behavioral health services. Utilizing a strengths-based, student-centered approach, school counselors can provide 1-1 counseling to learn more about the complex identities of each student, their lived experiences, and pertinent thoughts, feelings, and behaviors that may be causing distress or inhibiting wellness. School counselors are also well positioned to identify barriers that may be preventing students from being healthy, happy, and successful. Should the school counselor determine that a student is in need of longer-term counseling services, they may use a warm handoff to refer the student to the school psychologist.

Given their expertise in educational assessments, the school psychologist may determine that an educational or behavioral health assessment is warranted to determine individualized counseling goals. School psychologists can provide affirmative counseling services to support students while they are at school (NASP, 2017). Considering the caseloads of both school psychologists and school counselors, it is possible the SBMHP team may also determine that an individual student would benefit most from a more consistent, community-based mental health provider with expertise in sexual and gender identity development. In which case, school social workers are well positioned to connect students with community-based behavioral health providers. "Creating, developing, and sustaining partnerships with LGBTQ+ affirming community-based organizations (CBOs) allows school social workers to connect students to affirming and culturally responsive supports both on campus and in the community" (Mulkern, 2020, para 15). School social workers may also need to ensure that individual LGBTQ+ students have their basic needs met, particularly for students who may be displaced due to family turmoil. Similarly, school social workers may take the lead in assessing for and responding to acute student crises, while ensuring students have access to appropriate, consistent behavioral health supports.

FAMILY/COMMUNITY ENGAGEMENT

Connections between schools, families, and the community are essential components to support the well-being of LGBTQ+ students, and intentional efforts to engage family and community are necessary for fostering an inclusive school culture. With expertise in home-school-community linkages, school social workers are well positioned to take a lead on family and community engagement within interdisciplinary teams of SBMHPs (Frey et al., 2013). Although all SBMHPs must maintain a network of LGBTQ+ affirmative community-based partners, school social workers can take a leadership role to ensure these connections are well established, current, and truly affirmative for LGBTQ+ youth and families. School social workers can also develop an accessible and non-stigmatizing referral mechanism so LGBTQ+ students and families know how to access community-based providers. Similarly, school social workers may house relevant resources and referrals that are easily accessible for LGBTQ+ youth and families.

In addition to community connections, SBMHPs must commit to family education and outreach in order to ensure that LGBTQ+ youth have the support they need outside of school. With support from the SBMHPs team, school social workers can provide opportunities for caregivers (e.g., parents, guardians, family members) to partner with the school on LGBTQ+ affirmative events and celebrations as a way of communicating that the school supports, affirms, and empowers LGBTQ+ people. For example, the SBMHPs team can host an Allyship in Action event during Solidarity Week (GLSEN) to educate the school community about LGBTQ+ solidarity, allyship, and advocacy. With leadership from school social workers, the SBMHPs team may actively recruit LGBTQ+ caregivers and community members to participate in other school events such as career and college exploration days. Further, school social workers may offer educational groups for caregivers about sexual and gender diversity, identity development, and caring for LGBTQ+ youth. Such proactive family and community engagement is integral to an LGBTQ+ affirmative school culture that supports the needs of LGBTQ+ students.

Implications and Future Directions

As previously mentioned, an interdisciplinary team of SBMHPs is important for meeting the diverse educational and holistic health needs of LGBTQ+ youth. However, research remains limited regarding the roles, responsibilities, and actions of SBMHPs working with LGBTQ+ youth. It is clear the professional values of SBMHPs align with LGBTQ+ affirmative advocacy (ASCA, 2016; NASP, 2017; Paceley et al., 2018), and yet, a review of school counseling, school psychology, and school social work literature elucidates a substantive gap and an urgent need for LGBTQ+ affirmative research and practice. Moreover, future research is needed to explicate how SBMHPs can contribute to improved educational outcomes and reduced health disparities for LGBTQ+ youth. Research exploring the unique and collaborative efforts of SBMHPs will help practitioners structure their own advocacy efforts, ultimately contributing to improved outcomes for LGBTQ+ youth.

In addition to increased research and more intentional practice, SBMHPs must advocate for more LGBTQ+ affirmative policies and practices with school boards and school-, district-, and state-level administrators. At the school level, SBMHPs must advocate for nondiscriminatory school policies such as discrimination and bullying policies that explicitly name sexual and gender diversity and affirmative dress codes. School-level advocacy is also necessary so students have access to safe and affirmative spaces, such as bathrooms and locker rooms, and inclusive physical education and extracurricular activities. State-level legislative advocacy is also necessary as very few US states (i.e., California, Colorado, Illinois, New Jersey, Oregon) require the inclusion of LGBTQ+ curricula; in fact, the majority of states either provide no guidance or have explicit discriminatory laws prohibiting LGBTQ+ inclusivity in curricula (GLSEN, 2020). Even more concerning, approximately 60% of the United States does not include sexual orientation or gender identity in school discrimination laws and lack state-level policies regarding LGBTQ+ students (GLSEN, 2020). The collective efforts and expertise of SBMHPs make future policy advocacy a possibility and priority for fostering more affirmative schools.

Conclusion

In order to fully meet the needs of LGBTQ+ youth in pre-K–12 schools, it is essential that SBMHPs begin identifying their unique roles and responsibilities while establishing strategies to collaborate within an interdisciplinary team. Professional leadership and advocacy are necessary to ensure each school's team of SBMHPs are competent, confident, and informed to provide coordinated, inclusive services for LGBTQ+ students, while acknowledging and addressing the unique considerations for both sexual and gender diverse students. Through a strengths-based and intersectional approach, SBMHPs have the capacity to support the educational and holistic health needs of LGBTQ+ students. In particular, these student service providers may be more effective when they establish an interdisciplinary team that is committed to critical self-reflection, actionable advocacy, and coordinated service delivery through a multitiered system of supports framework. Relying on their unique and shared professional values, knowledge, and skills, SBMHPs can develop an LGBTQ+ affirmative foundation of inclusive policies and practices that make pre-K–12 schools more welcoming and effective for LGBTQ+ students and families.

KEY KNOWLEDGE FOR STUDENTS

- Learn risk and protective factors of LGBTQ+ youth in pre-K–12 schools
- Learn roles and responsibilities of educational stakeholders working with and for LGBTQ+ youth in pre-K–12 schools
- Gain key knowledge about the importance of an interdisciplinary approach to strengthen advocacy with and for LGBTQ+ youth in pre-K–12 schools
- Learn strategies for establishing an integrated, holistic, and interdisciplinary team to support LGBTQ+ youth in pre-K–12 schools
- Develop LGBTQ+ affirmative interventions through an interdisciplinary and multitiered system of supports framework

RECOMMENDATIONS FOR PRACTITIONERS AND PROFESSIONALS

- SBMHPs are encouraged to commit to intentional, critical self-reflection and competency assessments regarding sexual and gender diversity
- SBMHPs will benefit from interdisciplinary dialogue focused on identifying strengths, limitations, roles, and responsibilities of each SBMHP within a school in order to develop a coordinated and comprehensive LGBTQ+ affirmative advocacy plan
- SBMHPs can utilize a multitiered system of supports and ecological framework to guide actionable LGBTQ+ advocacy efforts
- Although recommendations have been provided, the configuration, roles, and responsibilities of SBMHPs will vary from school to school, and it is important to assign leadership tasks to ensure advocacy efforts are delivered with fidelity

References

American School Counselor Association. (2019). *ASCA national model: A framework for school counseling programs* (4th ed.). https://www.schoolcounselor.org/school-counselors-members/asca-national-model

American School Counselor Association. (2016). *The professional school counselor and LGBTQ youth*. ASCA Position Statements. https://schoolcounselor.org/asca/media/asca/Position Statements/PS_LGBTQ.pdf

Aragon, J., Arellano, L. M., Brazzel, P., Cardenas, J., Catalde, T., Cottrill, M., Giambona, M., Manos, S., McMillian, K., Parsons, J., Peevy, J., Pianta, R., Dalman-Schroeder, M., Sopp, T. J., Strear, M., Thomas, S., Topalian, J., Uresti, A., Weglarz, L. . . . Zavalza, O. (2020). *Fostering the whole child: A guide to school-based mental health professionals*. California Association of School Psychologists. https://casponline.org/pdfs/spw/SBMHP%20Guide%20Book%20v4.pdf

Arora, P. G., Kelly, J., & Goldstein, T. R. (2016). Current and future school psychologists' preparedness to work with LGT students: Role of education and gay-straight alliances. *Psychology in the Schools, 53*(7), 722–735. https://doi.org/10.1002/pits.21942

Beck, M. J. (2018). Lead by example: A phenomenological study of school counselor-principal team experiences with LGBT students. *Professional School Counseling, 21*(1), 1–13. https://doi.org/10.1177/ 2156759X18793838

Beck, M. J., & Wikoff, H. D. (2020). Professional development is really key: Experiences of school counselors engaging in professional development focused on LGBTQ youth. *Professional School Counseling, 24*(1), 1–11. https://doi.org/ 10.1177/2156759X20952062

Bronfenbrenner, U. (1979). *The ecology of human development*. Harvard University Press.

Bullard, J. R. (2020). *School social workers and perceived barriers when providing services to LGBTQ children* [Doctoral dissertation, Walden University]. https://scholarworks.waldenu.edu/dissertations/9539

Byrd, R., & Hays, D. G. (2013). Evaluating a safe space training for school counselors and trainees using a randomized control group design. *Professional School Counseling, 17*(1), 20–31. https://doi.org/10.1177/2156759X0001700103

Centers for Disease Control and Prevention. (2018). *HIV and youth*. https://www.cdc.gov/hiv/group/age/youth/index.html

Cerezo, A., & Bergfeld, J. (2013). Meaningful LGBTQ inclusion in schools: The importance of diversity representation and counterspaces. *Journal of LGBT Issues in Counseling, 7*(4), 355–371. https://doi.org/10.1080/15538605.2013.839341

Chan, R. C., & Mak, W. W. S. (2020). Liberating and empowering effects of critical reflection on collective action in LGBT and cisgender heterosexual individuals. *American Journal of Community Psychology, 65*(1–2), 63–77. https://doi.org/10.1002/ajcp.12350

Cowan, K. C., Vaillancourt, K., Rossen, E., & Pollitt, K. (2013). *A framework for safe and successful schools* [Brief]. National Association of School Psychologists.

Craig, S. L. (2013). Affirmative supportive safe and empowering talk (ASSET): Leveraging the strengths and resiliencies of sexual minority youth in school-based groups. *Journal of LGBT Issues in Counseling, 7*, 372–386. https://doi:10.1080/15538605.2013.839342

Crenshaw, K. (1991). Mapping the margins: Intersectionality, identity, politics, and violence against women of color. *Stanford Law Review, 43*(6), 1241–1299. https://doi.org/10.2307/1229039

DePaul, J., Walsh, M. E., & Dam, U. C. (2009). The role of school counselors in addressing sexual orientation in schools. *Professional School Counseling, 12*(4), 300–308.

Frank, D. A., & Cannon, E. P. (2010). Queer theory as pedagogy in counselor education: A framework for diversity training. *Journal of LGBT Issues in Counseling, 4*(1), 18–31. https://doi:10.1080/15538600903552731

Freire, P. (1970). *Pedagogy of the oppressed*. Penguin Group.

Frey, A. J., Alvarez, M. E., Dupper, D. R., Sabatino, C. A., Lindsey, B. C., Raines, J. C., Streeck, F., McInerney, A., & Norris, M. A. (2013). *School social work practice model*. School Social Work Association of America. http://sswaa.org/displaycommon.cfm?an=1&subarticlenbr=459

Frieden, T. R., Jaffe, H. W., Cono, J., Richards, C. L., & Iademarco, M. F. (2016). Sexual identity, sex of sexual contacts, and health-related behaviors among students in grades 9–12—United States and Selected Sites, 2015. MMWR Center for Surveillance, Epidemiology, and Laboratory Services, Centers for Disease Control and Prevention, 65, 1–202.

Gay, Lesbian and Straight Education Network. (2016). *Educational exclusion: Drop out, push out, and the school-to-prison pipeline among LGBTQ youth*. https://www.glsen.org/sites/default/files/2020-06/Separation%20and%20Stigma%20-%20Full%20Report.pdf

Gay, Lesbian and Straight Education Network. (2019). *Respect for all: Policy recommendations to support LGBTQ students: A guide for district and school leaders*. https://www.glsen.org/sites/default/files/2019-10/GLSEN-Respect-For-All-Policy-Resource.pdf

Gay, Lesbian and Straight Education Network. (2020, August). *Policy maps*. https://www.glsen.org/policy-maps

Gay, Lesbian and Straight Education Network. (n.d.). *Local school climate survey*. http://localsurvey.glsen.org

Gay, Lesbian and Straight Education Network, American School Counselor Association, American Council for School Social Work, & School Social Work Association of America. (2019). *Supporting safe and healthy schools for lesbian, gay, bisexual, transgender, and queer students: A national survey of school counselors, social workers, and psychologists*. GLSEN.

Gender Identity in U.S. Surveillance Group. (2014). *Best practices for asking questions to identify transgender and other gender minority respondents on population-based surveys*. J. L. Herman (Ed.). Williams Institute.

GLSEN. (2022). *LGBTQ history*. http://live-glsen-website.pantheonsite.io/lgbtq-history

Gonzalez, M. (2017). Advocacy for and with LGBT students: An examination of high school counselor experiences. *Professional School Counseling, 20*, 38–46. https://doi.org/10.5330/1096-2409-20.1a.38

Goodman-Scott, E., Betters-Bubon, J., Olsen, J., & Donohue, P. (2020). *Making MTSS work*. American School Counselor Association.

Goodrich, K. M. (2017). Exploring school counselors' motivations to work with LGBTQQI students in schools: A Q methodology study. *Professional School Counseling, 20*(1a), 5–12. https://doi.org/10. 5330/1096-2409-20.1a.5

Greytak, E. A., Kosciw, J. G., & Diaz, E. M. (2009). *Harsh realities: The experiences of transgender youth in our nation's schools*. GLSEN.

Griffith, M. (2018). What is the cost of providing students with adequate psychological support. NASP. https://www.nasponline.org/research-and-policy/policy-matters-blog/what-is-the-cost-of-providing-students-with-adequate-psychological-support

Hanson, T., Zhang, G., Cerna, R., Stern, A., & Austin, G. (2019). *Understanding the experiences of LGBTQ students in California*. WestEd.

Jackson, K. (2017). Supporting LGBTQ students in high school for the college transition: The role of school counselors. *Professional School Counseling, 20*(1a), 21–28. https://doi.org/10.5330/1096-2409-20.1a.21

Kosciw, J. G., Clark, C. M., Truong, N. L., & Zongrone, A. D. (2020). *The 2019 national school climate survey: The experiences of lesbian, gay, bisexual, transgender, and queer youth in our nation's schools*. GLSEN.

Kosciw, J. G., & Cullen, M. K. (2002). *The GLSEN 2001 national school climate survey: The school-related experiences of our nation's lesbian, gay, bisexual, and transgender youth*. GLSEN.

Learning for Justice. (2021). *Gender and sexual identity*. https://www.learningforjustice.org/topics/gender-sexual-identity

Mason, E. C. M., Springer, S. I., & Pugliese, A. (2017). Staff development as a school climate intervention to support transgender and gender nonconforming students: An integrated research partnership model for school counselors and counselor educators. *Journal of LGBT Issues in Counseling, 11*(4), 301–318. https://doi.org/10.1080/15538605.2017.1380552

Movement Advancement Project and GLSEN. (2017). *Separation and stigma: Transgender youth and school facilities*. https://www.lgbtmap.org/transgender-youth-school

Mulkern, P. (2020). *Supporting queer youth in schools using a multi-tiered approach*. https://www.sswaa.org/post/supporting-queer-youth-in-schools-using-an-multi-tiered-approach

Murphy, H. E. (2012). Improving the lives of students, gay and straight alike: Gay-straight alliances and the role of school psychologists. *Psychology in the Schools, 49*(9), 883–891. https://doi.org/10.1002.pits.21643

National Association of School Psychologists. (2017). *Safe and supportive schools for LGBTQ+ youth* (Position statement).

National Association of Social Workers. (2015). *Standards and indicators for cultural competence in social work practice*. NASW Press.

National Association of Social Workers. (2017). *Code of ethics of the National Association of Social Workers*. NASW Press.

Paceley, M. S., Goffnett, J., & Wagaman, M. A. (2018). *Promoting the well-being of LGBTQIA+ students*. School Social Work Association of America.

Palmer, N. A., Kosciw, J. G., & Bartkiewicz, M. J. (2012). *Strengths and silences: The experiences of lesbian, gay, bisexual and transgender students in rural and small-town schools*. GLSEN.

School Social Work Association of America. (2010). *Gay, lesbian, transgender, bisexual and questioning youth* (position statement). https://aab82939-3e7b-497d-8f30-a85373757e29.filesusr.com/ugd/486e55_bdd2e14be640470d9d125c09026ec24e.pdf

Simons, J. D., & Beck, M. J. (2020). Sexual and gender minority identity development: Recommendations for school counselors. *Journal of School Counseling, 18*(20). http://www.jsc.montana.edu/articles/v18n20.pdf

Simons, J. D., & Cuadrado, M. (2019). Narratives of school counselors regarding advocacy for LGBT students. *Professional School Counseling, 22*(1), 1–9. https://doi.org/10.1177/2156659X19861529

Simons, J. D., Hutchison, B., & Bahr, M. (2017). School counselor advocacy for lesbian, gay, and bisexual students: Intentions and practice. *Professional School Counseling, 20*, 29–37. https://doi.org/10.5330/1096-2409-20.1a.29

Singh, A. A., & Kosciw, J. G. (2017). School counselors transforming schools for lesbian, gay, bisexual, transgender, and queer (LGBTQ) students. *Professional School Counseling, 20*(1a), 1–4.

Skalski, A. K., Minke, K., Rossen, E., Cowan, K. C., Kelly, J., Armistead, R., & Smith, A. (2015). NASP Practice Model Implementation Guide. National Association of School Psychologists.

Smith-Millman, M., Harrison, S. E., Pierce, L., & Flaspohler, P. D. (2019). Ready, willing, and able: Predictors of school mental health providers' competency in working with LGBTQ youth. *Journal of LGBT Youth, 16*(4), 380–402. https://doi.org/10.1080/19361653.20191580759

Strear, M. M. (2017). Forecasting an inclusive future: School counseling strategies to deconstruct educational heteronormativity. *Professional School Counseling, 20*, 47–56. https://doi.org/10.5330/10962409-20.1a.47

Truong, N. L., Zongrone, A. D., & Kosciw, J. G. (2020a). *Erasure and resilience: The experiences of LGBTQ students of color, black LGBTQ youth in U.S. schools*. GLSEN.

Truong, N. L., Zongrone, A. D., & Kosciw, J. G. (2020b). *Erasure and resilience: The experiences of LGBTQ students of color, Asian American and pacific islander LGBTQ youth in U.S. schools*. GLSEN.

Whitaker, A., Torres-Guillén, S., Morton, M., Jordan, H., Coyle, S., Mann, A., & Sun, W-L. (2019). *Cops and no counselors: How the lack of school mental health staff is harming students*. https://www.aclu.org/report/cops-and-no-counselors

Willoughby, B. (2018). *Speak up at school: How to respond to everyday prejudice, bias, and stereotypes*. Southern Poverty Law Center.

Zaza, S., Kann, L., & Barrios, L. C. (2016). Lesbian, gay, and bisexual adolescents population estimate and prevalence of health behaviors. *Journal of American Medical Association, 316*(22), 2355–2356.

Zongrone, A. D., Truong, N. L., & Kosciw, J. G. (2020a). *Erasure and resilience: The experiences of LGBTQ students of color, Native American, American Indian, and Alaska native LGBTQ youth in U.S. schools*. GLSEN.

Zongrone, A. D., Truong, N. L., & Kosciw, J. G. (2020b). *Erasure and resilience: The experiences of LGBTQ students of color, Latinx LGBTQ youth in U.S. schools*. GLSEN.

CHAPTER 8

Serving LGBTQ+ Students at University and College Campuses

Jan E. Estrellado, PhD, & Saeromi Kim, PhD

Lesbian, gay, bisexual, transgender, queer, intersex, questioning, and asexual (LGBTQ+) college students reflect the diversity of the broader LGBTQ+ population in the United States, but the context of post-secondary education highlights special challenges. College students from diverse sexual orientations and gender identities are at particularly high risk for negative health outcomes, social isolation, and attrition. This chapter focuses on addressing four main topics: (1) the types of challenges LGBTQ+ college students face, or issues of special concern for this population that clinicians ought to know, especially as their sexual orientation and gender identity intersect with other important identities; (2) the need for providing LGBTQ-affirming services on college campuses; (3) the gaps in research concerning LGBTQ+ college students; and (4) clinical considerations and policy recommendations for providers working in college counseling centers.

Challenges Facing LGBTQ+ College Students

MENTAL HEALTH DISPARITIES

The mental health outcomes of LGBTQ+ college students are intimately linked to the structural and institutional forces with which they interact. Minority stress theory (MST) (Brooks, 1981; Meyer, 2003) is a framework that posits health disparities as sequelae of the chronic, systemic discrimination these populations face (rather than pathology inherent in the populations). Initially studied in lesbian, gay, and bisexual populations, MST has since been researched in gender diverse and transgender populations (Lefevor et al., 2019; Tan et al., 2019). MST is a useful frame for understanding the impact of interpersonal discrimination, familial rejection, and systemic bias LGBTQ+ students face (e.g., lack of visible LGBTQ+ faculty, institutional failure to accurately capture sexual orientation and gender identity data).

By the time LGBTQ+ students enter college, they may have already encountered discrimination. For example, in one study, more than half of transgender students in K–12 settings reported being verbally harassed, and almost one in five transgender students said that they were physically harassed (James et al., 2016). This trend appears to continue in college. LGBQ college students across gender identities were almost twice as likely (23% vs. 12%) to report verbal harassment as heterosexual college students (Rankin et al., 2010). In the same study, the majority of transmasculine respondents (87%) and transfeminine respondents (82%) reported being harassed based on their gender identity (versus 20% of men and 24% of women).

The mental health effects of discrimination, consistent with MST, are clear. Woodford and colleagues (2014) found that sexual minority college students overall were more likely to report moderate to high anxiety and depression symptoms when compared to their heterosexual counterparts. In addition, sexual minority college students' exposure to subtle forms of discrimination in the environment were associated with moderate to high rates of anxiety and depression symptoms. Bisexual students may be an especially vulnerable group. Bisexual college students, especially women, had an increased risk of using alcohol, tobacco, and other drugs in college and also experienced greater consequences related to their substance use (Kerr et al., 2014).

Given that suicide is the second leading cause of death among college students in general (Lamis & Lester, 2011), suicide risk among LGBTQ+ populations is worthy of examination. Prevalence rates of suicidality among all segments of the transgender population is staggeringly high. Approximately 41% of transgender people reported having made a suicide attempt in their lifetime (Grant et al., 2011), compared to 0.6% of all adults in the United States (Substance Abuse and Mental Health Services Administration, 2018). Among transgender college students, increased suicide rates in one study were predicted by race, household income, disability, and being denied access to appropriate housing or bathroom facilities due to their transgender status (Seelman, 2016). Russell and colleagues (2011) provided clinical recommendations to improve university social environments to reduce bias and prejudice in order to decrease the risk of suicidality for LGBT college students.

LGBTQ+ college students may also be at increased risk for suicidality. In one study, gay, lesbian, and bisexual college students reported more depression, feelings of loneliness, and fewer reasons for living compared to their heterosexual peers (Westefeld et al., 2001). In another study, gay, lesbian, bisexual, and questioning students were more likely than their heterosexual counterparts to say that they had thought about or attempted suicide (Oswalt & Wyatt, 2011).

The research literature suggests that LGBTQ+ students, starting in K–12 settings and continuing into post-secondary educational environments, face increased exposure to interpersonal and systemic discrimination (Fields & Wotipka, 2020). Increased rates of mental health symptoms, including depression (Lindquist et al., 2017) and suicidality (Fulginiti et al., 2020), tend to be associated with exposure to these various forms of discrimination, providing further support for MST.

IDENTITY DEVELOPMENT AS A MAJOR TASK OF LATE ADOLESCENCE AND EMERGING ADULTHOOD

For most traditionally aged students, college is a time of identity development and values exploration (Chickering & Reisser, 1993). Many students, especially if they move away from home for the first time, clarify their worldviews as separate from or congruent with their families of origin. In college, students are exposed to a diversity of ideas and worldviews that can be vastly different from those with which they were raised. A theoretical perspective on student identity development suggests that clarification of internally driven values allows students to delve into deeper meaning-making processes and may buffer against the various challenges of campus life (Abes & Jones, 2004). Identity development is a hallmark of a higher education experience. For LGBTQ+ students, a strengthened sense of sexual orientation and gender identity can be both powerful and painful, much of which is determined by the level of support their educational environment and institutional culture promote.

Acknowledging one's sexual orientation and/or gender identity to self and/or disclosing to others in college is often regarded as milestones in one's identity development process. While verbal disclosures of coming out may impact white versus ethnic minority students differently, some college students find coming out is helpful for naming oneself, particularly in relation to others and their environments (Villicana et al., 2016). Coming out may be associated with developmental growth, particularly if coming out was a stressful process that was overcome (Vaughan & Waehler, 2010); and may be one avenue for self-acceptance, which ideally is enhanced by access to visible resources that affirm one's identities (Stevens, 2004). Coming out also allows for opportunities for connection with others who identify similarly and/or who may have similar sociopolitical values.

Navigating sexual orientation and gender identities in the context of other salient identities often presents challenges to LGBTQ+ college students. For example, a genderqueer, transfeminine, nonbinary student who also identifies as Brazilian American would likely understand her gender identity in the context of being Brazilian American and her ethnicity in the context of her genderqueer identity. This has implications for how the student interacts in educational spaces. What are the various ways in which her gender, sexual orientation, and ethnic identities, as well as her immigration status, might impact how she is heard, acknowledged, or possibly dismissed or silenced in a gender studies class? An ethnic studies class? An organic chemistry class? How might faculty and her peers respond to her? Affirmation and acknowledgment of the student's multiple identities need to be approached with complexity and nuance by faculty, staff, and health care providers on campus to support her well-being and promote positive educational outcomes. The best-case scenario for this student would be that she receives validation, support, and access to resources, not only in health care provision, but in all aspects of student life (student affairs, residence life, student organizations, and student services) to support her academic success at the university.

ACCEPTANCE AND VISIBILITY OF LGBTQ+ STUDENTS ON CAMPUS

Acceptance, acknowledgment, and affirmation are experiences college students hope to find and many higher educational institutions aim to provide, as there is recognition that these experiences improve psychological well-being and educational outcomes.

In a study of 1,400 college students at a diverse, urban research university, a sense of belonging was closely associated with retention (Han et al., 2017), and retention stakes may be particularly high for students from diverse sexual orientations and gender identities.

LGBTQ+ students' beliefs about their campus environment affect their sense of belonging at the university. Tetreault and colleagues (2013) found that LGBTQ+ students who felt they could disclose their sexual orientation and gender identity, as well as students who found support after their disclosure, were more likely to report positive perceptions about their campus climate. LGBTQ+ students are likely to assess where they are physically and emotionally safe across the university campus: classrooms, libraries, student organizations, student support services, health centers, and residential facilities. Their level of safety would likely have a direct impact on their ability to focus on academic and social support endeavors.

How do LGBTQ+ students respond when they experience rejection? Fine's (2011) qualitative study on decreasing heterosexism and homophobia on college campuses suggests that LGB students are likely to minimize their sexual identities and the discrimination they encounter. Results from Fine's (2011) analysis showed that participants attempted to downplay the heterosexism and homophobia they encountered, in part because the bias they faced was normalized in their daily lives at their universities.

In response to challenges they face on college campuses, some LGBTQ+ students may develop a sense of resilience. More recent studies suggest that while barriers to academic and social belonging still occur, LGBTQ+ students may have protective factors that buffer the effects of discrimination and bias. In one study (Woodford et al., 2018), resilience was associated with lower risk for suicide attempts among cisgender LGBQ students who experienced microaggressions; a sense of pride was related to lower levels of depression. While transgender students reported higher rates of experiencing violence and feeling less safe on campus than their cisgender counterparts, there were no significant differences in their academic performances (Messman & Leslie, 2019). While these studies highlight some of the strengths LGBTQ+ college students engage in response to various challenges in their university settings, the costs of having to utilize these strengths is less understood in the research.

INTERSECTIONALITY AND MARGINALIZED IDENTITIES

Holding multiple marginalized identities often requires carrying multiple burdens. Not being [x identity] "enough," being hypervisible or invisible, feeling silenced or tokenized, and being asked to solve institutional diversity problems are some of the powerful ways that students from minority groups remain at the margins. For LGBTQ+ college students with multiple marginalized identities (including, but not limited to, students of color, international students, students with disabilities, and first-generation college students), these dynamics can be even more challenging due to potential experiences of rejection, lack of safety and support, and shaming from within one's own communities. The places from which students may seek support (an LGBTQ+ campus center, for example) might also be where students experience oppression. For example, a mostly white LGBTQ+ campus center staff that has difficulty understanding and/or talking openly about issues of race can alienate LGBTQ+ students of color by avoiding conversations related to race, being defensive when given race-related feedback from LGBTQ+ students of color, or expecting LGBTQ+ students of color to be responsible for discussing race in the center.

The experience of living at the intersections of multiple marginalized identities can have significant costs, including increased risk for being a target of violence. In a study of sexual assault victimization of college students in the past year (Coulter et al., 2017), transgender students were more likely to experience sexual assault than cisgender students and Black transgender students were at a particularly high risk for sexual assault. Their predicted probabilities of sexual assault were 57.7% (versus 2.6 to 2.9% for cisgender heterosexual Asian and Pacific Islander and white men).

The Need for Affirming LGBTQ+ College Student Services

As aforementioned, higher education affords both constraints and potential protections for LGBTQ+ individuals. The following section highlights these opportunities and challenges in areas such as student support services, faculty and peer relationships, and student health and counseling services.

STUDENT SUPPORT SERVICES

Higher education institutions in the United States strive and take pride in building inclusive, accessible, and active learning environments for their students. Student support services aim to increase college students' academic, emotional, and social connection to their campuses, consistent with the larger institutional goal of improving student retention and successful degree completion (Ciobanu, 2013). Throughout the past few decades, college campuses have gradually built in particular protections and supports for an increasingly diverse student body, which has benefitted LGBTQ+ students in many ways. Nevertheless, these support systems vary widely across the nation in relation to institution type (e.g., four-year, two-year, private, public) as well as geopolitical and sociohistorical contexts that impact state legislation, funding sources, board of regents, and other significant sustainability factors.

As previously mentioned, the significance of the educational context in shaping, both positively and negatively, LGBTQ+ students' well-being and success on college campuses is well documented. The presence and perception of affirming campus services and policies are linked to positive mental health and academic outcomes among sexual and gender minority college students (Goldberg et al., 2018; Rankin et al., 2010; Woodford et al., 2015). Alternatively, perceptions and experiences of hostile campus climates are linked to negative outcomes such as increased experiences of harassment, academic disengagement, and lower levels of identity disclosure, which in turn impact the ability to access campus and community support (Garvey & Rankin, 2015; Garvey et al., 2018; Woodford & Kulick, 2015).

Many relevant areas exist for LGBTQ+ student support services: Explicit nondiscrimination policies that include both sexual orientation and gender identity, campus resource centers and cocurricular campus programming, health and mental health access and competencies, LGBTQ+ inclusion in the classroom, and broader efforts to educate the campus community to increase awareness and acceptance of gender diversity and sexual minority experiences. The Campus Pride Index (https://www.campusprideindex.org) likely provides the most up-to-date and comprehensive accounting of which support services are offered by distinct US colleges.

Some glaring disparities are evident in institutional support systems for LGBTQ+ students in community colleges and for transgender students on most campuses. Students who attend two-year institutions make up more than a third of all undergraduates in the United States (National Center for Education Statistics, 2019). However, Garvey and colleagues (2015) posit that despite progressive efforts by community colleges to emphasize diversity and inclusion practices for historically marginalized and underrepresented populations, these efforts have not been extended to include LGBTQ+ students. LGBTQ+ community college students may perceive classroom climates as noninclusive (curricular) and largely indifferent (faculty interactions), which in turn is closely related to students' overall perception of an uninviting campus climate. Regarding negative or unsupportive faculty interactions, the authors suggest that inadequate investment in faculty retention and development in community colleges may contribute to their faculty's general disinterest or inability (due to scarcity of resources and time) to thoughtfully integrate LGBTQ+ curricular content and related issues in the classroom.

Transgender inclusive policies and services vary widely among college campuses. Few offer the means to change names in nonlegal college documents, comprehensive and trans-inclusive health care insurance policies, or discrimination policies that specifically protect trans students. Even in more resourced settings, most continue to operate at a bare minimum approach (Goldberg et al., 2018). For example, whereas more campuses are starting to offer gender inclusive bathrooms, they exist in concentrated areas, are poorly marked, or inconveniently located. Few campuses provide gender inclusive housing in which students can request a roommate of any gender (Nicolazzo et al., 2018), but, even if they do, these rooms are concentrated in one residence hall and not offered in the expected range of housing options (singles, doubles, suites, etc.). In addition, educational trainings are available but rarely mandated for faculty, staff, or students, which limits audiences to those who are already interested and concerned about trans inclusion on campus.

RELATIONSHIPS WITH FACULTY

The relationships between faculty and students are a core component of university life. Chickering and Gamson (1987) cited faculty and student contact as one of the seven best practices for undergraduate education. While there is a dearth of literature on the relationships between faculty and LGBTQ+ students, research on students from marginalized groups, including ethnic minority students (Castro Samayoa, 2018), students with disabilities (Markle et al., 2017), and women (Casto et al., 2005), suggest that relationships with faculty mentors may contribute to student success. For students at the intersections of multiple marginalized identities, access to faculty mentorship might be of particular importance.

The limited literature on the relationships between LGBTQ+ college students and faculty members suggests that mentorship is helpful. However, a quantitative study by Garvey and Inkelas (2012) found that lesbian, gay, and bisexual students reported increased satisfaction with their faculty and staff interactions than their heterosexual peers. Bisexual students were most likely to report being satisfied with their faculty and staff interactions. LGBTQ+ college students who were open about their identities and experiences with faculty members were more likely to have positive perceptions of their campus environment and were less likely to think about leaving campus (Tetreault et al., 2013). It is possible that given the negative campus environments LGBTQ+ students may face, they may turn to faculty support to successfully navigate the challenges of university life.

RELATIONSHIPS WITH PEERS

The college environment serves an essential role in facilitating social development in young adulthood. While clearly linked to sense of belonging and perceived social support, positive peer relationships are associated with academic achievement and persistence (Goguen et al., 2010). Alternatively, lack of social support and feelings of isolation can have detrimental effects on students' mental health and academic outcomes (Liu et al., 2019).

For many LGBTQ+ college students, the experience of having access and connections to similarly identifying students and communities may be unfamiliar yet deeply gratifying. This particular type of within-group social support is associated with positive mental health outcomes in LGBTQ+ populations. For example, Woodford and colleagues (2015) found that interpersonal factors played a moderating factor in decreased alcohol use among LGB college students.

Less studied are the deleterious effects of feeling isolated and excluded in communities where one expects and seeks acceptance and belonging. Despite the mission and intention to celebrate students across the queer and gender spectrum, campus centers and cocurricular programs may inadvertently exacerbate feelings of invisibility and exclusion for particular individuals. For example, transgender, bisexual, and asexual students have historically been casualties of exclusion in LGBTQ+ communities and may experience increased negative health outcomes compared to their gay and lesbian counterparts (Borgogna et al., 2019). Furthermore, community spaces may feel very different for individuals with varying intersectional identities, including people of color of distinct faiths and class identities, among many others. In the context of parental rejection and unsupportive environments, the impact of within-group disconnections can be devastating for some.

Additionally, access to inclusive communities and essential services may be obstructed for introverts, students with mental health disabilities, and people at different levels of outness.

Campus programming frequently favors extroverts and other people who can, by and large, manage their fear of navigating unfamiliar social spaces. Consequently, social anxiety among LGBTQ+ people (Reilly & Rudd, 2007; Wadsworth & Hayes-Skelton, 2015) may further pose barriers in developing close peer relationships in college settings. Furthermore, LGBTQ+ centers consistently grapple with the significant issue of how to reach students who may not feel safe disclosing their identities, who may be among the most vulnerable as well as the most likely to benefit from positive peer and community connections. By virtue of their increased sense of marginalization and decreased feelings of safety in college campuses, many transgender students do not openly disclose their identities and consequently may face higher barriers to reach other gender diverse students and supportive LGBTQ+ communities.

Another less known area is the extent and impact of cyberbullying and negative online interactions among college peers. The Pew Research Center (2014) identified 18- to 29-year-olds as more likely than any other age group to experience online harassment. Many studies have studied the relationships between social media use and psychological health (Rosen et al., 2013; Lou et al., 2012; Davila et al., 2012). Specifically, negative interactions in social media sites were associated with increased symptoms of depression and loneliness. Alternatively, social media provides an important digital platform to build and maintain social networks among LGBTQ+ students. More attention is needed to better understand the opportunities and costs related to the ubiquitous use of social media among college students.

HEALTH SERVICES ON CAMPUS

The two areas of health service provision that LGBTQ+ college students can access on campus are primary medical care and counseling and psychological services. Both positive and negative physical and mental health outcomes can have significant impact on student success, academic impairment, and campus safety (Larson et al., 2016; Keyes et al., 2012, Ruthig et al., 2011). Therefore, health and counseling centers serve as significant components of comprehensive retention efforts for all college and university students. These centers provide a wide range of interventions, such as treatment of acute illness and disorders, adjustment-related problems, and neurodevelopmental evaluations, as well as vital preventive services such as primary and specialized care, substance abuse and mental health screenings, and suicide prevention.

LGBTQ+ students can face several challenges accessing primary medical care on campus. Intake forms may not reflect a range of sexual orientation and gender identity options. Front service staff, nurses, and physicians may lack the adequate training necessary to serve transgender, nonbinary, and gender expansive (TNBGE) students specifically, such as using students' names and pronouns, recognizing the differences between names used and legal documentation, and asking about gender identity rather than assuming identity based on gender expression. Providers may ask questions about sexual orientation or gender identity out of curiosity, rather than out of medical necessity. Physicians may lack training to provide gender-affirming hormone therapy to TNBGE students, therefore limiting the type of basic medical care they can access on campus.

While sexual and gender minority college students report higher mental health service utilization, they continue to experience significant barriers such as lack of specific services for LGBQ+ and TNBGE students, variability in provider cultural competence, and past negative experiences in mental health care (Becker et al., 2017; Dunbar et al., 2017; Goldberg et al., 2018). Such barriers can pose serious consequences for students who may be seeking confidential mental health services in the absence of other peer, parent, cultural, and religion-based support. For TNBGE students, mental health access and quality of care can impact their ability to obtain gender-affirming health care with relevant referrals and letters of support.

Gaps in Research

While the research on LGBTQ+ college students is growing, there are a number of understudied areas in the college student research, LGBTQ+ research, or both. These less-researched areas offer multiple opportunities to better understand how these issues likely affect LGBTQ+ college students, and the sections below offer helpful questions for consideration, both for clinicians and areas for future research.

FIRST-GENERATION STUDENTS

The literature on the experiences of first-generation college students is well-established (see Ellis et al., 2019; Garriott & Nisle, 2018). However, there is a dearth of literature on the experiences of first-generation LGBTQ+ college students. How do these students navigate their sexual and gender identities when the stakes of graduating and succeeding are exceptionally high? How might these students' financial, caregiving, and other commitments to their families be affected when they may be rejected due to their sexual orientations and/or gender identities? The possibility of coming out during college might further contribute to the distance students may already feel if they are the first in their family to attend college. Mental health professionals serving first-generation LGBTQ+ students should accurately assess students' presenting problems and how these may or may not be related to being a first-generation student or being a LGBTQ+ student. They will want to acknowledge the potential dilemmas first-generation students may face related to family obligations, pressure to conform to familial expectations, and the need to be their whole, authentic selves as part of the LGBTQ+ community.

BISEXUAL AND FLUID STUDENTS

As discussed previously, bisexual students and those who have a fluid sexual orientation are at particularly high risk for adverse health outcomes. While the marginalization of bisexual people within the larger LGBT community is frequently acknowledged, it is unclear how these dynamics apply in the college setting. How do students navigate being a "minority within a minority," particularly if this is complicated by ethnicity, gender identity, and/or class? Given the importance of peer support during the college years, the lack of belonging bisexual students may experience likely contributes to some of the negative health outcomes seen in the literature.

TRANSGENDER, NONBINARY, AND GENDER EXPANSIVE (TNBGE) STUDENTS

As discussed throughout this chapter, TNBGE students experience substantial barriers in college settings. While recent works have highlighted a wide range of insufficient systems in place for transgender college students, improvements have been slow coming or altogether nonexistent. Among more than 4,000 degree-granting institutions (NCES, 2019), only about one quarter of them include gender identity and expression in their nondiscrimination policies, about 260 institutions offer gender inclusive housing, and less than 100 offer hormones and surgeries under their student insurance plans (Campus Pride Trans Policy Clearinghouse, 2022). More disturbingly, more than 100 religiously affiliated campuses have successfully implemented or are pursuing exemptions from federal civil rights protections to enact discriminatory actions against LGBTQ+ students (Campus Pride, 2016).

Among the many missing institutional policies and services for TNBGE students in college settings, access to TNBGE-affirming medical and mental health services is paramount for these populations, and particularly for those who seek to medically transition during their college years. Guidelines created by the American College Health Association (2015) underscore the importance of college health programs for transgender student retention and success, as well as the need to comply with Title IX guidelines that prohibit higher education institutions from discrimination based on gender identity. As summarized in this chapter's later section on policy recommendations, these guidelines include advances in access, information dissemination, insurance coverage, medical-form reviews, and provider trainings to increase competencies. Access to competent and responsive medical care, particularly for TNBGE students, may not only affect their physical health, but also their mental health and academic success as well.

Previous studies about the experiences of TNBGE students seeking health and counseling services at college and university settings have suggested that it is common for providers to be biased and to make incorrect assumptions. Goldberg and colleagues (2019) found that one third in a sample of 500 trans university students reported being misgendered "sometimes or often" while accessing on-campus health services. Study participants also reported several other negative experiences, including explicit invalidations of gender identity by therapists, overemphasis on gender identity in the understanding of the causes of the students' overall psychological distress, perceived lack of therapist competence in working with TNBGE students, and therapist avoidance of gender identity topics.

STEM STUDENTS

While the struggles of students of color, women, and people with disabilities in the science, technology, engineering, and mathematics (STEM) fields have received scholarly attention (National Science Foundation, 2017), sexual orientation and gender identity in the STEM fields have been less studied. Might LGBTQ+ students feel less comfortable disclosing their sexual orientation and/or gender identity if they perceive their faculty members and/or mentors in STEM fields to be conservative and/or rejecting? And what about for students whose sexual orientation and/or gender identity is assumed based on gender expression or "inability" to pass as heterosexual and/or cisgender? To understand these experiences, accurate sexual orientation and gender identity data would need to be captured in the STEM fields.

It would be important to understand potential factors contributing to the lack of diversity in the STEM field. For example, do LGBTQ+ college students self-select out of STEM majors due to a perceived lack of acceptance? And for those who do graduate with those majors, what are their experiences like as they enter STEM fields professionally, in graduate school, and in academia? The impact of the climate of this field is worth examining, particularly in the context of sexual orientation and gender identity.

IMMIGRATION STATUS

The intersection of immigration status and LGBTQ+ identities among college students requires heightened attention. Suárez-Orozco and colleagues (2015) catalogued a wide range of unique challenges that impact undocumented college students, including college affordability, significant mental health vulnerabilities, and campus climate concerns. While Deferred Action for Childhood Arrivals (DACA) resulted in many benefits for some undocumented students, these are greatly limited by its strict and arbitrary eligibility requirements, as well as the wide range of state and institutional policies that affect funding and other forms of support for all undocumented students, regardless of DACA status. Furthermore, while the conservative number of undocumented students in college is estimated to be in the upwards of 6,500 (Best Colleges, 2019), this number excludes students with mixed-status families who may face similar vulnerabilities as students who are classified as undocumented.

In 2013, the Center for American Progress published a report that focused on individuals who are at the intersection of these two marginalized populations. Despite the inevitability of inaccurate numbers due to risks related to disclosure, the report states that 30% of all LGBTQ+ immigrants (foreign born) are undocumented, and among this group, 49% are under the age of 30 (Gates et al., 2013). While college settings may offer some protections to LGBTQ+ undocumented students, higher education administrators and faculty must make intentional efforts in ensuring an inclusive environment for this population.

INTERNATIONAL STUDENTS

LGBTQ+ international students face increased barriers in multiple ways. Similar to other students, they may experience some freedom and space during their college years to explore and "come out" to themselves and others without the many pressures back home. However, the implications of coming out to international students may be exponentially more challenging for those whose home countries have repressive, oppressive, and/or even criminalizing stances against LGBTQ+ people (Nguyen et al., 2017). International students have very limited immigration options after completing their college degrees, and thus may feel increased anxiety and helplessness as they consider how to transition outside of what may have been a supportive, but time-limited space to be who they are (Oba & Pope, 2013). For a few, asylum visas may be the only option to consider, yet these processes are often expensive, lengthy, and susceptible to changing sociopolitical climates.

Family relationships often become a source of uncertainty and distress, as international students develop cultural flexibility and opportunities to question previous status quo assumptions as part of their learning experience in a new country (Quach et al., 2013). Meanwhile, most family members are not able to share this process with their adult child studying abroad and may blame the new environment for allowing expressions that challenge cultural constants in their lives. This growing distance may be even more pronounced as international students rarely get to visit home during the academic year as consistently and frequently as domestic students, and thus any changes may seem drastic and jarring, rather than being seen as the often slow progression of identity development.

Clinical and Policy Recommendations When Working with LGBTQ+ College Students

UNIVERSITY OR COLLEGE COUNSELING CENTERS

A primary function of clinicians who work with LGBTQ+ college students, regardless of setting, is to find multiple and unique ways to support a person's self-determination in their search for identity and well-being. Clinicians who are competent in delivering services to people with diverse sexual orientations and gender identities are skilled at establishing a therapeutic relationship that empowers clients to explore, examine, and express themselves in ways that are congruent with their values and worldviews.

When working with LGBTQ+ college students, primary areas to address may include coming out, language around their LGBTQ+ identities and experiences, the complexity of students' multiple identities, depathologizing symptoms, and advocacy for inclusion and human rights. These recommendations are best implemented when using a strengths-based approach, which includes attention to resilience and protective factors. In one study, character strengths such as hope, love, and gratitude were associated with well-being; and hope, zest, and self-regulation were inversely correlated with mental distress in LGBQ people (Antebi-Gruszka et al., 2020). Clinicians can highlight the inherent value of these character strengths and assist clients in increasing their expression and appreciation. Perrin and colleagues (2020) developed the minority strengths model, which identifies self-esteem, identity pride, social support, and community consciousness as predictors of positive mental and physical health, resilience, and positive health behaviors in LGBTQ+ people. Informed by this model, clinicians may deepen clients' understanding of the benefits of community engagement and their powerful reparative effect on internalized stigma. These positive psychology models acknowledge both the systemic barriers faced by LGBTQ+ college students and the individual- and community-based strategies used to overcome them.

The following section will provide recommendations on ways to address the aforementioned areas of clinical impact in working with LGBTQ+ clients. When applicable, potential pitfalls in clinical practice will be identified.

COMING OUT

Clinicians will likely work with LGBTQ+ college students who are at different stages of the coming out process. College is a time when students are likely to be engaged in various change-oriented processes related to their sense of self and beliefs about the people they interact with and the world in which they live. For LGBTQ+ students, coming out is one of these change processes they may be going through while attending college, so the topic is common in the context of psychotherapy. LGBTQ+ college student clients who are coming out may question what it means to be out or what it means to be part of a larger LGBTQ+ community. Depending on their previous exposure to people from diverse sexual orientations and gender identities, these students may wonder about whether their gender expression "should" change if they decide to adopt a gay, lesbian, bisexual, or some other sexual minority identity. Where might they meet potential partners? And how might they talk about their sexual orientation and gender identity with family members, roommates, peers, staff, and faculty members?

Clinically, there is no formula to follow here, perhaps with the exception of helping students identify actions they want to take that align with their values. Students may likely benefit from exploring their previous and current exposure to LGBTQ+ culture and communities, as these experiences can potentially be imbued with mainstream stereotypes and noninclusive representations. This exploration can then assist in addressing potential fears they have about being out, as well as considering strengths they could develop by becoming active in or involved with the community. Well-informed clinicians would discuss the pros and cons of being out as it relates to safety. What resources, if any, does the college campus and surrounding area have specifically for LGBTQ+ people? Ideally, the therapist would have connections to these resources and would be able to make a specific recommendation to the client (e.g., "You might contact Juan at the LGBT Resource Center on campus. He's very welcoming and has a lot of experience advising transgender students.").

For many students, coming out is filled with ambivalence and conflicting feelings. It is common for them to want to explore in therapy how to "be" themselves in the newly claimed "gay," "lesbian," or other sexual orientation and/or gender identity and how to communicate who they are to other people. Effective clinicians should be able to provide psychoeducation on the fluidity of sexual orientations, gender expressions, and gender identities as these could change over time. Clinicians who open the door for these possibilities allow their clients the freedom to explore their sexual orientation and gender identity, without any formula to follow, in the service of understanding and accepting themselves more deeply.

Clinicians likely have their own biases about coming out, no matter how they identify regarding sexual orientation and gender identity. For some, coming out could be considered a necessary step toward authenticity and self-realization. However, they should keep in mind some college students may not see the need to "come out." Rather, they might opt to continue to function in the world as their authentic selves without claiming an LGBTQ+ label or announcing their sexual orientation or gender identity to others.

Another potential bias or misconception clinicians may have is that coming out is a one-time, linear, finite process, when LGBTQ+ people don't come out to everyone in their lives at the same time. For instance, LGBTQ+ students may decide to be out to people on campus but not to people at home, or vice versa. Additionally, no matter how open one is about their LGBTQ+ identities, they are likely to have to come out again every time they meet new people in daily life, as they bring up their partner in conversation, their pronouns, or ways they choose to express gender. Coming out also can be a process that unfolds over a longer period, depending on safety concerns, worldviews, and emotional capacity of the individual to assert their identity publicly. These decisions can be shifted according to academic, social, and geographical contexts.

Grief and loss are common in the coming out process, not only for the college students themselves, but also for their parents, caregivers, and other family members. LGBTQ+ college students may have had a vision for themselves that aligned with what their family members wanted for them. For example, many parents envision a cisgender, heteronormative future for their adult children, where their children graduate from college, get married to a cisgender partner within a heterosexual relationship, and have their own children. LGBTQ+ students who come out may fear disappointing others, but they may also grieve the loss of future cisgender, heteronormative roles they may have wanted for themselves. Their future after coming out may be filled with uncertainty and fears. While clinicians would likely be able to provide psychoeducation about marriage and children, regardless of sexual orientation and gender identity, it would be important to open space in sessions for validation and acknowledgment of feelings of grief and worry. Avoiding these fears and other emotions might prevent a college student from coming out. Learning to manage and live with these feelings *is* part of a coming out process.

LANGUAGE

Using language that mirrors language the client uses is one of the most powerful tools for clinicians when working with LGBTQ+ people in general, and with college students in particular. Language expresses the ways a person understands themselves, so the competent clinician acknowledges this by using the language their client uses to describe themselves. There are myriad ways people can refer to their pronouns, sexual orientations, gender identities, sexual behaviors, and body parts. College students may be actively exploring these parts of themselves, and clinicians should flexibly meet their clients where they are to be effective in their role.

Use of inclusive language is important even before the client arrives at the therapy office. Intake forms that affirm a diversity of sexual orientations and gender identities allow for self-identification of sexual orientation and gender identity, name on their legal documentation, and name and pronouns the student uses. By the time clinicians see the student in their office, they should already have access to this information to be able to refer to the student in ways that will be perceived as welcoming and affirming. When discussing sexuality and sexual behaviors, clinicians should be familiar with a range of sexual practices and be able to discuss these comfortably with the client.

When working with transgender and nonbinary clients, the use of appropriate pronouns will likely be very important in establishing therapeutic rapport. Displaying confidence when asking what pronouns someone uses, if any, is the mark of a therapist who is comfortable working with this community. Therapists should use the pronouns their clients use and apologize when they inadvertently misgender their clients.

COMPLEXITY OF IDENTITIES

As mentioned previously, students typically attend college at a time in development when they are exploring multiple facets of their identities. Experiencing a shift in one identity can be a catalyst for shifts in other identities. For example, a student developing a stronger sense of himself as African American will likely feel the impact of this change in his sense of self as an African American bisexual man. He may navigate queer spaces wanting to find connection with other African American students, and he may wish to find other queer students in community spaces serving African American students. The possibility of politicization is often realized during college. Clinicians who affirm all aspects of one's identities, including the contradictions and nonlinear nature encompassed in identity development, have a higher chance of maintaining therapeutic rapport.

Individuals who identify with multiple marginalized communities often feel the need to "choose" which identity is most important to them. Fearing rejection from a particular community might become more salient after experiencing some form of "othering" by a member of that community (Jensen, 2011). Unfortunately, this othering can potentially occur in the therapeutic setting too. For example, a comment from a college counseling center therapist to a first-generation college student such as, "You'll be lying to yourself and to your family by staying in the closet" might negate the student's need to balance at least two parts of their identity: their sexual orientation (or gender identity) and their first-generation status. By pushing a student to come out, the therapist is inadvertently asking the student to choose their gender identity or sexual orientation by rendering their first-generation status invisible. The clinician may fail to recognize the stakes for this student when it comes to their family, may underestimate the family's ability to support the student's sexual orientation and/or gender identity, and further, may ignore the multiple options available to the student to "hold" both identities with similar levels of importance.

DEPATHOLOGIZING SYMPTOMS

When conceptualizing the nature of LGBTQ+ college students' problems, clinicians should consider the possibility of symptoms as a response to structural and systemic oppression, as minority stress theory (Brooks, 1981; Meyer, 2003) might suggest. Given the tenuous history between the mental health profession and LGBTQ+ people, mental health professionals should take great care to think about their clients' problems from multiple angles, not just problems that are endemic to the individual. How might this manifest in therapy? One example might be to over-inquire about the HIV status of a gay or bisexual man, or a transgender woman. Further, a less-informed clinician might inadvertently blame clients for their health status: the research literature suggests that providers demonstrate race-related implicit bias (Tajeu et al., 2018) and blame transgender people of color for their health issues (Lambda Legal, 2010).

How might a more effective, informed clinician proceed in this scenario? The intake paperwork of the clinic should have a section for clients to list medical conditions, including HIV status. In addition, the clinician needs to assess whether an exploration of HIV status is therapeutically indicated. Did the person come to therapy to address issues related to their health? Do they manage their health well? If the therapist finds that treatment related to a client's health status is relevant, the clinician can explore circumstances related to how HIV status was contracted, but more importantly, what it means to the individual to be living with HIV. How might their health status and subsequent coping mechanisms be related to a lack of older role models, many of whom were lost to the AIDS epidemic in the 1980s and 1990s? Understanding the cultural, social, and historical contexts of the LGBTQ+ community might offer more affirming clinical hypotheses to understand clients' problems.

ADVOCACY

The therapeutic relationship with LGBTQ+ college students is important not only for treatment, but also for the purposes of connecting students to other resources on their campus. If part of the college experience for many students is about broadening worldviews and engaging with a diversity of ideas, accessing multiple resources, especially ones that affirm multiple aspects of a person's identities, is a conduit for this process. Therapists might be the first stop on a longer path toward finding support and community for LGBTQ+ college students. Do therapists know a supportive person in the registrar's office who can assist with changing legal documentation to accurately reflect one's name and gender identity? Is there a particular residence hall that historically has been supportive to students of diverse sexual orientations and gender identities? Or perhaps the therapist can provide testimony that the health services center is in fact competent (or not) to provide hormone therapy.

Affirming clinicians have multiple avenues for advocacy regarding their LGBTQ+ college student clients. On college campuses, many departments and units must work in tandem to provide coordinated care for students. This may be particularly true for LGBTQ+ students who may be struggling with their identities and how to navigate resources on campus. Proactively, affirming clinicians would establish rapport with other service providers on campus who would interact with LGBTQ+ students.

POLICY RECOMMENDATIONS

These recommendations are compiled and informed by a growing body of work that addresses many, but not nearly all, the multiple barriers that affect LGBTQ+ students in college settings. Therefore, most of these recommendations emphasize the need for continuous assessment and creative approaches to meet a wide, dynamic, and complex range of students' needs.

Data Collection

Data collection is needed to inform best policies and practices. Administrators must determine how the data will be used and balance these institutional needs with the need to protect privacy. Processes must be designed keeping in mind that identity development and self-identification processes are fluid and dynamic. Therefore, rather than capturing data by means of one-time assessments, often in college applications or at matriculation, consider numerous data assessment points throughout students' time in college.

Institutional Policies

Institutional policies must be reviewed and revised to include nondiscrimination protections for all LGBTQ+ students, and especially for trans students who have not been afforded these rights at the state and federal level. Regardless of sociopolitical changes, college campuses have the responsibility to provide equitable access to education for all students.

Feedback Loops

Feedback loops can be implemented by designing targeted campus climate surveys, creating participatory research teams, and appointing student representatives in relevant campus committees and task forces that review hiring processes and policy proposals. In particular, feedback loops must be a consistent practice in student health and counseling centers in order to assess competency and issues of access.

Inclusivity

Inclusivity is an essential part of designing and improving all services. As described earlier in this chapter, more attention is needed for people with disabilities, including mental health disabilities. In addition, creative services can provide opportunities for introverted people and students who are at different levels of "outness" on their campus. Finally, trans students' needs cannot continue to be served at a bare minimum approach, and most colleges can and should actively work toward building and expanding trans inclusive support systems.

Dialogue Spaces

Dialogue spaces can provide important opportunities for young people to discuss current issues affecting LGBTQ+ people locally, nationally, and globally. Significant experiences of marginalization can result when such current events are ignored or addressed only as intellectual debates. Particular attention is needed regarding the ongoing immigration issues that clearly impact a significant number of students in college.

Intersectionality

Provide spaces or programs where intersectionality can be celebrated. While closed communities serve an essential function for underrepresented students, more effort is needed in bridging some of these communities by offering programs that address intersecting needs. For example, a self-care series designed for student activists can bring together students from multiple student groups. These spaces and programs can provide opportunities for solidarity and coalition, as well as increase feelings of belonging for students with multiple and intersecting identities.

Community LGBTQ+ Services

Expand services *for and about* LGBTQ+ students to educate all community members, rather than focusing on interventions for this underrepresented group. The emphasis must be consistently placed in effecting change in the community, campus environment, and relevant systems rather than intervening at the individual level.

Community Colleges

As community colleges are increasingly credited for providing educational access to underprivileged and underrepresented student groups, it is important to invest in creating and improving resources on these campuses. For example, building LGBTQ+ centers on these campuses may significantly increase visibility and a sense of belonging for queer and trans students.

Protective Factors

Link protective factors to programming. Consult the research literature on protective factors to design data-informed interventions, such as opportunities for social connections that can facilitate positive identity development.

Health Providers

Invest in professional development and *systemic support* for health providers, by providing time, resources, and access to essential adjunctive care practices such as case management. In addition, consistently review medical systems and processes such as intake forms and screening tools for affirming and inclusive language.

Counseling Centers

Support counseling centers, as they are uniquely poised to provide advocacy for some of the most vulnerable students in marginalized populations. Students who do not feel safe to come out in other spaces often share their experiences in individual or group therapy. While protecting confidentiality, counseling staff can provide important aggregate information about systemic barriers for marginalized communities.

Academic and Career Advisors

Develop LGBTQ+ relevant resources and training for academic and career advisors. Students greatly benefit from one-on-one advising regarding academic choices and career planning (McGill & Joslin, 2021). Advisors can increase their knowledge base and confidence in guiding LGBTQ+ college students by attending trainings about how particular issues and concerns may affect their academic path as well as their transition to work and professions post-graduation.

Conclusion

While LGBTQ+ college students are at a higher risk for negative health outcomes and attrition, there are a plethora of steps that both clinicians and educational institutions can take to help ensure their mental health and academic success. Campus communities that affirm students' multiple marginalized identities, provide relevant academic curricula, and equip its staff and faculty to competently serve students of diverse sexual orientations and gender identities aim to see LGBTQ+ college students thrive in their campus environments.

KEY KNOWLEDGE POINTS

- LGBTQ+ college students face a number of challenges that may affect their academic success, including limited access to adequate and responsive care and stigma related to their sexual orientation and gender identity.
- LGBTQ+ college students with intersecting marginalized identities may experience particular stressors as they navigate a sense of belonging in campus spaces that may reject one or more of their identities.
- There is a need for more empirical studies about the experiences of first-generation; bisexual and fluid; international; transgender, nonbinary, and gender expansive; undocumented; and STEM LGBTQ+ students.
- Members of the campus community with opportunities to support LGBTQ+ students include not only health service providers, but also faculty as well as staff of student affairs offices and student services.
- Recommendations for clinicians who work with LGBTQ+ students at university and college campus settings include using inclusive language, depathologizing symptoms, addressing whether to come out based on one's values, and engaging in campus advocacy on behalf of the students.
- Recommendations for policy changes to support LGBTQ+ students at university and college campuses include collection of accurate sexual orientation and gender identity data, collaboration between multiple campus entities, and inclusive institutional policies that protect both sexual orientation and gender identity categories.

RECOMMENDATIONS FOR PRACTITIONERS

- Evaluate the extent to which, if any, sexual orientation and gender identity affects LGBTQ+ students' reasons for seeking clinical services and their potential impact on students' academic successes.
- Understand the ways in which LGBTQ+ students' multiple identities may affect their sense of belonging and access to support on campus.
- Assess how campus policies and systems regarding sexual orientation and gender identity may adversely affect LGBTQ+ students.

References

Abes, E. S., & Jones, S. R. (2004). Meaning-making capacity and the dynamics of lesbian college students' multiple dimensions of identity. *Journal of College Student Development, 45*(6), 612–632. https://doi.org/10.1353/csd.2004.0065

American College Health Association. (2015). Trans-inclusive college health programs. https://www.acha.org/documents/Resources/Guidelines/Trans-Inclusive_College_Health_Programs.pdf

Antebi-Gruszka, N., Friedman, A. A., & Schrimshaw, E. W. (2020). Character strengths and their associations with well-being and mental distress among lesbian, gay, bisexual, and queer individuals. *Journal of Gay & Lesbian Social Services: The Quarterly Journal of Community & Clinical Practice.* https://doi.org/10.1080/10538720.2020.1859424

Becker, M. A. S., Roberts, S. F. N., Ritts, S. M., Branagan, W. T., Warner, A. R., & Clark, S. L. (2017). Supporting transgender college students: Implications for clinical intervention and campus prevention. *Journal of College Student Psychotherapy, 67*(2), 161–173. https://doi.org/10.1080/07448481.2018.1465060

Best Colleges. (2019). College guide for undocumented students. https://www.bestcolleges.com/resources/undocumented-students-guide/

Bilodeau, B. L., & Renn, K. (2005). Analysis of LGBT identity development models and implications for practice. *New Directions for Student Services, 25*–39.

Borgogna, N. C., McDermott, R. C., Aita, S. L., & Kridel, M. M. (2019). Anxiety and depression across gender and sexual minorities: Implications for transgender, gender nonconforming, pansexual, demisexual, asexual, queer, and questioning individuals. *Psychology of Sexual Orientation and Gender Diversity, 6*(1), 54–63. https://doi.org/10.1037/sgd0000306

Brooks, V. R. (1981). *Minority stress and lesbian women.* Lexington Books.

Burns, C., Garcia, A., & Wolgin, P. E. (2013). Living in dual shadows: LGBT undocumented immigrants. Center for American Progress. https://www.americanprogress.org/wp-content/uploads/2013/03/LGBTUndocumentedReport-5.pdf

Burton, C. M., Marshal, M. P., Chisolm, D. J., Sucato, G. S., & Friedman, M. S. (2013). Sexual minority-related victimization as a mediator of mental health disparities in sexual minority youth: A longitudinal analysis. *Journal of Youth and Adolescence, 42*(3), 394–402. https://doi.org/10.1007/s10964-012-9901-5

Campus Pride. (2016). *Shame list: The absolute worst campuses for LGBTQ youth.* https://www.campuspride.org/shamelist

Campus Pride Trans Policy Clearinghouse. (2022). https://www.campuspride.org/tpc/nondiscrimination/

Casto, C., Caldwell, C., & Salazar, C. F. (2005). Creating mentoring relationships between female faculty and students in counselor education: Guidelines for potential mentees and mentors. *Journal of Counseling & Development, 83*(3), 331.

Castro Samayoa, A. (2018). "People around me here, they know the struggle": Students' experiences with faculty member's mentorship at three Hispanic serving institutions. *Education Sciences, 8.*

Chickering, A. W., & Gamson, Z. F. (1987). Seven principles for good practice in undergraduate education. *American Association for Higher Education Bulletin, 3*, 3–7.

Chickering, A. W., & Reisser, L. (1993). *Education and identity.* Jossey-Bass.

Ciobanu, A. (2013). The role of student services in the improving of student experience in higher education. *Procedia—Social and Behavioral Sciences, 92*, 169–173.

Coulter, R. W. S., Mair, C., Miller, E., Blosnich, J. R., Matthews, D. D., & McCauley, H. L. (2017). Prevalence of past-year sexual assault victimization among undergraduate students: Exploring differences by and intersections of gender identity, sexual identity, and race/ethnicity. *Prevention Science, 18*(6), 726–736. https://doi.org/10.1007/s11121-017-0762-8

Davila, J., Hershenberg, R., Feinstein, B. A., Gorman, K., Bhatia, V., & Starr, L. R. (2012). Frequency and quality of social networking among young adults: Associations with depressive symptoms, rumination, and co-rumination. *Psychology of Popular Media Culture, 1*(2), 72–86.

Dunbar, M. S., Sontag-Padilla, L., Ramchand, R., Seelam, R., & Stein, B. D. (2017). Mental health service utilization among lesbian, gay, bisexual, and questioning or queer college students. *Journal of Adolescent Health, 61*(3), 294–301. https://doi.org/10.1016/j.jadohealth.2017.03.008

Ellis, J. M., Powell, C. S., Demetriou, C. P., Huerta-Bapat, C., & Panter, A. T. (2019). Examining first-generation college student lived experiences with microaggressions and microaffirmations at a predominately White public research university. *Cultural Diversity and Ethnic Minority Psychology, 25*(2), 266–279. https://doi.org/10.1037/cdp0000198

Fields, X., & Wotipka, C. M. (2020). Effect of LGBT anti-discrimination laws on school climate and outcomes for lesbian, gay, and bisexual high school students. *Journal of LGBT Youth.* https://doi.org/10.1080/19361653.2020.1821276

Fine, L. E. (2011). Minimizing heterosexism and homophobia: Constructing meaning of out campus LGB life. *Journal of Homosexuality, 58*(4), 521–546. https://doi.org/10.1080/00918369.2011.555673

Fulginiti, A., Goldbach, J. T., Mamey, M. R., Rusow, J., Srivastava, A., Rhoades, H., Schrager, S. M., Bond, D. W., & Marshal, M. P. (2020). Integrating minority stress theory and the interpersonal theory of suicide among sexual minority youth who engage crisis services. *Suicide and Life-Threatening Behavior.* https://doi.org/10.1111/sltb.12623

Garriott, P. O., & Nisle, S. (2018). Stress, coping, and perceived academic goal progress in first-generation college students: The role of institutional supports. *Journal of Diversity in Higher Education, 11*(4), 436–450. https://doi.org/10.1037/dhe0000068

Garvey, J. C., & Inkelas, K. K. (2012). Exploring relationships between sexual orientation and satisfaction with faculty and staff interactions. *Journal of Homosexuality, 59*(8), 1167–1190. https://doi.org/10.1080/00918369.2012.712846

Garvey, J. C., & Rankin, S. R. (2015). The influence of campus experiences on the level of outness among trans-spectrum and queer-spectrum students. *Journal of Homosexuality, 62*(3), 374–393. https://doi.org/10.1080/00918369.2014.977113

Garvey, J. C, Squire, D. D., Stachler, B., & Rankin, S. (2018). The impact of campus climate on queer-spectrum student academic success. *Journal of LGBT Youth, 15*(2), 89–105. https://doi.org/10.1080/19361653.2018.1429978

Garvey, J. C., Taylor, J. L., & Rankin, S. (2015). An examination of campus climate for LGBTQ community college students. *Community College Journal of Research and Practice, 39*(6), 527–541. https://doi.org/10.1080/10668926.2013.861374

Gates, G. J. (2013). LGBT adult immigrants in the United States. https://escholarship.org/uc/item/2cj0k29c

Goguen, L. M. S., Hiester, M. A., & Nordstrom, A. H. (2010). Associations among peer relationships, academic achievement, and persistence in college. *Journal of College Student Retention: Research, Theory, & Practice, 12*(3), 319–337. https://doi.org/10.2190/CS.12.3.d

Gold, S. P., & Stewart, D. L. (2011). Lesbian, gay, and bisexual students coming out at the intersection of spirituality and sexual identity. *Journal of LGBT Issues in Counseling, 5*(3–4), 237–258. https://doi.org/10.1080/15538605.2011.633052

Goldberg, A. E. (2018). Transgender students in higher education. Williams Institute. https://williamsinstitute.law.ucla.edu/wp-content/uploads/1808-Trans-Higher-Ed.pdf

Goldberg, A. E., Beemyn, G., & Smith, J. Z. (2018). What is needed, what is valued: Trans students' perspectives on trans-inclusive policies and practices in higher education. *Journal of Educational and Psychological Consultation, 29*(1), 27–67. https://doi.org/10.1080/10474412.2018.1480376

Goldberg, A. E., Kuvalanka, K. A., Budge, S. L., Benz, M. B., & Smith, J. Z. (2019). Health care experiences of transgender binary and nonbinary university students. *Counseling Psychologist.* https://doi.org/10.1177/0011000019827568

Grant, J. M., Mottet, L. A., Tanis, J., Harrison, J., Herman, J. L., & Keisling, M. (2011). *Injustice at every turn: A report of the national transgender discrimination survey.* National Center for Transgender Equality and National Gay and Lesbian Task Force.

Han, C., Farruggia, S. P., & Moss, T. P. (2017). Effects of academic mindsets on college students' achievement and retention. *Journal of College Student Development, 58*(8), 1119–1134. https://doi.org/10.1353/csd.2017.0089

Herek, G. M., & Garnets, L. D. (2007). Sexual orientation and mental health. *Annual Review of Clinical Psychology, 3*, 353–375. https://doi.org/10.1146/annurev.clinpsy.3.022806.091510

James, S. E., Herman, J. L., Rankin, S., Keisling, M., Mottet, L., & Anafi, M. (2016). *Report of the 2015 U.S. transgender survey.* National Center for Transgender Equality.

Jensen, S. (2011). Othering, identity formation and agency. *Qualitative Studies, 2*(2), 63–78. https://doi.org/10.7146/qs.v2i2.5510

Kann, L., Olsen, E. O., McManus, T., Harris, W. A., Shanklin, S. L., Flint, K. H., Queen, B., Lowry, R., Chyen, D., Whittle, L., Thornton, J., Lim, C., Yamakawa, Y., Brener, N., & Zaza, S. (2016). Sexual identity, sex of sexual contacts, and health-related behaviors among students in grades 9–12—United States and selected sites, 2015. *Morbidity and Mortality Weekly Report Surveillance Summaries, 65*(9), 1–202. http://dx.doi.org/10.15585/mmwr.ss6509a1

Kann, L., McManus, T., Harris, W. A., Shanklin, S. L., Flint, K. H., Queen, B., Lowry, R., Chyen, D., Whittle, L., Thornton, J., Lim, C., Bradford, D., Yamakawa, Y., Leon, M., Brener, N., & Ethier, K. A. (2018). Youth risk behavior surveillance—United States. *Morbidity and Mortality Weekly Report Surveillance Summaries, 67*(8), 1–114.

Kerr, D. L., Ding, K., & Chaya, J. (2014). Substance use of lesbian, gay, bisexual and heterosexual college students. *American Journal of Health Behavior, 38*(6), 951–962. https://doi.org/10.5993/AJHB.38.6.17

Keyes, C. L., Eisenberg, D., Perry, G. S., Dube, S. R., Kroenke, K, & Dhingra, S. S. (2012). The relationship of level of positive mental health with current mental disorders in predicting suicidal behavior and academic impairment in college students. *Journal of American College Health, 60*(2), 126–133. https://doi.org/10.1080/07448481.2011.608393

Lambda Legal. (2010). When health care isn't caring: Lambda Legal's survey of discrimination against LGBT people and people with HIV. www.lambdalegal.org/health-care-report

Lamis, D. A., & Lester, D. (Eds.) (2011). *Understanding and preventing college student suicide.* Charles C Thomas Publisher.

Larson, M., Orr, M., & Warne, D. (2016). Using student health data to understand and promote academic success in higher education settings. *College Student Journal, 50*(4), 590–602.

Lefevor, G. T., Boyd-Rogers, C. C., Sprague, B. M., & Janis, R. A. (2019). Health disparities between genderqueer, transgender, and cisgender individuals: An extension of minority stress theory. *Journal of Counseling Psychology.* https://doi.org/10.1037/cou0000339

Levin, M. E., & Levin, J. R. (1991). A critical examination of academic retention programs for at-risk minority college students. *Journal of College Student Development, 32*(4), 323–334. http://0-search.ebscohost.com.library.alliant.edu/login.aspx?direct=true&db=psyh&AN=1991-34613-001&site=ehost-live&scope=site

Lindquist, L. M., Livingston, N. A., Heck, N. C., & Machek, G. R. (2017). Predicting depressive symptoms at the intersection of attribution and minority stress theories. *Journal of Gay & Lesbian Mental Health, 21*(1), 32–50. https://doi.org/10.1080/19359705.2016.1217498

Liu, H., Zhang, M., Yang, Q., & Yu, B. (2019). Gender differences in the influence of social isolation and loneliness on depressive symptoms in college students: A longitudinal study. *Social Psychiatry and Psychiatric Epidemiology: The International Journal for Research in Social and Genetic Epidemiology and Mental Health Services.* https://doi.org/10.1007/s00127-019-01726-6

Lou, L. L., Yan, Z., Nickerson, A., & McMorris, R. (2012). An examination of the reciprocal relationship of loneliness and Facebook use among first-year college students. *Journal of Educational Computing Research, 46*(1), 105–117.

Markle, L., Wessel, R. D., & Desmond, J. (2017). Faculty mentorship program for students with disabilities: Academic success outcomes (practice brief). *Journal of Postsecondary Education and Disability, 30*(4), 385–392.

McGill, C. M., and Joslin, J. E. (2021). *Advising lesbian, gay, bisexual, transgender, and queer college students*. Stylus Publishing.

Messman, J. B., & Leslie, L. A. (2019). Transgender college students: Academic resilience and striving to cope in the face of marginalized health. *Journal of American College Health, 67*(2), 161–173. https://doi.org/10.1080/07448481.2018.1465060

Meyer, I. H. (2003). Prejudice, social stress, and mental health in lesbian, gay, and bisexual populations: Conceptual issues and research evidence. *Psychological Bulletin, 129*(5), 674–697. https://doi.org/10.1037/0033-2909.129.5.674

National Center for Education Statistics (NCES). (2019). Enrollment and employees in postsecondary institutions, fall 2017; and Financial statistics and academic libraries, fiscal year 2017: First look (provisional data). https://nces.ed.gov/pubs2019/2019021REV.pdf

National Science Foundation, National Center for Science and Engineering Statistics. (2017). *Women, minorities, and persons with disabilities in science and engineering: 2017.* Special Report NSF 17-310. www.nsf.gov/statistics/wmpd/

Nguyen, H., Grafsky, E., & Lambert-Shute, J. (2017). The experiences of lesbian, gay, bisexual, and queer international students. *Journal of Underrepresented & Minority Progress, 1*(1), 80–94. https://doi.org/10.32674/jump.v1i1.39

Nicolazzo, Z., Marine, S. B., & Wagner, R. (2018). From best to intentional practices: Reimagining implementation of gender-inclusive housing. *Journal of Student Affairs Research and Practice, 55*(2), 225–236. https://doi.org/10.1080/19496591.2018.1399896

Oba, Y., & Pope, M. (2013). Counseling and advocacy with LGBT international students. *Journal of LGBT Issues in Counseling, 7*, 185–193. https://doi.org/10.1080/15538605.2013.785468

Oswalt, S. B., & Wyatt, T. J. (2011). Sexual orientation and differences in mental health, stress, and academic performance in a national sample of US college students. *Journal of Homosexuality, 58*(9), 1255–1280. https://doi.org/10.1080/00918369.2011.605738

Perrin, P. B., Sutter, M. E., Trujillo, M. A., Henry, R. S., & Pugh, M. Jr. (2020). The minority strengths model: Development and initial path analytic validation in racially/ethnically diverse LGBTQ individuals. *Journal of Clinical Psychology, 76*(1), 118–136. https://doi.org/10.1002/jclp.22850

Pew Research Center. (2014). https://www.pewinternet.org/2014/10/22/online-harassment/

Quach, A. S., Todd, M. E., Hepp, B. W., & Doneker Mancini, K. L. (2013). Conceptualizing sexual identity development: Implications for GLB Chinese international students. *Journal of GLBT Family Studies, 9*, 254–272. https://doi.org/10.1080/1550428X.2013.781908

Rankin, S., Weber, G. N., Blumenfeld, W. J., & Frazer, S. (2010). *2010 state of higher education for lesbian, gay, bisexual and transgender people.* https://www.campuspride.org/wp-content/uploads/campuspride2010lgbtreportssummary.pdf

Reilly, A., & Rudd, N. A. (2007). Stress and dress: Investigating the relationship between social anxiety and appearance management among gay and straight men. *Journal of Homosexuality, 52*(3–4), 151–166. https://doi.org/10.1300/J082v52n03_07

Rosen, L. D., Whaling, K., Rab, S., Carrier, L. M., & Cheever, N. A. (2013). Is Facebook creating "iDisorders"? The link between clinical symptoms of psychiatric disorders and technology use, attitudes and anxiety. *Computers in Human Behavior, 29*, 1243–1254.

Russell, S. T., & Fish, J. N. (2016). Mental health in lesbian, gay, bisexual, and transgender (LGBT) youth. *Annual review of clinical psychology, 12*, 465–487. https://doi.org/10.1146/annurev-clinpsy-021815-093153

Russell, S. T., Van Campen, K. S., Hoefle, J. M., & Boor, J. K. (2011). Suicide risk and lesbian, gay, bisexual, and transgender college students. In D. A. Lamis & D. Lester (Eds.), *Understanding and preventing college student suicide.* (pp. 146–156). Charles C Thomas Publisher. http://0-search.ebscohost.com.library.alliant.edu/login.aspx?direct=true&db=psyh&AN=2011-27511-010&site=ehost-live&scope=site

Ruthig, J. C., Marrone, S., Hladkyi, S., & Robinson-Epp, N. (2011). Changes in college student health: Implications for academic performance. *Journal of College Student Development, 52*(3), 307–320. https://doi.org/10.1353/csd.2011.0038

Schmitz, R. M., & Tyler, K. A. (2019). "Life has actually become more clear": An examination of resilience among LGBTQ young adults. *Sexualities, 22*(4), 710–733. https://doi.org/10.1177/1363460718770451

Seelman, K. L. (2016). Transgender adults' access to college bathrooms and housing and the relationship to suicidality. *Journal of Homosexuality, 63*(10), 1378–1399. https://doi.org/10.1080/00918369.2016.1157998

Stevens, R. A. (2004). Understanding gay identity development within the college environment. *Journal of College Student Development, 45*(2), 185–206.

Strayhorn, T. L., Johnson, R. M., Henderson, T. S., & Tillman-Kelly, D. L. (2015). *Beyond coming out: New insights about GLBQ college students of color.* Center for Higher Education Enterprise, Ohio State University.

Suárez-Orozco, M. M., Teranishi, R., & Suárez-Orozco, C. E. (2015). In the shadows of the ivory tower: Undocumented undergraduates and the liminal state of immigration reform. *UCLA.* https://escholarship.org/uc/item/2hq679z4

Substance Abuse and Mental Health Services Administration. (2018). Key substance use and mental health indicators in the United States: Results from the 2017 National Survey on Drug Use and Health (HHS Publication No. SMA 18-5068, NSDUH Series H-53). Center for Behavioral Health Statistics and Quality, Substance Abuse and Mental Health Services Administration. https://www.samhsa.gov/data/

Tajeu, G. S., Halanych, J., Juarez, L., Stone, J., Stepanikova, I., Green, A., & Cherrington, A. L. (2018). Exploring the association of healthcare worker race and occupation with implicit and explicit racial bias. *Journal of the National Medical Association, 110*(5), 464–472. https://doi.org/10.1016/j.jnma.2017.12.001

Tan, K. K. H., Treharne, G. J., Ellis, S. J., Schmidt, J. M., & Veale, J. F. (2019). Gender minority stress: A critical review. *Journal of Homosexuality.* https://doi.org/10.1080/00918369.2019.1591789

Tetreault, P. A., Fette, R., Meidlinger, P. C., & Hope, D. (2013). Perceptions of campus climate by sexual minorities. *Journal of Homosexuality, 60*(7), 947–964. https://doi.org/10.1080/00918369.2013.774874

Torres, V., Jones, S. R., & Renn, K. A. (2009). Identity development theories in student affairs: Origins, current status, and new approaches. *Journal of College Student Development, 50*(6), 577–596. https://doi.org/10.1353/csd.0.0102

Vaughan, M. D., & Waehler, C. A. (2010). Coming out growth: Conceptualizing and measuring stress-related growth associated with coming out to others as a sexual minority. *Journal of Adult Development, 17*(2), 94–109. https://doi.org/10.1007/s10804-009-9084-9

Villicana, A. J., Delucio, K., & Biernat, M. (2016). "Coming out" among gay Latino and gay White men: Implications of verbal disclosure for well-being. *Self and Identity, 15*(4), 468–487. https://doi.org/10.1080/15298868.2016.1156568

Wadsworth, L. P., & Hayes-Skelton, S. A. (2015). Differences among lesbian, gay, bisexual, and heterosexual individuals and those who reported an other identity on an open-ended response on levels of social anxiety. *Psychology of Sexual Orientation and Gender Diversity, 2*(2), 181–187. https://doi.org/10.1037/sgd0000092

Westefeld, J. S., Maples, M. R., Buford, B., & Taylor, S. (2001). Gay, lesbian, and bisexual college students: The relationship between sexual orientation and depression, loneliness, and suicide. *Journal of College Student Psychotherapy, 15*(3), 71–82. https://doi.org/10.1300/J035v15n03_06

Woodford, M. R., Han, Y., Craig, S., Lim, C., & Matney, M. M. (2014). Discrimination and mental health among sexual minority college students: The type and form of discrimination does matter. *Journal of Gay & Lesbian Mental Health, 18*(2), 142–163. https://doi.org/10.1080/19359705.2013.833882

Woodford, M. R., & Kulick, A. (2015). Academic and social integration on campus among sexual minority students: The impacts of psychological and experiential campus climate. *American Journal of Community Psychology, 55*, 13–24.

Woodford, M. R., Kulick, A., & Atteberry, B. (2015). Protective factors, campus climate, and health outcomes among sexual minority college students. *Journal of Diversity in Higher Education, 8*(2), 73–87. http://dx.doi.org/10.1037/a0038552

Woodford, M. R., Weber, G., Nicolazzo, Z., Hunt, R., Kulick, A., Coleman, T., . . . Renn, K. A. (2018). Depression and attempted suicide among LGBTQ college students: Fostering resilience to the effects of heterosexism and cisgenderism on campus. *Journal of College Student Development, 59*(4), 421–438. https://doi.org/10.1353/csd.2018.0040

CHAPTER 9

Medical Care Centers as Beacons of Hope for LGBTQ+ Youth

Hiram Rivera-Mercado, PsyD, Kevin Carrión, PsyD, & Taymy J. Caso, PhD

Children's hospitals or children's clinics were created toward the nineteenth century, and the first one, Hôpital NeckerEnfants Malades in Paris, France, had 250 beds, was publicly funded, had gardens, and would divide their children by age, sex, and diseases (Casimir, 2019). Today in the United States, children's hospitals perform 97% of all pediatric organ transplants and 90% of all pediatric cancer care. However, only 1 in 20 hospitals is a children's hospital. There are about 250 children's hospitals in the United States, so they play a much greater regional role than general hospitals, especially for rare diseases, for which multidisciplinary follow-up is organized (Casimir, 2019).

In 2007, the Healthcare Equality Index began transforming healthcare for LGBTQ+ people by publishing their first report of 10 recommendations to create more welcoming environments and improve inclusivity of LGBTQ+ patients and families within healthcare facilities. Those recommendations included the following four foundational elements of LGBTQ+ patient-centered care: an LGBTQ+ inclusive patient nondiscrimination policy, an LGBTQ+ inclusive visitation policy, an LGBTQ+ inclusive employment nondiscrimination policy, and staff training in LGBTQ+ patient-centered care. Hospitals in the United States have recognized that minority groups face significant barriers to health care because of bias and discrimination, which has led them to examine their policies and practices to ensure that discrimination is prohibited, that recommendations for equitable and inclusive care are followed, and that staff are trained in this area (Meyer et al., 2016). More specifically to transgender individuals, hospitals found that adopting transgender inclusive health care practices can reduce the costs associated with complications that arise when patients are denied or delayed medical services (Meyer et al., 2016). Currently, children's hospitals are regular participants in the Healthcare Equality Index, with around 50 participating during the last few years (Ng & Hanneman, 2020). Therefore, by ensuring hospitals have inclusive policies, stakeholders ensure LGBTQ+ youth have increased access to quality healthcare, and hospitals reduce costs related to more complex patient health care situations for LGBTQ+ youth that can arise from poor access to health care (Ng & Hanneman, 2020).

Role of Hospitals in Serving LGBTQ+ Youth and Emerging Adults

Hospitals should have LGBTQ+ inclusive patient nondiscrimination policies, be teen-friendly, and ensure that health care providers do not make assumptions about sexual orientation and gender identity. LGBTQ+ inclusive policies and practices should be paired with ongoing staff training in LGBTQ+ patient-centered care. LGBTQ+ youth who do not receive affirming medical and mental health care are at higher risk for substance abuse, depression, homelessness, HIV infection, and suicide, compared to non-LGBTQ+ youth (Asakura, 2016; Ng & Hanneman, 2020). Further, a 2016 study revealed that as many as 30% of transgender youth attempt suicide at least once in their lifetime and 42% report self-harm (Ng, 2020).

Some Services Included

LGBTQ+ youth not only deal with the typical health and developmental challenges of puberty and growing up; they also face additional challenges associated with stigma and discrimination based on their sexual and gender identities, as well as other potential marginalized identities (Coker et al., 2010; Asakura, 2016). LGBTQ+ individuals live and navigate within a heterosexist and heteronormative society, which "others" them on a regular basis. These experiences of oppression, harassment, victimization, and discrimination often place LGBTQ+ individuals at elevated risk for psychological distress, which can negatively affect their overall well-being (Kort, 2008; Meyer, 2003). In order to meet the needs of LGBTQ+ youth and emerging adults, it is important that providers and staff in hospitals and medical facilities understand the unique challenges of this community. With this in mind, what types of services should hospitals and medical centers have at their disposal to provide appropriate and affirmative care to LGBTQ+ youth?

PRIMARY CARE

Primary care providers may serve as the first point of contact into the healthcare system for young people and/or their parents/guardians. As such, it is important that primary care providers are knowledgeable and competent in issues typically faced by LGBTQ+ youth in order not only to provide the proper care, but also to respond in an affirming manner that will engage the youth and their families within the healthcare system (Agana et al., 2019; Chulani et al., 2021; Knight & Jarrett, 2017). Primary care providers need up-to-date training regarding LGBTQ+ concepts, including knowledge and understanding regarding gender identity, sex assigned at birth, sexual orientation, gender expression, pronouns, heterosexism, and microaggressions, to name a few. Due to the complexities that LGBTQ+ youth face, these patients might need services that fall outside the scope of the primary care provider's role. This is where it becomes pivotal for primary care providers to consult and collaborate with other health professionals in order to connect LGBTQ+ youth to the appropriate services. Some of these additional services include the following.

PEDIATRIC ENDOCRINOLOGIST

A pediatric endocrinologist may be an essential component of the care team at a medical center, particularly for transgender or gender diverse youth. When a child's gender identity does not align with their sex assigned at birth, they might experience a degree of psychological distress, which is known as gender dysphoria. Not all transgender or gender diverse individuals experience distress related to their gender, and not all meet criteria for a gender dysphoria diagnosis. Variations in and a lack of gender dysphoria does not invalidate their identities. A young person may experience gender dysphoria at any point throughout their development or not at all. For some, gender dysphoria can worsen significantly during puberty as the young person begins to develop secondary sex characteristics that are typically associated with their assigned sex at birth (Ng, 2020). It is important to acknowledge the full spectrum of gender presentations and journeys and the validity of each and every one of these manifestations of gender identity and presentation.

The path toward gender affirmation is individualized and diverse, and it can be instrumental in alleviating gender dysphoria when it occurs (Murad et al., 2010). For some, the gender affirmation process may include social, legal, psychological, and/or medical aspects (Reisner et al., 2016; Vance et al., 2014). Some gender-affirming medical interventions that adolescents may explore include puberty suppression and/or hormone therapy.

Puberty suppression involves the use of hormones to "suppress estrogen or testosterone production and consequently delay the physical changes of puberty" (Coleman et al., 2012, p. 176). The use of puberty suppression is a medical intervention with guidelines from the World Professional Association for Transgender Health and the Endocrine Society, and these guidelines have been endorsed by national health organizations such as the US Department of Health and Human Services, the American Academy of Pediatrics, and the American Academy of Child and Adolescent Psychiatry. Puberty suppression provides a young person the ability to prevent undesired physical changes associated with puberty, while also giving the individual time to explore and make plans regarding the next steps in their gender journey (de Vries, 2020), which may or may not include further transition. Puberty suppression can be a helpful tool that can benefit the well-being of transgender and gender diverse youth. Turban and colleagues (2020) explored the association between puberty suppression and risk of suicidal ideation. Results highlighted that transgender adults who received puberty suppression during adolescence reported less suicidal ideation than transgender adults who wanted puberty suppression but did not receive it during their adolescence (Turban et al., 2020).

Gender-affirming hormone therapy seeks to bring about hormone-induced changes to the body, thus helping the person's body align more with their gender identity. Prescribing hormone therapy regimens requires specialized knowledge and training, and prescribing providers must also account for physical, emotional, and cognitive changes that occur during adolescence. Hormone therapy can be a useful intervention and help foster positive mental health outcomes for transgender and gender diverse youth. In a recent study, Kuper and colleagues (2020) explored the impact of hormone therapy on body dissatisfaction and mental health outcomes in transgender and gender diverse youth. Participants receiving hormone therapy reported large improvements in body dissatisfaction and mild to moderate improvements in depressive and anxiety symptoms (Kuper et al., 2020).

BEHAVIORAL HEALTH AND MENTAL HEALTH SERVICES

Providers in medical centers working with LGBTQ+ young people should also include a behavioral/mental health team who can provide high-quality and culturally appropriate care. It should be noted that not every LGBTQ+ person wants behavioral/mental health services. This is where a competent behavioral team who can accurately assess the patient's clinical needs will be an asset. LGBTQ+ youth are at a higher risk for poor mental health, including high rates of depression, anxiety, suicidal ideation, suicidal attempts, self-harm, and substance use (Ng, 2020; Trevor Project, 2020). However, it is important to highlight that these vulnerabilities or difficulties are not caused by the patients' identities, but rather that they stem from the environmental forces that surround the patient and their responses to the patient's identities (Rafferty, 2018). The minority stress model (Meyer, 2003) suggests that this higher prevalence of mental health concerns reported by LGBTQ+ individuals is caused by excess social stressors related to stigma and prejudice.

The mental health provider must have a comprehensive understanding of these realities and how they relate to sexual orientation and gender identities and help patients navigate the behavioral/mental health concerns that may arise when needed. An affirming therapist can assist the patient in exploring their gender and sexual identities, help manage gender dysphoria (when present), discuss disclosure of these identities in different settings (if desired), and build safety-enhancing skills. In addition, the therapist must be able to help patients navigate social interactions, including building relationships with peers and dating, which should also include discussions around sexual health—and what this looks like for LGBTQ+ individuals.

Comprehensive care for LGBTQ+ young people cannot be limited to individual-level work. Family work is essential when working with children and adolescents, as family dynamics have an impact on the youth's well-being. Studies show that positive parent-child relationships and effective parenting responses are linked to better health outcomes in children (Newcomb et al., 2019). However, compared to heterosexual cisgender peers, LGBTQ+ youth are more likely to experience family tension, conflicts, and/or rejection due to stigma based on sexual and/or gender identities. A study with LGB white and Latinx youth, for example, found that higher levels of family rejection were associated with a higher likelihood of depressive symptoms, suicidality, substance use, and sexual risk behaviors (Ryan et al., 2009). Family-focused therapy can help build more positive interactions between members, as well as improve mental health outcomes for LGBTQ+ youth (Diamond et al., 2012; Newcomb et al., 2019). Mental health providers need to work with families to educate them on sexual and/or gender identity development; process caregivers' feelings of disappointment, anger, confusion, and fears related to their child's identity; foster a path toward acceptance and validation of their child's identity; increase awareness around invalidating responses and modify these; and build resiliency to manage societal challenges (Coulter et al., 2019). When working with transgender and gender diverse youth, the family therapy space should be used to address management of gender dysphoria, facilitating discussions around social gender transition and decisions around how to manage gender transition (as appropriate) in different settings (school, community, extended family). A comprehensive behavioral health team for youth may also include a pediatric psychiatrist. Psychiatry services can be helpful resources to assist with psychiatric evaluations and psychotropic medication, when needed or desired by patients and their families.

Obstetrics and Gynecology

Obstetricians and gynecologists serve an important function in a clinic geared toward LGBTQ+ youth. Screening and preventive services are important for LGBTQ+ youth, just as with all other youth. When working with transgender and gender diverse individuals, one has to consider potential barriers that might prevent them from engaging in these routine visits with an OB/GYN provider. Potential barriers include discomfort presenting for services at a "women's health" program, worries and anticipation around misgendering by staff or others at the clinic, discomfort surrounding their anatomy, and potential reaction during an examination (Ng, 2020). Keeping this in mind, the clinic should establish a commitment to create a safe and affirming environment and hire LGBTQ+-competent providers, so that sexual and gender diverse youth's experiences with the gynecology department are as positive as possible.

In addition to these services, patients and families should also be offered reproductive health/fertility consultations, even when patients are not interested in these issues at present (Coleman et al., 2012). Both adolescent and adult patients need to be informed and engage in conversations about reproductive health and family planning considerations when exploring gender-affirming medical interventions. Yet, these conversations are not consistently or frequently happening. In a study with 158 transgender and gender diverse adolescents and young adults, only 20% reported having discussions around fertility in general, and only 13% had discussions about the effects that gender-affirming medical interventions, such as hormone therapy, could have on fertility. Furthermore, 60% of the participants expressed interest in learning more about fertility options (Rafferty, 2019). Studies suggest that semen cryopreservation is a viable and effective fertility preservation method in adolescent and young gender diverse adults and that it is also an option for patients who have started medically affirming interventions (Barnard et al., 2019). The use of fertility services by transgender and gender diverse youth and young adults is low, and potential factors tied to this include: 1) high cost of these services, as insurances often do not cover these; 2) limited availability of services; 3) collection procedures may cause dysphoria; 4) a desire not to delay initiation of gender-affirming medical interventions; and 5) low interest in fertility services in adolescents and young adults (Rafferty, 2019). The lack of interest or clarity regarding fertility goals can make fertility planning and family counseling difficult at times. A resource such as the Transgender Youth Fertility Attitudes Questionnaire can be helpful in exploring these topics with youth and their families (Strang et al., 2018).

An integrated-care health team composed of these different providers can increase access and engagement in services for LGBTQ+ youth and their families. A gender-affirming care model is best achieved through the integration of medical, mental health, and social services (Rafferty, 2018). Providers can work together to decrease stigma, provide education to families, enhance self-worth and empower youth in their identities, facilitate access to care, and help establish supports and create community connections.

While primary care, endocrinology, behavioral health, and reproductive health are important types of services for LGBTQ+ young people, the reality is the entire hospital needs to be a safe environment for sexual and gender diverse youth. Specialized teams of providers often are specifically tailored to the needs of LGBTQ youth, but these young people also seek other services (e.g., emergency care, physical therapy). As such, inclusive policies are needed that span the entire hospital setting.

Policies and Their Function

Hospitals should have affirming policies that create equal access to high-quality health care (Meyer et al., 2016). Existing recommended policies and practices for healthcare facilities are: 1) nondiscrimination and staff training, 2) patient services and support, 3) employee benefits and policies, and 4) patient and community engagement (Hanneman et al., 2022). A report on LGBTQ inclusion in children's hospitals noted that nondiscrimination policies for children's hospitals are not different from adult hospitals, however, there are unique considerations and challenges related to visitation policies (Ng & Hanneman, 2020). For example, it is important to consider how the facility is defining families, given the significant diversity of families that exist and the historic practice of using social work services to investigate families with alternative parental structures. Another unique issue is related to visitation refusal. Depending on age, maturity, and social circumstances of the LGBTQ patient, hospitals can allow youth to refuse visitation, even by a guardian or parent, which is important when caregivers are unsupportive of their identities (Ng & Hanneman, 2020).

Training of staff will be expanded further in the next section; however, it is important to point out that children's hospitals have the ability to use policies to make LGBTQ training required for their staff. Hospitals should deliver patient-centered, intersectional, and culturally sensitive training to their staff that includes a wide range of topics that impact LGBTQ+ youth, such as health disparities, identity development, and the impact of bullying, discrimination, and victimization. Last, children's hospitals can implement various strategies to deliver ongoing trainings for students/

trainees and staff and continuing education opportunities for licensed providers (Dowshen et al., 2016).

Developing policies that support delivery of affirming and inclusive services for LGBTQ+ youth is not without its challenges. Ng and Hanneman (2020) describe that addressing issues of sexuality and sexual orientation are hard to implement in children's hospitals, which result in gaps of care for LGBTQ+ youth. They discuss that pediatrician's attitudes and denial of adolescents as sexual beings, and the policing and shaming of sexual behaviors, contribute to disparities in care for LGBTQ youth. More specifically to transgender and gender diverse youth, they discuss issues related to rooming; clinical concerns such as fertility preservations services for adolescents considering hormone treatment; and the current political climate and the negative implications for health care facilities.

Also, although explored further in another section, patient and community-engagement policies are important in the delivery of care for LGBTQ+ youth. Through community engagement, hospitals are able to understand the needs of the patients they serve and their families (Hanneman et al., 2022). There are many strategies that can be implemented to achieve this, such as being present and supporting LGBTQ community events and activities, inviting LGBTQ community members to be part of hospital advisory committees and boards, taking public stances on state and federal regulations (Ng & Hanneman, 2020), and establishing a point person in the hospital who addresses LGBTQ+ concerns (e.g., the LGBTQ+ veteran care coordinator position that exists in every VHA hospital; US Department of Veterans Affairs, 2021).

Hadland, Yehia, and Makadon (2016) discuss systems-level principles for LGBTQ youth-friendly services. To optimize services focused on the biological, developmental, and psychosocial needs of children, adolescents, and young adults, particularly those who are LGBTQ, these services need to be available, accessible, acceptable, and equitable. Availability refers to the presence of providers with knowledge and competence in working with LGBTQ+ youth. Accessibility refers to the relative ease in which LGBTQ+ youth can obtain services. Acceptability indicates the extent to which clinical services are culturally competent and developmentally appropriate and that confidentiality is assured and protected. Equity is the degree to which clinical care is friendly to all LGBTQ+ youth regardless of race, ethnicity, language, ability to pay, housing status, insurance status, and so on.

Training of Personnel

Discrimination in a healthcare setting may include denial of care, disrespect and abuse, low-quality care, negative attitude and behavior of providers, and lack of confidentiality and privacy; therefore, it is important to train personnel in LGBTQ+ youth issues so that care is delivered in an affirming and equitable way (Sekoni et al., 2017). Studies have found that medical students and practicing healthcare providers receive minimal or no training on LGBT health issues (Parameshwaran et al., 2017). In a mixed-method systemic review, Sekoni and colleagues (2017) found that the content of training for LGBT curricula can be grouped under five topics: key terms and terminology, stigma and discrimination, sexuality and sexual dysfunction, sexual history taking, and LGBT-specific health and health disparities. They also found that the vast majority of trainings were hosted and developed by universities and the trainers were faculty in the institutions. There was a wide variation regarding allotted time, ranging from 1 to 42 hours, with the median being 11 hours. Additionally, they reported that there were changes in attitudes toward accepting sexuality, masturbation, and homosexuality as natural aspects of human experiences and in the level of comfort with and cultural competence in addressing those topics with patients. The most notable change was related to a positive attitude toward homosexuality, indicating that giving employees more access to training is an effective way to improve care for LGBTQ+ patients.

Community Partnerships and Resources

For LGBTQ+ communities disproportionately impacted by health disparities associated with structural and systemic issues, hospitals and medical centers often provide vital healthcare services, especially as initial points of contact for individuals in crisis. These services can include medical care, acute inpatient psychiatry, outpatient psychotherapy for emergency inpatient psychiatric needs and acute and severe mental health concerns, and referral services to other resources (e.g., housing, vocational rehabilitation programs, substance use recovery programs, etc.). LGBTQ+ youth experience increased mental health disparities associated with exposure to societal bias, homophobia, and transphobia, in addition to other forms of discrimination and victimization (Fulginiti et al., 2021). While hospitals and treatment centers aim to address these health disparities, they often lack information about unique community needs and how to provide affirming services to LGBTQ+ youth. As such, it is important for hospitals to form professional partnerships with local community agencies and stakeholders (Freda et al., 2018).

Developing strategic community partnerships from a community development framework informed by social and structural determinants of health can improve quality of service delivery and provider competency (Knight et al., 2014), provide better estimates of financial feasibility for programming, and enhance cultural responsiveness (Freda et al., 2018). Working from a health-equity lens can help build and foster trust between service providers and communities to improve treatment compliance, reduce barriers to care, and improve access to preventive services and programs (Michener et al., 2020). Moreover, these partnerships can center community strengths, foster resilience, and identify protective factors to empower community members to advocate for themselves while challenging structural inequities (Johns et al., 2019). This process can begin by developing community advisory boards to provide nuanced contextual knowledge about the needs of the targeted communities as well as how to best communicate and advertise services and identify implementation issues and appropriate forms of community-driven intervention outreach (e.g., open houses, walk-in informational sessions, presentations at local stakeholder agencies, etc.). Gathering this information while also taking into account the voices and experiences of local activists, advocates, and community resources can help make determinations concerning need-based allocation of resources (e.g., finances, distribution efforts, etc.), which can in turn foster long-term change in service provision in the targeted community.

Creating a Welcoming Environment

As discussed in previous sections of this chapter, LGBTQ+ individuals may encounter various barriers that might impact their access and/or willingness to seek medical care. Many LGBTQ+ individuals report having experienced some type of negative interaction with a medical provider/agency, such as discrimination, disdain, or a general lack of knowledge regarding specific LGBTQ+ realities (Lykens et al., 2018; Rossman et al., 2017; Trevor Project, 2020). Studies have shown that LGBTQ+ patients and their families often scan their surroundings, seeking signs within the environment that may indicate a perception of safety and acceptance for their identities (Joint Commission, 2011). Taking this into account, we must understand that an LGBTQ+ patient might approach a medical setting with a sense of hesitation, fear, and distrust. Thus, it is important that an LGBTQ+-focused medical facility take an active and intentional approach toward establishing a safe and affirming environment for everyone. Here are some considerations to take into account toward this goal.

PHYSICAL ENVIRONMENT

The physical spaces of the facility, such as the lobby, waiting room, and examination/consult rooms, can be used to indicate the facility's level of awareness and supportiveness for the LGBTQ+ population. Studies have shown that visual cues of LGBTQ+ affirmation such as LGBTQ+-themed stickers, pronoun pins, pride flags, and LGBTQ+-specific reading materials can foster a sense of acceptance and ease for LGBTQ+ patients (Quinn et al., 2020; McClain et al., 2015). Additional visual elements such as posters or marketing materials exhibiting same-sex couples or gender diverse people, as well as having brochures about LGBTQ+ concerns, such as safer sex, hormone therapy, mental health, substance use, and sexually transmitted infections, also can help build a more welcoming and affirming space for LGBTQ+ patients (National LGBTQIA+ Health Education Center, 2021). The inclusion of gender-neutral and/or one-person capacity restrooms within the facility also can help create a more comfortable environment for LGBTQ+ patients, especially for gender diverse individuals who might experience discomfort or distress related to using a binary-gendered and shared public bathroom (Quinn et al., 2020).

In a previous section, we discussed the importance of creating inclusive policies to guarantee appropriate care for sexual and gender diverse patients. Displaying the agency's nondiscrimination policy, patient's bill of rights, and grievance procedures to report discrimination or mistreatment in high-traffic areas around the office space also can help set a more positive tone for patients and their families.

REGISTRATION AND DOCUMENTATION PROCESSES

Registration offers an opportunity for LGBTQ+ patients to feel welcomed and validated by using inclusive language on the forms and documents provided. Forms should include options to report sexual orientation, gender identity, and chosen name and pronouns. These options can help communicate to patients that the agency recognizes and respects their identities. Questions on the intake forms should also be formulated in a gender inclusive manner, steering away from a heteronormative perspective. Some examples of these include:

- Relationship status: replacing questions about *marital status* with *relationship status* (ex., single, partnered, married, etc.). Including gender-neutral language when collecting this information, such as using the term *partner(s)* or *significant other(s)*, rather than *husband* or *wife*. (National LGBTQIA+ Health Education Center, 2021)
- Gender identity: including various gender diverse options in this section, such as man, woman, trans man, trans woman, gender nonconfirming, and other identity terms.
- Family/support network: expanding definitions to recognize how diverse family constellations can be, as well as allowing for the inclusion of chosen families. Incorporating an explicit definition around family that includes "individuals not legally related to the patient" (Joint Commission, 2011) communicates a sense of validation and allows the patient the opportunity to accurately identify their support network. Response options should also be worded in a gender-neutral manner, such as replacing *mother* and *father* with *parent* or *caregiver*.

LANGUAGE AND COMMUNICATION

McClain and colleagues (2015) found in their sample that some of the interpersonal factors that helped LGBTQ+ youth feel more welcomed and accepted in medical spaces included: 1) being treated with respect, 2) having a competent provider, 3) perceived appreciation of their own identities and validation of these identities, and 4) having providers who listened to them and understood their concerns. As a way to work toward these conditions, it is important to explore the communication dynamics, both verbal and nonverbal, that are occurring between staff and patients. Support staff, medical providers, security personnel, as well as any other employees working in the department are recommended to receive appropriate training regarding providing affirmative care for LGBTQ+ patients. Please refer to the previous section, "Training of Personnel," regarding specifics that should be covered in these trainings.

Instructing staff to use the patient's chosen name and pronouns, adopt gender-neutral language when referring to sexual and/or relationship partners, anatomy, and procedures, and refraining from making assumptions regarding a patient's identities can lead to more positive experiences between patients and staff (Baldwin et al., 2018). Staff can be asked to add identifiers to their attire, such as pins displaying their own pronouns, and taught how to ask questions in a sensitive manner. For example, when gathering information, staff can be instructed to disclose their own name and pronouns before asking the patient to share their name and pronouns (i.e., "My name is X, and my pronouns are Y. What name and pronouns would you like me to use?").

Baldwin and colleagues' (2018) study also found that provider's reactions to a patient's identity disclosure can impact the patient's experience of the encounter. When providers reacted in a neutral manner or treated the identity disclosure as routine, participants reported a better perception of the experience. Nonverbal cues can be just as impactful to patient-provider interactions. Hood and colleagues (2018) explored LGBTQ+ students' experiences with health services, and a common source for experiences of discrimination for participants was patient-provider interactions. One account in this study detailed the discomfort experienced after a patient disclosed their sexual identity and noticed the provider's lack of response and "shift" in demeanor. In Rossman and colleagues' (2017) study, participants reported that the most common reaction they received was this "lack of reaction" response, which some interpreted as a lack of care on the provider's part. Rossman and colleagues (2017) also reported that other emotional reactions such as confusion, surprise or disbelief from providers led to patients' feeling discomfort. Based on this, staff members need to build self-awareness around their body language, facial expressions, and other gestures that may be sending unintended microaggressive messages.

Conclusion

Our objective with this chapter was to highlight recommendations and steps that can be taken to provide quality care for LGBTQ+ youth within hospital settings. We hope that the information provided can help providers understand the importance of affirmative LGBTQ+ care and motivate them to address the particular challenges LGBTQ+ youth face in order to better meet the needs of these young people. We hope readers are willing to take stock of the behaviors and efforts they are currently engaging in, how effective they may or may not be for this population, and implement some of the strategies outlined in this chapter. Changes at the institutional level can include modifying existing policies to ensure they are LGBTQ+ inclusive and providing consistent staff training related to LGBTQ+ care, and changes at the micro level can involve adding an LGBTQ+-themed pin to your lapel or deciding to start every interaction with a patient by asking for their chosen names and pronouns. Healthcare is a universal need, and healthcare providers should be doing what they can to ensure that they are prepared to serve young people, regardless of their identities, with respect and dignity.

References

Agana, M. G., Greydanus, D. E., Indyk, J. A., Calles, J. L. Jr., Kushner, J., Leibowitz, S., Chelvakumar, G., & Cabral, M. D. (2019). Caring for the transgender adolescent and young adult: Current concepts of an evolving process in the 21st century. *Disease-a-Month, 65*(9), 303–356. https://doi.org/10.1016/j.disamonth.2019.07.004

Asakura, K. (2016). Extraordinary acts to "show up": Conceptualizing resilience of LGBTQ youth. *Youth & Society, 51*(2), 268–285. https://doi.org/10.1177/0044118x16671430

Baldwin, A., Dodge, B., Schick, V. R., Light, B., Scharrs, P. W., Herbenick, D., & Fortenberry, J. D. (2018). Transgender and genderqueer individuals' experiences with health care providers: What's working, what's not, and where do we go from here? *Journal of Health Care for the Poor and Underserved, 29*(4), 1300–1318. https://doi.org/10.1353/hpu.2018.0097

Barnard, E. P., Dhar, C. P., Rothenberg, S. S., Menke, M. N., Witchel, S. F., Montano, G. T., Orwig, K. E., & Valli-Pulaski, H. (2019). Fertility preservation outcomes in adolescent and young adult feminizing transgender patients. *Pediatrics, 144*(3). https://doi.org/10.1542/peds.2018-3943

Casimir, G. (2019). Why children's hospitals are unique and so essential. *Frontiers in Pediatrics, 7*, 1–5. https://dx.doi.org/10.3389%2Ffped.2019.00305

Chulani, V., Cooper, M. B., Reitman, D., & Warus, J. (2021). Medical care for adolescent males who have sex with males. *Current Pediatrics Reports, 9*(2), 30–26. https://doi.org/10.1007/s40124-021-00237-w

Coker, T. R., Austin, S. B., & Schuster, M. A. (2010). The health and health care of lesbian, gay, and bisexual adolescents. *Annual Review of Public Health, 31*, 457–477. https://doi.org/10.1146/annurev.publhealth.012809.103636

Coleman, E., Bockting, W., Botzer, M., Cohen-Kettenis, P., DeCuypere, G., Feldman, J., Fraser, L., Green, J., Knudson, G., Meyer, W. J., Monstrey, S., Adler, R. K., Brown, G. R., Devor, A. H., Ehrbar, R., Ettner, R., Eyler, E., Garofalo, R., Karasic, D. H., . . . Zucker, K. (2012). Standards of care for the health of transsexual, transgender, and gender-nonconforming people, version 7. *International Journal of Transgenderism, 13*(4), 165–232. https://doi.org/10.1080/15532739.2011.7008733

Coulter, R. W. S., Egan, J. E., Kinsky, S., Friedman, M. R., Eckstrand, K. L., Frankeberger, J., Folb, B. L., Mair, C., Markovic, N., Silvestre, A., Stall, R., & Miller, E. (2019). Mental health, drug, and violence interventions for sexual/gender minorities: A systematic review. *Pediatrics, 144*(3), e20183367. https://doi.org/10.1542/peds.2018-3367

de Vries, A. L. C. (2020). Challenges in timing puberty suppression for gender-nonconforming adolescents. *Pediatrics, 146*(4), e2020010611. https://doi.org/10.1542/peds.2020-010611

Diamond, G. M., Diamond, G. S., Levy, S., Closs, C., Ladipo, T., & Siqueland, L. (2012). Attachment-based family therapy for suicidal lesbian, gay, and bisexual adolescents: A treatment development study and open trial with preliminary findings. *Psychotherapy, 49*(1), 62–71. https://doi.org/10.1037/a0026247

Dowshen, N., Meadows, R., Byrnes, M., Hawkins, L., Eder, J., & Noonan, K. (2016). Policy perspective: Ensuring comprehensive care and support for gender nonconforming children and adolescents. *Transgender Health, 1*(1), 75–85. https://doi.org/10.1089/trgh.2016.0002

Freda, B., Kozick, D., & Spencer, A. (2018). Partnerships for health: Lessons for bridging community-based organizations and health care organizations. https://www.chcs.org/media/CBO-HCO_Partnership_update_032018.pdf

Fulginiti, A., Rhoades, H., Mamey, M. R., Klemmer, C., Srivastava, A., Weskamp, G., & Goldbach, J. T. (2021). Sexual minority stress, mental health symptoms, and suicidality among LGBTQ youth accessing crisis services. *Journal of Youth and Adolescence, 50*(5), 893–905. https://doi.org/10.1007/s10964-020-01354-3

Hadland, S. E., Yehia, B. R., & Makadon, H. J. (2016). Caring for lesbian, gay, bisexual, transgender, and questioning youth in inclusive and affirmative environments. *Pediatric Clinics of North America, 63*(6), 955–969. https://doi.org/10.1016/j.pcl.2016.07.001

Hanneman, T., Garcia, M. R., Touhey, S., & Steward, D. (2022). *Healthcare Equality Index 2022: Promoting equitable and inclusive care for lesbian, gay, bisexual, transgender, and queer patients and their families.* Human Rights Campaign Foundation.

Hood, L., Sherrell, D., Pfeffer, C. A., & Mann, E. S. (2018). LGBTQ college students' experiences with university health services: An exploratory study. *Journal of Homosexuality, 66*(6), 797–814. https://doi.org/10.1080/00918369.2018.1484234

Johns, M. M., Poteat, V. P., Horn, S. S., & Kosciw, J. (2019). Strengthening our schools to promote resilience and health among LGBTQ youth: Emerging evidence and research priorities from *The State of LGBTQ Youth Health and Wellbeing* Symposium. *LGBT Health, 6*(4), 146–155. https://doi.org/10.1089/lgbt.2018.0109

Joint Commission. (2011). *Advancing effective communication, cultural competence, and patient-and family-centered care for the lesbian, gay, bisexual, and transgender (LGBT) community: A field guide.* https://www.jointcommission.org/-/media/tjc/documents/resources/patient-safety-topics/health-equity/lgbtfieldguide_web_linked_verpdf.pdf?db=web&hash=FD725DC02CFE6E4F21A35EBD839BBE97&hash=FD725DC02CFE6E4F21A35EBD839BBE97

Knight, D. A., & Jarrett, D. (2017). Preventive health care for women who have sex with women. *American Family Physician, 95*(5), 314–321.

Knight, R. E., Shoveller, J. A., Carson, A. M., & Contreras-Whitney, J. G. (2014). Examining clinicians' experiences providing sexual health services for LGBTQ youth: Considering social and structural determinants of health in clinical practice. *Health Education Research, 29*(4), 662–670. https://doi.org/10.1093/her/cyt116

Kort, J. (2008). *Gay affirmative therapy for the straight clinician: The essential guide.* W.W. Norton & Co.

Kuper, L. E., Stewart, S., Preston, S., Lau, M., & Lopez, X. (2020). Body dissatisfaction and mental health outcomes of youth on gender-affirming hormone therapy. *Pediatrics, 145*(4), e20193006. https://doi.org/10.1542/peds.2019-3006

Lykens, J. E., LeBlanc, A. J., & Bockting, W. O. (2018). Healthcare experiences among young adults who identify as genderqueer or nonbinary. *LGBT Health, 5*(3), 191–196. https://doi.org/10.1089/lgbt.2017.0215

McClain, Z., Hawkins, L. A., & Yehia, B. R. (2015). Creating welcoming spaces for lesbian, gay, bisexual, and transgender (LGBT) patients: An evaluation of the health care environment. *Journal of Homosexuality, 63*(3), 387–393. https://doi.org/10.1080/00918369.2016.1124694

Meyer, E., Levasseur, M. D., Hanneman, T., & Snowden, S. (2016). *Creating equal access to quality health care for transgender patients: Transgender-affirming hospital policies.* Lambda Legal.

Meyer, I. H. (2003). Prejudice, social stress, and mental health in lesbian, gay, and bisexual populations: Conceptual issues and research evidence. *Psychological Bulletin, 129*(5), 674–697. https://doi.org/10.1037/0033-2909.129.5.674

Michener, L., Aguilar-Gaxiola, S., Alberti, P. M., Castaneda, M. J., Castrucci, B. C., Harrison, L. M., Hughes, L. S., Richmond, A., & Wallerstein, N. (2020). Engaging with communities—lessons (re)learned from COVID-19. *Preventing Chronic Disease, 17*, E65. https://doi.org/10.5888/pcd17.200250

Murad, M. H., Elamin, M. B., Garcia, M. Z., Mullan, R. J., Murad, A., Erwin, P. J., & Montori, V. M. (2010). Hormonal therapy and sex reassignment: A systematic review and meta-analysis of quality of life and psychosocial outcomes. *Clinical Endocrinology, 72*(2), 214–231. https://doi.org/10.1111/j.1365-2265.2009.03625.x

National LGBTQIA+ Health Education Center. (2021, May 4). *Ten strategies for creating inclusive health care environments for LGBTQIA+ people.* LGBTQIA+ Health Education Center. https://www.lgbtqiahealtheducation.org/publication/ten-strategies-for-creating-inclusive-health-care-environments-for-lgbtqia-people-2021/

Newcomb, M. E., LaSala, M. C., Bouris, A., Mustanski, B., Prado, G., Schrager, S. M., & Huebner, D. M. (2019). The influence of families on LGBTQ youth health: A call to action for innovation in research and intervention development. *LGBT Health, 6*(4), 139–145. https://doi.org/10.1089/lgbt.2018.0157

Ng, H. (2020). *Comprehensive care clinics for transgender & non-binary youth: Considerations and best practices.* Human Rights Campaign Foundation.

Ng, H., & Hanneman, T. (2020). *LGBTQ inclusion in children's hospitals: Lessons learned from the Healthcare Equality Index.* Human Rights Campaign Foundation.

Parameshwaran, V., Cockbain, B. C., Hillyard, M., & Price, J. R. (2017). Is the lack of specific lesbian, gay, bisexual, transgender and queer/questioning (LGBTQ) health care education in medical school a cause for concern? Evidence from a survey of knowledge and practice among UK medical students. *Journal of Homosexuality, 64*(3), 367–381. https://doi.org/10.1080/00918369.2016.1190218

Quinn, G. P., Alpert, A. B., Sutter, M., & Schabath, M. B. (2020). What oncologists should know about treating sexual and gender minority patients with cancer. *JCO Oncology Practice, 16*(6), 309–316. https://doi.org/10.1200/op.20.00036

Rafferty, J. (2018). Ensuring comprehensive care and support for transgender and gender-diverse children and adolescents. *Pediatrics, 142*(4), e20182162. https://doi.org/10.1542/peds.2018-2162

Rafferty, J. (2019). Fertility preservation outcomes and considerations in transgender and gender-diverse youth. *Pediatrics, 144*(3), e20192000. https://doi.org/10.1542/peds.2019-2000

Reisner, S. L., Poteat, T., Keatley, J., Cabral, M., Mothopeng, T., Dunham, E., Holland, C. E., Max, R., & Baral, S. D. (2016). Global health burden and needs of transgender populations: A review. *Lancet, 388*(10042), 412–436. https://doi.org/10.1016/S0140-6736(16)00684-X

Rossman, K., Salamanca, P., & Macapagal, K. (2017). A qualitative study examining young adults' experiences of disclosure and nondisclosure of LGBTQ identity to health care providers. *Journal of Homosexuality, 64*(10), 1390–1410. https://doi.org/10.1080/00918369.2017.1321379

Ryan, C., Huebner, D., Diaz, R. M., & Sanchez, J. (2009). Family rejection as a predictor of negative health outcomes in White and Latino lesbian, gay, and bisexual young adults. *Pediatrics, 123*(1), 346–352. https://doi.org/10.1542/peds.2007-3524

Sekoni, A. O., Gale, N. K., Manga-Atangana, B., Bhadhuri, A., & Jolly, K. (2017). The effects of educational curricula and training on LGBT-specific health issues for healthcare students and professionals: A mixed-method systematic review. *Journal of the International AIDS Society, 20*, 1–13. http://dx.doi.org/10.7448/IAS.20.1.21624

Strang, J. F., Jarin, J., Call, D., Clark, B., Wallace, G. L., Anthony, L. G., Kenworthy, L., & Gomez-Lobo, V. (2018). Transgender youth fertility attitudes questionnaire: Measure development in nonautistic and autistic transgender youth and their parents. *Journal of Adolescent Health, 62*(2), 128–135. https://doi.org/10.1016/j.jadohealth.2017.07.022

Trevor Project. (2020). *The Trevor Project national survey 2020.* https://www.thetrevorproject.org/survey-2020/

Turban, J. L., King, D., Carswell, J. M., & Keuroghlian, A. S. (2020). Pubertal suppression for transgender youth and risk of suicidal ideation. *Pediatrics, 145*(2). https://doi.org/10.1542/peds.2019-1725

US Department of Veterans Affairs. (2021, July 1). *Patient care services.* Retrieved from VA LGBTQ+ Policies: https://www.patientcare.va.gov/LGBT/VA_LGBT_Policies.asp

Vance, S. R. Jr., Ehrensaft, D., & Rosenthal, S. M. (2014). Psychological and medical care of gender nonconforming youth. *Pediatrics, 134*(6), 1184–1192. https://doi.org/10.1542/peds.2014-0772

CHAPTER 10

Improving Child Welfare and Foster Care Outcomes for LGBTQ+ Youth

Kellen Grayson, PsyD, LMFT, & Mira Krishnan, PhD, ABPP

When considering the lives and well-being of lesbian, gay, bisexual, transgender, and queer/questioning (LGBTQ+) youth, the conjunction of several factors makes consideration of the child welfare system of care of particular importance. First, LGBTQ+ youth are at increased risk for numerous factors that are known to predispose youth to contact with the child welfare system. These include higher rates of family rejection, increased risk of polyvictimization, and increased exposure to poverty (Jacobs & Freundlich, 2006; Sterzing et al., 2017). In addition, many youth experience daily microaggressions and stressors that impact their self-esteem and health outcomes (Jacobs & Freundlich, 2006). These stressors are present in the daily lives of LGBTQ+ youth, especially LGBTQ+ people who are non-white. This adversity becomes more prominent when experiencing minority stress both within their homes of origin, where they may be the only LGBTQ+ person in the family, and especially in out-of-home placements where they already are considered an "outsider" of the family system. The sexual and gender minority population experiences a magnification of stress compared to non-LGBTQ+ foster youth (Prince et al., 2021). LGBTQ+ foster youth of color face additional stress and rejection related to their intersecting racial and ethnic identities. These individuals encounter converging traumas due to exposure to intensive levels of homophobia, heterosexism, transphobia, racism, and xenophobia.

LGBTQ+ youth are *overrepresented* in child welfare settings and in out-of-home placements (Dettlaff et al., 2018). And yet, providers in these settings underemphasize gender and sexual diversity in terms of provider acumen and training (Dettlaff et al., 2018). This is further complicated by legal attempts to both disenfranchise LGBTQ+ people (and youth particularly) as well as legislative attempts to permit or even enshrine discrimination against LGBTQ+ youth in child welfare settings.

Recently, the Supreme Court made a ruling in the case of *Fulton et al. v. City of Philadelphia, Pennsylvania*, No. 19-123 (2021), confirming that religious organizations can discriminate against LGBTQ+ parents and children. Originally, a Pennsylvania chapter of Catholic Charities declined providing a lesbian couple an opportunity to be foster parents. After being denied, they sued Catholic Charities, with the case eventually being decided by the Supreme Court. On June 17, 2021, the Supreme Court decided that Catholic Charities can refuse to work with LGBTQ+ families who want to provide care to foster children in need. Despite the many families that could serve these youth, this religious agency decided that only heterosexual foster parents can serve youth (Fulton, 2021). Justice Roberts, writing on behalf of the court, found that "the contractual non-discrimination requirement burdens . . . religious exercise" (*Fulton et al., v. City of Philadelphia*, 2021). Under the guise of religious freedom, some foster agencies at least for now can refuse to work with LGBTQ+ families. Many foster agencies are privately funded, which allows them to undertake actions that would be considered illegal if they received federal funding. As a result, discrimination can be more bountiful in those agencies.

Family Rejection, Abuse, and Homophobia

Youth who have marginalized sexual and gender identities are so commonly rejected by their families of origin and also kicked out of their foster homes that homelessness is the very foundation and history of the LGBTQ+ experience for many youth (see McCann & Brown, 2019 for a recent review). It is such a common narrative that it is now both an expected and stereotypical concept when engaging with LGBTQ+ youth and adults. A typical question frequently asked by a non-queer person when hearing that a person is a part of the LGBTQ+ community is, "How is your relationship with your family?" or "What does your family think about your identity?" Many of these youth were given one-way tickets (if given anything at all) to major cities such as New York or San Francisco.

As a result of such abandonment and family cut off, LGBTQ+ youth and adults have historically created their own configurations known as a chosen family, which is a phenomenon that emerged in response to ongoing family rejection, abuse, and homelessness that queer youth face (Hammack et al., 2019). Hammack and colleagues (2019) attribute the paradigm of chosen family not only as a response to family rejection but also due to the legal and social denial of same-sex marriage and unions. This led naturally to LGBTQ+ youth and adults wishing to create alternatives to the nucleus family. This was particularly relevant during the AIDS crisis, when biological families regularly turned their backs on their dying sons, and thus community members, very often lesbians as well as other gay men, formed alternative families and took care of their own (Jackson Levin et al., 2020).

African American and Latino New York City LGBTQ+ youth in the 1980s created families by forming houses, mostly led by house mothers, who identified homeless queer youth and invited them in off the streets. Ballroom culture (Bailey, 2014) created a space for different expressions of identity, especially gender expansiveness. Ballroom culture is a historically safe environment where creativity, fashion, and voguing are performed with the form of gender expression (Bailey, 2014). Filmmaker Jennie Livingston's documentary *Paris Is Burning* (Livingston, 1990) captures how ballroom culture created a space for gender survival for its participants. Indeed, the film showcases how many LGBTQ+ youth, especially Black and Brown transgender people, are at great risk of harm and fight to survive every day. One of the film's older participants, a house mother, stated, "When they're undetectable and they can walk out of that ballroom into the sunlight and onto the subway and get home, and still have all their clothes and no blood running off their bodies—those are the femme realness queens . . . and usually it's a category for young queens" (*Paris Is Burning*, 1990).

The hit series POSE, which is in part based upon *Paris is Burning*, shows the narratives of homeless LGBTQ+ youth and how important creating community is when a family system is voided from a young person's life. During the pilot of POSE, the main elder in the series, Pray Tell, states, "Houses are homes to all the little boys and girls who never had one, and they keep comin' every day, just as sure as the sun rises" (POSE, 2018). LGBTQ+ kids arrive at shelters daily from all over the country after being rejected from their family homes for being LGBTQ+ identified (Ream & Forge, 2014).

LGBTQ+ Youth and Polyvictimization

Adversity in the lives of youth can take many forms, ranging from acute, discrete traumatizing events to chronic and lasting sources of traumatization, as well as in complex combinations of ongoing and acute stressors. Many models of adversity in the lives of youth view this in a dose-response fashion, such as in the case of cumulative adverse childhood events (ACEs), experienced by the time a youth attains age 18 (Hughes et al., 2017). In addition to evaluating the cumulative burden of trauma or adversity a youth faces, polyvictimization allows for a framework in which certain traumas can be seen as interrelated; for instance, a youth who is a victim of mugging may experience both trauma related to physical assault and adversity related to the violation against their property. This type of lens helps us better understand both the cumulative burden of trauma and patterns of traumatization. Baams (2018) investigated polyvictimization in LGBTQ+ youth using data from a 2016 student survey that sampled more than 81,000 students in Minnesota. While 80–85% of LGBTQ+ youth experienced "relatively low level abuse" in this study, 1–2% of youth in the full sample experienced polyvictimization. This study found that polyvictimization was 1.8–7.5 times more likely for nontrans-identified sexual minority youth (lesbian, gay, bisexual, or questioning) and 1.5–2.9 times more likely for transgender youth. An additional, independent study, which included a national US sample of gender and sexual minority youth (Sterzing et al., 2017), found much higher rates of polyvictimization, ranging from 33.0% for cisgender male sexual minority youth, to 63.4% for transgender female youth. These differences may reflect differences in sampling methodology, differences in means of assessing trauma history, or the lack of a consistent definition of polyvictimization, but the results show consistently elevated rates for gender and sexual minority youth.

Polyvictimization risk can also be affected by other factors, such as ethnic minority status. Foster youth who have cross-cultural identities along with being a sexual or gender minority are commonly present in the foster care system (Watt & Kim, 2019). African American children in particular are more likely to be placed outside of the home and encounter higher frequency of placement changes that often lack a suitable placement for prolonged periods of time. Sadly, some may never find a stable home (Courtney & Wong, 1996; Boyd, 2014). As in society, youth of color in the foster care system often are not given the same treatment as white children, which may include less referrals for psychotherapy and case management services (McMillen et al., 2004). As a result, society's most vulnerable individuals are left to struggle on their own to recover from traumatic events. Foster youth who do not receive adequate support, including mental health services, are more likely to then have encounters with the juvenile justice system.

Research has demonstrated that polyvictimization is also more common in youth who experience higher acuity care, such as referrals into child welfare and out-of-home placements, even when studies do not focus specifically on LGBTQ+ youth (Cyr et al., 2012). Polyvictimization in turn increases the risk of a range of adverse outcomes that extend through youth and well into adulthood. These include broadly poorer perception of physical and mental health and higher rates of anxiety, depression, substance abuse, and suicidality (Kassing et al., 2021).

Poverty and LGBTQ+ Youth Vulnerability

Another factor that merits consideration in terms of risk that LGBTQ+ youth face is economic impoverishment. Poverty among LGBTQ+ adults is well established. Badgett, Choi, and Wilson (2019), in a UCLA Williams Institute research briefing, noted a combined estimate of poverty for all LGBTQ+ adults of 21.6%, compared to a rate of 15.7% in cisgender, heterosexual adults. This included higher rates of poverty for sexual minority cisgender women than sexual minority cisgender men but particularly high rates of poverty for bisexual and transgender adults, with rates of 29.4% for cisgender, bisexual women and for transgender people. These findings were also overlaid on racial/ethnic disparities, with particularly high rates of poverty for Black and Native American LGBTQ+ people. Of note, the sample was also limited by an absence of sexual orientation and gender diversity data on poverty in 15 states. Finally, and of particular relevance, in adult samples, poverty is most concentrated among younger populations (representing both youth who have just reached adulthood and the young parents of many children)—this is true both in cisgender, heterosexual, and LGBTQ+ people, but this finding was more pronounced in the LGBTQ+ sample, with a peak poverty rate of 30.8% for the 18–24 age range. Kee Tobar, an attorney and fellow of the Stoneleigh Foundation, has called this a "closet to poverty pipeline" (2018). Brandon Robinson, a sociologist, worked alongside a sample of LGBTQ+ youth (three-quarters were also ethnic minorities) and cited a "context of family poverty shaped by instability, including parental incarceration, contact with [Child Protective Services], parental drug and alcohol abuse, and other stressful life events" as leading to particular instability in the lives of poor LGBTQ+ youth. While he noted that more affluent families also demonstrate homophobia and transphobia, the interplay of these factors led to more instability and increased risk of homelessness for the LGBTQ+ youth from poor families (Tobar, 2018).

Overrepresentation of LGBTQ+ Youth in Child Welfare Services

Although the cause is not completely clear, research has demonstrated that LGBTQ+ youth are more likely to be placed into child welfare services. Investigation of a national US sample that included nearly 1,100 youth who had been referred to child welfare services found a rate of sexual minority identification (lesbian, gay, or bisexual) of 15.5%, well above most estimates of community prevalence of sexual minority identities (Dettlaff et al., 2018). A subsequent study combined national US samples and found that sexual minority youth were 2.4 times as likely as heterosexual peers to be placed in foster care, with overall overrepresentation in child welfare, broadly, ranging from 2 to 2.5 times that for heterosexual peers, and in out-of-home placements at 3.7 to 4.7 times the rate for heterosexual peers.

The State of Foster Care and Child Welfare Systems

POLICIES AND PRACTICES IN CHILD WELFARE SERVICES

The child welfare system is overloaded with children that need homes, and not enough foster placements exist to care for them. When foster homes are available, children need to be placed with immediacy, which does not always allow for welfare system staff to align a match to a client's sociocultural needs. Often, the child welfare system must prioritize finding housing that is safe from child abuse when placements are limited. Due to the lack of housing placements, LGBTQ+ youth may be put into a home that does not fit their identity needs. However, for an LGBTQ+-identified youth, the lack of cultural competency in a home that can address their unique needs most likely will be devastating. Although such a home may meet agency standards for basic needs, it may still be an inadequate and even unsafe home for a vulnerable LGBTQ+ youth.

Unfortunately, negative experiences for LGBTQ+ youth are quite common in foster care. Mallon (2001) describes that 78% of young people and 88% of child welfare professionals report that it is not safe for foster youth to openly identify as a sexual minority when they are placed in the foster care system. When LGBTQ+ youth do disclose gender and sexuality differences in foster care despite the consequences, they encounter challenges that their cisgender and straight peers do not experience (Children's Bureau, 2013). Lack of specific training, foster parents' religious intolerance, conservative political viewpoints, as well as homophobia and transphobia, may create tension between a foster parent and a child. These issues can also arise in residential settings, where multiple youth reside together, and where bullying is present and dangerous. Typical issues related to friends, dating, choice of clothing, having access to community, and gender expression may magnify a youth's differences within their placements. Such tensions can lead to disagreements, punitive actions by foster parents, harmful practices such as conversion therapy, and possibly unsafe and/or self-destructive behaviors and acting out by the youth. They also mean that polyvictimization is not a static, baseline feature of gender and sexual minority youth when they "enter care," but a risk to which they continue to be exposed *during* care (Cyr et al., 2012). Not surprisingly, a failed placement can result, in which a youth is given a notice of removal from a home or group home.

Sadly, most LGBTQ+ youth are at risk of multiple placement failures while in foster care. In addition to receiving blatant discrimination, youth may also be overly scrutinized for age-normative behaviors. Foster parents have the right to give notice to a youth in their care for any reason, with the expectation the youth will be moved within days. While many agencies will try to work with a foster home to improve the situation before a notice is final, youth often prefer to have a removal occur rather than live in a rejecting environment. Tragically, in such situations, youth may actually re-experience the type of trauma they had in the primary home they were initially removed from. It's unsurprising that youth may also run away from intolerant foster parents and group homes, becoming AWOL (Absence without Leave), often ending up homeless and on the streets.

LGBTQ+ youth enter the foster care system for many of the same reasons as non-LGBTQ+ youth in care. These reasons often fall within the categories of physical and/or sexual abuse, neglect, and/or parental substance abuse. Most, if not all, youth in foster care have been impacted by significant amounts of trauma, including the trauma of removal from their birth families, even when abusive. They experience high amounts of grief and loss and require nurturance and acceptance to begin to heal. In addition to the tragic experiences these youth have suffered, LGBTQ+ youth have the added layer of trauma that comes from being rejected or mistreated by their caregivers because of their sexual orientation, gender identity, or gender expression.

In addition, LGBTQ+ youth in foster care are shown to have a higher level of victimization and mental health problems than their peers (Irvine & Canfield, 2016). When youth are not able to disclose their identity or are discriminated against as a result of doing so, they experience much higher levels of depression and are more likely to have an increase in suicidal ideation and engage in suicidal behaviors (Ryan et al., 2009). In fact, they are six times more likely to have serious depressive episodes, three times more likely to abuse illegal drugs (Ryan et al., 2009), and more than eight times as likely to attempt suicide (Children's Bureau, 2013).

Yet, studies are limited and vary in the accuracy of how many LGBTQ+ youth are actually in the child welfare system. Better tracking is needed to ensure consistent results and thus improve policy making, as well as increase the number of LGBTQ+-accepting homes. Pilot programs in some cities include utilizing LGBTQ+-savvy "host families" who are less monitored or less regulated than foster homes and more connected to LGBTQ+-specific resources in the community, such as LGBT centers and job training programs. These programs are driven by the communities in which they serve and are organized by LGBTQ+ community members, not child welfare. Rates of success and outcome tracking compared to traditional settings are not available yet because of their fairly new status and their nontraditional nature.

TRAINING AND OVERSIGHT OF FOSTER PARENTS AND CHILD WELFARE WORKERS

LGBTQ+ youth in foster care need the same validation from caregivers that all youth do, and their individual interests and skills should be encouraged. This does not always happen naturally in foster care. To become licensed foster care providers, potential foster parents must complete a multitude of steps including extensive background checks, home inspections, and a training process. A major component of the mandatory training is related to the specific issues of foster care children. Training topics include education around trauma-informed care practices, how to counter difficult behaviors, how best to navigate the foster care system, the legal and ethical standards of child abuse reporting, and sometimes a brief training on multicultural practices. Basic issues around LGBTQ+ identity may be included, but it may not be provided by expert practitioners or be in sufficient detail. When such training is offered, it should begin with an overview of the unique strengths of LGBTQ+ youth, rather than be focused on perceived maladaptive tendencies. Trainings for foster parents around LGBTQ+ issues need significant expansion and should include units on issues such as the importance of using gender-affirming names and pronouns, legal rights, medical transition for transgender teens, social transition for transgender children, and education on nonbinary gender identities. After training on validating strengths and core identities is presented, specific affiliated issues such as the common intersectionality between eating disorders and body dysphoria can be shared. All such topics should become standard practice.

Once training is completed and background checks are cleared, then foster parents are set to begin receiving children in their home. Experienced foster parents know that they can receive any type of child with any type of background. Yet, having a youth in one's home can be a different reality. Although experienced and inexperienced foster parents alike are excited to welcome their new foster child, most foster parents do not imagine, like many parents, that their child will be part of the LGBTQ+ community.

As a former supervisor (Dr. Kellen Grayson) working in a Child Protective Services care facility, I witnessed, multiple times, foster youth being rejected for being queer before placement was completed. Youth would anxiously await foster parents en route to the center to pick them up, but then the foster parent would see a youth who was perceived to be gender expansive, and the foster parent would turn around and not take them. The youth would be devastated as the rejection was immediate, and they would often internalize this rejection. Although foster parents were not supposed to engage in these types of actions, they did, and their rejecting behavior did not prevent them from still fostering other youth in their home.

Gaps in Care

TRANSITION-AGE YOUTH

Many sexual minority youth experience negative outcomes when exiting foster care and developing into young adulthood (Mallon, 1998). When a youth exits foster care, it can be an overwhelming experience, especially when youth do not have basic resources needed or enough foundational life skills to function successfully. Aftercare services are limited for transitional-age youth (TAY) and especially for gender and sexual minorities. In addition, many youth prefer to opt out of aftercare services altogether in order to protect themselves from harassment and discrimination (Wilber et al., 2006).

LGBTQ+ TAY youth struggle to attain self-sufficiency upon exiting foster care primarily due to a lack of support for post-secondary educational options, a lack of safe and affordable housing, a scarcity of job training facilities, poverty, mental health and/or substance abuse problems, a dearth of role models and mentors, and discrimination due to LGBTQ+ identity. These are often all compounded for youth of color. It is not uncommon for this population to have experienced educational disruption due to multiple foster placements, avoidance of school due to bullying or undiagnosed special needs such as ADHD or other learning issues, and ongoing discrimination while in the classroom. Disrupted education leads to not obtaining a high school diploma or GED, which impairs prospects for employment (Toro et al., 2007). When employment is limited, poverty is inevitable. Impoverishment is difficult to overcome as basic survival becomes the focus.

Lack of life skills are also attributed to multiple placement changes and lack of educational and vocational opportunities, as well as limited modeling and coaching from foster parents and/or group home staff. Foster youth who are transitioning to adulthood, often at or just before they turn age 18, are typically given resources, life skills courses, and vocational training to maintain sustainability. However, when LGBTQ+ foster youth transition into adulthood, they have experienced such abandonment and trauma, as well as a systemic neglect of their specific core identities, that they often opt out of services even when they are offered.

Community is an important factor in LGBTQ+ identity formation and often the key factor in creating a solid sense of self. LGBTQ+ foster youth can be denied community access when in placement and therefore become isolated. As discussed in the previous section, "Family Rejection, Abuse, and Homophobia," community structures may also differ for LGBTQ+ youth exiting care, including chosen family and other community, alternative, or hybrid support structures.

THE LANDSCAPE FOR CHANGE

There are serious concerns for the ability of child welfare services (broadly defined) to adequately support and empower LGBTQ+ youth. There are many potential avenues for improving these systems of care. Legislation can positively impact the change needed for LGBTQ+ foster youth. At the same time, caution is also needed, because systemic changes also have the potential to *worsen* the situation for these vulnerable youth. Recent legislation includes the Religious Freedom Restoration Act, the ruling from the Supreme Court case *Fulton et al. v. Pennsylvania* (2021), the Family First Prevention Services Act, and Every Student Succeeds Act.

RELIGIOUS FREEDOM RESTORATION ACTS AND CHILD WELFARE

The original Religious Freedom Restoration Act (RFRA) of 1993 was widely popular, passing the US House of Representatives on a voice vote basis and receiving overwhelming support in the Senate as well, where it passed 97-3 (Drinan & Huffman, 1993). Over time, however, religious freedom in some cases has transformed from a means of ensuring constitutional civil liberties to a means of providing legislative support for discrimination *using federal funding*, in areas such as adoption, foster care, and other child welfare services, when these services are provided by religious nonprofit organizations (see Lacy, 2021, for an overview). This is particularly concerning in parts of the country in which many service providers, or even a majority of service providers, are religious organizations. Even within and among these provider organizations, opinions on this type of policy vary. For instance, a large, Christian adoption provider, Bethany Christian Services, which is headquartered in Michigan, a state that passed such a law, recently announced their intention to begin actively allowing and working with LGBTQ+ parents in foster and adoption contexts (Shellnutt, 2021).

This type of legislation has a further "miasma" effect that reaches beyond the clear possibility that services are denied or provided in a non-affirming fashion. Blosnich and colleagues (2019) conducted a unique "natural experiment" by studying a large sample of sexual minority individuals before and after the passage of one such law (i.e., a high-profile RFRA-style law in Indiana). Their outcome measure involved asking individuals to report whether they experienced some combination of poor physical and/or mental health for more than 14 days within a given 30-day window. The rate was stable over the study year (2015) for sexual minority individuals who lived outside Indiana (about 20% of the sample reported feeling unhealthy more than 14 out of 30 days) but increased progressively over the year for those who lived in Indiana. By the end of the study year, this rate had risen to 60%, which was nearly three times the rate for the national sample.

CONSIDERATIONS FOR CLINICIANS

Clinicians working with LGBTQ+ youth in foster care must be culturally aware and sensitive to the needs of the foster youth, starting from the beginning of the assessment period, and even prior to meeting the youth. The first step is to evaluate one's own values and decide whether they can work with LGBTQ+ youth in foster care, even if they themselves identify as LGBTQ+. It is important for clinicians to know their blind spots and their own privileges when working with diverse youth. This includes being knowledgeable about using current language when addressing LGBTQ+ identities, since youth often are at the forefront of inclusive language change. When you are unaware of such language, it is imperative that clinicians do their own research to have a clear understanding of current concepts (Martin et al., 2006) and ensure they also ask the youth they work with what terminology they prefer for their own sexual orientation and gender identity, also known as SOGI.

For example, as the clinician reads through a referral, they should be aware of their own assumptions regarding this case and the client they will be meeting. As a clinician conducts the assessment, it is imperative they do not assume the client's SOGI, but rather, ask the client themselves. The report itself should be written with SOGI affirmative language that is non-pathologizing (SAMSHA, 2008). While assessing, it is also important to consider the youth's level of comfort with being out, as they may not feel safe disclosing their gender and sexual identities (SAMSHA, 2008), particularly to someone they are just meeting. It is important for the youth to have their own agency regarding their SOGI narrative. Assessment forms should include LGBTQ+ language and choices for self-identifications beyond the typical binary choices for sexuality and gender and limiting categories of race.

As youth progress through the system, it is important to connect them to additional services and communities where they can be in contact with peers who identify similarly to them. The agency waiting room and clinician's office should be welcoming environments, with inclusive posters, stickers, flyers, and/or therapeutic toys and items that reflect diversity and allyship. When the practice is in a building, the bathroom signs and options for restroom use should ideally reflect gender-neutral language and choices.

In treatment, clinicians should focus on building trust, fostering resiliency, modeling self-care and healthy habits, improving communication, encouraging the further development of a youth's own strengths and skills, future planning, linking youth to resources, and doing everything they can to infuse treatment with hope. Such factors are critical to the successful outcomes of LGBTQ+ foster youth. Clinicians who provide the above interventions in a clinically competent, safe environment can increase the youth's ability to develop self-agency, greater self-esteem, and overall better outcomes. When combined with access to affirming school environments, involvement in inclusive community events and spaces, and connection to positive mentors (Colpitts & Gahagan, 2016), the outcomes will only increase.

Conclusion

LGBTQ+ youth in foster care face a complex web of interwoven factors that place some of them at substantial risk. Disparities in wealth and poverty in the United States, and discrimination based on factors such as sexuality and gender, as well as racial and ethnic identities, result in LGBTQ+ people facing many unique risks, particularly in the form of family and/or community rejection. LGBTQ+ youth are at increased risk for a wide range of victimization, as well as multiple overlapping victimization experiences, or polyvictimization. This, in turn, places LGBTQ+ youth at a high risk for experiencing trauma, often resulting in health disparities such as mental illness, as well as for additional adverse outcomes of great consequence, such as homelessness and placement in out-of-home child welfare services. This risk is compounded by systemic and individual racism and heterosexism.

Although such risks can befall youth from many different backgrounds, LGBTQ+ youth are overrepresented across a spectrum of adverse outcomes, including involvement in the child welfare system. This renders negative experiences all too common for LGBTQ+ youth who encounter the child welfare system and are placed in foster care settings. Furthermore, as they approach adulthood, armed with fewer supportive resources and experiencing more barriers than cisgender, heterosexual peers, LGBTQ+ youth in foster care face unique challenges transitioning into independent, adult lives. They continue to face new threats, such as laws and regulations enfranchising discrimination in service provider settings, all along this path; and yet, as anyone who works with LGBTQ+ youth can attest, many survive this process with stunning resilience and strength of will. The mere act of reaching adulthood, having successfully mastered the lifelong process of self-actualization and fulfillment that gives life meaning to all human beings, should not be an outcome reserved for exceptional youth, but rather be the expectation for what every LGBTQ+ youth in care can achieve. Systemic changes as we have attempted to outline will not guarantee this, but they will transform our systems in the direction of what these youth need and deserve.

References

Baams, L. (2018). Disparities for LGBTQ+ and gender non-conforming adolescents. *Pediatrics, 141*, e20173004.

Baams, L., Wilson, B., & Russell, S. (2019). LGBTQ youth in unstable housing and foster care. *Pediatrics, 143*(3), e20174211.

Badgett, M. L., Choi, S.-K., & Wilson, B. D. M. (2019). LGBT poverty in the United States: A study of differences between sexual orientation and gender identity groups. Williams Institute. https://williamsinstitute.law.ucla.edu/wp-content/uploads/National-LGBT-Poverty-Oct-2019.pdf

Bailey, M. M. (2014). Engendering space: Ballroom culture and the spatial practice of possibility in Detroit. *Gender, Place & Culture: A Journal of Feminist Geography, 21*(4), 489–507.

Blosnich, J. R., Cassese, E. C., Friedman, M. R., Coulter, R. W. S., Sang, J. M., Matthews, D. D., & Mair, C. (2019). Religious Freedom Restoration Acts and sexual minority population health in the United States. *American Journal of Orthopsychiatry, 89*(6), 675–681.

Boyd, R. (2014). African American disproportionality and disparity in child welfare: Toward a comprehensive conceptual framework. *Children and Youth Services Review, 37*, 15–27.

Child Welfare Information Gateway. (2021). Child maltreatment 2019: *Summary of key findings*. US Department of Health and Human Services, Administration for Children and Families, Children's Bureau. https://www.childwelfare.gov/

Children's Bureau. (2013, May). *Supporting your LGBTQ+ youth: A guide for foster parents*. Child Welfare Information Gateway. https://www.childwelfare.gov/pubPDFs/LGBTQ+youth.pdf

Colpitts, E., Gahagan, J. (2016). The utility of resilience as a conceptual framework for understanding and measuring LGBTQ health. *International Journal of Equity Health, 15*, 60.

Courtney, M. E., & Wong, Y. (1996). Comparing the timing of exits from substitute care. *Children and Youth Services Review, 18*, 307–334.

Cyr, K., Chamberland, C., Lessard, G., Clément, M.-E., Wemmers, J.-A., Collin-Vézina, D., Gagné, M. H., & Damant, D. (2012). Polyvictimization in a child welfare sample of children and youths. *Psychology of Violence, 2*, 385–400.

Dettlaff, A. J., & Rycraft, J. R. (2008). Deconstructing disproportionality: Views from multiple community stakeholders. *Child Welfare, 87*(2), 37–58.

Dettlaff, A. J., Washburn, M., Carr, L. C., Vogel, A. N. (2018). Lesbian, gay, and bisexual (LGB) youth within in welfare: Prevalence, risk, and outcomes. *Child Abuse & Neglect, 80*, 183–193.

Drinan, R. F., & Huffman, J. I. (1993). "The Religious Freedom Restoration Act: A legislative history." *Journal of Law and Religion, 10*(2), 531–541.

Fulton et al. v. City of Philadelphia, Pennsylvania, No. 19-123, (2021).

Goodkind, S., Shook, J. J., Kim, K. H., Pohlig, R. T., & Herring, D. J. (2013). From child welfare to juvenile justice: Race, gender, and system experiences. *Youth Violence and Juvenile Justice*, 11, 249–272.

Hammack, P. L., Frost, D. M., & Hughes, S. D. (2019). Queer intimacies: A new paradigm for the study of relationship diversity. *Journal of Sex Research, 56*(4–5), 556–592.

Hughes, K., Bellis, M. A., Hardcastle, K. A., Sethi, D., Butchart, A., Mikton, C., Jones, L., & Dunne, M. P. (2017). The effect of multiple adverse childhood experiences on health: A systematic review and meta-analysis. *Lancet Public Health, 2*(8), 356–366.

Hunt, J., and Moodie-Mills, A. (2012). The unfair criminalization of gay and transgender youth: An overview of the experiences of LGBT youth in the juvenile justice system. The Center for American Progress.

Irvine, A., & Canfield, A. (2016). The overrepresentation of lesbian, gay, bisexual, questioning, gender non-conforming and transgender youth within the child welfare to juvenile justice crossover population. *Journal of Gender, Social Policy & the Law*.

Jackson Levin, N., Kattari, S. K., Piellusch, E. K., & Watson, E. (2020). "We just take care of each other": Navigating "chosen family" in the context of health, illness, and the mutual provision of care amongst queer and transgender young adults. *International Journal of Environmental Research and Public Health, 17*(19).

Jacobs, J., & Freundlich, M. (2006). Achieving permanency for LGBTQ+ youth. *Child Welfare 85*(2), 299–316.

Kassing, F., Casanova, T., Griffin, J. A., Wood, E., & Stepleman, L. M. (2021). The effects of polyvictimization on mental and physical health outcomes in an LGBTQ+ sample. *Journal of Traumatic Stress, 34*, 161–171.

Kosciw, J. G., Greytak, E. A., Palmer, N. A., & Boesen, M. J. (2013). The 2013 National School Climate Survey: The experiences of lesbian, gay, bisexual, and transgender youth in our nation's schools. GLSEN.

Lacy, A. (2021). How the Trump era encouraged publicly funded discrimination in adoption and foster care: The Biden administration can block a Trump rule codifying legal discrimination using federal funds, but 11 state-level measures remain intact. *The Intercept*. https://theintercept.com/2021/02/08/adoption-foster-discrimination-law

Livingston, J. (1990). *Paris Is Burning*. Off White Productions Inc.

Mallon, G. P. (1998). After care, then where? Evaluating outcomes of an independent living program. *Child Welfare, 77*(1), 61–78.

Mallon, G. P. (2001). Sticks and stones can break your bones: Verbal harassment and physical violence in the lives of gay and lesbian youth in child welfare settings. *Journal of Gay and Lesbian Social Services*, 13, 63–81.

Martin, M., Down, L., & Erney, R. (2016). *Out of the Shadows: Supporting LGBTQ+ youth in child welfare through cross-system collaboration*. Center for the Study of Social Policy.

McCann, E., & Brown, M. (2019). Homelessness among Youth Who Identify as LGBTQ+: A systematic review. *Journal of Clinical Nursing*, 28, 2061–2072.

McCormick, A. (Ed.) (2018). *LGBTQ+ youth in foster care: Empowering approaches for an inclusive system of care*. Routledge.

McMillen, J. C., Scott, L. D., Zima, B. T., Ollie, M. T., Munson, M. R., & Spitznagel, E. (2004). Use of mental health services among older youths in foster care. *Psychiatric Services, 55*(7), 811–817.

Paris Is Burning. (1990). Dire. Jenny Livingston. BBC Television, Miramax, Off White Productions.

POSE. (2018). FX. Color Force, Brad Falchuk Teley-Vision, Ryan Murphy Television, Fox 21 Television Studios, FXP.

Prince, D. M., Ray-Novak, M., Braveheart, G., Peterson, E. (2021). Sexual and gender minority youth in foster care: An evidence-based theoretical conceptual model of disproportionality and psychological comorbidities. *Trauma, Violence, & Abuse*, 1–15.

Ream, G. L., & Forge, N. (2014). Homeless lesbian, gay, bisexual and transgender (LGBT) youth in New York City: Insights from the field. *Child Welfare, 93*(2), 7–22.

Remlin Wilson, C., Currey Cook, Esq. M., & Erney, R. (2017). Safe havens closing the gap between recommended practice and reality for transgender and gender-expansive youth in out-of-home care.

Ryan, C., Huebner, D., Diaz, R. M., & Sanchez, J. (2009). Family rejection as a predictor of negative health outcomes in white and Latino lesbian, gay, and bisexual young adults. *Pediatrics, 123*(1), 346–352.

SAMSHA. (2008). Brief: Providing services and supports for youth who are LGBTQ+i2-S. Spring 2008.

SAMSHA. (2011). Learning from the field: Programs serving youth who are LGBTQ+i2-s and experiencing homelessness. https://www.samhsa.gov/sites/default/files/programs_campaigns/homelessness_programs_resources/learning-field-programs-serving-youth-LGBTQ+i2s-experiencing-homelessness.pdf

Shellnutt, K. (2021). Bethany Christian will allow LGBT parents to foster and adopt. *Christianity Today.* https://www.christianitytoday.com/news/2021/march/bethany-christian-services-adoption-foster-lgbt-same-sex.html

Sterzing, P. R., Ratliff, G. A, Gartner, R. E., McGeough, B. L., & Johnson, K. C. (2017). Social ecological correlates of polyvictimization among a national sample of transgender, genderqueer, and cisgender sexual minority adolescents. *Child Abuse & Neglect, 67*, 1–12.

Tobar, K. (2018). Ending the "closet to poverty pipeline" for LGBTQ+ youth. https://stoneleighfoundation.org/ending-closet-poverty-pipeline-LGBTQ+-youth/

Toro, P. A., Dworsky, A., Fowler, P. J. (2007). Homeless youth in the United States: Recent research findings and intervention approaches. Paper presented at the 2007 National Symposium on Homelessness Research.

Watt, T., & Kim, S. (2019). Race/ethnicity and foster youth outcomes: An examination of disproportionality using the national youth in transition database. *Children and Youth Services Review, 102*, 251–258.

Wilber, S., Reyes, C., & Marksamer, J. (2006). The model standards project: Creating inclusive systems for LGBT youth in out-of-home care. *Child Welfare, 85*(2), 133–149.

CHAPTER 11

LGBTQ+ Youth Experiencing Homelessness

Catherine Forbes, PhD, Carrie Mounier, LCSW, & Kaitlin Venema, PhD

Mental health (MH) clinicians working with LGBTQ+ youth experiencing homelessness (YEH) need to understand the homeless program and shelter context in order to provide effective mental health services. Knowledge of barriers to care, effective or promising services, and well-being-promoting and barrier-reducing policies are needed. In this chapter, we review literature about LGBTQ+ YEH regarding epidemiology of YEH, trajectories leading to homelessness, risk and protective factors, exacerbating factors/barriers to positive outcomes, and frameworks for understanding issues impacting LGBTQ+ YEH. We also review literature about existing shelter program models, mental health and substance abuse services and interventions that are promising or known to be effective for working with LGBTQ+ youth in the shelter/homelessness program context, and recommendations for programs and policies to promote the mental health of LGBTQ+ YEH.

Literature Review and Gaps in Research: LGBTQ+ Youth Experiencing Homelessness

Homelessness is a serious concern for youth, and particularly for LGBTQ+-identified young people. About 4.2 million youth in the United States experience homelessness each year, and of those, 20–40% identify as a sexual minority (Corliss et al., 2011; Morton, Dworsky et al., 2018). Compared to their heterosexual and cisgender peers, LGBTQ+ youth are at higher risk for homelessness and report longer durations of time experiencing homelessness (Choi et al., 2015). LGBTQ+ youth have more than twice the risk of homelessness than non-LGBTQ youth, and those who identify as both LGBTQ+ and Black or multiracial have even higher rates of homelessness (Morton, Dworsky et al., 2018). Within the LGBTQ+ youth community, transgender and nonbinary youth are the most at risk for homelessness (Choi et al., 2015; Corliss et al., 2011).

Some factors that propel LGBTQ+ youth into homelessness are shared by youth experiencing homelessness in general. History of trauma, foster care system involvement, and juvenile justice involvement are major risk factors for homelessness that are shared across all youth. More than 25% of former foster children become homeless within two to four years of leaving the system, and 50% of adolescents aging out of foster care and juvenile justice systems will be homeless within six months (Covenant House, 2017). Trauma is both a factor contributing to homelessness and a consequence of homelessness. Homeless youth have high rates of both childhood abuse prior to homelessness and victimization afterward; for example, in a study with homeless youth from three US cities, approximately 79% had experienced more than one type of childhood abuse and 28% had experienced more than two types of street victimizations (Bender et al., 2015).

Other risk factors for homelessness are unique to or exacerbated for LGBTQ+ youth. LGBTQ+ youth are at increased risk of experiencing trauma, which includes abuse and victimization, both prior and subsequent to homelessness (Russell & Fish, 2016). Many enter homeless programs with a significant history of trauma, mental health, and substance use concerns (Prock & Kennedy, 2020). Family rejection due to sexuality or gender identity is a risk factor for homelessness and is the most common reason for homelessness among LGBTQ+ youth. Compared to their heterosexual and cisgender peers, LGBTQ+ youth are also at increased risk of being the target of violence, victimization, and discrimination (Basile et al., 2020; Norris & Orchowski, 2020). Sexual minority youth have been found to be at higher risk for participation in survival sex (Walls & Bell, 2011; Marshall et al., 2010). After becoming homeless, LGBTQ+ youth have increased chances of victimization and of involvement in high-risk survival activities, such as sex work, which in turn increases their risk of substance use disorders, trauma, and violence (Cochran et al., 2002). Within the LGBTQ+ youth community, transgender youth compared to their cisgender LGB peers are at higher risk for trauma, bullying, and encountering barriers to services, both prior to and following homelessness (Coolhart & Brown, 2017). BIPOC (Black, Indigenous, and People of Color) sexual minority youth experience yet further increased risk of discrimination and negative effects on health outcomes (Thoma & Huebner, 2013). Compared to all youth experiencing homelessness, LGBTQ+ youth experiencing homelessness have more than twice the rate of early death (Morton, Dworsky, et al., 2018).

Once homeless, LGBTQ+ youth interact with homeless shelters that are not LGBTQ+ affirming (Shelton, 2015). A major concern is that shelters often utilize gender segregation as a general policy for decision making regarding placements, and this can be problematic and invalidating for LGBTQ+ youth. For example, cisgender LGB youth may be given the overt or implied message that they are "deviant" when they are not allowed to be with their identified gender group due to staff fears that they will engage in sexual behavior. Transgender youth are given similar messages, both direct and implied, that they are predators and dangerous to their cisgender peers; they often are not allowed to be housed with their identified gender group due to staff fears about predatory behavior and the safety of their cisgender peers; this is particularly problematic for trans feminine youth. A 2016 study found that many homeless shelter staff demonstrate unwelcoming attitudes or outright turn away transgender women seeking shelter (Rooney, 2016). Gender segregation also alienates nonbinary youth as they are forced to identify with a binary gender in order to be sheltered. Another major concern is that LGBTQ+ youth seeking homeless shelter services are often mistreated by homophobic and transphobic staff on the basis of the staffs' religious beliefs. LGBTQ+ youth who are homeless seek shelter for safety, but the reality is the safety of the LGBTQ+ youth can be more at risk in the shelters than at home or on the street. Non-LGBTQ+-affirming policies and practices in shelters lead to high anxiety, problems with other residents, conflicts with staff, and generally an experience where a place that is supposed to be safe ends up being just the opposite. LGBTQ+ YEH are very aware of these problems and risks, leading to a fear of mistreatment, which in turn is a barrier to seeking and receiving needed care and services.

What helps LGBTQ+ youth experiencing homelessness access shelters and services? Given that LGBTQ+ youth are underutilizing homelessness shelters and services even more than their cisgender peers and that they have even higher levels of mental health needs, it is important to identify factors that will reduce barriers and facilitate connection to needed services. A promising approach builds safety and trust whereby LGBTQ+ youth centers, as safe and trusted spaces, become bridges to accessing LGBTQ+-affirming shelter services. Integrated and holistic approaches to care are also

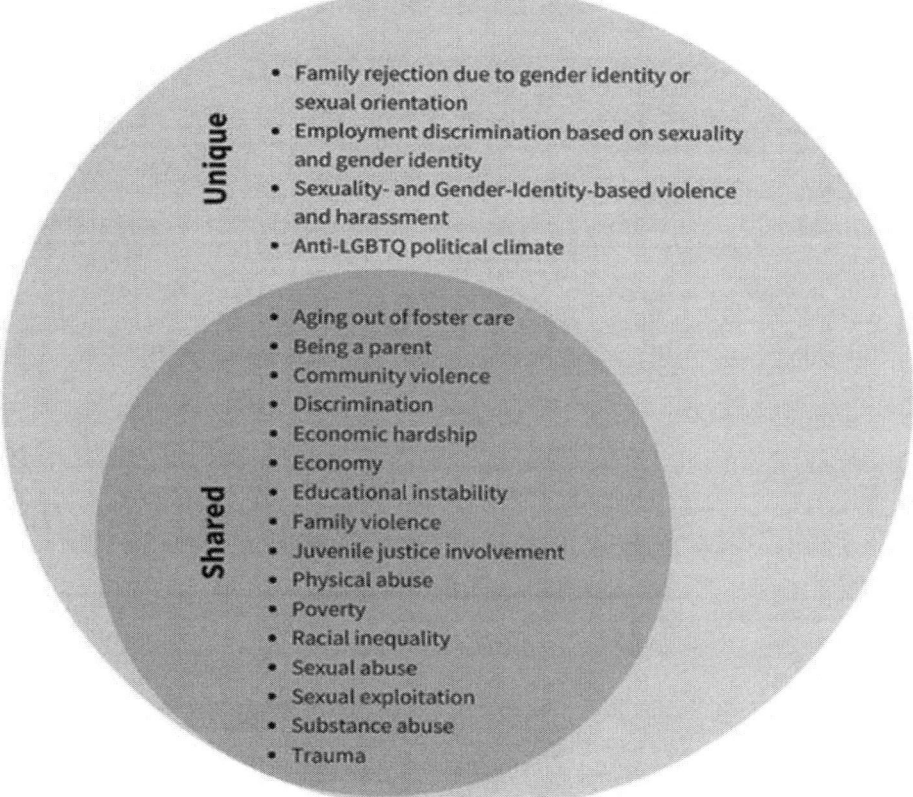

Figure 11.1. Risk factors for homelessness shared with cisgender/heterosexual youth and unique for LGBTQ+ youth (National Alliance to End Homelessness, n.d.; National Network for Youth, n.d.)

essential, seeing and valuing the LGBTQ+ YEH as a whole person. In addition, providers' and systems' willingness to work outside conventional methods and practices can decrease barriers to care and increase experiences of affirmation.

Several theories and frameworks are important and useful in expanding providers' and systems' understanding of the experiences and needs of LGBTQ+ YEH. While not an exhaustive list, the following theories and frameworks, some of which are discussed more comprehensively in other chapters, are recommended for guiding the work of clinicians: minority stress theory (see chapter 1), intersectionality (see chapter 2), interdisciplinary-holistic care (see chapter 3), social ecological model (Bronfenbrenner, 1979; Toro et al., 1991), social determinants of health (Braveman et al., 2011), and a structural violence and vulnerability lens (Farmer et al., 2006; Bourgois et al., 2017). Together, these provide the broad, flexible, and nuanced perspectives needed for mental health providers, and the systems within which they work, to more accurately understand individual and systemic factors propelling LGBTQ+ youth into homelessness and keeping them there. They can also inform intervention planning and implementation in order to promote their well-being and build skills for independent living.

The *social ecological model* (Bronfenbrenner, 1979) and more recent public health application of this theory, *social determinants of health* (Braveman et al., 2011; WHO, n.d.), provide another view of factors that impact LGBTQ+ youth. The World Health Organization (n.d.) defines social determinants of health as "the non-medical factors that influence health outcomes. They are the conditions in which people are born, grow, work, live, and age, and the wider set of forces and systems shaping the conditions of daily life. These forces and systems include economic policies and systems, development agendas, social norms, social policies and political systems." These models emphasize how individuals are parts of contexts and do not exist alone. These contexts include family, local community, institutions, and sociopolitical conditions.

The *structural vulnerability/structural violence/structural competency lens* also emphasizes the negative impact of systems and context on individuals. Structural vulnerability refers to the risks experienced by individuals when their intersectional location of self (age, race, ethnicity, skin color, sex assigned at birth, religion, sexual orientation and gender identity, living with disabilities, body size, and socioeconomic status) in the context of society's multiple overlapping and reinforcing power hierarchies constrains their choices and opportunities. The restriction of choices and opportunities amplifies risk and harm and results in negative health outcomes. Structural vulnerability is not caused by, nor can it be repaired solely by, individual agency or behaviors (Farmer et al., 2006; Bourgois et al., 2017).

Structural violence refers to the political, economic, and institutional arrangements of our social world that cause harm to people. It creates high levels of trauma across the population and a breakdown of social networks, prevents people and communities from meeting their basic needs, and threatens to undermine community protective factors. Structural violence is a primary cause of premature death and unnecessary disability in many communities. Structural competency is a holistic framework for understanding individual and community needs, bridging social determinants of health and clinical interventions, and using interdisciplinary and multilevel interventions to recognize and respond to health and illness as downstream effects of broad social, political, and economic structures (Bourgois et al., 2017).

As applied to LGBTQ+ youth experiencing homelessness, this framework highlights how structural vulnerability and structural violence: 1) lead some LGBTQ+ youth to become homeless; 2) influence experiences of homelessness (length of time, repeat episodes, experiences of victimization, mental and physical health outcomes); 3) impacts the practices of service organizations, specifically that some service organizations where LGBTQ+ YEH go to seek assistance display discriminatory and harmful attitudes, beliefs, and practices that are embedded in political and economic organizations and systems; and 4) must be understood and recognized by service agencies in order to understand and respond to existing needs.

Clinical Considerations and Recommendations for Practice in Mental Health and Substance Abuse Treatment

Within the homeless shelter environment, services that address mental health and substance use concerns and that adapt to meet the specific needs of LGBTQ+ YEH are crucial. A holistic and interdisciplinary approach that is LGBTQ+ affirming is essential in terms of building therapeutic relationships with LGBTQ+ YEH and increasing the utilization of available services that are often left underutilized. Although few interventions have been developed specifically to target the mental health needs of LGBTQ+ YEH, there are several interventions that appear promising in being adapted for this population, including Seeking Safety, Structured Psychotherapy for Adolescents Responding to Chronic Stress (SPARCS) and Trans-Affirming CBT (Cognitive-Behavioral Therapy) (Austin & Craig, 2015; DeRosa et al., 2006; Najavits et al., 1998). In working with this population, one must understand the significance and severity of the lived experiences of LGBTQ+ YEH prior to entering homelessness and in the shelter context (Prock & Kennedy, 2020), including sexual and physical victimization, mental health, substance use, health concerns, disrupted education, and employment difficulties. Providers establishing safe and affirming spaces is essential.

Understanding the mental health concerns faced by LGBTQ+ YEH is instrumental in developing interventions that target the unique needs of this population. LGBTQ+ youth are overrepresented among the homeless youth population (Choi et al., 2015). Compared to heterosexual YEH, lesbian, gay, and bisexual YEH tend to report more psychological symptoms and show significantly higher rates of depression, post-traumatic stress disorder, anxiety, suicidal ideation, and suicide attempts (Cochran et al., 2002; Prock & Kennedy, 2020; Whitbeck et al., 2004). Cochran and colleagues (2002) examined various differences across mental health domains for different youth groups and found that, compared to their heterosexual peers experiencing homelessness, LGBTQ+ YEH had higher rates of internalizing and externalizing symptoms including withdrawn behavior, somatic complaints, social problems, delinquency, and aggression. A challenge for understanding the psychological and behavioral problems of YEH is the uncertainty around whether these problems are due to being homeless or some other factor. The relationship between mental health and homelessness appears to be bidirectional, whereby homelessness can lead to or worsen mental health problems and mental health problems can lead to homelessness (Fraser et al., 2019). Homelessness among LGB youth has been found to have a direct relationship with increased substance abuse, more stressful life events, more negative social relationships, and less supportive friendships. which likely lead to worsening of existing psychological and behavioral symptoms of psychiatric and substance use conditions (Rosario et al., 2012). Findings demonstrating associations between various psychological and behavioral problems and negative social interactions and relationships for LGBTQ+ YEH suggest the need for interventions specifically targeting facilitation of social supports for LGBTQ+ YEH.

Experiences of victimization and trauma are highly prevalent amongst LGBTQ+ YEH. Compared to non-LGBTQ+ youth in transitional living programs (TLP), LGBTQ+ YEH have higher rates of lifetime sexual victimization, rejection, and abuse reported at intake to the TLP (Liu & Mustanski, 2012; Prock & Kennedy, 2020). According to Friedman and colleagues (2011), LGBTQ+ youth are 1.2 times more likely to report a history of physical abuse and 3.8 times more likely to have experienced sexual abuse from a parent/caregiver than non-LGBTQ+-identified peers prior to experiencing homelessness. Service providers working with this population reported higher rates of harassment, bullying, rejection, abuse, and intimate partner violence in their transgender clients leading to homelessness compared to cisgender LGBQ clients as it was reported to staff by the youth (Choi et al., 2015). In addition, transgender and gender expansive individuals with these higher loads of trauma may tend to blame themselves for these traumatic experiences, leading to exacerbated internalized stigma (Lange, 2020).

TRAUMA-INFORMED CARE

Due to the high rates of trauma experiences among LGBTQ+ YEH, there is a great need for all staff working with these youth to understand how the youth's trauma histories currently impact them and to provide trauma-informed care. Trauma-Informed Care (TIC) includes services that address how trauma impacts the individual with the eventual goal of reducing symptoms in order to support recovery (Hopper et al., 2010). TIC follows several basic principles of care, including: 1) *Trauma Awareness*, which involves helping clients understand that what they experienced was traumatic for them in order to gain perspective, which can be done through administering brief screenings, collecting a thorough history, and assessing for safety concerns; 2) *Emphasizing Safety*, which includes helping clients maintain healthy boundaries, clarifying roles, respecting privacy, upholding confidentiality, and seeking out cultural understanding; 3) *Providing Opportunities to Rebuild Control*, which involves establishing a predictable environment and allowing clients to make their own choices; and 4) *Adopting a Strength-Based Approach* to empower the individual by recognizing and validating their strengths. Using TIC with youth is associated with improved social relationships, increased safety, and improved self-esteem. Additionally, by utilizing TIC, staff are more likely to de-escalate critical situations when they occur and therefore decrease the need for crisis-based services.

One evidenced-informed practice to treat complex trauma in children and adolescents is the Attachment, Self-Regulation, and Competency (ARC) Framework (Arvidson et al., 2011; Blaustein & Kinniburgh, 2010). This flexible, component-based intervention identifies different skills and competencies that were negatively impacted by traumatic stressors and attachment systems. ARC's implementation targets the environment, staff training, and youth engagement. Many of the interventions in the ARC framework translate into ways in which youth homeless programming can be designed and implemented, including creating a predictable and structured environment, demonstrating unconditional respect and acceptance, training staff to manage strong emotions, training staff to support youth in identifying and labeling their feelings, creating a safe space for youth who are experiencing these strong emotions, and creating opportunities for youth to engage with peers and adults in a positive manner. One program that has adapted ARC concepts for use with YEH is Phoenix Rising, developed by Youth on Fire and the Trauma Center in Cambridge, Massachusetts (Dryden et al., 2010). Phoenix Rising has four main components: 1) staff training and consultation; 2) changes to creating a trauma-informed milieu based on the Trauma-Informed Facility Self-Assessment, which is a brief instrument designed to assess the degree to which a facility's physical space is trauma-informed (Hopper & Spinazzola, 2006); 3) risk counseling and services; and 4) group activities including community-building exercises and art therapy. Adapting Phoenix Rising or a similar program to meet the needs of LGBTQ+ youth would involve giving special consideration for the unique needs of LGBTQ+ youth who are homeless and have experienced trauma, where all staff (clinical and nonclinical) would learn about and understand their increased risk for victimization and abuse to be better equipped to address issues that may arise for these youth. For instance, having staff equipped to de-escalate a situation instead of the police being involved or a youth being psychiatrically hospitalized could significantly prevent further trauma for an LGBTQ+-identified individual if they had to interface with these systems. ARC is effective in addressing attachment concerns by training staff to support the youth in managing affect, increase attunement to the youth, provide consistent responses, and create structure, and it has the potential to create reparative, positive relationships that enhance the social support for LGBTQ+ YEH.

While many programs serving YEH offer a range of clinical services including individual therapy, group therapies, and case management, these services tend to be underutilized. An examination of the possible reasons for service underutilization is needed so that professionals involved in caring for these youth can make the necessary adaptations to increase engagement. Findings indicate that a distrust of service providers is a primary reason that youth are not actively seeking out these mental health services, which reflects the need for professionals to be adequately trained to work with LGBTQ+ YEH (Prock & Kennedy, 2020). Providers need to actively engage youth by forming a therapeutic relationship that emphasizes respect, understanding, empowerment, and affirmation. Engaging youth in milieu spaces prior to involving them in treatment is one way to build trust and also provides clinicians an opportunity to better understand barriers to accessing these services. For instance, speaking with youth in a nontherapeutic context (e.g., playing a game, working on an art project, listening to the youth's music) prior to a group therapy session can start to lay a relational foundation so that the youth may feel more comfortable joining the group or engaging in mental health services as trust is developed. Drop-in services are highly utilized by LGBTQ+ youth and non-LGBTQ+ YEH equally, as one study of YEH in Chicago and Los Angeles found that 58% of YEH accessed this service (Pergamit et al., 2010). YEH primarily use drop-in services to gain basic needs such as clothes, food, and showers and to charge electronics (Parast et al., 2019). A smaller percentage, 32–43%, use these drop-in services for clinical services such as mental health care and substance use treatment and to reduce HIV/STI risk (Parast et al., 2019). By working with YEH to reduce mental health stigma and promote positive attitudes toward mental health service utilization, youth may feel more comfortable engaging in higher-level services while getting their basic needs met. Drop-in centers also provide an opportunity for staff to interact with youth and screen for mental health needs, which can lead to the development of appropriate and affirming services of value to these youth.

INTERDISCIPLINARY PROGRAMS FOR LGBTQ+ YEH

Siloed services for YEH, which made it difficult for youth to navigate complex systems of care, are now shifting to more comprehensive and holistic programs that utilize an interdisciplinary team to provide a "one-stop shop" for YEH. The My Treatment Empowerment for Adolescents on the Move (iTEAM) is one such service specifically designed for LGBTQ+ youth and straight allies that included mental health and drug and alcohol services while also addressing housing, education, employment, and case management to link youth to medical services (Powell et al., 2016). The iTEAM program collaborated with a community-based mental health agency to provide individual crisis counseling on-site as needed along with Cognitive-Behavioral Therapy and Motivational Enhancement Therapy to target mental health symptoms and substance use. Given the challenges LGBTQ+ YEH youth face to secure affirming housing, intensive case management was offered by professionals specifically trained in working with LGBTQ+ youth. Sexual health education using the Street Smart evidence-based intervention (Rotheram-Borus et al., 1991) was incorporated into the program to reduce high-risk sexual behaviors. The iTEAM program had a positive impact on youth participants, with clinically significant improvements in housing access and stability, ability to secure employment, and testing for HIV; and decreases in frequency of traumatic memories, emotional problems and anxiety, and substance use. The documented success of this program in reaching and addressing the needs to LGBTQ YEH illustrates the importance of programs such as this and the need for making them available across the nation to improve the various aspects of life impacted by homelessness.

EVIDENCED-BASED LGBTQ+-AFFIRMING THERAPEUTIC SERVICES

In order to improve mental health symptoms that may be maintaining homelessness and creating barriers to engagement in education, employment, and housing, it is important that homeless shelters offer evidenced-based and LGBTQ+-affirming individual therapy services. There are a number of evidenced-based interventions for YEH, yet few are modified for sexual and gender minority youth. Cognitive-behavioral therapy (CBT) has been well studied in YEH and leads to improvements in depression as well as substance use and self-efficacy (Wang et al., 2019). A modified version of CBT, Trans-Affirming CBT (TA-CBT), delivers CBT interventions within an affirming and trauma-informed framework designed specifically for gender diverse individuals (Austin & Craig, 2015). TA-CBT uses a systemic approach to treatment by acknowledging and countering oppressive contexts, including macro and micro systems that impact the mental health of gender diverse people. This emphasis on examining oppressive systems is important when addressing minority stress and internalized transphobia, sexism, and racism within intersectional minority identities of many LBGTQ+ YEH. Providers practicing TA-CBT work to recognize and bring awareness to trans-specific sources of stress and adopt an affirming stance toward gender diversity. Specific interventions address self-regulation, psychoeducation, modifying negative thinking, and behavioral activation. With the high rates of trauma within LGBTQ+ youth, self-regulation strategies become imperative for YEH to have the ability to explore these traumatic experiences of transphobia by increasing their ability to manage strong emotions during the processing of trauma. Behavioral activation within this model seeks to reduce the sense of isolation and hopelessness by connecting individuals to the larger trans community. Providers should be aware of in-person and virtual local and national resources to offer the youth with limited financial means. Although not specifically designed for sexual minority youth, many of these interventions have the potential for being modified to target internalized messages of heteronormativity and homophobia and finding ways to connect individuals to the larger LGB-plus community.

Many evidenced-based practices that target trauma symptoms lack the inclusion of gender diverse individuals and may not adequately address trauma stemming from transphobia, minority stress, and internalized stigma. Trans-Affirming Narrative Exposure Therapy (TA-NET) seeks to utilize a framework that addresses these areas of trauma by supporting individuals in processing traumatic events in the context of their lives (Lange, 2020; Schauer et al., 2011). Like TA-CBT, TA-NET counters negative beliefs and self-assessment by increasing understanding of how these are formed by societal messaging. For LGBTQ+ YEH, this intervention during a developmental time period of identity formation may support the development of a positive self-identity. Modifications of Narrative Exposure Therapy include the exploration of gender-related experiences, emphasizing gender diversity as part of the human experience, and bringing awareness to a marginalized status in order to reframe this as a source of strength. TA-NET offers several strategies to incorporate in the work with LGBTQ YEH who have experienced trauma, although some limitations for this population include the homework of writing chapters and requiring 8–10 sessions, which may be difficult for youth particularly seeking services in drop-in centers. For some YEH who have experienced trauma, a narrative approach to processing trauma that relies on verbal or writing abilities may be challenging. These youth may benefit from less verbal or nonverbal approaches to trauma processing such as eye movement desensitization and reprocessing (EMDR), somatic processing of trauma, and trauma sensitive yoga.

GROUP THERAPY APPROACHES

Group therapy services support in reducing the sense isolation and fostering connection with others who may be experiencing similar challenges related to rejection, negative social interactions, and discrimination. Offering multiple types of groups including mental health, life skills, music therapy, and career development to treat the person holistically builds up competencies across areas of life to support a positive future. In terms of mental health groups, Structured Psychotherapy for Adolescents Responding to Chronic Stress (SPARCS) is a trauma-informed, 16-session group intervention for people who may be experiencing ongoing stress (DeRosa et al., 2006). SPARCS groups are commonly offered across sites that serve LGBTQ+ YEH (Ferguson & Maccio, 2015). SPARCS focuses on addressing problems with regulating emotions, somatization, physical health, attention and information processing, self-perception, relationships, and sense of meaning and purpose of life. The goal of this intervention is to increase awareness, learn effective coping strategies, connect with others, and create meaning and purpose. Staff being able to infuse SPARCS components into their interactions with LGBTQ+ YEH can support creating a trauma-informed way to relay information, establish rules of shelters, and create consequences for violation of these rules. Given that each of the 16 sessions review a particular component of the intervention, this style of group lends itself well to drop-in centers and shelters where participation in group may be variable and the youth can leave an individual group session with greater understanding and coping skills.

With the overlap between trauma and substance use among LGBTQ+ YEH, Seeking Safety is a manualized group psychotherapy that aligns with the needs of the population as it targets symptoms of PTSD and substance use disorders (Najavits et al., 1998). Seeking Safety covers 25 topics across cognitive, behavioral, and interpersonal domains with each topic offering a safe coping skill. Seeking Safety has been shown to be a promising intervention for adult transgender women of color (Takahashi et al., 2022) and adult transgender women living with HIV (Empson et al., 2017). Although Seeking Safety has not been modified for LGBTQ+ youth or YEH, the emphasis on making safety a first priority, including addressing risk concerns of suicidality and self-harm, reducing risky substance and sexual behaviors, and leaving dangerous relationships maps on well to the mental health and substance use concerns experienced by LGBTQ+ YEH. Substance use specific interventions, such as brief or group-based motivational interviewing, have been found to be effective in reducing non-marijuana substance use for YEH with additional findings demonstrating improvements from two brief sessions in a youth's readiness to change alcohol use (Thompson et al., 2017; Wang et al., 2019). With motivational interviewing techniques being effective in brief modules of treatment, it is an intervention that lends itself to the homeless shelter environment where youth may be sporadically engaging with services.

ALTERNATIVE PROGRAMMING FOR LGBTQ+ YEH

Incorporating unconventional interventions such as art, music, drama, and youth empowerment programming into group therapy at sites serving LGBTQ+ YEH is an opportunity to address mental health needs through alternative methods. Group programming that promotes youth empowerment by bringing awareness to systemic issues that impact well-being and includes community engagement/advocacy can support youth who are faced with discrimination. The social justice youth development framework is one that has been shown to enhance empowerment and well-being in LGBTQ+ youth (Wagaman, 2016). Art therapy that fosters creativity can promote resilience in LGBTQ+ YEH and offers an alternative method for youth to process their emotions and trauma through a technique that does not rely on verbal communication (Prescott et al., 2008). Music-based group therapy that involves collaborative group songwriting provides youth with an opportunity to process their experiences and has been found to increase hopefulness in children who have experienced family violence (Fairchild & McFerran, 2018). To better serve the needs of LGBTQ+ YEH, music therapy could incorporate aspects of queer music therapy, a type of music therapy that works to deconstruct binary power structures such as teacher/student, cis/trans, therapist/client; incorporates a diverse representation of music away from solely Western music styling; and confronts while challenging music that upholds systems of power and privilege (heternomativity, cisnormativity, white supremacy, and ableism) in order to create music that incorporates the variability, fluidity, and diversity of human experiences (Fansler et al., 2019). This inclusive and social-justice approach to music therapy may be an appropriate modification to benefit LGBTQ+ YEH (Bain et al., 2016). An offshoot of art therapy is drama therapy, where youth tell their stories, learn to solve problems, and express emotions. Considering drama therapy has been a powerful tool for exploring historically marginalized identities through narrative storytelling (Jen, 2016; Maynard, 2018; Yuksek, 2018), LGBTQ+ YEH may find this approach a helpful addition to trauma-based mental health services.

MEDICAL INTERVENTIONS

Targeting the physical health of LGBTQ+ YEH alongside the mental health symptoms is an important area of intervention for LGBTQ+ YEH. Due to higher engagement in survival sex, LGBTQ youth are at greater risk for HIV and STIs (Hein et al., 2018; van Leeuwen et al., 2006). Men who have sex with men (MSM) who are experiencing homelessness are at a high risk for engaging in HIV-risk behaviors (Keuroghlian et al., 2014). Trans youth experiencing homelessness have worse physical health outcomes compared to the broader LGBTQ+ community (van Leeuwen et al., 2006). A third of respondents to the Lambda Legal 2010 Survey who identify as transgender indicated that they fear that medical providers will treat them differently because of their gender identity and/or expression, creating a barrier for seeking out necessary medical treatment, and more than half of respondents expressed concerns around being refused medical services. In addition, access to gender-affirming medical interventions is essential for the well-being of trans youth (Hughto et al., 2020). Accessing Pre-Exposure Prophalaxis (PrEP) and Post-Exposure Prophylaxis (PEP) to lower the risk of contracting HIV along with regular testing and HIV medical treatment is also imperative to support the physical health of LGBTQ+ YEH.

One example of a model that effectively incorporated medical care into their services for LGBTQ+ YEH is the iTEAMS program, which was described earlier in this chapter. The iTEAMS program partnered with an AIDS service organization to provide weekly sexual health education and offer regular free HIV testing and counseling through the Street Smarts Intervention (Powell et al., 2016). Training these medical providers to utilize trauma-informed practices while delivering medical health services in an LGBTQ+-affirming space can greatly reduce the health disparities this population faces.

Addressing the unique needs of LGBTQ+ YEH through modifying and adapting current clinical practices has the potential to significantly impact mental health symptoms, substance use behaviors, and high-risk sexual behaviors in this population. While more promising individual and group therapy interventions are being developed, it is important to continue creating models of care that are integrative and address the whole being of these individuals. Including art, drama, and music while promoting positive youth empowerment takes a creative approach to targeting mental health needs that recognizes the impact of societal messages, discrimination, transphobia/homophobia, and victimization on well-being. Trauma-informed services and staff interactions are crucial in providing safe spaces for LGBTQ+ YEH to engage in critical mental health and substance use services that can support their ability to enroll in educational and employment services.

Structural Competency and Service Systems for LGBTQ+ YEH

When considering services for LGBTQ+ youth experiencing homelessness, it is essential to consider the settings designed for serving this population, as well as settings that have traditional service models, but where LGBTQ+ YEH accesses care. One example of this kind of service setting are traditional healthcare systems, which historically have not served LGBTQ+ YEH very well (Varcoe et al., 2019). There are multiple reasons for the lack of effective care, including lack of understanding of LGBTQ+ YEH needs, as well as a lack of economic incentive for making services more accessible and appropriate. "Implicit frameworks" of service providers can undermine care. These frameworks are the taken-for-granted lenses through which health professionals commonly understand health and wellness but that have the effect of blaming individuals for circumstances outside of their control (Farmer et al., 2006). These barriers to effective care are true for both LGBTQ+ and non-LGBTQ+ YEH, but they are exacerbated for LGBTQ+ YEH (Morton, Dworsky et al., 2018).

Youth and young adults experiencing homelessness face numerous structural barriers when trying to access medical, mental health, or other formal educational or social services. Some of these barriers include being asked for a permanent address (which they do not have), needing to arrive on time for appointments, needing proof of insurance and identification, and needing a "medical home" in order to access services. Another barrier comes in the form of "acceptable behavior." Since the young person may have difficulty making it to appointments and does not have other safe places to be, they may arrive early in the morning and try to sleep in the waiting room. They may try to groom themselves in the clinic restroom prior to appointments. If the young person happens to arrive hungry, or eating, or with poor hygiene, this may be viewed as an example of "inappropriate behavior," rather than being understood as a necessary aspect of serving young people experiencing homelessness (Pitcher et al., 2019). Additionally, there are logistical barriers such as being unable to bring your belongings with you into a medical clinic and needing to leave them somewhere else where they may or may not be secure. Under these circumstances, LGBTQ+ YEH may not know how long appointments are going to take, how long they will have to wait, and whether a provider is going to be helpful or not (Pitcher et al., 2019).

Because accessing health care is intermittent and potentially in different locations, it is unusual for there to be continuity in providers and providers are unlikely to have a substantial understanding of the young person's medical history. When the provider does meet with the young person, there are numerous potential pitfalls where services can become problematic.

The structural competency framework effectively describes the service needs of LGBTQ+ YEH. Structural competency approaches amplify and leverage LGBTQ+ YEH strengths to find solutions. Structural competency may look different depending on where it is being implemented, but it has common components: 1) recognizing the influence of structures on patient health; 2) recognizing the influences of structures on the clinical encounter, including implicit frameworks common in health care; 3) responding to structures in the clinic and beyond the clinic; and 4) structural humility, which is practicing collaboration with patients and populations in developing responses to structural vulnerability, rather than assuming that health professionals alone have all the answers, and includes awareness of interpersonal privilege and power hierarchies in healthcare (Neff et al., 2020).

Applying the structural competency framework to a case scenario will demonstrate how this framework improves understanding of how to better meet the needs of LGBTQ+ YEH. Consider this case: a 20-year-old African American transgender woman who is experiencing homelessness presents to a clinic for a mental health appointment but arrives with an acute medical issue—injury to lower leg resulting from assault on the street. She also presents with psychosis, substance use disorder, HIV, and PTSD.

There are multiple reasons and ways that services may not go well for this youth. Traditional health care would suggest providing first aid, prescribing estrogen to support affirmative gender care, prescribing antipsychotic medication to treat psychotic symptoms, and utilizing motivational interviewing to increase motivation to access treatment for substance use disorders or referring to Narcotics Anonymous groups. Anti-retroviral therapy would be used to treat HIV and reduce viral load to nondetectable levels, and creating a trauma narrative would be recommended to help reduce the impact of trauma. The next step would typically be to refer her to a shelter with the provider's role ending there. However, for this series of services to work, it will require scheduling a series of appointments with various specialties at different locations and require her to present on time, with different kinds of documentation, all of which is likely to present significant difficulties and barriers for her.

At the individual level, the separate interventions described above, while needed, miss the larger picture of this young person's needs. Without an understanding of structural vulnerability, structural violence, and structural competency, the above array of services represents a mismatch between what traditional systems offer and what is needed to effectively serve LGBTQ+ YEH (Bourgois et al., 2017).

IMPACT OF STRUCTURES ON PATIENT HEALTH

The young woman in our case scenario self-reports that she experiences exclusion and rejection everywhere she goes, that she has been harmed throughout her childhood by numerous systems and there have been few safe places or safe people. These experiences are related to her unique intersection of identities as an African American and a transgender young woman who did not receive gender-affirming care prior to the onset of puberty. When young transgender people do not receive gender-affirming hormone therapy prior to the development of secondary sex characteristics, many of these pubertal changes cannot be reversed without surgery. This results in individuals being more clearly recognizable as transgender and makes them at increased risk for transphobic hate-related violence (Begun & Kattari, 2016). As a result, although this young person currently uses gender-affirming hormone therapy, she continues to experience dysphoria with certain parts of her body and is frequently misgendered and "othered" by others.

She is in survival mode and is present-focused. This is both due to recent acute injury related to assault, which was very possibly transphobic violence, as well as the experience of surviving on the street. Being present-focused helps her to be constantly vigilant and prioritizes her immediate safety and basic needs. It also impacts her ability to plan or follow multistep instructions. This restricts her sense of agency and her ability to follow through with longer-term health-maintenance approaches (Morton, Samuels et al., 2018).

Given the trauma she has experienced throughout her whole life, the historical trauma that both African Americans and transgender individuals have experienced in medical systems, and her own experience with medical trauma, she is very guarded in her presentation to medical professionals. She has also been misgendered and disrespected in medical settings, amplifying this distrust. Because of this distrust of medical providers, she generally avoids medical clinics unless necessary. This causes her to present with multiple untreated health needs, rather than a single presenting issue. Hospitalization is likely to be terrifying for her, even if clinically recommended, because of loss of whatever stability she has been able to establish, potential loss of belongings, and fear of being held in a hostile environment (Pitcher et al. 2019).

She uses substances as her most reliable and available coping mechanism. She views it as a solution, not as a problem. It is always available, it never leaves her, it helps her stay awake, and it makes her feel more "normal," at least sometimes. She has survived on the street for a long time, and like many people experiencing homelessness, she has used survival sex, which is an exchange of sex for necessities such as food, clothing, shelter, or drugs (Morton Samuels et al., 2018). She does not have another viable source of income. Unfortunately, one of many occupational hazards of survival sex is exposure to STIs, including HIV. She does not have the ability, currently, to take HIV medication with any kind of consistency.

She experiences disorganized thinking and paranoia. This state may be a psychotic disorder, it may be a manifestation of complex trauma, it may be substance induced, or any combination of these options—and it is exacerbated by the fact that she does not have a safe and consistent place to sleep (Renard et al., 2017). She doesn't have a consistent way to take medication. She is suspicious about the effects of medication and is concerned that medications could make her sleepy, which would be unsafe for her on the street. Her memory is also inconsistent, and this affects self-report of medication adherence.

INFLUENCE OF STRUCTURES ON THE CLINICAL ENCOUNTER

From the entry into the clinic to the clinical encounter, LGBTQ+ YEH frequently experience "othering" by service providers. Like in larger society, clinic and service settings are places where white privilege confers benefits to individuals with lighter skin at the expense of those with darker skin. Homophobia, transphobia, sexism, anti-fat bias, adultism, anti-homelessness sentiment, and other types of bias and oppression can intersect with anti-Black racism and colorism and be present in a service setting. Barriers to services and structures that exclude or marginalize groups of people are often not acknowledged. Clinics may say "we want everyone to feel welcome" without acknowledging that while many feel welcome, many others may not. A space may be welcoming to LGBTQ+ persons, but not to Black, Indigenous, and People of Color. A space might be welcoming to Spanish speakers but not be welcoming to Spanish-speaking immigrant communities. A space might be welcoming to LGBTQ+ BIPOC experiencing homelessness but be less so for those who are also experiencing significant mental illness. Our identities and the ways we are welcomed into or excluded from public spaces are complicated and intersectional. Both implicit and explicit biases are manifestations of structural violence that have the effect of negatively impacting client care.

Will the service environment use the young person's asserted name and pronouns? What if the asserted name does not align with the legal name? Problems with individuals being misgendered, announced in the waiting room using the incorrect name (which potentially has the effect of "outing" them as LGBTQ+), and failing to recognize why asserted names and pronouns are essential for safe and effective care are common. Othering may come in various forms—racism, transphobia, and expressing judgment or stigma related to homelessness, substance use, HIV status, or use of survival sex. Young people may find themselves shamed or ignored (Pitcher et al. 2019). Service places that feel institutional (i.e., sterile, depersonalized, and controlling) contribute to BIPOC individuals feeling distrustful and apprehensive about engaging with service providers (Freeman et al., 2017).

The young person entering the clinic knows she is entering (another) rule-based bureaucracy. She has a long history with these kinds of systems failing to meet her needs. She expects to be mistreated or shamed and presents with her guard up. She anticipates she will be judged as wrong in some way, seen as behaving inappropriately, or will be exited from the clinic for some reason. Though she has numerous health care needs, she really avoids interacting with health care providers whenever possible (Pitcher et al., 2019).

Another challenge is the time allotted to the clinical encounter. Will there be adequate time for the provider to establish rapport with the young person, explain confidentiality and the exceptions to confidentiality, convey respect for the young person, and take a meaningful social history? Will the provider make heteronormative and cisnormative assumptions about the young person? Will the provider grasp the real-world restrictions experienced by the young person (such as lacking a place to store medication, limitations on food choice availability, needing to be able to stay awake at night because it is safer) that affect the ability to follow through on recommendations? Will the provider come in with an "individualizing framework"—that is, viewing the young person as primarily responsible for her own health regardless of external circumstances shaping those health outcomes? This may affect the provider's ability to understand risk behavior in the context of the young person's life. The need to prioritize immediate survival sometimes takes precedence over medium- or long-term health benefits. The provider may understand the need to take a harm-reduction approach, prioritizing the most urgent needs presented by the young person and the young person's own right to self-determination. If not, the encounter may become another experience where the young person is not understood and is told what to do and where the young person feels judged and disregarded. Providers may also come in with a "naturalizing inequality" point of view (i.e., you receive poor healthcare because you don't follow recommendations, you don't follow instructions, you don't behave appropriately, etc). Rather than viewing the young person as having a greater need and greater deservedness, the young person is viewed as less worthy (Farmer, 2004).

RESPOND TO STRUCTURES IN THE CLINIC

How could the clinic and the professionals involved attempt to respond to the impact of these structures within the clinic? The actions taken toward this end are limited only by service setting leadership and staff—their self-awareness, courage, willingness, and imagination. Are individuals aware of biases they experience toward YEH-, LGBTQ+-, and Black-identified individuals living with HIV, and how those biases are manifesting? Bias can manifest in an endless variety of ways, but here are some common examples:

unequal rule enforcement, lack of helpfulness, increased rigidity of providers, and increased tendency to involve law enforcement to resolve problems. All these forms of bias are well documented in health care settings (Shapiro, 2018). Assuming providers are self-aware, are they courageous enough to openly discuss these biases in the professional setting, to acknowledge disparities in care provided to BIPOC LGBTQ+ YEH, and to challenge hierarchies that undermine effective care? This may include clarifying values, communicating expectations openly, and providing safe opportunities for patients to give feedback. Is there willingness to change the ways services are provided, shift priorities, reallocate resources, and reimagine care models? For example, the clinic could commit to providing resources and support to staff who manage the waiting area to maintain safety and flexibility to all youth accessing care, including BIPOC LGBTQ+ YEH who may be presenting with complex needs. They could provide training to enhance the competence of providers to better service this client population. Medical providers could learn that their services should prioritize the young person's expressed needs and not come tied to a complex "to do" list. Services could be offered, but not required, to maximize client choice and autonomy. They could widely embrace harm-reduction approaches to risk behavior and commit to minimizing re-traumatization of BIPOC LGBTQ+ YEH in the clinic setting. The clinic could make a point of trying to address unmet needs such as hunger and the need for sleep by having a snack food cabinet accessible and relaxing rules related to sleeping in the waiting room. And is there creativity, imagination, flexibility, and ability to think outside the box and implement new approaches? This can be done in a range of ways, but they all require imagination, flexibility, and creativity (Neff et al., 2020).

RESPOND TO STRUCTURES BEYOND THE CLINIC

We need to recognize the bigger picture while prioritizing the services that will be most helpful and appropriate for young people experiencing homelessness. There is tension between the needs of LGBTQ+ YEH and societal demands. Examples include advocating for access to shelter that allows LGBTQ+ YEH to be housed with individuals with whom they feel safest and most comfortable, rather than based on rigid gender binaries. Shelters could match individual LGBTQ+ YEH's stage of change with housing options that offer maximum flexibility, such as advocating for allocation of greater resources for permanent supportive housing, addressing transphobic violence in the community, addressing violence toward LGBTQ+ YEH and anti-YEH sentiment in community, advocating for SSI eligibility, and addressing food insecurity. They could outreach and provide education to law enforcement to reduce criminalization and stigmatization of LGBTQ+ YEH. Providers can provide education and speak out against "no tolerance" policies that exclude people with substance use disorders from service environments. While the intention to have "drug free spaces" has value, it has the unintended consequence of pushing out the LGBTQ+ YEH who are most vulnerable and would most benefit from access to these services and institutions. They can advocate for reproductive justice, remembering that LGBTQ+ YEH have the right to choose when and how they wish to become parents, and that they have the right to parent their own children.

STRUCTURAL HUMILITY

Collaboration among different providers is necessary to help the young person in our scenario and be an advocate for her needs. Medical hierarchy creates numerous dynamics that pose barriers to effective collaboration. Medical hierarchy can have the effect of silencing providers who have valuable information (Orchard et al., 2005). There may be individuals who observe and recognize bias being manifested toward the African American transgender young woman seeking services in the case scenario. Individuals' locations on the medical hierarchy will influence whether they voice this observation, and if voiced, whether the individual will be praised or reprimanded, believed or shut down. The valuing of some professionals over others does not help with collaboration. Taking actions to flatten the hierarchy increases mutual respect between providers, which then lends itself toward greater respect for individual patients. Another consideration is the prioritized outcome of services. Providers do not have all the answers about the best or safest option for an individual youth. If the youth's problems were easy to solve, the youth would have figured out the best option already. Providers need to consult and collaborate with the youth to see if they have any ideas for improving their care. Respect for self-determination needs to be prioritized. In the words of Judith Herman (1997), "No intervention that takes power away from the survivor can possibly foster her recovery, no matter how much it appears to be in her immediate best interest" (p. 132).

Practice and Policy Recommendations

Services designed for LGBTQ+ YEH have the benefit of incorporating awareness of the psychosocial needs of the population and potentially having trained staff and resources that can be more responsive to these needs. Service models may differ, but what is needed is a service philosophy with specific underpinnings. Interventions targeting LGBTQ+ YEH need to be culturally sensitive, LGBTQ+ affirming, youth centered, accessible, and empowering. This means being voluntary, youth driven, low barrier, inclusive, people of color centered, and strength enhancing. Concepts useful for framing interventions with LGBTQ+ YEH include healing-centered engagement, restorative justice, positive youth development, and harm reduction.

HEALING-CENTERED ENGAGEMENT AND STRUCTURAL VIOLENCE

Both LGBTQ+ YEH and staff persons providing services are in a setting continuously affected by trauma, both past and present. Under the umbrella of trauma-informed care, healing-centered engagement refers to relationships developed within service settings, engaging with young people with the intention of nurturing healing, being cognizant of racism, sexism, and hetero- and cisnormative biases, which are a barrier to necessary healing, and working toward creating and maintaining safe spaces for all

LGBTQ+ YEH and staff persons. The emphasis is on understanding that individuals are affected by trauma, that it is a priority that service providers and settings avoid re-traumatization, and that services convey respect and emphasize client choice and autonomy. Services supporting healing and connection between people also have the effect of shifting norms to support safe and healthy behaviors. LGBTQ+ YEH need service environments that provide opportunities to experience mastery and success, see themselves in a positive way, develop positive relationships with adults and with each other, develop skills that support their transition to adulthood, and learn strategies that can help them navigate their way out of homelessness (Neff et al., 2020). This focus is intended to counter the symptoms of community trauma (Goodman, 2015).

RESTORATIVE JUSTICE AND STRUCTURAL VIOLENCE

Restorative justice refers to practices to help heal structural harm. Restorative justice is a concept usually referring to the criminal justice system, where crime is seen as harm caused by an individual. The aim is to facilitate that person's understanding of the harm they have caused, and the expected response is that the individual makes amends in various ways in order to "make things as right as possible." However, restorative justice can be understood in a broader, societal context, where the "crime" is the structural violence that violates and harms people and relationships, the aim is for the community to understand those harms, and the outcome is a community response to identify obligations, meet needs, and promote healing. Specific to service environments serving LGBTQ+ YEH, restorative justice means recognizing injustice and inequity experienced by marginalized young people, including those experiencing homelessness, and intervening to "make things as right as possible." Providers, administrators, and policy makers have a responsibility to see YEH, both LGBTQ+ and other, as young people who deserve to have been taken care of, but who have been harmed by structural violence. As a result, we can recognize our professional obligations to provide care, meet needs, and promote healing. Services settings, whether hospitals, schools, shelters, or drop-in centers, can be "restorative" by helping young people overcome the trauma of having been harmed, or "failed" by other service systems.

Restorative justice for LGBTQ+ youth, both housed and unhoused, can take many forms. One example is a program in a clinic serving transgender and nonbinary youth and young adults, both housed and experiencing homelessness. The program provides affirming health care, using informed consent rather than a gatekeeper model of care. There is an understanding that gender diverse young people are experts of their own experience and should be the leaders in their care and transition journey. They provide opportunities for young people to explore and share their gender journey, but without expectation that the young people have to "prove" their worthiness/eligibility for gender-affirming care. They provide targeted interventions to make sure young people know their rights to confidentiality and sensitive services (services youth can access without parental consent). They establish the expectation that in the clinic setting, parents who bring young people for services will use the asserted name and pronoun. They make sure that young people know about and have access to sexual and reproductive health care and support youth self-determination. They embrace sex-positive health care. They hire staff persons who share some of the identities as the youth served. All of these approaches attempt to center the needs of the LGBTQ+ youth being served, making their needs, their dignity, and their experience the priority in the service setting.

POSITIVE YOUTH DEVELOPMENT AND STRUCTURAL VIOLENCE

Positive youth development is a social-cultural-level approach that emphasizes building on youth strengths, providing supports and opportunities that will help young people achieve their goals and become positive actors in social change. Participation of youth in decision-making processes also counteracts ageism and paternalism, which are forms of structural violence. Decisions are often made for youth, not with them, resulting in a loss of their perspectives, insights, energy, and passion.

An example of a positive youth development intervention includes a leadership program organized by transgender and nonbinary youth that has the goals of empowering gender diverse people, both housed and homeless, and increasing visibility of transgender and nonbinary individuals. They create an annual calendar showcasing transgender and nonbinary youth, organize community events around the calendar distribution, and develop leadership skills through mentorship by leaders in the transgender community. The leadership program also helps facilitate community-led research. Participants are engaged in the process of creating the research proposal, facilitating visits, and dissemination of findings. Youth are also invited to participate in a youth community advisory board, where they can discuss program practices and provide recommendations for care, education, and the environment of care. This often serves as a bridge to employment opportunities in LGBTQ+ service settings.

HARM REDUCTION AND STRUCTURAL VIOLENCE

Harm reduction is a concept for helping young people be informed, safe, and empowered about substance use or other risk behaviors. Substance use disorders are complex biopsychosocial conditions that can and do cause harm to individuals and communities.

At the same time, substance use can also be viewed as one of many "survival tactics of the oppressed." For example, substance use can be a safer way of trying to maximize your safety and autonomy in environments hostile to your welfare, dignity, and very existence due to various forms of structural violence (CISUR, 2017). Young people need to be informed about a harm-reduction perspective in order to feel safe talking about substance use. When young people realize that they won't be penalized if they talk with their providers about substance use, it opens doors and creates opportunities.

Harm reduction means different things at different levels, but at its core it respects youth autonomy. It is a developmental approach that prioritizes an individualized partnership between the youth and the provider with the goal of working toward youth-identified needs and goals. It does not accept the status quo, instead allowing youth to consider their risk behaviors and the harms they experience and work toward reducing those harms in order to experience themselves in a different way. It creates space for young people to be both independent and dependent, both in terms of their risk behaviors and in their relationship with service providers. The opposite of harm reduction is when providers come in saying "do what I say," imparting wisdom but not collaborating and not considering the youth's current stages of change.

Harm reduction means programs use case-by-case flexibility rather than across-the-board zero-tolerance policies. For example, sometimes YEH will carry a weapon for self-protection. If a young person brings a weapon with them into a service environment, should they automatically be denied care? Should they be banned from the agency? A harm-reduction approach means there is not a one-size-fits-all response to a behavior. Providers would need to consider why the young person carries a weapon, whether they had intent to harm someone, and whether they have an alternate place to store the weapon during appointments. Another example of a harm-reduction approach would be providing services to YEH who arrive at a clinic while under the influence. Would they still be able to access services? It would depend on their ability to participate and benefit from a service, and whether it would cause any harm (to them or others) to provide the service while they are under the influence.

Each of these concepts—structural competency, healing-centered engagement, restorative justice, positive youth development, and harm reduction—interact and amplify each other. They are structural, multilevel interventions that shift resources and power away from institutions and hierarchies that enact structural violence and prioritize the healing and development of young people most vulnerable to structural violence, including but not limited to LGBTQ+ YEH. They create space for young people to be both independent and dependent—developing trust, making their own decisions, and asking for help when needed.

Gaps and Future Directions

While many important factors related to LGBTQ+ YEH have been identified and examined through research, there is a need for more information regarding the specific policies, interventions, and practices that LGBTQ+-affirming homelessness shelters, programs, and services should include. Additionally, more information is needed about how best to make the necessary changes in the homelessness program context. Regarding mental health services for LGBTQ+ YEH, more detailed information about the specifics of affirming mental health services in the homeless program or shelter context is needed. We know that good intentions are not enough, so what specifically is effective? Last, mental health providers can play very important roles as advocates for their LGBTQ+ youth clients in the homeless shelter and program context. However, more information is needed about how to effectively navigate shelter systems to advocate for the improvements and changes our clients need, as well as how to handle the challenges that often come up, because systems that are hostile to LGBTQ+ youth will also be hostile to the mental health providers who work with them and try to advocate for their needs.

References

Antrosio, Jason. "Is social inequality inevitable?" *Living Anthropologically* (blog), April 22, 2017. https://www.livinganthropologically.com/anthropology-2017/is-social-inequality-inevitable/

Arvidson, J., Kinniburgh, K., Howard, K., Spinazzola, J., Strothers, H., Evans, M., . . . Blaustein, M. E. (2011). Treatment of complex trauma in young children: Developmental and cultural considerations in application of the ARC intervention model. *Journal of Child & Adolescent Trauma, 4*(1), 34–51.

Austin, A., & Craig, S. L. (2015). Transgender affirmative cognitive behavioral therapy: Clinical considerations and applications. *Professional Psychology: Research and Practice, 46*(1), 21.

Bain, C. L., Grzanka, P. R., & Crowe, B. J. (2016). Toward a queer music therapy: The implications of queer theory for radically inclusive music therapy. *The Arts in Psychotherapy, 50*, 22–33.

Basile, K. C., Clayton, H. B., DeGue, S., Gilford, J. W., Vagi, K. J., Suarez, N. A., . . . Lowry, R. (2020). Interpersonal violence victimization among high school students—youth risk behavior survey, United States, 2019. *MMWR supplements, 69*(1), 28.

Begun, S., & Kattari, S. K. (2016). Conforming for survival: Associations between transgender visual conformity/passing and homelessness experiences. *Journal of Gay & Lesbian Social Services, 28*(1), 54–66. https://doi.org/10.1080/10538720.2016.1125821

Beharry, M., Harpin, S., Al Makadma, A., Ammerman, S., Eisenstein, E., Warf, C., Yeo, M., & Auerswald, C. L. (2018). The healthcare needs and rights of youth experiencing homelessness society for adolescent health and medicine. *Journal of Adolescent Health, 63*(3), 372–75.

Bender, K., Brown, S. M., Thompson, S. J., Ferguson, K. M., & Langenderfer, L. (2015). Multiple victimizations before and after leaving home associated with PTSD, depression, and substance use disorder among homeless youth. *Child Maltreatment, 20*(2), 115–124.

Blaustein, M. E., & Kinniburgh, K. M. (2010). *Treating traumatic stress in children and adolescents*. Guilford Press.

Bourgois, P., Holmes, S. M., Sue, K., & Quesada, J. (2017). Structural vulnerability: Operationalizing the concept to address health disparities in clinical care. *Academic Medicine: Journal of the Association of American Medical Colleges, 92*(3), 299.

Braveman, P., Egerter, S., & Williams, D. R. (2011). The social determinants of health: Coming of age. *Annual Review of Public Health, 32*(1), 381–398.

Bronfenbrenner, U. (1979). *The ecology of human development: Experiments by nature and design*. Harvard University Press.

Canadian Institute for Substance Use Research (CISUR). (2017). Understanding substance use: A health promotion perspective. https://www.heretohelp.bc.ca/infosheet/understanding-substance-use-a-health-promotion-perspective

Center for Substance Abuse Treatment (US). (2014). *Trauma-informed care in behavioral health services*. Substance Abuse and Mental Health Services Administration (US).

Choi, S. K., Wilson, B. D., Shelton, J., & Gates, G. J. (2015). Serving our youth 2015: The needs and experiences of lesbian, gay, bisexual, transgender, and questioning youth experiencing homelessness. https://escholarship.org/uc/item/1pd9886n

Cochran, B. N., Stewart, A. J., Ginzler, J. A., & Cauce, A. M. (2002). Challenges faced by homeless sexual minorities: Comparison of gay, lesbian, bisexual, and transgender homeless adolescents with their heterosexual counterparts. *American Journal of Public Health, 92*(5), 773–777.

Coolhart, D., & Brown, M. T. (2017). The need for safe spaces: Exploring the experiences of homeless LGBTQ youth in shelters. *Children and Youth Services Review, 82*, 230–238.

Corliss, H. L., Goodenow, C. S., Nichols, L., & Austin, S. B. (2011). High burden of homelessness among sexual-minority adolescents: Findings from a representative Massachusetts high school sample. *American Journal of Public Health, 101*(9), 1683–1689.

Covenant House. (2017). *Youth homelessness.* https://www.covenanthouse.org/homeless-issues/homeless-children-in-america

DeRosa, R., Habib, M., Pelcovitz, D., Rathus, J., Sonnenklar, J., Ford, J., . . . Kaplan, S. (2006). Structured psychotherapy for adolescents responding to chronic stress. *Unpublished manual.*

Dryden, E., Hyde, J., Livny, A., & Tula, M. (2010). Phoenix rising: Use of a participatory approach to evaluate a federally funded HIV, hepatitis and substance abuse prevention program. *Evaluation and Program Planning, 33*(4), 386–393.

Empson, S., Cuca, Y. P., Cocohoba, J., Dawson-Rose, C., Davis, K., & Machtinger, E. L. (2017). Seeking safety group therapy for co-occurring substance use disorder and PTSD among transgender women living with HIV: A pilot study. *Journal of Psychoactive Drugs, 49*(4), 344–351.

Fairchild, R., & McFerran, K. S. (2018). Understanding children's resources in the context of family violence through a collaborative songwriting method. *Children Australia, 43*(4), 255–266.

Fansler, V., Reed, R., bautista, e, Arnett, A. T., Perkins, F., & Hadley, S. (2019). Playing in the borderlands: The transformative possibilities of queering music therapy pedagogy. *Voices: A World Forum for Music Therapy, 19*(3). https://doi.org/10.15845/voices.v19i3.2679

Farmer, P. (2004). An anthropology of structural violence. *Current Anthropology, 45*(3), 305–325.

Farmer, P. E., Nizeye, B., Stulac, S., & Keshavjee, S. (2006). Structural violence and clinical medicine. *PLoS Medicine, 3*(10), e449.

Ferguson, K. M., & Maccio, E. M. (2015). Promising programs for lesbian, gay, bisexual, transgender, and queer/questioning runaway and homeless youth. *Journal of Social Service Research, 41*(5), 659–683.

Fraser, B., Pierse, N., Chisholm, E., & Cook, H. (2019). LGBTIQ+ homelessness: A review of the literature. *International Journal of Environmental Research and Public Health, 16*(15), 2677.

Freeman, R., Gwadz, M. V., Silverman, E., Kutnick, A., Leonard, N. R., Ritchie, A. S., . . . Martinez, B. Y. (2017). Critical race theory as a tool for understanding poor engagement along the HIV care continuum among African American/Black and Hispanic persons living with HIV in the United States: A qualitative exploration. *International Journal for Equity in Health, 16*(1), 1–14.

Friedman, M. S., Marshal, M. P., Guadamuz, T. E., Wei, C., Wong, C. F., Saewyc, E., & Stall, R. (2011). A meta-analysis of disparities in childhood sexual abuse, parental physical abuse, and peer victimization among sexual minority and sexual nonminority individuals. *American Journal of Public Health*, 101(8), 1481–1494. https://doi.org/10.2105/AJPH.2009.190009

Goodman, R. D. (2015). A liberatory approach to trauma counseling: Decolonizing our trauma-informed practices. In R. D. Goodman and P. C. Gorski (Eds.), *Decolonizing "multicultural" counseling through social justice* (pp. 55–72). Springer.

Gregg, J., & Saha, S. (2006). Losing culture on the way to competence: The use and misuse of culture in medical education. *Academic Medicine, 81*(6), 542–547.

Hein, L. C., Stokes, F., Greenberg, C. S., & Saewyc, E. M. (2018). Policy brief: Protecting vulnerable LGBTQ youth and advocating for ethical health care. *Nursing Outlook, 66*(5), 505–507.

Herman, J. L. (1997). *Trauma and recovery*. Basic Books.

Hollywood Homeless Youth Partnership. (2009). *10 reasons for integrating trauma-informed approaches in programs for runaway and homeless youth*. http://hhyp.org/wp-content/uploads/2012/02/HHYP_10Reasons_Flyer.pdf

Hollywood Homeless Youth Partnership. (n.d.). *The ARC framework (attachment, self-regulation, competency) for runaway and homeless youth serving agencies*. http://hhyp.org/wp-content/uploads/2012/02/HHYP_ARC_Framework.pdf

Hollywood Homeless Youth Partnership. (2012). *Trauma informed consequences for homeless youth*. http://hhyp.org/wp-content/uploads/2012/02/Trauma-Informed-Consequences.pdf

Hom, K. A., & Woods, S. J. (2013). Trauma and its aftermath for commercially sexually exploited women as told by front-line service providers. *Issues in Mental Health Nursing, 34*(2), 75–81.

Hopper, E. K., Bassuk, E. L., & Olivet, J. (2010). Shelter from the storm: Trauma-informed care in homelessness services settings. *Open Health Services and Policy Journal, 3*(1).

Hopper, E. K., & Spinazzola, J. (2006). *Trauma-informed facility assessment*. Trauma Center at Justice Resource Institute.

Hughto, J. M., Gunn, H. A., Rood, B. A., & Pantalone, D. W. (2020). Social and medical gender affirmation experiences are inversely associated with mental health problems in a US non-probability sample of transgender adults. *Archives of Sexual Behavior, 49*(7), 2635–2647.

Jen, W. (2016). The use of Image Theatre to examine the acculturation process of Taiwanese international performing arts students in New York City. *Drama Therapy Review, 2*(1), 79–97.

Keuroghlian, A. S., Shtasel, D., & Bassuk, E. L. (2014). Out on the street: A public health and policy agenda for lesbian, gay, bisexual, and transgender youth who are homeless. *American Journal of Orthopsychiatry, 84*(1), 66.

Lange, T. M. (2020). Trans-affirmative narrative exposure therapy (TA-NET): A therapeutic approach for targeting minority stress, internalized stigma, and trauma reactions among gender diverse adults. *Practice Innovations, 5*(3), 230.

Lavenda, R. H., & Schultz, E. A. (2013). *Anthropology: What does it mean to be human?* (p. 576). Oxford University Press.

Liu, R. T., & Mustanski, B. (2012). Suicidal ideation and self-harm in lesbian, gay, bisexual, and transgender youth. *American Journal of Preventive Medicine, 42*(3), 221–228.

Marlatt, G. A., & Witkiewitz, K. (2010). Update on harm-reduction policy and intervention research. *Annual Review of Clinical Psychology, 6*, 591–606.

Marshall, B. D., Shannon, K., Kerr, T., Zhang, R., & Wood, E. (2010). Survival sex work and increased HIV risk among sexual minority street-involved youth. *Journal of Acquired Immune Deficiency Syndromes (1999), 53*(5), 661.

Maynard, K. (2018). To be black. To be a woman. Can dramatherapy help black women to discover their true self despite racial and gender oppression? *Dramatherapy, 39*(1), 31–48. http://dx.doi.org/10.1080/02630672.2018.1432668

Metzl, J. M., & Hansen, H. (2014). Structural competency: Theorizing a new medical engagement with stigma and inequality. *Social Science & Medicine, 103*, 126–133.

Moore, J. (2013). Resilience and at-risk children and youth. *National Center for Homeless Education*.

Morton, M. H., Dworsky, A., Matjasko, J. L., Curry, S. R., Schlueter, D., Chávez, R., & Farrell, A. F. (2018). Prevalence and correlates of youth homelessness in the United States. *Journal of Adolescent Health, 62*(1), 14–21.

Morton, M. H., Samuels, G. M., Dworsky, A., & Patel, S. (2018). *Missed opportunities: LGBTQ youth homelessness in America.* Chapin Hall at the University of Chicago.

Najavits, L. M., Weiss, R. D., Shaw, S. R., & Muenz, L. R. (1998). "Seeking safety": Outcome of a new cognitive-behavioral psychotherapy for women with posttraumatic stress disorder and substance dependence. *Journal of Traumatic Stress: Official Publication of the International Society for Traumatic Stress Studies, 11*(3), 437–456.

National Alliance to End Homelessness (n.d.) *Who experiences homelessness? Youth and young adults.* https://endhomelessness.org/homelessness-in-america/who-experiences-homelessness/youth/

National Child Traumatic Stress Network. (2014). *Complex trauma: Facts for service providers working with homeless youth and young adults.* https://www.nctsn.org/resources/complex-trauma-facts-service-providers-working-homeless-youth-and-young-adults

National Child Traumatic Stress Network. (2013). *Complex trauma: Facts for service providers working with homeless youth and young adults.* http://hhyp.org/wp-content/uploads/2013/04/Complext-Trauma-Facts_Homeless-Youth_draft-4.pdf

National Health Care for the Homeless Council. (April 2016). *Using the social ecological model to examine how homelessness is defined and managed in rural East Tennessee.* www.nhchc.org

National Network for Youth (n.d.) *LGBTQ+ youth homelessness.* https://nn4youth.org/lgbtq-homeless-youth/

Neff, J., Holmes, S. M., Knight, K. R., Strong, S., Thompson-Lastad, A., McGuinness, C., . . . Nelson, N. (2020). Structural competency: Curriculum for medical students, residents, and interprofessional teams on the structural factors that produce health disparities. *MedEdPORTAL, 16*, 10888.

Nooe, R. M., & Patterson, D. A. (2010). The ecology of homelessness. *Journal of Human Behavior in the Social Environment, 20*(2), 105–152.

Norris, A. L., & Orchowski, L. M. (2020). Peer victimization of sexual minority and transgender youth: A cross-sectional study of high school students. *Psychology of Violence, 10*(2), 201.

Orchard, C. A., Curran, V., & Kabene, S. (2005). Creating a culture for interdisciplinary collaborative professional practice. *Medical Education Online, 10*(1), 4387.

Parast, L., Tucker, J. S., Pedersen, E. R., & Klein, D. (2019). Utilization and perceptions of drop-in center services among youth experiencing homelessness. *The Journal of Behavioral Health Services & Research, 46*(2), 234–248.

Pergamit, M. R., Ernst, M., & Hall, C. (2010). Runaway youth's knowledge and access of services. National Runaway Switchboard, Chicago. https://www.semanticscholar.org/paper/Runaway-Youth's-Knowledge-and-Access-of-Services-Pergamit/bb8824dafe04296a29119703b0e8964b1f530081

Pinderhughes, H., Davis, R., & Williams, M. (2015). Adverse community experiences and resilience: A framework for addressing and preventing community trauma.

Pitcher, C., Saewyc, E., Browne, A., & Rodney, P. (2019). Access to primary health care services for youth experiencing homelessness: "You shouldn't need a health card to be healthy." *Witness: The Canadian Journal of Critical Nursing Discourse, 1*(2), 73–92.

Powell, C., Ellasante, I., Korchmaros, J. D., Haverly, K., & Stevens, S. (2016). iTEAM: Outcomes of an affirming system of care serving LGBTQ youth experiencing homelessness. *Families in Society, 97*(3), 181–190.

Prescott, M. V., Sekendur, B., Bailey, B., & Hoshino, J. (2008). Art making as a component and facilitator of resiliency with homeless youth. *Art Therapy, 25*(4), 156–163.

Prock, K. A., & Kennedy, A. C. (2020). Characteristics, experiences, and service utilization patterns of homeless youth in a transitional living program: Differences by LGBQ identity. *Children and Youth Services Review, 116*, 105176.

Renard, S. B., Huntjens, R. J., Lysaker, P. H., Moskowitz, A., Aleman, A., & Pijnenborg, G. H. (2017). Unique and overlapping symptoms in schizophrenia spectrum and dissociative disorders in relation to models of psychopathology: A systematic review. *Schizophrenia Bulletin, 43*(1), 108–121.

Robjant, K., Roberts, J., & Katona, C. (2017). Treating posttraumatic stress disorder in female victims of trafficking using narrative exposure therapy: A retrospective audit. *Frontiers in Psychiatry, 8*, 63.

Rooney, C., Durso, L. E., & Gruberg, S. (2016) *Discrimination against transgender women seeking access to homeless shelters.* Center for American Progress. https://www.americanprogress.org/article/discrimination-against-transgender-women-seeking-access-to-homeless-shelters/

Rosario, M., Schrimshaw, E. W., & Hunter, J. (2012). Homelessness among lesbian, gay, and bisexual youth: Implications for subsequent internalizing and externalizing symptoms. *Journal of Youth and Adolescence, 41*(5), 544–560.

Rotheram-Borus, M. J., Koopman, C., Haignere, C., & Davies, M. (1991). Reducing HIV sexual risk behaviors among runaway adolescents. *Jama, 266*(9), 1237–1241.

Russell, S. T., & Fish, J. N. (2016). Mental health in lesbian, gay, bisexual, and transgender (LGBT) youth. *Annual Review of Clinical Psychology, 12*, 465.

Schauer, M., Neuner, F., & Elbert, T. (2011). *Narrative exposure therapy: A short-term treatment for traumatic stress disorders after war, terror, or torture.* Hogrefe Publishing.

Shapiro, J. (2018). "Violence" in medicine: Necessary and unnecessary, intentional and unintentional. *Philosophy, Ethics, and Humanities in Medicine, 13*(1), 1–8.

Shelton, J. (2015). Transgender youth homelessness: Understanding programmatic barriers through the lens of cisgenderism. *Children and Youth Services Review, 59*, 10–18.

Srivastava, A., Rusow, J. A., Holguin, M., Semborski, S., Onasch-Vera, L., Wilson, N., & Rice, E. (2019). Exchange and survival sex, dating apps, gender identity, and sexual orientation among homeless youth in Los Angeles. *Journal of Primary Prevention, 40*(5), 561–568.

Stajduhar, K. I., Mollison, A., Giesbrecht, M., McNeil, R., Pauly, B., Reimer-Kirkham, S., . . . Rounds, K. (2019). "Just too busy living in the moment and surviving": Barriers to accessing health care for structurally vulnerable populations at end-of-life. *BMC Palliative Care, 18*(1), 1–14.

Takahashi, L. M., Tobin, K., Li, F. Y., Proff, A., & Candelario, J. (2022). Healing transgender women of color in Los Angeles: A transgender-centric delivery of Seeking Safety. *International Journal of Transgender Health, 23*(1–2), 232–242.

Thoma, B. C., & Huebner, D. M. (2013). Health consequences of racist and antigay discrimination for multiple minority adolescents. *Cultural Diversity and Ethnic Minority Psychology, 19*(4), 404.

Thompson Jr., R. G., Elliott, J. C., Hu, M. C., Aivadyan, C., Aharonovich, E., & Hasin, D. S. (2017). Short-term effects of a brief intervention to reduce alcohol use and sexual risk among homeless young adults: Results from a randomized controlled trial. *Addiction Research & Theory, 25*(1), 24–31.

Toro, P. A., Trickett, E. J., Wall, D. D., & Salem, D. A. (1991). Homelessness in the United States: An ecological perspective. *American Psychologist, 46*(11), 1208.

van Leeuwen, J. M., Boyle, S., Salomonsen-Sautel, S., Baker, D. N., Garcia, J. T., Hoffman, A., & Hopfer, C. J. (2006). Lesbian, gay, and bisexual homeless youth: An eight-city public health perspective. *Child Welfare, 85*(2), 151–170.

Varcoe, C., van Roode, T., & Wilson Strosher, H. (2019) *Trauma- and violence-informed care: An orientation tool for service providers in the homelessness sector.* Public Health Agency of Canada. www.equiphealthcare.ca

Wagaman, M. A. (2016). Self-definition as resistance: Understanding identities among LGBTQ emerging adults. *Journal of LGBT Youth, 13*(3), 207–230.

Walls, N. E., & Bell, S. (2011). Correlates of engaging in survival sex among homeless youth and young adults. *Journal of Sex Research, 48*(5), 423–436.

Wang, J. Z., Mott, S., Magwood, O., Mathew, C., Mclellan, A., Kpade, V., . . . Andermann, A. (2019). The impact of interventions for youth experiencing homelessness on housing, mental health, substance use, and family cohesion: A systematic review. *BMC Public Health, 19*(1), 1–22.

Whitbeck, L. B., Chen, X., Hoyt, D. R., Tyler, K. A., & Johnson, K. D. (2004). Mental disorder, subsistence strategies, and victimization among gay, lesbian, and bisexual homeless and runaway adolescents. *Journal of Sex Research, 41*(4), 329–342.

World Health Organization (WHO). (n.d.). *Social determinants of health.* https://www.who.int/health-topics/social-determinants-of-health#tab=tab_1

Yosso, T. J. (2005). Whose culture has capital? A critical race theory discussion of community cultural wealth. *Race Ethnicity and Education, 8*(1), 69–91.

Yuksek, C. (2018). Dealing with stress using social theatre techniques with young Syrian students adapting to a new educational system in Turkey: A case study. *Intervention, 16*(2), 175. http://dx.doi.org/10.4103/INTV.INTV_38_18

CHAPTER 12

Gender Expansive and Sexual Minority Youth and the (In)Justice System

Macy Wilson, PsyD, Jessica Ward, MA, & Roberto L. Abreu, PhD

Incidence and Prevalence

Societal misunderstanding, prejudicial attitudes, discrimination, and a general mistrust of individual differences related to sexual orientation and gender diversity place lesbian, gay, bisexual, transgender, and queer (LGBTQ+) youth at a greater risk for involvement with the juvenile justice system. Research has identified LGBTQ+ youth as overrepresented in the juvenile justice system (Poteat et al., 2016; Snyder et al., 2016; Wilson et al., 2017), with a range between 12–15% (Irvine, 2010; Majd, 2009). However, these numbers may not be fully representative, as youth may hide, deny, or refuse to reveal their sexual or gender identity in these settings due to fear of discrimination and retaliation. Dank and colleagues (2015) report that LGBTQ+ youth are more likely than their heterosexual and cisgender counterparts to experience discriminatory practices and interventions in various stages of their juvenile justice system involvement. For example, the authors found that gender and sexually diverse youth may be subjected to interventions to "correct" or "change" their gender or sexual identities to meet the demands of cisgender and heteronormative social views and are more likely to be held in pretrial status for longer periods of time due to prostitution or sex for survival, violations of probation, warrants, truancy, or running away from home (Dank et al., 2015).

Risk Factors

LGBTQ+ identity has been described as a factor that mediates police and juvenile justice system contact for youth, whereby gender and sexually expansive identities explain the excessive contact these youth have with these systems (Dwyer, 2011). Ignorance, fear, and societal views of gender expression and sexuality have created an environment where LGBTQ+ people experience more police profiling, false or unnecessary arrests, and maltreatment within the juvenile justice system compared to their heterosexual counterparts (Snyder et al., 2016). The most common risk factors associated with LGBTQ+ youth contact in child welfare and juvenile justice systems include harsher and more frequent punishment in schools, expulsion from school, sex for survival, homelessness, familial instability, violence, and removal from the home due to abuse (Dank et al., 2015). LGBTQ+ youth involvement with the juvenile justice system has also been linked with engaging in risky behaviors, including alcohol and drug use and risky sexual behaviors (Allen et al., 2016). There is little empirical inquiry, beyond the literature listed here, into the further understanding of risk factors for LGBTQ+ youth with juvenile justice system involvement and how the experiences of this group compare to that of heterosexual youth.

School-to-Prison Pipeline

Differential and disproportionate school-based disciplinary practices for sexual minority and gender expansive youth have been well-documented throughout the literature. A substantial body of research has linked punitive educational measures, such as suspension, expulsion, and school-recommended legal prosecution, to LGBTQ+ youth entrance into the criminal and juvenile justice system, a pathway identified as the "school-to-prison pipeline" (Himmelstein & Bruckner, 2011). Pipeline entry can occur through a violation of academic achievement standards, safety, or discipline rules. These points of entry usually intersect and are applied concurrently, increasing the risk of transition from school to the juvenile justice system (Snapp et al., 2015). Tests used to make important decisions about student placement and to determine whether a student's academic abilities meet achievement standards, a greater number of police or safety officers on the school grounds, disregarding or sidestepping fairness in punitive actions, and higher rates of expulsion and suspension are common policies and practices utilized by schools that facilitate LGBTQ+ student entry into the pipeline (Glickman, 2016). The school-to-prison pipeline inconsistently affects marginalized youth, particularly youth with disabilities, youth of color, and LGBTQ+ and gender-nonconforming youth, who are propelled out of schools via policies and punitive actions and into the juvenile justice system (Snapp et al., 2015; Himmelstein & Bruckner, 2011). Higher rates of discipline for LGBTQ+ youth and juvenile justice system involvement have been associated with these youth experiencing harsher punishments, such as suspension and expulsion, than those received by their heterosexual counterparts for similar actions and behaviors, as well as being blamed for experiences of peer victimization (Poteat et al., 2016).

Snapp and colleagues (2015) found that LGBTQ+ youth may enter or be pushed into the pipeline through several school-based experiences, or pathways. These researchers found that LGBTQ+ youth receive greater administrative attention and punitive actions for publicly engaging in affection in school than their heterosexual and gender-conforming peers. Furthermore, sexual minority and gender diverse youth are often singled out based on their identification as belonging to this group, whereby these youth disproportionately receive more punitive actions when compared to their heterosexual counterparts. LGBTQ+ youth also receive disproportionate punishment for protecting themselves when they are victimized, often receiving blame for the victimization itself. Finally, entry into the school-to-prison pipeline for sexual minority and gender diverse youth is multifaceted, associated with factors such as mental health struggles, learning difficulties, and familial or home-life issues, which may sometimes be initially related to these negative experiences within the school and perpetuated by school curricula (Wilson et al., 2017).

"No Promo Homo" Laws and a Heterosexual-Cisgender School-Based Curriculum

School curricula often fail to include and address issues of minority populations. Implementation of anti-gay curricula promotes a heterosexual-cisgender school-based learning environment for youth. These curricula are often state mandated and typically require teachers of health and sex education to promote heterosexual relationships, known as "promo hetero" laws. For example, the states of Florida, Illinois, and North Carolina have legal statutes that require teachers of health, sexual, reproductive, and safety education to teach the benefits of traditional, monogamous, heterosexual relationships (Rosky, 2017). Abstinence-until-marriage state curriculum mandates require teachers to instruct students of the detriments of engaging in sexual activity before marriage, regardless of the sex of the persons involved. Though these mandates vary across states, they often require students to be educated on their state's anti-gay marriage decrees. Despite the 2015 Supreme Court ruling that concluded all 50 states must legally grant and recognize same-sex marriages (*Obergefell v. Hodges*, 2015), these anti-gay curricula and the acknowledgment of outdated state laws regarding same-sex marriage foster a learning environment that promotes heterosexual relationships and denounces same-sex marriage.

"Anti-gay" curricula are those that inhibit the inclusion of conversations, discussions, or learning materials related to LGBTQ+ persons and relevant issues and topics to this population. "No Promo Homo" (short for "no promotion of homosexuality") laws exist in various typologies and language in at least 20 US states (Eskridge, 2000; Rosky, 2017). The legal language used in these regulations has been identified as "negative," which commands teachers to speak of sexual orientation in an undesirable manner, and "neutral," which forbids teachers from speaking about nonheterosexual identities supportively (Lenson, 2015). Furthermore, the language of these mandates is considered discriminatory either indirectly, by using expressions that are not fundamentally anti-gay but are used in sodomy and anti-gay marriage laws, or directly, by specifically and explicitly discriminating against sexual minority and gender expansive persons (Barrett & Bound, 2015). Two states, South Carolina and Louisiana, employ "don't say gay" laws that require teachers to refrain from discussing diverse sexualities or showing images of persons who identify with these sexualities engaging in sexual activity. Similarly, in Arizona, teachers are forbidden to teach safe same-sex practices or speak of nonheterosexual identities in a positive way.

A Failed Welfare System

The lack of protection, compassion, and advocacy in the school setting works in conjunction with neglect within the welfare system. School-based LGBTQ+ youth are more likely than their heterosexual counterparts to enter the welfare system for truancy, running away from home, and struggles with parental conflict (Mallon, 2011). One study documented how gender and sexually diverse youth become involved in the child welfare system (Irvine & Canfield, 2016). LGBTQ+ youth are three times more likely to be removed from their homes and seven times more likely to be placed in a group or foster home than their heterosexual and cisgender counterparts. Furthermore, gender and sexually diverse youth are most likely to become involved with the child welfare system due to physical abuse, conflict with parents, running away, or being kicked out of their homes; this occurs at five times the rate it does for their heterosexual peers. Within the child welfare system, LGBTQ+ children often face harassment, bullying, rejection, teasing, and a lack of acceptance from caretakers and peers, as well as difficulty establishing permanent placement (McCormick et al., 2017). These oppressions and maltreatments often co-occur, are highly associated with each other, and are experienced prior to LGBTQ+ youth entering the juvenile justice system.

The (Il)legal System

Youth who are involved with both the child welfare and juvenile justice systems are referred to as "crossover" or "dually involved" (Herz et al., 2012). Involvement with both systems has been attributed to a variety of factors, including harsher school punishments for gender and sexually expansive youth, familial rejection, discriminatory practices within these systems, and inequitable societal treatment (Holsinger & Hodge, 2016). Institutionalized heterosexism, gender conformity expectations, and homophobia have created an environment that significantly impacts LGBTQ+ youth. This environment is comprised of more experiences of victimization, greater negative mental health outcomes, and higher rates of attempting suicide, running away, homelessness, substance abuse, and abuse (e.g., physical, sexual, emotional) for LGBTQ+ youth compared to their cisgender, heterosexual peers (Hunt & Moodie-Mills, 2012; Liu & Mustanski, 2012; Roberts et al., 2012).

DISPROPORTIONATE REPRESENTATION

LGBTQ+ youth are disproportionately represented both within the child welfare system and juvenile justice settings (Irvine & Canfield, 2016). Negative societal reactions to gender and sexually diverse youth, high rates of punishment in schools, and the criminalization of these behaviors have created a situation within the juvenile justice and child welfare systems where LGBTQ+ youth are disproportionately represented within these systems. Using a nationally representative sample of LGBTQ+

youth, Himmelstein and Bruckner (2011) compared the punishment experiences of heterosexual and gender and sexually diverse youth in juvenile justice settings. Their findings revealed that LGBTQ+ youth were more likely to be stopped and arrested by the police as youth and adults, and face conviction as juveniles and adults, regardless of engaging in illegal activities, than their heterosexual counterparts. For example, gender and sexually expansive youth may be pathologized, targeted, or viewed less favorably than cisgender and heterosexual youth based on sexual behavior or gender expression that is perceived as deviating from societal norms. LGBTQ+ youth may also be perceived more harshly than their heterosexual and gender-conforming peers in terms of tendency for engaging in risky or illegal behaviors that result in more severe punishments; combining this with societal and institutional views of gender and sexually diverse identity can lead the behavior of these youth to be more often attributed to, or labeled as, deviance (Wilson et al., 2017; Poteat et al., 2015).

UNEQUAL INJUSTICE

Shay and Strader (2012) recognized the lack of research and institutional focus on the experiences of LGBTQ+ people involved with the criminal justice system and argued for better addressing the many challenges these individuals experience within these systems, especially for persons with intersecting identities of gender, sexual diversity, and race. This need is especially apparent for LGBTQ+ youth in contact with or detained within the juvenile justice system. Not only do LGBTQ+ youth receive inequitable treatment before and during initial contact with the system, but also once involved with the juvenile justice system, gender and sexually expansive youth are often subjected to failures in protection, inadequate access to necessary and appropriate health and mental health services, and discriminatory or differential treatment (Estrada & Marksamer, 2006).

GENDER DIFFERENCES

For LGBTQ+ youth in contact with the juvenile justice system, disproportionate gender differences have emerged as important considerations. A study conducted by Wilson and colleagues (2017) found that a greater number of gender and sexually diverse youth who identify as girls (3.3 times the general population) were involved, detained, or in custody than gender and sexually diverse youth who identified as boys (about proportionally representative of boys in the general population). This indicates that gender and sexually expansive girls are disproportionately involved with the juvenile justice system, which may be based on structural, societal, and institutional bias toward LGBTQ+ girls. The researchers explained that this may be partially due to the current policy reform actions and research focused toward detained boys of color. There also exist gender-based differences in emotional and behavioral stereotypes for boys and girls who engage in illegal behavior and are punished within the juvenile justice system. Gender conformity has been speculated as an important factor that explains the higher rates of girls' involvement with juvenile justice systems (Wilkinson, 2008). Gender and sexually expansive girls may be viewed as violating societal norms and stereotypes related to femininity for girls who appear masculine or identify as such. However, more research is needed to better understand the interactions and intersection of gender and sexually expansive identities and gender presentation and conformity.

YOUTH OF COLOR

A recent study of youth residing within juvenile detention settings revealed that most of these youth were racial and/or ethnic minorities, with Black girls identified as the fastest growing group of youth involved with juvenile justice systems (Hockenberry, 2016; Crenshaw et al., 2015; Wilson et al., 2017). This finding suggests that racial and/or ethnic minority identity may be associated with higher risk for youth becoming involved with the juvenile justice system. Furthermore, youth of color are more likely to be incarcerated for longer periods of time compared to white youth. One study found Black youth were four times, Native American youth were three times, and Latinx youth were two times more likely to be engaged with the juvenile justice system than their white youth counterparts (Wilson et al., 2017). The disproportionate involvement of youth of color within the juvenile justice system has been explained as having a basis in racial and/or ethnic differences in engaging in activities that are criminalized and in the institutional, structural, and societal biases that lead to discrimination from police officers, judges, and corrections systems (Piquero, 2008). For example, youth of color are more likely than their white counterparts to receive harsher punishments (i.e., expulsion or prosecution) for fighting in school, which may be partially based on racial stereotypes such as youth of color being more aggressive than their white counterparts. This has been linked to disproportionate punishment in schools and social and health disparities for youth of color (Hunt & Moodie-Mills, 2012). Racial disparities within the school setting may directly push youth of color into the school-to-prison pipeline. This appears to be especially true for youth with intersectional identities at gender, sexual diversity, and race. Snapp and colleagues (2015) found that race-based discipline strategies combined with violence toward LGBTQ+ students account for the disproportionate contact of these students with the juvenile justice system. However, few studies have examined juvenile justice involvement, incarceration, and the criminalization of youth who identify at the intersection of race, gender, and sexually diverse identities. Future research should seek to better understand the experiences of LGBTQ+ youth of color who are involved with the juvenile justice system to better examine iniquitous treatment and disproportionate representation of these youth.

MICROAGGRESSIONS

LGBTQ+ youth also face microaggressions (i.e., subtle or indirect discrimination) within juvenile justice settings. This is an empirically under-examined phenomenon within the gender and sexually expansive youth population. One study conducted by

Holsinger and Hodge (2016) examined the experiences of LGBTQ+ girls detained within the juvenile justice system. These youth identified experiencing staff and administration addressing their sexuality or gender expression in passive and negative ways, feeling targeted via receiving more punishment and unfair treatment than their heterosexual peers, and not being able to discuss their relationships or identities during group activities. Similar experiences were reported in a case study with a gender nonconforming Latinx lesbian (Caraves, 2018). In this study, she reported experiencing multiple oppressions concerning her gender expression, sexual orientation, race, and ethnic identities. The author described that the youth's behavior, appearance, and sexuality were being criminalized based on others' perceptions of her identities and presentation as not aligning with expectation of the heteronormative and homophobic culture at large. Although more research is needed, it is likely that these findings are applicable across various LGBTQ+ identities for youth who are involved or detained within the juvenile justice system.

MEDIATING FACTORS

Although no existing literature specifically addresses factors that mediate the overrepresentation of LGBTQ+ youth in the child welfare and juvenile justice systems, much can be gleaned from the findings of the extant research. Irvine and Canfield (2016) paint a clear picture of how these youth move through these systems, beginning with familial rejection and moving through the school system, to contact with the child welfare system, to homelessness and survival acts, to juvenile justice system involvement. Important mediating factors may involve the assessment of violence, abuse, and polyvictimization at the youth's first contact with the child welfare system (Snyder et al., 2016). Using trauma- and victim-informed practices for working with gender and sexually diverse youth, the child welfare and criminal justice systems may help mediate negative outcomes associated with these realms for these youth. However, more research is needed to better understand the experiences of LGBTQ+ youth within these systems, how these systems have failed LGBTQ+ youth, and how these systems can be improved to serve this population appropriately.

Mental Health Behaviors While Incarcerated

First-time incarceration is difficult for many individuals. New routines, new people, limited freedoms, and strict rules and regulations coalesce and potentially lead to expressions of mental health issues. For incarcerated youth, the experience of incarceration is likely to exacerbate pre-existing symptoms of anxiety, depression, and suicidality, and this experience can be enough to trigger those concerns if they were not already present. Research has shown that social support and a general feeling of interpersonal connectedness act as buffers from negative experiences that may ordinarily lead to expressions of depression or aggression (Duong & Bradshaw, 2014).

For many LGBTQ+ youth, familial connectedness gets disturbed due to the family's unwillingness to accept the youth's identity. These types of estranged connections have the potential to disrupt attachment patterns and can cause youth to prematurely create attachments with other youth or staff in efforts to re-experience a feeling of security. Sometimes the youth's perception of security is evident via quickly forming multiple superficial relationships, appearing "clingy" with specific staff members, seeking romantic connections among peers, and/or engaging in high-risk sexual behavior. Harder and colleagues (2013) report that these adolescents often exhibit insecure attachment styles (see section "Aggression toward Others" below). This type of attachment may cause behavioral disruptions, interpersonal strife, confusion, and low self-esteem.

In addition to traumatic ruptures (i.e., estranged relationships within family dynamics), or stress due to internal identity struggles youth may have experienced prior to their incarceration, the process of being incarcerated (in itself) can be another form of trauma. Some of the behaviors exhibited by youth may resemble similar symptoms found in acute stress disorders or post-traumatic stress disorders (PTSD), such as nightmares, dissociative reactions, marked physiological reactions to internal or external cues that symbolize or resemble aspects of the disturbing event(s), avoidant behaviors, and negative alterations in mood (APA, 2013). Youth who endured distressing experiences related to their gender and/or sexual identities may also have trouble remembering aspects related to the event(s), persistent negative beliefs about one's self, diminished interest or participation in activities, irritability, hypervigilance, self-harming behaviors, and difficulty concentrating (APA, 2013).

It is also worth noting that many of the experiences of youth who identify as LGBTQ+ are often compounded by issues of race, given the additional layers of oppression (homophobia/transphobia, sexism, and racism). This is imperative for providers to consider, and attend to, given that a lack of attention to these critical oppressive experiences (-isms) can exacerbate feelings of isolation and contribute to symptoms of depression and/or suicidality. "In a study that examined an ethnically diverse transgender sample of 16 to 20-year-olds, the rate of prior suicide attempts was higher [than their non-ethnically diverse counterparts with rates between 9–30%] at 52%" (Janicka et al., 2018, p. 31). Factors that increase youths' risk for suicide include (but are certainly not limited to) repeated experiences of homophobia/transphobia and a perceived inability to advocate for one's self, family history of suicide, previous suicide attempts, substance abuse history, previous mental health diagnoses, poor distress tolerance, feelings of hopelessness/helplessness, impulsivity, chronic physical health issues, and a lack of social/familial support (Janicka et al., 2018).

SELF-HARMING BEHAVIORS

According to Liu and Mustanski (2012), suicide is the third-leading cause of death among adolescents. Additional studies have shown the risk for suicide increases in adolescents who identify as LGBTQ+ (Janicka et al., 2018; Levi & Connors, 2018; Morris & Brown, 2018). Notably, there is a key distinction between suicidal self-harm and non-suicidal self-injury (NSSI). The latter is defined as "a deliberate destruction of one's bodily tissue without the presence of suicidal intent" (Janicka et al., 2018, p. 30). Examples of NSSI include headbanging, cutting, burning, scratching, biting, and punching one's self. While some of these behaviors may also manifest with the presence of suicidal ideation, the functions of NSSI include attempts to tolerate distress and to regulate emotions, distract from (or suppress) negative emotions, rectify interpersonal upsets, and self-punish (Janicka et al., 2018). For example, individuals who experience interpersonal stressors and subsequently internalize blame or negative beliefs about self-worth, may engage in NSSI as a method to mitigate the intensity of the feelings associated with said interpersonal stressors. Factors that are predictive of suicidality for LGBTQ+ youth are the same for all youth and may include a history of/ongoing mental illness or previous suicidal ideation/attempts, loss of significant figures, various types of abuse, inadequate support systems, and poor coping skills (Janicka et al., 2018). Self-harm with suicidal intent and NSSI behaviors may be accompanied by emotions such as anger, frustration, sadness/depression, anxiety, confusion, isolation, hopelessness, and uncontrollable distress.

In the United Kingdom, a study of 68 transgender youth ages 17–25 was conducted to better understand experiences with NSSI (Arcelus & Bouman, 2015). Their study found that those who had more contact with transphobic ideas were at an increased risk of engaging in NSSI. For example, youth whose families of origin or communities were intolerant of transgender identities were found to be more likely to engage in NSSI. This finding may also be applicable to LGB youth who are exposed to homophobic and biphobic ideas within their families or communities (i.e., homophobic slurs, homophobic/biphobic discrimination, etc.). The researchers also found that self-harm was related more to their perceived inability to cope with transphobia, self-hatred, fear, and shame, rather than being related to gender. Notably, another study conducted by Dickey and colleagues (2015) examined 324 transgender adults and found that reported NSSI was higher in transgender men (58%) than in transgender women (26%). Though conducted with a non-incarcerated population, this finding may be due, in part, to possible underreporting of NSSI behaviors, however, this finding (along with similar studies of cisgender men and women) "suggest[s] that NSSI may be linked more to birth sex rather than asserted gender" (Janicka et al., 2018, pp. 30–31).

In heteronormative correctional settings, gender roles and constraints are often magnified, leaving little to no room for gender expression. For youth who may already struggle with emotional expression and/or internalizing or externalizing behavioral concerns, suicidal self-harm and NSSI may be amplified when they are in such settings with limited support.

AGGRESSION TOWARD OTHERS

Though many of the behaviors discussed in the published literature (regarding LGBTQ+ youth and mental health concerns) are related to internalizing behaviors, some youth exhibit externalizing behaviors in maladaptive attempts to navigate difficult emotions and situations. Prior to their incarceration, some LGBTQ+ youth may have been homeless and forced to survive through illegal means that may have included theft, sex work, and violence (to name a few illegal activities) to protect one's self from harm. There has been limited research on aggression among LGBTQ+ youth. However, a study by Duong and Bradshaw (2014) found that being a target of bullying was correlated with aggressive behavior among LGB youth. They noted that youth who identify as LGB report more frequent experiences with various types of violence, including being bullied about their sexual identities. Ongoing exposure to bullying behaviors eventually causes youth to reach a "breaking point," which may manifest as self-harm behaviors or as aggression (Duong & Bradshaw, 2014).

Another factor that may contribute to LGBTQ+ youth aggression is attachment style. Although Zegers and colleagues' (2006) research primarily focuses on behaviors of incarcerated youth, generally, their finding of insecure attachment styles being correlated with aggression is still relevant to the LGBTQ+ adolescent population due to experiences of trauma. In a study of 77 incarcerated adolescents, Zegers and colleagues (2008) examined various attachment representations and the responsiveness of caregivers. For the purposes of their study, Zegers and colleagues (2008) defined a preoccupied attachment representation as one in which an individual utilizes "a strategy of maximizing the display of attachment needs, as from the expectation that otherwise the response will be delayed and/or unsatisfactory" (p. 93). This may manifest with a child making a strong or loud request for attention or affection due to beliefs that the child will be ignored or that the child's needs will be inadequately met. Other attachment representations considered in this study included autonomous, dismissing, and unresolved/disorganized. The authors asserted an autonomous representation was one in which the child would make needs known and have those needs met in sufficient ways, thereby learning both independence and appropriate dependence on caregivers. Zegers and colleagues (2008) noted, "a dismissing attachment representation is indicative of a strategy of minimizing any signal of needing an attachment figure and thereby reducing chances of being rejected" (p. 93). They posited an unresolved/disorganized attachment representation was characterized by a predominance of fear instilled by the caregiver as a result of "attachment-related loss or abuse" (p. 92). The researchers found that institutionalized adolescents with preoccupied attachment representations appeared most problematic in the eyes of the group care workers as compared to adolescents with other attachment representations (Zegers et al., 2008). This difference was found across different forms of maladjustment, namely truancy, rule breaking, and externalizing problems.

The desire to protect one's self from additional harm through preemptive aggression may be rooted in traumatic exposures that lead to "emotional numbing" (Kerig et al., 2012). Abram and colleagues (2004) indicated that 93% of boys and 84% of girls who were incarcerated had experienced a traumatic situation during their lives. Existing research also suggests rates of PTSD for these populations range from 30–52% (Kerig et al., 2012). Exposure to trauma during childhood has been associated with adolescent involvement in the juvenile justice system, according to multiple studies (Becker & Kerig, 2011; Wood et al., 2002; Cernkovich et al., 2008; Feiring et al., 2007; Lansford et al., 2007). Emotional numbing has been explained as a phenomenon that contributes to "acquired callousness," wherein "youth who are exposed to trauma might intentionally cultivate emotional detachment as a method of coping with overwhelming distress" (Kerig et al., 2012, p. 272). A study by Allwood and colleagues (2011) identified that emotional numbing of fear and sadness, specifically, as a result of a traumatic experience was associated with youth aggression. This emotional numbing may help youth create distance between offending parties and feelings of disappointment, insensitivity, and/or rejection. While this can be considered a protective factor in some regards, emotional numbing is part of the same quality expressed in the psychopathic trait of "callous-unemotional," which is found in the Diagnostic and Statistical Manual of Mental Disorders (APA, 2013).

Kerig and colleagues (2012) conducted a study investigating the relationship between trauma exposure, emotional numbing, and callous-unemotional traits with 278 incarcerated youth (68 girls and 208 boys). The authors found that in situations where the trauma involved close relationships (such as rejection by family members), victims were more likely to disengage from their emotions, which allowed them to distance themselves from the emotional pain while preserving, or attempting to preserve, their perception of a positive relationship with the abuser. Such relationship preservation may be only a mental representation of the relationship; however, this allows the youth to defend one's self in the face of rejection. Additionally, avoiding acknowledgment of the abuse allows the youth to focus on other aspects of life. These findings are noteworthy, as history of traumatic experiences, both in the community and while incarcerated, have the capacity to increase aggressive behaviors in LGBTQ+ youth, particularly as their brain is not yet fully developed; and therefore, their ability to be introspective and to effectively communicate needs, fears, and desires may be limited. As clinicians, these factors are important foci in therapy if the goals are ultimately to help youth return to society better than when they left, and to maintain their safety while they are in the custody of the juvenile justice system.

Toward a Socially Just System: Ensuring Safety for LGBTQ+ Youth

A significant aspect of ensuring safety for LGBTQ+ youth is creating spaces that are inclusive and welcoming, while imposing consequences for behaviors that violate such an environment. In order to improve services for LGBTQ+ youth who are incarcerated, adults in these settings should focus on creating an organizational culture wherein respect is paramount and each youth's innate worth is always emphasized through the implementation of fair and equal treatment. In order to achieve this goal, training should be provided at all levels, and should be mandatory, while assuring staff that they are undoubtedly entitled to their beliefs as long as those beliefs do not interfere with the commitment to nondiscrimination while on the job. Such enforcement may be achieved through enhanced grievance procedures for youth and appropriate follow-through by staff, with adequate steps to protect confidentiality along the way.

As providers, the critical nature of confidentiality is key in all interactions with clients, however, this is sometimes nuanced in a correctional environment due to security concerns. As previously stated, there are occasionally situations that require sharing a youth's information with multidisciplinary teams for the purposes of coordinating care and maintaining the security/orderly running of the institution. One area, however, wherein confidentiality is essential is in meetings with mental health providers. It is important that youth understand the limits of confidentiality and that attempts are made to create a welcoming environment where youth feel comfortable to express their true selves. During initial intakes or first meetings with the youth, efforts should be taken to be intentional about the use of inclusive language. For example, this may involve questions such as: "Who lived in your home growing up?" instead of asking about the client's "parents" (who may or may not have been the primary caretakers) or assuming that they were raised by a married heterosexual couple (Mom and Dad). Regarding sexual orientation, one can ask such questions as, "Who are you [interested in] when it comes to romantic relationships?" instead of, "Are you primarily attracted to men, women, or both?" The latter question reinforces the gender binary, which can inadvertently alienate youth. Regarding race/ethnicity: "How do you racially/ethnically identify?" Also, rather than just asking if the client has experienced racism or prejudice, clinicians can word questions in the following manner: "Have you ever experienced any negative situations that you thought were because of your race? What was that like for you (support systems, coping skills, etc.)?" The phrasing of "negative situations" can help destigmatize and normalize their reactions to experiences of racism and allow them to be transparent if they did not necessarily believe the experience constituted racism. Concerning trauma, "Have you ever experienced anything that was especially upsetting for you or that you had a difficult time dealing with?" (Wilson, 2016, para. 24–27). Attention to the phrasing of questions fosters rapport and transparency.

INCORPORATING A HOLISTIC APPROACH TO CARE

According to the National Center for Biotechnology Information (NCBI) (Jasemi et al., 2017), the concept of holistic care integrates facets of holism and humanism. They define holistic care as the following:

> It [holistic care] refers to the provision of care to patients that are based on a mutual understanding of their physical, psychological, emotional, and spiritual dimensions. In addition, holistic care emphasizes the partnership between [healthcare provider] and patient and the negotiation of healthcare needs that lead to recovery. (Jasemi et al., 2017, p. 76)

For some youth, they may feel comfortable with staff whom they have identified as an ally and rely on them to advocate for needs related to their LGBTQ+ identities. While it is not appropriate to "out" youth without a clinical purpose, it is sometimes required to share information about a youth's identity when the youth has specific needs. Multidisciplinary teams are essential to fostering an environment wherein youth can thrive and receive quality care and continuity of care. If available, multidisciplinary teams should consist of all possible staff with whom the youth interact, such as the treating psychologist, physician, pharmacist, chaplain, education staff, social workers, and/or case managers.

Another consideration, specific to the correctional setting, is providing youth with the opportunity to shop from a transgender commissary list (or receive different laundry materials), if youth identify as transgender. Correctional staff in charge of this are required to know such information in order to provide them with the appropriate items. Maintaining confidentiality, building rapport (even through things as seemingly insignificant as laundry), and providing quality holistic care are all critical elements in successful outcomes for youth in corrections. Quality care aims to treat youth's problems and concerns (with their gender/sexual identity in mind) from a client-centered approach that enables staff to be more attentive in efforts to maintain their overall safety and well-being.

As clinicians, integrating a holistic approach includes consideration and exploration of the youth's various systems. This may encompass elements of physical health and access to appropriate medical care both within and outside the institution (health insurance), spiritual beliefs and the youth's perceptions of what their religion condemns or accepts regarding their LGBTQ identity, family dynamics and patterns, level of educational attainment/financial literacy, and access to educational resources, along with vocational training and access to vocational resources both within and outside the institution.

One of the more common treatment modalities within correctional settings is group therapy, as it enables clinicians to provide services to, and build rapport with, multiple individuals at once. Most often, in correctional settings, the treatment of choice is Cognitive-Behavioral Therapy (CBT) because it is evidence-based and empirically supported to engender positive outcomes. Group settings allow individuals the opportunity to learn from each other's experiences, and they also provide additional opportunities for the facilitator to tailor the treatment to address the more salient aspects of youths' lived experiences. Other modalities that have proven successful within correctional settings appear to stem from CBT, such as Dialectical Behavioral Therapy (DBT) and Rational Emotive Behavioral Therapy (REBT). This success has been recorded over several years and promoted by the Department of Justice:

> Cognitive behavioral therapy has been found to be effective with juvenile and adult offenders; substance abusing and violent offenders; and probationers, prisoners and parolees . . . in most cognitive behavioral therapy programs, offenders improve their social skills, means-ends problem solving, critical reasoning, moral reasoning, cognitive style, self-control, impulse management and self-efficacy. (Clark, 2010, p. 22)

Though these treatment modalities have evidence of positive outcomes for youth in correctional settings, special considerations must be taken when implementing this work with LGBTQ+ populations. For example, LGBTQ+ youth who have a greater tendency to mistrust others, or who demonstrate an inability to delay gratification (resulting in increased impulsivity), may benefit from treatment that encourages them to consider how certain automatic thoughts/beliefs are connected to negative experiences with others based on their identities as gender and sexually diverse individuals. Youth who struggle with making these connections may be seen in individual therapy for more focused exploration of these beliefs and experiences. Similarly, the CBT-based anger management protocol produced by the Substance Abuse and Mental Health Services Administration (SAMHSA, 2017) enables individuals to understand the myriad of emotions that may underlie angry or aggressive expressions (both internal and external)—an applied skill for numerous situations for both youth and adults.

Though group treatment is common in correctional settings, not all youth who identify as LGBTQ+ may be comfortable participating in therapy in a group format. If the group is specifically marketed toward LGBTQ+-identified youth, it is essentially requiring them to out themselves, if they have not already. Due to various stigmas and familial and societal dynamics, joining a group marketed as such could be triggering for some, result in increased group resistance, or lead to poor attendance, especially for those who have not achieved stability in their identities. This requires "safe spaces" to be established and communicated to youth prior to asking for enrollment in these groups. Such spaces must have strict standards of accountability, empathic staff, and fair/consistent consequences for violations of safe-space policies among all youth.

It is important to recognize, as mentioned before, that many of these youth do not have stable, supportive interpersonal and/or familial systems. With this in mind, intentional efforts must be made to acknowledge this and help them proactively prepare for a successful reentry into the community by providing resources, contact information, and general information on these issues. This is challenging but righteous work that has a far-reaching impact not only on clients served but also on the clinicians who are committed to such a worthy cause.

CONSTITUTIONAL RIGHTS

According to attorneys Estrada and Marksamer (2006), the right to safety for those in custody is the most fundamental civil right guaranteed to incarcerated individuals. This right is grounded in the Due Process clause of the Fourteenth Amendment to the US Constitution. They assert:

> These due process rights include the right to reasonably safe conditions of confinement, freedom from unreasonable bodily restraint, freedom from conditions that amount to punishment, access to treatment of mental and physical illnesses and injuries, and minimally adequate rehabilitation. These rights extend to children whether they are confined in juvenile detention centers, adult jails, training schools or other secure institutions for delinquent children. (Estrada & Marksamer, 2006, p. 5)

Youth have a right to safety, and the responsibility to maintain this falls on correctional staff, who have a duty to ensure juveniles are protected from harassment and violence (by both other youth and by staff). Once again, ensuring this aspect of youths' safety is more effectively achieved with up-to-date training for working effectively with these populations and by reinforcing nondiscrimination policies. The right to safety also encompasses the right to be free from sexual abuse. Risk of sexual victimization is an important factor to consider for LGBTQ+ youth who are incarcerated given that research findings indicate they are at higher risk of being sexually abused (Levi & Connors, 2018; National PREA Resource Center, 2013). Factors that increase odds of sexual abuse for LGBTQ+ incarcerated youth include having a previous history of being sexually assaulted; expressing concerns about safety while incarcerated; being small in stature; having developmental, mental, and/or medical disabilities; first time being incarcerated; and nonviolent criminal history; to name a few (National PREA Resource Center, 2013). While it is important to assess these risk factors, it is equally important to identify the youth's protective factors, which may include multiple incarcerations without a history of victimization; no history of childhood sexual victimization; large build; assertive presentation; violent criminal history; absence of developmental, mental, and/or medical disabilities; and denial of fear for safety while being incarcerated (National PREA Resource Center, 2013).

Youth also have a right to be free from unreasonably restrictive conditions of confinement, which is explicated as follows:

> Conditions that unduly restrict a youth's freedom of action and are not reasonably related to legitimate security or safety needs of the institution are unconstitutional. A restriction violates this standard if it is arbitrary, discriminatory, or purposeless, or if it is a substantial departure from accepted professional judgment. (Estrada & Marksamer, 2006, p. 6)

The use of isolation, also known as "segregation," special housing unit (SHU), or "the hole," falls into this category. There are inevitably times when the use of isolation is necessary for administrative or holdover purposes, or to protect others from the acts of a specific youth (this includes bullying behaviors toward LGBTQ+ youth and placing the perpetrators in isolation). There may also be times wherein a youth requests protective custody and is subsequently housed in an isolation unit. In such circumstances when the use of a special housing unit is warranted, attempts should be made to ensure the youth's duration there is not extended beyond what is necessary. Long-term use of an isolation unit as punishment can potentially "violate a youth's right to be free from unreasonably restrictive conditions of confinement and constitute impermissible punishment" (Estrada & Marksamer, 2006, p. 6). In addition, studies have shown that long-term placement in a segregation unit can have damaging effects on adults and children alike, leading to exacerbation (or initial onset) of symptoms of mental illness, including depression, anxiety, anger, and disruptive behavioral issues (Estrada & Marksamer, 2020; Levi & Connors, 2018).

LEGAL RIGHTS OF LGBTQ+ YOUTH IN THE JUSTICE SYSTEM

The case of *Kent v. United States* (1966) was predicated on a situation wherein a 16-year-old youth was tried as an adult without his counsel being provided relevant documentation or allowing a hearing to proceed. Because of this case, "the theory of the juvenile court is rooted in social welfare philosophy . . . The objectives [of the court] are to provide measures of guidance and rehabilitation for the child and protection for society, not to fix criminal responsibility, guilt and punishment" (Marksamer, 2008, p. 75). In order to effectively meet this mission, staff must also be keenly aware of the legal rights for incarcerated LGBTQ+ youth and make intentional efforts to ensure those rights are consistently granted.

It is a common misconception that youth who are incarcerated or are in the custody of the juvenile justice system have been "convicted" of crimes. In reality, youth are considered to be adjudicated: "once a young person is adjudicated, courts develop disposition orders rather than order sentences" (Marksamer, 2008, p. 75). This key distinction is not simply administrative; it sets the tone for how youth should be treated prior to and during incarceration. It is in the best interests of LGBTQ+ youth for attorneys and court systems to be knowledgeable of LGBTQ+ issues and how they impact one's identity and, potentially, affect youth's subsequent duration in custody. While incarcerated, youth continue to have the right to effective legal representation, and this is especially salient when abuses of other rights occur. While in custody, youths' right to equal protection remains in place, which includes equal treatment in the consideration of placements, services, and the right not to be harassed by others. Many youth are unaware that their legal representation extends throughout their incarceration; thus, many incidents of physical, verbal, emotional, and/or sexual abuse continue and are not reported verbally or in writing.

The Juvenile Delinquency Guidelines by the National Council of Juvenile and Family Court Judges (NCJFCJ) (Sickmund, 2017) indicate that judges for juveniles are legally and ethically responsible for monitoring and ensuring that all court-ordered services and requirements are met. This may include ordering specific services for rehabilitation or mental health, removing youth from placements, or intervening in other ways to ensure holistic treatment is being provided for successful reintegration to society. In efforts to effectively advocate for LGBTQ+ youth, and empower them to advocate for themselves, legal rights such as these should be reiterated frequently. Additionally, the guidelines set forth by the NCJFCJ (Sickmund, 2017) emphasize the importance of training all adults involved in the juvenile court system in matters of child and adolescent development, cultural nuances and expressions, and mental illness and its potential for comorbidity with substance use. It is important to provide training regarding the communities where these youth live, including awareness of available resources and services. It would also be beneficial for all involved to receive training specific to sexual orientation and gender identity, so youth feel heard and understood, and so that staff are better equipped to handle their unique needs.

Recommendations

Adolescence is, largely, a time of uncertainty, which is further exacerbated by incarceration for youth involved in the justice system. When working with this population, it is especially important to be cognizant of the language used with youth at all stages of the therapeutic process. For example, using jargon-free, developmentally appropriate language in our discourse allows us to be mindful of various developmental stages within this population and cultural differences that may ordinarily distance youth from anything therapy-related. Several studies indicate that LGBTQ+ youth of color report higher rates of physical and sexual abuse, homelessness, foster care placement, and group home involvement than their heterosexual and cisgender peers (Alvy et al., 2013; American Psychiatric Association, n.d.; Dank et al., 2014; Friedman et al., 2011; Irvine, 2010; Irvine & Canfield, 2016; Kann et al., 2016; Roberts et al., 2012; Walters et al., 2013). Though the word "trauma" is widely understood by many people, in the professional world and general population, this word can be triggering or confusing for some. Some survivors of traumatic experiences may find the word itself to be revictimizing and choose to use other words to describe their experiences in efforts to feel empowered. Perhaps more education around trauma is needed; however, when listening to these youth and attempting to fully understand their stories, our queries should be as jargon-free and as easily understandable as possible.

In working with youth who identify as transgender, it may be useful to familiarize one's self with Devor's 14-stage (2004) model of identity development for the purpose of understanding nuances of gender identity, while simultaneously understanding some youth may not relate to each category outlined. Similarly, there may be youth who feel a sense of empowerment in the process of coming out as a sexual and/or gender minority, while others do not wish to openly share this aspect of themselves. There are several factors to consider in coming out, including, but not limited to, racial and/or ethnic group membership, familial responses, the presence or absence of an understanding support system, along with legal and economic considerations. For many who identify as LGBTQ+, the presence of a support group (whether centered around mental health or education) can be enough to help one feel confident in one's identity and possibly facilitate the process of coming out. Unfortunately, this is not prioritized in many juvenile justice settings. As described by Trimble (2019), prison administrators often do not allow LGBTQ+ materials to be distributed. This is likely due to a general belief among administrators that "non-normative" identities related to sexual orientation and gender diversity are against the rules and cause disruption within a heteronormative and cisnormative environment. It is possible that groups specifically for this population could have the effect of inadvertently outing youth or creating further (unintentional) isolation. According to the Fenway Institute's Center (2018) for Prisoner Health and Human Rights, such groups should be facilitated by culturally competent clinicians and based on respect, professionalism, nondiscrimination, and privacy. It is recommended that training for clinicians be current and inclusive and that groups are conducted with transparent grievance procedures, should youth feel a need to utilize such a process.

Clinicians should attempt to identify cyclical, generational patterns that transpire within the frame of therapy. When possible, highlight ways these patterns may be manifesting for the adolescent and encourage the exploration of how those patterns may be affecting their current incarceration and life. Insight into these behaviors can help youth be more self-aware and contribute to feelings of self-confidence when guided by a therapist whose goal is to empower the youth to create lifelong change. In keeping with empowerment, therapy with this population should utilize a strengths-based perspective, especially given that correctional environments are often perceived as the antithesis of strengths-based. Some youth may not have family members who can offer this type of interaction and focus (for various reasons), and receiving that input in therapy may be the only source of positive regard they receive for a significant period.

- Use developmentally appropriate and jargon-free language when speaking with youth clients.
- Create safe spaces with consistent consequences for violations of the protections offered by such spaces.
- Consider using a systemic approach to holistic care. For example, how do the youth's familial dynamics, gender roles, medical issues, spiritual beliefs, and other factors play into current identity concerns?
- Integrate CBT/DBT interventions as a foundation, as these are evidence-based and proven to be highly effective in correctional settings.
- Prioritize multidisciplinary involvement in the youth's care, as each department likely has different relationships with/observations of the youth.

Key Knowledge Points

- The school-to-prison pipeline contributes to the oppression of gender expansive and sexual minority youth.
- The culture of oppression within the current welfare system contributes to gender expansive and sexual minority youths' introduction to the legal system.
- The varying experiences that gender expansive and sexual minority youth are exposed to within the legal system demonstrates the need to avoid treating sexual and gender minority groups as the same.
- Challenges include the lack of mental health services that gender expansive and sexual minority youth have within the legal system.

We need culturally appropriate recommendations for providing mental health services to gender expansive and sexual minority youth within the legal system.

References

Abram, K., Teplin, L., Charles, D., Longworth, S., McClelland, G., & Dulcan, M. (2004). Posttraumatic stress disorder and trauma in youth in juvenile detention. *Archives of General Psychiatry, 61*, 403–410.

Allen, S., Ruiz, M., & O'Rourke, A. (2016). Differences in the prevalence of risk behaviors between heterosexual and lesbian, gay, bisexual, and questioning (LGBQ) female adolescents in the juvenile justice system. *Journal of Gay & Lesbian Social Services, 28*, 171–175.

Allwood, M. A., Bell, D. J., & Horan, J. (2011). Posttrauma numbing of fear, detachment, and arousal predict delinquent behaviors in early adolescence. *Journal of Clinical Child and Adolescent Psychology, 40*(5), 659–667. https://doi.org/10.1080/15374416.2011.597081

Alvy, L., Hughes, T., Kristjanson, A., & Wilsnack, S. (2013). Sexual identity group differences in child abuse and neglect. *Journal of Interpersonal Violence, 28*, 2088–2111.

American Psychiatric Association (APA). (2013). Diagnostic and statistical manual of mental disorders (fifth edition). American Psychiatric Publishing.

American Psychiatric Association (APA). (n.d.). Best practice highlights: Lesbian, gay, bisexual, transgender and people who may be questioning their sexual orientation or sexual identity (LGBTQ). https://www.psychiatry.org/File%20Library/Psychiatrists/Cultural-Competency/Treating-Diverse-Populations/Best-Practices-LGBTQ-Patients.PDF

Arcelus, J., & Bouman, W. (2015). Current and future direction of gender dysphoria and gender incongruence research. *Journal of Sexual Medicine, 12*, 2226–2228.

Barrett, B., & Bound, A. (2015). A critical discourse analysis of *no promo homo* policies in US schools. *Educational Studies, 51*, 267–283.

Becker, S., & Kerig, P. K. (2011). Posttraumatic stress symptoms are associated with the frequency and severity of delinquency among detained boys. *Journal of Clinical Child and Adolescent Psychology, 40*, 765–771.

Caraves, J. (2018). Straddling the school-to-prison pipeline and gender non-conforming microagressions as a Latina lesbian. *Journal of LGBT Youth, 15*, 52–69.

Cernkovich, S., Lanctot, N., & Giordano, P. (2008). Predicting adolescent and adult antisocial behavior among adjudicated delinquent females. *Crime and Delinquency, 54*, 3–33.

Clark, P. (2010). *Preventing future crime with cognitive behavioral therapy*. National Institute of Justice.

Crenshaw, K., Ocen, P., & Nanda, J. (2015). Black girls' matter: Pushed out, overpoliced and underprotected. African American Policy Forum, Center for Intersectionality and Social Policy Studies.

Dank, M., Lachman, P., Zweig, J. M., & Yahner, J. (2014). Dating violence experiences of lesbian, gay, bisexual, and transgender youth. *Journal of Youth and Adolescence, 43*, 846–857.

Dank, M., Yahner, J., Madden, K., Banuelos, I., Yu, L., Ritchie, A., Mora, M., & Conner, B. (2015). Surviving the streets of New York: Experiences of LGBTQ youth, YMSM, and YWSW engaged in survival sex. https://doi.org/1015496/publication-8608

Devor, A. H. (2004). Witnessing and mirroring: A fourteen stage model of transsexual identity formation. *Journal of Gay & Lesbian Psychotherapy, 8*(1–2), 41–67.

Dickey, L., Reisner, S., & Juntunen, C. (2015). Non-suicidal self-injury in a large online sample of transgender adults. *Professional Psychology: Research and Practice, 46*, 3–11.

Duong, J., & Bradshaw, C. (2014). Associations between bullying and engaging in aggressive and suicidal behaviors among sexual minority youth: The moderating role of connectedness. *Journal of School Health, 84*, 636–645.

Dwyer, A. (2011). Policing lesbian, gay, bisexual, and transgender young people: A gap in the research literature. *Current Issues in Criminal Justice, 22*, 415–433.

Eskridge, W. (2000). No promo homo: The sedimentation of antigay discourse and the channeling effect of judicial review. *New York University Law Review, 75*, 1327–1411.

Estrada, R., & Marksamer, J. (2020). Lesbian, gay, bisexual and transgender young people in state custody: Making the child welfare and juvenile justice systems safe for all youth through litigation, advocacy, and education. *Temple Law Review, 79*, 415–438.

Estrada, R., & Marksamer, J. (2006). The legal rights of young people in state custody: What child welfare and juvenile justice professionals need to know when working with LGBT youth. *Child Welfare League of America, 85*, 1–16.

Feiring, C., Miller-Johnson, S., & Cleland, C. (2007). Potential pathways from stigmatization and internalizing symptoms to delinquency in sexually abused youth. *Child Maltreatment, 12*, 220–232.

Fenway Institute. (2018). Emerging best practices for the management and treatment of lesbian, gay, bisexual, transgender, questioning, and intersex youth in juvenile justice settings. https://fenwayhealth.org/wp-content/uploads/TFIP-21_BestPracticesForLGBTYouthIn JuvenileJustice_Brief_web.pdf

Friedman, M., Marshal, M., Guadamuz, T., Wei, C., Wong, C., Saewyc, E., & Stall, R. (2011). A meta-analysis to examine disparities in childhood sexual abuse, parental physical abuse, and peer victimization among sexual minority and sexual nonminority individuals. *American Journal of Public Health, 101*, 1481–1494.

Glickman, D. (2016). Fashioning children: Gender restrictive dress codes as an entry point for the trans school to prison pipeline. *American University Journal of Gender, Social Policy & the Law, 24*, 263–284.

Harder, A., Knorth, E., & Kalverboer, M. (2013). A secure base? The adolescent-staff relationship in secure residential youth care. *Child and Family Social Work, 18*(3), 305–317.

Herz, D., Lee, P., Lutz, L., Stewart, M., Tuell, J., & Wiig, J. (2012). Addressing the needs of multi-system youth: Strengthening the connection between child welfare and juvenile justice. Center for Juvenile Justice Reform.

Himmelstein, K., & Bruckner, H. (2011). Criminal justice and school sanctions against non-heterosexual youth: A national longitudinal study. *Pediatrics, 127*, 49–57.

Hockenberry, S. (2016). Juveniles in Residential Placement, 2013. US Department of Justice, Office of Justice Programs, Office of Juvenile Justice and Delinquency Prevention. http://www.ncjj.org/pdf/Juvenile%20Arrests%20Bulletins/249507.pdf

Holsinger, K., & Hodge, J. (2016). The experience of lesbian, gay, bisexual and transgender girls in juvenile justice systems. *Feminist Criminology, 11*, 23–47.

Hunt, J., & Moodie-Mills, A. (2012). The unfair criminalization of gay and transgender youth: An overview of the experiences of LGBT youth in the juvenile justice system. Center for American Progress. https://www.ncjrs.gov/App/Publications/abstract.aspx?ID=267708

Irvine, A. (2010). "We've had three of them": Addressing the invisibility of lesbian, gay, bisexual and gender nonconforming youths in the juvenile justice system. *Columbia Journal of Gender and Law, 19*, 675–701.

Irvine, A., & Canfield, A. (2016). The overrepresentation of lesbian, gay, bisexual, questioning, gender nonconforming and transgender youth within the child welfare to juvenile justice crossover population. *Journal of Gender, Social Policy & the Law, 24*, 243–261.

Janicka, A., Chung, K., & Reisner, S. (2018). Mental health and well-being of transgender youth: Clinical considerations. *International Journal of Pediatrics and Adolescent Medicine, 29*, 20–43.

Jasemi, M., Valizadeh, L., Zamanzadeh, V., & Keogh, B. (2017). A concept analysis of holistic care by hybrid model. *Indian Journal of Palliative Care, 23*(1), 71–80.

Kann, L., Olsen, E., McManus, T., Harris, W., Shanklin, S., & Flint, K., . . . Zaza, S. (2016). Sexual identity, sex of sexual contacts, and health-related behaviors among students in grades 9–12—United States and selected sites, 2015. *MMWR Surveillance Summaries, 65*, 1–202.

Kerig, P., Bennett, D., Thompson, M., & Becker, S. (2012). "Nothing really matters": Emotional numbing as a link between trauma exposure and callousness in delinquent youth. *Journal of Traumatic Stress, 25*, 272–279.

Lansford, J., Miller-Johnson, S., Berline, L., Dodge, K., Bates, J., & Petit, G. (2007). Early physical abuse and later violent delinquency: A prospective longitudinal study. *Child Maltreatment, 12*, 233–245.

Lenson, J. (2015). Litigation primer attacking state "no promo homo" laws: Why "don't say gay" is not ok. *Law and Sexuality: A Review of Lesbian, Gay, Bisexual & Transgender Legal Issues, 24*, 145–162.

Levi, J., & Connors, C. (2018). Transgender youth, medical professionals, and the law: What you should know. *International Journal of Pediatrics and Adolescent Medicine, 29,* 131–151.

Liu, R., & Mustanski, B. (2012). Suicidal ideation and self-harm in lesbian, gay, bisexual, and transgender youth. *American Journal of Preventive Medicine, 42,* 221–228.

Majd, K. (2009). *Hidden injustice: Lesbian, gay, bisexual, and transgender youth in juvenile courts.* Equity Project.

Mallon, G. (2011). Permanency for LGBTQ youth. *Protecting Children, 26,* 49–57.

Marksamer, J. (2008). And by the way, do you know he thinks he's a girl? The failures of law, policy, and legal representation for transgender youth in juvenile delinquency courts. *Sexuality Research and Social Policy, 5,* 72–92.

McCormick, A., Schmidt, K., & Tarrazas, S. (2017). LGBTQ youth in the child welfare system: An overview of research, practice, and policy. *Journal of Public Child Welfare, 11,* 27–39.

Morris, G., & Brown, J. (2018). Primary care for lesbian, gay, bisexual, transgender, and questioning youth. *International Journal of Pediatrics and Adolescent Medicine, 29,* 1–19.

National PREA Resource Center. (2013). *National Prison Rape Elimination Act Resource Center annual report 2012–2013.* National Council on Crime and Delinquency (NCCD). https://www.prearesourcecenter.org/sites/default/files/library/prc-annual-report-2013-final.pdf

Obergefell v. Hodges, 576 U.S. (2015). https://www.supremecourt.gov/opinions/14pdf/14-556_3204.pdf

Piquero, A. (2008). Disproportionate minority contact. *Future of Children, 18,* 59–79.

Poteat, V., Rivers, I., & Vecho, O. (2015). The role of peers in predicting students' homophobic behavior: Effects of peer aggression, prejudice, and sexual orientation identity importance. *School Psychology Review, 44,* 391–406.

Poteat, V., Scheer, J., & Chong, E. (2016). Sexual orientation-based disparities in school and juvenile justice discipline: A multiple group comparison of contributing factors. *Journal of Educational Psychology, 108,* 229–241. https://doi.org10.1037/edu0000058

Roberts, A., Rosario, M., Corliss, H., Koenen, K., & Austin, S. (2012). Childhood gender nonconformity: A risk indicator for childhood abuse and posttraumatic stress in youth. *Pediatrics, 129,* 410–417. https://doi.org/10.1542/peds.2011-1804

Rosky, C. (2017). Anti-gay curriculum laws. *Columbia Law Reviews, 117,* 1461–1541.

Shay, G., & Strader, K. (2012). Queer (in)justice: Mapping new gay (scholarly) agendas. *Journal of Criminal Law and Criminology, 102,* 171–193.

Sickmund, M. (2017). National council of juvenile and family court judges passes a set of practice reform resolutions. *Juvenile and Family Court Journal, 68*(4), 43–47.

Snapp, S., Hoenig, J., Fields, A., & Russell, S. (2015). Messy, butch, and queer: LGBTQ youth and the school-to-prison pipeline. *Journal of Adolescent Research, 30,* 57–82.

Snyder, S., Hartinger-Saunders, R., Brezina, T., Beck, E., Wright, E., Forge, N., & Bride, B. (2016). Homeless youth, strain, and justice system involvement: An application of general strain theory. *Children and Youth Services Review, 62,* 90–96.

Substance Abuse and Mental Health Services Administration (SAMHSA). (2017). *Key substance use and mental health indicators in the United States: Results from the 2016 National Survey on Drug Use and Health* (HHS Publication No. SMA 17-5044, NSDUH Series H-52). Center for Behavioral Health Statistics and Quality, Substance Abuse and Mental Health Services Administration. https://www.samhsa.gov/data

Trimble, P. E. (2019). Ignored LGBTQ prisoners: Discrimination in education, rehabilitation, and mental health services during incarceration. https://lgbtq.hkspublications.org/2019/05/22/ignored-lgbtq-prisoners-discrimination-in-education-rehabilitative-and-mental-health-services-during-incarceration/

Walters, M. L., Chen, J., & Breiding, M. J. (2013). The National Intimate Partner and Sexual Violence Survey (NISVS): 2010 findings on victimization by sexual orientation. National Center for Injury Prevention and Control, Centers for Disease Control and Prevention. https://www.cdc.gov/ViolencePrevention/pdf/NISVS_SOfindings.pdf (NCJ Publication No. 241083)

Wilkinson, W. (2008). Threatening the patriarchy: Testing an explanatory paradigm of anti-lesbian attitudes. *Sex Roles, 59*, 512–520.

Wilson, B., Jordan, S., Meyer, I., Flores, A., Stemple, L., & Herman, J. (2017). Disproportionality and disparities among sexual minority youth in custody. *Journal of Youth and Adolescence, 46*, 1547–1561.

Wilson, M. (2016). Cultural competence in therapy: Why we must see color. http://blog.time2track.com/cultural-competence-in-therapy-why-we-must-see-color

Wood, J., Foy, D., Goguen, C., Pynoos, R., & James, C. (2002). Violence exposure and PTSD among delinquent girls. *Journal of Aggression, Maltreatment, and Trauma, 6*, 79–108.

Zegers, M., Schuengel, C., & Van Ijzendoorn, M. (2006). Attachment representations of institutionalized adolescents and their professional caregivers: Predicting the development of therapeutic relationships. *American Journal of Orthopsychiatry, 76*, 325–334. https://doi.org/10.1037/0002-9432.76.3.325

Zegers, M., Schuengel, C., Van Ijzendoorn, M, & Janssens, M. (2008). Attachment and problem behavior of adolescents during residential treatment. *Attachment & Human Development, 10*, 91–103. https://doi.org/10.1080/14167 30701868621

CHAPTER 13

Services for Youth and Emerging Adults at LGBTQ+ Centers and Other Community-Based Organizations

Tangela Roberts, PhD, Zari Carpenter, MA, & Kat Schuette, MA

Authors' Note

A portion of these findings were presented as a poster at the 2019 American Psychological Association Convention, Chicago, Illinois, United States. We have no conflicts of interest to disclose. Address correspondence concerning this book chapter to Tangela Roberts, Department of Counselor Education Counseling Psychology, Western Michigan University, 1903 West Michigan Avenue, 3814 Sangren Hall, Kalamazoo, MI 49008. E-mail: tangela.roberts@wmich.edu

Despite recent progress toward acceptance and equality, LGBTQ+ people, and specifically LGBTQ+ youth and emerging adults, are experiencing a time in history where bearing witness to hate crimes (e.g., widespread violence against Black transgender women) and anti-LGBTQ+ legislation (e.g., Florida's *Don't Say Gay* bill) is a weekly, if not monthly, occurrence. While the experience or witness of anti-LGBTQ+ hate crimes and legislation are the tips of the individual and systemic oppression iceberg, LGBTQ+ centers and other community-based organizations are vital to supporting LGBTQ+ youth and emerging adults while serving as a source of advocacy, education, outreach, and prevention. LGBTQ+ community centers have the unique opportunity for primary prevention of the systemic level of oppression experienced by LGBTQ+ youth and emerging adults by providing exposure to positive information about LGBTQ+ individuals in classes or workshops, providing contact with other LGBTQ+ individuals, and working to institute nondiscrimination policies in work and school settings (Matthews & Adams, 2009). Given that LGBTQ+ community centers are uniquely positioned to address heterosexism, monosexism, cisgenderism, and other forms of oppression for LGBTQ+ youth and emerging adults, these centers remain the focus of the current chapter. This chapter will explore the number of services offered by 208 LGBTQ+ community centers to youth and emerging adults.

LGBTQ+ Youth and Emerging Adults of Color

Queer youth and emerging adults of color (QYAOC) have the undue experience of receiving racism, in the form of both microaggressions and overt racist actions, within primarily white LGBTQ+ spaces and heterosexism within largely cisgender and heterosexual racial minority communities. This experience of intersectional oppression can result in feelings of isolation, which can relate to QYAOC generally reporting higher rates of family rejection, bullying, physical and sexual violence, risky sexual behavior, and increased risk of alcohol and other drug abuse when compared to heterosexual racial minority communities and white LGBTQ+ communities (Arnold & Bailey, 2009; Balsam et al., 2011; Gamarel et al., 2014; Garnets & Kimmel, 2003; Johns et al., 2013; Needham & Austin, 2010). Supportive spaces specific to the intersection of racial and sexual orientation identities reduce isolation, create a stronger sense of community, increase visibility, and promote empowerment efforts for QYAOC. Additionally, QYAOC often view LGBTQ+ youth-centric organizations as a type of home or safe space that provides safety from discrimination and helps to foster a sense of pride and authenticity and general feelings of empowerment (Gamarel et al., 2014; Garnets & Kimmel, 2003). As such, LGBTQ+ community centers and other community-based organizations are in a prime position to protect the form of a safe space for QYAOC.

Transgender and Gender-Nonconforming (TGNC) Youth and Emerging Adults

Accepting an individual's gender identity is a prerequisite to support and a sense of belonging and community in society. The family system can be our first form of social support and provide a sense of connectedness and community. However, TGNC youth and emerging adults might not necessarily have a sense of community among their families of origin. For example, Le and colleagues (2016) reported that transfeminine youth perceive their parents as supportive but not fully accepting of their gender identity. The results mimic common social refrains of loving a person but not their identity. The limited ability of some parents to fully accept their transgender child's identity undoubtedly has many impacts on the perception of support. Additionally, Bauermeister and colleagues (2016) identified that although Black TGNC youth often receive the same amount of social support as Black non-TGNC youth, TGNC youth were more likely to experience daily harassment gender-related discrimination than non-TGNC youth. Again, we can see how LGBTQ+ community centers and other community-based organizations are uniquely positioned to provide the support and acceptance that many TGNC youth and emerging adults might not receive from traditional avenues of social support.

Challenges for LGBTQ+ Youth and Emerging Adults

HEALTH CARE CHALLENGES

Mental Health

Mental health is an essential aspect of psychological well-being for all human beings, and "it is important to note that LGBTQ+ youth are typically well adjusted and mentally healthy" (Institute of Medicine, 2011). However, sexual minority individuals are at increased risk for multiple mental health burdens than their heterosexual peers (Hatzenbuehler, 2009). Research has long indicated that mental health services are an especially crucial support for LGBTQ+ youth and emerging adults due to limited social support from peers and family as well as increased rates of victimization based on their sexual orientation and gender (D'Augelli & Hershberger, 1993; Hershberger & D'Augelli, 1995; Le et al., 2016; Mustanski et al., 2011; Painter et al., 2018). QYAOC individuals must also negotiate internalized racism and internalized heterosexism, and both internalized oppressions are significant negative predictors of self-esteem. In particular, Black youth and emerging adults often experience higher victimization levels than white peers (Mustanski et al., 2011). This further reiterates the importance of mental health services attuned to the complexities of racism and heterosexism for QYAOC.

Multiple factors impact the mental health of LGBTQ+ youth and emerging adults, and the relationships between these factors are often complex. Self-acceptance and family and peer support have long been identified as the most significant predictor of mental health for LGBTQ+ youth and emerging adults (D'Augelli & Hershberger, 1993; Hershberger & D'Augelli, 1995; Mustanski & Lui, 2013). Although capable of positive mental health impacts, social support alone does not eliminate the harmful effects of anti-LGBTQ+ oppression and victimization. In examining the risk factors of suicide in LGBTQ+ youth, Mustanski and Liu (2013) found symptoms of depression and conduct disorder, hopelessness, and impulsivity correlated with a lifetime history of suicide attempts. These results point to the need to advocate for LGBTQ+ people and address the root sources of mental distress: the broader heterosexist culture that incubates the victimization of LGBTQ+ youth and emerging adults.

When equipped with adequate mental health services, LGBTQ+ community centers and other community-based services are uniquely positioned to advocate for the affirmative mental health care of LGBTQ+ youth and emerging adults. This advocacy need not be as grand as macro-level political change or upheaval of maladaptive family dynamics. Advocacy can also be effective on a micro level. For instance, physicians can be attuned to potential mental health concerns in LGBTQ+ patients by taking comprehensive histories and physicals and making informed referrals to LGBTQ+-affirming mental health professionals. Faith leaders might serve LGBTQ+ youth by giving religious and spiritual support, acknowledging their strengths in the face of the unique stressors in their lives, and creating social spaces that affirm them (McCann et al., 2020). Teachers and mental health professionals are also players who can advocate for and support LGBTQ+ youth and emerging adults' interpersonal and intrapersonal development (Cerezo & Bergfeld, 2013; Haltom & Ratcliff, 2021; Hernandez & Fraynd, 2014; Kosciw et al., 2015; Snapp et al., 2015).

Sexual Health

Sexual health represents an essential prevention and treatment area to address for community centers, mental health professionals, and physicians. Lack of intimate and emotionally close relationships, unwanted status disclosure, shaming within LGBTQ+ communities, and general stigma around HIV status often leads to a host of negative impacts on the daily life of young LGBTQ+ people. LGBTQ+ youth and emerging adults who experience high levels of internalized homophobia and loneliness often report an increased number of sexual partners in the past year, drastically increasing the risk of contracting a sexually transmitted infection (DeLonga et al., 2011; Hubach et al., 2015). LGBTQ+ young women, in particular, are at increased risk of risky sexual practices (e.g., sharing sex toys), contracting a sexually transmitted infection (STI), sexual harassment, or sexual assault. Many LGBQ+ young women cited the limited general health and safe-sex specific messaging, noting an inaccurate belief that sex between cisgender women does not pose a significant STI risk (Herrick et al., 2010). LGBTQ+ community centers and other community-based organizations can address sexual health concerns among LGBTQ+ youth and emerging adults by developing targeted and developmentally appropriate programming. Centers with adjacent medical programs can also engage with LGBTQ+ specific health issues by adding inclusive sexual histories to their curriculum and practicum training of medical students (Lee et al., 2014).

INTERPERSONAL CHALLENGES

Coming Out

The age at which an LGBTQ+ identity is disclosed and same-sex sexual debut occur have been trending downward, regardless of gender. However, women are more likely to start the coming out process later (Grov et al., 2006). Race does not impede sexual identity development or affect same-sex sexual exploration. Regardless of age or gender, queer people of color are less likely to disclose their sexual orientation to their parents (Grov et al., 2006). This trend continues; Ratcliff and Haltom (2021) found that women continued to be more likely to publicly recognize and publicly come out about their sexual orientation at later ages. Although Black participants were more likely to realize their orientation earlier, their realizations did not correspond to disclosure. In addition, the authors found that LGBTQ+ emerging adults with a bachelor's degree were more likely to internally realize and publicly come out during traditional college years (ages 18–21). Perhaps counterintuitively, some studies have shown that religious affiliation and attendance alone do not significantly influence the internal or external coming out process (Ratcliff & Haltom, 2021). Additionally, in a study with men who experienced same-sex attraction, Hoffarth and Bogaert (2017) found openness to experience was the most significant factor to influence how soon private and public coming out occurs—more so than religiosity and whether or not the participants had embraced a masculine gender role as children.

Though coming out is often seen as an ongoing, dynamic process for LGBTQ+ people of all ages, many studies have reported on the unique coming out experiences of LGBTQ+ youth and emerging adults of today (Budge et al., 2018; Grov et al., 2006; Guittar & Rayburn, 2016; Robertson, 2014). LGBTQ+ youth often progress through an identity formation process involving violating compulsory heterosexuality, seeking out explanations, exploring sexuality, and identity negotiation (Robertson, 2014). For TGNC youth specifically, gender identity development may include a fluid process of conforming to expectations, experiential avoidance (e.g., avoidance of painful thoughts, emotions, and social experiences around gender, primarily through isolation and avoidance of introspection), seeking emotional relief (including self-injury), finding solace in enjoyable activities, building social support, and engaging actively in identity construction and community (Budge et al., 2018).

Regardless of sexual activity, some LGBTQ+ youth come out without claiming a distinct identity label and using their language to communicate their attractions. Many youths describe this decision as a first step because they are not ready to affirm a label, want to preserve a sense of normalcy, or have concerns about their safety and the threat their identity might pose to close relationships (Guittar, 2014). While older cohorts have tended to establish a fixed identity before coming out, younger cohorts are more likely to come out multiple times. Each change in identity is seen as a step toward their current sexuality (Guittar & Rayburn, 2016). This enduring, evolving process has been likened to a career requiring active management throughout one's life (Schmitz & Tyler, 2018; Guittar & Rayburn, 2016). Additionally, Savin-Williams and Cohen (2015) have cautioned that development research has not considered the complexity of sexual identity development, often ignoring lesser-known identity groups and disregarding experiences such as sexual fantasy, nonintercourse sexual contact, and infatuation.

The internet and social media have also provided new possibilities for LGBTQ+ youth who grapple with the challenges of coming out. An overwhelming majority of LGBTQ+ youth report using media, especially the internet, as a primary means of accessing resources and information on LGBTQ+ identities (Bond et al., 2009). Hillier and colleagues (2012) noted that in contrast to their heterosexual peers, LGBTQ+ youth regarded online information seeking and relationship exploration as reasonable and practical, given the relative lack of opportunity offline. LGBTQ+ youth also use online forums to engage in storytelling, give and receive validation, seek and build community, and advise others (Miller, 2016; Pascoe, 2011). Craig and McInroy (2014) found that LGBTQ+ youth tend to disclose their sexual orientation online first, thus, increasing self-acceptance and self-confidence before expanding the process into their "real lives." Many youths with accounts on social media sites such as Facebook report using multiple accounts, tracking their online image, and experiencing emotional and relational costs because of identity disclosure, particularly with family (McConnell et al., 2018).

Although outness may be protective against depression and increase well-being for LGBTQ+ youth (Kosciw et al., 2015), coming out may be unsafe, inadvisable, or come with the loss of meaningful relationships for some. Riley (2018) found that sexual minority youth experienced bullying from friends, family, peers at school, the media, their communities, and service providers, leading to self-harm, isolation, concealment of their identities, suicidal behavior, and denial of access to treatment. LGBTQ+ youth's early awareness of sexual orientation, disclosure to family, greater overall outness, and gender nonconformity are associated with higher physical, sexual, and emotional abuse (McGeough & Sterzing, 2018). There may be additional cultural considerations in navigating the coming out process for LGBTQ+ youth who belong to other marginalized groups, such as racial minorities. For example, African American lesbians may not hide their sexual orientation. Still, they may remain silent to retain family and community relationships and limit stress about claiming a different oppressed identity (Miller, 2011). Potocznik and colleagues (2009) noted that for queer people of color, the parental relationship is a source of support and a fundamental part of one's racial or ethnic self-identification and community. Therefore, potential damage to this relationship has additional meaning and weight. White racial/ethnic identity, nonimmigrant status, lower religious affiliation, and higher socioeconomic status have been linked to family acceptance (Ryan et al., 2010).

Social support from peers, family, friends, LGBTQ+ communities, and mental health professionals can be essential for the coming out process (Budge et al., 2018). LGBTQ+ centers are often a place of understanding. All stages of identity development are celebrated, and LGBTQ+ community members are given support to discover unique strengths and gifts that others may not have ever recognized. When trust and rapport are present in therapeutic relationships, mental health professionals can also provide a safe, confidential space for LGBTQ+ clients to share their identities and talk about the challenges and triumphs of the identity development process. Potocznik and colleagues (2009) noted that LGBTQ+ youth found peer support groups helpful in dealing with disclosure-related stress, whether online or face-to-face. For transgender individuals beginning to come out and explore gender presentation, Doan (2007) reported that support groups often assist in navigating these tasks and frequently meet at LGBTQ+ centers. Youth spaces play a critical role in providing access to resources and addressing sexual identity issues and salient issues for other marginalized identities (Robertson, 2014).

Building Community

A sense of community is a significant and multifaceted protective factor in LGBTQ+ youth and emerging adults' lives. LGBTQ+ community centers and other community-based organizations are uniquely positioned to increase the availability of supportive communities for LGBTQ+ youth and emerging adults. Using a constructivist phenomenological framework, Harper and colleagues (2012) explored gay and bisexual male youths' positive perceptions of their sexual orientation identity. One central theme emerged, connectedness. A sense of connectedness was expressed through identification and bonding with others in the gay community who had experienced similar hardships. The opposite of connectedness, lacking a sense of community, is often experienced as loneliness for LGBTQ+ young people. Specifically for Black LGBTQ+ youth and emerging adults, loneliness is related to higher rates of internalized homophobia, more sexual partners, and increased compulsive internet use (Delonga et al., 2011). There is a need to reduce feelings of loneliness for LGBTQ+ youth and emerging adults while simultaneously focusing on eradicating racial discrimination experienced by QYAOC.

Dating and Relationships

Romantic relationships are an essential part of development for most youth and emerging adults, and research suggests that some existing models of relationship development are insufficient to represent LGBTQ+ relationships. For sexual minority youth, the internet has facilitated experimentation with same-sex desires, connections with potential partners, and exploring long-distance relationships (DeHaan et al., 2013). Factors such as sexual identity, gender identity, social environment, family environment, overall development, and culture can affect LGBTQ+ individuals in relationships in complex ways that differ from their cisgender, heterosexual peers (Macapagal et al., 2015). It is also important to note that marriage equality at the federal level did not exist until very recently, which affected how LGBTQ+ individuals in relationships viewed certain milestones. For instance, cohabitation has been seen as a highly significant milestone for some LGBTQ+ individuals because it illustrates commitment, emotional support, a sense of family, and shared life, especially in states that have not legalized marriage equality (Haas & Whitton, 2015). After marriage equality became a reality in the United States, many LGBTQ+ individuals who married their partner to secure legal protections and social validation have reported that marriage did not change their emotional commitments to each other (Rostosky et al., 2016). LGBTQ+ youth now can conceptualize futures with romantic partners that include marriage. Coupled with the fact that sexual orientation disclosure is happening now, typically at earlier ages than before, the experiences and challenges the current generation of youth and emerging adults encounter in forming relationships will likely differ from previous generations (Frost et al., 2015).

In recognition of challenges such as these, LGBTQ+ youth have expressed interest in receiving education concerning relationships and sexual health, including sexual risk prevention, intimate partner violence (IPV) and family violence, building support systems, finding role models within the community, and enhancing communication with partners (Greene et al., 2015). After studying IPV rates among LGBTQ+ youth, Gillum (2017) also called for LGBTQ+-inclusive programs that focus on dating violence at younger ages. Evidence suggests that community-based organizations and centers can fill these needs and address some of these issues. Ford and colleagues (2013) studied a small sample of Los Angeles–based IPV professionals. They found that those professionals without connections to local LGBTQ+ agencies and community centers provided IPV awareness resources primarily aimed toward non-LGBTQ+ communities. Simultaneously, many of these professionals felt incompetent with specific populations, such as transgender community concerns and clinical work with cisgender male clients (Ford et al., 2013). This focus on training, competency, and culturally sensitive approaches is mirrored in studying community HIV prevention programs for transgender youth of color. Gelaude and colleagues (2013) reported that while striving to address the LGBTQ+ communities' needs, community-based organizations experienced difficulties creating safe spaces and trust, recruiting trained staff, and confronting interpersonal and structural transphobia. Some issues related to dating and relationships might also be addressed by affirming physicians, faith leaders, and mental health professionals, who can provide insight, education, and a safe space to discuss relationship dynamics, values, and physical health.

Intimate Partner Violence

Intimate partner violence (IPV) victimization and perpetration among LGBTQ+ youth have emerged as a significant area of concern in the literature. Compared to heterosexual youth, LGBTQ+ youth are at higher risk of perpetrating and being victimized by physical, psychological, and cyber abuse and are more likely to experience sexual coercion (Dank et al., 2014). Edwards and Sylaska (2013) reported that 30% of LGBTQ+ youth in their sample perpetrated IPV in their current relationship, with physical violence being the most common. Further research on LGBTQ+ youth and IPV has found that LGBTQ+ youth report being on both the side of perpetrator and victim of IPV in adolescent relationships. Gillum (2017), for example, reported LGBTQ+ youth perpetrating both psychological violence (88%) and physical violence (41%) during adolescent relationships. LGBTQ+ youth also reported experiencing IPV in physical violence (86%) and psychological violence (58%). Gillum (2017) further reported that many LGBTQ+ youths who experienced victimization later perpetrated violence continued to perpetuate IPV in subsequent interpersonal relationships. These findings suggest that LGBTQ+ youth and emerging adults who experience IPV may develop a skewed view of what constitutes a healthy relationship and, in turn, recapitulate those same abusive behaviors in future relationships. Whitton and colleagues (2019) reported that the experience of physical violence among LGBTQ+ youth was 76% more likely for those assigned female at birth when compared to other assigned genders. The same study also found that physical violence occurred twice as often for TGNC youth than for cisgender youth, three to four times as often for Black LGBTQ+ youth, and twice as likely for Latinx LGBTQ+ youth compared to white LGBTQ+ youth. Additionally, sexual violence was more than three times more likely for transgender youth and 75% more likely for bisexual and questioning youth when compared to their cisgender and monosexual peers, respectively.

Medical and behavioral health care providers can engage in interventions by making their IPV screening processes more inclusive of LGBTQ+ people, amending educational materials on IPV and clinical resources to include LGBTQ+-specific concerns, and making informed referrals for LGBTQ+ patients to community organizations (Ard & Makadon, 2011). In a study regarding LGBTQ+ youth's perceptions of IPV, Gillum and DiFulvio (2012) reported that youth saw challenges such as societal homophobia, internalized homophobia, the negotiation of gender roles within relationships, assumptions about female bonding and connection, lack of same-sex relationship models, and other related issues as critical reasons for the prevalence of IPV. Edwards and Sylaska (2013) found that among several minority stress variables, perpetration was most significantly influenced by internalized homonegativity. More positively, LGBTQ+ youth reported seeking help for IPV after the first incident within one day, more often than their heterosexual peers (Dank et al., 2014).

VOCATIONAL CHALLENGES

Career Development

Because life events and experiences influence career development, many career theorists have hypothesized that sexual and gender identity development can impact the career development process of LGBTQ+ youth (McFadden, 2015). Lyons and colleagues (2010) suggested that although most LGBTQ+ youths do not experience conflict between these two forms of development, some do and may prioritize one over the other. The authors noted that prioritizing *either* direction lowered career decision-making support or self-efficacy. The navigation of career tasks may be guided by self-awareness, as LGBTQ+ youth who have reported high self-awareness (i.e., awareness of strengths, weaknesses, feelings, and motivations) have also reported high career decision-making self-efficacy (Russon & Schmidt, 2014). Datti (2009) found that LGBTQ+ identity might discourage youth from pursuing careers in the military, educational institutions, ministry, and law enforcement. The same study indicates that geographic location can influence the range of safe and feasible career options for LGBTQ+ youth. Although there is a shortage of studies about the career development experiences of transgender youth, transgender individuals have reported increased levels of career decision self-efficacy post-transition, including self-appraisal, occupational information, planning, and problem-solving (dickey et al., 2016).

Employment Discrimination

Datti (2009) warned that LGBTQ+ youth might develop self-defeating generalizations and engage in career exploration with more caution based on previous negative experiences of discrimination, coming out, and others' homophobic remarks in response to career choices. In support of this, Schneider and Dimito (2010) found that LGBTQ+ individuals who endorsed more instances of discriminatory experiences also reported higher salience of sexual orientation in career choices and lower career satisfaction, and they perceived their career options as more limited. In a study about perceived barriers, LGBTQ+ youth ranked sexual orientation as the second most hindering and the third most anticipated career barrier (Parnell et al., 2012).

Due to a lack of employment nondiscrimination laws at the federal level, LGBTQ+ individuals may individually encounter or perceive discriminatory practices in hiring and their current workplaces. Transgender employees often face harassment, discrimination, and negative experiences on interpersonal, intrapersonal, systemic, and logistical levels, to which some transgender individuals respond with education and activism (Brewster et al., 2014). In the aftermath of these experiences, some LGBTQ+ employees reported displaying nonassertive responses, seeking social support, and engaging in confrontation (Chung et al., 2009). The same study reported that some transgender workers continually decide when to confront discrimination or microaggressions and may continue to endure them silently.

Workplace Identity Management

As workplace discrimination instances may occur without legal recourse, identity management can become a significant focus for LGBTQ+ individuals. Schneider and Dimito (2010) found that 29% of LGBTQ+ youth in their sample thought their identity would affect their career achievement and 62% endorsed some or high anxiety around their identity while completing job applications. Other LGBTQ+ youth have named decision making around outness as a career barrier and underscored the role of internalized homophobia in the process (Parnell et al., 2012). LGBTQ+ couples reported struggling with decision making to introduce their partners while attending work events, blending their work and personal lives, and building social support networks (O'Ryan & McFarland, 2010). McFadden (2015) elaborated that guardedness, caution, and difficulty establishing workplace relationships could result in coworkers' and superiors' perceptions that an LGBTQ+ individual is unfriendly, uncooperative, or hostile, affecting future opportunities for promotions performance reviews, relationships, and career development.

Lyons and colleagues (2010) noted that self-efficacy and social support might be important protective factors for LGBTQ+ youth navigating career, sexual identity, and gender identity development. Similarly, studies have noted that social support significantly influences career decisions and college adjustment, noting the importance of assisting transgender individuals in navigating employment records and documents, discussing gender identity and transition with coworkers, and dealing with workplace discrimination (Sangganjanavanich & Headley, 2016; Schmidt et al., 2011).

Method

The purpose of the current chapter was to review resources available to LGBTQ+ youth and emerging adults from 209 LGBTQ+ community centers in the United States. We utilized a social phenomenology framework to conduct an inductive thematic analysis of LGBTQ+ community center services for youth and emerging adults. Within this analytic frame, we identified six community center services offered to LGBTQ+ youth and emerging adults: physical health services, mental health services, queer and trans people of color (QTPOC) services, transgender-specific services, basic needs services, and auxiliary services. We employed Braun and Clarke's six-step thematic analysis (2006). In step 1 (*Familiarization*), we compiled a list of CenterLink–affiliated LGBTQ+ centers in the United States, explored each community center's website, and noted initial codes for the services offered. In step 2 (*Coding*), we input all of the information collected into a spreadsheet to ease the coding process.

We then identified features of the data such as region (Northeast, Midwest, South, and West), city/state, geographical region (urban or rural), site name, ages of the population served, type of site (physical community center, virtual community center, or satellite community center), availability of website and contact information, and specific services offered by each community center. In step 3 (*Generating Themes*), we analyzed the services offered and generated the following themes: mental health services, QTPOC services, transgender services, services for housing instability, other basic needs services, and auxiliary services. In steps 4 and 5 (*Reviewing* and *Defining Themes*, respectively), we conducted a cross-comparison of themes and combined services for housing instability and other basic needs services into the single theme "Basic Needs Services." Finally, in step 6 (*Writing*), we reported raw data and percentages of each type of service provided.

SAMPLE OF LGBTQ+ COMMUNITY CENTERS

Founded in 1994, CenterLink is a member-based alliance focused on supporting and developing LGBTQ+ community centers (CenterLink, n.d.). CenterLink's primary objective is to "help build the capacity of these centers to address the social, cultural, health, and political advocacy needs of LGBTQ+ community members across the country" (CenterLink, n.d.). Utilizing the CenterLink member directory from October 2018 to November 2018, we identified an initial list of 211 LGBTQ+ community centers within the United States.

Using an inductive, exploratory approach guided by social phenomenology, we gathered and analyzed content related to service provision for LGBTQ+ youth and emerging adults within these LGBTQ+ community centers. Procedurally, we looked for services and other readily available information to youth via the center's website or social media pages. This data-gathering process was used intentionally to mimic how youth and emerging adults access services from their local LGBTQ+ centers. This process is consistent with social phenomenology. We attempted to explore the social reality subjectively experienced by LGBTQ+ youth and emerging adults, such as how they go about their daily lives (Braun & Clarke, 2006). Centers that were a part of a college or a university, those whose information was not in English, and those whose sole focus was on adults or older populations were excluded from the final analysis. Given our research team's lack of Spanish-language fluency, our research team chose to exclude Spanish-speaking-only LGBTQ+ community centers (one) because we could not attest to the integrity of service provision. After these exclusions, 208 LGBTQ+ community centers remained. Data from the following LGBTQ+ community center types were analyzed: physical centers (N = 166), virtual centers (N = 18), satellite community centers, which were often connected to a more extensive network of LGBTQ+ centers (N = 16), three health centers, two counseling centers. Several centers (N = 14) either did not have resources and services listed on their website, did not have an active website, or had no website. We also identified three centers with information that appeared to be unclear/unknown. Given the lack of available information, these LGBTQ+ centers were excluded from the thematic analysis.

Table 13.1. Number of LGBTQ+ Community Centers in the United States by State

No Centers	1 LGBTQ+ Center	2-5 Centers	6-10 Centers	11-15 Centers	15+ Centers
Louisiana	Arkansas	Alabama (N = 3)	Illinois (N = 9)	Michigan (N = 11)	California (N = 35)
Minnesota	Alaska	Arizona (N = 2)	North Carolina (N = 8)	Pennsylvania (N = 14)	Florida (N = 16)
Montana	Delaware	Colorado (N = 5)	Ohio (N = 9)		New York (N = 19)
North Dakota	Hawaii	Connecticut (N = 3)	Texas (N = 10)		
West Virginia	Idaho	Washington, DC (N = 2)			
	Iowa	Georgia (N = 3)			
	Kansas	Indiana (N = 4)			
	Maine	Kentucky (N = 2)			
	Mississippi	Maryland (N = 3)			
	Nebraska	Massachusetts (N = 2)			
	New Mexico	Missouri (N = 4)			
	Oklahoma	Nevada (N = 2)			
	New Hampshire	New Jersey (N = 5)			
	Rhode Island	Oregon (N = 2)			
	South Dakota	South Carolina (N = 2)			
	Tennessee	Vermont (N = 3)			
	Utah	Virginia (N = 4)			
	Wyoming	Washington (N = 4)			
		Wisconsin (N = 4)			

Note: This table reflects states with LGBTQ+ community centers affiliated with CenterLink between October and November 2018.

To be included in the thematic analysis, LGBTQ+ community centers had to meet the following inclusion criteria: (a) LGBTQ+ community center with current CenterLink affiliation and (b) an active website with community center information listed primarily in English. Forty-five states and Washington, DC, had LGBTQ+ centers that met the inclusion criteria. Five states (Louisiana, Minnesota, Montana, North Dakota, and West Virginia) either did not have any LGBTQ+ center representation statewide or had LGBTQ+ centers that were not affiliated with CenterLink at the time of data collection and thus are not represented in the following results. Table 13.1 depicts the number of CenterLink–affiliated LGBTQ+ centers within each state. The LGBTQ+ community centers represented the following regions: Midwest (N = 45), Northeast (N = 49), South (N = 58), and West (N = 56). We also explored geographical representation among the LGBTQ+ community centers and found community centers in urban (N = 163) and rural (N = 45) areas.

Results

The types of services offered to LGBTQ+ youth and emerging adults were grouped into six categories: physical health services, mental health services, services directed toward LGBTQ+ youth and emerging adults of color, services directed toward transgender youth and emerging adults, services related to basic needs (shelter, food, and clothing), and innovative programming. Although we grouped services into these six categories, we acknowledge that categories are not discrete and that services could fall under more than one category. We encourage readers to conceptualize the results in a holistic framework that recognizes the interconnectivity of service provision.

PHYSICAL HEALTH SERVICES

Less than half of the LGBTQ centers (N = 81, 41.8%) advertised physical health services available to LGBTQ+ youth and young adults. The most popular were STD/STI testing focusing on HIV screenings. Of these centers that offer physical health services for youth and emerging adults, 18 centers (21%) advertised having information, counseling, or other services directed at the use of PEP/PrEP. Nine percent of centers offered general physical health services for LGBTQ+ youth and emerging adults. Three percent or less of community centers offered cancer screening, health insurance assistance, syringe exchange, gender-affirming hormone therapy, or provision of Narcan for substance use. Additional services included dental and health care access, assistance with public benefits, provision of showers and toiletries for homeless LGBTQ+ youth and emerging adults, and transportation assistance to and from medical appointments for individuals living with HIV. Less than three percent of LGBTQ+ centers also assisted with smoking cessation and drug risk reduction. While these specific programs were not explicitly advertised to youth and emerging adults, no information noted an explicit exclusion from these programs based on age. However, one center (N = 1, 0.5%) directly provided sober services for young adults.

MENTAL HEALTH SERVICES

Most LGBTQ+ community centers (N =171, 82%) offered youth and emerging adults mental health services. About 79% offered some peer or social support groups within these mental health services. These groups varied in topic, from groups for youth ages 13–18, groups for young adults ages 18–25 or in some cases up to 30 years old, to substance use and recovery groups, HIV-related groups, vocational groups, trauma groups, transgender groups, and Spanish-speaking groups. Several LGBTQ+ centers offered suicide prevention programs, meditation, polyamory support groups, and relationship skills that included information on safer sex practices, markers of unhealthy relationships, and domestic violence. Therapy groups for specific mental health concerns, such as anxiety, depression, and trauma, were also common.

Less than half of the centers (N = 90, 43%) offered psychotherapy services. Services offered included psychotherapy for individuals, couples, families, and various psychotherapy groups. These psychotherapy services were advertised as being led by a mental health professional, intern, or trainee, with available service providers ranging from one or two to 44 (including trainees). Research has long identified the general differences between psychotherapy and social support groups. In contrast, social support groups typically contain many discussions initiated by members sharing personal experiences. Support groups, however, lack the skills training, behavioral rehearsal, contracting, and psychotherapy homework assignments that are prevalent in psychotherapy groups (Koob et al., 1993).

SERVICES FOR QUEER YOUTH AND EMERGING ADULTS OF COLOR (QYAOC)

Only 48 centers (23%) advertised services explicitly geared toward LGBTQ+ people of color. Among these services, the following were the most prevalent: support groups for Latinx and Spanish-speaking youth, Black youth, Asian American/Pacific Islander youth, social dances and movie nights, queer women of color, as well as social support and psychotherapy groups for youth (ages 13–17) and emerging adults (ages 18–24). Interestingly, while many groups, in general, provided services for individuals with HIV, only one center specifically noted providing HIV counseling explicitly for queer people of color. Of those included in the sample, only four LGBTQ+ community centers were explicitly created to address the needs of queer and transgender people of color (QTPOC): Black Hills Center for Equality (SD), Latino Equality Alliance (CA), Ruth Ellis Center (MI), and the Mocha Center (NY).

SERVICES FOR TRANSGENDER AND GENDER-NONCONFORMING (TGNC) YOUTH AND EMERGING ADULTS

Emotional Support

Many LGBTQ+ community centers (N = 135, 65%) provided services for transgender or gender-nonconforming youth and young adults. These services generally included support groups for transgender youth (ages 11–18) and support groups for transgender young adults (ages 18–29). Groups tended to be labeled as binary gender categories (e.g., transgender women and transgender men). However, groups were presented as general transgender teen groups or groups for individuals identifying as gender nonconforming. Other ways of separating support for transgender youth were to have areas of support categorized by education level (e.g., middle school transgender group or high school transgender group).

Social Support

In addition to support groups, transgender-specific counseling, case management, family resources, voting information, online communities, workshops on various topics, and social events, such as game nights, were also offered. Several centers also offered information for transgender-friendly barbers/hairdressers and in-house services, such as makeup classes or gender-affirming clothing (e.g., binders and wings). Notably, many services related to transgender youth and young adults' basic needs such as housing support, employment and education assistance, and legal advocacy related to name changes, gender marker changes, hate crimes, and other forms of discrimination. A national transgender agency, such as the Transgender Law Center, was often identified as offering legal services for TGNC youth and emerging adults.

SERVICES RELATED TO THE PROVISION OF BASIC NEEDS

Housing Stability

Some LGBTQ+ centers (N = 39, 19%) assisted LGBTQ+ youth experiencing housing instability. Concerning physical placement, LGBTQ+ centers offer emergency shelter (some specifically for individuals experiencing domestic violence or other forms of abuse), transitional housing, short-term housing (such as host homes), and the occasional long-term housing option, such as the availability of housing facilities, which on average housed up to 23 LGBTQ+ youth. Several centers also indicated the provision of street outreach, case management, storage, showers, laundry, and toiletries for homeless youth. The focus was on housing instability for LGBTQ+ youth (under 18 years old) who were currently or at risk of becoming homeless.

Food Insecurity

Most housing assistance centers also offered nutritional assistance for LGBTQ+ youth and emerging adults. This support included offering an emergency food pantry, free community dinners (often themed around sexual orientation or gender identity communities), hot meal sites, nutrition coaching, cooking classes, and food justice projects. One center listed a food pantry specifically for individuals affected by HIV or AIDS.

SERVICES RELATED TO EDUCATIONAL AND VOCATIONAL ASSISTANCE

Many centers offered various education and vocation assistance programs for youth and emerging adults, including groups for LGBTQ+ youth and emerging adults with developmental or intellectual disabilities, computer labs, resource library, and mentoring. Regarding LGBTQ+ youth and emerging adults, centers offered supports directly related to LGBTQ+ youth experiences at school, such as after school programs that are LGBTQ+ focused and other safe learning environments, assistance with starting a Gender & Sexuality Alliance (GSA, formerly Gay-Straight Alliance) in middle and high schools, general school support, training and policy development for schools, tutoring, and back-to-school social events. Other supports for LGBTQ+ youth and emerging adults included youth summits, leadership programs, youth internships (both paid and unpaid), and scholarships.

Specific to LGBTQ+ emerging adults, the centers were focused on improving college experiences by providing information related to assistance in finding affirming study abroad programs, offering scholarships, supporting queer activism, college access and support services, and so on. LGBTQ+ centers also focus on the vocational development of LGBTQ+ emerging adults by providing employment placement programs, GED program support, job training and preparation workshops, young professionals groups, resume workshops, information on financial literacy, career fairs, and workshops on transgender-specific vocational concerns such as "being fired while trans" or transgender employment readiness workshops.

AUXILIARY SERVICES

When reviewing resources offered by LGBTQ+ centers to youth and emerging adults, we noted that some centers were offering resources not related to the previous categories. We labeled these resources "auxiliary services" because the nature of these programs at face value was dissimilar from prior thematic categories generated but lacked the numbers to account for separate categories in and of themselves. Common types of auxiliary services included support for youth in foster care, assistance in changing gender marker on state identification, life skills workshops, emergency financial assistance, resource libraries (both physical and online), local transportation assistance, as well as additional services offered in conjunction with local Planned

Parenthood centers. Three percent or less of LGBT community centers offered disability support services, immigration assistance, voting assistance, exercise and fitness resources, or sexual trauma recovery programs. Less than one percent of centers provided human trafficking recovery programs or mentoring through Big Brothers/Big Sisters of America.

Discussion

AREAS OF IMPROVEMENT IN SERVING LGBTQ+ YOUTH AND EMERGING ADULTS

Availability of Services by Geographical Region

When looking across regions, LGBTQ+ community centers were equally dispersed among the following four main US regions: South (N = 58, 28%), West (N = 56, 27%), Northeast (N = 49, 24%), and Midwest (N = 45, 22%). Within this equal regional split, the majority of LGBTQ+ community centers were largely located within the following states: California (N = 35, 17%), New York (N = 19, 9%), Florida (N = 16, 8%), Pennsylvania (N = 14, 7%), and Michigan (N = 11, 5%).

Of the 208 community centers, 163 were in urban areas (78%) and 45 were located in rural areas (21%). The regional breakdown within rural areas was as follows: nine LGBTQ+ centers were located within the rural West, nine centers were in the rural South, 17 were in the rural Northeast, and 10 were in the rural Midwest. This urban concentration of community center support puts LGBTQ+ youth and young adults who live in surrounding areas, with fewer means of transportation, at a grave disadvantage in accessing the care, support, and acceptance offered by LGBTQ+ community centers. Recently, research has begun to explore and amplify the lived experience of LGBTQ+ youth in rural areas. As a result, we have begun to see a clearer picture of rural LGBTQ+ youth not as wholly deprived of a community but as activists and community members advocating for visibility and acceptance that will appreciate their unique rural experiences (Gray, 2009; Greteman, 2012). The scarcity of LGBTQ+ centers in rural areas thus presents a severe disadvantage for LGBTQ+ youth and emerging adults who may want to explore ways to find or develop a connection to affirming LGBTQ+ communities in their area. However, since the beginning of the COVID-19 global pandemic, more services have shifted online and teletherapy has become more mainstream. More research is needed to learn how LGBTQ+ youth in rural areas adapt and possibly utilize the increased online support of nearby urban LGBTQ+ community centers.

Access to LGBTQ+ Community Centers

Seven percent of centers (N = 14) did not have resources and services listed on their website, did not have an active website, or had no website. This presents an interesting problem for LGBTQ+ youth and emerging adults who may have a growing interest in connecting to their local LGBTQ+ community center but cannot access information or find outdated information. Perhaps this sheds light on a more significant issue: the increased need for financial support for LGBTQ+ centers to adequately reach and provide efficient services for LGBTQ+ youth and emerging adults.

LGBTQ+ Youth and Emerging Adults of Color

Less than a fourth of LGBTQ+ centers (N = 48, 23%) explicitly stated that they offered LGBTQ+ people of color services. This lack of resources, community, and support for LGBTQ+ youth and emerging adults of color significantly disadvantages this population. Queer communities of color are needed for individuals to process their lived experiences at the intersection of multiple systems of oppression. For example, a queer person of color may experience racial microaggressions or hostility among their white LGBTQ+ counterparts when attempting to go to a local LGBTQ+ center for support. When resources provided by LGBTQ+ community centers and other community-based organizations attend not only to the experience of heterosexism but also to the experience of racism, they are positioned to intervene and decrease the high rates of adverse psychological outcomes (e.g., depression, suicidality, risky sexual practices, and anxiety), risk of incarceration, racial profiling, and physical violence experienced by QYAOC (Haltom & Ratcliff, 2021; Herrick et al., 2010; Potoczniak et al., 2009; Szymanski & Gupta, 2009).

CONSIDERATIONS FOR CLINICAL PRACTICE

As we have learned, LGBTQ+ community centers can be additional support that LGBTQ+ youth utilize to aid the development of healthy physical, emotional, and mental health. It is recommended that mental health providers learn about and connect with local LGBTQ+ community centers because of the opportunity for valuable information exchange. Mental health providers, equipped with knowledge of psychological distress and disparities, combined with LGBTQ+ community centers and bastions of social justice advocacy, are uniquely positioned to combine talents to better the overall well-being of LGBTQ+ youth and emerging adults. CenterLink is an excellent place to start. It can help clinicians find local centers online, check out their websites, and become familiar with the available resources. It can be valuable to know what support groups, populations served, physical health resources, virtual programming, and other resources are available and to contact the staff. It can be valuable to know what community resources are available and provide a website link or a phone number so clients may be able to get support in other aspects of their life outside the therapy hour. Clinicians may assist clients by referring them to LGBTQ+ community centers, and centers may refer clients to trusted clinicians. This integrative, interdisciplinary approach to care is becoming more recognized as needed by LGBTQ+ individuals (Hammer et al., 2019).

POLICY RECOMMENDATIONS

As previously mentioned, LGBTQ+ community centers need substantial financial backing to support LGBTQ+ youth and emerging adults and expand and innovate their current services. As mentioned, services directed toward LGBTQ+ people of color, people with disabilities, and transgender communities continue to be areas of increased need. Interestingly enough, many LGBTQ+ centers connected with their local Planned Parenthood to provide sexual health services for youth and emerging adults. Given the political landscape in terms of decreasing funding and access and closing physical Planned Parenthood clinics, one can only surmise that recent political challenges to reproductive rights might lead to unintended negative consequences on the sexual health of LGBTQ+ youth. Therefore, it is even more crucial for clinicians and LGBTQ+ community center leaders and staff to coordinate and collaborate on providing integrative, strengths-based, holistic services to LGBTQ+ youth and emerging adults.

References

Ard, K. L., & Makadon, H. J. (2011). Addressing intimate partner violence in lesbian, gay, bisexual, and transgender patients. *Journal of General Internal Medicine, 26*(8), 930–933. https://doi.org/10.1007/s11606-011-1697-6

Arnold, E. A., & Bailey, M. M. (2009). Constructing home and family: How the ballroom community supports African American GLBTQ youth in the face of HIV/AIDS. *Journal of Gay and Lesbian Social Services, 21*(2–3), 171–188. https://doi.org/10.1080/10538720902772006

Balsam, K. F., Molina, Y., Beadnell, B., Simoni, J. M., & Walters, K. (2011). Measuring multiple minority stress: The LGBT People of Color Microaggressions Scale. *Cultural Diversity and Ethnic Minority Psychology, 17*, 163–174.

Bauermeister, J. A., Goldenberg, T., Connochie, D., Jadwin-Cakmak, L., & Stephenson, R. (2016). Psychosocial disparities among racial/ethnic minority transgender young adults and young men who have sex with men living in Detroit. *Transgender Health, 1*, 279–290. https://doi.org/10.1089/trgh.2016.0027

Bond, B. J., Hefner, V., & Drogos, K. L. (2009). Information-seeking practices during the sexual development of lesbian, gay, and bisexual individuals: The influence and effects of coming out in a mediated environment. *Sexuality & Culture, 13*(1), 32–50. https://doi.org/10.1007/s12119-008-9041-y

Braun, V., & Clarke, V. (2006). Using thematic analysis in qualitative research. *Qualitative Research in Psychology, 3*(2), 77–101.

Brewster, M. E., Velez, B. L., Mennicke, A., & Tebbe, E. (2014). Voices from beyond: A thematic content analysis of transgender employees' workplace experiences. *Psychology of Sexual Orientation and Gender Diversity, 1*(2), 159–169.

Budge, S. L., Belcourt, S., Conniff, J., Parks, R., Pantalone, D. W., & Katz-Wise, S. L. (2018). A grounded theory study of the development of trans youths' awareness of coping with gender identity. *Journal of Child and Family Studies, 27*(5), 3048–3061. https://doi.org/10.1007/s10826-018-1136-y

CenterLink. (n.d.). CenterLink LGBTQ+ community center member directory. http://www.lgbtcenters.org/Centers/find-a-center.aspx

Cerezo, A., & Bergfeld, J. (2013). Meaningful LGBTQ inclusion in schools: The importance of diversity representation and counter spaces. *Journal of LGBT Issues in Counseling, 7*, 355–371. https://doi.org/10.1080/15538605.2013.839341

Chung, Y. B., Williams, W., & Dispenza, F. (2009). Validating work discrimination and coping strategy models for sexual minorities. *Career Development Quarterly, 58*(2), 162–170.

Craig, S. L., & McInroy, L. (2014). You can form a part of yourself online: The influence of new media on identity development and coming out for LGBTQ youth. *Journal of Gay & Lesbian Mental Health, 18*(1), 95–109. https://doi.org/10.1080/19359705.2013.777007

D'Augelli, A. R., & Hershberger, S. L. (1993). Lesbian, gay, and bisexual youth in community settings: Personal challenges and mental health problems. *American Journal of Community Psychology, 21*, 421–448. https://doi.org/10.1007/BF00942151

Dank, M., Lachman, P., Zweig, J. M., & Yahner, J. (2014). Dating violence experiences of lesbian, gay, bisexual, and transgender youth. *Journal of Youth and Adolescence, 43*(5), 846–857. https://doi.org/10.1007/s10964-013-9975-8

Datti, P. A. (2009). Applying the social learning theory of career decision-making to gay, lesbian, bisexual, transgender, and questioning young adults. *Career Development Quarterly, 58*(1), 54–64.

DeHaan, S., Kuper, L. E., Magee, J. C., Bigelow, L., & Mustanski, B. S. (2013). The interplay between online and offline explorations of identity, relationships, and sex: A mixed-methods study with LGBT youth. *Journal of Sex Research, 50*(5), 421–434. https://doi.org/10.1080/00224499.2012.661489

DeLonga, K., Torres, H. L., Kamen, C., Evans, S. N., Lee, S., Koopman, C., & Gore-Felton, C. (2011). Loneliness, internalized homophobia, and compulsive internet use: Factors associated with sexual risk behavior among a sample. *Sexual Addiction and Compulsivity, 18*(2), 61–74. https://doi.org/10.1080/10720162.2011.581897

dickey, l. m., Walinsky, D., Rofkahr, C., Richardson-Cline, K., & Juntunen, C. (2016). Career decision self-efficacy of transgender people: Pre- and post-transition. *Career Development Quarterly, 64*(4), 360–372. https://doi.org/10.1002/cdq.12071

Doan, P. L. (2007). Queers in the American city: Transgender perceptions of urban space. *Gender, Place, and Culture, 14*(1), 57–74. https://doi.org/10.1080/09663690601122309

Edwards, K. M., & Sylaska, K. M. (2013). The perpetuation of intimate partner violence among LGBTQ college youth: The role of minority stress. *Journal of Youth and Adolescence, 42*(11), 1721–1731. https://doi.org/10.1007/s10964-012-9880-6

Ford, C. L., Slavin, T., Hilton, K. L., & Holt, S. L. (2013). Intimate partner violence prevention services and resources in Los Angeles: Issues, needs, and challenges for assisting lesbian, gay, bisexual, and transgender clients. *Health Promotion Practice, 14*(6), 841–849. https://doi.org/10.1177/1524839912467645

Frost, D. M., Meyer, I. H., & Hammack, P. L. (2015). Health and well-being in emerging adults' same-sex relationships: Critical questions and directions for research in developmental science. *Emerging Adulthood, 3*(1), 3–13. https://doi.org/10.1177/2167696814535915

Gamarel, K. E., Reisner, S. L., Laurenceau, J. P., Nemoto, T., & Operario, D. (2014). Gender minority stress, mental health, and relationship quality: A dyadic investigation of transgender women and their cisgender male partners. *Journal of Family Psychology, 28*(4), 437–447. https://doi.org/10.1037/a0037171

Garnets, L. D., & Kimmel, D. C. (2003). Lesbian, gay male, and bisexual dimensions in the psychological study of human diversity. In L. D. Garnets & D. C. Kimmel (Eds.), *Psychological perspectives on lesbian, gay, and bisexual experiences* (pp. 1–21). Columbia University Press.

Gelaude, D. J., Sovine, M. L., Swayzer III, R., & Herbst, J. H. (2013). HIV prevention programs delivered by community-based organizations to young transgender persons of color:

Lessons learned to improve future program implementation. *International Journal of Transgenderism, 14*(3), 127–139. https://doi.org/10.1080/15532739.2013.824846

Gillum, T. L. (2017). Adolescent dating violence experiences among sexual minority youth and implications for subsequent relationship quality. *Child and Adolescent Social Work Journal, 34*(2), 137–145. https://doi.org/10.1007/s10560-016-0451-7

Gillum, T. L., & DiFulvio, G. (2012). "There's so much at stake": Sexual minority youth discuss dating violence. *Violence against Women, 18*(7), 725–745. https://doi.org/10.1177/1077801212455164

Gray, M. L. (2009). *Out in the country: Youth, media, and queer visibility in rural America*. New York University Press.

Greene, G. J., Fisher, K. A., Kuper, L., Andrews, R., & Mustanski, B. (2015). "Is this normal? Is this not normal? There is no set example": Sexual health intervention preferences of LGBT youth in romantic relationships. *Sexuality Research and Social Policy, 12*, 1–14. https://doi.org/10.1007/s13178-014-0169-2

Greteman, A. (2012). Country queers: Queer youth and the politics of rural America. *Journal of LGBT Youth, 9*(1), 63.

Grov, C., Bimbi, D. S., Nanín, J. E., & Parsons, J. T. (2006). Race, ethnicity, gender, and generational factors associated with the coming-out process among gay, lesbian, and bisexual individuals. *Journal of Sex Research, 43*(2), 115–121.

Guittar, N. A., & Rayburn, R. L. (2016). Coming out: The career management of one's sexuality. *Sexuality & Culture, 20*(2), 336–357. https://doi.org/10.1007/s12119-015-9325-y

Guittar, N. A. (2014). "At first, I just said 'I like girls'": Coming out with an affinity, not an identity. *Journal of LGBT Youth, 11*(4), 388–407. https://doi.org/10.1080/19361653.2014.910486

Haas, S. M., & Whitton, S. W. (2015). The significance of living together and importance of marriage in same-sex couples. *Journal of Homosexuality, 62*(9), 1241–1263. https://doi.org/10.1080/00918369.2015.1037137

Haltom, T. M., & Ratcliff, S. (2021). Effects of sex, race, and education on the timing of coming out among lesbian, gay, and bisexual adults in the US. *Archives of Sexual Behavior, 50*(3), 1107–1120. https://doi.org/10.1007/s10508-020-01776-x

Hammer, T. R., Crethar, H. C., & Hubach, R. D. (2019). The importance of an interdisciplinary approach in our work within the LGBTQ + community. *Journal of LGBT Issues in Counseling, 12*(4), 214–214. https://doi.org/10.1080/15538605.2018.1535469

Harper, G. W., Brodsky, A., & Bruce, D. (2012). What's good about being gay? Perspectives from youth. *Journal of LGBT Youth, 9*, 22–41. https://doi.org/10.1080/19361653.2012.628230

Hatzenbuehler, M. (2009). How does sexual minority stigma "Get under the skin"? A psychological mediation framework. *Psychological Bulletin, 135*, 707–730. https://doi.org/10.1037/a0016441

Hernandez, F., & Fraynd, D. J. (2014). Leadership's role in inclusive LGBTQ-supportive schools. *Theory into Practice, 53*, 115–122. https://doi.org/10.1080/00405841.2014.885811

Herrick, A. L., Matthews, A. K., & Garofalo, R. (2010). Health risk behaviors in an urban sample of young women who have sex with women. *Journal of Lesbian Studies, 14*(1), 80–92. https://doi.org/10.1080/10894160903060440

Hershberger, S. L., & D'Augelli, A. R. (1995). The impact of victimization on the mental health and suicidality of lesbian, gay, and bisexual youths. *Developmental Psychology, 31*, 65–74. https://doi.org/10.1037/0012-1649.31.1.65

Hillier, L., Mitchell, K. J., & Ybarra, M. L. (2012). The Internet as a safety net: Findings from a series of online focus groups with LGB and non-LGB young people in the United States. *Journal of LGBT Youth, 9*(3), 225–246.

Hoffarth, M. R., & Bogaert, A. F. (2017). Opening the closet door: Openness to experience, masculinity, religiosity, and coming out among same-sex attracted men. *Personality and Individual Differences, 109*, 215–219. https://doi.org/10.1016/j.paid.2017.01.011

Hubach, R. D., Dodge, B., Schick, V., Ramos, W. D., Herbenick, D., Li, M. J., … Reece, M. (2015). Experiences of HIV-positive gay, bisexual and other men who have sex with men residing in relatively rural areas. *Culture, Health & Sexuality, 17*(7), 795–809. https://doi.org/10.1080/13691058.2014.994231

Institute of Medicine. 2011. *The health of lesbian, gay, bisexual, and transgender people: Building a foundation for better understanding.* National Academies Press. https://doi.org/10.17226/13128

Johns, M. M., Pingel, E. S., Youatt, E. J., Soler, J. H., McClelland, S. I., & Bauermeister, J. A. (2013). LGBT community, social network characteristics, and smoking behaviors in young sexual minority women. *American Journal of Community Psychology, 52*(1), 141–154.

Koob, J. J., Brasfield, T. L., & Bernstein, B. M. (1993). The outcome of cognitive-behavioral and support group brief therapies for depressed, HIV-infected persons. *American Journal of Psychiatry, 150*(1), 1679–1686.

Kosciw, J. G., Palmer, N. A., Kull, R. M., & Greytak, E. A. (2013). The effect of negative school climate on academic outcomes for LGBT youth and the role of in-school supports. *Journal of School Violence, 12*, 45–63. https://doi.org/10.1080/15388220.2012.732546

Kosciw, J. G., Palmer, N. A., & Kull, R. M. (2015). Reflecting resiliency: Openness about sexual orientation and/or gender identity and its relationship to well-being and educational outcomes for LGBT students. *American Journal of Community Psychology, 55*(1–2), 167–178. https://doi.org/10.1007/s10464-014-9642-6

Le, V., Arayasirikul, S., Chen, Y-H., Jin, H., & Wilson, E. C. (2016). Types of social support and parental acceptance among transfemale youth and their impact on mental health, sexual debut, history of sex work, and condomless anal intercourse. *Journal of the International AIDS Society, 19*, 1–6. https://doi.org/10.7448/IAS.19.3.20781

Lee, R., Loeb, D., & Butterfield, A. (2014). Sexual history taking curriculum: Lecture and standardized patient cases. *MedEdPORTAL, 10*(1), 1–5. https://doi.org/10.15766/mep_2374-8265.9856

Lyons, H. Z., Brenner, B. R., & Lipman, J. (2010). Patterns of career and identity interference for lesbian, gay, and bisexual young adults. *Journal of Homosexuality, 57*(4), 503–524. https://doi.org/10.1080/00918361003608699

Macapagal, K., Greene, G. J., Rivera, Z., & Mustanski, B. (2015). "The best is always yet to come": Relationship stages and processes among young LGBT couples. *Journal of Family Psychology, 29*(3), 309–320.

Matthews, C. R., & Adams, E. M. (2009). Using a social justice approach to prevent the mental health consequences of heterosexism. *Journal of Primary Prevention, 30*, 11–26.

McCann, E., Donohue, G., & Timmins, F. (2020). An exploration of the relationship between spirituality, religion and mental health among youth who identify as LGBT+: A systematic literature review. *Journal of Religion and Health, 59*(2), 828–844. https://doi.org/10.1007/s10943-020-00989-7

McConnell, E., Néray, B., Hogan, B., Korpak, A., Clifford, A., & Birkett, M. (2018). "Everybody puts their whole life on Facebook": Identity management and the online social networks of LGBTQ youth. *International Journal of Environmental Research and Public Health, 15*(6), 1078–1097. https://doi.org/10.3390/ijerph15061078

McFadden, C. (2015). Lesbian, gay, bisexual, and transgender careers and human resource development: A systematic literature review. *Human Resource Development Review, 14*(2), 125–162. https://doi.org/10.1177/1534484314549456

McGeough, B. L., & Sterzing, P. R. (2018). A systematic review of family victimization experiences among sexual minority youth. *Journal of Primary Prevention, 39*(5). https://doi.org/10.1007/s10935-018-0523-x

Miller, B. (2016). A computer-mediated escape from the closet: Exploring identity, community, and disinhibited discussion on the internet coming out advice forums. *Sexuality & Culture, 20*(3), 602–625. https://doi.org/10.1007/s12119-016-9343-4

Miller, S. J. (2011). African-American lesbian identity management and identity development in the context of family and community. *Journal of Homosexuality, 58*(4), 547–563. https://doi.org/10.1080/00918369.2011.556937

Mustanski, B., & Liu, R. T. (2013). A longitudinal study of predictors of suicide attempts among lesbian, gay, bisexual, and transgender youth. *Archives of Sexual Behavior, 42*, 437–448. https://doi.org/10.1007/s10508-012-0013-9

Mustanski, B., Newcomb, M. E., & Garofalo, R. (2011). The mental health of lesbian, gay, and bisexual youths: A developmental resiliency perspective. *Journal of Gay & Lesbian Social Services, 23*, 204–225. https://doi.org/10.1080/10538720.2011.561474

Needham, B. L., & Austin, E. L. (2010). Sexual orientation, parental support, and health during the transition to young adulthood. *Journal of Youth and Adolescence, 39*(10), 1189–1198.

O'Ryan, L. W., & McFarland, W. P. (2010). A phenomenological exploration of the experiences of dual-career lesbian and gay couples. *Journal of Counseling and Development, 88*(1), 71–79.

Painter, K. R., Scannapieco, M., Blau, G., Andre, A., & Kohn, K. (2018). Improving the mental health outcomes of LGBTQ youth and young adults: A longitudinal study. *Journal of Social Service Research, 44*, 223–235. https://doi.org/10.1080/01488376.2018.1441097

Parnell, M. K., Lease, S. H., & Green, M. L. (2012). Perceived career barriers for gay, lesbian, and bisexual individuals. *Journal of Career Development, 39*(3), 248–268. https://doi.org/10.1177/0894845310386730

Pascoe, C. J. (2011). Resource and risk: Youth sexuality and new media use. *Sexuality Research and Social Policy, 8*(1), 5–17. https://doi.org/10.1007/s13178-011-0042-5

Potoczniak, D., Crosbie-Burnett, M., & Saltzburg, N. (2009). Experiences regarding coming out to parents among African American, Hispanic, and White gay, lesbian, bisexual, transgender, and questioning adolescents. *Journal of Gay & Lesbian Social Services, 21*(2), 189–205. https://doi.org/10.1080/10538720902772063

Ratcliff, S. M., & Haltom, T. M. (2021). The proverbial closet: Do faith and religiosity affect coming-out patterns? *Social Currents, 8*(3), 249–269. https://doi.org/10.1177/2329496521996056

Riley, E. (2018). Bullies, blades, and barricades: Practical considerations for working with adolescents expressing concerns regarding gender and identity. *International Journal of Transgenderism, 19*(2), 203–211. https://doi.org/10.1080/15532739.2017.1386150

Robertson, M. A. (2014). "How do I know I am gay?": Understanding sexual orientation, identity, and behavior among adolescents in an LGBT youth center. *Sexuality & Culture, 18*(2), 385–404. https://doi.org/10.1007/s12119-013-9203-4

Rostosky, S. S., Riggle, E. D. B., Rothblum, E. D., & Balsam, K. F. (2016). Same-sex couples' decisions and experiences of marriage in the context of minority stress: Interviews from a population-based longitudinal study. *Journal of Homosexuality, 63*(8), 1019–1040. https://doi.org/10.1080/00918369.2016.1191232

Russon, J. M., & Schmidt, C. K. (2014). Authenticity and career decision-making self-efficacy in lesbian, gay, and bisexual college students. *Journal of Gay & Lesbian Social Services, 872260*(2), 207–221. https://doi.org/10.1080/10538720.2014.891090

Ryan, C., Russell, S. T., Huebner, D., Diaz, R., & Sanchez, J. (2010). Family acceptance in adolescence and the health of LGBT young adults. *Journal of Child and Adolescent Psychiatric Nursing, 23*(4), 205–213.

Sangganjanavanich, V. F., & Headley, J. A. (2016). Career development of transgender college students pursuing gender transition. *Career Planning and Adult Development, 32*(1), 161–169.

Savin-Williams, R. C., & Cohen, K. M. (2015). Developmental trajectories and milestones of lesbian, gay, and bisexual young people. *International Review of Psychiatry, 27*(5), 357–366. https://doi.org/10.3109/09540261.2015.1093465

Schmidt, C. K., Raque-Bogdan, T. L., Piontkowski, S., & Schaefer, K. L. (2011). Putting the positive in health psychology: A content analysis of three journals. *Journal of Health Psychology, 16*(4), 607–620. https://doi.org/10.1177/1359105310384296

Schmitz, R. M., & Tyler, K. A. (2018). Contextual constraints and choices: Strategic identity management among LGBTQ youth. *Journal of LGBT Youth, 15*(3), 212–226. https://doi.org/10.1080/19361653.2018.1466754

Schneider, M. S., & Dimito, A. (2010). Factors influencing the career and academic choices of lesbian, gay, bisexual, and transgender people. *Journal of Homosexuality, 57*(10), 1355–1369. https://doi.org/10.1080/00918369.2010.517080

Snapp, S. D., McGuire, J. K., Sinclair, K. O., Gabrion, K., & Russell, S. T. (2015). LGBTQ-inclusive curricula: Why supportive curricula matter. *Sex Education, 15*, 580–596. https://doi.org/10.1080/14681811.2015.1042573

Szymanski, D. M., & Gupta, A. (2009). Examining the relationship between multiple internalized oppressions and African American lesbian, gay, bisexual, and questioning persons' self-esteem and psychological distress. *Journal of Counseling Psychology, 56*, 110–118. https://doi.org/10.1037/a0013317

Whitton, S. W., Newcomb, M. E., Messinger, A. M., Byck, G., & Mustanski, B. (2019). A longitudinal study of IPV victimization among sexual minority youth. *Journal of Interpersonal Violence, 34*(5), 912–945. https://doi.org/10.1177/0886260516646093

CHAPTER 14

Independent Practice

*Gary Howell, PsyD, Arlene Noriega, PhD,
& Julie Williams, MSEd, MA*

The landscape of mental health practice has evolved over the last decade. The emphasis on integrated care has significantly influenced independent practice and allowed clinicians to be part of a larger, more comprehensive delivery system for mental health services. The needs of LGBTQ+ children, adolescents, and emerging adults are often complicated by the ever-changing sociopolitical world we all inhabit as well as systems of oppression, barriers to care, and colonized practices. Regardless of the independent practice setting, there is a real need for affirmative practices for LGBTQ+ patients. According to Pachankis (2018), it is critical for clinicians to help LGBTQ+ patients gain insight into the role stigma plays in their mental health and have the knowledge and understanding of the unique experiences impacting LGBTQ+ individuals. This chapter will provide a glimpse into the distinct aspects of LGBTQ+-affirming independent practice settings and culturally competent approaches, and it will examine some of the challenges impacting care as well as gaps in the research and future directions.

Independent Practice

SOLO PRACTICES

Many clinicians work in independent practices where they are the sole practitioner. The challenge of practitioners in solo practices becomes staying connected to professional associations or with other practitioners and consultation groups, otherwise they run the risk of practicing in silos. The siloing has the potential of creating ethical challenges if clinicians are not staying current with evidence-based literature or connected with other professionals in clinical practice, especially when working with LGBTQ+ youth and emerging adults. In addition to clinicians having the complicated task of staying current on general practice issues, they must possess the knowledge, skills, and awareness in working with these patients and the complex world they navigate in their daily lives. The needs and experiences of LGBTQ+ youth patients are constantly in flux and require clinicians to stay abreast of their sometimes volatile social and interpersonal worlds. Those practicing in silos are often at risk of being out of touch with current practice standards, terminology, and evidence-based approaches unless they seek out continuing education opportunities on their own. Those who blend solo practice and academia have easier access to contemporary research and a colleague network within steps of their offices.

GROUP PRACTICES

Some clinicians choose to work in group practice models that include two or more practitioners, and the structures vary. According to Zimmerman (2017), some practices are co-op models that serve as more of an office-sharing process with a shared group brand. In an all-partner practice, all parties own the practice and decide jointly on matters. Partner and associate models involve a system in which the partners own the practice and the associates benefit from the structure without legal decision making for the group but may also vary in terms of how much power associates have. Multidisciplinary practices are inclusive of professionals from different backgrounds and have varying structures with less competitive settings. In many group practices, partners can provide peer-support and consultation for each other on a routine basis. It is important when working with LGBTQ+ youth and young adults that there be consideration of whom one is in practice with and if they can be a source of collaboration. Having partners with disparate areas of specialties leaves the practitioner working essentially in a solo practice. Whether in a group or in solo practice, there needs to be the additional considerations of how one keeps current with the issues important with any specific population, such as LGBTQ+ youth and young adults.

INTEGRATED PRACTICES

For the last several years, we have seen an influx of integrated practice models across the United States. As the Affordable Care Act was being rolled out under the Obama administration, the American Psychological Association (APA) dedicated resources to educating psychologists and advocating for psychologists to have a bigger role in the integrated healthcare industry. There are many ways for mental health practitioners to integrate their independent practices with the larger healthcare system. Some choose to co-locate their practices within a healthcare setting (primary care clinics, pediatric offices, etc.), and there are many variations of this process that allow a warm handoff to extend care beyond basic behavioral interventions. LGBTQ+ centers have grown to include more than social resources for the community and now include job skills training, psychotherapy and psychiatric services, as well as primary care and endocrinology services for transgender and nonbinary patients.

Nuances with LGBTQ+ Affirmative Practices

When working with LGBTQ+ patients, there are nuances that require additional competency and training. Affirming practitioners will often see patients who have negative experiences with other healthcare professionals (physicians, nurses, mental health providers, etc.) who were not affirming. It is not uncommon for affirming clinicians to hear about microaggressions and other discriminatory practices that have likely caused some harm or led to skepticism about seeking mental health treatment again. When working with LGBTQ+ youth and emerging adults, it is incredibly beneficial to have a clear understanding of what minority stress is and how it impacts this community. Much of the work on intersectionality and inclusive practices with the LGBTQ+ community has been informed by a growing body of research (e.g., Hatzenbuehler & Pachankis, 2016; Hendricks & Testa, 2012; Meyer, 2003) on minority stress.

In addition, clinicians working with transgender and nonbinary youth need to have a firm grounding in development and developmental trajectories and be able to identify possible neurodevelopmental disorders. While there is limited research, clinicians need awareness that transgender and nonbinary youth may present with challenges associated with neurodiversity that requires additional knowledge or training to avoid doing harm to patients (Nobili et al., 2018; Strang et al., 2020; Thrower et al., 2020). We have seen an increasing number of children and adolescents who may be diagnosed on the autism spectrum and struggling with gender dysphoria. There are specific nuances requiring a more delicate approach with these cases and competency in working with both challenges simultaneously. For clinicians with limited to no experience in working with autism spectrum disorder, it is important to work collaboratively with an experienced clinician or team of providers to provide specialty assessments and bolster the continuum of care.

Much of the work with LGBTQ+ youth involves parents or caregivers in some way and will require clinicians to navigate complicated family dynamics at times. In some cases, both or neither parent is on board with affirming treatment of their child, which presents a challenge for the clinician to create a space in their sessions for allowing the young patient to be as authentic as they can be while attending to the needs of the family. Practitioners in independent practice need to be particularly attuned in situations where parents are divorced as to who holds the decision-making power. It is important to work with parents to assist them in developing an affirming treatment of their child. However, in cases where that is not possible, a careful review of the child custody decree is essential in order to understand who has the final decision-making authority and communicate this to both parents in a manner that is not alienating to either parent. In situations like these, LGBTQ+ youth may be bounced between two homes where only one or neither may be affirming of their sexuality or gender, which causes significant distress for the youth.

An essential role for the practitioner is to assist the youth in developing the ability to manage their increasing dysphoria, particularly in situations when they are consistently misgendered and their deadname (i.e., a name they were assigned at birth but do not want to be called) is used by parents, caregivers, family, and/or teachers. Parents' attempts to control their own anxiety in these situations may manifest themselves in obvious and subtle ways to force or push the child into activities or presentations or engaging in conversations that are uncomfortable and distressing to the youth. For example, talking consistently about the youth's future heterosexual marriage. Independent practitioners can provide anticipatory guidance to parents regarding potential effects of these pressures to conform. Many of these pressures may be embedded in strict religious doctrine and/or strong cultural beliefs around gender roles. These are extremely important issues that may create situations of significant mental health risk for the LGBTQ+ child or adolescent. Clear assessments early on in the therapeutic relationship around these cultural and religious beliefs are critical elements to include that could give the clinician an indication of potential risk areas.

Consultative Roles

Independent practitioners often consult with other providers in the treatment of LGBTQ+ children, adolescents, and emerging adults. Letter writing for transgender and nonbinary folx is a common consultative role and often requires a unique skill set and knowledge of the risk factors associated with medical transition and an ability to thoroughly assess one's consent to treatment (World Professional Association for Transgender Health, 2012). The LGBTQ+ providers are often the proverbial "unicorns," especially those working with transgender and nonbinary individuals. They are often sought out for treatment as well as serving as an expert to other organizations or systems. An emerging area of focus for some independent practitioners is evaluating asylum seekers for LGBTQ+ youth and emerging adults who are escaping political or social danger in their countries (Cerezo et al., 2014; Nakamura & Pope, 2013).

LGBTQ+-affirming providers will likely encounter situations where youth and their parents experience roadblocks or barriers when navigating the educational system. Some systems are oppressive and dangerous for LGBTQ+ students. When consulting in these systems, providers often wear many hats and must advocate for their own patients as well as all LGBTQ+ youth. Providers may share their expertise with local school boards, city councils, and/or county governments (i.e., speaking as a licensed professional in support of banning sexual orientation and gender identity change efforts). These youth, regardless of their level of education, often need additional support. Providers may find opportunities to consult with colleges or universities when LGBTQ+ students are faced with mental health challenges that impact their ability to attend class, hand in assignments, transition safely, and so on. It is important for providers to engage in meaningful relationships with local LGBTQ+ centers and Gender and Sexuality Alliances (GSAs) as well.

Barriers to Care

Generally speaking, it is clear that marginalized communities are disparately impacted by inequity and discrimination in healthcare settings, which include independent practices. Mental health providers are also guilty of creating and perpetuating systems of oppression that lead to barriers and exclusionary practices that disenfranchise LGBTQ+ patients. There are also sociopolitical factors and social determinants of care that negatively impact the community. Patients deserve to have a provider who validates their experiences and works to eliminate barriers. There are other barriers (e.g., access, location, affordability, etc.) that impact patient care. Child and adolescent patients either may not serve as the decision makers for their medical care or have not yet had experience locating and initiating medical services before. They may be unaware that LGBTQ+-affirming and -niche practices exist or how to find them. Although many states allow minors to seek mental healthcare without parental consent, the patient may not seek treatment out of concerns about how they would pay for services, unaware that they may qualify for free or reduced-fee payment arrangements.

HEALTHCARE DISPARITIES

For those LGBTQ+-affirming providers working in the independent practice arena, there are often frequent complaints of non-affirming providers who have misgendered, deadnamed, or invalidated the experiences of transgender or nonbinary patients and who lack sensitivity toward or awareness of the challenges associated with one's sexual orientation. The non-affirming behaviors may cause folx to avoid seeking physical or mental healthcare services, which may lead to severe consequences. Independent practitioners who do not participate in insurance panels also create barriers for patients who need the services but cannot afford to pay out-of-pocket fees. In addition, insurance companies may create unnecessary hurdles, in the form of letters from mental health providers before initiating medical transitions and even services such as electrolysis.

SOCIOPOLITICAL FACTORS

This country saw a rollback of protections for LGBTQ+ patients of all ages from late 2016 through the end of 2020, and the National Center for Transgender Equality (2020) published a collection of more than 70 anti-LGBTQ+ actions taken during this time. The election occurred on the heels of the Pulse massacre on June 12, 2016, in Orlando, Florida. As the community was continuing to find a pathway to healing, an insidious undercurrent of bigotry toward the LGBTQ+ community was a significant part of the effort to erase the very rights that protected them. In 2021, planned and highly orchestrated tactics were used to discriminate and harm LGBTQ+ people in the United States. Some of these political moves were directed toward healthcare providers who treat transgender youth, and some efforts aimed to allow healthcare discrimination based on personal beliefs. In 2022, 238 anti-LGBTQ+ bills were proposed, 65% of which discriminated against transgender individuals (Lavietes & Ramos, 2022). In states such as Texas, Florida, Arizona, and Alabama, governors signed healthcare discriminations into law for transgender youth (Associated Press & Yurcaba, 2022; Atterbury, 2022; Caspani, 2022; Cole, 2022; Thoreson, 2022). While only some states have passed legislation, other states have begun to consider bills that would penalize healthcare providers, and in some cases parents, for providing gender-affirming care for transgender and nonbinary youth.

Holding multiple marginalized identities opens the door for more discrimination and racial trauma and creates vulnerability for LGBTQ+ youth and emerging adults. According to the US Department of Justice and FBI Hate Crime Report (2019), hate crimes against LGBTQ+ people skyrocketed after 2017 (United States Department of Justice, 2020). Independent practitioners are on the front lines of these issues, especially LGBTQ+-affirming providers, and are often tasked with creating a space to both contain and process the harsh realities of growing up LGBTQ+ in the United States.

SOCIAL DETERMINANTS OF CARE

Health disparities are often connected to or exacerbated by social determinants of care. Having one's basic needs met each day creates a foundation for the other social determinants. LGBTQ+ youth and emerging adults' opportunities to gain an education, to have access to financial support, and to secure work has a tremendous impact on their future successes. Depending on their geographic location, access to community resources (LGBTQ+ centers, queer+ally groups on campus, etc.) may be abundant or nonexistent. Many LGBTQ+ youth also experience a lack of social support and homelessness and are regularly exposed to violence. Experiences with racism and other discriminatory practices serve as a negative social determinant (Kronenfeld, 2013). Problem-solving with clients openly and in good faith about the cost involved in treatment and how the client can manage payment for services reduces unnecessary stress and bolsters therapist-client trust. The cost of services or a provider's refusal to accept insurance may be a barrier as well and exacerbate the mental and physical health concerns of the patient. Practitioners may need to assess their ability to offer pro-bono or sliding-scale fees or assist clients in determining if their insurance coverage includes out-of-network (OON) benefits, as this may be an additional way to increase access to care in an independent practice model. Independent practitioners must consider whether their own practices are exclusionary and increase mental health risks.

ELIMINATING BARRIERS TO CARE

Affirming LGBTQ+ providers should endeavor to break down barriers—not create them. Advocacy is a crucial part of this process. Using one's privilege to center intersectional voices and decolonize the systems we all inhabit helps eliminate barriers. Even independent practitioners may occasionally find themselves in advocacy-related situations, having to testify before local government boards to support more equitable treatment of LGBTQ+ patients, and/or standing before a school board to fight for inclusive trans and nonbinary voices. Providers need to consider all potential barriers when working with LGBTQ+ youth and emerging adults. Many factors may prevent these youth from engaging in needed services with independent practitioners. Not all patients are aware of the resources for finding clinicians. In some areas, there may be a unicorn effect—where the provider is the only affirming clinician in the area and often has no room for new patients. Some patients may not know how to search for and engage with affirming independent practitioners in private practice and may give up or end up working with non-affirming providers who may do harm due to their lack of knowledge or bigoted views of LGBTQ+ patients.

Cultural Competence

As independent practitioners, one's ability to effectively assess and treat LGBTQ+ children, adolescents, and young adults is dependent on one's ability to work in a culturally sound and effective manner. However, it is more than just being culturally competent or the cultural competency of the services delivered. Cultural competence is not a "one and done" technical skill you learn in a training or workshop—it is an ongoing developmental process. The holy trinity of cultural competence for decades has basically been the development of awareness, knowledge, and skills in delivering services to clients from diverse backgrounds. Cultural competence in the therapeutic relationship is predicated on the clinician's awareness of and understanding in addressing their own biases to prevent their unconscious influence on the therapeutic process. The more knowledge and exposure a clinician has had with a particular group, the greater the chance that overconfidence and thus wrong assumptions will arise. Cissexism, racism, homophobia, and transphobia are embedded in the societal narrative and no one is immune. Independent practitioners, who may not have the opportunity to be challenged by colleagues about their unrecognized biases, run the risk of unconsciously imposing these perceptions on their clients and families. Clinicians who identify as LGBTQ+ may face additional challenges being part of the community. For example, when the Pulse nightclub shooting occurred, many LGBTQ+ clinicians stepped up to provide services to the survivors and families of the victims. Some had been to the same nightclub, may have been once or twice removed from knowing victims personally, and were likely impacted by the immediate threat to their community but had to stay strong to support those in need. Another example is working with victims of anti-LGBTQ+ bullying and hate crimes as an LGBTQ+ clinician who may have experienced similar acts of bigotry and hatred. Issues related to countertransference and transference should be addressed as well. The independent practitioner is particularly vulnerable if opportunities to work on their own biases are unavailable or they are not motivated to engage in this difficult work.

The triad model (empathy, tolerance for ambiguity, and cultural competency) has been expanded by many diversity trainers to include other aspects such as attitude, which includes a way of perceiving diversity in the world around us and acknowledging differences of all kinds (Pedersen, 2000). However, this addition and others have not addressed the power differential in the therapeutic relationship, which mirrors the power differential in the social context in which many marginalized populations must navigate. By exclusively using a cultural competency model in a client-therapist relationship, the focus is on the clinician in the relationship and maintaining the power in the relationship with the clinician, which recapitulates the power differential marginalized communities experience daily in the social contexts in which they function. It is clinician-centered rather than a client-centered way of working with the cultural identities. In contrast, Hook and colleagues (2013) noted that cultural humility is the "ability to maintain an interpersonal stance that is other-oriented (or open to the other) in relation to aspects of cultural identity that are most important to the client" (p. 354). Cultural humility focuses on self-humility rather than achieving a state of knowledge or awareness. The power dynamic shifts from the therapist to the client in the client-therapist relationship. Many have postulated that the use of a model that incorporates both cultural competency as well as cultural humility is at the core of effective psychotherapy. Learning from our clients about their various intersecting identities and how they play out in the context of their daily functioning is an important application of being humble enough to allow our clients to teach us about their lived experience.

INTERSECTIONAL APPROACH

Therapists working with marginalized populations must be aware and address the multiple identities that clients hold. These identities are intricately woven, each carrying either a sense of privilege and power or marginalization and lack of power in the social context in which the client functions. Clinicians must consider the intersectional identities within the family unit as well in order to validate those vulnerabilities in treatment. If a therapist focuses only on one aspect of someone's identity such as sexual orientation and does not address intersectional issues related to gender, race, ethnicity, social class, and the like, then they may be missing important aspects of what the client may be struggling with. For example, consider a 20-year-old client who identifies as a Latinx, transgender man with cerebral palsy living with his mother, who does not accept her child being transgender, during a global pandemic. This young adult also goes to college and works part-time in retail. It is the intersection of these identities that provide the full picture of the complexity of this young person's lived experience. Isolating any one of his identities is an artificial process as the client does not experience the world through any one of their identities exclusively. To focus on any one in isolation is to deny important aspects of the individual sense of self.

CENTERING MARGINALIZED VOICES

A central goal of psychotherapy is to elevate the voices and experience of one's client, especially those who are marginalized. This is in essence the goal of using cultural humility as a way of the therapist understanding the client's worldview and agency over the psychotherapeutic process in a way that serves to empower the marginalized. Private practitioners serve on the front lines of many cultural and systemic barriers and have a unique opportunity to address things directly with the patient or on a more global scale.

ADVOCACY

An important aspect of working with marginalized populations is advocacy work. Advocacy as a mental health clinician can be done at the individual level, at the group or community level, or at a systems level. As mental health professionals, every aspect of our work is an opportunity to advocate for the marginalized voices that are not heard or respected, whether it be advocating for our individual clients as they try to navigate difficult systems or advocating for issues associated with the clinical work. As mental health providers, we have the skills to help educate systems (i.e., school systems, healthcare systems, courts, etc.) on important issues. Putting in educational pieces to clinical consultation reports is one aspect of advocacy. Most often, independent practitioners find themselves with the additional role of advocating for the safety of their clients within the educational system. Working with the school counselors and school administration, practitioners are challenged by unaware or rejecting school systems in creating safe spaces for their clients throughout their school day. From delineating safe spaces to taking care of biological needs to safety in vulnerable spaces such as gym locker rooms, the independent practitioner uses the ability to educate as their most valuable advocacy tool.

Integrated Approach

Mental healthcare from infancy through emerging adulthood requires an integrated approach across healthcare disciplines to ensure coordinated and comprehensive care. Health psychology research has long proven the influence of medical issues on mental health and vice versa (Petersen et al., 2011). The overlap between medical and mental healthcare needs increases exponentially when working with sexual orientation and gender minority youth throughout pivotal developmental years as they navigate crossover topics such as hormones, secondary sex characteristics, and body image. LGBTQ+ youth experience well-documented healthcare disparities as compared to their cisgender and heterosexual peers (US Department of Health and Human Services, 2016).

Approximately 30% of LGBTQ+ youth disclose their sexual orientation and/or gender identity minority status to doctors or other healthcare professionals as compared to 40% disclosure rates to teachers (Trevor Project, 2019). According to the same study, sexuality and gender have significant implications for physical and mental healthcare, so why do so few youth disclose this important information to their healthcare provider? Training for healthcare professionals on LGBT-specific health issues is sparse, especially for patients under the age of 18 (Hughes et al., 2017; Sekoni et al., 2017). Youth likely do not understand the impact their gender and sexuality may have on their physical or mental health, and providers with a heteronormative and cisgender assumption miss this important piece of the puzzle. Likewise, mental health practitioners who solely focus on the psychiatric needs of the patient can overlook integral medical aspects of care that interfere with the patient's ability to make progress in treatment. For example, an adolescent who experiences body dysmorphia due to gender dysmorphia may engage in extreme dieting or exercise. While they can benefit from a therapeutic conversation about nutrition and self-care in the context of addressing the mental and emotional effects of their dysmorphic symptoms, they may also benefit from a referral to a nutritionist or dietitian, who can provide healthy strategies for achieving their goals. In order for this adolescent client to develop a healthy body image and eating or exercise habits, they need an integrated-care approach.

To assist with coordination, some LGBTQ+-niche practices and some LGBTQ+-affirming practices develop fully integrated settings in which a patient may receive physical and mental healthcare in one place and their providers work as a treatment team for seamlessly coordinated care. Integrated-care-clinic models may include primary care, psychiatry, psychotherapy, lab services, pharmacy, and more. These practices are growing in popularity and may mean clinicians are co-located within other agencies as well.

Because solo practitioners may not have easy access to integrated-care settings, they would benefit from seeking ways to provide integrated care and independently foster relationships with affirming providers in the community to build a reliable referral and consultation network to better serve LGBTQ+ youth and emerging adults. In situations where there are limitations in access to care, such as in rural areas, consultation is an ethical obligation for clinicians.

In other cases, clinicians may have difficulty finding affirming providers or specialists with whom to network and consult in their local area. The clinician may spend time training and educating providers to understand the role of disparities among LGBTQ+ populations given their level of expertise. Providers can elicit trust from their LGBTQ+ clients by using inclusive language and non-assuming questions, especially when discussing sensitive topics such as sexual practices, alcohol and drug use, and exposure to violence.

IMPACT OF THE AFFORDABLE CARE ACT

Healthcare disparities of the LGBTQ+ community as compared to heterosexual adults has many explanations. The Affordable Care Act (ACA) passed in 2013 provided tax credits to help impoverished individuals to purchase private health insurance. The ACA also sought to ensure equitable access and patient protections for LGBT individuals. Many advances were made under the Obama administration; however, between 2016–2020, many of those efforts were under attack. Unfortunately, there was an active process during this time to repeal much of the ACA to prevent access specifically for the LGBTQ+ community (Kates et al., 2018).

IMPACT OF COVID

The Novel Coronavirus (2019-nCoV), known as COVID-19, evolved quickly into a global pandemic that impacted the United States in early 2020 and has changed access and delivery of healthcare services in ways no one could have imagined. Knowledge of the coronavirus influenced changes in guidelines for wearing masks, social distancing, and what groups of people were most at risk for serious reactions. National, state, and local mandates varied regarding the use of in-person healthcare services, resulting in many providers shifting their whole practices to telehealth. Some practices experienced a significant gap in services during the setting transition, while other practices chose to close indefinitely. Beyond mental healthcare, individuals experienced a generally more significant impact for medical care that was considered "nonessential" during the pandemic, such as gender-affirming procedures.

While the surge in telehealth services has reduced some barriers to treatment (e.g., transportation, childcare), it also has presented challenges specific to working within independent practices for LGBTQ+ children, adolescents, and emerging adults. To facilitate ready access to teleservices, the US Department of Health and Human Services issued a notice of enforcement discretion by the Office of Civil Rights (OCR) for the Health Insurance Portability Accountability Act of 1996 (HIPAA) and the Health Information Technology for Economic and Clinical Health (HITECH) Act from February 2020 until the present (US Department of Health and Human Services, 2020). Clinicians became tasked with researching telehealth platforms, developing or adapting intake processes, and investigating initiate services without in-person contact. As providers sought private physical environments to meet virtually with clients, some clients lacked available confidential spaces to speak openly to their therapist. Some clients attempted sessions in cars, parks, literal closets, and other unconventional places that influence the level of comfort and openness a client may feel in therapy. Whereas, other clients who may have never felt comfortable enough to sit in a physical waiting room and meet face-to-face with a therapist benefited from the opportunity to avoid this discomfort and meet exclusively through virtual means. For example, a client who identifies as nonbinary may agonize over meeting new people in novel social situations where they may have their gender identity questioned or criticized, such as a receptionist at an office or other clients in a waiting room. They may feel more free to exhibit a more authentic presentation through clothing and accessories if they know they are meeting only with their affirming clinician without interacting with anyone else. An additional challenge for some individuals who struggle with body dysphoria regarding facial features was that many telehealth platforms show both participants' videos, causing the client to see their image during the session. Clinicians have offered solutions such as recommending adjusting the position of the web browser window to span beyond the visible screen so that only the clinician's video is visible, to place a sticky note over the client's video, or to switch to a platform that allows the client to hide their self-view if preferred. During virtual group therapy, it has become common for new group members to leave their cameras off until they feel comfortable within the group. Where traditional practice may suggest that the clinician encourages the client to turn on their camera to see nonverbal communication, additional considerations for the client experience apply when working with this population.

Health insurance remains a concern for LGBTQ+ patients. Prior to the COVID-19 pandemic, few third-party payers covered the cost of telehealth services, resulting in unaffordable out-of-pocket fees. The Centers for Medicare and Medicaid Services (CMS) fought for a presidential executive order to include telehealth coverage in

August of 2020. Unfortunately, as the pandemic evolved, so did some state-level mandates for protection from COVID-19, which meant some areas were more devastated by the variants of the virus than others. Some states, such as Florida, ended mandates for coverage of telehealth services for patients, but healthcare practices or groups did not end their virtual-only services out of fear of prematurely returning to face-to-face services during a global pandemic. Unfortunately, the cost would be passed along to the patient in many cases.

SUCCESSES

Integrated care relies on pathways of collaboration and communication. Mental health providers can establish networks of LGBTQ+-affirming providers. The rapid expansion of telehealth services as a result of the COVID-19 global pandemic increases the parameters for collaboration. Clients who previously were unable to attend therapy services in their area have become more aware of telehealth options to identify providers who accept their insurance and best match their needs. As schools moved to online learning for K–12, undergraduate, and graduate programs during the COVID-19 pandemic, youth and their parents/guardians have developed more comfort with live video conferencing. National telehealth service providers such as Talkspace and Better Help launched marketing on television, radio, and social media to promote the use of mental health services and reduce the stigma of psychotherapy. Electronic Health Records (EHRs) continue to streamline exchanges of communication between patients and providers, as well as coordination between providers within integrated care.

CHALLENGES

Third-party funding for mental health care poses potential barriers for providers to afford the time required for comprehensive integrated care. Although providers may advertise as LGBTQ+ affirming, clinicians can avoid invalidating patient experiences by vetting providers before agreeing to coordinate with them. Medical providers tend to lead recommendations for hormone replacement therapy (HRT) and affirming surgical procedures, but true coordination demands the clinician demonstrate a basic understanding of the leading standards of LGBTQ+-affirming medical care to appropriately support patients during treatment. The pandemic also highlighted some vulnerabilities for LGBTQ+ youth who may have found school as a respite from tumultuous home environments but were forced to shelter in place in the earlier part of the pandemic. A major challenge for LGBTQ+ youth has been privacy and confidentiality in telemental health sessions given that it is often difficult to avoid being within an earshot of a parent, caregiver, or sibling, and this is an ongoing concern for clinicians. These youth and emerging adults already experience enough challenges and increased risk of suicide; however, the pandemic exacerbated these risks. The National Survey on LGBTQ Mental Health 2021 surveyed nearly 35,000 youth ages 13 to 24 across the United States, and 83% of LGBTQ respondents indicated that their living situation became more stressful during the COVID-19 pandemic (Trevor Project, 2021). The 2019 results of the same survey revealed 39% of LGBTQ youth seriously considered suicide in the previous 12 months (Trevor Project, 2019), but in 2021 that number rose to 43% (Trevor Project, 2021). In 2022, a major source of data that helps us understand the experiences of LGBTQ+ youth and other minority groups has come under attack in states where anti-LGBTQ+ efforts have been prioritized. From 1991–2019, the Youth Risk Behavior Surveillance System used a Youth Risk Behavior Survey to collect data from more than 4.9 million high school students in the United States. Survey data are used to design and monitor social support programs, to support policies geared toward better physical and mental health, for agencies seeking funding, and to further support for future federal funding. A loss of collecting such important data would be devastating to the efforts made to ensure that students are able to live their best lives and would silence LGBTQ+ youth voices. This survey has continually demonstrated that LGBTQ+ youth without supportive adults/parents in their lives are at risk of high-risk sexual behaviors, substance use, and suicide (Centers for Disease Control and Prevention, 2020).

Research Gaps and Future Directions

The mental healthcare of LGBTQ+ youth and emerging adults in independent practice rarely appears in research literature. For many years, research efforts reflected sociopolitical climates where LGBTQ+ identities were unacknowledged in major studies of mental and emotional functioning. Research questions surrounding the treatment of LGBTQ+ youth have evolved somewhat from the overpathologizing of sexuality other than strict heterosexuality, to battles over what age someone can identify their gender identity if it varies from one that aligns with their sex assigned at birth. Current legislative attempts to limit access to healthcare suggest that our society still has a long way to go with understanding and supporting our LGBTQ+ fellow citizens. Stigmas surrounding the experiences of LGBTQ+ community, but especially those who do not have legal power over their medical care, has limited opportunities for ethical research with this population. Institutional Review Boards (IRBs) identify individuals under the age of 18 as vulnerable populations, which increases the scrutiny of the application for research approval. Issues related to sexual practices may pose research risks that IRBs reject, which limits the possibilities for systematic study.

Beyond stigma, access to resources to conduct research can pose a barrier. Independent practitioners may not be afforded paid release time to conduct research tasks, have the necessary manpower or tools, or have access to a large enough sample of participants for robust data analysis. Some independent clinicians may discontinue their involvement in professional organizations or structured collaboration that may provide support and encouragement toward research efforts. Clinicians may also perceive that their research would not receive a warm welcome by major peer-reviewed journals or conferences due to political or other interfering dynamics.

If we do not overcome these barriers, research will continue to ignore the specific needs and recommendations for LGBTQ+ youth and emerging adults. Further research is needed to establish evidence-based practices that incorporate diverse gender identities and sexual orientations for individuals across the life span while considering other aspects of their intersectional identity. Investigation of the causes of healthcare disparities can assist with prevention and psychoeducation. Studies can also assist with issues of social and legislative advocacy.

Considerations for Practice

The need exists for independent LGBTQ+-niche or -affirming practices to address the significant healthcare disparities affecting youth and emerging adults with diverse gender identities or sexual orientations. Clinicians or students with an interest in developing an independent practice serving the LGBTQ+ youth and emerging adults should consider the unique needs of the patients and competencies needed when working with the challenges of this population.

Because this population may present with mental, emotional, or behavioral concerns that pertain to their sexuality, coming out issues, physical appearance, and even hormone levels, clinicians would benefit from becoming familiar with affirming physical and medical healthcare practices for LGBTQ+ patients. For patients with transgender identities, the World Professional Association for Transgender Health (WPATH) publishes a "Standards of Care" document that outlines best practices for trans-affirming healthcare. Unfortunately, not all providers who market themselves as LGBTQ+ affirming follow best practices or will offer services to minors. Before referring patients to community partners, clinicians should vet the referral to ascertain to what extent their services are actually affirming and supportive.

This work can be very rewarding but exhausting at times, which puts some clinicians at risk of vicarious trauma. Helping patients actualize a core aspect of their identity such as their gender or sexuality can become emotional for the client and clinician. Individuals within the LGBTQ+ community experience disproportionately higher levels of abuse and trauma, with sequelae such as self-injury and substance abuse and suicidal thoughts and attempts. Any provider who works with minors can tell stories about frustrations they experienced when a patient's parent(s) or caregiver(s) interferes or dismantles treatment progress. There will be times when you will feel helpless, hopeless, angry, and worried for your clients. There will also be moments when you get to celebrate with clients and feel their elation, pride, excitement, and hope. Clinicians interested in this work must maintain self-care practices to withstand the sometimes emotionally volatile nature of working with this population.

Key Knowledge Points

By the end of this chapter, students and clinicians will be able to:

- Describe the different types of independent practice structures and what advantages or disadvantages each pose to treatment of this unique population;

- Identify specific barriers to care that clients may experience and ways independent practitioners can address them;
- Discuss considerations for culturally competent independent practice that incorporates intersectional approaches to care and advocacy;
- Explain the necessities of integrated approaches to care when working with LGBTQ+ children, adolescents, and emerging adults in independent practice and how to coordinate integrated care for various settings;
- Summarize positive and negative influences of the COVID-19 pandemic on independent practice for LGBTQ+ children, adolescents, and emerging adults; and
- Examine the causes for gaps in the research literature about independent practice.

Recommendations for Practitioners

Recommendations for supporting the well-being of LGBTQ+ children, adolescents, and emerging adults in the independent practice setting:

- Foster consultative relationships with other clinicians who do this work. You may identify potential consultants through mutual membership in professional organizations, participation in social justice and community events supporting LGBTQ+ youth, social media, or word of mouth.
- Develop a network of affirming healthcare providers to which you can refer clients for comprehensive care. This may require providing training to local providers who express interest in developing competency in order to offer affirming care.
- Contribute to and be good consumers of contemporary research involving LGBTQ+ youth and emerging adults (e.g., social media use, bullying, etc).

References

Abbas, A. M., Fathy, S. K., Mohamed, A. M., Omar, F. A., & Fahmi, S. K. (2020). Effects of COVID-19 pandemic on children's mental health. *Archives of Health Science, 4*(1), 1–4. https://doi.org/10.31829/2641-7456/ahs2020-4(1)-130

Alvis, L. M., Douglas, R., Shook, N. J., & Oosterhoff, B. (Preprint). Associations between adolescents' prosocial experiences and mental health during the COVID-19 pandemic. https://www.researchgate.net/publication/341225361

Arafat, M. Y., Zaman, S., & Hawlader, M. D. H. (2021). Telemedicine improves mental health in COVID-19 pandemic. *Journal of Global Health, 11*, 1–4. https://doi.org/10.7189/jogh.11.03004

Associated Press, & Yurcaba, J. (2022, April 8). *Alabama governor signs bill criminalizing transgender healthcare for minors.* NBC News. https://www.nbcnews.com/nbc-out/out-politics-and-policy/alabama-governor-signs-bill-criminalizing-transgender-health-care-mino-rcna23674

Atterbury, A. (2022, March 28). *DeSantis signs Florida's contentious LGBTQ bill into law.* Politico. https://www.politico.com/news/2022/03/28/desantis-signs-floridas-contentious-lgbtq-bill-into-law-00020966

Balsam, K. F., Matsuno, E., Friedman, A., & Rana, V. (2020). Development and initial evaluation of the LGBTQ+ COVID-19 Concerns Scale. *Annals of LGBTQ Public and Population Health, 1*(4), 292–299. http://dx.doi.org/10.1891/LGBTQ-20-00047

Banerjee, D., & Nair, V. S. (2020). "The untold side of COVID-19": Struggle and perspectives of the sexual minorities. *Journal of Psychosexual Health, 2*(2), 113–120. https://doi.org/10.1177/2631831820939017

Bettinger, T. V. (2010). Ethical and methodolgocial complexities in research involving sexual minorities. *New Horizons in Adult Education and Human Resource Development, 24*(1), 43–58. http://education.fiu.edu/newhorizons

Caspani, M. (2022, April 29). Factbox: New U.S. state laws directed at transgender youth. Reuters. https://www.reuters.com/world/us/onslaught-us-laws-targeting-transgender-youth-2022-04-07/

Centers for Disease Control and Prevention. (2020). Youth risk behavior surveillance—United States, 2019. *MMWR Supplement, 69*(1), 1–88. https://www.cdc.gov/mmwr/volumes/69/su/pdfs/su6901-H.pdf

Cerezo, A., Morales, A., Quintero, D., & Rothman, S. (2014). Trans migrations: Exploring life at the intersection of transgender identity and immigration. *Psychology of Sexual Orientation and Gender Diversity,* (1), 170–180. https://doi.org/10.1037/sgd0000031

Cochran, S. D., Björkenstam, C., & Mays, V. M. (2017). Sexual orientation differences in functional limitations, disability, and mental health services use: Results from the 2013–2014 National Health Interview survey. *Journal of Counseling and Clinical Psychology, 85*(12), 1111–1121. http://dx.doi.org/10.1037/ccp0000243

Cole, D. (2022, March 30). *Arizona governor signs bill outlawing gender-affirming care for transgender youth and approves anti-trans sports ban.* CNN. https://www.cnn.com/2022/03/30/politics/arizona-transgender-health-care-ban-sports-ban/index.html

Dewey, J. M. (2013). Challenges of implementing collaborative models of decision making with trans-identified patients. *Health Expectations, 18,* 1508–1518. https://doi.org/10.1111/hex.12133

Fish, J. N., McInroy, L. B., Paceley, M. S., Williams, N. D., Henderson, S., Levine, D. S., & Edsall, R. N. (2020). "I'm kind of stuck at home with unsupportive parents right now": LGBTQ youths' experiences with COVID-19 and the importance of online support. *Journal of Adolescent Health, 67,* 450–452. https://doi.org/10.1016/j.jadohealth.2020.06.002

Gilbert, C., Siepser, C., Fink, A. E., & Johnson, N. L. (2020, October 15). Why LGBTQ+ campus resource centers are essential. *Psychology of Sexual Orientation and Gender Diversity, 8*(2), 245–249. http://dx.doi.org/10.1037/sgd0000451

Goldbach, C., Knutson, D., & Milton, D. C. (2020, December 31). LGBTQ+ people and COVID-19: The importance of resilience during a pandemic. *Psychology of Sexual Orientation and Gender Diversity, 8*(2), 123–132. http://dx.doi.org/10.1037/sgd0000463

Goldberg, S. B. (2020). COVID-19 and LGBT rights: Law in the time of COVID-19. *Columbia Law School.* https://scholarship.law.columbia.edu/faculty_scholarship/2687

Green, A. E., Price-Feeney, M., & Dorison, S. H. (2020). *Implications of COVID-19 for LGBTQ youth mental health and suicide prevention.* Trevor Project. https://www.thetrevorproject.org/2020/04/03/implications-of-covid-19-for-lgbtq-youth-mental-health-and-suicide-prevention/

Hamilton, A., Sala, G., Quereshi, O., & Eaton, J. (2020). Stories from the field: Mapping innovation in mental health during the COVID-19 pandemic. *Intervention, 18*(2), 159–165. https://doi.org/10.4103/INTV.INTV_22_20

Harkness, A., Gattamorta, K. A., Estrada, Y., Jimenez, D., Kanamori, M., Prado, G., & Behar-Zusman, V. (2020). Latinx health disparities research during COVID-19: Challenges and innovations. *Annals of Behavioral Medicine, 54,* 544–547. https://doi.org/10.1093/abm/kaaa054

Hatzenbuehler, M. L., & Pachankis, J. E. (2016). Stigma and minority stress as social determinants of health among lesbian, gay, gisexual, and transgender youth: Research evidence and clinical implications. *Pediatric Clinics of North America, 63*(6), 985–997. https://doi.org/10.1016/j.pcl.2016.07.003

Hawke, L. D., Hayes, E., Darnay, K., and Henderson, J. (2021). Mental health among transgender and gender diverse youth: An exploration of effects during the COVID-19 pandemic. *Psychology of Sexual Orientation and Gender Diversity, 8*(2), 180–187. http://dx.doi.org/10.1037/sgd0000467

Hendricks, M. L., & Testa, R. J. (2012). A conceptual framework for clinical work with transgender and gender nonconforming clients: An adaptation of the Minority Stress Model. *Professional Psychology: Research and Practice, 43*(5), 460–467. https://doi.org/10.1037/a0029597

Hook, J. N., Davis, D. E., Owen, J., Worthington Jr., E. L., & Utsey, S. O. (2013). Cultural humility: Measuring openness to culturally diverse clients. *Journal of Counseling Psychology, 60*(3), 353–366. https://doi.org/10.1037/a0032595

Hughes, R. L., Damon, C., & Heiden-Rootes, K. (2017). Where's the LGBT in integrated care research? A systematic review. *Families, Systems, & Health, 35*(3), 308–319. http://dx.doi.org/10.1037/fsh0000290

Iversen, J., Sabin, K., Chang, J., Thomas, R. M., Prestage, G., Strathdee, S. A., & Maher, L. (2020). COVID-19, HIV and key populations: Cross-cutting issues and the need for population-specific responses. *Journal of the International AIDS Society, 23,* 1–6. https://doi.org/10.1002/jia2.25632

Jones, B., Bowe, M., McNamara, N., Guerin, E., & Carter, T. (2021). Exploring the mental health experiences of young trans and gender diverse people during the coronavirus pandemic. *International Journal of Transgender Health* [preprint]. https://doi.org/10.1080/26895269.2021.1890301

Kates, J., Ranji, U., Beamesderfer, A., Salganicoff, A., & Dawson, L. (2018). *Health and access to care and coverage for lesbian, gay, bisexual, and transgender individuals in the U.S.* Henry Kaiser Family Foundation. http://files.kff.org/attachment/Issue-Brief-Health-and-Access-to-Care-and-Coverage-for-LGBT-Individuals-in-the-US

Keuroghlian, A. S. (2016). The importance of behavioral health integration for LGBT patients. [Presentation]. National LGBT Health Education Center: A Program of the Fenway Institute; National Center for Innovation in HIV Care. https://www.lgbtqiahealtheducation.org/wp-content/uploads/2016/09/Behavioral-Health-Integration-Webinar_Final.pdf

Kidd, J. D., Jackman, K. B., Barucco, R., Dworkin, J. D., Dolezal, C., Navalta, T. V., Belloir, J., & Bockting, W. O. (2021). Understanding the impact of the COVID-19 pandemic on the mental health of transgender and gender nonbinary individuals engaged in a longitudinal cohort study. *Journal of Homosexuality, 68*(4), 592–611. https://doi.org/10.1080/00918369.2020.1868185

Kline, N. S. (2020). Rethinking COVID-19 vulnerability: A call for LGBTQ+ im/migrant health equity in the United States during the pandemic. *Health Equity, 4*(1), 239–242. https://doi.org/10.1089/heq.2020.0012

Knutson, D., Kertz, S., Chambers-Baltz, S., Christie, M. B., Harris, E., & Perinchery, R. (2020, August 6). A pilot test of a text message-based transgender and nonbinary affirmative cognitive-behavioral intervention for anxiety and depression. *Psychology of Sexual Orientation and Gender Diversity, 8*(4), 440–450. http://dx.doi.org/10.1037/sgd0000438

Krause, K. D. (2021). Implications of the COVID-19 pandemic on LGBTQ communities. *Journal of Public Health Management and Practice, 27*(1), S69–S71. https://doi.org/10.1097/phh.0000000000001273

Kronenfeld, J. (2013). *Social determinants, health disparities and linkages to health and health care.* Emerald Group Publishing Limited.

Lavietes, M., & Ramos, E. (2022, March 20). *Nearly 240 anti-LGBTQ bills filed in 2022 so far, most of them targeting trans people.* NBC News. https://www.nbcnews.com/nbc-out/out-politics-and-policy/nearly-240-anti-lgbtq-bills-filed-2022-far-targeting-trans-people-rcna20418

Mandsager, P., Marier, A., Cohen, S., Fanning, M., Hauck, H., & Cheever, L. W. (2018). Reducing HIV-related health disparities in the health resources and service administration's Ryan White HIV/AIDS program. *American Journal of Public Health, Supplement 4, 108*(54), S246–S250. https://doi.org/10.2105/AJPH.2018.304689

Meyer, I. H. (2003). Prejudice, social stress, and mental health in lesbian, gay, and bisexual populations: Conceptual issues and research evidence. *Psychological Bulletin, 129*(5), 674–697. https://doi.org/10.1037/0033-2909.129.5.674

Mirza, S. A., & Baker, K. (2016, August 31). The impact of the Affordable Care Act on LGBTQ youth experiencing homelessness. *Center for American Progress.* https://cdn.americanprogress.org/wp-content/uploads/2016/08/30132612/LGBTQHomelessYouthBrief-FINALPDF.pdf?_ga=2.254054208.930158196.1616377535-968285068.1616377535

Nakamura, N., & Pope, M. (2013). Borders and margins: Giving voice to lesbian, gay, bisexual, and transgender immigrant experiences. *Journal of LGBT Issues in Counseling, 7*(2), 122–124. https://doi.org/10.1080/15538605.2013.785235

National Center for Transgender Equality. (2020, July). *The discrimination administration.* https://transequality.org/the-discrimination-administration

Nobili, A., Glazebrook, C., Bouman, W. P., Glidden, D., Baron-Cohen, S., Allison, C., Smith, P., & Arcelus, J. (2018). Autistic traits in treatment-seeking transgender adults. *Journal of Autism and Developmental Disorders, 48,* 3984–3994. https://doi.org/10.1007/s10803-018-3557-2

Pachankis, J. (2018). The scientific pursuit of sexual and gender minority mental health treatments: Toward evidence-based affirmative practice. *American Psychologist, 73*(9), 1207–1219. https://doi.org/10.1037/amp0000357

Pedersen, P. B. (2000). *Hidden messages in culture-centered counseling: A Triad Training Model.* Sage.

Petersen, S., Shrader, G., Hutchings, P., & Brake, K. (2011). Integrating health care: The clear advantage for underserved diverse populations. *Psychological Services, 8*(2), 69–81. https://doi.org/10.1037/a0023521

Phillips, G., Felt, D., Ruprecht, M. M., Wang, X., Xu, J., Perez-Bill, E., Bagnarol, R. M., Roth, J., Curry, C. W., & Beach, L. B. (2020). Addressing the disproportionate impacts of the COVID-19 pandemic on sexual and gender minority populations in the United States: Actions toward equity. *LGBT Health, 7*(6), 279–282. https://doi.org/10.1089/lgbt.2020.0187

Rettie, H., & Daniels, J. (2021). Coping and tolerance of uncertainty: Predictors and mediators of mental health during the COVID-19 pandemic. *American Psychologist, 76*(3), 427–437. http://dx.doi.org/10.1037/amp0000710

Rogers, B. G., Coats, C. S., Adams, E., Murphy, M., Stewart, C., Arnold, T., Chan, P. A., & Nunn, A. (2020). Development of telemedicine infrastructure at an LGBTQ+ clinic to support HIV prevention and care in response to COVID-19, Providence, RI. *AIDS and Behavior, 24*, 2743–2747. https://doi.org/10.1007/s10461-020-02895-1

Rosenbaum, S. (2011). The Patient Protection and Affordable Care Act: Implications for public health policy and practice. *Public health reports (Washington, DC: 1974), 126*(1), 130–135. https://doi.org/10.1177/003335491112600118

Salerno, J. P., Devadas, J., Pease, M., Nketia, B., & Fish, J. N. (2020). Sexual and gender minority stress amid the COVID-19 pandemic: Implications for LGBTQ young persons' mental health and well-being. *Public Health Reports, 135*(6), 721–727. https://doi.org/10.1177/0033354920954511

Salerno, J. P., Williams, N. D., & Gattamorta, K. A. (2020). LGBTQ populations: Psychologically vulnerable communities in the COVID-19 pandemic. *Psychological Trauma: Theory, Research, Practice, and Policy, 12*(1), 239–242. http://dx.doi.org/10.1037/tra0000837

Scroggs, B., Love, H. A., & Torgerson, C. (2020). COVID-19 and LGBTQ emerging adults: Risk in the face of social distancing. *Emerging Adulthood*, 1–6. https://doi.org/10.1177/2167696820968699

Sekoni, A. O., Gale, N. K., Manga-Atangana, B., Bhadhuri, A., & Jolly, K. (2017). The effects of educational curricula and training on LGBT-specific health issues for healthcare students and professionals: A mixed-method systematic review. *Journal of the International AIDS Society, 20*(21624), 1–13. http://dx.doi.org/10.7448/IAS.20.1.21624

Sibley, C. G., Greaves, L. M., Overall, N. C., Lee, C. H. J., Milojev, P., Houkamau, C. A., Wilson, M. S., Milfont, T. L., Duck, I. M., Vickers-Jones, R., & Barlow, F. K. (2020). *American Psychologist, 75*(5), 618–630. http://dx.doi.org/10.1037/amp00000662

Stanton, M. C., Ali, S., & Chaudhuri, S. (2017). Individual, social, and community-level predictors of wellbeing in a US sample of transgender and gender non-conforming individuals. *Culture, Health, & Sexuality, 19*(1), 32–49. http://dx.doi.org/10.1080/13691058.2016.1189596

Strang, J. F., Knaus, M., van der Misen, A., McGuire, J. K., Kenworthy, L., Caplan, R., Freeman, A., . . . Anthony, L. G. (2020). A clinical program for transgender and gender-diverse neurodiverse/Autistic adolescents developed through community-based participatory design. *Journal of Clinical Child & Adolescent Psychology, 50*(6), 730–745. https://doi.10.1080/15374416.2020.1731817

Substance Abuse and Mental Health Services Administration (SAMHSA). *Affordable Care Act enrollment assistance for LGBT communities: A resource for behavioral health providers.* https://www.samhsa.gov/sites/default/files/pep14-lgbtacaenrolla.pdf

Thoreson, R. (2022, February 25). *Texas officials threaten transgender children and families: Criminalizing medical care undermines rights.* Human Rights Watch. https://www.hrw.org/news/2022/02/25/texas-officials-threaten-transgender-children-and-families#

Thrower, E., Bretherton, I., Pang, K. C., Zajac, J. D., & Cheung, A. S. (2020). Prevalence of Autism Spectrum Disorder and Attention-Deficit Hyperactivity Disorder amongst individuals with Gender Dysphoria: A systematic review. *Journal of Autism and Developmental Disorders, 50*, 695–706. https://doi.org/10.1007/s10803-019-04298-1

Trevor Project. (2019). The National Survey on LGBTQ Youth Mental Health 2019. https://www.thetrevorproject.org/wp-content/uploads/2019/06/The-Trevor-Project-National-Survey-Results-2019.pdf

Trevor Project. (2021). The National Survey on LGBTQ Youth Mental Health 2019. https://www.thetrevorproject.org/survey-2021/

United States Department of Justice, Federal Bureau of Investigation. (2020, November). Hate Crime Statistics, 2019. https://ucr.fbi.gov/crime-in-the-u.s/2019/crime-in-the-u.s.-2019

US Department of Health and Human Services. (2020, February). Bulletin: HIPAA privacy and Novel Coronavirus. Office for Civil Rights. https://www.hhs.gov/sites/default/files/february-2020-hipaa-and-novel-coronavirus.pdf

US Department of Health and Human Services. (2016). *Advancing LGBT health and wellbeing: 2016 report of the HHS LGBT Policy Coordinating Committee.* https://www.hhs.gov/sites/default/files/2016-report-with-cover.pdf

World Professional Association for Transgender Health. (2012). Standards of care for the health of transsexual, transgender, and gender nonconforming people [7th Version]. https://www.wpath.org/publications/soc

Woznicki, N., Arriaga, A. S., Caporale-Berkowitz, N. A., & Parent, M. C. (2021). Parasocial relationships and depression among LGBQ emerging adults living with their parents during COVID-19: The potential for online support. *Psychology of Sexual Orientation and Gender Diversity, 8*(2), 228–237. http://dx.doi.org/10.1037/sgd0000458

Zimmerman, J. (2017). Models of private practice. Which practice is best? In S. Walfish, J. Barnett, & J. Zimmerman (Eds.), *Handbook of private practice: Keys to success for mental health practitioners* (pp. 15–21). Oxford.

Conclusion

INCREASING HEALTH AND WELL-BEING OF LGBTQ+ YOUTH AND EMERGING ADULTS: LESSONS LEARNED, QUESTIONS UNANSWERED

Richard A. Sprott, PhD, G. Nic Rider, PhD, LP, & Cristina L. Magalhães, PhD, LMHC

As noted by Dr. Eunice V. Avilés Faría in chapter 1, there is a need for further research about minority stress and its processes among children and adolescents, as much of the work on minority stress has been focused on adults. We also find that the field would benefit from emphasizing holistic health perspectives (i.e., the understanding that physical health impacts mental health and vice-versa), integrated-care approaches (i.e., care practices that value full integration of mental health with general health service delivery), and interdisciplinary team efforts targeting both the psychological and physical health needs of children, adolescents, and emerging adults. We intend this book to answer that need, by drawing our attention to the usefulness of minority stress theory, as well as multicultural, intersectional, and positive youth development frameworks. The focus on holistic health and integrated-care approaches prompted us to organize the book to address multiple systems of care and how mental health professionals face different challenges related to care integration in each system of care.

Summary of Findings and Lessons

Looking across the chapters in this book, we highlight some findings and lessons that stand out for us, in relation to the goals of the book.

- Minority stress theory continues to be a useful and productive framework for understanding the health needs of LGBTQ+ children, adolescents, and emerging adults, and the theory benefits from efforts to include intersectional factors in the theory's application to case conceptualization and treatment planning.
- Integrated care, both vertical and horizontal, incorporates a holistic approach to promoting optimum development and functioning of the whole person, which benefits LGBTQ+ children, adolescents, and emerging adults in effective ways, giving rise to new approaches to intervention across different systems of care.

- Care for transgender, nonbinary, and gender diverse youth is leading the way in modeling integrated care for LGBTQ+ youth and emerging adults and highlights the need for the field to approach the LGBTQ+ rainbow with awareness of the similarities and distinctiveness of each part of that rainbow.
- New opportunities for integrated care have developed as the American healthcare system adjusted to the Affordable Care Act. The need for mental health practice to become part of collaborative professional approaches to healthcare has also increased due to the COVID-19 pandemic.
- Radical healing as a framework draws our attention to both the distinctiveness of each part of the rainbow and other kinds of stigmatized identities, while emphasizing the commonality we all share for "an unconditional desire for human dignity, meaningful existence, and hope" (Ginwright, 2015, p. 35). It also calls attention to how systems of care might create or re-create power relations that silence the voices of LGBTQ+ adolescents and emerging adults and urges mental health providers to take action in helping remove institutional barriers to affirmative and client-centered care.
- LGBTQ+ children, adolescents, and emerging adults are resilient and have many strengths, which are essential to recognize and highlight in the course of treatment for providing effective care across different systems of health service delivery.

Gaps in our understanding and challenges in providing care are also apparent when viewing all of the chapters. In terms of theory, further work on understanding the mechanisms that lead to resilience and strengths when exposed to intersecting minority stressors would add to a more comprehensive theory of health and well-being for LGBTQ+ youth and emerging adults. Understanding how both intersectional minority stress mechanisms and resilience mechanisms change over the course of development as a function of changes in the individual and in the environment would have a beneficial impact on the provision of care as well.

Another area where we see the need for further work is the inclusion of an intersectionality framework in addressing the nuance and complexity of cases and situations. There is a critically important need to focus on how systems of care challenge, maintain, and perpetuate the stigma, discrimination, and marginalization individuals accessing healthcare services can experience and how the exposure to these stressors affect health. Tools that help guide and assist mental health practice in these complex cases are needed. Some of the recommendations offered by chapter authors point the way toward these needed professional developments in the field.

In terms of K–12 schools, we see the need for improving the resources that support the leadership in efforts to enhance integrated care in school settings. In colleges and universities, we need more resources for enhancing community engagement among LGBTQ+ students. In medical centers, we need more models and resources for how hospitals can engage with local LGBTQ+ communities to enhance their services and become better equipped to meet unique community needs. In child welfare and foster care systems, we also see the need for models and resources on how these systems can engage with local LGBTQ+ communities to facilitate youth's access to community supports. In homeless shelters, we see the need for integrated-care approaches and connections to LGBTQ+ community resources. In juvenile justice systems, a resilience and strengths-based approach is sought to address the needs of LGBTQ+ youth. LGBTQ+ community centers can also benefit from a resilience and strengths-based approach to providing services, as well as resources to develop services that would benefit collaboration with other systems of care. For mental health providers who are in private or independent practice, models and resources on how to increase collaboration and efforts to enhance integrated care would be of great benefit.

Chapter authors argued, in all of these systems of care, there is need for further training of personnel on issues that impact LGBTQ+ youth and emerging adults; need for addressing negative biases and assumptions held by clinicians, which often create obstacles in relationships between clinicians and clients and ultimately impact the quality of care provided to clients; and need for revisiting existing policies, procedures, and regulations that govern each institution and system, which may be interfering with care delivery in direct or indirect ways. Chapter authors also discussed how each system of care interacts with others, giving rise to questions on how to address the gaps that occur when each system is operating in its own silo.

A Possible Agenda for Research, Clinical Treatment, and Policy

MORE RESOURCES AND FUNDING

An agenda for addressing the gaps and cutting edges of our knowledge, the need for resources for clinical interventions, and the challenges in the institutional systems of care must include a general call for *more resources and funding*. Some systems of care are underfunded and struggle to provide mental health services. The funding mechanisms for research can be directed to address the gaps in knowledge that the chapter authors have identified. And funding for the development of clinical resources and the dissemination of those resources would enhance the care provided to LGBTQ+ youth and emerging adults. Addressing the need for funding and resources calls on mental health providers to be part of efforts to advocate for LGBTQ+ youth and emerging adults in policy arenas.

TRAIN MENTAL HEALTH PROVIDERS

In addition to funding and resources, *the training of more mental health providers* to address the complex and systemic aspects of the challenges and the strengths of LGBTQ+ youth and emerging adults needs to be on the agenda. We face many challenges to enhance integrated care and collaboration between systems of care. Training mental health providers to be effective leaders in integrated care and within and between systems of care will require new material and training resources to be developed. So the development and implementation of these trainings would help address the need for more skilled mental health providers.

SYSTEMS-BASED APPROACH REFINEMENT

Continued *refinement of a systems-based approach* will help address intersectional aspects of oppression that give rise to health disparities experienced by LGBTQ+ youth and emerging adults and include a focus on positive development, strengths, and resilience, as part of a coherent picture of the health and well-being of LGBTQ+ youth and emerging adults. The systems-based approach should inform research, clinical treatment, and policy. There are specific agenda items listed by the chapter authors, and we encourage the reader to examine relevant chapters for an expanded discussion of these specific items.

Summary

The overall purpose of the book is to improve the clinical practice of mental health professionals working within different systems of care, emphasizing integrated care in these contexts. The book aims to address three major gaps in the LGBTQ+ health literature, particularly in textbooks that can be used for training of mental health professionals: (1) information about the needs of children, adolescents, and emerging adults that are relevant to mental health clinicians (especially youth at younger stages of development); (2) frameworks for addressing LGBTQ+ clients' needs holistically (i.e., grounded in whole-person care principles that are based on an understanding that physical health impacts mental health and vice versa); and (3) practical recommendations for mental health clinicians working in different systems of care. The book is meant to be a teaching book; a presentation directed toward mental health care providers that orients the practitioner to current knowledge of health disparities for this population and best practices for competent care delivery in multiple systems of care.

The chapters on theoretical frameworks (section I) aim to (1) articulate major theoretical and/or practice frameworks that are relevant for mental health practice with this population, (2) provide a review of empirical studies that support these theories and/or frameworks, (3) identify gaps in the literature and future directions for clinically relevant research, and (4) discuss implications for mental health practice. Relevant theories and concepts that are included in section I chapters include: (1) minority stress theory, which helps clinicians understand unique types of challenges LGBTQ+ children, adolescents, and emerging adults face so clinicians can be prepared to address them in their practice; (2) intersectionality theory, which helps clinicians understand how structures of power and oppression affect LGBTQ+ people with multiple marginalized identities so they can practice competently with diverse clientele; (3) resilience-based frameworks, which help clinicians develop an appreciation for the importance of building strengths for coping with challenges and how this is important at all levels of preventive care (as opposed to focusing solely on fixing problems); (4) interdisciplinary frameworks, which help clinicians see themselves as part of a team of care providers who must work collaboratively to address the complex needs of their LGBTQ+ clients; and (5) a holistic approach to care, which helps clinicians stay attuned to the fact that mind and body are not separate entities and that psychological and physical wellness are interdependent.

The chapters on developmental stages/issues (section II) are less theoretical and more practice-focused than chapters in section I. Consistent with a holistic/integrated approach, they address physical and emotional well-being and emphasize interdisciplinary work. These chapters aim to (1) provide a review of relevant empirical- and practice-based literature for each of three developmental stages (childhood, adolescence, and emerging adulthood); (2) briefly discuss gaps and future directions for studies; (3) discuss implications for practice; and (4) include case studies, illustrating how issues might present and how principles of resilience-based practice, culturally sensitive care, and interdisciplinary work may be applied to meet the needs of the client and their family.

The chapters on site-specific contexts (section III) provide (1) a review of the literature covering pertinent issues/challenges or barriers to care for each setting; (2) a discussion about gaps in research and future directions; (3) a section for clinicians with considerations for practice; and (4) a section offering recommendations for policy making with the goal of improving quality of care in each specific setting, whenever applicable (e.g., hospitals, community-based agencies), and/or supporting the well-being of LGBTQ+ children, adolescents, and emerging adults in these settings (e.g., K–12 schools). Culturally competent, resilience-based, and holistic care approaches are emphasized in these chapters as well.

Working with the chapter authors has been a privilege. We have learned from each about their clinical practice and how they apply current approaches in mental health to their work with LGBTQ+ children, adolescents, and emerging adults. We hope that you, the reader, will learn something new, feel inspired to apply principles we cover in the book to your practice, and be encouraged to take the next step for you in addressing the health and well-being of LGBTQ+ children, adolescents, and emerging adults where you work and deliver care to your clients.

Reference

Ginwright, S. A. (2015). Radically healing black lives: A love note to justice. *New Directions for Student Leadership, 2015*(148), 33–44.

Appendix

LIST OF RESOURCES

This list includes resources recommended by chapter authors, organized by chapter and housed in three major sections: (1) books, articles, fact sheets, and presentations for professionals; (2) books for children; and (3) websites for professionals and clients.

Books, Articles, Fact Sheets, and Presentations for Professionals

CHAPTER 4

Berg, D., Tellawi, G., Anderson, S. O., & Rider, G. N. (2022). Beyond diagnosis: Prepubescent gender expansive children on the margins of clinical measures. *Infant and Child Development, 31*(3), e2311. https://doi.org/10.1002/icd.2311

Keo-Meier, C., & Ehrensaft, D. (Eds.) (2018). *The gender affirmative model: An interdisciplinary approach to supporting transgender and gender expansive children.* American Psychological Association.

Spencer, K. G., Berg, D. R., Bradford, N. J., Vencill, J., Tellawi, G., & Rider, G. N. (2021). The Gender Affirmative Lifespan Approach: A developmental model for clinical work with transgender and gender diverse children, adolescents, and adults. *Psychotherapy, 58*(1), 37–49. https://doi.org/10.1037/pst0000363

CHAPTER 8

Nicolazzo, Z. (2016). *Trans* in college: Transgender students' strategies for navigating campus life and the institutional politics of inclusion.* Stylus Publishing.

CHAPTER 12

DeWitt, P. (2012). *Dignity for all: Safeguarding LGBT students.* SAGE Publications.

GLSEN. (2016). *Educational exclusion: Drop out, push out, and the school-to-prison pipeline among LGBTQ youth.* https://www.glsen.org/sites/default/files/2019-11/Educational_Exclusion_2013.pdf

Mallett, C. (2015). *The school-to-prison pipeline: A comprehensive assessment.* Springer Publishing Company.

Meyer, E. (2010). *Gender and sexual diversity in schools.* Springer Netherlands.

Rider, G. N., & Abreu, R. (2017). *Cycles of injustices: LGBTQ youth in the juvenile justice system.* https://www.youtube.com/watch?v=lIkT5lFOHMc&ab_channel=AmericanPsychologicalAssociation

CHAPTER 14

American Psychological Association. (2020). *Guidelines for psychological practice with sexual minority persons.* Submitted to APA Council August 2020.

American Psychological Association. (2015). Guidelines for psychological practice with transgender and gender nonconforming people. *American Psychologist, 70*(9), 832– 864. https://www.apa.org/practice/guidelines/transgender.pdf

American Psychological Association. (2013). *Fact sheet: Gender diversity and transgender identity in children.* http://www.apadivisions.org/division-44/resources/advocacy/transgender-children.pdf

American Psychological Association. (2013). *Fact sheet: Gender diversity and transgender identity in adolescents.* http://www.apadivisions.org/division-44/resources/advocacy/transgender-adolescents.pdf

American Psychological Association. (2012). Guidelines for psychological practice with lesbian, gay, and bisexual clients. *American Psychologist, 67*(1), 10–42.

Brill, S., & Pepper, R. (2018). *The transgender teen: A handbook for families and professionals.* Cleis Press, Inc.

Downs, A. (2006). *The velvet rage: Overcoming the pain of growing up gay in a straight man's world* (second ed.). Hachette Publishing.

Coleman et al. (2011). World Professional Association for Transgender Health (WPATH) Standards of Care (SOC) for the health of transsexual, transgender, and gender-nonconforming people, Version 7. *International Journal of Transgenderism, 13,* 165–232.

Frankel, L. (2017). *This is how it always is: A novel.* Flatiron Books.

Singh, A. (2018). *The queer and transgender resilience workbook: Skills for navigating sexual orientation and gender expression.* New Harbinger.

Skinta, M., & Curtin, A. (2016). *Mindfulness and acceptance for gender and sexual minorities: A clinician's guide to fostering compassion, connection and equity using contextual strategies.* Context Press.

Storck, K. (2018). *The gender identity workbook for kids: A guide to exploring who you are.* Harbinger Publications.

Books for Children

CHAPTER 4

Bergman, S. B. (2012). *The adventures of Tulip, birthday wish fairy* (S. Malik, illus). Flamingo Rampant.

dePaola, T. (1979). *Oliver Button is a sissy*. Harcourt Mifflin.
Ewert, M. (2008). *10,000 dresses* (R. Ray, illus). Triangle Square.
Fabikant, A. (2013). *When Kayla was Kyle* (J. Levine, illus). Avid Readers Publishing.
Hall, M. (2018). *Red: A crayon's story*. Greenwillow Books.
Herthel, J., & Jennings, J. (2014). *I am Jazz* (S. McNicholas, illus). Dial.
Hoffman, S., & Hoffman, I. (2014). *Jacob's new dress* (C. Case, illus). Albert Whitman & Company.
Keo-Meier, C. (2017). *Stacy's not a girl* (J. Yang, illus). Self-published.
Kiernan-Johnson, E. (2013). *Roland Humphrey is wearing a what?* (K. Revenaugh, illus). Huntley Rahara Press.
Kilodavis, C. (2010). *My princess boy* (S. DeSimone, illus). KD Talent LLC.
LaBelle, S. (2015). *The genderific coloring book*. AssignedMale.
Love, J. (2018). *Julian is a mermaid*. Candlewick.
Parr, T. (2016). *Be who you are*. Little, Brown.
Rothblatt, P. (2011). *All I want to be is me*. CreateSpace Publishing.
Silverberg, C., & Smyth, F. (2015). *Sex is a funny word: A book about bodies, feelings, and you*. Seven Stories Press.
Simon, R. (2020). *The every body book: The LGBTQ+ inclusive guide for kids about sex, gender, bodies and families* (N. Grigni, illus). Jessica Kingsley Publishers.
Thorn, T. (2019). *It feels good to be yourself: A book about gender identity* (N. Grigni, illus). Henry Holt.
Walton, J. (2018). *Introducing Teddy* (D. MacPherson, illus). Bloomsbury.

Websites for Professionals and Clients

CHAPTER 3

National Center for Transgender Equality (https://transequality.org/)
Scarleteen: Sex Ed for the Real World (https://www.scarleteen.com/)
Transgender Law Center Resources (https://transgenderlawcenter.org/resources/youth)
Trans Lifeline (https://translifeline.org/)
Trans Student Educational Resources (https://www.facebook.com/transstudent/)

CHAPTER 4

Amaze: Sex Ed for Young Adolescents (www.amaze.org)
Amaze Jr.: Sex Ed for Young Children (www.amaze.org/jr)
Gender Wheel (www.genderwheel.com)

CHAPTER 6

American Academy of Pediatrics: LGBTQ+ Health and Wellness (https://www.aap.org/en/patient-care/lgbtq-health-and-wellness/)
American Psychological Association: LGBT Resources for Practitioners (https://www.apa.org/pi/lgbt/resources/practitioner/)

American Psychological Association: Practice Guidelines for LGB Clients (https://www.apa.org/pi/lgbt/resources/guidelines)
CDC: LGBTQ Youth Resources (https://www.cdc.gov/lgbthealth/youth-resources.htm)
Planned Parenthood: Info and Resources for LGBTQ Teens and Allies (https://www.plannedparenthood.org/learn/teens/lgbtq/info-and-resources-lgbtq-teens-and-allies)

CHAPTER 7

Gender Spectrum (https://genderspectrum.org/)
GLSEN: Gay Lesbian Straight Education Network (https://www.glsen.org/)
Welcoming Schools (https://welcomingschools.org/)

CHAPTER 8

Campus Pride (https://www.campuspride.org/)
Consortium of Higher Education LGBT Resource Professionals (https://www.lgbtcampus.org/)

CHAPTER 14

APA: LGBT Resources and Publications (https://www.apa.org/pi/lgbt/resources)
PFLAG (Parents, Families, and Friends of Lesbians and Gays) (https://www.pflag.org)
Society for the Psychology of Sexual Orientation and Gender Identity (https://www.apadivisions.org/division-44)
Trans Youth Family Allies (http://www.imatyfa.org/)
Trevor Project (https://www.thetrevorproject.org/)

Bibliography

Abbas, A. M., Fathy, S. K., Mohamed, A. M., Omar, F. A., & Fahmi, S. K. (2020). Effects of COVID-19 pandemic on children's mental health. *Archives of Health Science, 4*(1), 1–4. https://doi.org/10.31829/2641-7456/ahs2020-4(1)-130

Abes, E. S., & Jones, S. R. (2004). Meaning-making capacity and the dynamics of lesbian college students' multiple dimensions of identity. *Journal of College Student Development, 45*(6), 612–632. https://doi.org/10.1353/csd.2004.0065

Abram, K., Teplin, L., Charles, D., Longworth, S., McClelland, G., & Dulcan, M. (2004). Posttraumatic stress disorder and trauma in youth in juvenile detention. *Archives of General Psychiatry, 61*, 403–410.

Abreu, R. L., Rosenkrantz, D. E., Ryser-Oatman, J. T., Rostosky, S. S., & Riggle, E. D. (2019). Parental reactions to transgender and gender diverse children: A literature review. *Journal of GLBT Family Studies, 15*(5), 461–485. https://doi.org/10.1080/1550428X.2019.1656132

Academy of Integrative Health and Medicine. (2021). AIHM core values. https://aihm.org/vision

Achenbach, T. M., & Rescorla, L. A. (2001). *Manual for the ASEBA school-age forms & profiles.* University of Vermont, Research Center for Children, Youth, & Families.

Agana, M. G., Greydanus, D. E., Indyk, J. A., Calles, J. L. Jr., Kushner, J., Leibowitz, S., Chelvakumar, G., & Cabral, M. D. (2019). Caring for the transgender adolescent and young adult: Current concepts of an evolving process in the 21st century. *Disease-a-Month, 65*(9), 303–356. https://doi.org/10.1016/j.disamonth.2019.07.004

Aguayo-Romero, R. A. (2021). (Re)centering black feminism into intersectionality research. *American Journal of Public Health, 111*(1), 101–103. https://doi.org/10.2105/AJPH.2020.306005

Allen, S., Ruiz, M., & O'Rourke, A. (2016). Differences in the prevalence of risk behaviors between heterosexual and lesbian, gay, bisexual, and questioning (LGBQ) female adolescents in the juvenile justice system. *Journal of Gay & Lesbian Social Services, 28*, 171–175.

Allwood, M. A., Bell, D. J., & Horan, J. (2011). Posttrauma numbing of fear, detachment, and arousal predict delinquent behaviors in early adolescence. *Journal of Clinical Child and Adolescent Psychology, 40*(5), 659–667. https://doi.org/10.1080/15374416.2011.597081

Almeida, J., Johnson, R. M., Corliss, H. L., Molnar, B. E., & Azrael, D. (2009). Emotional distress among LGBT youth: The influence of perceived discrimination based on sexual orientation. *Journal of Youth and Adolescence, 38*(7), 1001–1014. https://doi.org/10.1007/s10964-009-9397-9

Alvis, L. M., Douglas, R., Shook, N. J., & Oosterhoff, B. (Preprint). Associations between adolescents' prosocial experiences and mental health during the COVID-19 pandemic. https://www.researchgate.net/publication/341225361

Alvy, L., Hughes, T., Kristjanson, A., & Wilsnack, S. (2013). Sexual identity group differences in child abuse and neglect. *Journal of Interpersonal Violence, 28*, 2088–2111.

American College Health Association. (2015). Trans-inclusive college health programs. https://www.acha.org/documents/Resources/Guidelines/Trans-Inclusive_College_Health_Programs.pdf

American Psychiatric Association (APA). (n.d.). Best practice highlights: Lesbian, gay, bisexual, transgender and people who may be questioning their sexual orientation or sexual identity (LGBTQ). https://www.psychiatry.org/File%20Library/Psychiatrists/Cultural-Competency/Treating-Diverse-Populations/Best-Practices-LGBTQ-Patients.PDF

American Psychiatric Association. (1987). *Diagnostic and statistical manual of mental disorders* (3rd ed., revised). American Psychiatric Association.

American Psychiatric Association. (2000). *Diagnostic and statistical manual of mental disorders* (4th ed.). American Psychiatric Association.

American Psychiatric Association. (2013). Diagnostic and statistical manual of mental disorders (5th ed.). American Psychiatric Association

American Psychological Association. (2013). Guidelines for psychological practice in health care delivery systems. *American Psychologist, 68*(1), 1–6. https://www.apa.org/pubs/journals/features/delivery-systems.pdf

American Psychological Association. (2016). Stress in America: The impact of discrimination. Stress in America™ Survey. https://www.apa.org/news/press/releases/stress/2015/impact-of-discrimination.pdf

American School Counselor Association. (2016). *The professional school counselor and LGBTQ youth*. ASCA Position Statements. https://schoolcounselor.org/asca/media/asca/PositionStatements/PS_LGBTQ.pdf

American School Counselor Association. (2019). *ASCA national model: A framework for school counseling programs* (4th ed.). https://www.schoolcounselor.org/school-counselors-members/asca-national-model

Ansara, Y. G., & Hegarty, P. (2012). Cisgenderism in psychology: Pathologizing and misgendering children from 1999 to 2008. *Psychology & Sexuality, 3*, 1–24. https://doi.org/10.1080/19419899.2011.576696

Antebi-Gruszka, N., Cain, D., Millar, B. M., Parsons, J. T., & Rendina, H. J. (2021). Stress-related growth among transgender women: Measurement, correlates, and insights for clinical interventions. *Journal of Homosexuality*, 1–24. https://doi.org/10.1080/00918369.2021.1921511

Antebi-Gruszka, N., Friedman, A. A., & Schrimshaw, E. W. (2020). Character strengths and their associations with well-being and mental distress among lesbian, gay, bisexual, and queer individuals. *Journal of Gay & Lesbian Social Services: The Quarterly Journal of Community & Clinical Practice*. https://doi.org/10.1080/10538720.2020.1859424

Antrosio, Jason. "Is social inequality inevitable?" *Living Anthropologically* (blog), April 22, 2017. https://www.livinganthropologically.com/anthropology-2017/is-social-inequality-inevitable/

Arafat, M. Y., Zaman, S., & Hawlader, M. D. H. (2021). Telemedicine improves mental health in COVID-19 pandemic. *Journal of Global Health, 11*, 1–4. https://doi.org/10.7189/jogh.11.03004

Aragon, J., Arellano, L. M., Brazzel, P., Cardenas, J., Catalde, T., Cottrill, M., Giambona, M., Manos, S., McMillian, K., Parsons, J., Peevy, J., Pianta, R., Dalman-Schroeder, M., Sopp, T. J., Strear, M., Thomas, S., Topalian, J., Uresti, A., Weglarz, L. . . . Zavalza, O. (2020).

Fostering the whole child: A guide to school-based mental health professionals. California Association of School Psychologists. https://casponline.org/pdfs/spw/SBMHP%20Guide%20Book%20v4.pdf

Aragon, S. R., Poteat, V. P., Espelage, D. L., & Koenig, B. W. (2014). The influence of peer victimization on educational outcomes for LGBTQ and non-LGBTQ high school students. *Journal of LGBT Youth, 11*(1), 1–19. https://doi.org/10.1080/19361653.2014.840761

Arcelus, J., & Bouman, W. (2015). Current and future direction of gender dysphoria and gender incongruence research. *Journal of Sexual Medicine, 12*, 2226–2228.

Ard, K. L., & Makadon, H. J. (2011). Addressing intimate partner violence in lesbian, gay, bisexual, and transgender patients. *Journal of General Internal Medicine, 26*(8), 930–933. https://doi.org/10.1007/s11606-011-1697-6

Arnett, J. J. (2000). Emerging adulthood: A theory of development from the late teens through the twenties. *American Psychologist, 55*(5), 469–480. https://doi.org/10.1037/0003-066X.55.5.469

Arnold, E. A., & Bailey, M. M. (2009). Constructing home and family: How the ballroom community supports African American GLBTQ youth in the face of HIV/AIDS. *Journal of Gay and Lesbian Social Services, 21*(2–3), 171–188. https://doi.org/10.1080/10538720902772006

Arora, P. G., Kelly, J., & Goldstein, T. R. (2016). Current and future school psychologists' preparedness to work with LGT students: Role of education and gay-straight alliances. *Psychology in the Schools, 53*(7), 722–735. https://doi.org/10.1002/pits.21942

Arvidson, J., Kinniburgh, K., Howard, K., Spinazzola, J., Strothers, H., Evans, M., . . . Blaustein, M. E. (2011). Treatment of complex trauma in young children: Developmental and cultural considerations in application of the ARC intervention model. *Journal of Child & Adolescent Trauma, 4*(1), 34–51.

Asakura, K. (2016). Extraordinary acts to "show up": Conceptualizing resilience of LGBTQ youth. *Youth & Society, 51*(2), 268–285. https://doi.org/10.1177/0044118x16671430

Asakura, K. (2019). Extraordinary acts to "show up": Conceptualizing resilience of LGBTQ youth. *Youth & Society, 51*(2), 268–285. https://doi.org/10.1177/0044118X16671430

Ashley, F. (2019). Gatekeeping hormone replacement therapy for transgender patients is dehumanising. *Journal of Medical Ethics, 45*(7), 480 LP–482. https://doi.org/10.1136/medethics-2018-105293

Associated Press, & Yurcaba, J. (2022, April 8). *Alabama governor signs bill criminalizing transgender healthcare for minors.* NBC News. https://www.nbcnews.com/nbc-out/out-politics-and-policy/alabama-governor-signs-bill-criminalizing-transgender-health-care-mino-rcna23674

Atterbury, A. (2022, March 28). *DeSantis signs Florida's contentious LGBTQ bill into law.* Politico. https://www.politico.com/news/2022/03/28/desantis-signs-floridas-contentious-lgbtq-bill-into-law-00020966

Austin, A., & Craig, S. L. (2015). Transgender affirmative cognitive behavioral therapy: Clinical considerations and applications. *Professional Psychology: Research and Practice, 46*(1), 21.

Baams, L. (2018). Disparities for LGBTQ and gender nonconforming adolescents. *Pediatrics, 141*(5), e20173004.

Baams, L., Grossman, A. H., & Russell, S. T. (2015). Minority stress and mechanisms of risk for depression and suicidal ideation among lesbian, gay, and bisexual youth. *Developmental Psychology, 51*(5), 688–696. https://doi.org/10.1037/a0038994

Baams, L., & Russell, S. T. (2021). Gay-Straight Alliances, and mental health: Associations for students of color and LGBTQ students. *Youth & Society, 53*(2), 211–229. https://doi.org/10.1177/0044118X20951045

Baams, L., Wilson, B., & Russell, S. (2019). LGBTQ youth in unstable housing and foster care. *Pediatrics, 143*(3), e20174211.

Badgett, M. L., Choi, S.-K., & Wilson, B. D. M. (2019). LGBT poverty in the United States: A study of differences between sexual orientation and gender identity groups. Williams Institute. https://williamsinstitute.law.ucla.edu/wp-content/uploads/National-LGBT-Poverty-Oct-2019.pdf

Bailey, M. M. (2014). Engendering space: Ballroom culture and the spatial practice of possibility in Detroit. *Gender, Place & Culture: A Journal of Feminist Geography, 21*(4), 489–507.

Bain, C. L., Grzanka, P. R., & Crowe, B. J. (2016). Toward a queer music therapy: The implications of queer theory for radically inclusive music therapy. *The Arts in Psychotherapy, 50,* 22–33.

Baldwin, A., Dodge, B., Schick, V. R., Light, B., Scharrs, P. W., Herbenick, D., & Fortenberry, J. D. (2018). Transgender and genderqueer individuals' experiences with health care providers: What's working, what's not, and where do we go from here? *Journal of Health Care for the Poor and Underserved, 29*(4), 1300–1318. https://doi.org/10.1353/hpu.2018.0097

Balsam, K. F., Matsuno, E., Friedman, A., & Rana, V. (2020). Development and initial evaluation of the LGBTQ+ COVID-19 Concerns Scale. *Annals of LGBTQ Public and Population Health, 1*(4), 292–299. http://dx.doi.org/10.1891/LGBTQ-20-00047

Balsam, K. F., Molina, Y., Beadnell, B., Simoni, J. M., & Walters, K. (2011). Measuring multiple minority stress: The LGBT People of Color Microaggressions Scale. *Cultural Diversity and Ethnic Minority Psychology, 17,* 163–174.

Banerjee, D., & Nair, V. S. (2020). "The untold side of COVID-19": Struggle and perspectives of the sexual minorities. *Journal of Psychosexual Health, 2*(2), 113–120. https://doi.org/10.1177/2631831820939017

Barba, A., Mooney, M., Giovanni, K., Clarke, M., Grady, J. B., & Cohen, J. A. (n.d.). *Identifying the intersection of trauma and sexual orientation and gender identity part I: Key considerations.* National Center for Child Traumatic Stress.

Barger, B. T., Obedin-Maliver, J., Capriotti, M. R., Lunn, M. R., & Flentje, A. (2021). Characterization of substance use among underrepresented sexual and gender minority participants in the Population Research in Identity and Disparities for Equality (PRIDE) study. *Substance Abuse, 41*(1), 1–12. https://doi.org/10.1080/08897077.2019.1702610

Barnard, E. P., Dhar, C. P., Rothenberg, S. S., Menke, M. N., Witchel, S. F., Montano, G. T., Orwig, K. E., & Valli-Pulaski, H. (2019). Fertility preservation outcomes in adolescent and young adult feminizing transgender patients. *Pediatrics, 144*(3). https://doi.org/10.1542/peds.2018-3943

Barrett, B., & Bound, A. (2015). A critical discourse analysis of *no promo homo* policies in US schools. *Educational Studies, 51,* 267–283.

Basile, K. C., Clayton, H. B., DeGue, S., Gilford, J. W., Vagi, K. J., Suarez, N. A., . . . Lowry, R. (2020). Interpersonal violence victimization among high school students—youth risk behavior survey, United States, 2019. *MMWR supplements, 69*(1), 28.

Bauermeister, J. A., Goldenberg, T., Connochie, D., Jadwin-Cakmak, L., & Stephenson, R. (2016). Psychosocial disparities among racial/ethnic minority transgender young adults and young men who have sex with men living in Detroit. *Transgender Health, 1,* 279–290. https://doi.org/10.1089/trgh.2016.0027

Baumeister, R. F., & Leary, M. R. (1995). The need to belong: Desire for interpersonal attachments as a fundamental human motivation. *Psychological Bulletin, 117*(3), 497–529.

Bearse, M. L. (2012). Becoming who we are meant to be: Native Americans with two-spirit, LGBT, and/or related tribal identities. In S. K. Fisher, J. M. Poirier, & G. M. Blau (Eds.), *Improving emotional & behavioral outcomes for LGBT youth: A guide for professionals* (pp. 87–109). Brookes Publishing.

Beck, M. J. (2018). Lead by example: A phenomenological study of school counselor-principal team experiences with LGBT students. *Professional School Counseling, 21*(1), 1–13. https://doi.org/10.1177/ 2156759X18793838

Beck, M. J., & Wikoff, H. D. (2020). Professional development is really key: Experiences of school counselors engaging in professional development focused on LGBTQ youth. *Professional School Counseling, 24*(1), 1–11. https://doi.org/ 10.1177/2156759X20952062

Becker, M. A. S., Roberts, S. F. N., Ritts, S. M., Branagan, W. T., Warner, A. R., & Clark, S. L. (2017). Supporting transgender college students: Implications for clinical intervention and campus prevention. *Journal of College Student Psychotherapy, 67*(2), 161–173. https://doi.org/10.1080/07448481.2018.1465060

Becker, S., & Kerig, P. K. (2011). Posttraumatic stress symptoms are associated with the frequency and severity of delinquency among detained boys. *Journal of Clinical Child and Adolescent Psychology, 40*, 765–771.

Beckwith, N., McDowell, M. J., Reisner, S. L., Zaslow, S., Weiss, R. D., Mayer, K. H., & Keuroghlian, A. S. (2019). Psychiatric epidemiology of transgender and nonbinary adult patients at an urban health center. *LGBT Health, 6*(2), 51–61. https://doi.org/10.1089/lgbt.2018.0136

Begun, S., & Kattari, S. K. (2016). Conforming for survival: Associations between transgender visual conformity/passing and homelessness experiences. *Journal of Gay & Lesbian Social Services, 28*(1), 54–66. https://doi.org/10.1080/10538720.2016.1125821

Beh, H. G., & Diamond, M. (2000). An emerging ethical and medical dilemma: Should physicians perform sex assignment surgery on infants with ambiguous genitalia. *Michigan Journal of Gender & Law, 7*(1), 1–63.

Beharry, M., Harpin, S., Al Makadma, A., Ammerman, S., Eisenstein, E., Warf, C., Yeo, M., & Auerswald, C. L. (2018). The healthcare needs and rights of youth experiencing homelessness society for adolescent health and medicine. *Journal of Adolescent Health, 63*(3), 372–75.

Bender, K., Brown, S. M., Thompson, S. J., Ferguson, K. M., & Langenderfer, L. (2015). Multiple victimizations before and after leaving home associated with PTSD, depression, and substance use disorder among homeless youth. *Child Maltreatment, 20*(2), 115–124.

Berg, D., & Edwards-Leeper, L. (2018). Child and family assessment. In C. Keo-Meier & D. Ehrensaft (Eds.), *The gender affirmative model: An interdisciplinary approach to supporting transgender and gender expansive children* (pp. 101–124). American Psychological Association.

Berg, D., Spencer, K., McGuire, J., Becker-Warner, R., Vencill, J. A., & Catalpa, J. (2017, January). The Gender Affirmative Lifespan Approach: Promoting positive identity by building resiliency, increasing gender literacy, moving beyond the binary, and developing sex-positive pleasure and satisfaction. In G. Knudson (Chair), *WPATH presents: The inaugural USPATH scientific conference*. Symposium conducted at the meeting of the United States Professional Association of Transgender Health, Los Angeles, CA.

Berlan, E., Corliss, H., Field, A., Goodman, E., & Austin, S. (2010). Sexual orientation and bullying among adolescents in growing up today study. *Journal Adolescent Health, 46*(4), 366–371.

Best Colleges. (2019). College guide for undocumented students. https://www.bestcolleges.com/resources/undocumented-students-guide/

Bettinger, T. V. (2010). Ethical and methodolgocial complexities in research involving sexual minorities. *New Horizons in Adult Education and Human Resource Development, 24*(1), 43–58. http://education.fiu.edu/newhorizons

Bhattacharya, T. (2017). Introduction: Mapping social reproduction theory. In *Social reproduction theory: Remapping class, recentering oppression* (pp. 1–20). Pluto Press. http://doi.org/10.2307/j.ctt1vz494j

Bidell, M. P., & Stepleman, L. M. (2017). An interdisciplinary approach to lesbian, gay, bisexual, and transgender clinical competence, professional training, and ethical care: Introduction to the special issue. *Journal of Homosexuality, 64*(10), 1305–1329. https://doi.org/10.1080/00918369.2017.1321360

Bilodeau, B. L., & Renn, K. (2005). Analysis of LGBT identity development models and implications for practice. *New Directions for Student Services, 25*–39.

Blaustein, M. E., & Kinniburgh, K. M. (2010). *Treating traumatic stress in children and adolescents*. Guilford Press.

Blondeel, K., de Vasconcelos, S., García-Moreno, C., Stephenson, R., Temmerman, M., & Toskin, I. (2018). Violence motivated by perception of sexual orientation and gender identity: A systematic review. *Bulletin of the World Health Organization, 96*(1), 29–41L. https://doi.org/10.2471/BLT.17.197251

Blosnich, J. R., Cassese, E. C., Friedman, M. R., Coulter, R. W. S., Sang, J. M., Matthews, D. D., & Mair, C. (2019). Religious Freedom Restoration Acts and sexual minority population health in the United States. *American Journal of Orthopsychiatry, 89*(6), 675–681.

Bockting, W. O. (2014). Transgender identity development. In D. L. Tolman & L. Diamond (Eds.), *APA handbook of sexuality and psychology, vol. 1: Person-based approaches* (pp. 739–758). American Psychological Association.

Bockting, W. O. (2015). Internalized transphobia. In A. Bolin & P. Whelehan (Eds.), *International encyclopedia of human sexuality*. https://doi.org/10.1002/9781118896877.wbiehs236

Bockting, W. O., Miner, M. H., Swinburne Romine, R. E., Hamilton, A., & Coleman, E. (2013). Stigma, mental health, and resilience in an online sample of the US transgender population. *American Journal of Public Health, 103*(5), 943–951. https://doi.org/10.2105/AJPH.2013.301241

Bond, B. J., Hefner, V., & Drogos, K. L. (2009). Information-seeking practices during the sexual development of lesbian, gay, and bisexual individuals: The influence and effects of coming out in a mediated environment. *Sexuality & Culture, 13*(1), 32–50. https://doi.org/10.1007/s12119-008-9041-y

Borgogna, N. C., McDermott, R. C., Aita, S. L., & Kridel, M. M. (2019). Anxiety and depression across gender and sexual minorities: Implications for transgender, gender nonconforming, pansexual, demisexual, asexual, queer, and questioning individuals. *Psychology of Sexual Orientation and Gender Diversity, 6*(1), 54–63. https://doi.org/10.1037/sgd0000306

Boskey, E. R. (2014). Understanding transgender identity development in childhood and adolescence. *American Journal of Sexuality Education, 9*(4), 445–463. https://doi.org/10.1080/15546128.2014.973131

Bourgois, P., Holmes, S. M., Sue, K., & Quesada, J. (2017). Structural vulnerability: Operationalizing the concept to address health disparities in clinical care. *Academic Medicine: Journal of the Association of American Medical Colleges, 92*(3), 299.

Bowleg, L. (2012). The problem with the phrase women and minorities: Intersectionality—an important theoretical framework for public health. *American Journal of Public Health, 102*(7), 1267–1273. https://doi.org/10.2105/AJPH.2012.300750

Bowleg, L. (2017). Intersectionality: An underutilized but essential theoretical framework for social psychology. In B. Gough (Ed.), *Palgrave handbook of critical social psychology* (pp. 507–530). MacMillan Publishers Ltd.

Bowleg, L. (2020). We're not all in this together: On COVID-19, intersectionality, and structural inequality. *American Journal of Public Health, 110*(7), 917. https://doi.org/10.2105/AJPH.2020.305766

Bowleg, L. (2021). Evolving intersectionality within public health: From analysis to action. *American Journal of Public Health, 111*(1), 88–90. https://doi.org/10.2105/AJPH.2020.306031

Boyd, R. (2014). African American disproportionality and disparity in child welfare: Toward a comprehensive conceptual framework. *Children and Youth Services Review, 37*, 15–27.

Bradford, N. J., DeWitt, J., Decker, J., Berg, D. R., Spencer, K. G., & Ross, M. W. (2018). Sex education and transgender youth: 'Trust means material by and for queer and trans people.' *Sex Education.* https://doi.org/10.1080/14681811.2018.1478808

Braun, V., & Clarke, V. (2006). Using thematic analysis in qualitative research. *Qualitative Research in Psychology, 3*(2), 77–101.

Braveman, P., Egerter, S., & Williams, D. R. (2011). The social determinants of health: Coming of age. *Annual Review of Public Health, 32*(1), 381–398.

Brennan, J. M., Dunham, K. J., Bowlen, M., Davis, K., Ji, G., & Cochran, B. N. (2021). Inconcealable: A cognitive–behavioral model of concealment of gender and sexual identity and associations with physical and mental health. *Psychology of Sexual Orientation and Gender Diversity, 8*(1), 80–93. https://doi.org/10.1037/sgd0000424

Breslow, A. S., Brewster, M. E., Velez, B. L., Wong, S., Geiger, E., & Soderstrom, B. (2015). Resilience and collective action: Exploring buffers against minority stress for transgender individuals. *Psychology of Sexual Orientation and Gender Diversity, 2*(3), 253–265. https://doi.org/10.1037/sgd0000117

Brewster, M. E., Velez, B. L., Mennicke, A., & Tebbe, E. (2014). Voices from beyond: A thematic content analysis of transgender employees' workplace experiences. *Psychology of Sexual Orientation and Gender Diversity, 1*(2), 159–169.

Bronfenbrenner, U. (1979). *The ecology of human development: Experiments by nature and design.* Harvard University Press.

Bronfenbrenner, U. (1999). Environments in developmental perspective: Theoretical and operational models. In S. L. Friedman & T. D. Wachs (Eds.), *Measuring environment across the life span: Emerging methods and concepts* (pp. 3–28). American Psychological Association Press.

Bronfenbrenner, U. (2001). The bioecological theory of human development. In N. J. Smelser & P. B. Baltes (Eds.), *International encyclopedia of the social and behavioral sciences* (Vol. 10, pp. 6963–6970). Elsevier.

Brooks, S. (2016). Staying in the hood: Black lesbian and transgender women and identity management in North Philadelphia. *Journal of Homosexuality, 63*(12), 1573–1593. https://doi.org/10.1080/00918369.2016.1158008

Brooks, V. R. (1981). *Minority stress and lesbian women.* Lexington Books.

Brown, A. M. (2017). *Emergent strategy: Shaping change.* AK Press.

Brownfield, J. M., Brown, C., Jeevanba, S. B., & VanMattson, S. B. (2018). More than simply getting bi: An examination of coming out growth for bisexual individuals. *Psychology of Sexual Orientation and Gender Diversity, 5*(2), 220–232. https://doi.org/10.1037/sgd0000282

Bruce, D., Harper, G. W., & Bauermeister, J. A. (2015). Minority stress, positive identity development, and depressive symptoms: Implications for resilience among sexual minority male youth. *Psychology of Sexual Orientation and Gender Diversity, 2*(3), 287–296. https://doi.org/10.1037/sgd0000128

Budge, S. L. (2015). Psychotherapists as gatekeepers: An evidence-based case study highlighting the role and process of letter writing for transgender clients. *Psychotherapy, 52*(3), 287–297. https://doi.org/10.1037/pst0000034

Budge, S. L., Belcourt, S., Conniff, J., Parks, R., Pantalone, D. W., & Katz-Wise, S. L. (2018). A grounded theory study of the development of trans youths' awareness of coping with gender identity. *Journal of Child and Family Studies, 27*(5), 3048–3061. https://doi.org/10.1007/s10826-018-1136-y

Buikstra, E., Ross, H., King, C. A., Baker, P. G., Hegney, D., McLachlan, K., & Rogers, C. C. (2010). The components of resilience-Perceptions of an Australian rural community. *Journal of Community Psychology, 38*(8), 975.

Bullard, J. R. (2020). *School social workers and perceived barriers when providing services to LGBTQ children* [Doctoral dissertation, Walden University]. https://scholarworks.waldenu.edu/dissertations/9539

Burns, C., Garcia, A., & Wolgin, P. E. (2013). Living in dual shadows: LGBT undocumented immigrants. Center for American Progress. https://www.americanprogress.org/wp-content/uploads/2013/03/LGBTUndocumentedReport-5.pdf

Burton, C. M., Marshal, M. P., Chisolm, D. J., Sucato, G. S., & Friedman, M. S. (2013). Sexual minority-related victimization as a mediator of mental health disparities in sexual minority youth: A longitudinal analysis. *Journal of Youth and Adolescence, 42*(3), 394–402. https://doi.org/10.1007/s10964-012-9901-5

Byrd, R., & Hays, D. G. (2013). Evaluating a safe space training for school counselors and trainees using a randomized control group design. *Professional School Counseling, 17*(1), 20–31. https://doi.org/10.1177/2156759X0001700103

Campus Pride Trans Policy Clearinghouse. (2022). https://www.campuspride.org/tpc/nondiscrimination/

Campus Pride. (2016). *Shame list: The absolute worst campuses for LGBTQ youth.* https://www.campuspride.org/shamelist

Canadian Institute for Substance Use Research (CISUR). (2017). Understanding substance use: A health promotion perspective. https://www.heretohelp.bc.ca/infosheet/understanding-substance-use-a-health-promotion-perspective

Caraves, J. (2018). Straddling the school-to-prison pipeline and gender non-conforming microagressions as a Latina lesbian. *Journal of LGBT Youth, 15*, 52–69.

Carney, V. (2017). Community connectedness within the LGBT* community. *Honors Projects.* https://scholarworks.bgsu.edu/honorsprojects/240

Carpenter, C. S., Eppink, S. T., & Gonzales, G. (2020). Transgender status, gender identity, and socioeconomic outcomes in the United States. *ILR Review, 73*(3), 573–599. https://doi.org/10.1177/0019793920902776

Carrión-Santiago, K., Francia-Martínez, M., Esteban, C., & Rivera-Mercado, H. (2016). Familias homoparentales: Mitos y realidades. In M. Vázquez-Rivera, A. Martínez-Taboas, M. Francia-Martínez, & J. Toro-Alfonso (Eds.), *LGBT 101: Una mirada introductoria al colectivo* (pp. 227–246). Publicaciones Puertorriqueñas Inc.

Carter, J. W. Jr. (2013). *Giving voice to black gay and bisexual men in the south: Examining the influences of religion, spirituality, and family on the mental health and sexual behaviors of black gay and bisexual men* (Doctoral dissertation). Retrieved from ProQuest Dissertations and Theses Full Text: The Humanities and Social Sciences Collection.

Casey, L. S., Reisner, S. L., Findling, M. G., Blendon, R. J., Benson, J. M., Sayde, J. M., & Miller, C. (2019). Discrimination in the United States: Experiences of lesbian, gay, bisexual, transgender, and queer americans. *Health Services Research, 54*(6), 1454–1466. https://doi.org/10.1111/1475-6773.13229

Casimir, G. (2019). Why children's hospitals are unique and so essential. *Frontiers in Pediatrics, 7*, 1–5. https://dx.doi.org/10.3389%2Ffped.2019.00305

Caspani, M. (2022, April 29). Factbox: New U.S. state laws directed at transgender youth. Reuters. https://www.reuters.com/world/us/onslaught-us-laws-targeting-transgender-youth-2022-04-07/

Casto, C., Caldwell, C., & Salazar, C. F. (2005). Creating mentoring relationships between female faculty and students in counselor education: Guidelines for potential mentees and mentors. *Journal of Counseling & Development, 83*(3), 331.

Castro Samayoa, A. (2018). "People around me here, they know the struggle": Students' experiences with faculty member's mentorship at three Hispanic serving institutions. *Education Sciences, 8*.

Center for Substance Abuse Treatment (US). (2014). *Trauma-informed care in behavioral health services*. Substance Abuse and Mental Health Services Administration (US).

CenterLink. (n.d.). CenterLink LGBTQ+ community center member directory. http://www.lgbtcenters.org/Centers/find-a-center.aspx

Centers for Disease Control and Prevention (CDC). (1997). *Principles of community engagement*. Centers for Disease Control and Prevention.

Centers for Disease Control and Prevention. (2018). *HIV and youth*. https://www.cdc.gov/hiv/group/age/youth/index.html

Centers for Disease Control and Prevention. (2020). Youth risk behavior surveillance—United States, 2019. *MMWR Supplement, 69*(1), 1–88. https://www.cdc.gov/mmwr/volumes/69/su/pdfs/su6901-H.pdf

Cerezo, A., & Bergfeld, J. (2013). Meaningful LGBTQ inclusion in schools: The importance of diversity representation and counter spaces. *Journal of LGBT Issues in Counseling, 7*, 355–371. https://doi.org/10.1080/15538605.2013.839341

Cerezo, A., Cummings, M., Holmes, M., & Williams, C. (2020). Identity as resistance: Identity formation at the intersection of race, gender identity, and sexual orientation. *Psychology of Women Quarterly, 44*(1), 67–83. https://doi.org/10.1177/0361684319875977

Cerezo, A., Morales, A., Quintero, D., & Rothman, S. (2014). Trans migrations: Exploring life at the intersection of transgender identity and immigration. *Psychology of Sexual Orientation and Gender Diversity,* (1), 170–180. https://doi.org/10.1037/sgd0000031

Cernkovich, S., Lanctot, N., & Giordano, P. (2008). Predicting adolescent and adult antisocial behavior among adjudicated delinquent females. *Crime and Delinquency, 54*, 3–33.

Chan, C. D., Ngadjui, O. T., Jackson, T., & Steen, S. (2021). Unsettling complex inequities on school climate for males of color: School counseling applications from an intersectionality-based policy analysis. *Professional School Counseling, 25*, 1–14. https://doi.org/10.1177/2156759X211040029

Chan, R. C., & Mak, W. W. S. (2020). Liberating and empowering effects of critical reflection on collective action in LGBT and cisgender heterosexual individuals. *American Journal of Community Psychology, 65*(1–2), 63–77. https://doi.org/10.1002/ajcp.12350

Charlton, B. M., Gordon, A. R., Reisner, S. L., Sarda, V., Samnaliev, M., & Austin, S. B. (2018). Sexual orientation-related disparities in employment, health insurance, healthcare access and health-related quality of life: A cohort study of US male and female adolescents and young adults. *BMJ Open, 8*(6), e020418. http://dx.doi.org/10.1136/bmjopen-2017-020418

Chavez-Dueñas, N. Y., Adames, H. Y., Perez-Chavez, J. G., & Salas, S. P. (2019). Healing ethno-racial trauma in Latinx immigrant communities: Cultivating hope, resistance, and action. *American Psychologist, 74*(1), 49–62. https://doi.org/10.1037/amp0000289

Chen, D., Hidalgo, M. A., & Garofalo, R. (2017). Parental perceptions of emotional and behavioral difficulties among prepubertal gender-nonconforming children. *Clinical Practice in Pediatric Psychology, 5*, 342–352. https://doi.org/10.1037/cpp0000217

Chickering, A. W., & Gamson, Z. F. (1987). Seven principles for good practice in undergraduate education. *American Association for Higher Education Bulletin, 3*, 3–7.

Chickering, A. W., & Reisser, L. (1993). *Education and identity*. Jossey-Bass.

Child Welfare Information Gateway. (2021). Child maltreatment 2019: *Summary of key findings*. US Department of Health and Human Services, Administration for Children and Families, Children's Bureau. https://www.childwelfare.gov/

Children's Bureau. (2013, May). *Supporting your LGBTQ+ youth: A guide for foster parents*. Child Welfare Information Gateway. https://www.childwelfare.gov/pubPDFs/LGBTQ+youth.pdf

Chmielewski, J. F., Belmonte, K. M., Fine, M., & Stoudt, B. G. (2016). Intersectional inquiries with LGBTQ and gender nonconforming youth of color: Participatory research on discipline disparities at the race/sexuality/gender nexus. In R. Skiba, K. Mediratta, & M. Rausch (Eds.), *Inequality in school discipline*. Palgrave Macmillan.

Choi, S. K., Wilson, B. D., Shelton, J., & Gates, G. J. (2015). Serving our youth 2015: The needs and experiences of lesbian, gay, bisexual, transgender, and questioning youth experiencing homelessness. https://escholarship.org/uc/item/1pd9886n

Chulani, V., Cooper, M. B., Reitman, D., & Warus, J. (2021). Medical care for adolescent males who have sex with males. *Current Pediatrics Reports, 9*(2), 30–26. https://doi.org/10.1007/s40124-021-00237-w

Chung, Y. B., Williams, W., & Dispenza, F. (2009). Validating work discrimination and coping strategy models for sexual minorities. *Career Development Quarterly, 58*(2), 162–170.

Cicero, E. C., Reisner, S. L., Merwin, E. I., Humphreys, J. C., & Silva, S. G. (2020). The health status of transgender and gender nonbinary adults in the United States. *PloS one, 15*(2), e0228765. https://doi.org/10.1371/journal.pone.0228765

Cicero, E. C., Reisner, S. L., Silva, S. G., Merwin, E. I., & Humphreys, J. C. (2019). Health care experiences of transgender adults: An integrated mixed research literature review. *Advances in Nursing Science, 42*(2), 123–138. https://doi.org/10.1097/ANS.0000000000000256

Ciobanu, A. (2013). The role of student services in the improving of student experience in higher education. *Procedia—Social and Behavioral Sciences, 92*, 169–173.

Clark, B. A., Veale, J. F., Greyson, D., & Saewyc, E. (2018). Primary care access and foregone care: A survey of transgender adolescents and young adults. *Family Practice, 35*(3), 302–306. https://doi.org/10.1093/fampra/cmx112

Clark, C. M., & Kosciw, J. G. (2021). Engaged or excluded: LGBTQ youth's participation in school sports and their relationship to psychological well-being. *Psychology in the Schools* (March 2020), 1–20. https://doi.org/10.1002/pits.22500

Clark, P. (2010). *Preventing future crime with cognitive behavioral therapy*. National Institute of Justice.

Cochran, B. N., Stewart, A. J., Ginzler, J. A., & Cauce, A. M. (2002). Challenges faced by homeless sexual minorities: Comparison of gay, lesbian, bisexual, and transgender homeless adolescents with their heterosexual counterparts. *American Journal of Public Health, 92*(5), 773–777.

Cochran, S. D., Björkenstam, C., & Mays, V. M. (2017). Sexual orientation differences in functional limitations, disability, and mental health services use: Results from the 2013–2014 National Health Interview survey. *Journal of Counseling and Clinical Psychology, 85*(12), 1111–1121. http://dx.doi.org/10.1037/ccp0000243

Cogan, C. M., Scholl, J. A., Lee, J. Y. and Davis, J. L. (2021). Potentially traumatic events and the association between gender minority stress and suicide risk in a gender-diverse sample. *Journal of Traumatic Stress, 34*(5), 977–984. https://doi.org/10.1002/jts.22728

Cohen-Kettenis, P. T., Owen, A., Kaijser, V. G., Bradley, S. J., & Zucker, K. J. (2003). Demographic characteristics, social competence, and behavior problems in children with gender identity disorder: A cross-national, cross-clinic comparative analysis. *Journal of Abnormal Child Psychology, 31*, 41–53. http://dx.doi.org/10.1023/A:1021769215342

Coker, T. R., Austin, S. B., & Schuster, M. A. (2010). The health and health care of lesbian, gay, and bisexual adolescents. *Annual Review of Public Health, 31*, 457–477. https://doi.org/10.1146/annurev.publhealth.012809.103636

Cole, D. (2022, March 30). *Arizona governor signs bill outlawing gender-affirming care for transgender youth and approves anti-trans sports ban*. CNN. https://www.cnn.com/2022/03/30/politics/arizona-transgender-health-care-ban-sports-ban/index.html

Coleman, E., Bockting, W., Botzer, M., Cohen-Kettenis, P., DeCuypere, G., Feldman, J., Fraser, L., Green, J., Knudson, G., Meyer, W. J., Monstrey, S., Adler, R. K., Brown, G. R., Devor, A. H., Ehrbar, R., Ettner, R., Eyler, E., Garofalo, R., Karasic, D. H., . . . Zucker, K. (2012). Standards of care for the health of transsexual, transgender, and gender-nonconforming people, version 7. *International Journal of Transgenderism, 13*(4), 165–232. https://doi.org/10.1080/15532739.2011.700873

Collins, P. H. (1990). *Black feminist thought: Knowledge, consciousness, and the politics of empowerment.* Unwin Hyman.

Colpitts, E., Gahagan, J. (2016). The utility of resilience as a conceptual framework for understanding and measuring LGBTQ health. *International Journal of Equity Health, 15*, 60.

Combahee River Collective. (1977/1995). Combahee River Collective statement. In B. Guy-Sheftall (Ed.), *Words of fire: An anthology of African American feminist thought* (pp. 232–240). New Press.

Coolhart, D., & Brown, M. T. (2017). The need for safe spaces: Exploring the experiences of homeless LGBTQ youth in shelters. *Children and Youth Services Review, 82*, 230–238.

Corliss, H. L., Goodenow, C. S., Nichols, L., & Austin, S. B. (2011). High burden of homelessness among sexual-minority adolescents: Findings from a representative Massachusetts high school sample. *American Journal of Public Health, 101*(9), 1683–1689.

Coulter, R. W. S., Egan, J. E., Kinsky, S., Friedman, M. R., Eckstrand, K. L., Frankeberger, J., Folb, B. L., Mair, C., Markovic, N., Silvestre, A., Stall, R., & Miller, E. (2019). Mental health, drug, and violence interventions for sexual/gender minorities: A systematic review. *Pediatrics, 144*(3), e20183367. https://doi.org/10.1542/peds.2018-3367

Coulter, R. W. S., Jun, H. J., Calzo, J. P., Truong, N. L., Mair, C., Markovic, N., . . . Corliss, H. L. (2018). Sexual-orientation differences in alcohol use trajectories and disorders in emerging adulthood: Results from a longitudinal cohort study in the United States. *Addiction, 113*(9), 1619–1632. https://doi.org/10.1111/add.14251

Coulter, R. W. S., Mair, C., Miller, E., Blosnich, J. R., Matthews, D. D., & McCauley, H. L. (2017). Prevalence of past-year sexual assault victimization among undergraduate students: Exploring differences by and intersections of gender identity, sexual identity, and race/ethnicity. *Prevention Science, 18*(6), 726–736. https://doi.org/10.1007/s11121-017-0762-8

Courtney, M. E., & Wong, Y. (1996). Comparing the timing of exits from substitute care. *Children and Youth Services Review, 18*, 307–334.

Covenant House. (2017). *Youth homelessness.* https://www.covenanthouse.org/homeless-issues/homeless-children-in-america

Cowan, K. C., Vaillancourt, K., Rossen, E., & Pollitt, K. (2013). *A framework for safe and successful schools* [Brief]. National Association of School Psychologists.

Craig, A. (2009). How do you feel—now? The anterior insula and human awareness. *Nature Reviews Neuroscience, 10*(1), 59–70. https://doi.org/10.1038/nrn2555

Craig, S. L. (2013). Affirmative supportive safe and empowering talk (ASSET): Leveraging the strengths and resiliencies of sexual minority youth in school-based groups. *Journal of LGBT Issues in Counseling, 7*, 372–386. https://doi:10.1080/15538605.2013.839342

Craig, S. L., Austin, A., Levenson, J., Leung, V. W. Y., Eaton, A. D., & D'Souza, S. A. (2020). Frequencies and patterns of adverse childhood events in LGBTQ+ youth. *Child Abuse & Neglect, 107*(June), 104623. https://doi.org/10.1016/j.chiabu.2020.104623

Craig, S. L., & McInroy, L. (2014). You can form a part of yourself online: The influence of new media on identity development and coming out for LGBTQ youth. *Journal of Gay & Lesbian Mental Health, 18*(1), 95–109. https://doi.org/10.1080/19359705.2013.777007

Crenshaw, K. W. (1989). Demarginalizing the intersection of race and sex: A Black feminist critique of antidiscrimination doctrine, feminist theory, and antiracist politics. *University of Chicago Legal Forum, 139*(1), 139–167. Retrieved from http://chicagounbound.uchicago.edu/uclf/vol1989/iss1/8

Crenshaw, K. (1991). Mapping the margins: Intersectionality, identity, politics, and violence against women of color. *Stanford Law Review, 43*(6), 1241–1299. https://doi.org/10.2307/1229039

Crenshaw, K. (1997). Intersectionality and identity politics: Learning from violence against women of color. In M. L. Shanley & U. Narayan (Eds.), *Reconstructing political theory: Feminist perspectives.* (pp. 178–193). Pennsylvania State University Press.

Crenshaw, K., Ocen, P., & Nanda, J. (2015). Black girls' matter: Pushed out, overpoliced and underprotected. African American Policy Forum, Center for Intersectionality and Social Policy Studies.

Cserni, R. T., & Talmud, I. (2015). To know that you are not alone: The effect of internet usage on LGBT youth's social capital. *Studies in Media and Communications, 9*, 161–182. https://doi.org/10.1108/S2050-206020150000009007

Cyr, K., Chamberland, C., Lessard, G., Clément, M. E., Wemmers, J. A., Collin-Vézina, D., Gagné, M. H., & Damant, D. (2012). Polyvictimization in a child welfare sample of children and youths. *Psychology of Violence, 2*, 385–400.

D'Augelli, A. R., Grossman, A. H., & Starks, M. T. (2006). Childhood gender atypicality, victimization, and PTSD among lesbian, gay, and bisexual youth. *Journal of Interpersonal Violence, 21*(11), 1462–1482. https://doi.org/10.1177/0886260506293482

D'Augelli, A. R., & Hershberger, S. L. (1993). Lesbian, gay, and bisexual youth in community settings: Personal challenges and mental health problems. *American Journal of Community Psychology, 21*, 421–448. https://doi.org/10.1007/BF00942151

Dahlen, S. (2020). De-sexing the medical record? An examination of sex versus gender identity in the general medical council's trans healthcare ethical advice. *The New Bioethics: A Multidisciplinary Journal of Biotechnology and the Body, 26*(1), 38–52. https://doi.org/10.1080/20502877.2020.1720429

Daniels, R. S. (2019). The evolution of attitudes on same-sex marriage in the United States, 1988–2014. *Social Science Quarterly (Wiley-Blackwell), 100*(5), 1651–1663. https://doi.org/10.1111/ssqu.12673

Dank, M., Lachman, P., Zweig, J. M., & Yahner, J. (2014). Dating violence experiences of lesbian, gay, bisexual, and transgender youth. *Journal of Youth and Adolescence, 43*(5), 846–857. https://doi.org/10.1007/s10964-013-9975-8

Dank, M., Yahner, J., Madden, K., Banuelos, I., Yu, L., Ritchie, A., Mora, M., & Conner, B. (2015). Surviving the streets of New York: Experiences of LGBTQ youth, YMSM, and YWSW engaged in survival sex. https://doi.org/1015496/publication-8608

Datti, P. A. (2009). Applying the social learning theory of career decision-making to gay, lesbian, bisexual, transgender, and questioning young adults. *Career Development Quarterly, 58*(1), 54–64.

Davila, J., Hershenberg, R., Feinstein, B. A., Gorman, K., Bhatia, V., & Starr, L. R. (2012). Frequency and quality of social networking among young adults: Associations with depressive symptoms, rumination, and co-rumination. *Psychology of Popular Media Culture, 1*(2), 72–86.

Day, J. K., Fish, J. N., Grossman, A. H., & Russell, S. T. (2020). Gay-straight alliances, inclusive policy, and school climate: LGBTQ youths' experiences of social support and bullying. *Journal of Research on Adolescence, 30*, 418–430. https://doi.org/10.1111/jora.12487

Day, J. K., Fish, J. N., Perez-Brumer, A., Hatzenbuehler, M. L., & Russell, S. T. (2017). Transgender youth substance use disparities: Results from a population-based sample. *Journal of Adolescent Health, 61*(6), 729–735. https://doi.org/10.1016/j.jadohealth.2017.06.024

de Graaf, N. M., & Carmichael, P. (2019). Reflections on emerging trends in clinical work with gender diverse children and adolescents. *Clinical Child Psychology and Psychiatry, 24*(2), 353–364. https://doi.org/10.1177/1359104518812924

de Vries, A. L. C. (2020). Challenges in timing puberty suppression for gender-nonconforming adolescents. *Pediatrics, 146*(4), e2020010611. https://doi.org/10.1542/peds.2020-010611

de Vries, A. L., & Cohen-Kettenis, P. T. (2012). Clinical management of gender dysphoria in children and adolescents: The Dutch approach. *Journal of Homosexuality, 59*(3), 301–320.

de Vries, A. L. C., Kreukels, B. P. C., Steensma, T. D., & McGuire, J. K. (2014). Gender identity development: A biopsychosocial perspective. In B. P. C. Kreukels, T. D. Steensma, & A. L. C. de Vries (Eds.), *Gender dysphoria and disorders of sex development: Progress in care and knowledge*. Springer. https://doi.org/10.1007/978-1-4614-7441-8_3

de Vries, A. L. C., McGuire, J. K., Steensma, T. D., Wagenaar, E. C. F., Doreleijers, T. A. H., & Cohen-Kettenis, P. T. (2014). Young adult psychological outcome after puberty suppression and gender reassignment. *Pediatrics, 134*(4), 696–704. https://doi.org/10.1542/peds.2013-2958

de Vries, A. L., Steensma, T. D., Cohen-Kettenis, P. T., VanderLaan, D. P., & Zucker, K. J. (2016). Poor peer relations predict parent- and self-reported behavioral and emotional problems of adolescents with gender dysphoria: A cross-national, cross-clinic comparative analysis. *European Child & Adolescent Psychiatry, 25*(6), 579–588. https://doi.org/10.1007/s00787-015-0764-7

Deaux, K. (1993). Reconstructing social identity. *Personality and Social Psychology Bulletin, 19*(1), 4–12.

DeHaan, S., Kuper, L. E., Magee, J. C., Bigelow, L., & Mustanski, B. S. (2013). The interplay between online and offline explorations of identity, relationships, and sex: A mixed-methods study with LGBT youth. *Journal of Sex Research, 50*, 421–434. https://doi.org/10.1080/00224499.2012.661489

DeLamater, J., & Friedrich, W. N. (2002). Human sexual development. *Journal of Sex Research, 39*, 10–14. https://doi.org/10.1080/00224490209552113

DeLonga, K., Torres, H. L., Kamen, C., Evans, S. N., Lee, S., Koopman, C., & Gore-Felton, C. (2011). Loneliness, internalized homophobia, and compulsive internet use: Factors associated with sexual risk behavior among a sample. *Sexual Addiction and Compulsivity, 18*(2), 61–74. https://doi.org/10.1080/10720162.2011.581897

DePaul, J., Walsh, M. E., & Dam, U. C. (2009). The role of school counselors in addressing sexual orientation in schools. *Professional School Counseling, 12*(4), 300–308.

DeRosa, R., Habib, M., Pelcovitz, D., Rathus, J., Sonnenklar, J., Ford, J., . . . Kaplan, S. (2006). Structured psychotherapy for adolescents responding to chronic stress. *Unpublished manual*.

Dessel, A. B., Goodman, K. D., & Woodford, M. R. (2017). LGBT discrimination on campus and heterosexual bystanders: Understanding intentions to intervene. *Journal of Diversity in Higher Education, 10*(2), 101–116. https://doi.org/10.1037/dhe0000015

Dettlaff, A. J., & Rycraft, J. R. (2008). Deconstructing disproportionality: Views from multiple community stakeholders. *Child Welfare, 87*(2), 37–58.

Dettlaff, A. J., Washburn, M., Carr, L. C., Vogel, A. N. (2018). Lesbian, gay, and bisexual (LGB) youth within in welfare: Prevalence, risk, and outcomes. *Child Abuse & Neglect, 80*, 183–193.

Devor, A. H. (2004). Witnessing and mirroring: A fourteen stage model of transsexual identity formation. *Journal of Gay & Lesbian Psychotherapy, 8*(1–2), 41–67.

Dewey, J. M. (2013). Challenges of implementing collaborative models of decision making with trans-identified patients. *Health Expectations, 18*, 1508–1518. https://doi.org/10.1111/hex.12133

Diamond, G. M., Diamond, G. S., Levy, S., Closs, C., Ladipo, T., & Siqueland, L. (2012). Attachment-based family therapy for suicidal lesbian, gay, and bisexual adolescents: A treatment development study and open trial with preliminary findings. *Psychotherapy, 49*(1), 62–71. https://doi.org/10.1037/a0026247

Diamond, L. M. (2020). Gender fluidity and nonbinary gender identities among children and adolescents. *Child Development Perspectives, 14*(2), 110–115. https://doi.org/10.1111/cdep.12366

Diamond, L. M., Pardo, S. T., Butterworth, M. R. (2011). Transgender experience and identity. In S. J. Shwartz, K. Luyckx, & V. L. Vignoles (Eds.), *Handbook of identity theory and research* (pp. 629–647). Springer.

Diaz, E. M., & Kosciw, J. G. (2009). *Shared differences: The experiences of lesbian, gay, bisexual, and transgender students of color in our nation's schools.* GLSEN.

Dickey, L., Reisner, S., & Juntunen, C. (2015). Non-suicidal self-injury in a large online sample of transgender adults. *Professional Psychology: Research and Practice, 46*, 3–11.

dickey, l. m., Walinsky, D., Rofkahr, C., Richardson-Cline, K., & Juntunen, C. (2016). Career decision self-efficacy of transgender people: Pre- and post-transition. *Career Development Quarterly, 64*(4), 360–372. https://doi.org/10.1002/cdq.12071

Diemer, M. A., Rapa, L. J., Park, C. J., & Perry, J. C. (2017). Development and validation of the Critical Consciousness Scale. *Youth & Society, 49*(4), 461–483. https://doi.org/10.1177/0044118X14538289

DiFulvio, G. T. (2011). Sexual minority youth, social connection and resilience: From personal struggle to collective identity. *Social Science & Medicine, 72*(10), 1611–1617. https://doi.org/10.1016/j.socscimed.2011.02.045

Ding, C., Chen, X., Wang, W., Yu, B., Yang, H., Li, X., Deng, S., Yan, H., & Li, S. (2020). Sexual minority stigma, sexual orientation concealment, social support and depressive symptoms among men who have sex with men in China: A moderated mediation modeling analysis. *AIDS and Behavior, 24*, 8–17. https://doi.org/10.1007/s10461-019-02713-3

Doan, P. L. (2007). Queers in the American city: Transgender perceptions of urban space. *Gender, Place, and Culture, 14*(1), 57–74. https://doi.org/10.1080/09663690601122309

Dover, K. J. (1978 [1989]). *Greek homosexuality.* Harvard University Press.

Dowshen, N., Meadows, R., Byrnes, M., Hawkins, L., Eder, J., & Noonan, K. (2016). Policy perspective: Ensuring comprehensive care and support for gender nonconforming children and adolescents. *Transgender Health, 1*(1), 75–85. https://doi.org/10.1089/trgh.2016.0002

Drabble, L. A., Wootton, A. R., Veldhuis, C. B., Perry, E., Riggle, E. D. B., Trocki, K. F., & Hughes, T. L. (2020). It's complicated: The impact of marriage legalization among sexual minority women and gender diverse individuals in the United States. *Psychology of Sexual Orientation and Gender Diversity.* https://doi.org/10.1037/sgd0000375

Dreger, A. (2009). Gender identity disorder in childhood: Inconclusive advice to parents. *The Hastings Center Report, 39*(1), 26–29.

Drescher, J. (2014). Gender identity diagnoses: History and controversies. In *Gender dysphoria and disorders of sex development* (pp. 137–150). Springer.

Drinan, R. F., & Huffman, J. I. (1993). "The Religious Freedom Restoration Act: A legislative history." *Journal of Law and Religion, 10*(2), 531–541.

Drummond, K. D., Bradley, S. J., Peterson-Badali, M., & Zucker, K. J. (2008). A follow-up study of girls with gender identity disorder. *Developmental Psychology, 44*(1), 34. https://doi.org/10.1037/0012-1649.44.1.34

Dryden, E., Hyde, J., Livny, A., & Tula, M. (2010). Phoenix rising: Use of a participatory approach to evaluate a federally funded HIV, hepatitis and substance abuse prevention program. *Evaluation and Program Planning, 33*(4), 386–393.

Dunbar, M. S., Sontag-Padilla, L., Ramchand, R., Seelam, R., & Stein, B. D. (2017). Mental health service utilization among lesbian, gay, bisexual, and questioning or queer college students. *Journal of Adolescent Health, 61*(3), 294–301. https://doi.org/10.1016/j.jadohealth.2017.03.008

Duong, J., & Bradshaw, C. (2014). Associations between bullying and engaging in aggressive and suicidal behaviors among sexual minority youth: The moderating role of connectedness. *Journal of School Health, 84*, 636–645.

Dwyer, A. (2011). Policing lesbian, gay, bisexual, and transgender young people: A gap in the research literature. *Current Issues in Criminal Justice, 22*, 415–433.

Earnshaw, V. A., Bogart, L. M., Poteat, V. P., Reisner, S. L., & Schuster, M. A. (2016). Bullying among lesbian, gay, bisexual, and transgender youth. *Pediatric Clinics of North America, 63*(6), 999–1010. https://doi.org/10.1016/j.pcl.2016.07.004

Edwards, K. M., & Sylaska, K. M. (2013). The perpetuation of intimate partner violence among LGBTQ college youth: The role of minority stress. *Journal of Youth and Adolescence, 42*(11), 1721–1731. https://doi.org/10.1007/s10964-012-9880-6

Edwards-Leeper, L., & Spack, N. P. (2012). Psychological evaluation and medical treatment of transgender youth in an interdisciplinary "gender management service" (GeMS) in a major pediatric center. *Journal of Homosexuality, 59*(3), 321–336. https://doi.org/10.1080/00918369.2012.653302

Egan, S. K., & Perry, D. G. (2001). Gender identity: A multidimensional analysis with implications for psychosocial adjustment. *Developmental Psychology, 37*(4), 451. https://doi.org/10.1037//0012-1649.37.4.451

Ehrensaft, D. (2020). Treatment paradigms for prepubertal children. In M. Forcier, G. van Schalkwyk, & J. L. Turban (Eds.), *Pediatric gender identity: Gender-affirming care for transgender & gender diverse youth*. Springer Cham. https://doi.org/10.1007/978-3-030-38909-3_13

Eisenberg, M. E., Erickson, D. J., Gower, A. L., Kne, L., Watson, R. J., Corliss, H. L., & Saewyc, E. M. (2020). Supportive community resources are associated with lower risk of substance use among lesbian, gay, bisexual, and questioning adolescents in Minnesota. *Journal of Youth and Adolescence, 49*(4), 836–848. https://doi.org/10.1007/s10964-019-01100-4

Eisenberg, M. E., Gower, A. L., Brown, C., Nam, Y. S., Rider, G. N., & Ramirez, M. (2021). "It was never really bullying, but . . .": Stigmatized adolescents' experiences with microaggressions in school. *International Journal of Bullying Prevention*. https://doi.org/10.1007/s42380-021-00103-9

Eisenberg, M. E., Gower, A. L., & McMorris, B. J. (2016). Emotional health of lesbian, gay, bisexual and questioning bullies: Does it differ from straight bullies? *Journal of Youth and Adolescence, 45*(1), 105–116. https://doi.org/10.1007/s10964-015-0316-y

Eisenberg, M. E., Gower, A. L., Watson, R. J., Porta, C. M., & Saewyc, E. M. (2020). LGBTQ youth-serving organizations: What do they offer and do they protect against emotional distress? *Annals of LGBTQ Public and Population Health, 1*(1), 63–79.

Eisenberg, M. E., & Resnick, M. D. (2006). Suicidality among gay, lesbian and bisexual youth: The role of protective factors. *The Journal of Adolescent Health, 39*(5), 662–668. https://doi.org/10.1016/j.jadohealth.2006.04.024

Ellis, J. M., Powell, C. S., Demetriou, C. P., Huerta-Bapat, C., & Panter, A. T. (2019). Examining first-generation college student lived experiences with microaggressions and microaffirmations at a predominately White public research university. *Cultural Diversity and Ethnic Minority Psychology, 25*(2), 266–279. https://doi.org/10.1037/cdp0000198

Ellison, E. R., & Langhout, R. E. (2020). Embodied relationship praxis in intersectional organizing: Developing intersectional solidarity. *Journal of Social Issues, 76*(4), 949–970. https://doi.org/10.1111/josi.12402

Empson, S., Cuca, Y. P., Cocohoba, J., Dawson-Rose, C., Davis, K., & Machtinger, E. L. (2017). Seeking safety group therapy for co-occurring substance use disorder and PTSD among transgender women living with HIV: A pilot study. *Journal of Psychoactive Drugs, 49*(4), 344–351.

English, D., Boone, C. A., Carter, J. A., Talan, A. J., Busby, D. R., Moody, R. L., Cunningham, D. J., Bowleg, L., & Rendina, H. J. (2022). Intersecting structural oppression and suicidality among black sexual minority male adolescents and emerging adults. *Journal of Research on Adolescence, 32*(1), 226–243. https://doi.org/10.1111/jora.12726

Erickson-Schroth, L. (2013). Update on the biology of transgender identity. *Journal of Gay & Lesbian Mental Health, 17*(2), 150–174. https://doi.org/10.1080/19359705.2013.753393

Erickson-Schroth, L., & Glaeser, E. (2017). The role of resilience and resilience characteristics in health promotion. In K. Eckstrand & J. Potter (Eds), *Trauma, resilience and health promotion in LGBT patients* (pp. 51–56). Springer International Publishing.

Eskridge, W. (2000). No promo homo: The sedimentation of antigay discourse and the channeling effect of judicial review. *New York University Law Review, 75*, 1327–1411.

Esteban, C., & Díaz-Medero, L. X. (2019). Una reflexión sobre prácticas adecuadas: Integración ética de las creencias religiosas/espirituales y las identidades sexuales y de género diversas (Sección especial). *Revista Ciencias de la Conducta, 22*(1), 97–134.

Estrada, R., & Marksamer, J. (2006). The legal rights of young people in state custody: What child welfare and juvenile justice professionals need to know when working with LGBT youth. *Child Welfare League of America, 85*, 1–16.

Estrada, R., & Marksamer, J. (2020). Lesbian, gay, bisexual and transgender young people in state custody: Making the child welfare and juvenile justice systems safe for all youth through litigation, advocacy, and education. *Temple Law Review, 79*, 415–438.

Fairchild, R., & McFerran, K. S. (2018). Understanding children's resources in the context of family violence through a collaborative songwriting method. *Children Australia, 43*(4), 255–266.

Fansler, V., Reed, R., bautista, e, Arnett, A. T., Perkins, F., & Hadley, S. (2019). Playing in the borderlands: The transformative possibilities of queering music therapy pedagogy. *Voices: A World Forum for Music Therapy, 19*(3). https://doi.org/10.15845/voices.v19i3.2679

Farmer, L. B., & Byrd, R. (2015). Genderism in the LGBTQQIA community: An interpretative phenomenological analysis. *Journal of LGBT Issues in Counseling, 9*(4), 288–310. https://doi.org/10.1080/15538605.2015.1103679

Farmer, P. (2004). An anthropology of structural violence. *Current Anthropology, 45*(3), 305–325.

Farmer, P. E., Nizeye, B., Stulac, S., & Keshavjee, S. (2006). Structural violence and clinical medicine. *PLoS Medicine, 3*(10), e449.

Fast, A. A., & Olson, K. R. (2018). Gender development in transgender preschool children. *Child development, 89*(2), 620–637.

Fausto-Sterling, A. (2019). The dynamic development of gender variability. In A. Slomowitz & A. Feit (Eds.), *Homosexuality, Transsexuality, Psychoanalysis and Traditional Judaism* (pp. 155–182). Routledge.

Fausto-Sterling, A. (2000). Sexing the body: Gender politics and the construction of sexuality. Basic Books.

Feinstein, B. A., Dyar, C., Li, D. H., Whitton, S. W., Newcomb, M. E., & Mustanski, B. (2019). The longitudinal associations between outness and health outcomes among gay/lesbian versus bisexual emerging adults. *Archives of Sexual Behavior, 48*(4), 1111–1126. https://doi.org/10.1007/s10508-018-1221-8

Feiring, C., Miller-Johnson, S., & Cleland, C. (2007). Potential pathways from stigmatization and internalizing symptoms to delinquency in sexually abused youth. *Child Maltreatment, 12,* 220–232.

Felner, J. K., Wisdom, J. P., Williams, T., Katuska, L., Haley, S. J., Jun, H.-J., & Corliss, H. L. (2020). Stress, coping, and context: Examining substance use among LGBTQ young adults with probable substance use disorders. *Psychiatric Services, 71*(2), 112–120. https://doi.org/10.1176/appi.ps.201900029

Fenway Institute. (2018). Emerging best practices for the management and treatment of lesbian, gay, bisexual, transgender, questioning, and intersex youth in juvenile justice settings. https://fenwayhealth.org/wp-content/uploads/TFIP-21_BestPracticesForLGBTYouthInJuvenileJustice_Brief_web.pdf

Fergus, S., & Zimmerman, M. (2005). Adolescent resilience: A framework for understanding healthy development in the face of risk. *Annual Review of Public Health, 26,* 399–419. https://doi.org/10.1146/annurev.publhealth.26.021304.144357

Ferguson, K. M., & Maccio, E. M. (2015). Promising programs for lesbian, gay, bisexual, transgender, and queer/questioning runaway and homeless youth. *Journal of Social Service Research, 41*(5), 659–683.

Fernandez, J. R., & Birnholtz, J. (2019). "I don't want them to not know": Investigating decisions to disclose transgender identity on dating platforms. *Proceedings of the ACM on Human-Computer Interaction, 3*(CSCW), 1–21.

Field, T. L., & Mattson, G. (2016). Parenting transgender children in PFLAG. *Journal of GLBT Family Studies, 12*(5), 413–429.

Fields, E. L., Morgan, A. R., Malebranche, D. J., Smith, K. C., Ellen, J. M., & Sanders, R. A. (2015). The role of virtual venues among young black men who have sex with men (YBMSM): Exploration of patterns of use from 2001–2011. *Journal of Adolescent Health, 56*(2), S118–S119. https://doi.org/10.1016/j.jadohealth.2014.10.237

Fields, X., & Wotipka, C. M. (2020). Effect of LGBT anti-discrimination laws on school climate and outcomes for lesbian, gay, and bisexual high school students. *Journal of LGBT Youth.* https://doi.org/10.1080/19361653.2020.1821276

Fine, L. E. (2011). Minimizing heterosexism and homophobia: Constructing meaning of out campus LGB life. *Journal of Homosexuality, 58*(4), 521–546. https://doi.org/10.1080/00918369.2011.555673

Fish, J. N., Mcinroy, L. B., Paceley, M. S., Williams, N. D., Henderson, S., Levine, D. S., & Edsall, R. N. (2020). "I'm kinda stuck at home with unsupportive parents right now": LGBTQ youths' experiences with COVID-19 and the importance of online support. *Journal of Adolescent Health, 67*(3), 450–452. https://doi.org/10.1016/j.jadohealth.2020.06.002

Fish, J. N., Moody, R. L., Grossman, A. H., & Russell, S. T. (2019). LGBTQ youth-serving community-based organizations: Who participates and what difference does it make? *Journal of Youth and Adolescence, 48,* 2418–2431. https://doi.org/10.1007/s10964-019-01129-5

Fisher, C. B., Fried, A. L., Desmond, M., Macapagal, K., & Mustanski, B. (2017). Facilitators and barriers to participation in PrEP HIV prevention trials involving transgender male and female adolescents and emerging adults. *AIDS Education and Prevention, 29*(3), 205–217. https://doi.org/10.1521/aeap.2017.29.3.205

Flentje, A., Heck, N. C., Brennan, J. M., & Meyer, I. H. (2020). The relationship between minority stress and biological outcomes: A systematic review. *Journal of Behavioral Medicine, 43*(5), 673–694. https://doi.org/10.1007/s10865-019-00120-6

Fletcher, J. K. (1999). *Disappearing acts: Gender, power, and relational practice at work.* M.I.T. Press. https://doi.org/10.7551/mitpress/2440.001.0001

Flores, A. R., Herman, J. L., Gates, G. J., & Brown, T. N. T. (2016). *How many adults identify as transgender in the United States?* Williams Institute.

Ford, C. L., Slavin, T., Hilton, K. L., & Holt, S. L. (2013). Intimate partner violence prevention services and resources in Los Angeles: Issues, needs, and challenges for assisting lesbian, gay, bisexual, and transgender clients. *Health Promotion Practice, 14*(6), 841–849. https://doi.org/10.1177/1524839912467645

Forster, M., Vetrone, S., Grigsby, T. J., Rogers, C., & Unger, J. B. (2020). The relationships between emerging adult transition themes, adverse childhood experiences, and substance use patterns among a community cohort of Hispanics. *Cultural Diversity and Ethnic Minority Psychology, 26*(3), 378–389. https://doi.org/10.1037/cdp0000304

Foucault, M. (1980). *The history of sexuality. Volume one: An introduction.* Robert Hurley (trans.). Vintage Books.

Frank, D. A., & Cannon, E. P. (2010). Queer theory as pedagogy in counselor education: A framework for diversity training. *Journal of LGBT Issues in Counseling, 4*(1), 18–31. https://doi:10.1080/15538600903552731

Fraser, B., Pierse, N., Chisholm, E., & Cook, H. (2019). LGBTIQ+ homelessness: A review of the literature. *International Journal of Environmental Research and Public Health, 16*(15), 2677.

Freda, B., Kozick, D., & Spencer, A. (2018). Partnerships for health: Lessons for bridging community-based organizations and health care organizations. https://www.chcs.org/media/CBO-HCO_Partnership_update_032018.pdf

Fredriksen-Goldsen, K. I., Hoy-Ellis, C. P., & Brown, M. (2015). Addressing behavioral cancer risk from LGBT health equity perspective. In U. Boehmer & R. Elk (Eds.), *Cancer and the LGBT community: Unique perspectives from risk to survivorship* (pp. 37–62). Springer.

Fredriksen-Goldsen, K. I., Simoni, J. M., Kim, H.-J., Lehavot, K., Walters, K. L., Yang, J., Hoy-Ellis, C. P., & Muraco, A. (2014). The health equity promotion model: Reconceptualization of lesbian, gay, bisexual, and transgender (LGBT) health disparities. *American Journal of Orthopsychiatry, 84*(6), 653–663. https://doi.org/10.1037/ort0000030

Freeman, R., Gwadz, M. V., Silverman, E., Kutnick, A., Leonard, N. R., Ritchie, A. S., . . . Martinez, B. Y. (2017). Critical race theory as a tool for understanding poor engagement along the HIV care continuum among African American/Black and Hispanic persons living with HIV in the United States: A qualitative exploration. *International Journal for Equity in Health, 16*(1), 1–14.

Freire, P. (1970). *Pedagogy of the oppressed.* Penguin Group.

French, B. H., Lewis, J. A., Mosley, D. V., Adames, H. Y., Chavez-Dueñas, N. Y., Chen, G. A., & Neville, H. A. (2020). Toward a psychological framework of radical healing in communities of color. *Counseling Psychologist, 48*(1), 14–46. https://doi.org/10.1177/0011000019843506

Frey, A. J., Alvarez, M. E., Dupper, D. R., Sabatino, C. A., Lindsey, B. C., Raines, J. C., Streeck, F., McInerney, A., & Norris, M. A. (2013). *School social work practice model*. School Social Work Association of America. http://sswaa.org/displaycommon.cfm?an=1&subarticlenbr=459

Frey, J. H., & Fontana, A. (1991). The group interview in social research. *Social Science Journal, 28*(2), 175–187. https://doi.org/10.1016/0362-3319(91)90003-M

Frieden, T. R., Jaffe, H. W., Cono, J., Richards, C. L., & Iademarco, M. F. (2016). Sexual identity, sex of sexual contacts, and health-related behaviors among students in grades 9–12—United States and Selected Sites, 2015. MMWR Center for Surveillance, Epidemiology, and Laboratory Services, Centers for Disease Control and Prevention, 65, 1–202.

Friedman, M. S., Marshal, M. P., Guadamuz, T. E., Wei, C., Wong, C. F., Saewyc, E., & Stall, R. (2011). A meta-analysis of disparities in childhood sexual abuse, parental physical abuse, and peer victimization among sexual minority and sexual nonminority individuals. *American Journal of Public Health, 101*(8), 1481–1494. https://doi.org/10.2105/AJPH.2009.190009

Frost, D. M., Lehavot, K., & Meyer, I. H. (2015). Minority stress and physical health among sexual minority individuals. *Journal of Behavioral Medicine, 38*(1), 1–8. https://doi.org/10.1007/s10865-013-9523-8

Frost, D. M., & Meyer, I. H. (2012). Measuring community connectedness among diverse sexual minority populations. *Journal of Sex Research, 49*(1), 36–49. https://doi.org/10.1080/00224499.2011.565427

Frost, D. M., Meyer, I. H., & Hammack, P. L. (2015). Health and well-being in emerging adults' same-sex relationships: Critical questions and directions for research in developmental science. *Emerging Adulthood, 3*(1), 3–13. https://doi.org/10.1177/2167696814535915

Fuist, T. N. (2017). "It just always seemed like it wasn't a big deal, yet I know for some people they really struggle with it": LGBT religious identities in context. *Journal for the Scientific Study of Religion, 55*(4), 770–786. https://doi.org/10.1111/jssr.12291

Fulginiti, A., Goldbach, J. T., Mamey, M. R., Rusow, J., Srivastava, A., Rhoades, H., Schrager, S. M., Bond, D. W., & Marshal, M. P. (2020). Integrating minority stress theory and the interpersonal theory of suicide among sexual minority youth who engage crisis services. *Suicide and Life-Threatening Behavior*. https://doi.org/10.1111/sltb.12623

Fulginiti, A., Rhoades, H., Mamey, M. R., Klemmer, C., Srivastava, A., Weskamp, G., & Goldbach, J. T. (2021). Sexual minority stress, mental health symptoms, and suicidality among LGBTQ youth accessing crisis services. *Journal of Youth and Adolescence, 50*(5), 893–905. https://doi.org/10.1007/s10964-020-01354-3

Fulton et al. v. City of Philadelphia, Pennsylvania, No. 19-123, (2021).

Gamarel, K. E., Reisner, S. L., Laurenceau, J. P., Nemoto, T., & Operario, D. (2014). Gender minority stress, mental health, and relationship quality: A dyadic investigation of transgender women and their cisgender male partners. *Journal of Family Psychology, 28*(4), 437–447. https://doi.org/10.1037/a0037171

Gamarel, K. E., Walker, J. J., Rivera, L., & Golub, S. A. (2014). Identity safety and relational health in youth spaces: A needs assessment with LGBTQ youth of color. *Journal of LGBT Youth, 11*, 289–314. https://doi.org/10.1080/19361653.2013.879464

Gardner, M., & Sandberg, D. E. (2018). Navigating surgical decision making in disorders of sex development (DSD). *Frontiers in Pediatrics, 6*, 339.

Garmulewicz, A., & Ireland, L. (2010). The Canadian Youth Climate Change Conference (YC3) as a model for effective youth and adult engagement in promoting environmental and social justice. In W. Linds, L. Goulet, & A. Sammel (Eds.), *Emancipatory practices: Adult/youth engagement for social and environmental justice* (pp. 145–164). Brill. https://doi.org/10.1163/9789460911538_013

Garnets, L. D., & Kimmel, D. C. (2003). Lesbian, gay male, and bisexual dimensions in the psychological study of human diversity. In L. D. Garnets & D. C. Kimmel (Eds.), *Psychological perspectives on lesbian, gay, and bisexual experiences* (pp. 1–21). Columbia University Press.

Garofalo, R., Deleon, J., Osmer, E., Doll, M., & Harper, G. W. (2006). Overlooked, misunderstood and at-risk: Exploring the lives and HIV risk of ethnic minority male-to-female transgender youth. *Journal of Adolescent Health, 38*(3), 230–236. https://doi.org/10.1016/j.jadohealth.2005.03.023

Garriott, P. O., & Nisle, S. (2018). Stress, coping, and perceived academic goal progress in first-generation college students: The role of institutional supports. *Journal of Diversity in Higher Education, 11*(4), 436–450. https://doi.org/10.1037/dhe0000068

Garvey, J. C., & Inkelas, K. K. (2012). Exploring relationships between sexual orientation and satisfaction with faculty and staff interactions. *Journal of Homosexuality, 59*(8), 1167–1190. https://doi.org/10.1080/00918369.2012.712846

Garvey, J. C., Mobley, S. D., Summerville, K. S., & Moore, G. T. (2019). Queer and trans students of color: Navigating identity disclosure and college contexts. *Journal of Higher Education, 90*(1), 150–178. https://doi.org/10.1080/00221546.2018.1449081

Garvey, J. C., & Rankin, S. R. (2015). The influence of campus experiences on the level of outness among trans-spectrum and queer-spectrum students. *Journal of Homosexuality, 62*(3), 374–393. https://doi.org/10.1080/00918369.2014.977113

Garvey, J. C, Squire, D. D., Stachler, B., & Rankin, S. (2018). The impact of campus climate on queer-spectrum student academic success. *Journal of LGBT Youth, 15*(2), 89–105. https://doi.org/10.1080/19361653.2018.1429978

Garvey, J. C., Taylor, J. L., & Rankin, S. (2015). An examination of campus climate for LGBTQ community college students. *Community College Journal of Research and Practice, 39*(6), 527–541. https://doi.org/10.1080/10668926.2013.861374

Gates, G. J. (2013). LGBT adult immigrants in the United States. https://escholarship.org/uc/item/2cj0k29c

Gay and Lesbian Medical Association. (2010). *Healthy people 2020: Companion document for lesbian, gay, bisexual, and transgender (LGBT) health*. https://jnccn.org/doi/10.6004/jnccn.2017.0169

Gay, Lesbian and Straight Education Network. (n.d.). *Local school climate survey*. http://localsurvey.glsen.org

Gay, Lesbian and Straight Education Network. (2016). *Educational exclusion: Drop out, push out, and the school-to-prison pipeline among LGBTQ youth*. https://www.glsen.org/sites/default/files/2020-06/Separation%20and%20Stigma%20-%20Full%20Report.pdf

Gay, Lesbian and Straight Education Network. (2019). *Respect for all: Policy recommendations to support LGBTQ students: A guide for district and school leaders*. https://www.glsen.org/sites/default/files/2019-10/GLSEN-Respect-For-All-Policy-Resource.pdf

Gay, Lesbian and Straight Education Network. (2020, August). *Policy maps*. https://www.glsen.org/policy-maps

Gay, Lesbian and Straight Education Network, American School Counselor Association, American Council for School Social Work, & School Social Work Association of America. (2019). *Supporting safe and healthy schools for lesbian, gay, bisexual, transgender, and queer students: A national survey of school counselors, social workers, and psychologists*. GLSEN.

Gee, G. C., Hing, A., Mohammed, S., Tabor, D. C., & Williams, D. R. (2019). Racism and the life course: Taking time seriously. *American Journal of Public Health, 109*(S1), S43–S47. https://doi.org/10.2105/AJPH.2018.304766

Gelaude, D. J., Sovine, M. L., Swayzer III, R., & Herbst, J. H. (2013). HIV prevention programs delivered by community-based organizations to young transgender persons of color:

Lessons learned to improve future program implementation. *International Journal of Transgenderism, 14*(3), 127–139. https://doi.org/10.1080/15532739.2013.824846

Gender Identity in U.S. Surveillance Group. (2014). *Best practices for asking questions to identify transgender and other gender minority respondents on population-based surveys.* J. L. Herman (Ed.). Williams Institute.

Giammattei, S. V. (2015). Beyond the binary: Trans-negotiations in couple and family therapy. *Family Process, 54*(3), 418–434. https://doi.org/10.1111/famp.12167

Gibbs, J. J., & Goldbach, J. (2015). Religious conflict, sexual identity, and suicidal behaviors among LGBT young adults. *Archives of Suicide Research, 19*(4), 472–488. https://doi.org/10.1080/13811118.2015.1004476

Gilbert, C., Siepser, C., Fink, A. E., & Johnson, N. L. (2020, October 15). Why LGBTQ+ campus resource centers are essential. *Psychology of Sexual Orientation and Gender Diversity, 8*(2), 245–249. http://dx.doi.org/10.1037/sgd0000451

Gil-Hernández, G. (2007). El proceso de resiliencia en el desarrollo de la identidad gay, lesbiana y bisexual. *Vector Plus: Miscelánea científico—Cultural, 30*, 64–73.

Gillum, T. L. (2017). Adolescent dating violence experiences among sexual minority youth and implications for subsequent relationship quality. *Child and Adolescent Social Work Journal, 34*(2), 137–145. https://doi.org/10.1007/s10560-016-0451-7

Gillum, T. L., & DiFulvio, G. (2012). "There's so much at stake": Sexual minority youth discuss dating violence. *Violence against Women, 18*(7), 725–745. https://doi.org/10.1177/1077801212455164

Ginicola, M. M., Smith, C., & Filmore, J. M. (2017). *Affirmative counseling with LGBTQI+ people.* American Counseling Association.

Ginwright, S. (2010). *Black youth rising: Activism and racial healing in urban America.* Teachers College Press.

Ginwright, S. A. (2015). Radically healing black lives: A love note to justice. *New Directions for Student Leadership, 2015*(148), 33–44.

Glickman, D. (2016). Fashioning children: Gender restrictive dress codes as an entry point for the trans school to prison pipeline. *American University Journal of Gender, Social Policy & the Law, 24*, 263–284.

GLSEN. (2022). *LGBTQ history.* http://live-glsen-website.pantheonsite.io/lgbtq-history

Goguen, L. M. S., Hiester, M. A., & Nordstrom, A. H. (2010). Associations among peer relationships, academic achievement, and persistence in college. *Journal of College Student Retention: Research, Theory, & Practice, 12*(3), 319–337. https://doi.org/10.2190/CS.12.3.d

Gold, S. P., & Stewart, D. L. (2011). Lesbian, gay, and bisexual students coming out at the intersection of spirituality and sexual identity. *Journal of LGBT Issues in Counseling, 5*(3–4), 237–258. https://doi.org/10.1080/15538605.2011.633052

Goldbach, C., Knutson, D., & Milton, D. C. (2020, December 31). LGBTQ+ people and COVID-19: The importance of resilience during a pandemic. *Psychology of Sexual Orientation and Gender Diversity, 8*(2), 123–132. http://dx.doi.org/10.1037/sgd0000463

Goldbach, J. T., & Gibbs, J. J. (2017). A developmentally informed adaptation of minority stress for sexual minority adolescents. *Journal of Adolescence, 55*, 36–50. https://doi.org/10.1016/j.adolescence.2016.12.007

Goldberg, A. E. (2018). Transgender students in higher education. Williams Institute. https://williamsinstitute.law.ucla.edu/wp-content/uploads/1808-Trans-Higher-Ed.pdf

Goldberg, A. E., Beemyn, G., & Smith, J. Z. (2018). What is needed, what is valued: Trans students' perspectives on trans-inclusive policies and practices in higher education. *Journal of Educational and Psychological Consultation, 29*(1), 27–67. https://doi.org/10.1080/10474412.2018.1480376

Goldberg, A. E., Kuvalanka, K. A., Budge, S. L., Benz, M. B., & Smith, J. Z. (2019). Health care experiences of transgender binary and nonbinary university students. *Counseling Psychologist*. https://doi.org/10.1177/0011000019827568

Goldberg, S. B. (2020). COVID-19 and LGBT rights: Law in the time of COVID-19. *Columbia Law School*. https://scholarship.law.columbia.edu/faculty_scholarship/2687

Gonzalez, M. (2017). Advocacy for and with LGBT students: An examination of high school counselor experiences. *Professional School Counseling, 20*, 38–46. https://doi.org/10.5330/1096-2409-20.1a.38

Gonzalez, M. C. (2010). *Gender now coloring book: A learning adventure for children and adults*. Reflection Press.

Gonzalez, M., Kokozos, M., Byrd, C. M., & McKee, K. E. (2020). Critical positive youth development: A framework for centering critical consciousness. *Journal of Youth Development, 15*(6), 24–43. https://doi.org/10.5195/jyd.2020.859

González-Rivera, J. A., Rosario-Rodríguez, A., & Santiago-Torres, L. E. (2019). Depresión e ideación suicida en personas de la comunidad LGBT con y sin pareja: Un estudio exploratorio. *Revista Puertorriqueña de Psicología, 30*(2), 254–267.

Goodkind, S., Shook, J. J., Kim, K. H., Pohlig, R. T., & Herring, D. J. (2013). From child welfare to juvenile justice: Race, gender, and system experiences. *Youth Violence and Juvenile Justice*, 11, 249–272.

Goodman, R. D. (2015). A liberatory approach to trauma counseling: Decolonizing our trauma-informed practices. In R. D. Goodman and P. C. Gorski (Eds.), *Decolonizing "multicultural" counseling through social justice* (pp. 55–72). Springer.

Goodman-Scott, E., Betters-Bubon, J., Olsen, J., & Donohue, P. (2020). *Making MTSS work*. American School Counselor Association.

Goodrich, K. M. (2017). Exploring school counselors' motivations to work with LGBTQQI students in schools: A Q methodology study. *Professional School Counseling, 20*(1a), 5–12. https://doi.org/10. 5330/1096-2409-20.1a.5

Gower, A. L., Forster, M., Gloppen, K., Johnson, A. Z., Eisenberg, M. E., Connett, J. E., & Borowsky, I. W. (2017). School practices to foster LGBT-supportive climate: Associations with adolescent bullying involvement. *Prevention Science, 19*, 813–821. https://doi.org/10.1007/s11121-017-0847-4

Gower, A. L., Rider, G. N., Brown, C., McMorris, B. J., Coleman, E., Taliaferro, L. A., & Eisenberg, M. E. (2018). Supporting transgender and gender diverse youth: Protection against emotional distress and substance use. *American Journal of Preventive Medicine, 55*, 787–794. https://doi.org/10.1016/j.amepre.2018.06.030

Gower, A. L., Rider, G. N., McMorris, B. J., & Eisenberg, M. E. (2018). Bullying victimization among LGBTQ youth: Critical issues and future directions. *Current Sexual Health Reports, 10*(4), 246–254. https://doi.org/10.1007/s11930-018-0169-y

Grant, J. M., Mottet, L. A., Tanis, J., Harrison, J., Herman, J. L., & Keisling, M. (2011). Injustice at every turn: A report of the national transgender discrimination survey. Washington: National Center for Transgender Equality and National Gay and Lesbian Task Force. https://www.transequality.org/sites/default/files/docs/resources/NTDS_Report.pdf

Grant Smith, N. (2017). Resilience across life span: Adulthood. In: K. Eckstrand & J. Potter, (Eds), *Trauma, resilience and health promotion in LGBT patients* (pp. 77–88). Springer International Publishing AG.

Gray, A. J. (2002). Stigma in psychiatry. *Journal of the Royal Society of Medicine, 95*(2), 72–76. https://doi.org/10.1258/jrsm.95.2.72

Gray, M. L. (2009). *Out in the country: Youth, media, and queer visibility in rural America*. New York University Press.

Gray, N., Mendelsohn, D., & Omoto, A. (2015). Community connectedness, challenges, and resilience among gay Latino immigrants. *American Journal of Community Psychology, 55*(1–2), 202–214. https://doi.org/10.1007/s10464-014-9697-4

Green, A. E., Price-Feeney, M., & Dorison, S. H. (2020). *Implications of COVID-19 for LGBTQ youth mental health and suicide prevention.* Trevor Project. https://www.thetrevorproject.org/2020/04/03/implications-of-covid-19-for-lgbtq-youth-mental-health-and-suicide-prevention/

Greene, G. J., Fisher, K. A., Kuper, L., Andrews, R., & Mustanski, B. (2015). "Is this normal? Is this not normal? There is no set example": Sexual health intervention preferences of LGBT youth in romantic relationships. *Sexuality Research and Social Policy, 12*, 1–14. https://doi.org/10.1007/s13178-014-0169-2

Gregg, J., & Saha, S. (2006). Losing culture on the way to competence: The use and misuse of culture in medical education. *Academic Medicine, 81*(6), 542–547.

Greteman, A. (2012). Country queers: Queer youth and the politics of rural America. *Journal of LGBT Youth, 9*(1), 63.

Greytak, E. A., Kosciw, J. G., & Diaz, E. M. (2009). *Harsh realities: The experiences of transgender youth in our nation's schools.* GLSEN.

Griffin-Tomas, M., Cahill, S., Kapadia, F., & Halkitis, P. N. (2019). Access to health services among young adult gay men in New York City. *American Journal of Men's Health, 13*(1), 155798831881868. https://doi.org/10.1177/1557988318818683

Griffith, M. (2018). *What is the cost of providing students with adequate psychological support.* NASP. https://www.nasponline.org/research-and-policy/policy-matters-blog/what-is-the-cost-of-providing-students-with-adequate-psychological-support

Grov, C., Bimbi, D. S., Nanín, J. E., & Parsons, J. T. (2006). Race, ethnicity, gender, and generational factors associated with the coming-out process among gay, lesbian, and bisexual individuals. *Journal of Sex Research, 43*(2), 115–121.

Gruenewald, J. (2012). Are anti-lgbt homicides in the United States unique? *Journal of Interpersonal Violence, 27*(18), 3601–3623. https://doi.org/10.1177/0886260512462301

Guidi, J., Lucente, M., Sonino, N., & Fava, G. A. (2020). Allostatic load and its impact on health: A systematic review. *Psychotherapy and Psychosomatics*, 1–17. Advance online publication. https://doi.org/10.1159/000510696

Guittar, N. A. (2014). "At first, I just said 'I like girls'": Coming out with an affinity, not an identity. *Journal of LGBT Youth, 11*(4), 388–407. https://doi.org/10.1080/19361653.2014.910486

Guittar, N. A., & Rayburn, R. L. (2016). Coming out: The career management of one's sexuality. *Sexuality & Culture, 20*(2), 336–357. https://doi.org/10.1007/s12119-015-9325-y

Haas, S. M., & Whitton, S. W. (2015). The significance of living together and importance of marriage in same-sex couples. *Journal of Homosexuality, 62*(9), 1241–1263. https://doi.org/10.1080/00918369.2015.1037137

Hadland, S. E., Yehia, B. R., & Makadon, H. J. (2016). Caring for lesbian, gay, bisexual, transgender, and questioning youth in inclusive and affirmative environments. *Pediatric Clinics of North America, 63*(6), 955–969. https://doi.org/10.1016/j.pcl.2016.07.001

Hafeez, H., Zeshan, M., Tahir, M. A., Jahan, N., & Naveed, S. (2017). Health care disparities among lesbian, gay, bisexual, and transgender youth: A literature review. *Cureus, 9*(4), e1184. https://doi.org/10.7759/cureus.1184

Hagai, E. B., Annechino, R., Young, N., & Antin, T. (2020). Intersecting sexual identities, oppressions, and social justice work: Comparing LGBTQ Baby Boomers to Millennials who came of age after the 1980s AIDS epidemic. *Journal of Social Issues, 76*(4), 971–992. https://doi.org/10.1111/josi.12405

Halkitis, P. N., Maiolatesi, A. J., & Krause, K. D. (2020). The health challenges of emerging adult gay men: Effecting change in health care. *Pediatric Clinics of North America, 67*(2), 293–308. https://doi.org/10.1016/j.pcl.2019.12.003

Hall, W. J. (2018). Psychosocial risk and protective factors for depression among lesbian, gay, bisexual, and queer youth: A systematic review. *Journal of Homosexuality, 65*(3), 263–316. https://doi.org/10.1080/00918369.2017.1317467

Haltom, T. M., & Ratcliff, S. (2021). Effects of sex, race, and education on the timing of coming out among lesbian, gay, and bisexual adults in the US. *Archives of Sexual Behavior, 50*(3), 1107–1120. https://doi.org/10.1007/s10508-020-01776-x

Hamilton, A., Sala, G., Quereshi, O., & Eaton, J. (2020). Stories from the field: Mapping innovation in mental health during the COVID-19 pandemic. *Intervention, 18*(2), 159–165. https://doi.org/10.4103/INTV.INTV_22_20

Hammack, P. L., Frost, D. M., & Hughes, S. D. (2019). Queer intimacies: A new paradigm for the study of relationship diversity. *Journal of Sex Research, 56*(4–5), 556–592.

Hammer, T. R., Crethar, H. C., & Hubach, R. D. (2019). The importance of an interdisciplinary approach in our work within the LGBTQ + community. *Journal of LGBT Issues in Counseling, 12*(4), 214–214. https://doi.org/10.1080/15538605.2018.1535469

Han, C., Farruggia, S. P., & Moss, T. P. (2017). Effects of academic mindsets on college students' achievement and retention. *Journal of College Student Development, 58*(8), 1119–1134. https://doi.org/10.1353/csd.2017.0089

Hanneman, T., Garcia, M. R., Touhey, S., & Steward, D. (2022). *Healthcare Equality Index 2022: Promoting equitable and inclusive care for lesbian, gay, bisexual, transgender, and queer patients and their families.* Human Rights Campaign Foundation.

Hanson, T., Zhang, G., Cerna, R., Stern, A., & Austin, G. (2019). *Understanding the experiences of LGBTQ students in California.* WestEd.

Harder, A., Knorth, E., & Kalverboer, M. (2013). A secure base? The adolescent-staff relationship in secure residential youth care. *Child and Family Social Work, 18*(3), 305–317.

Harkness, A., Gattamorta, K. A., Estrada, Y., Jimenez, D., Kanamori, M., Prado, G., & Behar-Zusman, V. (2020). Latinx health disparities research during COVID-19: Challenges and innovations. *Annals of Behavioral Medicine, 54*, 544–547. https://doi.org/10.1093/abm/kaaa054

Harper, G. W., Brodsky, A., & Bruce, D. (2012). What's good about being gay? Perspectives from youth. *Journal of LGBT Youth, 9*, 22–41. https://doi.org/10.1080/19361653.2012.628230

Harris, M., & Fallot, R. D. (Eds.). (2001). *Using trauma theory to design service systems.* Jossey-Bass/Wiley.

Hatchel, T., & Marx, R. (2018). Understanding intersectionality and resiliency among transgender adolescents: Exploring pathways among peer victimization, school belonging, and drug use. *International Journal of Environmental Research and Public Health, 15*(6), 1289. https://doi.org/10.3390/ijerph15061289

Hatchel, T., Polanin, J. R., & Espelage, D. L. (2019). Suicidal thoughts and behaviors among LGBTQ youth: Meta-analyses and a systematic review. *Archives of Suicide Research, 25*(1), 1–37. https://doi.org/10.1080/13811118.2019.1663329

Hatzenbuehler, M. (2009). How does sexual minority stigma "Get under the skin"? A psychological mediation framework. *Psychological Bulletin, 135*, 707–730. https://doi.org/10.1037/a0016441

Hatzenbuehler, M. L. (2011). The social environment and suicide attempts in lesbian, gay, and bisexual youth. *Pediatrics, 127*(5), 896–903. https://doi.org/10.1542/peds.2010-3020

Hatzenbuehler, M. L., Flores, A. R., & Gates, G. J. (2017). Social attitudes regarding same sex marriage and LGBT health disparities: Results from a National Probability Sample. *Journal of Social Issues, 73*(3), 508–528. https://doi.org/10.1111/josi.12229

Hatzenbuehler, M. L., Keyes, K. M., & Hasin, D. S. (2009). State-level policies and psychiatric morbidity in lesbian, gay, and bisexual populations. *American Journal of Public Health, 99*(12), 2275–2281. https://doi.org/10.2105/AJPH.2008.153510

Hatzenbuehler, M. L., & Pachankis, J. E. (2016). Stigma and minority stress as social determinants of health among lesbian, gay, gisexual, and transgender youth: Research evidence and clinical implications. *Pediatric Clinics of North America, 63*(6), 985–997. https://doi.org/10.1016/j.pcl.2016.07.003

Hatzenbuehler, M. L., Shen, Y., Vandewater, E. A., & Russell, S. T. (2019). Proposition 8 and homophobic bullying in California. *Pediatrics, 143*(6), e20182116. https://doi.org/10.1542/peds.2018-2116

Hawke, L. D., Hayes, E., Darnay, K., and Henderson, J. (2021). Mental health among transgender and gender diverse youth: An exploration of effects during the COVID-19 pandemic. *Psychology of Sexual Orientation and Gender Diversity, 8*(2), 180–187. http://dx.doi.org/10.1037/sgd0000467

Hein, L. C., Stokes, F., Greenberg, C. S., & Saewyc, E. M. (2018). Policy brief: Protecting vulnerable LGBTQ youth and advocating for ethical health care. *Nursing Outlook, 66*(5), 505–507.

Hendricks, M. L., & Testa, R. J. (2012). A conceptual framework for clinical work with transgender and gender nonconforming clients: An adaptation of the Minority Stress Model. *Professional Psychology: Research and Practice, 43*(5), 460–467. https://doi.org/10.1037/a0029597

Henry, R. S., Perrin, P. B., Sawyer, A., & Pugh, M. (2020). Health conditions, access to care, mental health, and wellness behaviors in lesbian, gay, bisexual, and transgender adults. *International Journal of Chronic Diseases, 2020*, 1–8. https://doi.org/10.1155/2020/9094047

Herek, G. M., Chopp, R., & Strohl, D. (2012). Sexual stigma: putting sexual minority health issues in context. In: I. H. Meyer & M. E. Northridge (Eds.), *The health of sexual minorities: Public health perspectives on lesbian, gay, bisexual, and transgender populations* (pp. 171–208). Springer.

Herek, G. M., & Garnets, L. D. (2007). Sexual orientation and mental health. *Annual Review of Clinical Psychology, 3*, 353–375. https://doi.org/10.1146/annurev.clinpsy.3.022806.091510

Herman, J. L. (1997). *Trauma and recovery*. Basic Books.

Herman, J. L. (2015). *Trauma and recovery: The aftermath of violence—from domestic abuse to political terror*. Hachette.

Hernandez, F., & Fraynd, D. J. (2014). Leadership's role in inclusive LGBTQ-supportive schools. *Theory into Practice, 53*, 115–122. https://doi.org/10.1080/00405841.2014.885811

Herrick, A. L., Matthews, A. K., & Garofalo, R. (2010). Health risk behaviors in an urban sample of young women who have sex with women. *Journal of Lesbian Studies, 14*(1), 80–92. https://doi.org/10.1080/10894160903060440

Hershberger, S. L., & D'Augelli, A. R. (1995). The impact of victimization on the mental health and suicidality of lesbian, gay, and bisexual youths. *Developmental Psychology, 31*, 65–74. https://doi.org/10.1037/0012-1649.31.1.65

Herz, D., Lee, P., Lutz, L., Stewart, M., Tuell, J., & Wiig, J. (2012). Addressing the needs of multi-system youth: Strengthening the connection between child welfare and juvenile justice. Center for Juvenile Justice Reform.

Hesse-Biber, S. (2016). Doing interdisciplinary mixed methods health care research: Working the boundaries, tensions, and synergistic potential of team-based research. *Qualitative Health Research, 26*(5), 649–658. https://doi.org/10.1177/1049732316634304

Hicks Peterson, T. (2018). Self-awareness and radical healing. In *Student Development and Social Justice.* https://doi.org/10.1007/978-3-319-57457-8_3

Hidalgo, M. A., & Chen, D. (2019). Experiences of gender minority stress in cisgender parents of transgender/gender-expansive prepubertal children: A qualitative study. *Journal of Family Issues, 40*(7), 865–886. https://doi.org/10.1159/000355235

Hidalgo, M. A., Ehrensaft, D., Tishelman, A. C., Clark, L. F., Garofalo, R., Rosenthal, S. M., Spack, N. P., & Olson, J. (2013). The gender affirmative model: What we know and what we aim to learn. *Human Development, 56*(5), 285–290.

Hill, R. M., Rooney, E. E., Mooney, M. A., Kaplow, J. B., Hill, R. M., Rooney, E. E., & Mooney, M. A. (2017). Links between social support, thwarted belongingness, and suicide ideation among lesbian, gay, and bisexual college students. *Journal of Family Strengths, 17*(2). http://digitalcommons.library.tmc.edu/jfs/vol17/iss2/6

Hillier, L., Mitchell, K. J., & Ybarra, M. L. (2012). The Internet as a safety net: Findings from a series of online focus groups with LGB and non-LGB young people in the United States. *Journal of LGBT Youth, 9*(3), 225–246.

Himmelstein, K., & Bruckner, H. (2011). Criminal justice and school sanctions against non-heterosexual youth: A national longitudinal study. *Pediatrics, 127,* 49–57.

Hines, M. (2000). Gonadal hormones and sexual differentiation of human behavior: Effects on psycho-social and cognitive development. In A. Matsumoto (Ed.), *Sexual differentiation of the brain* (pp. 257–278). CRC Press.

Hines, M. (2005). *Brain Gender.* Oxford University Press.

Hines, M. (2009). Gonadal hormones and sexual differentiation of human brain and behavior. In D. W. Pfaff, A. P. Arnold, A. M. Etgen, S. E. Fahrbach, & R. T. Rubin (Eds.), *Hormones, brain and behavior* (2nd ed., pp. 1869–1909). Academic.

Hockenberry, S. (2016). Juveniles in Residential Placement, 2013. US Department of Justice, Office of Justice Programs, Office of Juvenile Justice and Delinquency Prevention. http://www.ncjj.org/pdf/Juvenile%20Arrests%20Bulletins/249507.pdf

Hoffarth, M. R., & Bogaert, A. F. (2017). Opening the closet door: Openness to experience, masculinity, religiosity, and coming out among same-sex attracted men. *Personality and Individual Differences, 109,* 215–219. https://doi.org/10.1016/j.paid.2017.01.011

Hoffman, S., & Hoffman, I. (2014). *Jacob's new dress* (C. Case, Illus). Albert Whitman & Company.

Hollywood Homeless Youth Partnership. (n.d.). *The ARC framework (attachment, self-regulation, competency) for runaway and homeless youth serving agencies.* http://hhyp.org/wp-content/uploads/2012/02/HHYP_ARC_Framework.pdf

Hollywood Homeless Youth Partnership. (2009). *10 reasons for integrating trauma-informed approaches in programs for runaway and homeless youth.* http://hhyp.org/wp-content/uploads/2012/02/HHYP_10Reasons_Flyer.pdf

Hollywood Homeless Youth Partnership. (2012). *Trauma informed consequences for homeless youth.* http://hhyp.org/wp-content/uploads/2012/02/Trauma-Informed-Consequences.pdf

Holsinger, K., & Hodge, J. (2016). The experience of lesbian, gay, bisexual and transgender girls in juvenile justice systems. *Feminist Criminology, 11,* 23–47.

Hom, K. A., & Woods, S. J. (2013). Trauma and its aftermath for commercially sexually exploited women as told by front-line service providers. *Issues in Mental Health Nursing, 34*(2), 75–81.

Hood, L., Sherrell, D., Pfeffer, C. A., & Mann, E. S. (2018). LGBTQ college students' experiences with university health services: An exploratory study. *Journal of Homosexuality, 66*(6), 797–814. https://doi.org/10.1080/00918369.2018.1484234

Hook, J. N., Davis, D. E., Owen, J., Worthington Jr., E. L., & Utsey, S. O. (2013). Cultural humility: Measuring openness to culturally diverse clients. *Journal of Counseling Psychology, 60*(3), 353–366. https://doi.org/10.1037/a0032595

Hopper, E. K., Bassuk, E. L., & Olivet, J. (2010). Shelter from the storm: Trauma-informed care in homelessness services settings. *Open Health Services and Policy Journal, 3*(1).

Hopper, E. K., & Spinazzola, J. (2006). *Trauma-informed facility assessment.* Trauma Center at Justice Resource Institute.

Hubach, R. D., Dodge, B., Schick, V., Ramos, W. D., Herbenick, D., Li, M. J., . . . Reece, M. (2015). Experiences of HIV-positive gay, bisexual and other men who have sex with men residing in relatively rural areas. *Culture, Health & Sexuality, 17*(7), 795–809. https://doi.org/10.1080/13691058.2014.994231

Hughes, K., Bellis, M. A., Hardcastle, K. A., Sethi, D., Butchart, A., Mikton, C., Jones, L., & Dunne, M. P. (2017). The effect of multiple adverse childhood experiences on health: A systematic review and meta-analysis. *Lancet Public Health, 2*(8), 356–366.

Hughes, R. L., Damon, C., & Heiden-Rootes, K. (2017). Where's the LGBT in integrated care research? A systematic review. *Families, Systems, & Health, 35*(3), 308–319. http://dx.doi.org/10.1037/fsh0000290

Hughto, J. M., Gunn, H. A., Rood, B. A., & Pantalone, D. W. (2020). Social and medical gender affirmation experiences are inversely associated with mental health problems in a US non-probability sample of transgender adults. *Archives of Sexual Behavior, 49*(7), 2635–2647.

Hulko, W., & Hovanes, J. (2018). Intersectionality in the lives of LGBTQ youth: Identifying as LGBTQ and finding community in small cities and rural towns. *Journal of Homosexuality, 65*(4), 427–455. https://doi.org/10.1080/00918369.2017.1320169

Human Rights Campaign. (2021). Violence against the transgender and gender non-conforming community in 2021. https://www.hrc.org/resources/fatal-violence-against-the-transgender-and-gender-non-conforming-community-in-2021

Hunt, J., & Moodie-Mills, A. (2012). The unfair criminalization of gay and transgender youth: An overview of the experiences of LGBT youth in the juvenile justice system. Center for American Progress. https://www.ncjrs.gov/App/Publications/abstract.aspx?ID=267708

Hyde, J. S. (2005). The gender similarities hypothesis. *American Psychologist, 60*(6), 581–592. https://doi.org/10.1037/0003-066X.60.6.581

Hyde, J. S., Bigler, R. S., Joel, D., Tate, C. C., & van Anders, S. M. (2019). The future of sex and gender in psychology: Five challenges to the gender binary. *American Psychologist, 74*(2), 171–193. https://doi.org/10.1037/amp0000307

Institute of Medicine. (2011). *The health of lesbian, gay, bisexual, and transgender people: Building a foundation for better understanding.* National Academies Press. https://doi.org/10.17226/13128

Institute of Medicine. (2013). *Interprofessional education for collaboration: Learning how to improve health from interprofessional models across the continuum of education to practice: Workshop summary.* National Academies Press.

International Institute of Restorative Practices. (2021). *Restorative practices in schools.* IIRP Graduate School. Retrieved from https://www.iirp.edu/resources/restorative-practices-in-schools-k-12-education.

Irvine, A. (2010). "We've had three of them": Addressing the invisibility of lesbian, gay, bisexual and gender nonconforming youths in the juvenile justice system. *Columbia Journal of Gender and Law, 19*, 675–701.

Irvine, A., & Canfield, A. (2016). The overrepresentation of lesbian, gay, bisexual, questioning, gender nonconforming and transgender youth within the child welfare to juvenile justice crossover population. *Journal of Gender, Social Policy & the Law, 24*, 243–261.

Iversen, J., Sabin, K., Chang, J., Thomas, R. M., Prestage, G., Strathdee, S. A., & Maher, L. (2020). COVID-19, HIV and key populations: Cross-cutting issues and the need for population-specific responses. *Journal of the International AIDS Society, 23*, 1–6. https://doi.org/10.1002/jia2.25632

Jackson, K. (2017). Supporting LGBTQ students in high school for the college transition: The role of school counselors. *Professional School Counseling, 20*(1a), 21–28. https://doi.org/10.5330/1096-2409-20.1a.21

Jackson Levin, N., Kattari, S. K., Piellusch, E. K., & Watson, E. (2020). "We just take care of each other": Navigating "chosen family" in the context of health, illness, and the mutual provision of care amongst queer and transgender young adults. *International Journal of Environmental Research and Public Health, 17*(19).

Jackson, S. D., Mohr, J. J., Sarno, E. L., Kindahl, A. M., & Jones, I. L. (2020). Intersectional experiences, stigma-related stress, and psychological health among Black LGBQ individuals. *Journal of Consulting and Clinical Psychology, 88*(5), 416–428. https://doi.org/10.1037/ccp0000489

Jacobs, J., & Freundlich, M. (2006). Achieving permanency for LGBTQ+ youth. *Child Welfare 85*(2), 299–316.

James, S. E., Herman, J. L., Rankin, S., Keisling, M., Mottet, L., & Anafi, M. (2016). *The report of the 2015 US transgender survey*. National Center for Transgender Equality. http://www.transequality.org/

James, S. E., & Salcedo, B. (2017). *2015 U.S. transgender survey: Report on the experiences of Latino/a respondent*. www.USTransSurvey.org

Jamil, O. B., Harper, G. W., & Fernandez, M. I. (2009). Sexual and ethnic identity development among gay/bisexual/questioning (GBQ) male ethnic minority adolescents. *Cultural Diversity & Ethnic Minority Psychology, 15*(3), 203–214. https://doi.org/10.1037/a0014795

Janicka, A., Chung, K., & Reisner, S. (2018). Mental health and well-being of transgender youth: Clinical considerations. *International Journal of Pediatrics and Adolescent Medicine, 29*, 20–43.

Jasemi, M., Valizadeh, L., Zamanzadeh, V., & Keogh, B. (2017). A concept analysis of holistic care by hybrid model. *Indian Journal of Palliative Care, 23*(1), 71–80.

Jemal, A. (2017). Critical consciousness: A critique and critical analysis of the literature. *Urban Review, 49*(4), 602–626. https://doi.org/10.1007/s11256-017-0411-3

Jen, W. (2016). The use of Image Theatre to examine the acculturation process of Taiwanese international performing arts students in New York City. *Drama Therapy Review, 2*(1), 79–97.

Jensen, S. (2011). Othering, identity formation and agency. *Qualitative Studies, 2*(2), 63–78. https://doi.org/10.7146/qs.v2i2.5510

Joel, D., Berman, Z., Tavor, I., Wexler, N., Gaber, O., Stein, Y., . . . Assaf, Y. (2015). Sex beyond the genitalia: The human brain mosaic. Proceedings of the National Academy of Sciences of the United States of America, 112, 15468–15473. https://doi.org/10.1073/pnas.1509654112

Johns, M. M., Pingel, E. S., Youatt, E. J., Soler, J. H., McClelland, S. I., & Bauermeister, J. A. (2013). LGBT community, social network characteristics, and smoking behaviors in young sexual minority women. *American Journal of Community Psychology, 52*(1), 141–154.

Johns, M. M., Poteat, V. P., Horn, S. S., & Kosciw, J. (2019). Strengthening our schools to promote resilience and health among LGBTQ youth: Emerging evidence and research priorities from *The State of LGBTQ Youth Health and Wellbeing* Symposium. *LGBT Health, 6*(4), 146–155. https://doi.org/10.1089/lgbt.2018.0109

Johnson, A. H. (2016). Transnormativity: A new concept and its validation through documentary film about transgender men. *Sociological Inquiry, 86*(4), 465–491. https://doi.org/10.1111/soin.12127

Joint Commission. (2011). *Advancing effective communication, cultural competence, and patient-and family-centered care for the lesbian, gay, bisexual, and transgender (LGBT) community: A field guide.* https://www.jointcommission.org/-/media/tjc/documents/resources/patient-safety-topics/health-equity/lgbtfieldguide_web_linked_verpdf.pdf?db=web&hash=FD725DC02CFE6E4F21A35EBD839BBE97&hash=FD725DC02CFE6E4F21A35EBD839BBE97

Jones, B., Bowe, M., McNamara, N., Guerin, E., & Carter, T. (2021). Exploring the mental health experiences of young trans and gender diverse people during the coronavirus pandemic. *International Journal of Transgender Health* [preprint]. https://doi.org/10.1080/26895269.2021.1890301

Jones, T. (2017). Evidence affirming school supports for Australian transgender and gender diverse students. *Sexual Health, 14*(5), 412–416. https://doi.org/10.1071/SH17001

Jones, T., Smith, E., Ward, R., Dixon, J., Hillier, L., & Mitchell, A. (2016). School experiences of transgender and gender diverse students in Australia. *Sex Education, 16*(2), 156–171. https://doi.org/10.1080/14681811.2015.1080678

Juster, R. (2019). *Sex × gender and sexual orientation in relation to stress hormones and allostatic load.* SAGE Publications. https://doi.org/10.1177/2470289719862555

Kabat-Zinn, J. (2013). *Full catastrophe living: Using the wisdom of your body and mind to face stress, pain and illness.* Delacorte.

Kail, B. L., Acosta, K. L., & Wright, E. R. (2015). State-level marriage equality and the health of same-sex couples. *American Journal of Public Health, 105*(6), 1101–1105. https://doi.org/10.2105/AJPH.2015.302589

Kann, L., McManus, T., Harris, W. A., Shanklin, S. L., Flint, K. H., Queen, B., Lowry, R., Chyen, D., Whittle, L., Thornton, J., Lim, C., Bradford, D., Yamakawa, Y., Leon, M., Brener, N., & Ethier, K. A. (2018). Youth risk behavior surveillance—United States. *Morbidity and Mortality Weekly Report Surveillance Summaries, 67*(8), 1–114.

Kann, L., Olsen, E. O., McManus, T., Harris, W. A., Shanklin, S. L., Flint, K. H., Queen, B., Lowry, R., Chyen, D., Whittle, L., Thornton, J., Lim, C., Yamakawa, Y., Brener, N., & Zaza, S. (2016). Sexual identity, sex of sexual contacts, and health-related behaviors among students in grades 9–12—United States and selected sites, 2015. *Morbidity and Mortality Weekly Report Surveillance Summaries, 65*(9), 1–202. http://dx.doi.org/10.15585/mmwr.ss6509a1

Kassing, F., Casanova, T., Griffin, J. A., Wood, E., & Stepleman, L. M. (2021). The effects of polyvictimization on mental and physical health outcomes in an LGBTQ+ sample. *Journal of Traumatic Stress, 34*, 161–171.

Kates, J., Ranji, U., Beamesderfer, A., Salganicoff, A., & Dawson, L. (2018). *Health and access to care and coverage for lesbian, gay, bisexual, and transgender individuals in the U.S.* Henry Kaiser Family Foundation. http://files.kff.org/attachment/Issue-Brief-Health-and-Access-to-Care-and-Coverage-for-LGBT-Individuals-in-the-US

Katz-Wise, S. L., Ehrensaft, D., Vetters, R., Forcier, M., & Austin, S. B. (2018). Family functioning and mental health of transgender and gender-nonconforming youth in the Trans Teen and Family Narratives Project. *The Journal of Sex Research, 55*, 582–590. https://doi.org/10.1080/00224499.2017.1415291

Kelly, J., Davis, C., & Schlesinger, C. (2015). Substance use by same sex attracted young people: Prevalence, perceptions and homophobia. *Drug and Alcohol Review, 34*(4), 358–365. https://doi.org/10.1111/dar.12158

Kent, M. (2006). Gender differentiation. *Oxford Dictionary of Sports Science & Medicine.* Oxford University Press. https://www.oxfordreference.com/view/10.1093/acref/9780198568506.001.0001/acref-9780198568506-e-2832

Keo-Meier, C., & Ehrensaft, D. E. (2018). *The gender affirmative model: An interdisciplinary approach to supporting transgender and gender expansive children.* American Psychological Association.

Kerig, P., Bennett, D., Thompson, M., & Becker, S. (2012). "Nothing really matters": Emotional numbing as a link between trauma exposure and callousness in delinquent youth. *Journal of Traumatic Stress, 25*, 272–279.

Kerr, D. L., Ding, K., & Chaya, J. (2014). Substance use of lesbian, gay, bisexual and heterosexual college students. *American Journal of Health Behavior, 38*(6), 951–962. https://doi.org/10.5993/AJHB.38.6.17

Keuroghlian, A. S. (2016). The importance of behavioral health integration for LGBT patients. [Presentation]. National LGBT Health Education Center: A Program of the Fenway Institute; National Center for Innovation in HIV Care. https://www.lgbtqiahealtheducation.org/wp-content/uploads/2016/09/Behavioral-Health-Integration-Webinar_Final.pdf

Keuroghlian, A. S., Shtasel, D., & Bassuk, E. L. (2014). Out on the street: A public health and policy agenda for lesbian, gay, bisexual, and transgender youth who are homeless. *American Journal of Orthopsychiatry, 84*(1), 66.

Keyes, C. L., Eisenberg, D., Perry, G. S., Dube, S. R., Kroenke, K, & Dhingra, S. S. (2012). The relationship of level of positive mental health with current mental disorders in predicting suicidal behavior and academic impairment in college students. *Journal of American College Health, 60*(2), 126–133. https://doi.org/10.1080/07448481.2011.608393

Kidd, J. D., Jackman, K. B., Barucco, R., Dworkin, J. D., Dolezal, C., Navalta, T. V., Belloir, J., & Bockting, W. O. (2021). Understanding the impact of the COVID-19 pandemic on the mental health of transgender and gender nonbinary individuals engaged in a longitudinal cohort study. *Journal of Homosexuality, 68*(4), 592–611. https://doi.org/10.1080/00918369.2020.1868185

Klemmer, C. L., Rusow, J., Goldbach, J., Kattari, S. K., & Rice, E. (2021). Socially assigned gender nonconformity and school violence experience among transgender and cisgender adolescents. *Journal of Interpersonal Violence, 36*(15–16), NP8567-NP8589. https://doi.org/10.1177/0886260519844781

Kline, N. S. (2020). Rethinking COVID-19 vulnerability: A call for LGBTQ+ im/migrant health equity in the United States during the pandemic. *Health Equity, 4*(1), 239–242. https://doi.org/10.1089/heq.2020.0012

Knight, D. A., & Jarrett, D. (2017). Preventive health care for women who have sex with women. *American Family Physician, 95*(5), 314–321.

Knight, R. E., Shoveller, J. A., Carson, A. M., & Contreras-Whitney, J. G. (2014). Examining clinicians' experiences providing sexual health services for LGBTQ youth: Considering social and structural determinants of health in clinical practice. *Health Education Research, 29*(4), 662–670. https://doi.org/10.1093/her/cyt116

Knutson, D., Kertz, S., Chambers-Baltz, S., Christie, M. B., Harris, E., & Perinchery, R. (2020, August 6). A pilot test of a text message-based transgender and nonbinary affirmative cognitive-behavioral intervention for anxiety and depression. *Psychology of Sexual Orientation and Gender Diversity, 8*(4), 440–450. http://dx.doi.org/10.1037/sgd0000438

Kohlberg, L. (1966). A cognitive developmental analysis of children's sex role concepts and attitudes. In E. E. Maccoby (Ed.), *The development of sex differences* (pp. 82–172). Stanford University Press.

Kolbuck, V. D., Muldoon, A. L., Rychlik, K., Hidalgo, M. A., & Chen, D. (2019). Psychological functioning, parenting stress, and parental support among clinic-referred prepubertal gender-expansive children. *Clinical Practice in Pediatric Psychology, 7*(3), 254. https://doi.org/10.1037/cpp0000293

Koob, J. J., Brasfield, T. L., & Bernstein, B. M. (1993). The outcome of cognitive-behavioral and support group brief therapies for depressed, HIV-infected persons. *American Journal of Psychiatry, 150*(1), 1679–1686.

Korchmaros, J. D., Ybarra, M. L., & Mitchell, K. J. (2015). Adolescent online romantic relationship initiation: Differences by sexual and gender identification. *Journal of Adolescence, 40*, 54–64. https://doi,org/10.1016/j.adolescence.2015.01.004

Kort, J. (2008). *Gay affirmative therapy for the straight clinician: The essential guide.* W.W. Norton & Co.

Kosciw, J. G., Clark, C. M., Truong, N. L., & Zongrone, A. D. (2019). *The 2019 National School Climate Survey: The experiences of lesbian, gay, bisexual, transgender, and queer youth in our nation's schools.* GLSEN. www.glsen.org/research

Kosciw, J. G., & Cullen, M. K. (2002). *The GLSEN 2001 national school climate survey: The school-related experiences of our nation's lesbian, gay, bisexual, and transgender youth.* GLSEN.

Kosciw, J. G., Greytak, E. A., Palmer, N. A., & Boesen, M. J. (2013). The 2013 National School Climate Survey: The experiences of lesbian, gay, bisexual, and transgender youth in our nation's schools. GLSEN.

Kosciw, J. G., Greytak, E. A., Zongrone, A. D., Clark, C. M., & Truong, N. L. (2018). The 2017 National School Climate Survey: The experiences of lesbian, gay, bisexual, and queer youth in our nation's schools. GLSEN.

Kosciw, J. G., Palmer, N. A., & Kull, R. M. (2015). Reflecting resiliency: Openness about sexual orientation and/or gender identity and its relationship to well-being and educational outcomes for LGBT students. *American Journal of Community Psychology, 55*(1–2), 167–178. https://doi.org/10.1007/s10464-014-9642-6

Kosciw, J. G., Palmer, N. A., Kull, R. M., & Greytak, E. A. (2013). The effect of negative school climate on academic outcomes for LGBT youth and the role of in-school supports. *Journal of School Violence, 12*, 45–63. https://doi.org/10.1080/15388220.2012.732546

Krause, K. D. (2021). Implications of the COVID-19 pandemic on LGBTQ communities. *Journal of Public Health Management and Practice, 27*(1), S69–S71. https://doi.org/10.1097/phh.0000000000001273

Kronenfeld, J. (2013). *Social determinants, health disparities and linkages to health and health care.* Emerald Group Publishing Limited.

Kuper, L. E., Stewart, S., Preston, S., Lau, M., & Lopez, X. (2020). Body dissatisfaction and mental health outcomes of youth on gender-affirming hormone therapy. *Pediatrics, 145*(4), e20193006. https://doi.org/10.1542/peds.2019-3006

Kuper, L., Wright, L., & Mustanski, B. (2018). Gender identity development among transgender and gender nonconforming emerging adults: An intersectional approach. *International Journal of Transgenderism, 19*(4), 436–455. https://doi.org/10.1080/15532739.2018.1443869

Kuvalanka, K. A., Gardner, M., & Munroe, C. (2019). All in the family: How extended family relationships are influenced by children's gender diverse and transgender identities. *Families in transition: Parenting gender-diverse children, adolescents, and young adults*, 102–117.

Kuvalanka, K. A., Weiner, J. L., & Mahan, D. (2014). Child, family, and community transformations: Findings from interviews with mothers of transgender girls. *Journal of GLBT Family Studies, 10*(4), 354–379.

Kuvalanka, K. A., Weiner, J. L., Munroe, C., Goldberg, A. E., & Gardner, M. (2017). Trans and gender-nonconforming children and their caregivers: Gender presentations, peer relations, and well-being at baseline. *Journal of Family Psychology, 31*(7), 889–899. https://doi.org/10.1037/fam0000338

Kwate, N., & Meyer, I. H. (2010). The myth of meritocracy and African American health. *American Journal of Public Health, 100*, 1831–1834. http://dx.doi.org/10.2105/AJPH.2009.186445

Labelle, S. (2015). *The genderific coloring book*. AssignedMale.

Lacy, A. (2021). How the Trump era encouraged publicly funded discrimination in adoption and foster care: The Biden administration can block a Trump rule codifying legal discrimination using federal funds, but 11 state-level measures remain intact. *The Intercept*. https://theintercept.com/2021/02/08/adoption-foster-discrimination-law

Lagos, D. (2018). Looking at population health beyond "male" and "female": Implications of transgender identity and gender nonconformity for population health. *Demography, 55*(6), 2097–2117. https://doi.org/10.1007/s13524-018-0714-3

Lakey, B., & Cohen, S. (2000). Social support theory and measurement. In S. Cohen, L. G. Underwood, & B. H. Gottlieb (Eds.), *Social support measurement and intervention: A guide for health and social scientists* (pp. 29–52). Oxford University Press.

Lambda Legal. (2010). When health care isn't caring: Lambda Legal's survey of discrimination against LGBT people and people with HIV. https://www.lambdalegal.org/publications/when-health-care-isnt-caring

Lamis, D. A., & Lester, D. (Eds.) (2011). *Understanding and preventing college student suicide*. Charles C Thomas Publisher.

Lange, T. M. (2020). Trans-affirmative narrative exposure therapy (TA-NET): A therapeutic approach for targeting minority stress, internalized stigma, and trauma reactions among gender diverse adults. *Practice Innovations, 5*(3), 230.

Lansford, J., Miller-Johnson, S., Berline, L., Dodge, K., Bates, J., & Petit, G. (2007). Early physical abuse and later violent delinquency: A prospective longitudinal study. *Child Maltreatment, 12*, 233–245.

Larson, M., Orr, M., & Warne, D. (2016). Using student health data to understand and promote academic success in higher education settings. *College Student Journal, 50*(4), 590–602.

Lavenda, R. H., & Schultz, E. A. (2013). *Anthropology: What does it mean to be human?* (p. 576). Oxford University Press.

Lavietes, M., & Ramos, E. (2022, March 20). *Nearly 240 anti-LGBTQ bills filed in 2022 so far, most of them targeting trans people*. NBC News. https://www.nbcnews.com/nbc-out/out-politics-and-policy/nearly-240-anti-lgbtq-bills-filed-2022-far-targeting-trans-people-rcna20418

Lazarus, R. S., & Folkman, S. (1984). *Stress, appraisal, and coping*. Springer.

Le, V., Arayasirikul, S., Chen, Y-H., Jin, H., & Wilson, E. C. (2016). Types of social support and parental acceptance among transfemale youth and their impact on mental health, sexual debut, history of sex work, and condomless anal intercourse. *Journal of the International AIDS Society, 19*, 1–6. https://doi.org/10.7448/IAS.19.3.20781

Learning for Justice. (2021). *Gender and sexual identity*. https://www.learningforjustice.org/topics/gender-sexual-identity

Lee, C., & Ostergard, C. R. (2017). Measuring discrimination against LGBTQ people: A cross-national analysis. *Human Rights Quarterly, 39*, 37–72.

Lee, H. Y., & Mutz, D. C. (2019). Changing attitudes toward same-sex marriage: A three-wave panel study. *Political Behavior, 41*(3), 701–722. https://doi.org/10.1007/s11109-018-9463-7

Lee, R., Loeb, D., & Butterfield, A. (2014). Sexual history taking curriculum: Lecture and standardized patient cases. *MedEdPORTAL, 10*(1), 1–5. https://doi.org/10.15766/mep_2374-8265.9856

Lefevor, G. T., Boyd-Rogers, C. C., Sprague, B. M., & Janis, R. A. (2019). Health disparities between genderqueer, transgender, and cisgender individuals: An extension of minority stress theory. *Journal of Counseling Psychology, 66*(4), 385–395. https://doi.org/10.1037/cou0000339

Lehavot, K., & Simoni, J. M. (2011). The impact of minority stress on mental health and substance use among sexual minority women. *Journal of Consulting and Clinical Psychology, 79*(2), 159–170. https://doi.org/10.1037/a0022839

Lenson, J. (2015). Litigation primer attacking state "no promo homo" laws: Why "don't say gay" is not ok. *Law and Sexuality: A Review of Lesbian, Gay, Bisexual & Transgender Legal Issues, 24*, 145–162.

lesbian, gay, bisexual, transgender, and queer (LGBTQ) students. *Professional School*

Levi, J., & Connors, C. (2018). Transgender youth, medical professionals, and the law: What you should know. *International Journal of Pediatrics and Adolescent Medicine, 29*, 131–151.

Levin, M. E., & Levin, J. R. (1991). A critical examination of academic retention programs for at-risk minority college students. *Journal of College Student Development, 32*(4), 323–334. http://0-search.ebscohost.com.library.alliant.edu/login.aspx?direct=true&db=psyh&AN=1991-34613-001&site=ehost-live&scope=site

Liang, C. T. H., Rocchino, G. H., Gutekunst, M. H. C., Paulvin, C., Li, K. M., & Elam-Snowden, T. (2020). Perspectives of respect, teacher-student relationships, and school climate among boys of color: A multifocus group study. *Psychology of Men & Masculinities, 21*(3), 345–356.

Liben, L. (2017). Gender development: A constructivist-ecological perspective. In N. Budwig, E. Turiel, & P. Zelazo (Eds.), *New perspectives on human development* (pp. 143–144). Cambridge University Press.

Liben, L. S., & Bigler, R. S. (2002). The developmental course of gender differentiation: Conceptualizing, measuring, and evaluating constructs and pathways. *Monographs of the Society for Research in Child Development, 67*(2), vii–147.

Lindquist, L. M., Livingston, N. A., Heck, N. C., & Machek, G. R. (2017). Predicting depressive symptoms at the intersection of attribution and minority stress theories. *Journal of Gay & Lesbian Mental Health, 21*(1), 32–50. https://doi.org/10.1080/19359705.2016.1217498

Linehan, M. M. (2014). *DBT training manual*. Guilford Press.

Liu, H., Zhang, M., Yang, Q., & Yu, B. (2019). Gender differences in the influence of social isolation and loneliness on depressive symptoms in college students: A longitudinal study. *Social Psychiatry and Psychiatric Epidemiology: The International Journal for Research in Social and Genetic Epidemiology and Mental Health Services.* https://doi.org/10.1007/s00127-019-01726-6

Liu, J. X., & Choi, K. H. (2013). Emerging gay identities in China: The prevalence and predictors of social discrimination against men who have sex with men. In P. Liamputtong (Ed.), *Stigma, discrimination and living with HIV/AIDS* (pp. 271–287). Springer.

Liu, R. T., & Mustanski, B. (2012). Suicidal ideation and self-harm in lesbian, gay, bisexual, and transgender youth. *American Journal of Preventive Medicine, 42*(3), 221–228.

Livingston, J. (1990). *Paris Is Burning*. Off White Productions Inc.

Livingston, N. A., Berke, D., Scholl, J., Ruben, M., & Shipherd, J. C. (2020). Addressing diversity in PTSD treatment: Clinical considerations and guidance for the treatment of

PTSD in LGBTQ populations. *Current Treatment Options in Psychiatry*, 1–17. Advance online publication. https://doi.org/10.1007/s40501-020-00204-0

Logan, C., & Carter, A. (2017). Coming out and gay identity development. In C. B. Roland & L. D. Burlew (Eds.), *Counseling LGBTQ adults during life span* (pp. 3–5). American Counseling Association.

Lombardi, E. L., Wilchins, R. A., Priesing, D., & Malouf, D. (2001). Gender violence: Transgender experiences with violence and discrimination. *Journal of Homosexuality, 42*(1), 89–101. https://doi.org/10.1300/j082v42n01_05

Lou, L. L., Yan, Z., Nickerson, A., & McMorris, R. (2012). An examination of the reciprocal relationship of loneliness and Facebook use among first-year college students. *Journal of Educational Computing Research, 46*(1), 105–117.

Luong, C. T., Rew, L., & Banner, M. (2018). Suicidality in young men who have sex with men: A systematic review of the literature. *Issues in Mental Health Nursing, 39*(1), 37–45. https://doi.org/10.1080/01612840.2017.1390020

Lykens, J. E., LeBlanc, A. J., & Bockting, W. O. (2018). Healthcare experiences among young adults who identify as genderqueer or nonbinary. *LGBT Health, 5*(3), 191–196. https://doi.org/10.1089/lgbt.2017.0215

Lykens, J., Pilloton, M., Silva, C., Schlamm, E., Wilburn, K., & Pence, E. (2019). Google for sexual relationships: Mixed-methods study on digital flirting and online dating among adolescent youth and young adults. *Journal of Medical Internet Research, 5*, e10695. https://doi.org/10.2196/10695

Lyons, H. Z., Brenner, B. R., & Lipman, J. (2010). Patterns of career and identity interference for lesbian, gay, and bisexual young adults. *Journal of Homosexuality, 57*(4), 503–524. https://doi.org/10.1080/00918361003608699

Ma, J., Korpak, A. K., Choukas-Bradley, S., & Macapagal, K. (2021). Patterns of online relationship seeking among transgender and gender diverse adolescents: Advice for others and common inquiries. *Psychology of Sexual Orientation and Gender Diversity*. Advance online publication. http://dx.doi.org/10.1037/sgd0000482

Macapagal, K., Bhatia, R., & Greene, G. J. (2016). Differences in healthcare access, use, and experiences within a community sample of racially diverse lesbian, gay, bisexual, transgender, and questioning emerging adults. *LGBT Health, 3*(6), 434–442. https://doi.org/10.1089/lgbt.2015.0124

Macapagal, K., Greene, G. J., Rivera, Z., & Mustanski, B. (2015). "The best is always yet to come": Relationship stages and processes among young LGBT couples. *Journal of Family Psychology, 29*(3), 309–320. https://doi.org/10.1037/fam0000094

Macapagal, K., Kraus, A., Moskowitz, D. A., & Birnholtz, J. (2020). Geosocial networking application use, characteristics of app-met sexual partners, and sexual behavior among sexual and gender minority adolescents assigned male at birth. *Journal of Sex Research, 57*(8), 1078–1087. https://doi.org/10.1080/00224499.2019.1698004

Macapagal, K., Moskowitz, D. A., Li, D. H., Carrión, A., Bettin, E., Fisher, C. B., & Mustanski, B. (2018). Hookup app use, sexual behavior, and sexual health among adolescent men who have sex with men in the United States. *Journal of Adolescent Health, 62*(6), 708–715. https://doi.org/10.1016/j.jadohealth.2018.01.001

Magette, A. L., Durtschi, J. A., & Love, H. A. (2018). Lesbian, gay, and bisexual substance use in emerging adulthood moderated by parent-child relationships in adolescence. *American Journal of Family Therapy, 46*(3), 272–286. https://doi.org/10.1080/01926187.2018.1493958

Majd, K. (2009). *Hidden injustice: Lesbian, gay, bisexual, and transgender youth in juvenile courts.* Equity Project.

Mallon, G. (2011). Permanency for LGBTQ youth. *Protecting Children, 26*, 49–57.

Mallon, G. P. (1998). After care, then where? Evaluating outcomes of an independent living program. *Child Welfare, 77*(1), 61–78.

Mallon, G. P. (2001). Sticks and stones can break your bones: Verbal harassment and physical violence in the lives of gay and lesbian youth in child welfare settings. *Journal of Gay and Lesbian Social Services*, 13, 63–81.

Mallory, C., Brown, T. N., Russell, S. T., & Sears, B. (2017). *The impact of stigma and discrimination against LGBT people in Texas*. Williams Institute.

Malpas, J. (2011). Between pink and blue: A multi-dimensional family approach to gender nonconforming children and their families. *Family Process, 50*(4), 453–470. https://doi.org/10.1111/j.1545-5300.2011.01371.x

Mandsager, P., Marier, A., Cohen, S., Fanning, M., Hauck, H., & Cheever, L. W. (2018). Reducing HIV-related health disparities in the health resources and service administration's Ryan White HIV/AIDS program. *American Journal of Public Health, Supplement 4, 108*(54), S246–S250. https://doi.org/10.2105/AJPH.2018.304689

Markle, L., Wessel, R. D., & Desmond, J. (2017). Faculty mentorship program for students with disabilities: Academic success outcomes (practice brief). *Journal of Postsecondary Education and Disability, 30*(4), 385–392.

Marksamer, J. (2008). And by the way, do you know he thinks he's a girl? The failures of law, policy, and legal representation for transgender youth in juvenile delinquency courts. *Sexuality Research and Social Policy, 5*, 72–92.

Marlatt, G. A., & Witkiewitz, K. (2010). Update on harm-reduction policy and intervention research. *Annual Review of Clinical Psychology, 6*, 591–606.

Marshall, B. D., Shannon, K., Kerr, T., Zhang, R., & Wood, E. (2010). Survival sex work and increased HIV risk among sexual minority street-involved youth. *Journal of Acquired Immune Deficiency Syndromes (1999), 53*(5), 661.

Martin, M., Down, L., & Erney, R. (2016). *Out of the Shadows: Supporting LGBTQ+ youth in child welfare through cross-system collaboration*. Center for the Study of Social Policy.

Mason, E. C. M., Springer, S. I., & Pugliese, A. (2017). Staff development as a school climate intervention to support transgender and gender nonconforming students: An integrated research partnership model for school counselors and counselor educators. *Journal of LGBT Issues in Counseling, 11*(4), 301–318. https://doi.org/10.1080/15538605.2017.1380552

Masten, A. (2007). Resilience in developing systems: Progress and promise as the fourth wave rises. *Development and Psychopathology, 19*(3), 921–930. doi:10.1017/S0954579407000442

Masten, A. S. (2014). Global Perspectives on Resilience in Children and Youth. *Child Development, 85*, 6–20. https://doi.org/10.1111/cdev.12205

Masten, A. S. (2014). *Ordinary magic: Resilience in development*. Guilford Press.

Masten, A. S. (2018). Resilience theory and research on children and families: Past, present, and promise. *Journal of Family Theory & Review, 10*(1), 12–31. https://doi.org/10.1111/jftr.12255

Masten, A. S., Cutuli, J. J., Herbers, J. E., & Reed, M. G. (2009). Resilience in Development. In Lopez, S. J., & Snyder, C. R. (Eds.), *Oxford handbook of positive psychology* (pp. 74–88). Oxford University Press

Masten, A. S., & Tellegen, A. (2012). Resilience in developmental psychopathology: Contributions of the Project Competence Longitudinal Study. *Development and Psychopathology, 24*(2), 345–361. https://doi.org/10.1017/S095457941200003X

Matthews, C. R., & Adams, E. M. (2009). Using a social justice approach to prevent the mental health consequences of heterosexism. *Journal of Primary Prevention, 30*, 11–26.

May, V. M. (2015). *Pursuing intersectionality, unsettling dominant imaginaries*. Routledge.

Maynard, K. (2018). To be black. To be a woman. Can dramatherapy help black women to discover their true self despite racial and gender oppression? *Dramatherapy, 39*(1), 31–48. http://dx.doi.org/10.1080/02630672.2018.1432668

McCann, E., & Brown, M. (2019). Homelessness among Youth Who Identify as LGBTQ+: A systematic review. *Journal of Clinical Nursing, 28,* 2061–2072.

McCann, E., Donohue, G., & Timmins, F. (2020). An exploration of the relationship between spirituality, religion and mental health among youth who identify as LGBT+: A systematic literature review. *Journal of Religion and Health, 59*(2), 828–844. https://doi.org/10.1007/s10943-020-00989-7

McClain, Z., Hawkins, L. A., & Yehia, B. R. (2015). Creating welcoming spaces for lesbian, gay, bisexual, and transgender (LGBT) patients: An evaluation of the health care environment. *Journal of Homosexuality, 63*(3), 387–393. https://doi.org/10.1080/00918369.2016.1124694

McConnell, E. A., Clifford, A., Korpak, A. K., Phillips, G., & Birkett, M. (2017). Identity, victimization, and support: Facebook experiences and mental health among LGBTQ youth. *Computers in Human Behavior, 76,* 237–244. https://doi.org/10.1016/j.chb.2017.07.026

McConnell, E. A., Janulis, P., Phillips, G. II, Truong, R., & Birkett, M. (2018). Multiple minority stress and LGBT community resilience among sexual minority men. *Psychology of Sexual Orientation and Gender Diversity, 5*(1), 1–12. https://doi.org/10.1037/sgd0000265

McConnell, E., Néray, B., Hogan, B., Korpak, A., Clifford, A., & Birkett, M. (2018). "Everybody puts their whole life on Facebook": Identity management and the online social networks of LGBTQ youth. *International Journal of Environmental Research and Public Health, 15*(6), 1078–1097. https://doi.org/10.3390/ijerph15061078

McCormick, A. (Ed.) (2018). *LGBTQ+ youth in foster care: Empowering approaches for an inclusive system of care.* Routledge.

McCormick, A., Schmidt, K., & Tarrazas, S. (2017). LGBTQ youth in the child welfare system: An overview of research, practice, and policy. *Journal of Public Child Welfare, 11,* 27–39.

McCormick, C. M., Kuo, S. I., & Masten, A. S. (2011). Developmental tasks across the lifespan. In K. L. Fingerman, C. A. Berg, J. Smith, & T. C. Antonucci (Eds.), *Handbook of Lifespan Development* (pp. 117–139). Springer.

McDermott, E., Hughes, E., & Rawlings, V. (2018). The social determinants of lesbian, gay, bisexual and transgender youth suicidality in England: A mixed methods study. *Journal of Public Health (Oxford, England), 40,* e244–e251.

McEwen, B. S. (1998). Protective and damaging effects of stress mediators. *New England Journal of Medicine, 338*(3), 171–179. https://doi.org/10.1056/NEJM199801153380307

McEwen, B. S. (2004). Protection and damage from acute and chronic stress: Allostasis and allostatic overload and relevance to the pathophysiology of psychiatric disorders. *Annals of the New York Academy of Sciences, 1032,* 1–7. https://doi.org/10.1196/annals.1314.001

McEwen, B. S. (2020). The untapped power of allostasis promoted by healthy lifestyles. *World Psychiatry: Official Journal of the World Psychiatric Association (WPA), 19*(1), 57–58. https://doi.org/10.1002/wps.20720

McEwen, B. S., & Stellar, E. (1993). Stress and the individual: Mechanisms leading to disease. *Archives of Internal Medicine, 153*(18), 2093–2101.

McFadden, C. (2015). Lesbian, gay, bisexual, and transgender careers and human resource development: A systematic literature review. *Human Resource Development Review, 14*(2), 125–162. https://doi.org/10.1177/1534484314549456

McGeough, B. L., & Sterzing, P. R. (2018). A systematic review of family victimization experiences among sexual minority youth. *Journal of Primary Prevention, 39*(5). https://doi.org/10.1007/s10935-018-0523-x

McGill, C. M., and Joslin, J. E. (2021). *Advising lesbian, gay, bisexual, transgender, and queer college students.* Stylus Publishing.

McGuire, J. K., Anderson, C. R., Toomey, R. B., & Russell, S. T. (2010). School climate for transgender youth: A mixed method investigation of student experiences and school responses. *Journal of Youth and Adolescence, 39*(10), 1175–1188. https://doi.org/10.1007/s10964-010-9540-7

McGuire, J. K., & Morrow, Q. J. (2020). Pathways of gender development. In M. Forcier, G. Van Schalkwyk, & J. Turban (Eds.), *Pediatric gender identity.* Springer Cham. https://doi.org/10.1007/978-3-030-38909

McHale, S. M., Crouter, A. C., & Whiteman, S. D. (2003). The family contexts of gender development in childhood and adolescence. *Social Development, 12*(1), 125–148. https://doi.org/10.1111/1467-9507.00225

McIntosh, C. A. (2016). Interdisciplinary care for transgender patients. In K. L. Eckstrand & J. M. Ehrenfeld (Eds.), *Lesbian, gay, bisexual, and transgender healthcare* (pp. 339–350). Springer Cham. https://doi.org/10.1007/978-3-319-19752-4_18

McLeroy, K., Bibeau, D., Steckler, A., & Glanz, K. (1988). An ecological perspective on health promotion programs. *Health Education & Behavior, 15,* 351–377.

McMillen, J. C., Scott, L. D., Zima, B. T., Ollie, M. T., Munson, M. R., & Spitznagel, E. (2004). Use of mental health services among older youths in foster care. *Psychiatric Services, 55*(7), 811–817.

McNeil, J., Ellis, S. J., & Eccles, F. J. R. (2017). Suicide in trans populations: A systematic review of prevalence and correlates. *Psychology of Sexual Orientation and Gender Diversity, 4*(3), 341–353. https://doi.org/10.1037/sgd0000235

Mereish, E. H., Parra, L. A., Watson, R. J., & Fish, J. N. (2021). Subtle and intersectional minority stress and depressive symptoms among sexual and gender minority adolescents of color: Mediating role of self-esteem and sense of mastery. *Prevention Science.* https://doi.org/10.1007/s11121-021-01294-9

Mereish, E. H., & Poteat, V. P. (2015). A relational model of sexual minority mental and physical health: The negative effects of shame on relationships, loneliness, and health. *Journal of Counseling Psychology, 62*(3), 425–437. https://doi.org/10.1037/cou0000088

Messman, J. B., & Leslie, L. A. (2019). Transgender college students: Academic resilience and striving to cope in the face of marginalized health. *Journal of American College Health, 67*(2), 161–173. https://doi.org/10.1080/07448481.2018.1465060

Metzl, J. M., & Hansen, H. (2014). Structural competency: Theorizing a new medical engagement with stigma and inequality. *Social Science & Medicine, 103,* 126–133.

Meyer, E., Levasseur, M. D., Hanneman, T., & Snowden, S. (2016). *Creating equal access to quality health care for transgender patients: Transgender-affirming hospital policies.* Lambda Legal.

Meyer, E. J., Tilland-Stafford, A., & Airton, L. (2016). Transgender and gender-creative students in PK–12 schools: What we can learn from their teachers. *Teachers College Record, 118*(8), 1–50. https://doi.org/10.1177/016146811611800806

Meyer, I. H. (1995). Minority stress and mental health in gay men. *Journal of Health and Social Behavior, 36*(1), 38–56. http://www.jstor.org/stable/2137286

Meyer, I. H. (2003). Prejudice, social stress, and mental health in lesbian, gay, and bisexual populations: Conceptual issues and research evidence. *Psychological Bulletin, 129*(5), 674–697. https://doi.org/10.1037/0033-2909.129.5.674

Meyer, I. H. (2015). Resilience in the study of minority stress and health of sexual and gender minorities. *Psychology of Sexual Orientation and Gender Diversity, 2*(3), 209–213. https://doi.org/10.1037/sgd0000132

Meyer, I. H., Brown, T. N., Herman, J. L., Reisner, S. L., & Bockting, W. O. (2017). Demographic characteristics and health status of transgender adults in select US regions: Behavioral risk factor surveillance system, 2014. *American Journal of Public Health, 107*(4), 582–589. https://doi.org/10.2105/AJPH.2016.303648

Meyer, I. H., & Dean, L. (1998). Internalized homophobia, intimacy, and sexual behavior among gay and bisexual men. In G. M. Herek (Ed.), *Psychological perspectives on lesbian and gay issues, Vol. 4. Stigma and sexual orientation: Understanding prejudice against lesbians, gay men, and bisexuals* (pp. 160–186). Sage Publications, Inc. https://doi.org/10.4135/9781452243818.n8

Meyer, I. H., & Frost, D. M. (2013). Minority stress and the health of sexual minorities. In C. J. Patterson & A. R. D'Augelli (Eds.), *Handbook of psychology and sexual orientation* (pp. 252–266). Oxford University Press.

Meyer, I. H., Russell, S. T., Hammack, P. L., Frost, D. M., & Wilson, B. (2021). Minority stress, distress, and suicide attempts in three cohorts of sexual minority adults: A U.S. probability sample. *PloS one, 16*(3), e0246827. https://doi.org/10.1371/journal.pone.0246827

Meyer, I. H., Wilson, B. D. M., & O'Neill, K. (2021). LGBTQ People in the US: Select findings from the generations and transpop studies. Los Angeles: The Williams Institute. https://williamsinstitute.law.ucla.edu/publications/generations-transpop-toplines/

Meyer, W., Bockting, W. O., Cohen-Kettenis, P., Coleman, E., DiCeglie, D., Devor, H., Gooren, L., Hage, J. J., Kirk, S., Kuiper, B., Laub, D., Lawrence, A., Menard, Y., Patton, J., Schaefer, L., Webb, A., & Wheeler, C. C. (2001). Harry Benjamin International Gender Dysphoria Association's: The standards of care for gender identity disorders—sixth version. *Journal of Psychology & Human Sexuality, 13*(1), 1–30. https://doi.org/10/1300/J056v13n01_01

Michener, L., Aguilar-Gaxiola, S., Alberti, P. M., Castaneda, M. J., Castrucci, B. C., Harrison, L. M., Hughes, L. S., Richmond, A., & Wallerstein, N. (2020). Engaging with communities—lessons (re)learned from COVID-19. *Preventing Chronic Disease, 17*, E65. https://doi.org/10.5888/pcd17.200250

Miller, B. (2016). A computer-mediated escape from the closet: Exploring identity, community, and disinhibited discussion on the internet coming out advice forums. *Sexuality & Culture, 20*(3), 602–625. https://doi.org/10.1007/s12119-016-9343-4

Miller, J. (1988). *The holistic curriculum*. OISE Press.

Miller, S. J. (2011). African-American lesbian identity management and identity development in the context of family and community. *Journal of Homosexuality, 58*(4), 547–563. https://doi.org/10.1080/00918369.2011.556937

Miller, S. J., Mayo, C., & Lugg, C. A. (2017). Sex and gender in transition in US schools: Ways forward. *Sex Education, 18*(34), 1–15. https://doi.org/10.1080/14681811.2017.1415204

Mirza, S. A., & Baker, K. (2016, August 31). The impact of the Affordable Care Act on LGBTQ youth experiencing homelessness. *Center for American Progress*. https://cdn.americanprogress.org/wp-content/uploads/2016/08/30132612/LGBTQHomelessYouthBrief-FINALPDF.pdf?_ga=2.254054208.930158196.1616377535-968285068.1616377535

Moody, C., Fuks, N., Peláez, S., & Smith, N. G. (2015). "Without this, I would for sure already be dead": A qualitative inquiry regarding suicide protective factors among trans adults. *Psychology of Sexual Orientation and Gender Diversity, 2*(3), 266–280. http://dx.doi.org/10.1037/sgd0000130

Moon, A., & Diamond, K. D. (2018). *Girl Sex 101*. Lunatic Ink.

Moore, J. (2013). Resilience and at-risk children and youth. *National Center for Homeless Education.*

Moraga, C., & Anzaldúa, G. (1983). *This bridge called my back: Writings by radical women of color* (2nd ed.). Kitchen Table Press.

Morandini, J., Blaszczynski, A., Dar-Nimrod, I., & Ross, M. (2015). Minority stress and community connectedness among gay, lesbian and bisexual Australians: A comparison of rural and metropolitan localities. *Australian and New Zealand Journal of Public Health, 39*(3), 260–266.

Morgan, E. M. (2020). Same-sex relationships and LGBTQ youth. In S. Hupp & J. D. Jewell (Eds.), *Encyclopedia of Child and Adolescent Development.* John Wiley & Sons. https://doi.org/10.1002/9781119171492.wecad488

Morris, G., & Brown, J. (2018). Primary care for lesbian, gay, bisexual, transgender, and questioning youth. *International Journal of Pediatrics and Adolescent Medicine, 29,* 1–19.

Morton, M. H., Dworsky, A., Matjasko, J. L., Curry, S. R., Schlueter, D., Chávez, R., & Farrell, A. F. (2018). Prevalence and correlates of youth homelessness in the United States. *Journal of Adolescent Health, 62*(1), 14–21.

Morton, M. H., Samuels, G. M., Dworsky, A., & Patel, S. (2018). *Missed opportunities: LGBTQ youth homelessness in America.* Chapin Hall at the University of Chicago.

Mosley, D. V., Neville, H. A., Chavez-Dueñas, N. Y., Adames, H. Y., Lewis, J. A., & French, B. H. (2020). Radical hope in revolting times: Proposing a culturally relevant psychological framework. *Social and Personality Psychology Compass, 14*(1), 1–12. https://doi.org/10.1111/spc3.12512

Movement Advancement Project. (2019). *Where we call home: Transgender people in rural America.* https://www.lgbtmap.org/file/Rural-Trans-Report-Nov2019.pdf

Movement Advancement Project and GLSEN. (2017). *Separation and stigma: Transgender youth and school facilities.* https://www.lgbtmap.org/transgender-youth-school

Mulkern, P. (2020). *Supporting queer youth in schools using a multi-tiered approach.* https://www.sswaa.org/post/supporting-queer-youth-in-schools-using-an-multi-tiered-approach

Munro, L., Travers, R., & Woodford, M. R. (2019). Overlooked and invisible: Everyday experiences of microaggressions for LGBTQ adolescents. *Journal of Homosexuality, 66*(10), 1439–1471. https://doi.org/10.1080/00918369.2018.1542205

Murad, M. H., Elamin, M. B., Garcia, M. Z., Mullan, R. J., Murad, A., Erwin, P. J., & Montori, V. M. (2010). Hormonal therapy and sex reassignment: A systematic review and meta-analysis of quality of life and psychosocial outcomes. *Clinical Endocrinology, 7*(2), 214–231. https://doi.org/10.1111/j.1365-2265.2009.03625.x

Murphy, H. E. (2012). Improving the lives of students, gay and straight alike: Gay-straight alliances and the role of school psychologists. *Psychology in the Schools, 49*(9), 883–891. https://doi.org/10.1002.pits.21643

Mustanski, B., Andrews, R., & Puckett, J. A. (2016). The effects of cumulative victimization on mental health among lesbian, gay, bisexual, and transgender adolescents and young adults. *American Journal of Public Health, 106*(3), 527–533. https://doi.org/10.2105/AJPH.2015.302976

Mustanski, B., & Espelage, D. L. (2020). Why are we not closing the gap in suicide disparities for sexual minority youth? *Pediatrics, 145*(3), e20194002. https://doi.org/10.1542/peds.2019-4002

Mustanski, B., & Liu, R. T. (2013). A longitudinal study of predictors of suicide attempts among lesbian, gay, bisexual, and transgender youth. *Archives of Sexual Behavior, 42,* 437–448. https://doi.org/10.1007/s10508-012-0013-9

Mustanski, B., Newcomb, M. E., & Garofalo, R. (2011). The mental health of lesbian, gay, and bisexual youths: A developmental resiliency perspective. *Journal of Gay & Lesbian Social Services, 23*, 204–225. https://doi.org/10.1080/10538720.2011.561474

Nagata, J. M., Ganson, K. T., & Austin, S. B. (2020). Emerging trends in eating disorders among sexual and gender minorities. *Current Opinion in Psychiatry, 33*(6), 562–567. https://doi.org/10.1097/YCO.0000000000000645

Najavits, L. M., Weiss, R. D., Shaw, S. R., & Muenz, L. R. (1998). "Seeking safety": Outcome of a new cognitive-behavioral psychotherapy for women with posttraumatic stress disorder and substance dependence. *Journal of Traumatic Stress: Official Publication of the International Society for Traumatic Stress Studies, 11*(3), 437–456.

Nakamura, N., & Pope, M. (2013). Borders and margins: Giving voice to lesbian, gay, bisexual, and transgender immigrant experiences. *Journal of LGBT Issues in Counseling, 7*(2), 122–124. https://doi.org/10.1080/15538605.2013.785235

National Association of School Psychologists. (2017). *Safe and supportive schools for LGBTQ+ youth* (Position statement).

National Association of Social Workers. (2015). *Standards and indicators for cultural competence in social work practice*. NASW Press.

National Association of Social Workers. (2017). *Code of ethics of the National Association of Social Workers*. NASW Press.

National Center for Education Statistics (NCES). (2019). Enrollment and employees in postsecondary institutions, fall 2017; and Financial statistics and academic libraries, fiscal year 2017: First look (provisional data). https://nces.ed.gov/pubs2019/2019021REV.pdf

National Center for Transgender Equality. (2020, July). The discrimination administration. https://transequality.org/the-discrimination-administration

National Child Traumatic Stress Network. (2014). *Complex trauma: Facts for service providers working with homeless youth and young adults*. https://www.nctsn.org/resources/complex-trauma-facts-service-providers-working-homeless-youth-and-young-adults

National Health Care for the Homeless Council. (April 2016). *Using the social ecological model to examine how homelessness is defined and managed in rural East Tennessee*. www.nhchc.org

National Institute of Health, Sexual and Gender Minority Research Office. (2021). Sexual & gender minority health disparities research framework. https://dpcpsi.nih.gov/sites/default/files/NIH-SGM-Health-Disparities-Research-Framework-FINAL_508c.pdf

National Institute on Minority Health and Health Disparities. (2018). National institute on minority health and health disparities research framework. https://www.nimhd.nih.gov/about/overview/research-framework/nimhd-framework.html

National LGBTQIA+ Health Education Center. (2021, May 4). *Ten strategies for creating inclusive health care environments for LGBTQIA+ people*. LGBTQIA+ Health Education Center. https://www.lgbtqiahealtheducation.org/publication/ten-strategies-for-creating-inclusive-health-care-environments-for-lgbtqia-people-2021/

National PREA Resource Center. (2013). *National Prison Rape Elimination Act Resource Center annual report 2012–2013*. National Council on Crime and Delinquency (NCCD). https://www.prearesourcecenter.org/sites/default/files/library/prc-annual-report-2013-final.pdf

National Science Foundation, National Center for Science and Engineering Statistics. (2017). *Women, minorities, and persons with disabilities in science and engineering: 2017*. Special Report NSF 17-310. www.nsf.gov/statistics/wmpd/

Needham, B. L., & Austin, E. L. (2010). Sexual orientation, parental support, and health during the transition to young adulthood. *Journal of Youth and Adolescence, 39*(10), 1189–1198.

Neff, J., Holmes, S. M., Knight, K. R., Strong, S., Thompson-Lastad, A., McGuinness, C., . . . Nelson, N. (2020). Structural competency: Curriculum for medical students, residents, and interprofessional teams on the structural factors that produce health disparities. *MedEdPORTAL, 16*, 10888.

Newcomb, M. E., LaSala, M. C., Bouris, A., Mustanski, B., Prado, G., Schrager, S. M., & Huebner, D. M. (2019). The influence of families on LGBTQ youth health: A call to action for innovation in research and intervention development. *LGBT Health, 6*(4), 139–145. https://doi.org/10.1089/lgbt.2018.0157

Ng, H. (2020). *Comprehensive care clinics for transgender & non-binary youth: Considerations and best practices*. Human Rights Campaign Foundation.

Ng, H., & Hanneman, T. (2020). *LGBTQ inclusion in children's hospitals: Lessons learned from the Healthcare Equality Index*. Human Rights Campaign Foundation.

Nguyen, H., Grafsky, E., & Lambert-Shute, J. (2017). The experiences of lesbian, gay, bisexual, and queer international students. *Journal of Underrepresented & Minority Progress, 1*(1), 80–94. https://doi.org/10.32674/jump.v1i1.39

Nicolazzo, Z., Marine, S. B., & Wagner, R. (2018). From best to intentional practices: Reimagining implementation of gender-inclusive housing. *Journal of Student Affairs Research and Practice, 55*(2), 225–236. https://doi.org/10.1080/19496591.2018.1399896

Nobili, A., Glazebrook, C., Bouman, W. P., Glidden, D., Baron-Cohen, S., Allison, C., Smith, P., & Arcelus, J. (2018). Autistic traits in treatment-seeking transgender adults. *Journal of Autism and Developmental Disorders, 48*, 3984–3994. https://doi.org/10.1007/s10803-018-3557-2

Nogueira de Lira, A., & Araujo de Morais, N. (2018). Resilience in lesbian, gay, and bisexual (LGB) populations: An integrative literature review. *Sexuality Research and Social Policy, 3*(15), 272–282. https://doi.org/10.1007/s13178-017-0285-x

Nooe, R. M., & Patterson, D. A. (2010). The ecology of homelessness. *Journal of Human Behavior in the Social Environment, 20*(2), 105–152.

Norman, D., Hunter, Q., & O'Hara, M. (2017). Career development. In C. B. Roland & L. D. Burlew (Eds.), *Counseling LGBTQ adults during life span* (pp. 6–9). American Counseling Association.

Norris, A. L., & Orchowski, L. M. (2020). Peer victimization of sexual minority and transgender youth: A cross-sectional study of high school students. *Psychology of Violence, 10*(2), 201.

Noyola, N., Sánchez, M., & Cardemil, E. V. (2020). Minority stress and coping among sexual diverse Latinxs. *Journal of Latinx Psychology, 8*(1), 58–82. https://doi.org/10.1037/lat0000143

O'Ryan, L. W., & McFarland, W. P. (2010). A phenomenological exploration of the experiences of dual-career lesbian and gay couples. *Journal of Counseling and Development, 88*(1), 71–79.

Oba, Y., & Pope, M. (2013). Counseling and advocacy with LGBT international students. *Journal of LGBT Issues in Counseling, 7*, 185–193. https://doi.org/10.1080/15538605.2013.785468

Obergefell v. Hodges, 576 U.S. (2015). https://www.supremecourt.gov/opinions/14pdf/14-556_3204.pdf

Oberheim, S. T., DePue, M. K., & Hagedorn, W. B. (2017). Substance use disorders (SUDs) in transgender communities: The need for trans-competent SUD counselors and facilities. *Journal of Addictions and Offender Counseling, 38*(1), 33–47. https://doi.org/10.1002/jaoc.12027

Olson, K. R., Durwood, L., DeMeules, M., & McLaughlin, K. A. (2016). Mental health of transgender children who are supported in their identities. *Pediatrics, 137*(3), e20153223. https://doi.org/10.1542/peds.2015-3223

Olson, K. R., Key, A. C., & Eaton, N. R. (2015). Gender cognition in transgender children. *Psychological Science, 26*, 467–474. https://doi.org/10.1177/0956797614568156

Orchard, C. A., Curran, V., & Kabene, S. (2005). Creating a culture for interdisciplinary collaborative professional practice. *Medical Education Online, 10*(1), 4387.

Orel, N. A., & Coon, D. W. (2016). The challenges of change: How can we meet the care needs of the ever-evolving LGBT family? *Generations, 40*(2), 41–45.

Oswalt, S. B., & Wyatt, T. J. (2011). Sexual orientation and differences in mental health, stress, and academic performance in a national sample of US college students. *Journal of Homosexuality, 58*(9), 1255–1280. https://doi.org/10.1080/00918369.2011.605738

Ouch, S., & Moradi, B. (2019). Cognitive and affective expectation of stigma, coping efficacy, and psychological distress among sexual minority people of color. *Journal of Counseling Psychology, 66*(4), 424–436. https://doi.org/10.1037/cou0000360

Paceley, M. S., Goffnett, J., & Wagaman, M. A. (2018). *Promoting the well-being of LGBTQIA+ students*. School Social Work Association of America.

Pachankis, J. (2018). The scientific pursuit of sexual and gender minority mental health treatments: Toward evidence-based affirmative practice. *American Psychologist, 73*(9), 1207–1219. https://doi.org/10.1037/amp0000357

Padilla, M. B., Rodríguez-Madera, S., Varas-Díaz, N., & Ramos-Pibernus, A. (2016). Transmigrations: Border-crossing and the politics of body modification among Puerto Rican transgender women. *International Journal of Sexual Health, 28*(4), 261–277. https://doi.org/10.1080/19317611.2016.1223256

Painter, K. R., Scannapieco, M., Blau, G., Andre, A., & Kohn, K. (2018). Improving the mental health outcomes of LGBTQ youth and young adults: A longitudinal study. *Journal of Social Service Research, 44*, 223–235. https://doi.org/10.1080/01488376.2018.1441097

Palmer, N. A., Kosciw, J. G., & Bartkiewicz, M. J. (2012). *Strengths and silences: The experiences of lesbian, gay, bisexual and transgender students in rural and small-town schools*. GLSEN.

Panter-Brick, C., & Leckman, J. F. (2013). Editorial commentary: Resilience in child development—interconnected pathways to wellbeing. *Journal of Child Psychology and Psychiatry, 54*(4), 333–336. https://doi.org/10.1111/jcpp.12057

Parameshwaran, V., Cockbain, B. C., Hillyard, M., & Price, J. R. (2017). Is the lack of specific lesbian, gay, bisexual, transgender and queer/questioning (LGBTQ) health care education in medical school a cause for concern? Evidence from a survey of knowledge and practice among UK medical students. *Journal of Homosexuality, 64*(3), 367–381. https://doi.org/10.1080/00918369.2016.1190218

Parast, L., Tucker, J. S., Pedersen, E. R., & Klein, D. (2019). Utilization and perceptions of drop-in center services among youth experiencing homelessness. *The Journal of Behavioral Health Services & Research, 46*(2), 234–248.

Parent, M. C., Arriaga, A. S., Gobble, T., & Wille, L. (2019). Stress and substance use among sexual and gender minority individuals across the lifespan. *Neurobiology of Stress, 10*(December), 100146. https://doi.org/10.1016/j.ynstr.2018.100146

Paris Is Burning. (1990). Dire. Jenny Livingston. BBC Television, Miramax, Off White Productions.

Pariseau, E. M., Chevalier, L., Long, K. A., Clapham, R., Edwards-Leeper, L., & Tishelman, A. C. (2019). The relationship between family acceptance-rejection and transgender youth psychosocial functioning. *Clinical Practice in Pediatric Psychology, 7*(3), 267–277. https://doi.org/10.1037/cpp0000291

Parnell, M. K., Lease, S. H., & Green, M. L. (2012). Perceived career barriers for gay, lesbian, and bisexual individuals. *Journal of Career Development, 39*(3), 248–268. https://doi.org/10.1177/0894845310386730

Parra, L. A., Bell, T. S., Benibgui, M., Helm, J. L., & Hastings, P. D. (2018). The buffering effect of peer support on the links between family rejection and psychosocial adjustment in LGB emerging adults. *Journal of Social and Personal Relationships, 35*(6), 854–871. https://doi.org/10.1177/0265407517699713

Pascoe, C. J. (2011). Resource and risk: Youth sexuality and new media use. *Sexuality Research and Social Policy, 8*(1), 5–17. https://doi.org/10.1007/s13178-011-0042-5

Pearlin, L. I., Schieman, S., Fazio, E. M., & Meersman, S. C. (2005). Stress, health, and the life course: Some conceptual perspectives. *Journal of Health and Social Behavior, 46*(2), 205–219. https://doi.org/10.1177/002214650504600206

Pedersen, P. B. (2000). *Hidden messages in culture-centered counseling: A Triad Training Model*. Sage.

Perez-Brumer, A., Day, J. K., Russell, S. T., & Hatzenbuehler, M. L. (2017). Prevalence and correlates of suicidal ideation among transgender youth in California: Findings from a representative, population-based sample of high school students. *Journal of the American Academy of Child & Adolescent Psychiatry, 56*(9), 739–746. https://doi.org/10.1016/j.jaac.2017.06.010

Pergamit, M. R., Ernst, M., & Hall, C. (2010). Runaway youth's knowledge and access of services. National Runaway Switchboard, Chicago. https://www.semanticscholar.org/paper/Runaway-Youth's-Knowledge-and-Access-of-Services-Pergamit/bb8824dafe04296a29119703b0e8964b1f530081

Perrin, P. B., Sutter, M. E., Trujillo, M. A., Henry, R. S., & Pugh, M. Jr. (2020). The minority strengths model: Development and initial path analytic validation in racially/ethnically diverse LGBTQ individuals. *Journal of Clinical Psychology, 76*(1), 118–136. https://doi.org/10.1002/jclp.22850

Petersen, S., Shrader, G., Hutchings, P., & Brake, K. (2011). Integrating health care: The clear advantage for underserved diverse populations. *Psychological Services, 8*(2), 69–81. https://doi.org/10.1037/a0023521

Peterson, C., Matthews, A., Copps-Smith, E., & Conrad, L. (2016). Suicidality, self-harm, and body dissatisfaction in transgender adolescents and emerging adults with gender dysphoria. *Suicide and Life-Threatening Behavior, 47*, 475–482. https://doi.org/10.1111/sltb.12289

Pettigrew, T. F. (1967). Social evaluation theory: Convergences and applications. In *Nebraska symposium on motivation* (pp. 241–304). University of Nebraska Press.

Pew Research Center. (2014). https://www.pewinternet.org/2014/10/22/online-harassment/

Pflum, S. R., Testa, R. J., Balsam, K. F., Goldblum, P. B., & Bongar, B. (2015). Social support, trans community connectedness, and mental health symptoms among transgender and gender nonconforming adults. *Psychology of Sexual Orientation and Gender Diversity, 2*(3), 281–286. https://doi.org/10.1037/sgd0000122

Phillips, G., Felt, D., Ruprecht, M. M., Wang, X., Xu, J., Perez-Bill, E., Bagnarol, R. M., Roth, J., Curry, C. W., & Beach, L. B. (2020). Addressing the disproportionate impacts of the COVID-19 pandemic on sexual and gender minority populations in the United States: Actions toward equity. *LGBT Health, 7*(6), 279–282. https://doi.org/10.1089/lgbt.2020.0187

Pinderhughes, H., Davis, R., & Williams, M. (2015). Adverse community experiences and resilience: A framework for addressing and preventing community trauma.

Pinto, R. M., Melendez, R. M., & Spector, A. Y. (2008). Male-to-female transgender individuals building social support and capital from within a gender-focused network. *Journal of Gay & Lesbian Social Services, 20*(3), 203–220. https://doi.org/10.1080/10538720802235179

Piquero, A. (2008). Disproportionate minority contact. *Future of Children, 18*, 59–79.

Pitcher, C., Saewyc, E., Browne, A., & Rodney, P. (2019). Access to primary health care services for youth experiencing homelessness: "You shouldn't need a health card to be healthy." *Witness: The Canadian Journal of Critical Nursing Discourse, 1*(2), 73–92.

Pleak, R. R. (2011). Gender-variant children and transgender adolescents. *Child and Adolescent Psychiatric Clinics, 20*(4), xv–xx. https://doi.org/10.1016/j.chc.2011.08.007

Porta, C. M., Singer, E., Mehus, C. J., Gower, A. L., Saewyc, E., Fredkove, W., & Eisenberg, M. E. (2017). LGBTQ youth's views on Gay-Straight Alliances: Building community, providing gateways, and representing safety and support. *Journal of School Health, 87*(7), 489–497. https://doi.org/10.1111/josh.12517

POSE. (2018). FX. Color Force, Brad Falchuk Teley-Vision, Ryan Murphy Television, Fox 21 Television Studios, FXP.

Poteat, T. C., Divsalar, S., Streed, C. G. Jr., Feldman, J. L., Bockting, W. O., & Meyer, I. H. (2021). Cardiovascular disease in a population-based sample of transgender and cisgender adults. *American Journal of Preventive Medicine*, S0749-3797(21)00350-0. Advance online publication. https://doi.org/10.1016/j.amepre.2021.05.019

Poteat, V. P., Calzo, J. P., Yoshikawa, H., Rosenbach, S. B., Ceccolini, C. J., & Marx, R. A. (2019). Extracurricular settings as a space to address sociopolitical crises: The case of discussing immigration in gender-sexuality alliances following the 2016 U.S. presidential election. *American Educational Research Journal, 56*, 2262–2294. https://doi.org/10.3102/0002831219839033

Poteat, V. P., Godfrey, E. B., Brion-Meisels, G., & Calzo, J. P. (2020). Development of youth advocacy and sociopolitical efficacy as dimensions of critical consciousness within Gender-Sexuality Alliances. *Developmental Psychology, 56*(6), 1207–1219.

Poteat, V., Rivers, I., & Vecho, O. (2015). The role of peers in predicting students' homophobic behavior: Effects of peer aggression, prejudice, and sexual orientation identity importance. *School Psychology Review, 44*, 391–406.

Poteat, V., Scheer, J., & Chong, E. (2016). Sexual orientation-based disparities in school and juvenile justice discipline: A multiple group comparison of contributing factors. *Journal of Educational Psychology, 108*, 229–241. https://doi.org10.1037/edu0000058

Poteat, V. P., Scheer, J. R., Marx, R. A., Calzo, J. P., & Yoshikawa, H. (2015). Gay-straight alliances vary on dimensions of youth socializing and advocacy: Factors accounting for individual and setting-level differences. *American Journal of Community Psychology, 55*, 422–432. https://doi.org/10.1007/s10464-015-9722-2.Gay-Straight

Poteat, V. P., Sinclair, K. O., DiGiovanni, C. D., Koenig, B. W., & Russell, S. T. (2013). Gay-straight alliances are associated with student health: A multischool comparison of LGBTQ and heterosexual youth. *Journal of Research on Adolescence, 23*(2), 319–330. https://doi.org/10.1111/j.1532-7795.2012.00832.x

Potoczniak, D., Crosbie-Burnett, M., & Saltzburg, N. (2009). Experiences regarding coming out to parents among African American, Hispanic, and White gay, lesbian, bisexual, transgender, and questioning adolescents. *Journal of Gay & Lesbian Social Services, 21*(2), 189–205. https://doi.org/10.1080/10538720902772063

Powell, C., Ellasante, I., Korchmaros, J. D., Haverly, K., & Stevens, S. (2016). iTEAM: Outcomes of an affirming system of care serving LGBTQ youth experiencing homelessness. *Families in Society, 97*(3), 181–190.

Prescott, M. V., Sekendur, B., Bailey, B., & Hoshino, J. (2008). Art making as a component and facilitator of resiliency with homeless youth. *Art Therapy, 25*(4), 156–163.

Preston, A. M. (2020, September 9). The anatomy of transmisogynoir. *Harper's Bazaar*. https://www.harpersbazaar.com/culture/features/a33614214/ashlee-marie-preston-transmisogynoir-essay/

Price, C. J., & Hooven, C. (2018). Interoceptive awareness skills for emotion regulation: Theory and approach of mindful awareness in body-oriented therapy (MABT). *Frontiers in Psychology, 9*, 798. https://doi.org/10.3389/fpsyg.2018.00798

Prince, D. M., Ray-Novak, M., Braveheart, G., Peterson, E. (2021). Sexual and gender minority

Prock, K. A., & Kennedy, A. C. (2020). Characteristics, experiences, and service utilization patterns of homeless youth in a transitional living program: Differences by LGBQ identity. *Children and Youth Services Review, 116*, 105176.

Prunas, A. (2019). The pathologization of trans-sexuality: Historical roots and implications for sex counselling with transgender clients. *Sexologies, 28*(3), e54–e60. https://doi.org/10.1016/j.sexol.2019.06.002

Puckett, J. A., Cleary, P., Rossman, K., Mustanski, B., & Newcomb, M. E. (2018). Barriers to gender-affirming care for transgender and gender nonconforming individuals. *Sexuality Research and Social Policy, 15*(1), 48–59. https://doi.org/10.1007/s13178-017-0295-8

Puckett, J. A., Maroney, M. R., Wadsworth, L. P., Mustanski, B., & Newcomb, M. E. (2020). Coping with discrimination: The insidious effects of gender minority stigma on depression and anxiety in transgender individuals. *Journal of Clinical Psychology* 76: 176–194. https://doi.org/10.1002/jclp.22865

Pullen Sansfaçon, A., Robichaud, M. J., & Dumais-Michaud, A. A. (2015). The experience of parents who support their children's gender variance. *Journal of LGBT Youth, 12*(1), 39–63. https://doi.org/10.1080/19361653.2014.935555

Quach, A. S., Todd, M. E., Hepp, B. W., & Doneker Mancini, K. L. (2013). Conceptualizing sexual identity development: Implications for GLB Chinese international students. *Journal of GLBT Family Studies, 9*, 254–272. https://doi.org/10.1080/1550428X.2013.781908

Quinn, G. P., Alpert, A. B., Sutter, M., & Schabath, M. B. (2020). What oncologists should know about treating sexual and gender minority patients with cancer. *JCO Oncology Practice, 16*(6), 309–316. https://doi.org/10.1200/op.20.00036

Rafferty, J. (2018). Ensuring comprehensive care and support for transgender and gender-diverse children and adolescents. *Pediatrics, 142*(4), e20182162. https://doi.org/10.1542/peds.2018-2162

Rafferty, J. (2019). Fertility preservation outcomes and considerations in transgender and gender-diverse youth. *Pediatrics, 144*(3), e20192000. https://doi.org/10.1542/peds.2019-2000

Ramos-Pibernus, A. G., Rivera-Segarra, E. R., Rodríguez-Madera, S. L., Varas-Díaz, N., & Padilla, M. (2020). Stigmatizing experiences of trans men in Puerto Rico: Implications for health. *Transgender Health, 5*(4), 234–240. https://doi.org/10.1089/trgh.2020.0021

Rankin, S., Weber, G. N., Blumenfeld, W. J., & Frazer, S. (2010). *2010 state of higher education for lesbian, gay, bisexual and transgender people.* https://www.campuspride.org/wp-content/uploads/campuspride2010lgbtreportssummary.pdf

Rashid, T. (2015). Positive psychotherapy: A strength-based approach. *Journal of Positive Psychology, 10*(1), 25–40. https://doi.org/10.1080/17439760.2014.920411

Ratcliff, S. M., & Haltom, T. M. (2021). The proverbial closet: Do faith and religiosity affect coming-out patterns? *Social Currents, 8*(3), 249–269. https://doi.org/10.1177/2329496521996056

Ream, G. L. (2019). What's unique about lesbian, gay, bisexual, and transgender (LGBT) youth and young adult suicides? Findings from the National Violent Death Reporting System. *Journal of adolescent health: Official Publication of the Society for Adolescent Medicine, 64*(5), 602–607. https://doi.org/10.1016/j.jadohealth.2018.10.303

Ream, G. L., & Forge, N. (2014). Homeless lesbian, gay, bisexual and transgender (LGBT) youth in New York City: Insights from the field. *Child Welfare, 93*(2), 7–22.

Reback, C. J., Clark, K., Holloway, I. W., & Fletcher, J. B. (2018). Health disparities, risk behaviors and healthcare utilization among transgender women in Los Angeles county: A comparison from 1998–1999 to 2015–2016. *AIDS and Behavior, 22*(8), 2524–2533. https://doi.org/10.1007/s10461-018-2165-7

Reeves, S., Pelone, F., Harrison, R., Goldman, J., & Zwarenstein, M. (2017). Interprofessional collaboration to improve professional practice and healthcare outcomes. *Cochrane Database of Systematic Reviews*, (6). https://doi.org/10.1002/14651858.CD000072.pub3

Reilly, A., & Rudd, N. A. (2007). Stress and dress: Investigating the relationship between social anxiety and appearance management among gay and straight men. *Journal of Homosexuality, 52*(3–4), 151–166. https://doi.org/10.1300/J082v52n03_07

Reisner, S. L., Greytak, E. A., Parsons, J. T., & Ybarra, M. L. (2015). Gender minority social stress in adolescence: Disparities in adolescent bullying and substance use by gender identity. *Journal of Sex Research, 52*(3), 243–256. https://doi.org/10.1080/00224499.2014.886321

Reisner, S. L., Poteat, T., Keatley, J., Cabral, M., Mothopeng, T., Dunham, E., Holland, C. E., Max, R., & Baral, S. D. (2016). Global health burden and needs of transgender populations: A review. *Lancet, 388*(10042), 412–436. https://doi.org/10.1016/S0140-6736(16)00684-X

Remlin Wilson, C., Currey Cook, Esq. M., & Erney, R. (2017). Safe havens closing the gap between recommended practice and reality for transgender and gender-expansive youth in out-of-home care.

Renard, S. B., Huntjens, R. J., Lysaker, P. H., Moskowitz, A., Aleman, A., & Pijnenborg, G. H. (2017). Unique and overlapping symptoms in schizophrenia spectrum and dissociative disorders in relation to models of psychopathology: A systematic review. *Schizophrenia Bulletin, 43*(1), 108–121.

Rettie, H., & Daniels, J. (2021). Coping and tolerance of uncertainty: Predictors and mediators of mental health during the COVID-19 pandemic. *American Psychologist, 76*(3), 427–437. http://dx.doi.org/10.1037/amp0000710

Richmond, J. R., Edmonds, K. A., Rose, J. P., & Gratz, K. L. (2020). Examining the impact of online rejection among emerging adults with borderline personality pathology: Development of a novel online group chat social rejection paradigm. *Personality Disorders: Theory, Research, and Treatment, 11*(5), 301–311. https://doi.org/10.1037/per0000381.supp

Rider, G. N., McMorris, B. J., Gower, A. L., Coleman, E., & Eisenberg, M. E. (2018). Health and care utilization of transgender and gender nonconforming youth: A population-based study. *Pediatrics, 141*(3), e20171683. https://doi.org/10.1542/peds.2017-1683

Rider, G. N., Vencill, J. A., Berg, D. R., Becker-Warner, R., Candelario-Pérez, L., & Spencer, K. G. (2019). The gender affirmative lifespan approach (GALA): A framework for competent clinical care with nonbinary clients. *International Journal of Transgenderism, 20*(2–3), 275–288. https://doi.org/10.1080/15532739.2018.1485069

Riggle, E. D. B., Rostosky, S. S., Black, W. W., & Rosenkrantz, D. E. (2017). Outness, concealment, and authenticity: Associations with LGB individuals' psychological distress and well-being. *Psychology of Sexual Orientation and Gender Diversity, 4*(1), 54–62. https://doi.org/10.1037/sgd0000202

Riggs, D. W., & Bartholomaeus, C. (2017). Transgender young people's narratives of intimacy and sexual health: Implications for sexuality education. *Sex Education, 18*(4), 376–390. https://doi.org/10.1080/14681811.2017.1355299

Rijn, A. B. V., Steensma, T. D., Kreukels, B. P., & Cohen-Kettenis, P. T. (2013). Self-perception in a clinical sample of gender variant children. *Clinical Child Psychology and Psychiatry, 18*(3), 464–474. https://doi.org/10.1177/1359104512460621

Riley, E. (2018). Bullies, blades, and barricades: Practical considerations for working with adolescents expressing concerns regarding gender and identity. *International Journal of Transgenderism, 19*(2), 203–211. https://doi.org/10.1080/15532739.2017.1386150

Rivas, D. (2020). Resiliencia: ¿Debemos hablar de ella? *Boletín Diversidad.* https://www.boletindiversidad.org/articulo3

Rivas, J. (2015). Half of young people believe gender isn't limited to male and female. Splinter. https://splinternews.com/halfof-young-people-believe-gender-isnt-limited-to-mal-1793844971

Roberts, A. L., Rosario, M., Corliss, H. L., Koenen, K. C., & Austin, S. B. (2012). Childhood gender nonconformity: A risk indicator for childhood abuse and posttraumatic stress in youth. *Pediatrics, 129*, 410–417. https://doi.org/10.1542/peds.2011-1804

Roberts, A. L., Rosario, M., Slopen, N., Calzo, J. P., & Austin, S. B. (2013). Childhood gender nonconformity, bullying victimization, and depressive symptoms across adolescence and early adulthood: An 11-year longitudinal study. *Journal of the American Academy of Child & Adolescent Psychiatry, 52*(2), 143–152. https://doi.org/10.1016/j.jaac.2012.11.006

Robertson, M. A. (2014). "How do I know I am gay?": Understanding sexual orientation, identity, and behavior among adolescents in an LGBT youth center. *Sexuality & Culture, 18*(2), 385–404. https://doi.org/10.1007/s12119-013-9203-4

Robjant, K., Roberts, J., & Katona, C. (2017). Treating posttraumatic stress disorder in female victims of trafficking using narrative exposure therapy: A retrospective audit. *Frontiers in Psychiatry, 8*, 63.

Roe, S. L. (2015). Examining the role of peer relationships in the lives of gay and bisexual adolescents. *Children & Schools, 37*(2), 117–124. https://doi.org/10.1093/cs/cdv001

Rogers, B. G., Coats, C. S., Adams, E., Murphy, M., Stewart, C., Arnold, T., Chan, P. A., & Nunn, A. (2020). Development of telemedicine infrastructure at an LGBTQ+ clinic to support HIV prevention and care in response to COVID-19, Providence, RI. *AIDS and Behavior, 24*, 2743–2747. https://doi.org/10.1007/s10461-020-02895-1

Rogers, C. R. (1957). The necessary and sufficient conditions of therapeutic personality change. *Journal of Consulting Psychology, 21*(2), 95–103. https://doi.org/10.1037/h0045357

role of school counselors. *Professional School Counseling, 20*(1a), 21–28. https://doi.org/10.5330/1096-2409-20.1a.21

Romanelli, M., & Hudson, K. D. (2017). Individual and systemic barriers to health care: Perspectives of lesbian, gay, bisexual, and transgender adults. *American Journal of Orthopsychiatry, 87*(6), 714–728. https://doi.org/10.1037/ort0000306

Rood, B. A., Maroney, M. R., Puckett, J. A., Berman, A. K., Reisner, S. L., & Pantalone, D. W. (2017). Identity concealment in transgender adults: A qualitative assessment of minority stress and gender affirmation. *American Journal of Orthopsychiatry, 87*(6), 704–713. https://doi-org.colby.idm.oclc.org/10.1037/ort0000303

Rood, B. A., Reisner, S. L., Surace, F. I., Puckett, J. A., Maroney, M. R., & Pantalone, D. W. (2016). Expecting rejection: Understanding the minority stress experiences of transgender and gender-nonconforming individuals. *Transgender Health, 1*(1), 151–164. https://doi.org/10.1089/trgh.2016.0012

Rooney, C., Durso, L. E., & Gruberg, S. (2016) *Discrimination against transgender women seeking access to homeless shelters.* Center for American Progress. https://www.americanprogress.org/article/discrimination-against-transgender-women-seeking-access-to-homeless-shelters/

Rosario, M., Corliss, H. L., Koenen, K. C., & Austin, S. B. (2011). Childhood gender nonconformity: A risk indicator for childhood abuse and posttraumatic stress in youth. *Pediatrics, 129*(3), 410–417. https://doi.org/10.1542/peds.2011-1804

Rosario, M., Schrimshaw, E. W., & Hunter, J. (2012). Homelessness among lesbian, gay, and bisexual youth: Implications for subsequent internalizing and externalizing symptoms. *Journal of Youth and Adolescence, 41*(5), 544–560.

Rose, A. J., & Smith, R. L. (2018). Gender and peer relationships. In W. M. Bukowski, B. Laursen, & K. H. Rubin (Eds.), *Handbook of peer interactions, relationships, and groups* (pp. 571–589). Guilford Press.

Rosen, L. D., Whaling, K., Rab, S., Carrier, L. M., & Cheever, N. A. (2013). Is Facebook creating "iDisorders"? The link between clinical symptoms of psychiatric disorders and technology use, attitudes and anxiety. *Computers in Human Behavior, 29*, 1243–1254.

Rosenbaum, S. (2011). The Patient Protection and Affordable Care Act: Implications for public health policy and practice. *Public health reports (Washington, DC: 1974), 126*(1), 130–135. https://doi.org/10.1177/003335491112600118

Rosenkrantz, D. E., Black, W. W., Abreu, R. L., Aleshire, M. E., & Fallin-Bennett, K. (2017). Health and health care of rural sexual and gender minorities: A systematic review. *Stigma and Health, 2*(3), 229–243. https://doi.org/10.1037/sah0000055.supp (Supplemental)

Rosenthal, L., Earnshaw, V. A., Carroll-Scott, A., Henderson, K. E., Peters, S. M., McCaslin, C., & Ickovics, J. R. (2015). Weight- and race-based bullying: Health associations among urban adolescents. *Journal of Health Psychology, 20*(4), 401–412. https://doi.org/10.1177/1359105313502567

Rosky, C. (2017). Anti-gay curriculum laws. *Columbia Law Reviews, 117*, 1461–1541.

Rossman, K., Salamanca, P., & Macapagal, K. (2017). A qualitative study examining young adults' experiences of disclosure and nondisclosure of LGBTQ identity to health care providers. *Journal of Homosexuality, 64*(10), 1390–1410. https://doi.org/10.1080/00918369.2017.1321379

Rostosky, S. S., Riggle, E. D. B., Rothblum, E. D., & Balsam, K. F. (2016). Same-sex couples' decisions and experiences of marriage in the context of minority stress: Interviews from a population-based longitudinal study. *Journal of Homosexuality, 63*(8), 1019–1040. https://doi.org/10.1080/00918369.2016.1191232

Rotheram-Borus, M. J., Koopman, C., Haignere, C., & Davies, M. (1991). Reducing HIV sexual risk behaviors among runaway adolescents. *Jama, 266*(9), 1237–1241.

Ruble, D. N., Martin, C. L., & Berenbaum, S. A. (2006). Gender development. In N. Eisenberg (Ed.), *Handbook of child psychology: Vol. 3, Personality and social development* (pp. 858–932).

Ruble, D. N., Taylor, L. J., Cyphers, L., Greulich, F. K., Lurye, L. E., & Shrout, P. E. (2007). The role of gender constancy in early gender development. *Child Development, 78*, 1121–1136. https://doi.org/10.1111/j.1467-8624.2007.01056.x

Russell, S. T., & Fish, J. N. (2016). Mental health in lesbian, gay, bisexual, and transgender (LGBT) youth. *Annual review of clinical psychology, 12*, 465–487. https://doi.org/10.1146/annurev-clinpsy-021815-093153

Russell, S., Ryan, C., Toomey, R., Diaz, R., & Sanchez, J. (2011). Lesbian, gay, bisexual and transgender adolescent school victimization implications for young adult health and adjustment. *Journal of School Health, 81*(5), 223–230.

Russell, S. T., Sinclair, K. O., Poteat, V. P., & Koenig, B. W. (2012). Adolescent health and harassment based on discriminatory bias. *American Journal of Public Health, 102*(3), 493–495. https://doi.org/10.2105/AJPH.2011.300430

Russell, S. T., Toomey, R. B., Ryan, C., & Diaz, R. M. (2014). Being out at school: The implications for school victimization and young adult adjustment. *American Journal of Orthopsychiatry, 84*(6), 635–643.

Russell, S. T., Van Campen, K. S., Hoefle, J. M., & Boor, J. K. (2011). Suicide risk and lesbian, gay, bisexual, and transgender college students. In D. A. Lamis & D. Lester (Eds.), *Understanding and preventing college student suicide.* (pp. 146–156). Charles C Thomas Publisher. http://0-search.ebscohost.com.library.alliant.edu/login.aspx?direct=true&db=psyh&AN=2011-27511-010&site=ehost-live&scope=site

Russon, J. M., & Schmidt, C. K. (2014). Authenticity and career decision-making self-efficacy in lesbian, gay, and bisexual college students. *Journal of Gay & Lesbian Social Services, 872260*(2), 207–221. https://doi.org/10.1080/10538720.2014.891090

Ruthig, J. C., Marrone, S., Hladkyi, S., & Robinson-Epp, N. (2011). Changes in college student health: Implications for academic performance. *Journal of College Student Development, 52*(3), 307–320. https://doi.org/10.1353/csd.2011.0038

Ryan, C., Huebner, D., Diaz, R. M., & Sanchez, J. (2009). Family rejection as a predictor of negative health outcomes in white and Latino lesbian, gay, and bisexual young adults. *Pediatrics, 123*(1), 346–352.

Ryan, C., Russell, S. T., Huebner, D., Diaz, R., & Sanchez, J. (2010). Family acceptance in adolescence and the health of LGBT young adults. *Journal of Child and Adolescent Psychiatric Nursing, 23*(4), 205–213.

Saewyc, E. M., Li, G., Gower, A. L., Watson, R. J., Erickson, D., Corliss, H. L., & Eisenberg, M. E. (2020). The link between LGBTQ-supportive communities, progressive political climate, and suicidality among sexual minority adolescents in Canada. *Preventive Medicine, 139*, 106191. https://doi.org/10.1016/j.ypmed.2020.106191

Saewyc, E. M., Skay, C. L., Pettingell, S. L., Reis, E. A., Bearinger, L., Resnick, M., Murphy, A., & Combs, L. (2006). Hazards of stigma: The sexual and physical abuse of gay, lesbian, and bisexual adolescents in the United States and Canada. *Child Welfare, 85*(2), 195–213.

Safer, J. D., Coleman, E., Feldman, J., Garofalo, R., Hembree, W., Radix, A., & Sevelius, J. (2016). Barriers to healthcare for transgender individuals. *Current Opinion in Endocrinology & Diabetes and Obesity, 23*(2), 168–171. https://doi.org/10.1097/MED.0000000000000227

Salerno, J. P., Devadas, J., Pease, M., Nketia, B., & Fish, J. N. (2020). Sexual and gender minority stress amid the COVID-19 pandemic: Implications for LGBTQ young persons' mental health and well-being. *Public Health Reports, 135*(6), 721–727. https://doi.org/10.1177/0033354920954511

Salerno, J. P., Williams, N. D., & Gattamorta, K. A. (2020). LGBTQ populations: Psychologically vulnerable communities in the COVID-19 pandemic. *Psychological Trauma: Theory, Research, Practice, and Policy, 12*(1), 239–242. http://dx.doi.org/10.1037/tra0000837

SAMSHA. (2008). Brief: Providing services and supports for youth who are LGBTQ+i2-S. Spring 2008.

SAMSHA. (2011). Learning from the field: Programs serving youth who are LGBTQ+i2-s and experiencing homelessness. https://www.samhsa.gov/sites/default/files/programs_campaigns/homelessness_programs_resources/learning-field-programs-serving-youth-LGBTQ+i2s-experiencing-homelessness.pdf

Sangganjanavanich, V. F., & Headley, J. A. (2016). Career development of transgender college students pursuing gender transition. *Career Planning and Adult Development, 32*(1), 161–169.

Santelli, J., Ott, M. A., Lyon, M., Rogers, J., Summers, D., & Schleifer, R. (2006). Abstinence and abstinence-only education: A review of U.S. policies and programs. *Journal of Adolescent Health, 38*(1), 72–81. https://doi.org/10.1016/j.jadohealth.2005.10.006

Savin-Williams, R. C., & Cohen, K. M. (2015). Developmental trajectories and milestones of lesbian, gay, and bisexual young people. *International Review of Psychiatry, 27*(5), 357–366. https://doi.org/10.3109/09540261.2015.1093465

Schauer, M., Neuner, F., & Elbert, T. (2011). *Narrative exposure therapy: A short-term treatment for traumatic stress disorders after war, terror, or torture.* Hogrefe Publishing.

Schmidt, C. K., Raque-Bogdan, T. L., Piontkowski, S., & Schaefer, K. L. (2011). Putting the positive in health psychology: A content analysis of three journals. *Journal of Health Psychology, 16*(4), 607–620. https://doi.org/10.1177/1359105310384296

Schmitz, R. M., Robinson, B. A. & Sanchez, J. (2020). Intersectional family systems approach: LGBTQ+ Latino/a youth, family dynamics, and stressors. *Family Relations, 69,* 832–848. https://doi.org/10.1111/fare.12448

Schmitz, R. M., Robinson, B. A., Tabler, J., Welch, B., & Rafaqut, S. (2020). LGBTQ+ Latino/a young people's interpretations of stigma and mental health: An intersectional minority stress perspective. *Society and Mental Health, 10*(2), 163–179. https://doi.org/10.1177/2156869319847248

Schmitz, R. M., & Tabler, J. (2019). Health services and intersections of care: Promises and pitfalls experienced by LGBTQ + Latino/a emerging adults. *Journal of LGBT Youth, 0*(0), 1–22. https://doi.org/10.1080/19361653.2019.1684416

Schmitz, R. M., & Tyler, K. A. (2018). Contextual constraints and choices: Strategic identity management among LGBTQ youth. *Journal of LGBT Youth, 15*(3), 212–226. https://doi.org/10.1080/19361653.2018.1466754

Schmitz, R. M., & Tyler, K. A. (2019). "Life has actually become more clear": An examination of resilience among LGBTQ young adults. *Sexualities, 22*(4), 710–733. https://doi.org/10.1177/1363460718770451

Schnarrs, P. W., Stone, A. L., Salcido, R., Georgiou, C., Zhou, X., & Nemeroff, C. B. (2020). The moderating effect of resilience on the relationship between adverse childhood experiences (ACEs) and quality of physical and mental health among adult sexual and gender minorities. *Behavioral Medicine, 46*(3–4), 366–374. https://doi.org/10.1080/08964289.2020.1727406

Schneider, M. S., & Dimito, A. (2010). Factors influencing the career and academic choices of lesbian, gay, bisexual, and transgender people. *Journal of Homosexuality, 57*(10), 1355–1369. https://doi.org/10.1080/00918369.2010.517080

School Social Work Association of America. (2010). *Gay, lesbian, transgender, bisexual and questioning youth (position statement).* https://aab82939-3e7b-497d-8f30-a85373757e29.filesusr.com/ugd/486e55_bdd2e14be640470d9d125c09026ec24e.pdf

Schrager, S. M., Latkin, C. A., Weiss, G., Kubicek, K., & Kipke, M. D. (2014). High-risk sexual activity in the House and Ball community: Influence of social networks. *American Journal of Public Health, 104*(2), 326–331. https://doi.org/10.2105/AJPH.2013.301543

Schulz, S. L. (2018). The informed consent model of transgender care: An alternative to the diagnosis of gender dysphoria. *Journal of Humanistic Psychology, 58*(1), 72–92. https://doi.org/10.1177/0022167817745217

Scott, J., & Marshall, G. (2009). *Dominant culture. A Dictionary of Sociology.* Oxford University Press. https://www.oxfordreference.com/view/10.1093/acref/9780199533008.001.0001/acref-9780199533008-e-634

Scroggs, B., Love, H. A., & Torgerson, C. (2020). COVID-19 and LGBTQ emerging adults: Risk in the face of social distancing. *Emerging Adulthood,* 1–6. https://doi.org/10.1177/2167696820968699

Seelman, K. L. (2016). Transgender adults' access to college bathrooms and housing and the relationship to suicidality. *Journal of Homosexuality, 63*(10), 1378–1399. https://doi.org/10.1080/00918369.2016.1157998

Sekoni, A. O., Gale, N. K., Manga-Atangana, B., Bhadhuri, A., & Jolly, K. (2017). The effects of educational curricula and training on LGBT-specific health issues for healthcare students and professionals: A mixed-method systematic review. *Journal of the International AIDS Society, 20*(21624), 1–13. http://dx.doi.org/10.7448/IAS.20.1.21624

Shapiro, J. (2018). "Violence" in medicine: Necessary and unnecessary, intentional and unintentional. *Philosophy, Ethics, and Humanities in Medicine, 13*(1), 1–8.

Shapiro, L. A. S., & Margolin, G. (2014). Growing up wired: Social networking sites and adolescent psychosocial development. *Clinical Child and Family Psychology Review, 17*, 1–18. https://doi.org/10.1007/s10567-013-0135-1

Shay, G., & Strader, K. (2012). Queer (in)justice: Mapping new gay (scholarly) agendas. *Journal of Criminal Law and Criminology, 102*, 171–193.

Shellnutt, K. (2021). Bethany Christian will allow LGBT parents to foster and adopt. *Christianity Today*. https://www.christianitytoday.com/news/2021/march/bethany-christian-services-adoption-foster-lgbt-same-sex.html

Shelton, J. (2015). Transgender youth homelessness: Understanding programmatic barriers through the lens of cisgenderism. *Children and Youth Services Review, 59*, 10–18.

Shilo, G., Antebi, N., & Mor, Z. (2015). Individual and community resilience factors among lesbian, gay, bisexual, queer, and questioning youth and adults in Israel. *American Journal of Community Psychology, 55*(1), 215–227.

Shipherd, J. C., Kauth, M. R., Firek, A. F., Garcia, R., Mejia, S., Laski, S., Walden, B., Perez-Padilla, S., Lindsay, J. A., Brown, G., Roybal, L., Keo-Meier, C. L., Knapp, H., Johnson, L., Reese, R. L., & Byne, W. (2016). Interdisciplinary transgender veteran care: Development of a core curriculum for VHA providers. *Transgender Health, 1*(1), 54–62. https://doi.org/10.1089/trgh.2015.0004

Sibley, C. G., Greaves, L. M., Overall, N. C., Lee, C. H. J., Milojev, P., Houkamau, C. A., Wilson, M. S., Milfont, T. L., Duck, I. M., Vickers-Jones, R., & Barlow, F. K. (2020). *American Psychologist, 75*(5), 618–630. http://dx.doi.org/10.1037/amp00000662

Sickmund, M. (2017). National council of juvenile and family court judges passes a set of practice reform resolutions. *Juvenile and Family Court Journal, 68*(4), 43–47.

Silenzio, V. M., Pena, J. B., Duberstein, P. R., Cerel, J., & Knox, K. L. (2007). Sexual orientation and risk factors for suicidal ideation and suicide attempts among adolescents and young adults. *American Journal of Public Health, 97*(11), 2017–2019. https://doi.org/10.2105/AJPH.2006.095943

Simons, J. D., & Beck, M. J. (2020). Sexual and gender minority identity development: Recommendations for school counselors. *Journal of School Counseling, 18*(20). http://www.jsc.montana.edu/articles/v18n20.pdf

Simons, J. D., & Cuadrado, M. (2019). Narratives of school counselors regarding advocacy for LGBT students. *Professional School Counseling, 22*(1), 1–9. https://doi.org/10.1177/2156659X19861529

Simons, J. D., Hutchison, B., & Bahr, M. (2017). School counselor advocacy for lesbian, gay, and bisexual students: Intentions and practice. *Professional School Counseling, 20*, 29–37. https://doi.org/10.5330/1096-2409-20.1a.29

Simons, L., Schrager, S. M., Clark, L. F., Belzer, M., & Olson, J. (2013). Parental support and mental health among transgender adolescents. *Journal of Adolescent Health, 53*(6), 791–793. https://doi.org/10.1016/j.jadohealth.2013.07.019

Singh, A. A. (2013). Transgender youth of color and resilience: Negotiating oppression and finding support. *Sex Roles, 68*, 690–702. https://doi.org/10.1007/s11199-012-0149-z

Singh, A. A., & Kosciw, J. G. (2017). School counselors transforming schools for

Skalski, A. K., Minke, K., Rossen, E., Cowan, K. C., Kelly, J., Armistead, R., & Smith, A. (2015). NASP Practice Model Implementation Guide. National Association of School Psychologists.

Smith, A. (2014). *African Americans and technology use*. Pew Research Center.

Smith, C. P., Cunningham, S. A., & Freyd, J. J. (2016). Sexual violence, institutional betrayal, and psychological outcomes for LGB college students. *Translational Issues in Psychological Science, 2*(4), 351–360. https://doi-org.colby.idm.oclc.org/10.1037/tps0000094

Smith, L., Webber, R., & DeFrain, J. (2013). Spiritual well-being and its relationship to resilience in young people: A mixed methods case study. *Sage Journals, 1*, 1–16. http://doi.org/10.1177/2158244013485582

Smith, S. K., & Turell, S. C. (2017). Perceptions of healthcare experiences: Relational and communicative competencies to improve care for LGBT people. *Journal of Social Issues, 73*(3), 637–657. https://doi.org/10.1111/josi.12235

Smith-Millman, M., Harrison, S. E., Pierce, L., & Flaspohler, P. D. (2019). Ready, willing, and able: Predictors of school mental health providers' competency in working with LGBTQ youth. *Journal of LGBT Youth, 16*(4), 380–402. https://doi.org/10.1080/19361653.20191580759

Snyder, S., Hartinger-Saunders, R., Brezina, T., Beck, E., Wright, E., Forge, N., & Bride, B. (2016). Homeless youth, strain, and justice system involvement: An application of general strain theory. *Children and Youth Services Review, 62*, 90–96.

Snapp, S., Hoenig, J., Fields, A., & Russell, S. (2015). Messy, butch, and queer: LGBTQ youth and the school-to-prison pipeline. *Journal of Adolescent Research, 30*, 57–82.

Snapp, S. D., McGuire, J. K., Sinclair, K. O., Gabrion, K., & Russell, S. T. (2015). LGBTQ-inclusive curricula: Why supportive curricula matter. *Sex Education, 15*, 580–596. https://doi.org/10.1080/14681811.2015.1042573

Sørlie, A. (2019). The right to trans-specific healthcare in Norway: Understanding the health needs of transgender people. *Medical Law Review, 27*(2), 295–317. https://doi.org/10.1093/medlaw/fwy029

Sotto-Santiago, S. (2019). Time to reconsider the word minority in academic medicine. *Journal of Best Practices in Health and Professions Diversity, 12*(1), 72–78.

Southwick, S. M., Bonanno, G. A., Masten, A. S., Panter-Brick, C., & Yehuda, R. (2014). Resilience definitions, theory, and challenges: Interdisciplinary perspectives. *European Journal of Psychotraumatology, 5*(1), 25338. https://doi.org/10.3402/ejpt.v5.25338

Spencer, K. G., Berg, D. R., Bradford, N. J., Vencill, J., Tellawi, G., & Rider, G. N. (2021). The gender affirmative lifespan approach: A developmental model for clinical work with transgender and gender diverse children, adolescents, and adults. *Psychotherapy, 58*(1), 37–49. https://doi.org/10.1037/pst0000363

Spencer, K. G., & Vencill, J. A. (2017). Body beyond: A pleasure-based, sex-positive group therapy curriculum for transfeminine adults. *Psychology of Sexual Orientation and Gender Diversity, 4*(4), 392–402. http://dx.doi.org/10.1037/sgd0000248

Srivastava, A., Rusow, J. A., Holguin, M., Semborski, S., Onasch-Vera, L., Wilson, N., & Rice, E. (2019). Exchange and survival sex, dating apps, gender identity, and sexual orientation among homeless youth in Los Angeles. *Journal of Primary Prevention, 40*(5), 561–568.

Stajduhar, K. I., Mollison, A., Giesbrecht, M., McNeil, R., Pauly, B., Reimer-Kirkham, S., . . . Rounds, K. (2019). "Just too busy living in the moment and surviving": Barriers to accessing health care for structurally vulnerable populations at end-of-life. *BMC Palliative Care, 18*(1), 1–14.

Staller, K. (2004). Runaway youth system dynamics: A theoretical framework for analyzing runaway and homeless youth policy. *Families in Society: The Journal of Contemporary Social Services, 85*(3), 379–390. https://doi.org/10.1606/1044-3894.1499

Stanton, M. C., Ali, S., & Chaudhuri, S. (2017). Individual, social, and community-level predictors of wellbeing in a US sample of transgender and gender non-conforming individuals.

Culture, Health, & Sexuality, 19(1), 32–49. http://dx.doi.org/10.1080/13691058.2016.1189596

Steensma, T. D., McGuire, J. K., Kreukels, B. P. C., Beekman, A. J., & Cohen-Kettenis, P. T. (2013). Factors associated with desistence and persistence of childhood gender dysphoria: A quantitative follow-up study. *Journal of the American Academy of Child and Adolescent Psychiatry, 52*(6), 582–590. https://doi.org/10.1016/j.jaac.2013.03.016

Sterling, P. & Eyer, J. (1988). Allostasis: A new paradigm to explain arousal pathology. In S. Fisher & J. Reason (Eds.), *Handbook of life stress, cognition, and health* (pp. 629–649). John Wiley & Sons

Sterzing, P. R., Ratliff, G. A, Gartner, R. E., McGeough, B. L., & Johnson, K. C. (2017). Social ecological correlates of polyvictimization among a national sample of transgender, genderqueer, and cisgender sexual minority adolescents. *Child Abuse & Neglect, 67*, 1–12.

Stevens, R. A. (2004). Understanding gay identity development within the college environment. *Journal of College Student Development, 45*(2), 185–206.

Strang, J. F., Jarin, J., Call, D., Clark, B., Wallace, G. L., Anthony, L. G., Kenworthy, L., & Gomez-Lobo, V. (2018). Transgender youth fertility attitudes questionnaire: Measure development in nonautistic and autistic transgender youth and their parents. *Journal of Adolescent Health, 62*(2), 128–135. https://doi.org/10.1016/j.jadohealth.2017.07.022

Strang, J. F., Knaus, M., van der Misen, A., McGuire, J. K., Kenworthy, L., Caplan, R., Freeman, A., . . . Anthony, L. G. (2020). A clinical program for transgender and gender-diverse neurodiverse/Autistic adolescents developed through community-based participatory design. *Journal of Clinical Child & Adolescent Psychology, 50*(6), 730–745. https://doi.10.1080/15374416.2020.1731817

Strayhorn, T. L., Johnson, R. M., Henderson, T. S., & Tillman-Kelly, D. L. (2015). *Beyond coming out: New insights about GLBQ college students of color.* Center for Higher Education Enterprise, Ohio State University.

Strear, M. M. (2017). Forecasting an inclusive future: School counseling strategies to deconstruct educational heteronormativity. *Professional School Counseling, 20*, 47–56. https://doi.org/10.5330/10962409-20.1a.47

Strelnik, O. N., & Strelnik, S. N. (2020). Interdisciplinary research of self-consciousness on the base of phenomenology of Karl Jaspers. *RUDN Journal of Philosophy, 24*(3), 410–418. doi: 10.22363/2313-2302-2020-24-3-410-418

Suárez-Orozco, M. M., Teranishi, R., & Suárez-Orozco, C. E. (2015). In the shadows of the ivory tower: Undocumented undergraduates and the liminal state of immigration reform. *UCLA.* https://escholarship.org/uc/item/2hq679z4

Substance Abuse and Mental Health Services Administration (SAMHSA). (n.d.) *Affordable Care Act enrollment assistance for LGBT communities: A resource for behavioral health providers.* https://www.samhsa.gov/sites/default/files/pep14-lgbtacaenrolla.pdf

Substance Abuse and Mental Health Services Administration (SAMHSA). (2017). *Key substance use and mental health indicators in the United States: Results from the 2016 National Survey on Drug Use and Health* (HHS Publication No. SMA 17-5044, NSDUH Series H-52). Center for Behavioral Health Statistics and Quality, Substance Abuse and Mental Health Services Administration. https://www.samhsa.gov/data

Substance Abuse and Mental Health Services Administration. (2018). Key substance use and mental health indicators in the United States: Results from the 2017 National Survey on Drug Use and Health (HHS Publication No. SMA 18-5068, NSDUH Series H-53). Center for Behavioral Health Statistics and Quality, Substance Abuse and Mental Health Services Administration. https://www.samhsa.gov/data/

Suzuki, L. A., Shaughnessy, T. A. O., Roysircar, G., Ponterotto, J. G., & Carter, R. T. (2019). Counseling Psychology and the amelioration of oppression: Translating our knowledge into action. *Counseling Psychologist, 47*, 826–872. https://doi.org/10.1177/0011000019888763

Szymanski, D. M., & Gupta, A. (2009). Examining the relationship between multiple internalized oppressions and African American lesbian, gay, bisexual, and questioning persons' self-esteem and psychological distress. *Journal of Counseling Psychology, 56*, 110–118. https://doi.org/10.1037/a0013317

Tajeu, G. S., Halanych, J., Juarez, L., Stone, J., Stepanikova, I., Green, A., & Cherrington, A. L. (2018). Exploring the association of healthcare worker race and occupation with implicit and explicit racial bias. *Journal of the National Medical Association, 110*(5), 464–472. https://doi.org/10.1016/j.jnma.2017.12.001

Tajfel, H. (1974). Social identity and intergroup behaviour. *Social Science Information, 13*(2), 65–93. https://doi.org/10.1177/053901847401300204

Takahashi, L. M., Tobin, K., Li, F. Y., Proff, A., & Candelario, J. (2022). Healing transgender women of color in Los Angeles: A transgender-centric delivery of Seeking Safety. *International Journal of Transgender Health, 23*(1–2), 232–242.

Taliaferro, L. A., Gloppen, K. M., Muehlenkamp, J. J., & Eisenberg, M. E. (2018). Depression and suicidality among bisexual youth: A nationally representative sample. *Journal of LGBT Youth, 15*(1), 16–31. https://doi.org/10.1080/19361653.2017.1395306

Tan, K. K. H., Treharne, G. J., Ellis, S. J., Schmidt, J. M., & Veale, J. F. (2020). Gender minority stress: A critical review, *Journal of Homosexuality, 67*(10), 1471–1489. doi: 10.1080/00918369.2019.1591789

Tan, P. (2005). The importance of spirituality among gay and lesbian individuals. *Journal of Homosexuality, 49*, 135–144. http://dx.doi.org/10.1300/J082v49n02_08

Tate, Charlotte. (2016, October). *Self-categorization dynamics for transgender spectrum and cisgender adults.* Presented at the Gender Development Research Conference, San Francisco.

Tebbe, E. A., & Moradi, B. (2016). Suicide risk in trans populations: An application of minority stress theory. *Journal of Counseling Psychology, 63*(5), 520–533. https://doi.org/10.1037/cou0000152

Testa, R. J., Habarth, J., Peta, J., Balsam, K., & Bockting, W. (2015). Development of the gender minority stress and resilience measure. *Psychology of Sexual Orientation and Gender Diversity, 2*(1), 65–77. https://doi.org/10.1037/sgd0000081

Tetreault, P. A., Fette, R., Meidlinger, P. C., & Hope, D. (2013). Perceptions of campus climate by sexual minorities. *Journal of Homosexuality, 60*(7), 947–964. https://doi.org/10.1080/00918369.2013.774874

Theodore, P. S., & Chiasson, J. (2021). Evolving strategies to counter school bullying of gender and sexually diverse students. In M. C. Lytle & R. A. Sprott (Eds.), Supporting gender identity and sexual orientation diversity in K–12 Schools (pp. 71–96). *American Psychological Association.* http://www.jstor.org/stable/j.ctv19wx7zq.8

Thoma, B. C., & Huebner, D. M. (2013). Health consequences of racist and antigay discrimination for multiple minority adolescents. *Cultural Diversity and Ethnic Minority Psychology, 19*(4), 404.

Thompson Jr., R. G., Elliott, J. C., Hu, M. C., Aivadyan, C., Aharonovich, E., & Hasin, D. S. (2017). Short-term effects of a brief intervention to reduce alcohol use and sexual risk among homeless young adults: Results from a randomized controlled trial. *Addiction Research & Theory, 25*(1), 24–31.

Thoreson, R. (2022, February 25). *Texas officials threaten transgender children and families: Criminalizing medical care undermines rights.* Human Rights Watch. https://www.hrw.org/news/2022/02/25/texas-officials-threaten-transgender-children-and-families#

Thorne, N., Witcomb, G., Nieder, T., Nixon, E., Yip, A., & Arcelus, J. (2018). A comparison of mental health symptomatology and levels of social support in young treatment seeking transgender individuals who identify as binary and non-binary. *International Journal of Transgenderism, 20*(2–3), 241–250. https://doi.org/10.1080/15532739.2018.1452660

Thrower, E., Bretherton, I., Pang, K. C., Zajac, J. D., & Cheung, A. S. (2020). Prevalence of Autism Spectrum Disorder and Attention-Deficit Hyperactivity Disorder amongst individuals with Gender Dysphoria: A systematic review. *Journal of Autism and Developmental Disorders, 50*, 695–706. https://doi.org/10.1007/s10803-019-04298-1

Tjale, A. A., & Bruce, J. (2007). A concept analysis of holistic nursing care in paediatric nursing. *Curationis, 30*(4), 45–52. https://doi.org/10.4102/curationis.v30i4.1116

Tobar, K. (2018). Ending the "closet to poverty pipeline" for LGBTQ+ youth. https://stoneleighfoundation.org/ending-closet-poverty-pipeline-LGBTQ+-youth/

Toomey, R. B., Ryan, C., Diaz, R. M., & Russell, S. T. (2011). High school gay-straight alliances (GSAs) and young adult well-being: An examination of GSA presence, participation, and perceived effectiveness. *Applied Developmental Science, 15*(4), 175–185. https://doi.org/10.1080/10888691.2011.607378

Toro, P. A., Dworsky, A., Fowler, P. J. (2007). Homeless youth in the United States: Recent research findings and intervention approaches. Paper presented at the 2007 National Symposium on Homelessness Research.

Toro, P. A., Trickett, E. J., Wall, D. D., & Salem, D. A. (1991). Homelessness in the United States: An ecological perspective. *American Psychologist, 46*(11), 1208.

Torres, V., Jones, S. R., & Renn, K. A. (2009). Identity development theories in student affairs: Origins, current status, and new approaches. *Journal of College Student Development, 50*(6), 577–596. https://doi.org/10.1353/csd.0.0102

Trần, N. L. (2016). Calling-in: A less disposable way of holding each other accountable. In M. McKenzie (Ed.), *The solidarity struggle: How people of color succeed and fail at showing up for each other in the fight for freedom.* BGD Press.

Trent, M., Dooley, D. G., & Dougé, J. (2019). The impact of racism on child and adolescent health. *Pediatrics, 144*(2), e20191765. https://doi.org/10.1542/peds.2019-1765

Trevor Project. (2019). The National Survey on LGBTQ Youth Mental Health 2019. https://www.thetrevorproject.org/wp-content/uploads/2019/06/The-Trevor-Project-National-Survey-Results-2019.pdf

Trevor Project. (2020). *The Trevor Project national survey 2020.* https://www.thetrevorproject.org/survey-2020/

Trevor Project. (2021). The National Survey on LGBTQ Youth Mental Health 2019. https://www.thetrevorproject.org/survey-2021/

Trimble, P. E. (2019). Ignored LGBTQ prisoners: Discrimination in education, rehabilitation, and mental health services during incarceration. https://lgbtq.hkspublications.org/2019/05/22/ignored-lgbtq-prisoners-discrimination-in-education-rehabilitative-and-mental-health-services-during-incarceration/

Truong, N. L., Zongrone, A. D., & Kosciw, J. G. (2020). *Erasure and resilience: The experiences of LGBTQ students of color, black LGBTQ youth in U.S. schools.* GLSEN.

Truong, N. L., Zongrone, A. D., & Kosciw, J. G. (2020). *Erasure and resilience: The experiences of LGBTQ students of color, Asian American and pacific islander LGBTQ youth in U.S. schools.* GLSEN.

Truszczynski, N., Singh, A. A., & Hansen, N. (2020). The discrimination experiences and coping responses of non-binary and trans people. *Journal of Homosexuality, 69*(4), 741–755. https://doi.org/10.1080/00918369.2020.1855028

Turban, J. L., Beckwith, N., Reisner, S. L., & Keuroghlian, A. S. (2020). Association between recalled exposure to gender identity conversion efforts and psychological distress and suicide attempts among transgender adults. *JAMA Psychiatry, 77*(1), 68–76.

Turban, J. L., King, D., Carswell, J. M., & Keuroghlian, A. S. (2020). Pubertal suppression for transgender youth and risk of suicidal ideation. *Pediatrics, 145*(2). https://doi.org/10.1542/peds.2019-1725

Turner, R. J., & Roszell, P. (1994). Psychosocial resources and the stress process. In W. R. Avison & I. H. Gotlib (Eds.), *Stress and mental health, contemporary issues and prospects for the future* (pp. 179–210). Plenum Press

Turner, W. B. (2000). *A genealogy of queer theory*. Temple University Press.

Twist, J., Barker, M.-J., Nel, P. W., & Horley, N. (2017). Transitioning together: A narrative analysis of the support accessed by partners of trans people. *Sexual & Relationship Therapy, 32*(2), 227–243. https://doi.org/10.1080/14681994.2017.1296568

UN General Assembly. (1948). *Universal declaration of human rights*. United Nations.

UN General Assembly. (1966). *International covenant on civil and political rights*. United Nations.

UN General Assembly. (2006). *Convention on the rights of persons with disabilities*. United Nations.

United States Department of Justice, Federal Bureau of Investigation. (2020, November). Hate Crime Statistics, 2019. https://ucr.fbi.gov/crime-in-the-u.s/2019/crime-in-the-u.s.-2019

US Department of Health and Human Services. (2016). *Advancing LGBT health and well-being: 2016 report of the HHS LGBT Policy Coordinating Committee*. https://www.hhs.gov/sites/default/files/2016-report-with-cover.pdf

US Department of Health and Human Services. (2020, February). Bulletin: HIPAA privacy and Novel Coronavirus. Office for Civil Rights. https://www.hhs.gov/sites/default/files/february-2020-hipaa-and-novel-coronavirus.pdf

US Department of Veterans Affairs. (2021, July 1). *Patient care services*. Retrieved from VA LGBTQ+ Policies: https://www.patientcare.va.gov/LGBT/VA_LGBT_Policies.asp

Vaitses-Fontanari, A. M., Fagundes-Pase, P., Churchill, S., Machado-Borba Soll, B., Schwarz, K., Schneider, M. A., . . . Rodrigues-Lobato, M. I. (2019). Dealing with gender-related and general stress: Substance use among Brazilian transgender youth. *Addictive Behaviors Reports, 9*(November 2018), 100166. https://doi.org/10.1016/j.abrep.2019.100166

Valentijn, P. P., Schepman, S. M., Opheij, W., & Bruijnzeels, M. A. (2013). Understanding integrated care: A comprehensive conceptual framework based on the integrative functions of primary care. *International Journal of Integrated Care, 13*, e010. https://doi.org/10.5334/ijic.886

van Beusekom, G., Bos, H. M. W., Overbeek, G., & Sandfort, T. G. M. (2015). Same-sex attraction, gender nonconformity, and mental health: The protective role of parental acceptance. *Psychology of Sexual Orientation and Gender Diversity, 2*(3), 307–312. https://doi.org/10.1037/sgd0000118

Van Bewer, V. (2017). Transdisciplinarity in health care: A concept analysis. *Nursing Forum, 52*(4), 339–347. https://doi.org/10.1111/nuf.12200

Van Dyke, M. E., Baumhofer, N. K., Slopen, N., Mujahid, M. S., Clark, C. R., Williams, D. R., & Lewis, T. T. (2020). Pervasive discrimination and allostatic load in African American and white adults. *Psychosomatic Medicine, 82*(3), 316–323. https://doi.org/10.1097/PSY.0000000000000788

van Leeuwen, J. M., Boyle, S., Salomonsen-Sautel, S., Baker, D. N., Garcia, J. T., Hoffman, A., & Hopfer, C. J. (2006). Lesbian, gay, and bisexual homeless youth: An eight-city public health perspective. *Child Welfare, 85*(2), 151–170.

Vance, S. R. Jr., Ehrensaft, D., & Rosenthal, S. M. (2014). Psychological and medical care of gender nonconforming youth. *Pediatrics, 134*(6), 1184–1192. https://doi.org/10.1542/peds.2014-0772

Vance, T. A., Klein, S. L., Nikiforova, Y., Rubin, L. R., & Lopez, F. G. (2021). The health and wellbeing of transgender and gender non-conforming people of colour in the United States: A systematic literature search and review. *Journal of Community & Applied Social Psychology*, 1–29. https://doi.org/10.1002/casp.2555

Varcoe, C., van Roode, T., & Wilson Strosher, H. (2019) *Trauma- and violence-informed care: An orientation tool for service providers in the homelessness sector.* Public Health Agency of Canada. www.equiphealthcare.ca

Vaughan, M. D., & Waehler, C. A. (2010). Coming out growth: Conceptualizing and measuring stress-related growth associated with coming out to others as a sexual minority. *Journal of Adult Development, 17*(2), 94–109. https://doi.org/10.1007/s10804-009-9084-9

Veale, J. F., Watson, R. J., Peter, T., & Saewyc, E. M. (2017). Mental health disparities among Canadian transgender youth. *Journal of Adolescent Health, 60*(1), 44–49. https://doi.org/10.1016/j.jadohealth.2016.09.014

Villarreal, L., Charak, R., Schmitz, R. M., Hsieh, C., & Ford, J. D. (2020). The relationship between sexual orientation outness, heterosexism, emotion dysregulation, and alcohol use among lesbian, gay, and bisexual emerging adults. *Journal of Gay and Lesbian Mental Health.* Advance online publication. https://doi.10.1080\\19359705.2020.1809588

Villicana, A. J., Delucio, K., & Biernat, M. (2016). "Coming out" among gay Latino and gay White men: Implications of verbal disclosure for well-being. *Self and Identity, 15*(4), 468–487. https://doi.org/10.1080/15298868.2016.1156568

Wadsworth, L. P., & Hayes-Skelton, S. A. (2015). Differences among lesbian, gay, bisexual, and heterosexual individuals and those who reported an other identity on an open-ended response on levels of social anxiety. *Psychology of Sexual Orientation and Gender Diversity, 2*(2), 181–187. https://doi.org/10.1037/sgd0000092

Wagaman, M. A. (2016). Self-definition as resistance: Understanding identities among LGBTQ emerging adults. *Journal of LGBT Youth, 13*(3), 207–230.

Wagaman, M. A., Watts, K. J., Lamneck, V., Souza, S. A. D., Mcinroy, L. B., Eaton, A. D., & Craig, S. (2020). Managing stressors online and offline: LGBTQ+ youth in the Southern United States. *Children and Youth Services Review, 110*, 104799. https://doi.org/10.1016/j.childyouth.2020.104799

Wallace, B. C., & Santacruz, E. (2017). Health disparities and LGBT populations. In R. Ruth & E. Santacruz (Eds.), *LGBT psychology and mental health: Emerging research and advances* (pp. 177–196). Praeger.

Wallace, R., & Russell, H. (2013). Attachment and shame in gender-nonconforming children and their families: Toward a theoretical framework for evaluating clinical interventions. *International Journal of Transgenderism, 14*(3), 113–126.

Wallien, M. S., Veenstra, R., Kreukels, B. P., & Cohen-Kettenis, P. T. (2010). Peer group status of gender dysphoric children: A sociometric study. *Archives of Sexual Behavior, 39*(2), 553–560.

Walls, N. E., & Bell, S. (2011). Correlates of engaging in survival sex among homeless youth and young adults. *Journal of Sex Research, 48*(5), 423–436.

Walters, M. L., Chen, J., & Breiding, M. J. (2013). The National Intimate Partner and Sexual Violence Survey (NISVS): 2010 findings on victimization by sexual orientation. National Center for Injury Prevention and Control, Centers for Disease Control and Prevention. https://www.cdc.gov/ViolencePrevention/pdf/NISVS_SOfindings.pdf (NCJ Publication No. 241083)

Wang, C. C., Lin, H. C., Chen, M. H., Ko, N. Y., Chang, Y. P., Lin, I. M., & Yen, C. F. (2018). Effects of traditional and cyber homophobic bullying in childhood on depression, anxiety, and physical pain in emerging adulthood and the moderating effects of social support among gay and bisexual men in Taiwan. *Neuropsychiatric Disease and Treatment, Volume 14*, 1309–1317. https://doi.org/10.2147/NDT.S164579

Wang, J. Z., Mott, S., Magwood, O., Mathew, C., Mclellan, A., Kpade, V., . . . Andermann, A. (2019). The impact of interventions for youth experiencing homelessness on housing, mental health, substance use, and family cohesion: A systematic review. *BMC Public Health, 19*(1), 1–22.

Watt, T., & Kim, S. (2019). Race/ethnicity and foster youth outcomes: An examination of disproportionality using the national youth in transition database. *Children and Youth Services Review, 102*, 251–258.

Westefeld, J. S., Maples, M. R., Buford, B., & Taylor, S. (2001). Gay, lesbian, and bisexual college students: The relationship between sexual orientation and depression, loneliness, and suicide. *Journal of College Student Psychotherapy, 15*(3), 71–82. https://doi.org/10.1300/J035v15n03_06

Westwater, J. J., Riley, E. A., & Peterson, G. M. (2019). What about the family in youth gender diversity? A literature review. *International Journal of Transgenderism, 20*(4), 351–370. https://doi.org/10.1080/15532739.2019.1652130

Whitaker, A., Torres-Guillén, S., Morton, M., Jordan, H., Coyle, S., Mann, A., & Sun, W-L. (2019). *Cops and no counselors: How the lack of school mental health staff is harming students.* https://www.aclu.org/report/cops-and-no-counselors

Whitbeck, L. B., Chen, X., Hoyt, D. R., Tyler, K. A., & Johnson, K. D. (2004). Mental disorder, subsistence strategies, and victimization among gay, lesbian, and bisexual homeless and runaway adolescents. *Journal of Sex Research, 41*(4), 329–342.

Whitton, S. W., Newcomb, M. E., Messinger, A. M., Byck, G., & Mustanski, B. (2019). A longitudinal study of IPV victimization among sexual minority youth. *Journal of Interpersonal Violence, 34*(5), 912–945. https://doi.org/10.1177/0886260516646093

Wilber, S., Reyes, C., & Marksamer, J. (2006). The model standards project: Creating inclusive systems for LGBT youth in out-of-home care. *Child Welfare, 85*(2), 133–149.

Wilkinson, W. (2008). Threatening the patriarchy: Testing an explanatory paradigm of anti-lesbian attitudes. *Sex Roles, 59*, 512–520.

Williams, S. L., Job, S. A., Todd, E., & Braun, K. (2020). A critical deconstructed quantitative analysis: Sexual and gender minority stress through an intersectional lens. *Journal of Social Issues, 76*, 859– 879. https://doi.org/10.1111/josi.12410

Willis, P., Dobbs, C., Evans, E., Raithby, M., & Bishop, J. (2020). Reluctant educators and self-advocates: Older trans adults' experiences of health-care services and practitioners in seeking gender-affirming services. *Health Expectations: An International Journal of Public Participation in Health Care & Health Policy.* https://doi.org/10.1111/hex.13104

Willoughby, B. (2018). *Speak up at school: How to respond to everyday prejudice, bias, and stereotypes.* Southern Poverty Law Center.

Wilson, B., Jordan, S. P., Meyer, I. H., Flores, A. R., Stemple, L., & Herman, J. L. (2017). Disproportionality and disparities among sexual minority youth in custody. *Journal of Youth and Adolescence, 46*(7), 1547–1561. https://doi.org/10.1007/s10964-017-0632-5

Wilson, M. (2016). Cultural competence in therapy: Why we must see color. http://blog.time2track.com/cultural-competence-in-therapy-why-we-must-see-color

Wong, C. F., Schrager, S. M., Holloway, I. W., Meyer, I. H., & Kipke, M. D. (2014). Minority stress experiences and psychological well-being: The impact of support from and connection to social networks within the Los Angeles House and Ball communities. *Prevention*

Science: The Official Journal of the Society for Prevention Research, 15(1), 44–55. https://doi.org/10.1007/s11121-012-0348-4

Wong, W. I., van der Miesen, A. I. R., Li, T. G. F., MacMullin, L. N., & VanderLaan, D. P. (2019). Childhood social gender transition and psychosocial well-being: A comparison to cisgender gender-variant children. *Clinical Practice in Pediatric Psychology, 7*(3), 241–253. https://doi.org/10.1037/cpp0000295

Wood, A. W., & Conley, A. H. (2014). Loss of religious or spiritual identities among the LGBT population. *Counseling and Values, 59*(1), 95–111. https://doi.org/10.1002/j.2161-007X.2014.00044.x

Wood, J., Foy, D., Goguen, C., Pynoos, R., & James, C. (2002). Violence exposure and PTSD among delinquent girls. *Journal of Aggression, Maltreatment, and Trauma, 6*, 79–108.

Wood, S. M., Salas-Humara, C., & Dowshen, N. L. (2016). Human immunodeficiency virus, other sexually transmitted infections, and sexual and reproductive health in lesbian, gay, bisexual, transgender youth. *Pediatric Clinics of North America, 63*(6), 1027–1055. https://doi.org/https://doi.org/10.1016/j.pcl.2016.07.006

Woodford, M. R., Han, Y., Craig, S., Lim, C., & Matney, M. M. (2014). Discrimination and mental health among sexual minority college students: The type and form of discrimination does matter. *Journal of Gay & Lesbian Mental Health, 18*(2), 142–163. https://doi.org/10.1080/19359705.2013.833882

Woodford, M. R., & Kulick, A. (2015). Academic and social integration on campus among sexual minority students: The impacts of psychological and experiential campus climate. *American Journal of Community Psychology, 55*, 13–24.

Woodford, M. R., Kulick, A., & Atteberry, B. (2015). Protective factors, campus climate, and health outcomes among sexual minority college students. *Journal of Diversity in Higher Education, 8*(2), 73–87. http://dx.doi.org/10.1037/a0038552

Woodford, M. R., Weber, G., Nicolazzo, Z., Hunt, R., Kulick, A., Coleman, T., . . . Renn, K. A. (2018). Depression and attempted suicide among LGBTQ college students: Fostering resilience to the effects of heterosexism and cisgenderism on campus. *Journal of College Student Development, 59*(4), 421–438. https://doi.org/10.1353/csd.2018.0040

World Health Organization (WHO). (n.d.). *Social determinants of health*. https://www.who.int/health-topics/social-determinants-of-health#tab=tab_1

World Health Organization. (2010). *Framework for action on interprofessional education and collaborative practice*. World Health Organization.

World Health Organization. (2012). What are the social determinants of health? Retrieved from http://www.who.int/social_determinants/sdh_definition/en/

World Professional Association for Transgender Health. (2012). Standards of care for the health of transsexual, transgender, and gender nonconforming people [7th Version]. https://www.wpath.org/publications/soc

Woznicki, N., Arriaga, A. S., Caporale-Berkowitz, N. A., & Parent, M. C. (2021). Parasocial relationships and depression among LGBQ emerging adults living with their parents during COVID-19: The potential for online support. *Psychology of Sexual Orientation and Gender Diversity, 8*(2), 228–237. http://dx.doi.org/10.1037/sgd0000458

Wright, A., & Stern, S. (2016). The role of spirituality in sexual minority identities. *Psychology of Sexual Orientation and Gender Diversity, 3*(1), 71–79.

Xavier, J. M., Bradford, J., & Honnold, J. (2007). *The health, health-related needs, and lifecourse experiences of transgender Virginians*. Virginia Department of Health.

Ybarra, M. L., Mitchell, K. J., Kosciw, J. G., & Korchmaros, J. D. (2015). Understanding linkages between bullying and suicidal ideation in a national sample of LGB and heterosexual youth in the United States. *Prevention Science, 16*(3), 451–462. https://doi.org/10.1007/s11121-014-0510-2

Ybarra, M. L., Mitchell, K. J., Palmer, N. A., & Reisner, S. L. (2015). Online social support as a buffer against online and offline peer and sexual victimization among U.S. LGBT and non-LGBT youth. *Child Abuse & Neglect, 39*, 123–136. https://doi.org/10.1016/j.chiabu.2014.08.006

Yosso, T. J. (2005). Whose culture has capital? A critical race theory discussion of community cultural wealth. *Race Ethnicity and Education, 8*(1), 69–91.

youth in foster care: An evidence-based theoretical conceptual model of disproportionality and psychological comorbidities. *Trauma, Violence, & Abuse*, 1–15.

Yuksek, C. (2018). Dealing with stress using social theatre techniques with young Syrian students adapting to a new educational system in Turkey: A case study. *Intervention, 16*(2), 175. http://dx.doi.org/10.4103/INTV.INTV_38_18

Yunger, J. L., Carver, P. R., & Perry, D. G. (2004). Does gender identity influence children's psychological well-being? *Developmental Psychology, 40*(4), 572.

Zautra, J., Hall, J. S., & Murray, K. E. (2010). Resilience: A new definition of health for people and communities. In J. W. Reich, A. J. Zautra & J. S. Stuart (Eds.), *Handbook of adult resilience* (pp. 3–29). Guilford Press.

Zaza, S., Kann, L., & Barrios, L. C. (2016). Lesbian, gay, and bisexual adolescents population estimate and prevalence of health behaviors. *Journal of American Medical Association, 316*(22), 2355–2356.

Zegers, M., Schuengel, C., & Van Ijzendoorn, M. (2006). Attachment representations of institutionalized adolescents and their professional caregivers: Predicting the development of therapeutic relationships. *American Journal of Orthopsychiatry, 76*, 325–334. https://doi.org/10.1037/0002-9432.76.3.325

Zegers, M., Schuengel, C., Van Ijzendoorn, M, & Janssens, M. (2008). Attachment and problem behavior of adolescents during residential treatment. *Attachment & Human Development, 10*, 91–103. https://doi.org/10.1080/1416730701868621

Zimmerman, J. (2017). Models of private practice. Which practice is best? In S. Walfish, J. Barnett, & J. Zimmerman (Eds.), *Handbook of private practice: Keys to success for mental health practitioners* (pp. 15–21). Oxford.

Zimmerman, L., Darnelle, D., Rhew, I., Lee, C., & Kaysen, D. (2015). Resilience in community: A social ecological development model for young adult sexual minority women. *American Journal of Community Psychology, 55*(1), 179–190. https://doi.org/10.1007/s10464-015-9702-6

Zongrone, A. D., Truong, N. L., & Kosciw, J. G. (2020). *Erasure and resilience: The experiences of LGBTQ students of color, Native American, American Indian, and Alaska native LGBTQ youth in U.S. schools*. GLSEN.

Zongrone, A. D., Truong, N. L., & Kosciw, J. G. (2020). *Erasure and resilience: The experiences of LGBTQ students of color, Latinx LGBTQ youth in U.S. schools*. GLSEN.

Zosky, D. L., & Alberts, R. (2016). What's in a name? Exploring use of the word queer as a term of identification within the college-aged LGBT community. *Journal of Human Behavior in the Social Environment, 26*(7–8), 597–607. https://doi.org/10.1080/10911359.2016.1238803

Zucker K. J. (2017). Epidemiology of gender dysphoria and transgender identity. *Sexual Health 14*, 404–411.

Zucker, K. J., & Bradley, S. J. (1995). *Gender identity disorder and psychosexual problems in children and adolescents*. Guilford Press.

Zucker, K. J., Bradley, S. J., Kuksis, M., Pecore, K., Birkenfeld-Adams, A., Doering, R. W., ... Wild, J. (1999). Gender constancy judgments in children with gender identity disorder: Evidence for a developmental lag. *Archives of Sexual Behavior, 28,* 475–502.

Zucker, K. J., Wood, H., Singh, D., & Bradley, S. J. (2012). A developmental, biopsychosocial model for the treatment of children with gender identity disorder. *Journal of Homosexuality, 59*(3), 369–397.

Zucker, K. J., Wood, H., & VanderLaan, D. P. (2014). Models of psychopathology in children and adolescents with gender dysphoria. In: B. P. C. Kreukels, T. D. Steensma, A. L. C. de Vries (Eds.), *Gender dysphoria and disorders of sex development: Progress in care and knowledge* (pp. 171–192). Springer Science + Business Media.

Index

Page numbers in italics indicate figures and tables.

ableism, 32
   gender diverse children and, 68, 86
ACEs. *See* adverse childhood events
activism movements. *See* youth activism movement
adolescence, in LGBTQ+ populations
   American Academy of Child and Adolescent Psychiatry, 185
   among BIPOC populations, 95–96, 100–102
   bullying during, 95, 100, 105
   case studies for, 104–6
   community support during, 101–2
   during COVID-19 pandemic, 99
   as critical development period, 31
   cyberbullying during, 102
   developmental considerations during, 103–4
   discrimination and, 95
   family rejection and, 95, 99
   friendships during, 97–98
   Gay-Straight Alliances during, 101, 104, 106
   gender-affirming providers, 105
   gender dysphoria during, 95
   gender identity during, 65
   geospatial networking applications and, 98
   identity development during, 103–4
   Internet/online support during, 102–3
   interpersonal relationships during, 97–99
   intersectional microaggressions during, 100
   in LGBTQ+-supportive political climates, 102
   mental health outcomes during, 33
   minority stress model and, 97
   minority stressors during, 95, 98
   online participation during, 98, 102–3
   parental relationships during, 99
   PFLAG groups and, 99
   positive youth development approaches during, 96–97
   protective factors during, 95–97
   radical healing and, 95–97
   risk factors during, 95–97
   romantic relationships during, 98
   in school contexts, 100–101
   social media use and, 34
   socioecological contexts for, 97
   suicidality and, 95
   transgender individuals during, 104
   trauma-informed approaches to, 34
adults. *See* emerging adulthood
adverse childhood events (ACEs), 199–200
affirmation. *See also specific topics*
   through affirming LGBTQ+ services, on colleges and universities, 161–65
   of gender identity, 12–13
   in hospital policies, 188–89
   medical, of gender identity, 13
   social, of gender identity, 13

affirmative care. *See also* LGBTQ+
    affirmative; transaffirmative care
    as framework, 3–4
    Trans-Affirmative CBT, 219
Affirmative Support Safe and Empowering
    Talk (ASSET) model, 149
Affordable Care Act, U.S., 286, 294
aftercare, for transitional age youth, 204
age-normative behaviors, 202
allostasis, 16
allostatic load framework, 15
American Academy of Child and Adolescent
    Psychiatry, 185
American College Health Association, 166
American Council for School Social Work,
    142–43
American Psychological Association, 286
anti-bullying policies, 74, 142
anti-gay policies, 13, 31, 52, 116–17
    "No Homo Promo" laws, 241
anti-transgender behaviors, homicides and, 13
anti-transgender legislation, 105
anxiety disorders, 15
    emerging adulthood and, 120
    in gender diverse children, 71
ARC Framework. *See* Attachment, Self-
    Regulation, and Competency
    Framework
art therapy, 221
ASCA National Model, 140, 143–44, 147
ASD. *See* Autism Spectrum Disorder
ASSET model. *See* Affirmative Support Safe
    and Empowering Talk model
Attachment, Self-Regulation, and
    Competency Framework (ARC
    Framework), 217
attachment-related issues, 246–49
authenticity, radical healing and, 97
Autism Spectrum Disorder (ASD), 52–53
autonomy, of YEH, 231

behavioral health services, in hospitals,
    186–88
Better Health, 296
bias-based bullying, 100
binary identity, overrepresentation of, 68
biopsychosocial needs, 19, 230
biopsychosociocultural model, 45
biphobic behaviors, 247

BIPOC populations, in LGBTQ+
    populations, during adolescence,
    95–96, 100–102
bisexual individuals
    at college and universities, 158, 163, 166
    poverty and, 200
Black. *See* minority identities; minority stress
    model; minority stress theory
Black children, polyvictimization of,
    199–200
Black LGBTQ+ populations. *See also*
    BIPOC populations
    coming out for, 264
    connectedness for, 267
    in House and Ball community, 18, 18n1
    in juvenile justice system, 244
    sexual assault against, 161
    youth experiencing homelessness among,
    225–27
breastfeeding, 84
broadscale longitudinal studies, on gender
    identity, 86
Bronfenbrenner, U., 144–45, 214
Brooks, V. R., 11
bullying. *See also* anti-bullying policies;
    stigma-based bullying
    during adolescence, 95, 100, 105
    bias-based, 100
    in school contexts, 100, 137

calling-in, 35–36
calling-out, 35
Campus Pride Index, 163
career advisors, 175
CBC. *See* Child Behavior Checklist
CBT. *See* Cognitive Behavioral Therapy
Centers for Disease Control and Prevention
    (CDC), 150
Centers for Medicare and Medicaid Services
    (CMS), 295–96
Child Behavior Checklist (CBC), 67
childcare, 295
children's hospitals, 183
child welfare settings, LGBTQ+ youth in.
    See also foster care systems
    clinician considerations for, 205–6
    community support in, 204
    as crossover system, with juvenile justice
    system, 242

demographics for, 202
during emerging adulthood, 203–4
Every Student Succeeds Act and, 204
exposure to poverty and, 197
Family First Prevention Services Act and, 204
family rejection and, 197
Fulton et al. v. City of Philadelphia, Pennsylvania, No. 19-123, 197, 204
gaps in care for, 203–6
juvenile justice system and, 239, 242
overrepresentation of, 197, 201–6
oversight and training in, 203
policies and practices in, 201–2
polyvictimization and, 197
referrals for, 200
under Religious Freedom Restoration Act, 205
sexism in, 206
for transition-age youth, 203–4
chosen family, 114
cisgender individuals, poverty and, 200
cisgenderism
    intersectionality and, 32
    presumed, among children, 66
cisheterosexual relationships, 127
cisnormative assumptions, about YEH, 226
cissexism
    against gender diverse adults, 116
    gender diverse children and, 68, 86
    against transgender individuals, 116
clinical practice. *See* independent practice
CMS. *See* Centers for Medicare and Medicaid Services
cocurricular programming, 162–63
Code of Ethics of the National Association of Social Workers (National Association of Social Workers), 141
cofounding, of longitudinal studies, 104
Cognitive Behavioral Therapy (CBT), 218–19
    in juvenile justice system, 251
    Trans-Affirmative CBT, 219
college and universities, LGBTQ+ populations at
    academic advisors for, 175
    acceptance of, 159–60
    advocacy strategies for, 172–73
    affirming LGBTQ+ services, 161–65

bisexual students, 158, 163, 166
campus health services and, 164–65
Campus Pride Index, 163
career advisors for, 175
clinical recommendations for, 168–75
coming out disclosures, 159, 169–70
community colleges, 174
community services for, 174
counseling centers, 168–69, 175
cyberbullying of, 164
data collection for, 173
Deferred Action for Childhood Arrivals benefits, 167
depathologization of, 172
dialogue spaces for, 174
discrimination and, 157
emerging adulthood and, 114–15
exclusion of, 163
faculty relationships, 162–63
family relationships for, 168
feedback loops for, 173–74
for first-generation students, 165
fluid students, 166
gender expression for, 165
healthcare providers for, 164–65, 175
identity development for, 158–59
identity disclosure for, 161–62
immigration status for, 167–68
inclusive policies for, 162, 174
institutional policies for, 173
international students, 168
intersectionality and, 159–61, 171–72, 174
language use for, in clinical settings, 171
marginalized identities for, 160–61
mental health disparities for, 157–58
microaggressions against, 160
minority stress theory and, 157
misgendering of, 166
nondiscrimination policies for, 163
peer relationships, 163–64
policy recommendations for, 173–75
protective factors for, 159–60, 175
research on, gaps in, 165–68
resilience skills for, 160, 169
sexual assault of, 161
social rejection of, 159–60
social support for, 163
STEM students, 167

strengths-based approach to, 169
student support services for, 161–62
suicidality and, 158
Title IX guidelines, 166
for transgender, nonbinary, and gender expansive students, 164–67
transgender individuals, 157–58
visibility of, 159–60
co-location of clinicians, 294
colonialism, intersectionality and, 32
coming out
    for Black LGBTQ+ youth, 264
    at college and universities, 159, 169–70
    by gender, 264–65
    grief as element, 170
    Internet and, 264
    National Coming Out Day, 146
    social media and, 264
    for transgender individuals, 266
    for whites compared to minority students, 159
coming out growth, 20
community building and support, for LGBTQ+ populations
    during adolescence, 101–2
    in child welfare settings, 204
    community centers, 271, *272,* 273
    constructivist phenomenological frameworks for, 266
    during emerging adulthood, 123–24
    in foster care systems, 204
    in hospitals, 189
    intersectionality and, 34–35
    medical care centers and, 190–91
    school-based mental health professionals and, 150–51
community centers, for LGBTQ+ populations, 271, *272,* 273
    access to, 277–78
    availability of services through, by geographical region, 277
    clinical practice considerations for, 278
    policy considerations for, 279
community colleges, 174
community groups and services, for LGBTQ+ populations
    in colleges and universities, 174
    purpose of, 261
    for queer youth and emerging adults of color, 262
community-level interventions, for resilience, 19
community resilience
    House and Ball community, 18, 18n1
    self-identification in LGBTQ+ community, 18
connectedness, 123–24
    for Black LGBTQ+ populations, 267
    during emerging adulthood, 123–24, 266–67
    for LGBTQ+ youth, 266–67
consent. *See* informed consent; parental consent
Constitution, US, 252–53
conversion therapy, gender identity and, 69
coping skills. *See also* resilience
    intersectionality and, 32
counseling centers, at colleges and universities, 168–69, 175
counselors. *See* school counselors
countercultural norms, 45
COVID-19 pandemic, 1
    adolescence during, 99
    economic inequality during, 31
    independent practice impacted by, 294–96
    teletherapy during, 31
coworkers, workplace identity management among, 270
critical consciousness, radical healing and, 96–97, 102–3
cross-cultural identities, 199
culture
    during emerging adulthood, 127
    intersectionality theory and, 5
    resilience influenced by, 72
cyberbullying
    during adolescence, 102
    at college and universities, 164

DACA benefits. *See* Deferred Action for Childhood Arrivals benefits
Day of Silence, 146
DBT. *See* Dialectical Behavioral Therapy
deadname, 287
decision making
    data driven, 139

for LGBTQ+ youth, 270
logical, 95
in placement policies, 212
decision-making tools, for school-based mental health professionals, 139
Deferred Action for Childhood Arrivals (DACA) benefits, 167
depathologization, of LGBTQ+ populations, at college and universities, 172
depression, 15
emerging adulthood and, 116, 120
in gender diverse children, 71
Diagnostic and Statistical Manual of Mental Disorders, 5th Edition (DSM-5), 69, 249
Dialectical Behavioral Therapy (DBT), 20, 251
dialogue spaces, 174
Diamond, K. D., 53
differences of sexual development (DSD), 66
discrimination, 32
during adolescence, 95
at college and universities, 157
during emerging adulthood, 115
employment, 269–70
distal stressors, in minority stress processes
intersecting minority status, 13
life-threatening experiences, 13
negative experiences in healthcare, 14
social approval/stigma, 13
social institutions and, lack of acknowledgment by, 13
systemic racism, 13
for transgender individuals, 44–45
violence and harassment, 13
white privilege, 13
diversity training, intersectionality theory and, 4
dominant culture, minority stress theory and, 11
drama therapy, 221
dropouts, from school, 99, 101
DSD. *See* differences of sexual development
DSM-5. *See Diagnostic and Statistical Manual of Mental Disorders*

eating disorders, 15
Ecological Model of Human Development, 144–45

EHRs. *See* electronic health records
elderly LGBTQ+ populations, healthcare for, 2
electronic health records (EHRs), 296
emerging adulthood, in LGBTQ+ populations. *See also* adolescence
anxiety and, 120
auxiliary services for, 276–77
career development for, 269
case studies, 126–27
in child welfare settings, 203–4
chosen family and, 114
clinical implications for, 125
in college and university settings, 114–15
coming out for, 264–66
community building for, 266–67
community engagement during, 123–24
connectedness and, 123–24, 266–67
as critical development period, 31
cultural contexts during, 127
definition of, 113–14
depression and, 116, 120
discrimination during, 115
educational assistance for, 276
employment discrimination against, 269–70
familial conflict during, 114
family constructs for, 114
family rejection during, 123
food insecurity for, 276
foster care systems, 203–4
future research on, 124–25
for gender diverse individuals, 115
government institutions and, policies for, 116
healthcare services during, 115, 119
heterocisnormative family structures and, 114
HIV incidence rates and, 119
housing stability for, 275
identity formation as part of, 113–14
instability as part of, 113
institutional challenges for, 114–16
interpersonal challenges for, 116–18
among Latinx populations, 127
LGBTQ+-affirming religious institutions and, 115, 118, 123
marriage issues in, 116–17
medical care centers for, 184–90

mental health challenges for, 263–64
mental health issues during, 120–21
mental health services for, 274
methodological approaches to, 270–73
parental consent and, for transitioning medical services, 115
peer support during, 117
personal challenges for, 118–21
physical health issues for, 118–20
physical health services for, 273–74
protective factors for, 121–24
religious affiliations during, 115, 117–18
reproductive challenges in, 114
resilience skills, 121–22, 124
risk behaviors during, 118
romantic and sexual relationships during, 116, 267–68
romantic relationships for, challenges with, 267–68
self-esteem issues during, 122–23
self-focus as part of, 113
self-sufficiency skills as part of, 114
sexual health challenges, 264
sexually-transmitted infection rates for, 119
in socially conservative settings, 122
social support during, 122–23
structural stigma and, 116
substance abuse issues during, 119–20
suicidality and, 116, 120–21
transgender and gender-nonconforming youth and, 262
for transgender individuals, 115
vocational assistance for, 276
vocational challenges for, 269–70
workplace identity management, 270
emotional numbing, 248
emotion regulation, resilience and, 17
empiricism
in Gender Affirmative Lifespan Approach, 45
gender diverse children and, approaches to, 78
employment discrimination, 269–70
equity, in hospitals, 189
essentialism. *See* gender essentialism
Eurocentrism, gender identity influenced by, 68
Every Student Succeeds Act, U.S., 204

evidence-based LGBTQ+-affirming services, 219–20

familialism, 127
Family First Prevention Services Act, U.S., 204
family-focused therapy, 186–87
family rejection, 1
during adolescence, 95, 99
child welfare settings and, 197
during emerging adulthood, 123
foster care systems and, 198–99
family resilience, 73–74
family support
colleges and universities and, 168
during emerging adulthood, 114, 123
for gender diverse children, 73–74
nonsupportive family members, 74, 125
school-based mental health professionals and, 150–51
feedback loops, 173–74
first-generation students, 165
fluid students, 166
follow through, on patient health structures, 224, 226
foster care systems, LGBTQ+ youth in
clinician considerations for, 205–6
community support in, 204
during emerging adulthood, 203–4
entrance into, 202
family rejection and, 198–99
gaps in care for, 203–6
heterosexism in, 206
homophobia in, 198–99
House and Ball communities and, 198–99
negative experiences in, 201
oversight and training in, 203
placement failures, 201–2
policies and practices in, 201–2
polyvictimization in, 199–200
sexism in, 206
sexual abuse and, 198–99
transition-age youth in, 203–4
Fourteenth Amendment, US Constitution, 252–53
friendships, during adolescence, 97–98
Fulton et al. v. City of Philadelphia, Pennsylvania, No. 19-123, 197, 204

GALA. *See* Gender Affirmative Lifespan Approach
gatekeeping, in Gender Affirmative Lifespan Approach, by psychotherapists, 47–48
Gay, Lesbian and Straight Education Network (GLSEN), 137–38, 142–44, 147
   Solidarity Week, 151
Gay-Straight Alliance (GSAs), 104, 106
   in schools, 101
gender
   coming out experiences and, 264–65
   definition of, 66
   differences of sexual development and, 66
   gender diverse children and, 66
   juvenile justice system treatment by, 243–44
gender affirmation
   during adolescence, by medical providers, 105
   for gender diverse children, 76–77
   through hormone therapy, 185–86
   in individual-level interventions, 20
   pediatric endocrinologists and, 185–86
   during puberty, 185
gender affirmative healthcare, 42–44, 47
   for trans youth, 51
Gender Affirmative Lifespan Approach (GALA), 42, 56–57
   Autism Spectrum Disorder and, 52–53
   biopsychosociocultural model and, 45
   case studies with, 48–56
   definition of, 45
   developmental differences across lifespan, 45–46
   empiricism in, 45
   gender diverse children and, 76–78, 80, 85, 87
   gender dysphoria and, treatment strategies for, 51–52
   gender literacy in, 46–47
   health insurance advocacy case, 50–52
   hormone providers as part of, 48
   interdisciplinary approach in, 45–47
   intersectionality and, 45–46
   medical interventions as part of, 46–48
   philosophical foundations of, 45–46
   pleasure-oriented positive sexuality in, 46–47
   psychotherapists as gatekeepers in, 47–48
   resilience strategies, 46–47
   sex education in, 48–50, 53–54
   transaffirmative care, 45–46
   transdisciplinarity in, 56
   transparency in, 46, 54
   Unicorn Youth Project and, 49
   WPATH Standards of Care, 48, 51–52
   for youth experiencing homelessness, 54–56
gender affirmative models. *See* Gender Affirmative Lifespan Approach
gender atypicality, 71
gender-competent pediatricians, 47
gender-competent professionals
   health providers, 77
   pediatricians, 47
   psychotherapists, 47
gender conformity, 95, 242–43
gender constructivist theories, 70
gender creative, 42
gender differentiation, 68
gender diverse adults
   during emerging adulthood, 115
   romantic and sexual relationships for, 116
gender diverse children
   ableism and, 68, 86
   anxiety in, 71
   case studies, 77–85
   Child Behavior Checklist and, 67
   cissexism and, 68, 86
   classism and, 68, 86
   clinical implications for, 72–77
   clinical interventions for, 75–76
   collaborative treatment planning for, 79–80
   community contexts for, 74–77
   definition of, 65–66
   depression in, 71
   empiricism in approaches to, 78
   family support for, 73–74
   future approaches to, 85–86
   Gender Affirmative Lifespan Approach, 76–78, 80, 85, 87
   gender affirmative models for, 76–77
   gender atypicality and, 71
   gender dysphoria for, 71, 75–76
   gender expression among, 67–68
   gender identity for, 66–67

gender incongruence in, 71
gender literacy for, 78–79, 81, 86
gender nonconformity for, 71
Gender-Sexuality Alliances and, 74
healthcare settings for, 75–77
heterosexism and, 68, 86
historical context for, 67–68
initial experiences for, 74
interdisciplinary approaches to, 77
interpersonal contexts for, 73–74
intersectionality and, 77, 85
Jacob's New Dress, 82
across lifespan, 77
Live in Your Own Skin approach, 76
in medical settings, 75
mental health in, 70–71
in mental health settings, 75–77
models of care for, 76
Multidimensional Family Approach, 76–77
overrepresentation of, 68
peer group support for, 73
pleasure-oriented positive sexuality and, 78
positive outcomes for, 74
presumed cisgender children, 66
racism and, 68
resilience in, 72–78, 81
role-playing for, 81–82
school support systems for, 74–75
sex and gender for, 66
social climate for, 65
social context for, 67–68
social stigma for, 73
therapeutic process models for, 76, 80–84
transformative processes for, 74
Trans*Kids Project and, 71, 74
transparency in approaches to, 77
TransYouth Project and, 71
Watchful Waiting approach, 76
gender dysphoria
during adolescence, 95
for gender diverse children, 71, 75–76
gender identity and, 69
treatment strategies for, 51–52
gender environmentalist theories, 69–70
gender essentialism, 69
gender expansive individuals
in college and universities, 164–65
in justice system, 239–56
in juvenile justice system, 239–56
gender exploration, 72, 77–78
gender expression
at colleges and universities, 165
among gender diverse children, 67–68
in hospitals, 184
gender identity
during adolescence, 65
affirmation of, 12–13
broadscale longitudinal studies on, 86
concealment of, 12–15
conversion therapy and, 69
as developmental task, 65
development of, 68–70, 158–59
in *Diagnostic and Statistical Manual of Mental Disorders,* 69
Eurocentric influences on, 68
gender constructivist theories and, 70
for gender diverse children, 66–67
gender dysphoria and, 69
gender environmentalist theories, 69–70
gender essentialism and, 69
in hospitals, 184
legitimization of, 66
nonaffirmation of, 12
as proximal stressor, 14
sexual orientation and gender identity, 205–6
social influences on, 70
suicidality and, 15
gender inclusive, 75, 81, 162, 166, 192
gender incongruence, 71
gender literacy, 46–47
for gender diverse children, 78–79, 81, 86
gender-neutral, 191–92
language as, 192, 206
gender nonbinary individuals
health outcomes for, 16
homicides of, 13
minority stress processes for, 12–15
nonaffirmation for, 12
gender nonconformity
for gender diverse children, 71
transgender and gender-nonconforming youth, 262
genderqueer, 45, 138, 159
gender-related. *See specific topics*
Gender-Sexuality Alliances (GSAs), 276

gender diverse children and, 74
school-based mental health professionals
    and, 142
Gender Spectrum, 144, 147
Girl Sex 101 (Moon, A., and Diamond, K.
    D.), 53
GLSEN. *See* Gay, Lesbian and Straight
    Education Network
government policies, for LGBTQ+
    populations
    anti-LGBTQ policies, 31
    emerging adulthood and, 116
Grayson, Kellen, 203
group-level interventions, for resilience, 19
group therapy, for youth experiencing
    homelessness, 220–21
GSA. *See* Gay-Straight Alliance; Gender
    Sexuality Alliance
GSAs. *See* Gender-Sexuality Alliances
gynecology, 187–88

harm reduction strategies, for YEH, 230–31
healing-centered engagement, with YEH,
    214–15, 228–29
health care. *See* hospitals; medical care
    centers; *specific professionals*
healthcare. *See also specific topics*
    at colleges and universities, for LGBTQ+
        populations, 164–65, 175
    under Conventions on the Rights of
        Persons with Disabilities, 43
    during emerging adulthood, 115, 119
    gender affirmative, 42–44, 47
    Gender Affirmative Lifespan Approach,
        42, 45–47
    gender clinics, 43–44
    for gender diverse children, 75–77
    informed consent clinics, 43–44
    integrated, 41–43
    integrated-care health teams, 188
    interdisciplinary, 41–43
    under International Covenant on Civil
        and Political Rights, 43
    in international human rights law, 43–44
    LGBTQ+-competent providers, 187
    negative experiences in, 14
    for transgender individuals, approaches
        to, 42–44

    under Universal Declaration of Human
        Rights, 43
    WPATH Standards of Care, 48, 51–52
Healthcare Equality Index, 183
health disparities
    for gender nonbinary individuals, 16
    for LGBTQ+ populations, 2
    for transgender males, 16
Health Information Technology for
    Economic and Clinical Health Act
    (HITECH), U.S. (2020), 295
health insurance, 295–96
health insurance advocacy, 50–52
Health Insurance Portability Accountability
    Act (HIPAA), U.S. (1996), 295
health-promoting behaviors, 5, 16–17
Herman, Judith, 228
heterocisnormative structures
    emerging adulthood and, 114
    school-based curriculum based on, 241
heteronormative assumptions, about
    YEH, 226
heterosexism
    in child welfare settings, 206
    gender diverse children and, 68, 86
    in hospital settings, 184
    institutionalization of, 242
    intersectionality and, 32
heterosexual. *See* heterocisnormative;
    heteronormative
HIPAA. *See* Health Insurance Portability
    Accountability Act
HITECH Act. *See* Health Information
    Technology for Economic and
    Clinical Health Act
HIV incidence rates, 16
    emerging adulthood and, 119
    among transgender individuals, 119
    treatment strategies for youth
        experiencing homelessness,
        221–22, 224
Hoffman, I., 82
Hoffman, S., 82
holistic approach, 151. *See also* whole-person
    approaches
    interdisciplinary-holistic care, for
        YEH, 214
    to juvenile justice system, 250–52

homeless shelters. *See* non-LGBTQ+
  affirming homeless shelters
homophobia
  in foster care systems, 198–99
  internalized, 14
  in juvenile justice system, 246
  against youth experiencing
    homelessness, 213
hormone replacement therapy, 296
hormone therapy
  in Gender Affirmative Lifespan
    Approach, hormone providers as
    part of, 48
  gender-affirming, 185–86
Hospital NeckerEnfants Malades, 183
hospitals, LGBTQ+ populations and
  acceptability in, 189
  affirming policies, 188–89
  availability in, 189
  behavioral health services in, 186–88
  community engagement policies, 189
  equity in, 189
  family-focused therapy in, 186–87
  gender-affirming medical interventions,
    185–88
  gender expression in, 184
  gender identity in, 184
  gynecology, 187–88
  heterosexism and, 184
  integrated-care health teams, 188
  mental health services in, 186–88
  microaggressions in, 184
  obstetrics, 187–88
  personnel training in, 188–90
  women's health programs, 187
  youth-friendly services in, 189
House and Ball community
  foster care systems and, 198–99
  resilience in, 18, 18n1
human ecology theory, resilience and, 72
Human Rights Campaign, 144
hyperfocusing, on individual resilience, 18

identity. *See also* gender identity
  cross-cultural, 199
  during emerging adulthood, formation of,
    113–14
  marginalized, 160–61
  non-cisgender, 66, 138
  non-normative, 202
  transnormative, 68
ILI. *See* individual-level interventions
immigration status, at colleges and
  universities, 167–68
inclusive policies. *See also* gender inclusive;
  LGBTQ+ inclusive; noninclusive;
  transgender inclusive
  at college and universities, for LGBTQ+
    populations, 162, 174
  in medical care centers, 192–93
independent practice, for clinicians, for
  LGBTQ+ populations
  advocacy as part of, 293
  under Affordable Care Act, 286, 294
  American Psychological Association
    and, 286
  barriers to care, 288–91
  Centers for Medicare and Medicaid
    Services and, 295–96
  consultative roles in, 288
  COVID-19 pandemic and, impacts of,
    294–96
  cultural competence and, 291–93
  electronic health records and, 296
  future approaches to, 297–98
  group practices, 286
  healthcare disparities in, 289
  under Health Information Technology
    for Economic and Clinical Health
    Act, 295
  health insurance issues, 295–96
  under Health Insurance Portability
    Accountability Act, 295
  hormone replacement therapy and, 296
  integrated practices, 286, 293–97
  intersectional approach in, 292
  LGBTQ+-affirmative practices, 287–88
  marginalized identities and, centering
    of, 292
  multidisciplinary practices, 286
  nuances with, 287–88
  research gaps for, 297–98
  social determinants of care, 290
  sociopolitical factors for, 289–90
  solo practices, 285–86
  standards of care guidelines, 298
  telehealth services as part of, 296
  triad model of, 291–92

Indigenous youth, among YEH, 225
individual-level interventions (ILI)
  coming out growth, 20
  Dialectical Behavioral Therapy and, 20
  gender-affirming interventions, 20
  interdisciplinary approach to, 20–21
  mindfulness-based interventions and, 20
  stress-related growth, 20
  for transgender women, 20
  as trauma-informed, 19
individual resilience, 17–18, 122
  hyperfocusing on, 18
inequality. *See also* structural inequality
  during COVID-19 pandemic, 31
  in minority stress theory, as stressor, 11
  socioeconomic, for transgender individuals, 14, 21
informed consent, clinics, 43–44
institutional systems. *See also* oppressive institutional systems
  at college and universities, 173
  emerging adulthood and, challenges for, 114–16
  resilience influenced by, 72
  youth experiencing homelessness and, 224–28
integrated-care approaches, 305–6
  by health teams, 188
integrated healthcare
  functional elements of, 41–42
  macro level, 41
  meso level, 41
  micro level, 41
  for transgender individuals, 42–43
intelligence, resilience and, 17
interdisciplinary approaches, 5–6
  in Gender Affirmative Lifespan Approach, 45–47
  to gender diverse children, 77
  to individual-level interventions, 20–21
  by school-based mental health professionals, 144–45
  to youth experiencing homelessness, 218
interdisciplinary-holistic care, for YEH, 214
internalized homophobia. *See* homophobia
internalized transphobia, 12
international students, 168
International Transgender Day of Visibility, 146

Internet. *See also* online communities
  coming out and, 264
  cyberbullying on, 102
  geospatial networking applications, 98
  online support on, during adolescence, 102–3
interrelated approaches, to trauma, 199
intersectionality, 306
  ableism and, 32
  advocacy considerations with, 35–36
  calling-in, 35–36
  cisgenderism and, 32
  college and universities and, 159–61, 171–72, 174
  colonialism and, 32
  community building and, 34–35
  coping strategies and, 32
  Gender Affirmative Lifespan Approach and, 45–46
  for gender diverse children, 77, 85
  heterosexism and, 32
  independent practice and, 292
  institutional systems of oppression and, 32
  matrix perspective, 33
  with minority status, 4, 13
  minority stress theory and, 32
  poverty and, 32
  power and, 32–33
  racism and, 32–33
  radical healing and, 36
  in school systems, intersectional microaggressions during adolescence, 100
  sexism and, 32
  in solidarity framework, 35
  stigma-based bullying and, 1–2, 33
  structural inequality and, 31–33
  as transformative framework, 34
  trauma-informed approaches and, 34, 36
  among youth experiencing homelessness, 214
intersectionality theory
  culture and, 5
  diversity training and, 4
  life experiences and, 5
  minority identities in, 4
  sociodemographic factors in, 5
intersectional minority stress frameworks, 32

intimate partner violence (IPV), LGBTQ+ youth and, 267–69
iTEAM service. *See* My Treatment Empowerment for Adolescents on the Move service

Jacob's New Dress (Hoffman, S., and Hoffman, I.), 82
juvenile justice system, LGBTQ+ youth in, 306–7. *See also* restorative justice
   aggressive behaviors, 247–49
   attachment-related issues, 246–49
   for Black LGBTQ+ individuals, 244
   callousness and, development of, 249
   child welfare systems and, 239, 242
   Cognitive Behavioral Therapy in, 251
   constitutional rights for, 252–53
   as crossover system, with child welfare system, 242
   Dialectical Behavioral Therapy in, 251
   disproportionate representation of, 242–43
   emotional numbing and, 248
   gender differences for, 243–44
   gender expansive individuals and, 239–56
   heterocisnormative school-based curriculum and, 241
   holistic approaches to, 250–52
   homophobia in, 246
   incidence rates for, 239
   Kent v. United States, 253–54
   for Latinx LGBTQ+ individuals, 244
   mediating factors within, 245
   mental health behaviors in, 245–49
   microaggressions within, 244–45
   minority youth in, 240–41
   National Council of Juvenile and Family Court Judges guidelines for, 254
   non-suicidal self-injury and, 247
   "No Promo Homo" laws, 241
   policy recommendations for, 254–56
   post-traumatic stress disorder and, 246
   prevalence rates for, 239
   Prisoner Health and Human Rights and, 255
   racism in, 244
   Rational Emotive Behavioral Therapy in, 251
   risk factors for, 239–40

   safe spaces in, 252
   safety reforms for, 249–54
   school-to-prison pipeline and, 240–41
   segregation mechanisms in, 239, 242
   self-harming behaviors for, 246–47
   suicide rates and, 246–47
   transphobia in, 246
   trauma-informed approaches in, 245
   unequal treatment of, 243
   in United Kingdom, 247

K-12 settings. *See* school systems
Kent v. United States, 253–54

language use
   in colleges and universities, for LGBTQ+ populations, 171
   gender-neutral, 192, 206
   in medical care centers, 192–93
   non-pathologizing, 206
Latinx LGBTQ+ populations. *See also* House and Ball community; minority stress model; minority stress processes; minority stress theory
   emerging adulthood in, 127
   in House and Ball community, 18, 18n1
   in juvenile justice system, 244
   sexually diverse populations among, 32
Learning for Justice, 147
lesbians, psychopathology in, 44
LGBTQ+ affirmative systems
   during emerging adulthood, religious institutions and, 115, 118, 123
   independent practices as, 287–88
   religious institutions as, 115, 118, 123
LGBTQ+-affirming environments. *See also* non-LGBTQ+-affirming
   schools as, 34
LGBTQ+-competent providers, 187
LGBTQ+ inclusive policies
   in college and universities, 162
   for transgender students, 162
LGBTQ+-niche, 289, 294, 298
LGBTQ+ populations. *See also* lesbians; transgender males; transgender women; *specific topics*
   affirmative care framework, 3–4
   conceptual frameworks for, 3–6
   depathologization of, 116

elderly, 2
  healthcare for, 2, 151
  health disparities for, 2
  holistic health needs for, 151
  methodological approaches to, 2–4, 6–7
  negative health outcomes for, 145
  training for, increased demands for, 3
LGBTQ+-rights, anti-LGBTQ policies and, 31
LGBTQ+-supportive political climates, 102
LGBTQ+ youth. *See also* adolescence; child welfare settings; emerging adulthood; foster care systems; juvenile justice system; school systems; youth experiencing homelessness; *specific topics*
  auxiliary services for, 276–77
  career development for, 269
  coming out for, 264–66
  community building for, 266–67
  connectedness for, 266–67
  decision making for, 270
  educational assistance for, 276
  employment discrimination against, 269–70
  food insecurity for, 276
  healthcare challenges for, 263–64
  housing stability for, 275
  interpersonal challenges for, 264–69
  intimate partner violence and, 267–69
  mental health challenges for, 263–64
  mental health services for, 274
  methodologic approaches to, 270–73
  physical health services for, 273–74
  positive youth development and, 96–97, 230
  poverty and, 200
  queer youth and emerging adults of color, 262
  romantic relationships for, challenges with, 267–68
  sexual health challenges, 264
  transitional-age youth, 203–4
  vocational assistance for, 276
  vocational challenges for, 269–70
  workplace identity management, 270
life experiences, intersectionality theory and, 5
lifespan. *See also* Gender Affirmative Lifespan Approach

developmental differences across, in GALA, 45–46
  for gender diverse children, 77
life-threatening experiences, as distal stressor, 13
Live in Your Own Skin approach, 76
Livingston, Jennie, 198–99
Local School Climate Survey, 146

marginalized identities
  at colleges and universities, 160–61
  independent practices and, centering of, 292
marriage. *See also* same-sex marriage
  emerging adulthood and, 116–17
Masten, Ann, 72
master's degrees, for school counseling services, 139
MDFA. *See* Multidimensional Family Approach
medical affirmation, of gender identity, 13
medical care centers, 306
  children's hospitals, 183
  communication strategies in, 192–93
  community partnerships with, 190–91
  documentation processes for, 192
  for emerging adults, 184–90
  environment setting, 191–93
  Hospital NeckerEnfants Malades, 183
  hospitals, 184–90
  inclusive language use in, 192–93
  personnel training in, 189–90
  physical environments for, 191
  registration processes for, 192
  resources for, 190–91
  in United States, 183
mental health. *See also specific topics*
  at college and universities, disparities in, 157–58
  during emerging adulthood, 120–21
  in gender diverse children, 70–71
  in youth experiencing homelessness, interventions for, 215–22
mental health services. *See* independent practice; *specific services; specific topics*
Meyer, Han H., 11
microaggressions
  in colleges and universities, 160
  in hospital settings, 184

intersectional, 100
    within juvenile justice system, 244–45
    under-examination of, 244–45
microaggressive messaging, 193
mindfulness-based interventions, 20
minority, as obsolete term, 32
minority coping skills, 18
minority identities, in intersectionality
    theory, 4, 13
minority status. *See also* Black LGBTQ+
        populations; Latinx LGBTQ+
        populations; Native American
        LGTBQ+
    polyvictimization and, 199–200
minority strengths model, adolescence
    and, 97
Minority Stress and Lesbian Women
    (Brooks), 11
minority stress model
    empirical support for, 21
    future research on, 21
    psychopathogenic effects of social
        environments in, 44
minority stress processes
    during adolescence, 95, 98
    cognitive appraisal in, 12
    as continuum, 12
    distal stressors, 12–14
    for gender nonbinary individuals, 12–15
    intersectional, 32
    negative social attitudes, 12
    objective events, 12
    proximal stressors, 12, 14–15
    resilience pathways and, 45
    socialization and, 12
    for transgender individuals, 12–15, 44–45
minority stress theory, 305
    college and universities and, 157
    dominant culture and, role in, 11
    inequality as stressor, 11
    intersectionality and, 32
    intrapersonal dynamics in clinical
        assessment, 4
    mental health and, 15
    multiple levels in, 7
    physical health and, 16–17
    post-traumatic stress disorder and, 15
    prejudice as stressor, 11
    resilience in, 17–21

minority youths. *See also* Black LGBTQ+
        populations; Latinx LGBTQ+
        populations; Native American
        LGTBQ+
    in juvenile justice system, 240–41
misgendering, at college and universities, 166
misogynoir. *See* transmisogynoir
models of care, for gender diverse children, 76
mood disorders, 15
Moon, A., 53
Motivational Enhancement Therapy, 218
motivation to succeed, resilience and, 17
Movement Advancement Project, 138
MTSS framework. *See* multi-tiered system of
        support framework
Multidimensional Family Approach
    (MDFA), 76–77
multiple systems of care, 1
multi-tiered system of support (MTSS)
        framework, 145–51
    intensified support in, 149–50
    school counselors in, 146
    supplemental support in, 148–49
    universal support in, 146–48
music-based group therapy, 221
myocardial infarction, incidence rates for, 16
My Treatment Empowerment for
    Adolescents on the Move (iTEAM)
    service, 218, 222

NASP. *See* National Association of School
    Psychologists
NASW. *See* National Association of Social
    Workers
National Association of School Psychologists
    (NASP), 140, 142, 143–44
National Association of Social Workers
    (NASW), 141
National Center for Biotechnology
    Information, 250
National Coming Out Day, 146
National Council of Juvenile and Family
    Court Judges, 254
National School Climate Survey, 138,
    147–48
Native American LGTBQ+, 33. *See also*
    minority identities; minority stress
    model; minority stress theory; two-
    spirit youth

negative social attitudes, 12
neurodiverse individuals, 54, 68
"No Homo Promo" laws, 241
non-affirmation
    for gender nonbinary individuals, 12
    for transgender individuals, 12
No-Name Calling Week, 146
non-assuming questions, 294
nonbinary individuals
    definition of, 1
    qualitative research on, 68
    romantic and sexual relationships for, 116
non-cisgender identity, 66, 138
nonclinical staff, 217
nonconforming. See transgender and gender-nonconforming youth
nondiscrimination policies, at college and universities, 163
non-dominant narratives, 137
nonheterosexual. See LGBTQ+ populations
non-incarcerated population, 247
noninclusive
    classrooms, 162
    representations, 169
nonintercourse sexual contact, 265
non-LGBTQ+ affirming homeless shelters, 212–13
non-normative identities, 202
non-pathologizing language, 206
nonprofit organizations, 51, 205
non-queer, 198
non-stigmatizing referral mechanisms, 151
non-suicidal self-injury (NSSI), 1, 247
nonsupportive family members, 74, 125
nontherapeutic contexts, 218
"No Promo Homo" laws, 241
NSSI. See non-suicidal self injury

obstetrics, 187–88
online communities
    during adolescence, participation in, 98, 102–3
    during COVID-19 pandemic, 31
    geospatial networking applications, 98
    web-based mental health services, 31
oppression-related research, 31–32
oppressive institutional systems. See also structural inequality
    intersectionality and, 32

overrepresentation, of LGBTQ+ populations
    of binary identities, 68
    in child welfare settings, 197, 201–6
    of gender diverse children, 68

Pacific Islanders
    mental health services for, 274
    sexual assault and, 161
parental consent, for transitioning medical services, 115
parental relationships. See also family support
    during adolescence, 99
Parents, Families, and Friends of Lesbians and Gays (PFLAG), 99
Paris is Burning, 198–99
pediatric endocrinologists, 185–86
pediatricians, gender-competent, 47
peer groups, as support. See also friendships
    at colleges and universities, 163–64
    during emerging adulthood, 117
    for gender diverse children, 73
personal agency, resilience and, 17
PFLAG. See Parents, Families, and Friends of Lesbians and Gays
physical health
    allostatic load framework and, 16
    minority stress as influence on, 16–17
    for transgender males, 16
planfulness, resilience and, 17
Planned Parenthood, 279
pleasure-oriented positive sexuality, 46–47
    gender diverse children and, 78
polyvictimization
    adverse childhood events and, 199–200
    of Black children, 199–200
    in child welfare settings, 197
    in foster care systems, 199–200
    minority status as factor for, 199–200
POSE, 199
positive psychology, 5
positive self-talk, 5
positive youth development (PYD)
    radical healing and, 96–97
    for youth experiencing homelessness, 230
post-graduate training, 3
post-traumatic stress disorder (PTSD), 15
    juvenile justice system and, 246
poverty
    child welfare influenced by, 197

intersectionality and, 32
LGBTQ+ youth and, vulnerability to, 200
power, intersectionality and, 32–33
prejudice, as stressor, 11
prepubertal social transition, 75, 85
presumed cisgender, among children, 66
primary care providers, 184–85
Prisoner Health and Human Rights, 255
problem-solving skills, resilience and, 17
proximal stressors, in minority stress processes, 12
  distal stressors mediated by, 15
  gender identity concealment, 14
  internalized homophobia, 14
  internalized transphobia and, 15
  suicidal ideation and, 15
  for transgender individuals, 15, 45
psychoeducation, 20, 170, 219, 298
psychologists. *See* school psychologists
psychosocial needs, 47, 71, 189, 228. *See also* biopsychosocial
psychotherapeutic processes, 48, 292
psychotherapists, as gatekeepers, in Gender Affirmative Lifespan Approach, 47–48
PTSD. *See* post-traumatic stress disorder
puberty. *See also* prepubertal social transition
  differences of sexual development and, 66
  gender affirmation during, 185
  gender identity and, 65
puberty suppression
  American Academy of Child and Adolescent Psychiatry and, 185
  gender affirmation during, 185
  medications for, 44, 51, 185–86
  pediatric endocrinologists and, 185–86
  World Professional Association for Transgender Health and, 185
Pulse Nightclub massacre, 289
pushout, from school, 100–101
PYD. *See* positive youth development

QAYOC. *See* queer youth and emerging adults of color
QTPOC. *See* queer and trans people of color
queer. *See* lesbians; LGBTQ+ populations; transgender individuals; *specific topics*
queer and trans people of color (QTPOC), 270

queer youth and emerging adults of color (QAYOC), 262
  services for, 274

racism
  gender diverse children and, 68
  intersectionality and, 32–33
  in juvenile justice system, 244
  in school systems, against LGBTQ+ populations, 138
  systemic, 13
radical healing, 306
  during adolescence, 95–97
  adolescence and, 95–97
  authenticity as component of, 97
  critical consciousness and, 96–97, 102–3
  definition of, 95
  intersectionality and, 36
  positive youth development and, 96–97
  in United States, 96–97
Rational Emotive Behavioral Therapy (REBT), 251
Religious Freedom Restoration Act, U.S. (1993), 205
religious organizations and systems, emerging adulthood LGBTQ+ populations and, 115, 117–18
reproductive issues, during emerging adulthood, 114
research approaches
  for college and universities, gaps in, 165–68
  to emerging adulthood, 124–25
  funding for, 307
  for independent practices, 297–98
  for mental health training, 307–8
  to minority stress model, 21
  to nonbinary individuals, qualitative research on, 68
  oppression-related, 31–32
  systems-based approach refinements, 308
  underfunding of, 49, 307
  to youth experiencing homelessness, gaps in, 211–15
resilience, 5
  characteristics of, 17
  at college and universities, 160, 169
  community, 18, 18n1
  community-level interventions, 19

cultural influences on, 72
definition of, 17, 72, 121–22
development of, strategies for, 21
emerging adulthood and, 121–22, 124
emotion regulation and, 17
family, 73–74
in Gender Affirmative Lifespan Approach, 46–47
in gender diverse children, 72–78, 81
governmental systems as influence on, 72
group-level interventions, 19
human ecology theory and, 72
individual, 17–18, 122
individual-level interventions, 19–21
intelligence and, 17
mental health outcomes and, 33
minority coping and, 18
minority stress processes and, 45
motivation to succeed and, 17
personal agency and, 17
planfulness and, 17
problem-solving skills and, 17
progressive development of, 17
self-control and, 17
self-efficacy and, 17
societal-level interventions, 19
systems theory and, 72
restorative justice, 229–30
restrooms, 84, 206
re-traumatization, 227, 229
rights. *See also* LGBTQ+-rights
Prisoner Health and Human Rights, 255
risk-taking
during adolescence, 95–97
during emerging adulthood, 118
Robinson, Brandon, 200
role-playing, for gender diverse children, 81–82
role-plays, 82
romantic and sexual relationships
during adolescence, 98
during emerging adulthood, 116, 267–68

safe spaces, in juvenile justice system, 252
same-sex marriage
anti-gay legislation against, 117
legalization of, 116
school-based mental health professionals (SBMHPs), 138–52

Affirmative Support Safe and Empowering Talk model, 149
ASCA National Model, 140, 143–44, 147
collaborations among, 142–43
in community-based organizations, 150
community engagement and, 150–51
decision-making tools for, 139
Ecological Model of Human Development and, 144–45
effectiveness of, 139
family engagement and, 150–51
future directions for, 151–52
Gender-Sexuality Alliance and, 142
Gender Spectrum and, 144, 147
Human Rights Campaign and, 144
implications for, 151–52
interdisciplinary teams for, 144–45
Learning for Justice and, 147
Local School Climate Survey, 146
in multi-tiered system of support framework, 145–51
National Association of School Psychologists, 140, 142
professional values of, 151
recommendations for, 143–45
school counselors, 139–41, 146, 150
school-level advocacy by, 152
school psychologists, 139–40, 142, 150
school social workers, 139–42, 150–51
School Social Work Practice Model, 140
state-level legislative advocacy by, 152
strength-based approach by, 152
student access to, 139
Welcoming Schools and, 144, 147
Youth Risk Behavior Study, 150
school counselors, 139–41, 146, 150
school psychologists, 139–40, 142, 150
school social workers, 139–42, 150–51
School Social Work Practice Model, 140
school systems, LGBTQ+ populations in, 306
during adolescence, 100–101
bullying in, 100, 137
Day of Silence in, 146
dropouts, 99, 101
Gay, Lesbian and Straight Education Network and, 137–38, 142–44, 147, 151

Gay-Straight Alliance in, 101
for gender diverse children, 74–75
gender diverse youth in, 138
International Transgender Day of
   Visibility, 146
intersectional microaggressions in, during
   adolescence, 100
intervention strategies in, 137–38
Movement Advancement Project, 138
National Coming Out Day in, 146
National School Climate Survey, 138,
   147–48
No-Name Calling Week in, 146
noninclusive classrooms, 162
psychoeducation in, 20, 170, 219, 298
pushout from, 100–101
racism in, 138
school-based mental health professionals
   in, 138–52
socioeconomic status and, 141
transgender youth in, 138
school-to-prison pipeline, 240–41
school-wide practices, 140, 145–47
science, technology, engineering, and
   mathematics (STEM) fields, 167
Seeking Safety psychotherapy, 220
self-control, resilience and, 17
self-efficacy, resilience and, 17
self-esteem, during emerging adulthood,
   122–23
self-harming behaviors, juvenile justice
   system and, 246–47
self-injurious behaviors. See non-suicidal self-
   injury
semi-structured interviews, 49, 79
sex assigned at birth in, 184
sex education, in Gender Affirmative
   Lifespan Approach, 48–50, 53–54
sexism. See also cissexism
   in child welfare settings, 206
   in foster care systems, 206
   intersectionality and, 32
sexual abuse, in foster care systems, 198–99
sexual assault
   at colleges and universities, 161
   Pacific Islanders and, 161
sexual diversive populations, among Latinx
   populations, 32
sexually-expansive individuals, 242–44

sexually-transmitted infections (STIs), during
   emerging adulthood, 119
sexual orientation and gender identity
   (SOGI), 205–6
sexual relationships. See romantic and sexual
   relationships
sex work, among youth experiencing
   homelessness, 212
shaming. See calling-out
skill sets. See also resilience
   coping, 32
social affirmation, of gender identity, 13
social attitudes, negative, 12
social-cultural approaches, 76, 230
social determinants of health, 17
   independent practice and, 290
   for youth experiencing homelessness, 214
social ecological model, for youth
   experiencing homelessness, 214
socialization, minority stress processes
   and, 12
social media
   adolescent use of, 34
   coming out and, 264
social stigma
   as distal stressor, 13
   for gender diverse children, 73
social support
   at colleges and universities, 163
   during emerging adulthood, 122–23
   lack of, 1
   for transgender and gender-
      nonconforming youth, 275
   within-group, 163
social workers. See school social workers
societal-level interventions, for resilience, 19
sociocultural factors, 4, 13, 18–19, 76,
   119, 201
sociodemographics, intersectionality theory
   and, 5
socioecological contexts, during
   adolescence, 97
socioeconomic status
   in school systems, 141
   for transgender individuals, 14, 21
socio-emotional domains, 5
sociopolitical factors/issues, 34, 121, 159,
   168, 173, 214
   in independent practice, 289–90

Index 395

socio-structural factors, 33, 36
SOGI. *See* sexual orientation and gender identity
Solidarity Week, 151
SPARCS. *See* Structured Psychotherapy for Adolescents Responding to Chronic Stress
Standards and Indicators for Cultural Competence in Social Work Practice (National Association of Social Workers), 141
STEM fields. *See* science, technology, engineering, and mathematics fields
stigma. *See* social stigma; structural stigma
stigma-based bullying, 1–2
    intersectionality and, 33
STIs. *See* sexually-transmitted infections
Street Smarts Intervention, for YEH, 222
strength-focused approaches, 5
    at colleges and universities, 169
    by school-based mental health professionals, 152
    in trauma-informed care, 216–17
stress-related growth, 20
structural competence lens, for YEH, 214–15, 222–24
structural inequality
    distal stressors and, in minority stress processes, lack of institutional acknowledgment as, 13
    intersectionality and, 31
structural stigma, emerging adulthood and, 116
structural violence lens, for YEH, 214–15, 228–31
structural vulnerability lens, for YEH, 214–15
Structured Psychotherapy for Adolescents Responding to Chronic Stress (SPARCS), 220
student support services, 161–62
subdisciplines, 42
subgroups, 119. *See also specific groups*
substance abuse, 15
    during emerging adulthood, 119–20
    treatment interventions for, among youth experiencing homelessness, 215–22
    among youth experiencing homelessness, 212

suicidal ideation and behaviors. *See also* non-suicidal self-injury
    during adolescence, 95
    at colleges and universities, 158
    from concealment of gender identity, 15
    during emerging adulthood, 116, 120–21
    juvenile justice system and, 246–47
    proximal stressors and, 15
syndemic, between groups, 119
systemic racism, as distal stressor, 13
systems theory, resilience and, 72

TA-CBT. *See* Trans-Affirmative CBT
Talkspace, 296
TA-NET. *See* Trans-Affirming Narrative Exposure Therapy
TAY. *See* transitional-age youth
telehealth services, 296
teletherapy, during COVID-19 pandemic, 31
TGNC youth. *See* transgender and gender-nonconforming youth
Title IX guidelines, at colleges and universities, 166
TNBGE students. *See* nonbinary individuals; transgender, nonbinary, and gender expansive students; transgender individuals
Tobar, Kee, 200
transaffirmative care
    in Gender Affirmative Lifespan Approach, 45–46
    Trans-Affirming Narrative Exposure Therapy, 219
Trans-Affirmative CBT, 219
Trans-Affirming Narrative Exposure Therapy (TA-NET), 219
transdisciplinarity, in Gender Affirmative Lifespan Approach, 56
transgender, nonbinary, and gender expansive (TNBGE) students, 164–67
transgender and gender-nonconforming (TGNC) youth, 262
    emotional support for, 275
    services for, 275
    social support for, 275
transgender healthcare, 42–44
    HIV infection rates, 119
    puberty-suppressing medications, 44, 51
transgender inclusive, nonaffirmation for, 12

transgender individuals. *See also* adolescence;
    emerging adulthood; gender
    affirmation; transgender males;
    transgender women; trans youth
  during adolescence, 104
  cissexism and, 116
  at college and universities, 157–58
  coming out for, 266
  distal stressors for, 44–45
  emerging adulthood for, 115
  employment discrimination against,
    269–70
  Gender Affirmative Lifespan Approach,
    42, 45–47
  healthcare approaches to, 42–43
  HIV infection rates, 119
  internalized transphobia and, 12, 15
  minority stress processes for, 12–15,
    44–45
  pediatric endocrinologists and, 185–86
  poverty and, 200
  proximal stressors for, in minority stress
    processes, 15, 45
  queer and trans people of color, 270
  romantic and sexual relationships for,
    challenges for, 116
  in school systems, 138
  socioeconomic outcomes for, inequality
    in, 14, 21
  transgender and gender-nonconforming
    youth, 262
  World Professional Association for
    Transgender Health, 185
  among youth experiencing
    homelessness, 212
transgender males. *See also specific topics*
  health outcomes for, 16
transgender women. *See also specific topics*
  individual-level interventions for, 20
transitional-age youth (TAY), 203–4
  aftercare for, 204
Trans*Kids Project, gender diverse children
  and, 71, 74
transmisogynoir, 105
transnormative identity, 68
transparency
  in Gender Affirmative Lifespan Approach,
    46, 54
  with gender diverse children, 77

transphobia
  internalized, 12
  in juvenile justice system, 246
  as proximal stressor, in minority stress
    processes, 15
  against youth experiencing
    homelessness, 213
transracial adoptions, 83
trans youth. *See also* transgender individuals
  sexual health outcomes with, 49
TransYouth Project, 71
trauma-informed approaches
  to adolescent interventions, 34
  in individual-level interventions, 19
  intersectionality and, 34, 36
  in juvenile justice system, 245
trauma-informed care, for YEH, 216–18
  Attachment, Self-Regulation, and
    Competency Framework, 217
  Facility Assessment in, 217
  principles of, 216–17
  strength-based approach to, 216–17
triad model, in independent practice,
    291–92
two-spirit youth, 33

under-examination, of microaggressions,
    244–45
underfunded research, 49, 307
Unicorn Youth Project, 49
United Kingdom, juvenile justice system in,
    247
United States (U.S.)
  Affordable Care Act, 286, 294
  Every Student Succeeds Act, 204
  Family First Prevention Services Act, 204
  Fourteenth Amendment, US
    Constitution, 252–53
  Health Information Technology for
    Economic and Clinical Health
    Act, 295
  Health Insurance Portability
    Accountability Act, 295
  medical care centers in, 183
  "No Homo Promo" laws in, 241
  radical healing in, 96–97
  Religious Freedom Restoration Act, 205

violence and harassment, as distal stressor, 13

Watchful Waiting approach, 76
Welcoming Schools, 144, 147
welfare systems. *See* child welfare settings
wellbeing, 141
white privilege, 13
white supremacy, 13, 18n1
whole-person approaches, 5–6
　case conceptualization perspective with, 5
within-group differences, 138
within-group social support, 163
women's health programs, 187
word of mouth, 299
workplace identity management, 270
World Professional Association for Transgender Health (WPATH), 185, 298
worldviews, 113, 159, 168, 170, 172
WPATH. *See* World Professional Association for Transgender Health
WPATH Standards of Care, 48, 51–52

YEH. *See* youth experiencing homelessness
youth activism movement, 50
youth experiencing homelessness (YEH), among LGBTQ+ populations
　alternative programming for, 221
　anti-homeless sentiments and, 227
　art therapy for, 221
　autonomy of, respect for, 231
　for Black youth, 225–27
　cisnormative assumptions about, 226
　clinical considerations for, 215–22
　clinical encounters with, 225–26
　Cognitive Behavioral Therapy for, 218–19
　demographics for, 211–12
　drama therapy for, 221
　evidence-based LGBTQ+-affirming services for, 219–20
　future approaches to, 231–32
　gaps in research on, 211–15
　Gender Affirmative Lifespan Approach for, 54–56
　group therapy approaches to, 220–21
　harm reduction strategies for, 230–31
　healing-centered engagement with, 214–15, 228–29
　heteronormative assumptions about, 226
　HIV treatment for, 221–22, 224
　holistic approaches to, 213–14
　homophobia against, 213
　for Indigenous youth, 225
　institutional structures and, impact of, 224–28
　integrated approaches to, 213–14
　interdisciplinary-holistic care for, 214
　interdisciplinary programs for, 218
　intersectionality among, 214
　medical hierarchies for, 228
　medical interventions for, 221–22
　mental health interventions for, 215–22
　Motivational Enhancement Therapy for, 218
　motivational interviewing techniques for, 220–21
　music-based group therapy for, 221
　My Treatment Empowerment for Adolescents on the Move service, 218, 222
　in non-LGBTQ+ affirming homeless shelters, 212–13
　policy recommendations for, 228
　positive youth development and, 230
　restorative justice mechanisms, 229–30
　risk factors for, 212, *213*
　Seeking Safety psychotherapy, 220
　service systems for, 222–24
　sex work and, 212
　social determinants of health and, 214
　social ecological model for, 214
　Street Smarts Intervention for, 222
　structural competence lens for, 214–15, 222–24
　structural violence lens for, 214–15, 228–31
　structural vulnerability lens for, 214–15
　Structured Psychotherapy for Adolescents Responding to Chronic Stress, 220
　substance abuse among, 212
　substance abuse treatment interventions for, 215–22
　among transgender youth, 212
　transphobia against, 213
　trauma-informed care for, 216–18
　trauma risks for, 212
youth-friendly services, in hospitals, 189
Youth Risk Behavior Study, 150

About the Authors

Roberto L. Abreu, PhD (he/him/él) is assistant professor of counseling psychology and the director of the Collective Healing and Empowering VoicEs through Research and Engagement (¡Chévere!) in the Department of Psychology at the University of Florida (UF). Dr. Abreu's research seeks to explore how systemic oppression (e.g., restrictions to resources, sociopolitical events, laws, and policies) impacts the well-being of marginalized communities; how Latinx communities use cultural values and beliefs to accept, affirm, and celebrate their LGBTQ people; and how culturally affirming interventions promote collective well-being among Latinx and LGBTQ people and communities. Dr. Abreu's work is guided by decolonial principles, social justice values, person–environment interactions, growth, resilience, and resistance.

Eunice V. Avilés Faría, PsyD, LMHC, LPC is a trans and human rights advocate, educator, and policy influencer informed by 15+ years of clinical practice with a wide variety of trans, gender diverse, and queer individuals across the life span. She is the founder of Transcending Identities, an organization committed to improving the quality of life for transgender and gender nonbinary individuals through research, human rights advocacy, professional training, and consulting in the United States, in her natal Puerto Rico, and abroad. She continues to work toward her life's goal of ensuring that these individuals are treated with dignity and respect.

Matthew J. Beck, PhD, LCPC, NCC, ACS is a counselor educator and the school counseling clinical coordinator at Western Illinois University-Quad Cities. Prior to his position as associate professor, he worked in public education for 12 years as a teacher and professional school counselor at the elementary, middle, and high school settings in Illinois. He is a licensed clinical professional counselor (LCPC) in the state of Illinois, an approved clinical supervisor (ACS), and a national certified counselor (NCC), and he holds licensure as a professional school counselor in Illinois. Matthew's research interests include school counselor advocacy, professional identity development for school counselors, and the needs of LGBTQ+ students in K–12 settings.

Rachel Becker-Warner, PsyD, LP (she/they) is a former assistant professor at the Institute for Sexual and Gender Health (ISGH) at the University of Minnesota Medical School and currently a sexual and gender health specialist at Health Partners of Minnesota. Dr. Becker-Warner specializes in sexual health and gender care focused on helping individuals across the age span establish and renew their sexual, emotional, and gender health and relational well-being. Her research and practice interests include the intersection of neuro and gender diversity, the neurobiological impact of trauma, and the development of gender identity for gender diverse people.

Dianne Berg, PhD, LP is associate professor and licensed psychologist at the Institute for Sexual and Gender Health (ISGH) at the University of Minnesota Medical School. She has been working clinically with gender diverse children and transgender adolescents for more than 20 years and is the founder and coordinator of Child and Adolescent Gender Services at the Sexual and Gender Health Clinic affiliated with ISGH. Dr. Berg is a member of the WPATH Standards of Care Version 8 Child Chapter Workgroup as well as co-founder and staff member of the National Center for Gender Spectrum Health (NCGSH), a philanthropic initiative of the ISGH. The mission of the NCGSH is to 1) promote scholarship by those who are trans-identified; 2) forward empiricism that is based on the real lived experience of trans and gender diverse people across the life span; 3) challenge cisnormativity in healthcare; and 4) promote pleasure and positive sexuality for all bodies. Dr. Berg is co-author of the Gender Affirmative Lifespan Approach (GALA), the theoretical framework guiding the clinical-research program of the NCGSH.

Nova J. Bradford, MSW is a psychotherapist, a PhD student in Health Policy at Stanford University, and a Knight-Hennessy Scholars fellow. Nova's research aims to reduce health disparities and improve access to healthcare for marginalized communities. Nova has earned master's of social work and bachelor of arts in psychology degrees from the University of Minnesota. She previously worked as a researcher for the University of Minnesota Medical School, where she studied the health outcomes of sexual and gender minority populations.

Leonardo Candelario-Pérez, PhD, LP is a licensed psychologist and sexual health consultant in the urology department, a therapist in Gender Services, and a co-chair for Adolescent Care at Health Partners Minnesota. Additionally, they are co-educational consultant at the National Center for Gender Spectrum Health. Their clinical, administrative, and research interests include sexual and gender health and wellness, mental health as it relates to issues of sexuality and gender identity, language and LGBTQI identity formation, and the intersections of race/ethnicity, gender, and sexual orientation.

Zari K. Carpenter, MA is a doctoral student in counseling psychology at Western Michigan University. Her research interests center on race, LGBTQ+, and understanding power and oppression. Zari's dissertation research examines how white counseling psychology trainees communicate about whiteness with white clients. She aims for a career deconstructing the relationship between identity and power in clinical, educational, and community settings.

Kevin Carrión, PsyD is a clinical psychologist currently working at Behavioral Health Services, Advocate Illinois Masonic Medical Center, located in Chicago, Illinois. Dr. Carrión received his PsyD degree from Carlos Albizu University, San Juan, Puerto Rico. He completed his internship at the Institute of Child and Family Health and completed a child-focused fellowship at Under the Rainbow, Mount Sinai Hospital, in Chicago. Dr. Carrión has always been passionate about working with LGBTQ+ populations as well as expanding knowledge around LGBTQ+ realities. Some professional highlights include: leading a gender and sexual orientation group focused on providing seminars and trainings to graduate students; dissertation project focusing on creating a short story–based protocol for school-age children regarding gender identity; membership of the committee of LGBT affairs of the Puerto Rico Psychological Association; and chapter contribution toward *LGBT 101: An Introductory View to the Collective* (Vázquez-Rivera et al., 2016). He continues to be involved in training of future mental health professionals, offering didactics to practicum students around LGBTQ+ clinical concerns.

Taymy J. Caso, PhD (they/them) is assistant professor in educational psychology at the University of Alberta and a lecturer at New York University and the University of Minnesota Medical School. Dr. Caso completed a postdoctoral fellowship in transgender health in the Institute for Sexual and Gender Health and maintains a research affiliation at the National Center for Gender Spectrum Health. They hold degrees in counseling and clinical psychology from New York University and Columbia University, Teachers College. Their research focuses on minority health disparities, intersectionality, identity-based marginalization within LGBTQ+ BIPOC communities, gender and sexual fluidity, and social determinants of health. Their advocacy work utilizes decolonizing pedagogy to deconstruct institutional and systemic barriers to equity and develop community-based interventions for underserved communities. They have been the recipient of several grants and awards that recognize scholarship, service, advocacy, and activism supporting and empowering marginalized and underrepresented communities.

Jennifer J. Connor, PhD, LMFT is associate professor and licensed marriage and family therapist at the Institute for Sexual and Gender Health (ISGH) at the University of Minnesota Medical School. She is also the director of clinical services at ISGH. She provides therapeutic services for gender diverse individuals across the life span, with a particular interest in providing care to younger children and their support systems using the Gender Affirmative Lifespan Approach.

Luis Díaz-Medero, MS is currently a PhD candidate in clinical psychology at Ponce Health Sciences University in Puerto Rico. He has contributed to the development of other book chapters, such as: "LGBTAIQ+ research in Puerto Rico: What has been documented" and "Affirmative integration of religious and spiritual identities with sexual and gender identities." He was also a member on the Sex, Gender and Sexual Orientation Diversity Committee of Puerto Rico's Psychological Association and has co-authored research articles under the guidance of Dr. Caleb Esteban.

Marla E. Eisenberg, ScD, MPH is professor in pediatrics in the Division of General Pediatrics and Adolescent Health at the University of Minnesota. Her research focuses on multilevel social influences on health, behavior, and well-being among adolescents and young adults, with an emphasis on LGBTQ+ young people.

Caleb Esteban, PhD is assistant professor in the School of Behavioral and Brain Sciences at the Ponce Health Sciences University. He was an independent postdoctoral researcher in a research faculty development program focused on human intersexuality at the University of Puerto Rico, Medical Sciences Campus. He completed three postdoctoral certifications in distance education facilitator, LGBT-affirmative psychotherapy, and sexual therapy. Dr. Esteban's research focuses on biopsychosocial health, health disparities, and health barriers among Hispanic LGBTAQI+ adults. Dr. Esteban interests also include the construction, translation, adaptation, and validation of psychology instruments measuring LGBTAQI+ issues.

Jan E. Estrellado, PhD (responds to all pronouns, do not default to she/her) is associate professor in the PsyD program at the California School of Professional Psychology, Alliant International University, San Diego campus. Dr. Estrellado's research areas examine race, ethnicity, sexual orientation, and gender identity in trauma therapy. Dr. Estrellado's scholarly interests connect multicultural psychology and trauma psychology, with the goal of providing quantitative and qualitative evidence for effective, culturally informed supervision and training of graduate students. Dr. Estrellado was a leadership fellow with the Asian American Psychological Association and an alum of the Minority Fellowship Program with the American Psychological Association. Dr. Estrellado runs a private practice dedicated to trauma recovery and is also a consultant to the Avellaka Program, a federally funded anti-violence program serving the La Jolla Band of Luiseño Indians.

Catherine Forbes, PhD is a licensed clinical psychologist who has worked in community mental health, private practice, and college counseling during her 20+-year career. She has focused on working with adolescents and young adults, with specialized training and experience with transgender youth. She received her BA in psychology and French studies from Smith College and her MPhil and PhD in clinical and community psychology from the George Washington University. She has published several articles and conducted numerous presentations, trainings, and workshops focused on gender-affirming care for youth. She has also been a clinical supervisor for psychology interns and postdoctoral trainees for more than 15 years. Her clinical and scholarly interests include gender-affirming care, adolescent and young adult development, cognitive behavioral therapy, trauma-informed care, and intersectional systemic impacts on mental health.

About the Authors

Amy Gower, PhD is a research associate in the Division of General Pediatrics and Adolescent Health in the Department of Pediatrics at the University of Minnesota. Her research focuses on the well-being of LGBTQ+ adolescents, with a focus on the ways schools, communities, and policies influence health.

Kellen R. Grayson, PsyD, LMFT is a trans-identified clinician who has worked with children, youth, families, and adults for more than 25 years. Educated at Ohio State University, New College of California, and Alliant International University, he is the former president of the Northern California Society for Psychoanalytic Psychology. Dr. Grayson now serves as the clinic director of Golden Gate Integral Counseling Clinic at the California Institute of Integral Studies in San Francisco, as well as the clinical director of Pathways to Wellness, an agency of several psychiatric clinics across the San Francisco Bay area. He is an experienced supervisor and private practitioner who has provided consultation, training, and public speaking on gender affirmative care. He is an ongoing member of the University of California San Francisco Mind the Gap group and has worked with children, youth, and adults with complex trauma. He is a proud father and foster parent who works with LGBTQ foster children and is also serving as a foreign exchange home for international students.

Gary Howell, PsyD (he/him/his) is the owner and chief psychologist of his group practice, Center for Psychological Growth. He also founded and serves as the director of the Institute for LGBT Health and Wellbeing nonprofit in Tampa, Florida. As a licensed clinical psychologist in Illinois and Florida, he has spent most of his career working with LGBTQ+ patients and created the nonprofit as a mechanism to provide more pro bono services and support groups for trans youth, trans adults, and the parents of trans people as well. He is also the director of practicum training and associate professor at Florida School of Professional Psychology at National Louis University, and he mentors students interested in sexual and gender minority research. He is a former APA Division 44 president and dedicates a lot of time to social justice and advocacy work around amplifying marginalized voices.

Astrid Irizarry-Rodríguez, MS is a fifth-year clinical psychology student enrolled in the PhD Program of the School of Behavioral and Brain Sciences at the Ponce Health Sciences University, where she completed her master's degree in clinical psychology as well. For various years, she has been working as a research assistant on projects that focus on sexual orientation, sexual health, stigma, and sexual violence. She also has received two competitive grants from Fundación Intellectus to carry out research projects on sexual violence, including the development of a sexual consent scale that was validated for the Puerto Rican population. She's currently working on her doctoral dissertation, which aims to explore the experiences of LGBT+ individuals who have survived sexual aggression. She has been a member of the Sex, Gender and Sexual Orientation Diversity Committee of the Puerto Rican Psychology Association since 2020 and was recognized with the Graduate Student of the Year Award by the Puerto Rican Psychological Association in 2021.

Saeromi Kim, PhD (she/they) is assistant clinical director at UCLA's Counseling and Psychological Services (CAPS). Their work focuses on campus climate, community engagement, and culturally responsive care in higher education settings. At CAPS, she oversees prevention efforts and community outreach to underserved populations, including international, Asian American and Pacific Islander, first-generation college, undocumented, and LGBTQ+ students. Dr. Kim is the founder and co-chair of the interdisciplinary Trans Wellness Team at UCLA and a member of the University of California–wide Transgender Care team.

Mira Krishnan, PhD, ABPP is a board-certified clinical neuropsychologist in private practice. Her clinical practice is focused on autism and other neurodevelopmental conditions, as well as traumatic brain injury. She serves as a board advisor to the Association of Children's Residential & Community Centers (ACRC), where she has authored multiple position papers advocating for high-quality care for youth in out-of-home settings. She is a past president of Division 44 of the American Psychological Association, the Society for the Psychology of Sexual Orientation and Gender Diversity. She is a clinical assistant professor in the Department of Psychiatry at Michigan State University. She is based in the Grand Rapids, Michigan area, where she lives with her husband and their cat.

Cristina L. Magalhães, PhD, LMHC (she/her) is professor of clinical psychology, director of the Clinical PsyD Program, and coordinator of the Rockway Certificate in LGBTQ Mental Health and Human Services at the California School of Professional Psychology (CSPP) at Alliant International University, Los Angeles. Dr. Magalhães has served on various committees and task forces charged with addressing the needs of LGBTQ+ people and communities. She is founding editor of PERSPECTIVES (2014–2021)—the newsletter of APA Division 35 Section IV on gender and sexual minority concerns—and currently serves as president-elect of the same professional organization. Dr. Magalhães began her training as a psychologist in Brazil in the late 1980s, became licensed as a mental health counselor in Florida in 2002, and obtained her license as a psychologist in California in 2010. She has experience working with LGBTQ+ couples, families, and individuals across the life span in community mental health centers, residential settings, social service agencies, and private practice.

Caroline Maykut, PhD is a psychologist in private practice in Ontario, Canada. She was previously a clinical postdoctoral fellow at the Institute for Sexual and Gender Health (ISGH) at the University of Minnesota Medical School, where she worked clinically with gender diverse children, transgender adolescents, and their families. She is a member of the World Professional Association for Transgender Health and continues to contribute to research and scholarship on sexuality and gender.

Carrie Mounier, LCSW is a licensed clinical social worker working across multiple programs at the Division of Adolescent and Young Adult Medicine at Children's Hospital Los Angeles. For more than 20 years, she has developed expertise in providing clinical services to youth and young adults with a high degree of clinical complexity.

Specialties include: young people experiencing homelessness; LGBTQIA+ youth; and youth with complex trauma, serious mental illness, and co-occurring substance use disorder. Mounier coordinates the social work internship training and is clinical faculty for the Leadership Education in Adolescent Health program at Children's Hospital Los Angeles. Current areas of interest include: medication-assisted-treatment for youth and young adults with opiate use disorders, the intersection of structural competency and interdisciplinary practice to advance antiracism, and using eye movement desensitization and reprocessing (EMDR) and neurofeedback to address complex trauma in community mental health. She is a passionate advocate for youth and young adults from disadvantaged backgrounds.

Arlene Noriega, PhD has been a practicing psychologist for more than 30 years and has spent the past 22 years in independent practice in Atlanta, Georgia. Dr. Noriega has worked with the Latinx community in the context of independent practice at a time where there were very few culturally and linguistically appropriate clinical services for the Latinx community in Atlanta. Dr. Noriega focuses on the development of empowerment and resilience with her clients.

Alixida Ramos-Pibernus, PhD is assistant professor at the School of Behavioral and Brain Sciences of the Ponce Health Sciences University. She is also a researcher, licensed clinical psychologist, and rehabilitation counselor by training. Dr. Ramos-Pibernus completed her postdoctoral training at the Department of Global and Sociocultural Studies, School of International and Public Affairs at Florida International University. Dr. Ramos-Pibernus has dedicated her entire career to understanding the role of social, cultural, and environmental factors that foster the health disparities experienced by Latinx transgender and nonconforming populations. Her research, which has been supported by the American Cancer Society and the National Cancer Institute, aims to understand and address the interrelated and multilevel factors that foster cancer-related health disparities (cervical and breast) among Latinx transgender women and transgender men in the United States and the Caribbean. Dr. Alixida Ramos-Pibernus received recognition as Psychologist of the Year in Academia in 2020 by the Puerto Rico Psychological Association.

G. Nic Rider, PhD, LP is assistant professor at the Institute for Sexual and Gender Health at the University of Minnesota Medical School and director at the National Center for Gender Spectrum Health. Dr. Rider's scholarly work often focuses on social and structural factors affecting the lived experiences of historically marginalized communities and resilience/strengths identified by these communities. Their professional interests are in the areas of intersectionality, improving various health disparities, decolonizing healing justice, systems change, and social justice advocacy. They currently serve as co-chair for the Asian American Psychological Association's Division on LGBTQQ and participate on committees advocating for sexual and gender diverse individuals globally.

Hiram Rivera-Mercado, PsyD is a clinical psychologist who currently works as the first LGBTQ+-focused staff psychologist in the Michael E. DeBakey Veterans Affairs Medical Center in Houston, Texas. Dr. Rivera-Mercado is also the LGBTQ+ veteran care coordinator at the Houston VA and focuses on developing services for LGBTQ+-identified veterans and training staff to be culturally sensitive in delivering evidenced-based care. Dr. Rivera-Mercado also serves as the national coordinator for the LGBTQ+ psychology fellowships for the entire Veterans Affairs and serves as primary clinical supervisor in LGBTQ+ psychology rotations in the Houston VA for interns and fellows. Dr. Rivera-Mercado received a PsyD from Carlos Albizu University, San Juan, Puerto Rico, and he completed his internship at the Boston University School of Medicine Center for Multicultural Training in Psychology and a fellowship in LGBTQ+ healthcare from Edward Hines, Jr. VA in Chicago.

Tangela Roberts, PhD is assistant professor of counseling psychology in the Department of Counselor Education and Counseling Psychology at Western Michigan University. As a researcher, she explores the mental health of LGBTQ+ communities to (1) highlight intersectionalities and resiliencies and (2) better understand the overall psychological and physiological challenges faced by these communities. As an educator, she uses multicultural-feminist pedagogies to assist future mental health professionals develop a critical understanding of the individual, institutional, and structural marginalization within the field and practice of counseling psychology. Related to clinical work, she focuses on clinical training, psychological assessment, and psychotherapy from a psychodynamic-integrative framework.

Catherine Schaefer, MS is a graduate student in the Family Social Sciences program at the University of Minnesota. Her main research interests include the development of gender identity and cognitive processes of gender development in an inclusive population. She served as a coordinator for the National Center for Gender Spectrum Health and received her MS in developmental psychology from Pennsylvania State University.

Kat Schuette, MA is a mental health counselor who received her graduate education in the counseling psychology program at Western Michigan University. She was born and raised on the outskirts of Chicagoland but has enjoyed moving to various places. Her clinical interests currently include incorporating dialectical behavior therapy (DBT) and acceptance and commitment therapy (ACT) to treat anxiety and personality disorders. Her research interests lie in better understanding and advocating for the needs of underserved, marginalized, and oppressed populations. She currently works as an assistant behavioral health provider for active-duty military service members.

Kayden J. Schumacher, BA, MSc, MSEd, LSC is currently an experiential learning licensed school counselor in Minneapolis, Minnesota, running a district-wide credit recovery program and advocacy efforts for LGBTQ+ students in education within Minneapolis public schools. Kayden previously has worked as a licensed middle school counselor in Milwaukee, Wisconsin, and as a licensed elementary Montessori school counselor in River Falls, Wisconsin. They earned one of their master of science degrees in education: school counseling from Concordia University-Wisconsin, and the other master of science degree in social and applied psychology from the University of Kent-Canterbury, United Kingdom. Kayden earned their bachelor of arts degree from Lawrence University in psychology and gender studies. Their work specializes in LGBTQ+ equity and inclusion in schools and educational environments especially as it relates to sexuality and gender education within social and emotional learning and body image.

Katherine G. Spencer, PhD is assistant professor, licensed psychologist, and certified sex therapist at the Institute for Sexual and Gender Health and a staff member of the National Center for Gender Spectrum Health. Her clinical practice primarily involves working with queer and gender diverse communities on sexual pleasure, trauma, healing, and relationships. Dr. Spencer and her colleague, Dr. Dianne Berg, are co-authors of the Gender Affirmative Lifespan Approach (GALA™).

Richard A. Sprott, PhD received his doctoral degree in developmental psychology from University of California Berkeley in 1994. His early work was on social and language development in early childhood. He was president of the Society for the Psychology of Sexual Orientation and Gender Diversity for 2021–2022 (APA Division 44). For more than 12 years, he co-chaired the Children, Youth and Families Committee of Society for the Psychology of Sexual Orientation and Gender Diversity. He is co-editor on a newly released book from APA Books entitled *Supporting Gender Identity and Sexual Orientation Diversity in K–12 Schools*. He is also the co-author of *Sexual Outsiders: Understanding BDSM Sexualities and Communities* (Rowman & Littlefield, 2013). Along with Dr. Elisabeth Sheff, he is also co-editor of a new book series, *Diverse Sexualities, Genders, and Relationships*, from Rowman & Littlefield. He is currently directing research projects focused on identity development and health/well-being in people who express alternative sexualities and nontraditional relationships, with a special emphasis on kink/BDSM sexuality and polyamory or consensual non-monogamy. Richard currently teaches courses in the Department of Human Development and Women's Studies at California State University, East Bay.

Molly M. Strear, PhD, NCC is associate professor in the Department of Counseling at San Francisco State University in the School Counseling and Pupil Personnel Services specialization. Molly completed her doctoral degree in counselor education and supervision from the University of Northern Colorado with emphases in school counseling and counseling children and adolescents. Molly has been working on the intersection of education and mental health for almost 20 years through mentoring programs, elementary education, school and clinical mental health counseling, and as a counselor educator and supervisor. Molly's scholarship focuses on transforming school counseling to meet the needs of students historically marginalized in educational environments such as LGBTQ+ students, which recently included co-authorship of a unit plan on gender diversity for the Teachers of Psychology in Secondary Schools (TOPSS) of the American Psychological Association.

Kaitlin Venema, PhD is a gender specialist treating children and adolescents at Kaiser Permanente in Northern California. She completed her doctoral degree at Palo Alto University and a postdoctoral fellowship at Children's Hospital Los Angeles. During her two-year fellowship, she worked with transitional-aged LGBTQ youth experiencing homelessness in a drop-in center and in transitional housing.

Jessica Ward, MA is a doctoral candidate in the counseling psychology program at Tennessee State University. She is currently completing her doctoral internship in community mental health at Family Service and Guidance Center in Topeka, Kansas. Her research interests focus on the immediate and enduring effects of early life trauma and the experiences of youth with diverse gender and sexual identities. The major focus of her clinical work is on serving oppressed and underprivileged children, adolescents, and families.

Julie Williams, MSEd, MA (she/her/hers) is a licensed mental health counselor (LMHC) and qualified supervisor in Tampa, Florida, where she co-owns the private practice Thrive Counseling & Consultation, LLC with her husband, Demetrius. She specializes in the treatment of interpersonal trauma and LGBTQ+ issues from an intersectional lens with adolescents and adults. She is also completing a PsyD in clinical psychology at the Florida School of Professional Psychology at National Louis University, and her current research focus is on the assessment and treatment of perpetrators of sex trafficking.

Macy Wilson, PsyD is a licensed clinical psychologist employed by the Federal Bureau of Prisons. Macy's research interests include masculinity, rape culture, misogynoir, cultural awareness, adolescents, and working with underserved populations. Macy is the LGBTQ program affairs manager at her institution, which involves educating staff about LGBTQ+ issues and promoting opportunities for individuals who identify as LGBTQ+, along with providing information and programs to further these initiatives. Much of her clinical work within the institution also involves providing treatment and support to transgender inmates.

Made in the USA
Monee, IL
10 April 2025

15500434R10236